QUANTITATIVE APPROACHES TO MANAGEMENT

QUANTITATIVE APPROACHES TO MANAGEMENT

Fourth Edition

Richard I. Levin, Ph.D.
Charles A. Kirkpatrick, D.C.S.

Graduate School of
Business Administration
University of North Carolina

McGraw-Hill Book Company

New York   St. Louis   San Francisco   Auckland   Bogotá   Düsseldorf
Johannesburg   London   Madrid   Mexico   Montreal   New Delhi
Panama   Paris   São Paulo   Singapore   Sydney   Tokyo   Toronto

QUANTITATIVE APPROACHES TO MANAGEMENT

34567890   VHVH   7832109

This book was set in Souvenir Light by Monotype Composition
Company, Inc. The editors were Donald E. Chatham, Jr., and
Annette Hall; the designer was Joseph Gillians; the production
supervisor was Dennis J. Conroy. New drawings were done by
Fine Line Illustrations, Inc.; chapter-opening illustrations were done
by Joseph Gillians.
Von Hoffmann Press, Inc., was printer and binder.

Library of Congress Cataloging in Publication Data

Levin, Richard I
     Quantitative approaches to management.

     Includes bibliographies and index.
     1. Operations research.   I.   Kirkpatrick, Charles
Atkinson, joint author.   II.   Title.
T57.6.L48   1978   658.4'03   78-4615
ISBN 0-07-037423-6

To Charlotte and Irma

Contents

Preface

It's always been fun writing *Quantitative Approaches to Management,* from the first edition in 1965 to this, the fourth edition. When we came out with the first edition, there weren't *any* books available which approached quantitative topics at a level and in a manner which made it possible for persons with modest mathematical backgrounds to benefit from this discipline. Today there are over a dozen books following our original strategy . . . making difficult things understandable. We're also happy that writers, publishers, and adopters have decided that nonmathematicians deserve a chance to study management science and if we've had a small part in leading the way, we're even happier.

Those who are familiar with our first three editions will see that our original strategy has not changed—we are still committed to helping students understand how to use quantitative methods without excessive or complex mathematical notation. Our goal for the last 13 years has been to explain *how, why,* and *where* the newer quantitative techniques are used without sacrificing pedagogical soundness. We have always taught students that intuitive understanding by managers of when to use management science and how to "get the numbers" would produce more successful applications than detailed mathematical proofs and complex notation . . . and that's exactly the way we write.

Four things are *new* in this edition. A quick word about each of them:

1. The Topical Coverage Has Been Greatly Expanded. Readers will find an entirely new chapter on *understanding and using probability distributions.* We've added a new chapter devoted exclusively to *forecasting methods,* all the way from simple least-squares projections through trend-adjusted exponential smoothing. Our *decision theory* material now includes a thorough treatment of decision criteria such as maximin, maximax, minimax regret, criterion of realism, criterion of rationality, and the maximum likelihood criterion. Our material on *inventory theory* presents a complete treatment of the backorder problem. We've added to the discussion on *linear programming* more material on duality, an entirely new section on linear programming applications, plus an extensive section on sensitivity which includes right-hand-side ranging and changes in objective function coefficients.

We've taken our material on branch and bound and made it into a separate chapter to which we've added material on *integer programming, goal programming,* and *dynamic programming.* Another new feature of this edition is an entire chapter devoted to *simulation* using both hand-computed and computer approaches. The *queuing theory* chapter has been expanded to cover multiple-channel queuing problems. In our *networking* chapter, we've added treatment of the minimal spanning tree problem, the maximal flow problem, the shortest route problem, and a linear programming solution method for crashing CPM networks. Finally, our *Markov analysis* chapter now contains an extensive treatment of accounting uses of this technique.

2.   The Thrust of the Entire Book Is Toward Applications. In this edition you will find numerous problems and narratives from our consulting experience in applying quantitative methods; in each of these situations we share with you some of the problems we've had in applying management science techniques to organizations. In this edition we spend more time worrying about "where to get the numbers" and "how to deal with the folks who have the numbers." After all, this is the greatest hassle in management science today. We feel that if we share with you, for example, the problems we had dealing with a manager of a sausage plant (Chapter 10), you will come away with a much better intuitive notion about what linear programming really does.

3.   This Edition Brings a Number of New Pedagogical Aids to Teaching and Learning. *Marginal notes* which help you locate specific topics for study purposes appear for the first time. At the end of *each* chapter you'll find a section called *Review of Equations.* Here we list all the equations introduced in that chapter, explain each, and give the page number on which it was first used. This should make studying a lot more effective. Each chapter also has its own *glossary* where each technical term used in that chapter is defined—this, too, will minimize hunting all over the chapter before quizzes. And, for the first time, we're making available a *Workbook and Study Guide*—a separate paperback for students with study hints for each chapter, over 250 worked-out problems to supplement the textbook, true-false and multiple-choice questions for each chapter, and a set of thoughtful essay-type questions as well. All this is designed to help students increase their learning efficiency.

4.   The Problems Are the Fourth Significant Change on This Edition. We've expanded the number of problems by over 60 percent, and the majority of problems are new to this edition. Appendix 9 of this book is a *functional area problem index.* There each problem in the text is classified according to the functional area (finance, education, marketing, organizational behavior, accounting, transportation, etc.) from which it comes. Thus, if you want to look at a linear programming application in education, a glance at this index finds such a problem for you in a second. And, finally, over a third of the problems in this edition come from the public sector of our economy. You'll find welfare examples, education examples, city planning examples, public transportation examples, and many more examples from the not-for-profit sector. After all, many of the consequential problems that exist today are not confined to just the private sector of our economy.

There are some folks who deserve special mention. First is my dear friend Charles A. Kirkpatrick, who continues to provide advice, understanding, and friendship year after year. His fine hand is not as evident in this edition, but his heart is still on every page. David Rubin leaves his special mark on this effort. His combination of quantitative brilliance and extraordinary teaching ability shows through in so many places in this edition; I am truly grateful for his contributions. John Gwin led the crew that checked problem answers and has assured me errors will be at a minimum. Please write us when you find one so that we can correct it as quickly as possible. And finally, I owe thanks to Don Chatham, my long-suffering editor; Joel Stinson, who has left his influence in many parts of this book; Annette Hall, whose eagle eye catches everything and whose patient ear is always a comfort; and Lisa Levin, who struggled long and hard over the index.

We hope you like what we've done.

Richard I. Levin

Charles A. Kirkpatrick

Introduction

1

The key managerial responsibility

Decision making is a key managerial responsibility. The process is initiated whenever a manager observes a problem. Perhaps unconsciously, the manager first defines the problem and then formulates the objective, recognizes the constraints, and evaluates the alternatives. After that, he or she selects the apparent "best" course of action—the one which will lead to the optimum solution.

This process of analysis is formal or informal, and it takes two basic forms: qualitative and quantitative.

Qualitative and quantitative analysis

Using only a qualitative approach, a manager would rely on personal judgment or past experience with similar problems. Such an intuitive "feel" for the situation may be sufficient for making a decision.

Yet managers may require quantitative analyses. This would be the case when they have no experience with similar problems. Or it would occur when a problem is so important and complex that it requires à thorough analysis (if a great deal of money or a perplexing set of variables is involved). Or the problem may be repetitive and simple, and a quantitative procedure can save the manager's time.

Skills in qualitative analysis are inherent in the manager and generally increase with experience.

Acquiring skills in quantitative analysis

Skills in *quantitative analysis* can be acquired by study of mathematical "tools" such as those introduced in this book. Using these tools, managers can maximize their decision-making effectiveness. They can compare and combine the qualitative *and* the quantitative information at their disposal and thus make the best decisions possible.

1. Operations Research: The Quantitative Approach to Management Decision Making

Operations research (commonly called OR) provides managers with quantitative bases for decision making. OR enhances a manager's ability to make long-range plans and to solve the *everyday* problems of running a business, a government unit, or a private institution.

Operations research

If you were hired as an *operations researcher,* management would ask you to gather and interpret data, build and experiment with mathematical models predict future operations, and then make recommendations. Your activities would be summarized in the following six steps, which constitute the *scientific methodology* of operations research.

What operations researchers do

Analyzing and Defining the Problem

As a first step, you would determine your research objectives; that is, you would define the problem by its type and the form of its solution. As a result, you could determine which factors were relevant to the solution and could isolate those under the control of management.

The first of six steps in operations research

Suppose, for example, a manager looks at comparative income statements and notes that profits decreased last year. An examination of the figures shows that a reduction in sales volume—not an increase in costs—is the explanation. The manager asks you to discover *why* this occurred.

You analyze the company's products, prices, and promotion. You discover that promotion is the problem area. You realize that you must investigate the advertising variables to discern which is responsible for reduced sales. The culprit could be the amount of money spent, the media used, the advertising theme, the timing, or a combination of any of these.

Notice your methodology. First, you have isolated the problem area, and then you have formulated the problem as an interconnected series of factors within the manager's control.

At this point, then, you can report back to the manager, indicating the problem and a *cost/benefit analysis*—that is, an estimate of the cost of the solution and the economic returns if the study is successful. You can conclude the report with a firm recommendation: to pursue the analysis as originally proposed, to abandon the study because its costs outweigh the potential benefits, or to scale down the project to increase the anticipated returns.

With this information, a manager is in a good position to decide whether the project is worthwhile.

Developing a Model

Once the project is approved, your next step will be to construct a model which represents, mathematically, the situation you are studying. You can construct

Step two

models to show the relation and the interrelation between an action and a reaction or between a cause and effect. Your task is to produce a model which enables you to forecast the effect of factors crucial to the solution of your problem.

An iconic model
Models are either iconic or symbolic. An *iconic model* is concrete. It is a physical representation of some real life object on a different scale (an airplane model) or in idealized form (a photographer's model).

Symbolic models
Operations research deals with *symbolic,* or abstract, *models.* A simple demand curve in economics is a symbolic model predicting buyers' behavior at different price levels. Equations are the mathematical models commonly used in operations research. A profit-and-loss statement is a model familiar to business managers. Often just one sheet of paper, this model summarizes a year of a company's existence in a manner which measures the success of its operations. The statement does not re-create every action which took place during the year; instead, it shows the net result of all activities. Obviously, last year's profit-and-loss statement and the budget for next year are both symbolic models.

A chart showing what a company did with the typical dollar of sales revenue is a graphic model. A drawing of what might happen if your automobile were in a collision while your seat belt was unfastened is a pictorial model. A firm's organization chart—showing, perhaps, the vice-president of production reporting to the executive vice-president and the sales manager reporting to the vice-president of marketing—is another kind of model called an organogram.

The symbolic models of interest to us usually take the form of figures, symbols, and mathematics. We use them because they are concise and precise. They are not easily misconstrued. They are easy to manipulate. They are easier to "see" than words are. We can, for example, grasp "273/146" much more quickly than the words "two hundred seventy-three divided by one hundred forty-six."

It will not be easy to find the best representation of your real world problem. You will need to test and refine whatever model you choose. Often, this testing and refining will turn out to be the most time-consuming part of the OR project.

Selecting the Inputs

Collecting data required by the model
Once you construct an appropriate model, you are ready to collect the data required by that model. This information can come from well-kept records, from current tests and experiments, or even from hunches based on experience.

Suppose, for example, a high school dean of students is preparing next year's class schedules in anticipation of spring registration. Already, she has amassed the following inputs: the number of students, the number of teachers and their specialties, the number of required and elective courses, the number of rooms grouped by their seating capacity, the number of class periods available daily and weekly, and last year's enrollments. Another important input gained from last year's experience is the dean's awareness that the honors chemistry and junior English classes cannot be scheduled for the same period.

Obviously, data collection is not a trivial step in the decision-making process.

It can affect your model's output significantly. Never assume that you have solved the problem once you define your objectives and develop the model. A moderate-sized linear programming model with 50 decision variables and 25 constraints will have over 1300 data elements which must be identified. It takes time to prepare these data if you wish to reduce the possibility of data collection errors.

Coming Up with a Solution

Once you have collected and prepared your inputs, you can solve the model. Under the conditions represented by the model, the solution provides an answer to the problem you are researching.

Solving the model

Suppose, for example, the owner of an ice cream parlor is trying to decide what quantity of ice cream he needs and when to order it for the summer season. He sets up an inventory model and calculates the inputs (that is, the ordering costs, carrying costs, and stockout costs—as we shall discover later). If he sticks to that solution when he enters the winter season, he may be overstocked and short of cash.

Often you will simplify your models to facilitate a solution. But if you do, remember that the solution generally will work only under those simplified assumptions. Therefore, once you have a solution, try altering the inputs and the model and watch what happens to the output. The general term for this procedure is *sensitivity testing*. Perform the tests to discover not only the magnitude of these reactions but also their direction.

Sensitivity testing

Qualifying the Model and the Solution

The next step is to explain your findings to management. Here it is important that you specify those conditions under which the solution can be used. Point out any weaknesses of your underlying assumptions so that management will know what risks they are taking when they employ your model to generate results. Attempt to set limits within which the results obtained from using the model are valid. Define those conditions under which the model will *not* work.

State when the model will work

An arts administrator, for example, might write off labor unions as potential sources of financial support because audience surveys show a low proportion of blue-collar workers in performing arts audiences. Her conclusion appears to be valid because she assumes the unions will support the arts only if their membership demands it. Yet labor unions *are* sources of contributions: some clothing unions have a long history of interest in the arts; the AFL-CIO made sizable contributions to the Kennedy Center; and unions in New York bought quantities of Lincoln Center bonds.[1] Why? The leaders of these labor unions feel that the arts *should* be available to their membership. If the arts administrator will change her assumptions, she may be able to broaden her base of economic support.

[1] William J. Baumol and William G. Bowen, *Performing Arts—The Economic Dilemma,* Cambridge, Mass: The M.I.T. Press, 1966, pp. 335–336.

Putting the Model to Work

The final step is to "sell" your findings to management. The key here is to secure the involvement of operating managers and their commitment to use your findings.

The use of models is not new. Models abound in every organization. The budget for next year is a model of how we expect to operate and how much we may need to spend in each category. A job description is a model of what a person should be accomplishing over a period of time. The income statement is a model of a company's performance over time; the balance sheet, a model of the financial condition of a company. What is new about operations research models is that they enable us to combine many factors at one time and, by using mathematics, come up with solutions to complex problems which might not have been solved with more conventional approaches.

Perhaps the most useful part of an operations research model is that it lets us experiment without making "real" mistakes. Having constructed our model, we can perform sensitivity analysis by altering the inputs and watching what happens to the output—without disrupting the operation we are trying to model. We can determine which factors are the more important ones and how our model will behave over time with changing conditions. It is this ability to vary conditions mathematically that makes operations research an effective tool for dealing with fast-moving, *dynamic* situations.

2. The Development of Scientific Management: From Industrial Engineering to Operations Research

Much of humanity's progress in the last few centuries can be traced to the application of the scientific method to problems where custom, inertia, and tradition had previously ruled. Scientific methodology, prominent earlier in the natural sciences, is now being applied more and more to management—to the planning, organizing, and controlling of operations.

Industrial engineering was born when the scientific method was applied to management problems, but the date of birth is not certain. Individual instances in which the essence of scientific method appears to have been used to solve management problems have been found in writings thousands of years old. Moses' father-in-law, Jethro, is credited with a treatise on organization principles in Chapter 18 of the Book of Exodus. The ancient ships of Venice were reconditioned and refitted for sea duty using an extremely ingenious assembly line; each ship was moved (floated) along the assembly line where a group of skilled workers performed a specific operation at each station in the line. Much more recently (1832), Charles Babbage wrote *On the Economy of Machinery and Manufacturers,* showing much industrial engineering insight.

In the late nineteenth century, Frederick W. Taylor converted industrial engineering into a profession; he can, with some justification, be considered the father of scientific management. Taylor's shovel study is an excellent example of the application of the scientific method to a management problem, namely, the productivity of men shoveling ore. Management had always assumed that the largest shovel a man could fill and carry was the size to maximize output. Even though this seems to be a reasonable assumption, Taylor questioned it and designed a series of experiments to prove or disprove it. After testing all variables that seemed relevant, Taylor determined that only one variable was really significant, namely, the combined weight of the shovel and its load. Too much weight on the shovel, and the worker tired easily and moved slowly. Too little, and he had to make too many trips. For a "first-class man" the proper load turned out to be about 20 pounds. Since the density of ores differs greatly, a shovel was designed for each ore so as to assume the proper weight when the shovel was correctly filled. Productivity rose substantially after this change.

Another man of the early scientific management era was Henry L. Gantt, best known perhaps for his work in scheduling production. Most work-scheduling methods prior to Gantt were rather haphazard. A machining job, for instance, might run through one stage of its production with no trouble and then wait for days for acceptance in the next machine center. Gantt mapped each job from machine to machine, allowing for and minimizing every delay. It is possible to plan machine loadings months in advance with the Gantt procedure and to quote delivery dates accurately. While Taylor was interested in the "one best way" to accomplish a single task, Gantt took a broader point of view; he looked at the various phases or steps in a complete operation.

H. L. Gantt

This shift of interest away from the minutiae of management toward broader considerations was actually a transfer of emphasis from industrial engineering to operations research, a multidisciplinary approach to complex problems. It can be said that operations research emerged as a separate field when (1) industrial engineers became interested in the overall operations of the firm and (2) natural and social scientists became interested in management problems. The blending of ideas, methods, and techniques from the basic sciences, from engineering, and from the newer discipline of management was not accidental. Those persons who were catalysts in the development of operations research recognized the need to have specialists, each highly skilled in his or her own field of knowledge, brought together to work in closely integrated research teams in order to experiment with entire systems rather than with single elements of a system.

Emergence of operations research

3. Early Operations Research

Pre-World War II
Scientists and engineers have been involved with military activities for at least as long as recorded history. One of the best-known individual instances in ancient history occurred in 212 B.C., when the city of Syracuse employed Archimedes (who was then a man of 75 years) to devise means of breaking the naval siege of the city, which was then under attack by the Romans.

Archimedes and the siege of Syracuse

The scientists and engineers who brought about the development of the submarine, the machine gun, the wireless telegraph, and the airplane were, however, more interested in the instrumentalities than the process of war.

The germination of the concept of operations research, from the military standpoint, occurred on both sides of the Atlantic Ocean during World War I.

F. W. Lanchester's equations tested

In England, in the years 1914–1915, F. W. Lanchester attempted to treat military operations quantitatively. He obtained equations relating the outcome of a battle to both the relative numerical strength of the combatants and their relative firepower.

Lanchester's equations suggested that the overall power of fighting forces was proportional to the square of the numerical strength of those forces; he tested his theory against Admiral Nelson's plan at the Battle of Trafalgar and determined that Nelson's plan had been optimal. Whether it was Nelson or Lanchester who was right is not really discernible; what *is* important, however, is that Lanchester "modeled" a situation involving strategic choices and then tested that model against a known real world situation. Ever since that time, operations researchers have been doing precisely that.

T. A. Edison's statistics on submarine warfare

During the period when Lanchester was pioneering military operations research in Great Britain, Thomas Alva Edison in America was studying the process of antisubmarine warfare. He collected statistics to be used in analyzing maneuvers whereby surface ships could evade and destroy submarines. He devised a war game to be used for simulating problems of naval maneuver. He even analyzed the merits of "zigzagging" as a submarine countermeasure for merchant ships.

We have shown previously that, in the late nineteenth century, pioneers in management consulting and industrial engineering were proving the value of scientific techniques in the fields of production and planning—specifically, Frederick W. Taylor's techniques, which operations research was to refine and extend.

F. W. Taylor in production and planning

Taylor was important in ways directly germane to operations research. His contributions, great as they were as techniques, were even more valuable in demonstrating the value of creating groups within organizations whose mission was to analyze the organizations themselves, that is, to form organizations for research on operations.

Another point of resemblance between Taylor's work and operations research concerns the mixed or multidisciplinary teams which have been said to be central to operations research. For example, Taylor had at least 12 colleagues in his metalworking studies and had this to say about three of them:

> Mr. White (Maunsel White) is undoubtedly a much more accomplished metallurgist than any of the rest of us; Mr. Gantt (H. L. Gantt) is a better all around manager, and the writer of this paper has perhaps the faculty of holding on tighter with his teeth than any of the others. . . . Mr. Barth (Carl G. Barth), who is a very much better mathematician than any of the rest of us, has devoted a large part of his time . . . to carrying on the mathematical work.[2]

---

[2]   Taylor, On the Art of Cutting Metals, *Transactions of the American Society of Mechanical Engineers,* vol. 28, p. 35, 1916.

Operations research also involves the development of mathematical models to represent the operations under study. One could say that the slide rule developed by Carl Barth to perform metalworking evaluations appears to be a mathematical model, too, representative of the operations it portrays.

In 1917, A. K. Erlang, a Danish mathematician working with the Copenhagen telephone company, published his most important work, "Solutions of Some Problems in the Theory of Probabilities of Significance in Automatic Telephone Exchanges"; it contained his formulas for waiting time which he had developed on the basis of statistical principles. These now well-known formulas are of fundamental importance to the theory of telephone traffic. A few years after its appearance, his formula for the probability of loss was accepted by the British Post Office as the basis for calculations concerning circuit facilities.

A. K. Erlang's early work in waiting time

Erlang grappled with various technical problems, the first of which was to measure stray currents in the manholes of the streets of Copenhagen. Erlang's ideas and work anticipated by almost half a century the modern concepts of waiting-line or queuing theory.

In the area of inventory control, the well-known economic lot size models have a long genealogy. While it has been reported that G. D. Babcock developed a model stated in the form of a cubic equation, his technique was never published. The first published inventory economic lot size model is generally attributed to Ford W. Harris, who described his model in 1915. Other early contributors to the development of inventory control models include H. S. Owen (1925), Benjamin Cooper (1926), and R. H. Wilson and W. A. Mueller (1926–1927). Mathematical techniques of inventory control are, therefore, among the oldest of the operations research tools.

F. W. Harris develops the first inventory model

The theory of probability and statistical inference has been a part of management theory for a relatively short time. Walter Shewhart made the earliest recorded applications of statistical inference in 1924, when he introduced the concept of quality control charts. Much of the theory he outlined is still used today.

Walter Shewhart applies statistical inference

The utilization of statistical inference and probability theory was aided by the work of H. F. Dodge and H. G. Romig, coworkers with Shewhart at Bell Telephone Laboratories. They developed the technique of sampling inspection in connection with quality control and published statistical sampling tables which, although slowly accepted at first, are now widely used.

Another engineer at Bell Laboratories, T. C. Fry, made additional significant contributions toward the statistical foundations of queuing theory. A series of lectures presented by Fry in 1928 concerning the engineering applications of probability theory became the basis for his important book on the subject.

Of course, the work of Sir Ronald Fisher dealing with various modern statistical methods must be included in any survey of the development of operations research. At the time it was written, Fisher's work had little direct effect on management thought; but it is the basis for most of the applied statistical theory in use today. An early model widely applied is the breakeven chart, developed by Walter Rautenstrauch, an industrial engineer, in the 1930s.

R. Fisher and modern statistical methods

The development of models to allocate scarce resources among competing activities to achieve some desired output (now referred to as "linear programming") originated around 1760, when economists first began to describe economic systems in mathematical terms. The problem was first treated in the *Tableau Économique* of Quesnay, who attempted to interrelate the roles of the landlord, the peasant, and the artisan. The use of a linear-type model seems next to have appeared, as a part of the Walrasian system, in the 1870s. But the concern with interindustry input-output theories and measurements (brought about by the Great Depression of the 1930s) stimulated the work of Wassily Leontieff, a Harvard professor, who developed a linear programming model representing the entire United States economy. Many military and industrial applications of linear programming models have resulted from these early efforts.

Quesnay, forerunner of linear modeling

W. Leontieff develops a linear programming model

One of the first proponents of business operations research in the United States was Horace C. Levinson, an astronomer who began his operations research in the decade of 1920–1930. He applied the methods of science to the problems of commerce—and studied such problems as the relationship between advertising *and* sales, and the relationship between customers' incomes and home locations *and* types of articles purchased.

H. C. Levinson does operations research work in the decade 1920–1930

One of Levinson's best-known studies involved customers' refusals to accept c.o.d. packages ordered from a mail-order house. These rejections averaged over 30 percent of gross sales and were having bad effects on profits. Two variables turned out to be significant. First, as would be expected, the more expensive orders were frequently refused. Another factor proved easier to deal with than this. Analysis of a very large sample of orders revealed that the time between receipt of the order and shipment of the merchandise was quite important. It was so important, in fact, that shipment 5 days after the placement of the order was not worthwhile. On the average, orders older than 5 days did not break even. From this point, it was relatively easy to compare the cost of rejections with the cost of faster shipping and thus determine the optimum shipping effort. Levinson retired in 1946 as vice-president of L. Bamberger and Company.

World War II

Early British operations research group

As Britain was at war 2 years before the United States, it was almost inevitable that the first effective military operations research should occur there. In 1939, according to one historian, "there was a nucleus of a British operational research organization already in existence,"[3] and its contributions were quickly followed and augmented in various important ways: in improving the early-warning radar system, in antiaircraft gunnery, in antisubmarine warfare, in civilian defense, in the determination of convey size, and in the conduct of bombing raids upon Germany.[4]

---

[3]   Florence N. Trefethen, "A History of Operations Research," in Joseph F. McCloskey and Florence N. Trefethen (eds.), *Operations Research for Management*, Baltimore: The Johns Hopkins Press, 1954, vol. 1, pp. 3–35.

[4]   Ibid., pp. 5–10.

One of the most publicized of Britain's operations research groups was that under the direction of Professor P. M. S. Blackett of the University of Manchester, a Fellow of the Royal Society, Nobel Laureate, and former naval officer. "Blackett's circus," as the group was called, included "three physiologists, two mathematical physicists, one astrophysicist, one Army officer, one surveyor, one general physicist, and two mathematicians."[5] The value of the mixed-team approach was effectively demonstrated over and over again by this group.

Blackett's circus

Two Americans who were instrumental in the development of operations research in the United States during World War II were James B. Conant, then Chairman of the National Defense Research Committee, and Vannevar Bush, Chairman of the Committee on New Weapons and Equipment, Joint Chiefs of Staff. These gentlemen had observed such groups in England in 1940 and in 1942, respectively.[6]

In October 1942, at the request of General Spaatz, Commanding General of the Eighth Air Force, General Arnold (then Chief of Staff) sent a letter to all commanding generals of Air Force commands, recommending that they include in their staffs "operations analysis groups."[7] The first such operations analysis team was assigned to the Eighth Bomber Command, stationed in England. Almost simultaneously, the U.S. Navy formed operations research teams (in two organizations—the Naval Ordnance Laboratory and the Tenth Fleet). The Tenth Fleet group was under the direction of Philip M. Morse of the Massachusetts Institute of Technology, while the Naval Ordnance group was directed by Ellis A. Johnson.

Early United States operations research groups

Post-World War II

Operations research activity was considered to be so valuable by American military leaders that such functions were not discontinued at the end of the war. The Army continued its operations research functions through the agency of the Operations Research Office (later called the Research Analysis Corporation), in Chevy Chase, Maryland, with Ellis A. Johnson as Director. The Navy established the Operations Evaluation Group under the direction of Professor Morse at MIT. The Air Force continued to employ operations analysis groups as a part of the various commands under its Operations Analysis Division. Additionally, the Air Force established Project RAND, administered by the RAND Corporation, for long-range studies of aerial warfare.

Army and Navy postwar operations research

At the close of the war, the industrial climate on both sides of the Atlantic was ripe for the introduction of operations research into business planning. As some of the formerly "top secret" indications of its value were released, its possible contributions to the business world became more apparent. Industry needed to revamp its production and organization to service peacetime needs quickly. In the United States the question of competition was paramount. In Great Britain, a

[5] Ibid., p. 6.

[6] Ibid., p. 12.

[7] Ibid., p. 13.

critical economic situation demanded drastic increase of efficiency in production and in the development of new markets.

Differences in British and United States development of operations research

Industrial operations research in Great Britain and in the United States developed along different lines. In Britain the nationalization of a few industries provided a fertile field for experimentation with operations research techniques in industries as a whole. In government, operations research studies for the Ministry of Food surveyed food consumption and expenditure patterns to predict the effects of government food and price policies on nutrition and the family budget. Operations research groups exist in Great Britain for the iron and steel industry and for coal, road and rail transport, textiles, agriculture, brickmaking, shoes, etc., with most but not all of them under government sponsorship.

The reaction was much different in the United States. Management consulting in this country dated back at least to F. W. Taylor, and managers had seen many fads come and go. Communication between managers and scientists (in contrast to communication between managers and consultants) was quite difficult because neither spoke the other's language. What little message the scientists could get across to managers sounded like no innovation at all. And managers were inclined to turn to established consulting firms to get done the research recommended by the scientists. Furthermore, to some managers, the scientists did not seem completely reliable or respectable.

It was not until a few of our bolder companies tried operations research with considerable success and word began to leak out about its World War II accomplishments that civilian operations research began to make any real headway in the United States. Scientists and managers began to learn how to achieve two-way communication.

4. Operations Research Today

Operations research activities have grown rapidly in business, government units, and private institutions. Simultaneously, the scope of the problems addressed by operations research practitioners has expanded as well.

ORSA and TIMS

In the early 1950s, groups of people interested in operations research organized the Operations Research Society of America (ORSA) and The Institute of Management Sciences (TIMS). Since 1952, ORSA has published the journal *Operations Research;* since 1953, TIMS has published the journal *Management Science.* Two decades later, the two societies are cooperating to produce *Interfaces,* a quarterly publication of papers and articles concerned with the operational problems of using management science and operations research, and *OR/MS Today,* a bimonthly newsletter for the two organizations.

In 1948 in England, people interested in operations research formed the Operational Research Club. Since then, they have changed the name to the Operational Research Society of the United Kingdom. In 1950, the British launched the *Operational Research Quarterly,* a publication which has the distinction of being the first periodical in the field.

More recently, operations research societies have been formed in France, Italy, Israel, and Austria, each with its own journal or bulletin. The most recent American entry into this field was the American Institute of Decision Sciences in 1971.

AIDS

5. Relationship between the Quantitative Specialist and the Manager

Earlier, you assumed the role of an operations researcher and learned the six steps of the scientific methodology of operations research. From that exercise, you gained a "feel" for the relationship between the operations research specialist and the manager. Let us examine that relationship more closely.

In short, the role of the operations research specialist is to help the manager make better decisions. Decision making is still a key *managerial* responsibility.

Major role of the operations research specialist

Now and in the future, managers need operations research specialists because the size of organizations is increasing to the point where they are becoming un-manageable by traditional methods. Even without this problem, managers face enormously complicated and fast-changing situations. Creative and workable solutions to these problems require the cooperative involvement of quantitative specialists and managers.

Figure 1-1 illustrates one suggested division of work between these two organizational members. The roles evolve naturally from the six steps discussed earlier.

Such close association between the operations research specialist and the managerial generalist means that managers need some understanding of the quantitative tools which specialists use. They need, for example, enough under-standing to be able to describe a problem and then provide pertinent data for its solution.

Management's need to understand quantitative analysis

It is not necessary that the manager be able to execute each intricate step of the mathematics used by operations researchers. Yet, as a future manager, you will benefit from the familiarity with these intricacies which you can gain from studying this book.

6. Typical Applications of Operations Research

To give you a preview of the challenges and approaches introduced in this book, we have collected a few examples.

An Inventory and Production Problem

Think of a manufacturer of a wide line of beer products—including premium, budget, light, draft, canned, and bottled—which vary by cost, containers, and taste. The firm's breweries are located in several states, and there are differences

A distribution problem

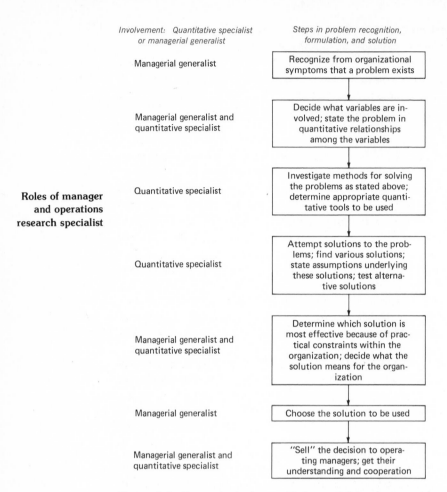

Involvement: Quantitative specialist or managerial generalist

Steps in problem recognition, formulation, and solution

Managerial generalist — Recognize from organizational symptoms that a problem exists

Managerial generalist and quantitative specialist — Decide what variables are involved; state the problem in quantitative relationships among the variables

Roles of manager and operations research specialist

Quantitative specialist — Investigate methods for solving the problems as stated above; determine appropriate quantitative tools to be used

Quantitative specialist — Attempt solutions to the problems; find various solutions; state assumptions underlying these solutions; test alternative solutions

Managerial generalist and quantitative specialist — Determine which solution is most effective because of practical constraints within the organization; decide what the solution means for the organization

Managerial generalist — Choose the solution to be used

Managerial generalist and quantitative specialist — "Sell" the decision to operating managers; get their understanding and cooperation

Figure 1-1 Proposed roles for quantitative specialist and managerial generalist.

among them with regard to the availability and price of ingredients, the age of machines, the cost of labor, and the expenses associated with shipping. The products are sold in several hundred cities and in all 50 states. Inventories consist of thousands of items. Forecasting sales is difficult. The manufacturers can reduce the total costs involved with purchasing, storing, manufacturing, and marketing if they are aware of the operations research techniques treated in Chapters 7 and 8.

A Maximization Problem

Suppose we manage a machine shop and a manufacturer of a line of small engines is interested in buying crankshafts from us. He is buying for inventory and will accept up to 175 power lawnmower crankshafts, up to 65 motor scooter crankshafts, and up to 160 golf cart crankshafts. They will pay $15.75 each for lawnmower crankshafts, $24.50 each for motor scooter crankshafts, and $20 each for golf cart crankshafts.

Our estimate is that material costs for the three kinds, in order, are $1, $6, and $5.50. These crankshafts would pass through three machine centers for which we expect no other orders in the near future. The first is the forge, which has 360 hours available. Here direct labor costs are $2.25 per hour. The next center is the lathe section, in which 240 machine-hours are available; here, direct labor costs amount to $2.50 per hour. Finally, there is the grinding department, which has 480 machine-hours available. Direct labor costs in this department are $2.75 per hour.

Product mix which generates greatest profit

From past experience with these crankshafts, we know the machine time needed for each type. A lawnmower crankshaft requires 3 hours in the forge, 2 hours lathe time, and 1 hour of grinding. A motor scooter crankshaft requires 4 hours of forge work, 1 hour of lathe time, and 3 hours of grinding. A golf cart crankshaft requires 2 hours in each of these three departments. The problem? What *one* combination of the three types of crankshafts will net us the greatest profits?

With traditional mathematical and statistical tools, this problem in the maximization of profit is time-consuming because there are so many variables and combinations. Our customer will not buy more of each type than stated. Our profit on each of the three types is different. We have a limited amount of time in each of the three machine centers, and each of the crankshaft types has its own needs for machine time. And, of course, there are three products rather than one. How can we approach a solution? You will see when we learn about linear programming, a procedure explained in Chapters 9 and 10.

A Work-Force Planning Problem

A hospital has a support staff of 1000 employees. Seventy percent are "old" employees; that is, they have worked for the hospital for more than a year. The other 30 percent are "new" employees with this attrition record:

Within the first 4 months of their employment, 50 percent leave.

Within the second 4 months, 20 percent leave.

Within the next 4 months, 10 percent leave.

Work-force planning with operations research

Only 20 percent make it through the first year; they become "old" employees.

Among the old employees, the attrition rate is 30 percent a year (or 10 percent every 4 months).

With these rates in mind, how should the company approach the problem of determining that hiring rate which will (1) maintain a stable work force, (2) reduce the work force by any given percentage rate annually, or (3) increase the work force by any given percentage rate annually? The methods discussed in Chapters 2 and 3 fit this problem and many others similar to it.

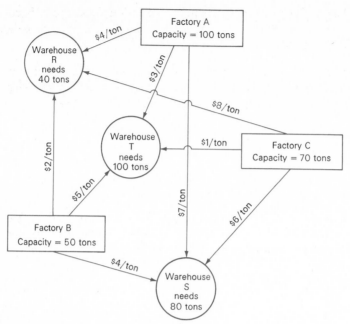

Figure 1-2 Possible shipping combinations.

A Minimization Problem

Minimizing the total cost of shipping

Operations research models can help managers reduce their transportation costs. Suppose, for example, you are the transportation manager of a company which produces ceramic tile in several factories and ships the finished products to several warehouses. Shipping costs from each factory to each warehouse are different. Therefore, your problem is to minimize total shipping costs in view of the total capacity of the factories and the total needs of the warehouses.

Figure 1-2 shows your situation. The rectangles contain the capacity of each factory for the forthcoming week; the circles, the weekly needs for each of the three warehouses. You must decide which factory will supply which warehouse so that you can minimize costs.

The relationship among capacity, needs, and shipping costs can be expressed as in Table 1-1. Obviously, the number of possible combinations of warehouses

Table 1-1 Possible Shipping Combinations

Factory	Capacity, tons	Shipping cost per ton		
		To R	To S	To T
A	100	$4	$7	$3
B	50	2	4	5
C	70	8	6	1
Needs this week		40 tons	80 tons	100 tons

and factories is very large. Each different shipping combination involves a different total shipping cost for the coming week. Take, for example, two of the many possible solutions to the problem facing you:

1. You could let factory A supply warehouse T's needs; then let factory B ship 40 tons to warehouse R and 10 tons to warehouse S; factory C would then ship all its output to warehouse S. Total shipping cost of this decision is $840:

One alternative

$100 \times \$3$	$300
$40 \times \$2$	80
$10 \times \$4$	40
$70 \times \$6$	420
	$840

2. You could let factory C ship 70 tons to warehouse T; then factory B could ship 30 tons to warehouse T and 20 tons to warehouse S; factory A then ships 60 tons to warehouse S and 40 tons to warehouse R. Total shipping cost of this decision is $880:

A second alternative

$70 \times \$1$	$ 70
$30 \times \$5$	150
$20 \times \$4$	80
$60 \times \$7$	420
$40 \times \$4$	160
	$880

There are, of course, many other possibilities, each with a different total shipping cost. You must find the optimum combination which, in this instance, is the lowest total shipping cost. To enumerate all the possible combinations by hand would require days of work. There is, however, a quantitative method which will yield the optimum answer in a few minutes; we shall discuss this type of problem and others in Chapter 11.

A Waiting-Line Example

For the administrator of a hospital, the theory of waiting lines and waiting-line behavior will hold the answer to many practical problems besetting hospitals today. Take, for instance, the operation of an emergency room which experiences, on average, 18 calls each night for service. If the patients arrive for emergency service in random fashion, the administrator must decide on an appropriate level of staffing for the emergency room. If too many medical professionals are assigned, their time is wasted; if too few are assigned, patients arrive and wait too long for service, which may endanger lives. If the administrator knows the average time it takes to treat an emergency room case, it is possible for her to apply waiting-line models to the situation. She would be interested not only in how long the waiting line might become but also in answers to questions such as "How long does the average patient wait?" and "What is the greatest number of patients we can expect to see in the waiting line at any one time?" Operations research techniques can be of great help in this situation.

Application of operations research to the emergency room

7. Quantitative Methods to Be Discussed

A brief comment about each of the techniques of operations research we will cover in this book may indicate more specifically some of the types of analyses available and some of the problems to which they can be applied.

Probability concepts

Probability concepts are useful when coping with an uncertain environment. Methods are indicated for computing and using probabilities. Bayesian statistics develops a powerful method for making decisions when only limited information is available. We also present a representative sampling of the many possible uses of probability theory. Problems are included involving sampling, military strategy, and replacement of items which fail over time.

Forecasting

Forecasting is an unavoidable responsibility of management. Faced with uncertainty concerning the future, management looks to past behavior as an indicator of what is to come. Among the topics to be treated in this chapter are moving averages, exponential smoothing, trend-adjusted exponential smoothing, trend line fitting, and causal forecasting with multiple regression.

Decision theory

Decision theory is concerned with making sensible decisions under both conditions of complete uncertainty about future outcomes and under conditions where you can make some probability statements about what you think will happen in the future. Methods are presented by which probability theory can be coupled with financial data to generate valuable decision algorithms. We examine conditions in which utility would be used instead of expected monetary value. Developed within this broad category are decision trees—an effective method of combining probability concepts and expected value (or utility) in the solution of complex problems involving both uncertainty *and* a large number of alternatives. Included in this topic is a treatment of cost-volume-profit analysis under conditions of uncertainty as to the behavior of both demand and cost.

Inventory models

Inventory models aid in controlling total inventory costs; these approaches can successfully reduce the total cost of purchasing inventory, carrying inventory, and being out of stock of inventory. Methods useful in dealing with discount evaluation, joint ordering of items from the same vendor, and making inventory decisions in the absence of complete information are also discussed at some length. Here we will also develop a model which intentionally suggests that being "out of stock" of an item may be a better alternative than always being able to supply demand; in this context we shall indicate how to calculate the appropriate out-of-stock condition for several situations.

Linear programming

Linear programming is of value when a choice must be made from alternatives too numerous to evaluate with conventional methods. Using linear programming, we can determine optimum combinations of the resources of a firm to achieve a certain objective. Graphic and simplex methods of applying this technique are discussed.

Special-purpose algorithms

Special-purpose algorithms are linear programming techniques useful when working with a certain type of problem. We illustrate the transportation method and the assignment method, two approaches that are useful when management is confronted with problems concerning the best distribution alternative or the optimum method of assigning operators to machines, accountants to audit teams, and even students to schools.

Integer programming, the branch and bound method, dynamic programming, and *goal programming* are methods for choosing among alternatives in situations where answers may have to be found in whole numbers, where the decision confronting management is one involving many consecutive stages, or where organizational objectives have to be stated in more than simple numerical terms. All these techniques provide us with additional flexibility in analyzing decision processes.

Simulation is a procedure that studies a problem by creating a model of the process involved in that problem and then, through a series of organized trial-and-error solutions, attempting to determine a better solution to that problem. Simulation is one of the most widely used quantitative techniques today.

Queuing theory studies random arrivals at a servicing or processing facility of limited capacity. Models allow management to calculate lengths of future waiting lines, average time spent in line by a person awaiting service, and needed facility additions. This technique is studied, first, using various formulas useful in the solution of waiting-line problems, then by using the technique of simulation to generate a solution.

Networking theory enables managers to cope with the complexities involved in large projects; the use of this technique has significantly reduced the time necessary to plan and produce complex products. Techniques covered in this section include PERT (Program Evaluation Review Technique), CPM (Critical Path Method), PERT/Cost, and Scheduling with Resource Limitations. Both the time and cost dimensions of the planning and control of large, complex projects are discussed.

Markov analysis permits one to predict changes over time when information about the behavior of a system is known. Although the best-known use of this technique is in predicting brand loyalties (the brand behavior of consumers over time), Markov analysis also has considerable use in the areas of accounting (movement of credit customers from one classification of collectibility to another) and general financial management (the movement of companies from one state of financial viability to another).

The *future direction* of the quantitative disciplines developed in this book is the subject of a final section. Here we shall report on current research into the direction that applications seem to be taking, the implications of the further development of these techniques for operating managers, and some of the "roadblocks" which may limit the effective, continued, profitable use of these techniques.

Integer programming, the branch and bound method, dynamic programming, goal programming

Simulation

Queuing theory

Networks

Markov analysis

A look ahead

Glossary

1. **Operations research** Systematic study of a problem involving gathering data, building a mathematical model, experimenting with the model, predicting future operations, and getting the support of management for the use of the model.

2. **Cost/benefit analysis** A comparison of both the cost of a solution and the economic benefits which would result from that solution.

3. **Iconic model**   Physical representation of some real life object.

4. **Symbolic model**   An abstract model, generally using mathematical symbols.

5. **Sensitivity testing**   Altering the inputs to a model and watching what happens to the output.

6. **Industrial engineering**   Study of managerial problems using the scientific method.

7. **Blackett's circus**   Early British operations research group under the leadership of P. M. S. Blackett of the University of Manchester.

8. **ORSA**   Operations Research Society of America.

9. **TIMS**   The Institute of Management Sciences.

10. **AIDS**   American Institute of Decision Sciences.

Exercises

1-1. Distinguish between qualitative and quantitative analyses in decision making. Give two examples of each.

1-2. What activities would you find yourself doing as an operations researcher?

1-3. What six steps constitute the scientific methodology of operations research?

1-4. Give two kinds of models, define each, and give three examples of each.

1-5. Comment on the makeup of Blackett's circus. What specific problem-solving skills would such a group offer?

1-6. Does the fact that operations research takes the organizational point of view instead of the individual problem-centered point of view appear to generate any constraints on its increased usage?

1-7. It appears that some early managerial decision making actually used an operations research approach. To what do you attribute the fact that it has taken about 50 years for operations research to come into accepted usage in industry?

1-8. Comment on the methodology of pre-World War II approaches to operations research. How would you compare the work done in this period with later operations research efforts?

1-9. What were the significant characteristics of operations research applications during World War II? What caused the discipline of operations research to take on these characteristics during that period?

1-10. Relate the scientific methodology of operations research to that of the scientific method. What are the major similarities and differences?

1-11. In section 6 (Typical Applications of Operations Research), five applications of operations research are given. Pick any three of these and determine (1) what are the relevant variables in the problem, (2) what data would be required as input to the solution of the problem, and (3) what form the output or answer to the problem would take.

Bibliography

Beer, S.: *Management Sciences: The Business Use of Operations Research* (Garden City, N.Y.: Doubleday & Company, Inc., 1968).

Churchman, C. W., R. L. Ackoff, and **E. L. Arnoff:** *Introduction to Operations Research* (New York: John Wiley & Sons, Inc., 1957).

Hillier, F. S., and **G. J. Lieberman:** *Introduction to Operations Research* (San Francisco: Holden-Day, Inc., Publisher, 1974).

Miller, David W., and **Martin K. Starr:** *Executive Decisions and Operations Research,* 2d ed. (Englewood Cliffs, N.J.: Prentice-Hall, Inc., 1969).

Waddington, C. H.: *OR in World War II: Operational Research against the U-Boat* (London: Elek Books, Ltd., 1973).

Probability I: basic concepts

2

1. Introduction to Probability

Decisions and certainty

If it were possible to predict the future with complete certainty, the structure of managerial decisions would be radically different from what it is. A wrong decision would be simply the result of failure to consider all the relevant information; there would be no excess production, no clearance sales, no speculation in the stock market, and business failure would be a rarity.

Use of probabilities in decision making

Of course, we do not live in a world of complete certainty, and our desire to cope with the uncertainty we face in decision making leads us to the study and use of probability theory. Often, managers have some knowledge about the possible outcomes in a decision situation; by organizing this information and considering it systematically, they usually reach a sounder decision than they would if they simply guessed.

Historical uses of probability theory

Probability theory was successfully applied at gambling tables as early as the eighteenth century and—more relevant to this text—was eventually used to guide managerial decisions. The insurance industry, which emerged in the nineteenth century, required exact knowledge about the risk of loss in order to calculate premiums. By the middle of the nineteenth century, many universities were studying probability theory as a basis for understanding social phenomena. Today, probability theory forms the basis for many approaches to managerial decision making.

Probability becomes a part of most decisions

The concept of probability is a part of our everyday lives in both personal and managerial situations. Whether we admit it or not, we do use probability theory when we face uncertainty. When the weather forecast is 60 percent chance

24

of rain, we change our plans for the day from backpacking to a movie. Those who play bridge tend to make some probability estimate before trying a finesse; managers who must manage inventories of highly styled women's clothing wonder whether sales will reach or exceed certain levels, and they make estimates of those chances. Managers in government agencies who must deal with the delivery of health care consider seriously the probabilities associated with the spread of disease; and, of course, students who face a test as a part of this course wonder what the chances are that the instructor will give a quiz on a certain day. All these decision makers benefit from their own assessments of the chances that certain things will happen.

2. Basic Probability Concepts

Probability is the chance that something will happen. Probabilities are expressed as fractions (¼, ½, ¾) or as decimals (.25, .50, .75) between 0 and 1. When you assign a probability of 0, you mean that something can *never* happen; when you assign a probability of 1, you mean that something will *always* happen.

Probability defined

Events and Experiments

In probability theory, an *event* is one or more of the possible outcomes of doing something. If we toss a coin, getting a tail would be an event; getting a head would be still another event. The activity that produces an event is referred to in probability theory as an *experiment*. Using this language, we could ask, "In a coin-toss experiment, what is the probability of the event *heads?*" In this case, we would answer, "½ or .5." Most managers are much less excited about tossing coins than they are in the answers to questions like, "What are the chances of that shipment arriving by Friday?" or "What are our chances of reaching a break-even volume on that product this year?" or "Will that new piece of equipment be likely to reduce fly ash from our smokestack sufficiently?"

An event

Mutually Exclusive and Collectively Exhaustive Events   Events are *mutually exclusive* if one and only one of them can take place at a time. Consider again the example of the coin toss. We have two possible outcomes, heads and tails. On any single toss, either heads or tails may turn up, but not both. Accordingly, the events *heads* and *tails* on a single toss are said to be *mutually exclusive*. Similarly, if you consider for a moment the possible outcomes of your taking this course, you will either pass it, fail it, or drop it without a grade. Only one of these three outcomes will occur; they are mutually exclusive events. The crucial question we ask in determining whether events are really mutually exclusive is, "Can two or more of these events occur at one time?" If we answer "Yes," the events are *not* mutually exclusive.

Mutually exclusive events

When you make a list of the possible events that can result from an experiment and this list includes every possible outcome, you have a *collectively exhaustive*

Collectively exhaustive events

list. In our previous coin-toss example, the list "head and tail" is collectively exhaustive (unless, of course, the coin happens to land on its edge). In a political campaign, the list "Democratic candidate and Republican candidate" is *not* a collectively exhaustive list, since there could be candidates who see themselves as Independents, Socialists, States Righters, Pacifists or "others."

3. Three Types of Probability

Approaches to probability: three different ways

There are three ways of classifying probability. These represent different conceptual approaches to the study of probability theory; in fact, experts disagree over which approach it is proper to use. We will examine these three approaches to probability:

1. The *classical* approach

2. The *relative frequency* approach

3. The *subjective* approach

Classical Probability

Classical probability defines the probability that an event will occur as:

$$\text{The probability of an event} = \frac{\text{number of outcomes favorable to the occurrence of the event}}{\text{total number of possible outcomes}} \quad (2\text{-}1)$$

The classical approach to defining probabilities

In order for Eq. (2-1) to be valid, each of the outcomes must be equally likely. Equation (2-1) may be a somewhat complex way of defining something that is intuitively obvious to us, but we can use it to express our coin-toss example in symbolic form. First, let us illustrate the question, "What is the probability of getting heads on one toss?":

$$P(\text{heads}) = \frac{1}{1+1}$$

The number of outcomes of one toss favorable to the occurrence of the event (in this case, the number that will produce heads)

Total number of possible outcomes of one toss (in this case, heads and tails)

$$= 1/2$$

Let us try one more example using the definition of classical probability. Suppose the question now is, "What is the probability of rolling a 5 on one die?" We would calculate the answer this way:

$$P(5) = \frac{1}{1+1+1+1+1+1}$$

The number of outcomes of one roll of the die which will produce a 5

Total number of possible outcomes of one roll of the die (getting a 1, a 2, a 3, a 4, a 5, or a 6)

$$= 1/6$$

Classical probability is often called *a priori* probability because—if we keep using these orderly examples of fair coins, unbiased dice, or decks of cards—we can state the answer in advance (a priori) *without ever tossing a coin, rolling a die, or drawing a card.* We do not even have to perform experiments to make probability statements about fair coins, unbiased dice, or decks of cards. Rather, we can make probability statements based on logical reasoning before any experiment takes place.

Assessing probabilities without experiments

If you are interested in dealing with coins, dice, or cards, this approach to probability is useful; but it has serious shortcomings when we attempt to apply it to the less orderly world of managerial decision making. The classical approach to probability assumes a world that really does not exist; it assumes away situations which, although very unlikely, could conceivably happen. Situations like a coin landing on its edge, a nuclear accident which would destroy an entire city, the simultaneous appearance of 50 identical new products from 50 different companies, or the simultaneous demise of all five suppliers of aircraft to the government are all extremely unlikely but not impossible. Nevertheless, the classical approach assumes them away. Classical probability also assumes a kind of symmetry about the world which can get us into trouble in managerial decision making. For example, although we define a fair coin as one having a probability of heads equal to .5, or symbolically $P(\text{heads}) = .5$, would you bet everything you possess on the chance that, of the next 10 tosses of a fair coin, 5 will be heads? The real world situation which confronts managerial decision makers, disorderly and unstructured as it is, makes it quite useful for us to define probabilities in other than classical ways.

Shortcomings of the classical approach

Relative Frequency of Occurrence

To introduce this definition of probability, let us ask ourselves questions such as, "What is the probability that I will live to 100?" or "What are the chances that a new paper plant on the river near town will produce a significant fish kill?" or "What is the chance that turning up a 200-watt amplifier wide open will blow one of my speakers?" In all these situations we can quickly see that we probably cannot state these probabilities without experimentation. Thus approaches other than the classical one will probably be more useful in answering these questions.

The relative frequency approach to assigning probabilities

In the nineteenth century, British statisticians became interested in calculating risk of losses in life insurance and commercial insurance; therefore they began to define probabilities from statistical data on births and deaths. Today, we call this approach *relative frequency of occurrence.* It defines probability either as

1. The proportion of times that an event occurs in the long run when conditions are stable, or

2. The observed relative frequency of an event in a very large number of trials

This method of defining probability uses the relative frequencies of past occurrences as probabilities. To predict the probability that something will happen in the future, we determine how often it happened in the past. Let us look at an example. Suppose that your college admissions office knows from past data that

Using past history to assign probabilities

about 50 of its 1000 entering freshmen usually leave school for academic reasons by the end of the first semester. Using this method, the school would estimate the probability of a freshman leaving school for academic reasons as:

$$\frac{50}{1000} \quad \text{or} \quad .05$$

Relationship between number of observations and accuracy of relative frequency probabilities

Another characteristic of probabilities which are calculated using this method based on the relative frequency of occurrence can be illustrated by tossing one of our fair coins, say, 500 times. Figure 2-1 illustrates the outcomes of these 500 tosses. In this illustration, we can see that although the proportion of heads was not .5 in the first 100 tosses, it seemed to stabilize and approach .5 as the number of tosses approached 500. If we wanted to use appropriate probability language, we would say that the relative frequency becomes stable as the number of tosses becomes large. Thus, when we use the relative frequency approach to establish probabilities, our probability values will gain accuracy as we increase the number of observations. Of course, this increased accuracy is not without its cost; the manager who will not act before seeing the market-research results of 500 different trial introductions may find that the market for that product is already supplied by a competitor who acted on less information.

On the other hand, however, one of the problems with the method based on the relative frequency of occurrence is that people sometimes use it *without* evaluating a sufficient number of outcomes. Suppose our marketing manager of the previous example test marketed a new product on just five persons, found from the test that four of the five persons liked the product, and on the basis of *their* acceptance or rejection authorized production of 10 million units of that product; we could criticize this manager for not basing the decision on enough evidence. Put in more proper language, the manager did not have sufficient data (reaction of five persons) to establish a probability based on relative frequency of occurrence.

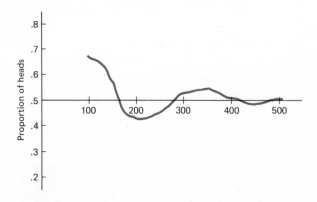

FIGURE 2-1 Proportion of heads in 500 tosses of a fair coin.

Subjective Probabilities

Subjective probabilities are based on the personal belief or feelings of the person who makes the probability estimate. We can define *subjective probability* as the probability assigned to an event on the basis of whatever evidence is available. This evidence may be data about relative frequency of occurrence or it may be nothing more than a good guess. The assignment of subjective probabilities gives us the greatest flexibility of any of the three methods we have discussed. The decision makers can use whatever *evidence* is available and temper this with their own personal feelings about the situations.

Managers generally assign probabilities subjectively when events occur only once or at most a very few times. Suppose it is your responsibility to select a new assistant and you have narrowed the choice down to three persons. All three have an attractive appearance, an apparent high level of energy, high self-confidence, and equally impressive records of past accomplishments. What are the chances that each of these candidates will make a good assistant? Answering this question and choosing one from the three requires you to assign a subjective probability to each person's potential.

Suppose we look at one more example of assigning probabilities subjectively. A cabinet-level officer is deciding whether to permit the operation of a supersonic jet transport at a metropolitan airport; there is some evidence that such operation will not only produce excessive noise (and thus inconvenience residents of that area) but also tend to deplete the ozone layer in the atmosphere. The officer must consider the question, "What is the probability that these operations will produce an atmospheric condition injurious to the health of a great many people?" The fact that there are no data on the relative frequency of occurrence of such an outcome at this location does not allow the officer to avoid deciding the issue. The decision must rest on whatever scientific evidence is available plus the officer's best judgment in trying to determine the probability of such a potentially disastrous event.

4. Probability Rules

Most managers who use probabilities are concerned with two situations: (1) the case where one event *or* another will occur and (2) the case where two or more events will *both* occur.

We are expressing an interest in the first case when we ask questions like, "What is the probability that our water supply will permit the plant to operate today?" If we wanted to illustrate the second case, we could ask, "What is the probability that our water supply will permit the plant to operate today *and* that plant absenteeism will exceed 5 percent?" In the material which follows, we shall illustrate methods of determining answers to questions similar to these under a variety of conditions.

Using personal feelings to assign probabilities

Frequency of occurrence suggests use of subjective method

Evidence and judgment are both used to assign probabilities

Situations in which probabilities are useful

Some Commonly Used Symbols, Definitions, and Rules

Marginal probability

Symbol for a Marginal Probability   In probability theory, symbols are used to simplify the presentation of ideas. For example, the probability of a single event A would be expressed symbolically as

$$P(A) \qquad\qquad \underline{\text{Probability}} \text{ of } \underline{\text{event } A} \text{ happening}$$

Example of a marginal probability

A *single* probability means that only one event can take place. It is called a *marginal* or *unconditional probability*. To illustrate, let us suppose that 10 computer programmers have an equal chance of being promoted to programming supervisor. Any one of these programmers could calculate his or her chance of getting the promotion by this formulation:

$$P(\text{promotion}) = \frac{1}{10}$$
$$= .1$$

In this situation, a programmer's chance is 1 in 10 because we are certain that the possible events are mutually exclusive; that is to say, only one programmer can get promoted to supervisor at a time.

Adding the probabilities of events that are mutually exclusive

Addition Rule for Mutually Exclusive Events   Often, however, we are interested in the probability that one thing *or* another will occur. If these two events are mutually exclusive, we can express this probability using the addition rule for mutually exclusive events. This rule is expressed symbolically as

$$P(A \text{ or } B) \qquad\qquad \underline{\text{Probability}} \text{ of either } A \text{ or } B \underline{\text{ happening}}$$

and is calculated as follows:

$$P(A \text{ or } B) = P(A) + P(B) \tag{2-2}$$

Examples of addition of probabilities of events which are mutually exclusive

Let us use this formula in an example. Five equally satisfactory brands of light trucks are being considered by a city government. It has announced that it will choose one of the five by random drawing. If our brands are Chevrolet, Dodge, Ford, GMC, and International and our question is, "What is the probability that Dodge will be chosen?" we can use Eq. (2-1), originally introduced on page 26, and calculate the answer as follows:

$$P(\text{Dodge}) = \frac{1}{5}$$
$$= .2$$

If, however, we ask this question, "What is the probability of either Dodge *or* International being chosen?" we would use Eq. (2-2):

$$P(\text{Dodge or International}) = P(\text{Dodge}) + P(\text{International})$$
$$= \quad 1/5 \quad + \quad 1/5$$
$$= \quad 2/5$$
$$= \quad .4$$

Let us do one more example. These are the experience data for welders in a fabrication shop:

Years of experience	Number	Probability
0–2	5	$5/50 = 1/10 = .1$
3–5	10	$10/50 = 1/5 = .2$
6–8	15	$15/50 = 3/10 = .3$
More than 8	20	$20/50 = 2/5 = .4$
Total	50	

What is the probability that a welder selected at random will have 6 or more years of experience? Using Eq. (2-2), we can calculate the answer as

$$P(\text{6 or more}) = P(\text{6 to 8}) + P(\text{more than 8})$$
$$= \quad .3 \quad + \quad .4$$
$$= \quad .7$$

Addition Rule for Events That Are Not Mutually Exclusive If two events are not mutually exclusive, it is possible for both events to occur together. In such cases, the addition rule must be modified. Let us use the example of a deck of cards to introduce this idea. What is the probability of drawing either an ace *or* a spade from a deck of cards? Obviously the events *ace* and *spade* can occur together because we could draw the ace of spades; thus ace and spade are *not* mutually exclusive. We must adjust Eq. (2-2) to avoid double counting; specifically, we have to *reduce* the probability of drawing either an ace or a spade by the chance that we could draw them both together. As a result, the correct equation to use for the probability of one or more of two events that are not mutually exclusive is

Avoiding double counting in events which are not mutually exclusive

Probability of A happening

Probability of A and B happening together

$$P(A \text{ or } B) = P(A) + P(B) - P(A \text{ and } B) \tag{2-3}$$

Probability of A or B happening when A and B are not mutually exclusive

Probability of B happening

Using Eq. (2-3) to calculate the probability of drawing either an ace *or* a spade, we get:

$$P(\text{ace or spade}) = P(\text{ace}) + P(\text{spade}) - P(\text{ace and spade})$$
$$= \ 4/52 + \ 13/52 \ - \ \ \ \ \ \ 1/52$$
$$= 16/52$$
$$= \ 4/13$$

Suppose we do another example. The city council of Chapel Hill, North Carolina, is composed of the following 5 persons:

Example of addition of probabilities of events which are not mutually exclusive

Person	Sex	Age
1	Male	31
2	Male	33
3	Female	46
4	Female	29
5	Male	41

If the members of the council decide to elect a chairperson by random draw (say, by drawing the names from a hat), what is the probability that the chairperson will be *either* female *or* over 35? To solve this, we can use Eq. (2-3) and set up the solution like this:

$$P(\text{female or over 35}) = P(\text{female}) + P(\text{over 35}) - P(\text{female and over 35})$$
$$= \ \ \ \ 2/5 \ \ \ + \ \ \ \ 2/5 \ \ \ - \ \ \ \ \ \ \ 1/5$$
$$= \ \ \ \ 3/5$$
$$= \ \ \ \ .6$$

You can check this quickly by noting that of the 5 council members, 3 would fit the requirement of being *either* female *or* over 35.

5. Probabilities under Conditions of Statistical Independence

Statistical independence: three types of probabilities

When events are statistically independent, the occurrence of one event has no effect on the probability of the occurrence of any *other* event. There are three types of probabilities under statistical independence: (1) marginal, (2) joint, and (3) conditional.

Marginal Probabilities under Statistical Independence

Marginal probabilities under statistical independence

Marginal probability is the simple probability of the occurrence of an event.

Example 1   In the fair coin example, we have $P(H) = .5$ and $P(T) = .5$; that is, the probability of heads equals .5 and the probability of tails equals .5. This is true for *every* toss, no matter how many tosses may precede it or what their outcomes may be. Every event (toss) stands alone and is in no way connected with any other event (toss). Thus *each* toss of a fair coin is a *statistically independent event.*

Example 2 Assume that we have a biased or unfair coin which has been altered in such a way that heads occurs .90 of the time and tails .10 of the time. On each individual toss, $P(H) = .90$ and $P(T) = .10$. The outcome of any particular toss is completely unrelated to the outcomes of the tosses which may precede it as well as to the outcomes of any which may follow. The tosses of *this* coin, too, are therefore statistically independent, even though the coin is biased.

Joint Probabilities under Statistical Independence
The probability of two or more *independent* events occurring together or in succession is the product of their marginal probabilities. Mathematically, this is defined as

$$P(AB) = P(A) \times P(B) \tag{2-4}$$

where $P(AB)$ = probability of events A and B occurring together or in succession; this is known as a *joint probability*
$P(A)$ = marginal probability of event A occurring
$P(B)$ = marginal probability of event B occurring

In terms of the fair coin example, the probability of heads on two successive tosses is the probability of heads on the first toss (shown as H_1) times the probability of heads on the second toss (shown as H_2). That is, $P(H_1H_2) = P(H_1) \times P(H_2)$. We have shown previously that the events are statistically independent because the probability of any outcome is not affected by any preceding outcome. Therefore, the probability of heads on any toss is .5; then, $P(H_1H_2) = .5 \times .5 = .25$; thus the probability of heads on two successive tosses is .25 (or ¼, or 25 percent).

Joint probabilities under statistical independence

Likewise, the probability of getting three heads on three successive tosses is $P(H_1H_2H_3) = .5 \times .5 \times .5 = .125$ (or ⅛, or 12.5 percent).

Assume that we are going to toss an unfair coin which has $P(H) = .9$ and $P(T) = .1$. The events (outcomes) are *independent* because the probabilities of all tosses are exactly the same. That is, the individual tosses are completely separate and in no way affected by any other toss or outcome.

What is the probability of getting three heads on three successive tosses?

$$P(H_1H_2H_3) = P(H_1) \times P(H_2) \times P(H_3) = .9 \times .9 \times .9 = .729$$

What is the probability of getting three tails on three successive tosses?

$$P(T_1T_2T_3) = P(T_1) \times P(T_2) \times P(T_3) = .1 \times .1 \times .1 = .001$$

FIGURE 2-2

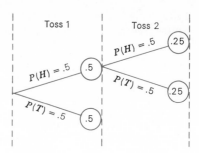

FIGURE 2-3

Note that these two probabilities do not add up to 1 because $P(H_1 H_2 H_3)$ and $P(T_1 T_2 T_3)$ do not constitute a collectively exhaustive list. They *are* mutually exclusive because if one occurs, the other cannot.

As further illustration, construct a *probability tree* showing the possible outcomes and their respective probabilities of three tosses of a fair coin.

For toss 1 we have two possible outcomes, heads and tails, each with probability of .5. This is shown in Figure 2-2.

Assume that the outcome of toss 1 is heads. We toss again. The second toss has two possible outcomes, heads and tails, each with probability of .5. In Figure 2-3 we add these two branches of the tree.

Illustrating the probability of outcomes with a probability tree

Next we consider the possibility that the outcome of toss 1 is tails. Then the second toss must stem from the second branch of toss 1. Thus we add two more branches to the tree in Figure 2-4.

Notice that on two tosses we have four possible outcomes: $H_1 H_2$, $H_1 T_2$, $T_1 H_2$, $T_1 T_2$. (The subscripts indicate the toss number; for example, T_2 means tails on toss 2.) Thus, after two tosses, we may arrive at any one of four possible points. Since we are going to toss three times, we must add more branches to the tree.

Assuming that we have had heads on the first two tosses, we are now ready to begin adding branches for the third toss. As before, the two possible outcomes are heads and tails, each with a probability of .5. The first step is shown in Figure 2-5.

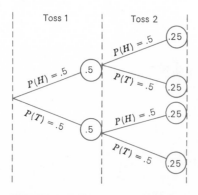

FIGURE 2-4 Two tosses illustrated.

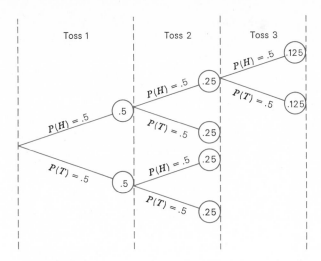

FIGURE 2-5

The additional branches are added in exactly the same manner. The completed probability tree is given in Figure 2-6.

Adding additional branches

Note that both heads and tails have a probability of .5 of occurring no matter how far from the origin (first toss) any particular toss may be. This follows from our definition of *independence; that is, no event is affected by the events preceding or following it.*

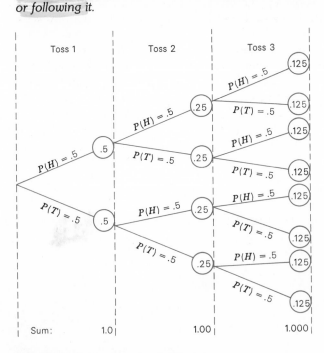

FIGURE 2-6 Completed probability tree.

Suppose we are going to toss a fair coin and want to know the probability that all three tosses will result in heads. Expressing the problem symbolically, we want to know $P(H_1H_2H_3)$. From the mathematical definition of the joint probability of independent events, we know that

$$P(H_1H_2H_3) = P(H_1) \times P(H_2) \times P(H_3) = .5 \times .5 \times .5 = .125$$

Reading answers directly from the tree

We could have read this answer from the probability tree by following the branches giving $H_1H_2H_3$.

Here are other brief examples using the probability tree.

Example 1   What is the probability of getting tails, heads, tails *in that order* on three successive tosses of a fair coin? $P(T_1H_2T_3) = P(T_1) \times P(H_2) \times P(T_3) = .125$. Following the prescribed path on the probability tree will give us the same answer.

Examples of probability questions answered with a probability tree

Example 2   What is the probability of getting tails, tails, heads *in that order* on three successive tosses of a fair coin? If we follow the branches giving tails on the first toss, tails on the second toss, and heads on the third toss, we arrive at the probability of .125. Thus $P(T_1T_2H_3) = .125$.

It is important to note that the probability of arriving at a given point by a given route is *not* the same as the probability of, say, heads on the third toss. $P(H_1T_2H_3) = .125$, but $P(H_3) = .5$. The first is a case of *joint probability,* that is, the probability of getting heads on the first toss, tails on the second, and heads on the third. The latter, by contrast, is simply the *marginal probability* of getting heads on a particular toss, in this instance toss 3.

Note that the sum of the probabilities of all the possible outcomes for each toss is 1. This results from the fact that we have mutually exclusive and collectively exhaustive lists of outcomes. These are given in Table 2-1.

Again referring to the probability tree, consider the following examples.

Table 2-1   Lists of Outcomes

Toss 1		Toss 2		Toss 3	
Possible outcomes	Probability	Possible outcomes	Probability	Possible outcomes	Probability
H_1	.5	H_1H_2	.25	$H_1H_2H_3$	.125
T_1	.5	H_1T_2	.25	$H_1H_2T_3$	.125
	1.0	T_1H_2	.25	$H_1T_2H_3$	.125
		T_1T_2	.25	$H_1T_2T_3$	.125
			1.00	$T_1H_2H_3$	.125
				$T_1H_2T_3$	.125
				$T_1T_2H_3$	.125
				$T_1T_2T_3$	.125
					1.000

Example 3 What is the probability of *at least* two heads on three tosses? Recalling that the probabilities of mutually exclusive independent events are additive, we can note the possible ways that at least two heads on three tosses can occur and we can sum their individual probabilities. The outcomes which satisfy the requirement are $H_1H_2H_3$, $H_1H_2T_3$, $H_1T_2H_3$, and $T_1H_2H_3$. Since each of these has an individual probability of .125, the sum is .5. Thus the probability of at least two heads on three tosses is .5.

Example 4 What is the probability of *at least* one tail on three tosses? There is only one case in which no tails occur, namely, $H_1H_2H_3$. Therefore we can simply subtract for the answer:

$$1 - P(H_1H_2H_3) = 1 - .125 = .875$$

The probability of at least one tail occurring in three successive tosses is .875.

Example 5 What is the probability of *at least* one head on two tosses? The possible ways a head may occur are H_1H_2, H_1T_2, T_1H_2. Each of these has a probability of .25. Therefore the probability of at least one head on two tosses is .75. Alternatively, we could consider the case in which no head occurs, namely, T_1T_2, and subtract its probability from 1, that is,

$$1 - P(T_1T_2) = 1 - .25 = .75$$

Two methods to get the same answer

Conditional Probabilities under Statistical Independence

Thus far we have considered two types of probabilities, *marginal* (or unconditional) probability and *joint* probability. Symbolically, marginal probability is $P(A)$ and joint probability is $P(AB)$. There is only one other type of probability, known as *conditional* probability. Symbolically, conditional probability is written $P(A|B)$ and is "the probability of event A, *given that event B has occurred*."

Conditional probability

For *statistically independent* events, the conditional probability of event B has occurred is simply the probability of event A. At first glance this may seem contradictory. However, by definition, independent events are those whose probabilities are *in no way* affected by the occurrence of any other events. In fact, statistical independence is symbolically defined as the condition in which

Conditional probabilities for statistically independent events

$$P(A|B) = P(A) \tag{2-5}$$

Example What is the probability that the second toss of a fair coin will result in heads, given that heads resulted on the first toss? Symbolically this is written as $P(H_2|H_1)$. Remember that for two independent events, the results of the first toss have absolutely no effect on the results of the second toss. Since the probabilities of heads and tails are identical for every toss, the probability of heads on the second toss is .5; thus, we must say that $P(H_2|H_1) = P(H) = .5$.

Table 2-2 Probabilities under Statistical Independence

Type of probability	Symbol	Formula
1. Marginal (or unconditional)	$P(A)$	$P(A)$
2. Joint	$P(AB)$	$P(A) \times P(B)$
3. Conditional	$P(A|B)$	$P(A)$

For a summary of the three types of probabilities and their mathematical formulas under conditions of statistical independence, see Table 2-2.

6. Probabilities under Conditions of Statistical Dependence

Statistical dependence defined

Statistical dependence exists when the probability of some event is *dependent upon* or *affected by* the occurrence of some other event. Just as with independent events, the types of probabilities under statistical dependence are (1) marginal, (2) conditional, and (3) joint.

Marginal Probabilities under Statistical Dependence

Marginal probability

The marginal probability of a statistically dependent event is exactly the same as that of a statistically independent event. This is not difficult to see if we note that a marginal probability is symbolized $P(A)$. *One* and only one probability is involved; a marginal probability refers to only one of them.

Conditional Probabilities under Statistical Dependence

Conditional probability under statistical dependence

Conditional and joint probabilities under statistical dependence are somewhat more involved than marginal probabilities. Conditional probabilities will be treated first, because the concept of joint probabilities is best illustrated using conditional probabilities as a basis.

Assume that we have one urn containing 10 balls distributed as follows:

3 are red and dotted.

1 is red and striped.

2 are green and dotted.

4 are green and striped.

The probability of drawing any particular ball from this urn is .1, since there are 10 balls, each with equal probability of being drawn. The discussion of the following examples will be facilitated by reference to Table 2-3.

Table 2-3 Color and Patterns on 10 Balls

Examples of
determining
conditional
probabilities under
statistical
dependence

Event	Probability of event	
1	.1 ⎫	
2	.1 ⎬	Red and dotted
3	.1 ⎭	
4	.1 }	Red and striped
5	.1 ⎫	Green and dotted
6	.1 ⎭	
7	.1 ⎫	
8	.1 ⎬	Green and striped
9	.1 ⎪	
10	.1 ⎭	

Example 1 Suppose someone draws a ball from the urn and tells us it is red. What is the probability that it is dotted? The question then can be expressed symbolically as $P(D|R)$, or "What is the conditional probability that this ball is dotted, given that it is red?"

Our question can be expressed diagrammatically as shown in Figure 2-7.

We have been told that the ball drawn is red. Therefore, to calculate the probability that the ball is dotted, we completely ignore all the green balls and concern ourselves with red only. Diagrammatically, we consider only what is shown in Figure 2-8.

From the statement of the problem, we know that there are 4 red balls, 3 of which are dotted and 1 of which is striped. Our problem is now broken down to one of finding the simple probabilities of dotted and striped. To do so we divide the number of balls in each category by the total number of red balls:

$$P(D|R) = \frac{3}{4} = .75$$

$$P(S|R) = \frac{1}{4} = \frac{.25}{1.00}$$

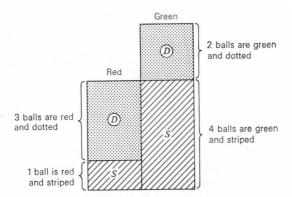

FIGURE 2-7 Contents of urn shown.

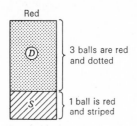

Red

3 balls are red
and dotted

1 ball is red
and striped

FIGURE 2-8　Probability of
dotted and of striped, given red.

In other words, three-fourths of the red balls are dotted and one-fourth of the red balls are striped. Thus the probability of dotted, given that the ball is red, is .75. Likewise, the probability of striped, given that the ball is red, is .25.

Now that we have calculated the answer, let us observe how our reasoning will enable us to develop the formula for conditional probability under statistical dependence. We can first assure ourselves that these events *are* statistically dependent by observing that the color of the balls determines the probabilities that they are either striped or dotted; for example, a green ball is more likely to be striped than a red ball. Since color affects the probability of striped or dotted, these two events can be said to be dependent.

To calculate the probability of dotted given red, $P(D|R)$, we divided the probability of *red and dotted* balls (3 out of 10, or .3) by the probability of red balls (4 out of 10, or .4). Thus

$$P(D|R) = \frac{P(DR)}{P(R)}$$

or, expressed as a general formula using the letters A and B to represent the two events,

**The general formula
for conditional
probability under
statistical
dependence**

$$P(A|B) = \frac{P(AB)}{P(B)} \qquad (2\text{-}6)$$

This is a formula for conditional probability under statistical dependence.

Example 2　What is $P(D|G)$? $P(S|G)$?

$$P(D|G) = \frac{P(DG)}{P(G)} = \frac{.2}{.6} = \frac{1}{3}$$

$$P(S|G) = \frac{P(SG)}{P(G)} = \frac{.4}{.6} = \frac{2}{3}$$

The problem is shown diagrammatically in Figure 2-9.

**Examples using the
conditional
probability formula**

The total probability of green is .6 (6 out of 10 balls). To determine the probability that the ball (which we know is green) will be dotted, divide the probability of green and dotted (.2) by the probability of green (.6), or $.2/.6 = ⅓$. Similarly,

Green

2 balls are green and dotted each with probability of .1

4 balls are green and striped, each with probability of .1

FIGURE 2-9 Probability of dotted and of striped, given green.

to determine the probability that the ball will be striped, divide the probability of green and striped (.4) by the probability of green (.6), or $.4/.6 = \frac{2}{3}$.

Example 3 Calculate $P(R|D)$ and $P(G|D)$.

See Figure 2-10. Having been told that the ball drawn is dotted, we disregard striped entirely and consider only dotted.

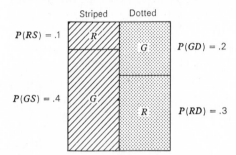

Striped   Dotted

$P(RS) = .1$

$P(GS) = .4$

$P(GD) = .2$

$P(RD) = .3$

FIGURE 2-10

Now see Figure 2-11, showing the probabilities of red and green, given dotted. Notice that the relative proportions of the two are as .4 is to .6.

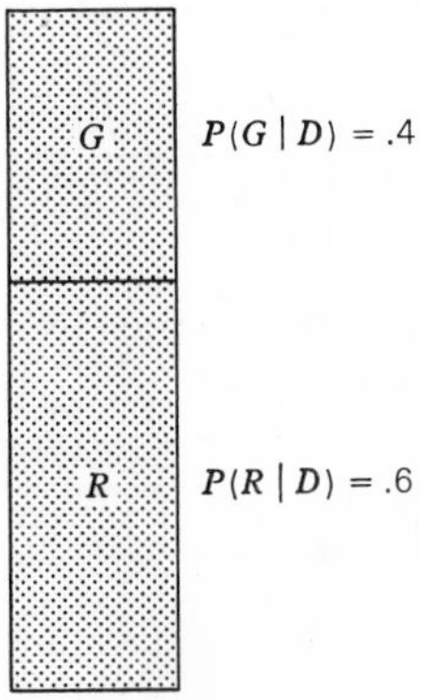

$P(G|D) = .4$

$P(R|D) = .6$

FIGURE 2-11   Probability of red and of green, given dotted. (Probability of striped = 0.)

$$P(G|D) = \frac{P(GD)}{P(D)} = \frac{.2}{.5} = \quad .4$$

$$P(R|D) = \frac{P(RD)}{P(D)} = \frac{.3}{.5} = \quad .6$$

$$\overline{\quad 1.0 \quad}$$

Example 4   Calculate $P(R|S)$ and $P(G|S)$.

$$P(R|S) = \frac{P(RS)}{P(S)} = \frac{.1}{.5} = .2$$

$$P(G|S) = \frac{P(GS)}{P(S)} = \frac{.4}{.5} = .8$$
$$\overline{\hspace{2em}1.0}$$

Joint probabilities under statistical dependence

Joint Probabilities under Statistical Dependence

We have shown that the formula for conditional probability under conditions of statistical dependence is $P(A|B) = P(AB)/P(B)$. If we solve this formula for $P(AB)$—and this can be done simply by cross multiplication—we find that:

$$P(AB) = P(A|B) \times P(B) \tag{2-7}$$

Joint probabilities under independence and dependence compared

This is the formula for joint probability under conditions of statistical dependence. It is read "the joint probability of events A and B equals the probability of event A, given that event B has occurred, times the probability of event B." Notice that this formula is *not* $P(AB) = P(A) \times P(B)$, as it would be under conditions of statistical independence.

Converting the general formula $P(AB) = P(A|B) \times P(B)$ to terms of red, green, dotted, and striped, we have $P(RD) = P(R|D) \times P(D)$, or $P(RD) = .6 \times .5 = .3$, where .6 is the probability of red given dotted (computed in example 3 above) and .5 is the probability of dotted (also computed in example 3).

$P(RD) = .3$ can be verified in Table 2-3, where we originally arrived at the probability by inspection. (There are 3 red and dotted balls among a total of 10 balls.)

The following joint probabilities are computed in the same manner and can also be substantiated by reference to Table 2-3.

$$P(RS) = P(R|S) \times P(S) = .2 \times .5 = .1$$
$$P(GD) = P(G|D) \times P(D) = .4 \times .5 = .2$$
$$P(GS) = P(G|S) \times P(S) = .8 \times .5 = .4$$

Computing Marginal Probabilities under Statistical Dependence

Note that the marginal probability of the event *red* can be computed by summing the probabilities of the joint events in which red is contained:

An alternative method to compute marginal probabilities under dependence

$$P(R) = P(RD) + P(RS) = .3 + .1 = .4$$

Similarly, the marginal probability of the event *green* can be computed by summing the probabilities of the joint events in which green is contained:

$$P(G) = P(GD) + P(GS) = .2 + .4 = .6$$

Similarly, the marginal probability of the event *dotted* can be computed by summing the probabilities of the joint events in which dotted is contained:

$$P(D) = P(RD) + P(GD) = .3 + .2 = .5$$

And finally, the marginal probability of the event *striped* can be computed by summing the probabilities of the joint events in which striped is contained:

$$P(S) = P(RS) + P(GS) = .1 + .4 = .5$$

These four marginal probabilities $P(R) = .4$, $P(G) = .6$, $P(D) = .5$, and $P(S) = .5$ can be verified by inspection of Table 2-3.

We have just considered the three types of probability—*marginal, conditional,* and *joint*—under conditions of statistical dependence. Table 2-4 provides a résumé.

Summary of probabilities under dependence

Table 2-4   Probabilities under Statistical Dependence

Type of probability	Symbol	Formula
1. Marginal (or unconditional)	$P(A)$	$P(A)$
2. Joint	$P(AB)$	$P(A|B) \times P(B)$
3. Conditional	$P(A|B)$	$\dfrac{P(AB)}{P(B)}$

An Example of Marginal Probabilities under Statistical Dependence   A two-person internal management audit team has begun an examination of the internal security system of one of the divisions of a large company. Each person works independently of the other. Past audit experience seems to indicate that each auditor has a .6 probability of finding a system deficiency during the audit period. If both auditors find such a deficiency, chances are .8 that the system needs to be redesigned. If either of the auditors finds a deficiency, the chances are .5 that the system needs to be redesigned. If neither finds a deficiency, there is still a small chance (.2) that the system needs to be redesigned. What is the probability that, after any given two-person audit, the system will have to be redesigned?

To answer this question, it is useful to set up the information like this:

P(first auditor finding a deficiency) $= .6$
P(second auditor finding a deficiency) $= .6$
P(first auditor not finding a deficiency) $= .4$
P(second auditor not finding a deficiency) $= .4$

Next, it will be useful to compute the joint probabilities of the auditors finding two deficiencies, one deficiency, or no deficiency. These probabilities are calculated like this:

$$P(\text{both auditors finding a deficiency}) \quad = \quad .6 \times .6 = \quad .36$$
$$P(\text{only one auditor finding a deficiency}) = \quad .6 \times .4 = \quad .24$$
$$+.4 \times .6 = +.24 \Big\} = .48$$
$$P(\text{neither auditor finding a deficiency}) \quad = \quad .4 \times .4 = \quad .16$$

Two ways an outcome can occur

In the case of the joint probability of *one* auditor finding a system deficiency, we were required to sum *two* probabilities, because a deficiency can be found in two ways (the first auditor finds it and the second one does not *or* the second auditor finds it and the first one does not).

Summing joint probabilities to get marginal probabilities

The answer we are looking for is the probability of having to redesign the system. Earlier in this chapter, we illustrated how this *marginal* probability could be found by summing the joint probabilities of all the joint events in which the marginal event is found. These joint probabilities are:

$$P(\text{system redesign and two deficiencies}) = .8 \times .36 = .288$$
$$P(\text{system redesign and one deficiency}) \; = .5 \times .48 = .240$$
$$P(\text{system redesign and no deficiency}) \quad = .2 \times .16 = .032$$
$$P(\text{system redesign}) = .560$$

Thus we see that after any given two-person audit, there is a bit better than a 50-50 chance that the security system will have to be redesigned.

This concludes our treatment of probability under conditions of both independence and dependence. Table 2-5 is a quick reference for the appropriate formulas in both cases.

Table 2-5 Probabilities under Statistical Independence and Dependence

Type of probability	Symbol	Formula under statistical independence	Formula under statistical dependence
1. Marginal	$P(A)$	$P(A)$	$P(A)$
2. Joint	$P(AB)$	$P(A) \times P(B)$	$P(A|B) \times P(B)$
3. Conditional	$P(A|B)$	$P(A)$	$\dfrac{P(AB)}{P(B)}$

Summary of probabilities under independence and dependence

7. Revising Prior Estimates of Probabilities: Bayes' Theorem

Using new information to revise a priori probabilities

When the NFL season opens, the supporters of last year's winner think that their team has a terrific chance to win the title again. But the season goes on, injuries sideline the first-string quarterback, the defensive team's pass defense begins to falter, and the team begins to lose games. Late in the season, the team rooters find they must alter their prior probabilities (their a priori probabilities) of winning.

A similar situation often occurs in managerial decision making. A manager of a fashion boutique finds that the pink and purple ski jackets she ordered early in the season are not selling; she must now alter her prior probabilities and reorder a different color combination. A financial officer of a large corporation makes an assessment of the money market for the coming year and elects to work with his investment banker for an equity issue. As the year progresses, economic news worsens and the market begins to decline; the financial officer must reassess his initial probabilities of a successful equity offering in light of new information.

In all these cases, probabilities are altered after the people involved got additional information. These new probabilities are known as revised or *posterior* probabilities. Because probabilities *can* be revised as new information becomes available, probability theory is of consequential value in decision making.

Posterior probabilities have value in decision making

The origin of the concept of obtaining posterior probabilities with limited information is credited to the Reverend Thomas Bayes (1702–1761), and the basic formula for conditional probability under dependence,

Origin of posterior probabilities

$$P(A\,|\,B) = \frac{P(AB)}{P(B)} \qquad\qquad (2\text{-}6)$$

is called *Bayes' theorem.*

Bayes, an Englishman, was a Presbyterian minister and a competent mathematician. He sought a way to prove the existence of God by examining the evidence of the world around him. Attempting to show "that the Principle End of the Divine Providence . . . is the Happiness of His Creatures," Bayes used mathematics to study God. Unfortunately, the theological implications of his findings so alarmed the good Reverend Bayes that he refused to permit publication of his work during his lifetime. Nevertheless, his work outlived him, and modern decision theory is often called *Bayesian decision theory* in his honor.

Bayes' theorem

Bayes' theorem offers us a powerful statistical method of evaluating new information and revising our prior estimates (based on limited information only) of the probability that things are in one state or another. If correctly used in managerial decision making, it eliminates the need for gathering masses of data over long periods of time in order to make decisions based on probabilities.

The value of Bayes' theorem in decision making

Calculating Posterior Probabilities

As a first example of revising prior probabilities, assume that we have two types of deformed (biased or weighted) dice in an urn. On half of them, ace (or one dot) comes up 30 percent of the time; $P(\text{ace}) = .3$. On the other half, ace comes up 60 percent of the time; $P(\text{ace}) = .6$. Let us call the former type 1 and the latter type 2. One is drawn, rolled once, and comes up ace. What is the probability that it is a type 1 die? Knowing there is the same number of both types, we might answer that the probability is one-half; but we can do better than this. To answer the question more intelligently, we set up Table 2-6.

Example of revising former probabilities using Bayes' theorem

The sum of the probabilities of the elementary events is 1.0 because there are only two types of dice; the probability of each type is .5. The two types constitute a mutually exclusive and collectively exhaustive list.

Table 2-6

Elementary event	Probability of elementary event	P(ace | elementary event)	P(ace, event)
Type 1	.5	.3	$.3 \times .5 = .15$
Type 2	.5	.6	$.6 \times .5 = \underline{.30}$
	$\overline{1.0}$		$P(\text{ace}) = .45$

The sum of P(ace|elementary event) does *not* equal 1.0. The figures .3 and .6 simply represent the conditional probabilities of getting an ace, given type 1 and type 2, respectively.

The fourth column is the joint probability of ace and type 1 occurring together, $.3 \times .5 = .15$, and the joint probability of ace and type 2 occurring together, $.6 \times .5 = .30$. The sum of these joint probabilities (.45) is the marginal probability of getting an ace. Note that in each case the joint probability was obtained by using the formula

$$P(AB) = P(A|B) \times P(B) \qquad (2\text{-}7)$$

To find the probability that the die we have drawn is type 1, we use the formula for conditional probability under statistical dependence:

$$P(A|B) = \frac{P(AB)}{P(B)} \qquad (2\text{-}6)$$

Converting to our problem, we have

$$P(\text{type 1}|\text{ace}) = \frac{P(\text{type 1, ace})}{P(\text{ace})}$$

or

$$P(\text{type 1}|\text{ace}) = \frac{.15}{.45} = \frac{1}{3}$$

Thus the probability that we have drawn a type 1 die is ⅓.

Let us compute the probability that the die is type 2.

$$P(\text{type 2}|\text{ace}) = \frac{P(\text{type 2, ace})}{P(\text{ace})} = \frac{.30}{.45} = \frac{2}{3}$$

Using new information effectively   What have we accomplished with the one additional piece of information made available to us; what inferences have we been able to draw from one roll of the die? Before we rolled this die, the best we could say was that there is a .5 chance it is a type 1 die and a .5 chance it is a type 2 die. However, after rolling the die and noticing its behavior, we have been able to alter or revise our prior probability estimate; our new posterior estimate is that there is a higher probability (⅔) that the die we have in our hand is a type 2 than a type 1 (only ⅓).

Posterior Probabilities with More Information

We may feel that one roll of the die is not sufficient to indicate its characteristics (whether it is type 1 or type 2). In this case, unlike many situations, obtaining additional information (rolling the die again) requires only a moment of our time. Assume that the same die is rolled a second time and again comes up ace. What is the further revised probability that the die is type 1? See Table 2-7.

Adding more information

Table 2-7

Elementary event	Probability of elementary event	P(ace | elementary event)	P(2 aces | elementary event)	P(2 aces, elementary event)
Type 1	.5	.3	.09	$.09 \times .5 = .045$
Type 2	.5	.6	.36	$.36 \times .5 = .180$
	1.0			$P(\text{2 aces}) = .225$

We have one new column for the table, $P(2\text{ aces} \mid \text{elementary event})$. This gives the *joint* probability of 2 aces on two successive rolls if the die is type 1 and if it is type 2; that is, $P(2\text{ aces} \mid \text{type 1}) = .3 \times .3 = .09$ and $P(2\text{ aces} \mid \text{type 2}) = .6 \times .6 = .36$. The joint probabilities of 2 aces on two successive rolls and the elementary events (type 1 and type 2) are given in the last column; that is, $P(2\text{ aces, type 1})$ equals the probability of type 1 times $P(2\text{ aces} \mid \text{type 1})$, or $.09 \times .5 = .045$, and $P(2\text{ aces} \mid \text{type 2})$ equals the probability of type 2 times $P(2\text{ aces} \mid \text{type 2})$, or $.36 \times .5 = .180$. The sum of these (.225) is the marginal probability of 2 aces on two successive rolls.

We are now ready to compute the probability that the die we have drawn is type 1, given an ace on each of two successive rolls. Using the same general formula as before, we convert to

$$P(\text{type 1} \mid \text{2 aces}) = \frac{P(\text{type 1,2 aces})}{P(\text{2 aces})} = \frac{.045}{.225} = .2$$

Similarly,

$$P(\text{type 2} \mid \text{2 aces}) = \frac{P(\text{type 2,2 aces})}{P(\text{2 aces})} = \frac{.180}{.225} = .8$$

What have we accomplished with two rolls? When we first drew the die, all we knew was that there was a probability of .5 that it was type 1 and a probability of .5 that it was type 2. Stated alternatively, there was a 50-50 chance that it was

Our reaction to new information

either type 1 or type 2. After rolling the die once, we revised these original probabilities to the following:

Probability that it is type 1 = ⅓
Probability that it is type 2 = ⅔

After the second roll, we revised the probabilities again:

Probability that it is type 1 = .2
Probability that it is type 2 = .8

Conclusion with more information

We have thus changed the original probabilities from .5 for each type to .2 for type 1 and .8 for type 2. This means that in view of the new information gained from rolling the die twice, we can be 80 percent certain that the die is type 2. Alternatively, if we were to bet that a die which turns up ace on two successive rolls is of type 2, we would be right 80 percent of the time over a long series of draws and rolls.

Considering the cost of new information

In both the experiments completed, new information was gained free; that is, we were able to roll the die twice, observe its behavior, and draw inferences from that behavior without any monetary cost. Obviously, there are few situations where this is true, and decision makers must not only understand how to utilize new information to revise prior probabilities, but also be able to determine *how much that information is worth* to them before the fact. In many cases, the value of the information obtained may be considerably less than its cost. Methods for determining the value of new information will be developed in Chapter 4.

A Problem with Three Observations

Revising prior probabilities with three observations

As a more practical problem, consider the case of a manufacturer who has an automatic machine which produces ball bearings. If the machine is correctly set up—that is, properly adjusted—it will produce 90 percent acceptable parts. If it is incorrectly set up, it will produce 40 percent acceptable parts. Past experience indicates that 70 percent of the setups are correctly done. After a certain setup, the machine produces 3 acceptable bearings as the first 3 pieces. What is the revised probability that the setup has been correctly done? See Table 2-8.

We are now ready to compute the revised probability that the machine is correctly set up. We convert the general formula $P(A|B) = P(AB)/P(B)$ to

$$P(\text{correct}|3 \text{ good parts}) = \frac{P(\text{correct, 3 good parts})}{P(3 \text{ good parts})} = \frac{.5103}{.5295} = .9637$$

Conclusion after revision

The posterior probability that the machine is correctly set up is .9637, or 96.37 percent. We have thus revised our original probability of a correct setup from 70 to 96.37 percent, based on 3 parts produced.

Table 2-8 Posterior Probabilities with Joint Events

Event	P(event)	P(1 good part | event)	P(3 good parts | event)	P(event, 3 good parts)
Correct	.70	.90	.729	$.729 \times .70 = .5103$
Incorrect	.30	.40	.064	$.064 \times .30 = \underline{.0192}$
	$\overline{1.00}$			P(3 good) = .5295

The table headings are interpreted as follows:
P(event) means the individual probabilities of correct and incorrect; that is, P(correct) = .70 (as given in the problem) and P(incorrect) = $1.00 - P$(correct) = $1.00 - .70 = .30$.

P(1 good part \| event) means the probability of a good part, given that the setup is correct or incorrect. These probabilities are given in the problem.

P(3 good parts \| event) is the probability of getting 3 good parts on 3 successive tries, given the event, that is, given correct or incorrect. The probabilities are computed as follows:
P(3 good parts \| correct) $= .9 \times .9 \times .9 = .729$
P(3 good parts \| incorrect) $= .4 \times .4 \times .4 = .064$

P(event, 3 good parts) is the probability of the joint occurrence of the event (correct or incorrect) and 3 good parts. The probabilities are computed as follows:
P(correct, 3 good parts) $= .729 \times .70 = .5103$
P(incorrect, 3 good parts) $= .064 \times .30 = .0192$

Notice that the last two probabilities conform to the general mathematical formula for joint probabilities under conditions of dependence: $P(AB) = P(A|B) \times P(B)$.

Posterior Probabilities with Inconsistent Outcomes

In each of the problems illustrated to this point, the behavior of the die (or the ball bearings) was consistent; that is, the die came up ace on two successive rolls and the automatic machine produced three acceptable ball bearings as the first three pieces. In most situations, the observer would expect a less consistent distribution of outcomes; for example, in the case of the ball bearings, we might observe the first five units of output and find them to be: acceptable, unacceptable,

Handling new information that is inconsistent

Table 2-9 Posterior Probabilities with Inconsistent Outcomes

Event	P(event)	$P(A$/event)	$P(AUAAA$/event)	P(event, $AUAAA$)
Correct	.70	.90	$.9 \times .1 \times .9 \times .9 \times .9 = .06561$	$.06561 \times .70 = .045927$
Incorrect	.30	.40	$.4 \times .6 \times .4 \times .4 \times .4 = .01536$	$.01536 \times .30 = \underline{.004608}$
	$\overline{1.00}$			$P(AUAAA) = .050535$

$$P(\text{correct setup}/AUAAA) = \frac{P(\text{correct setup}, AUAAA)}{P(AUAAA)}$$
$$= \frac{.045927}{.050535}$$
$$= .9088$$

acceptable, acceptable, acceptable. Calculating our *posterior* probability that the machine is correctly set up in this case is really no more difficult than with a set of perfectly consistent outcomes. Using the notation A = acceptable ball bearing and U = unacceptable ball bearings, we have solved this example in Table 2-9.

Posterior Probabilities with More Than Two Elementary Events
Consider the case of a manufacturing company which, because of the volume required, has four different suppliers for the same component part. Records kept over the past few years yield the following information:

Supplier	Percent of total use supplied	Percent defective (over time)
A	40	20
B	30	10
C	20	30
D	10	40

Revising prior probabilities with multiple elementary events

On a certain morning, the quality control staff examines a newly arrived batch of component parts produced by one of the suppliers. They test the first four components they open and find the last one to be defective. We want to know the likelihood that B supplied this batch. To help us solve this problem, let us set up Table 2-10.

Table 2-10 Posterior Probabilities with Multiple Elementary Events

Event	P(event)	P(good part | event)	P(bad part | event)	P(3 good, 1 bad | event)	P(3 good, 1 bad and event)
A	.4	.8	.2	$(.8^3) \times .2 = .1024$	$.1024 \times .4 = .04096$
B	.3	.9	.1	$(.9^3) \times .1 = .0729$	$.0729 \times .3 = .02187$
C	.2	.7	.3	$(.7^3) \times .3 = .1029$	$.1029 \times .2 = .02058$
D	.1	.6	.4	$(.6^3) \times .4 = .0864$	$.0864 \times .1 = .00864$
					$P(3 \text{ good}, 1 \text{ bad}) = .09205$

From Table 2-10 we can now compute the following probabilities:

Conclusion after revision

$$P(B \mid 3 \text{ good}, 1 \text{ bad}) = \frac{P(B, 3 \text{ good}, 1 \text{ bad})}{P(3 \text{ good}, 1 \text{ bad})} = \frac{.02187}{.09205} = .237$$

The probability that B supplied this batch is about .24.

Glossary

1. **Probability**   The chance that something will happen.
2. **Event**   One or more of the possible outcomes of doing something, or one of the possible outcomes of an experiment.
3. **Experiment**   The activity that produces an event.
4. **Mutually exclusive events**   Events which cannot happen together.
5. **Collectively exhaustive events**   The list of events that represents all of the possible outcomes of an experiment.
6. **Classical probability**   The number of outcomes favorable to the occurrence of an event divided by the total number of possible outcomes.
7. **Relative frequency of occurrence**   The proportion of times that an event occurs in the long run when conditions are stable, or the observed relative frequency of an event in a very large number of trials.
8. **Subjective probability**   Probabilities based on the personal beliefs of the person who makes the probability estimate.
9. **Marginal probability**   The unconditional probability of one event occurring; the probability of a single event.
10. **Statistical independence**   The condition when the occurrence of one event has no effect upon the probability of the occurrence of any other event.
11. **Joint probability**   The probability of two events occurring together or in succession.
12. **Conditional probability**   The probability of one event occurring given that another event has occurred.
13. **Statistical dependence**   The condition when the probability of some event is dependent upon or affected by the occurrence of some other event.
14. **A priori probability**   Probability estimate prior to receiving new information.
15. **Bayes' theorem**   The basic formula for conditional probability under conditions of statistical dependence.
16. **Posterior probability**   A probability that has been revised after new information was obtained.

Review of Equations

Page 26

$$\text{The probability of an event} = \frac{\text{number of outcomes favorable to the occurrence of the event}}{\text{total number of possible outcomes}} \qquad (2\text{-}1)$$

This is the definition of *classical* probability. In the use of this equation, each of the outcomes must be equally likely.

Page 30

$$P(A \text{ or } B) = P(A) + P(B) \qquad (2\text{-}2)$$

This is the addition rule in probability for mutually exclusive events. It refers to the case where we are interested in the probability of *either* A or B happening.

Page 31

$$P(A \text{ or } B) = P(A) + P(B) - P(A \text{ and } B) \tag{2-3}$$

This is the correct equation to use to calculate the probability of one or more of two events (A and B) when these events are *not* mutually exclusive.

Page 33

$$P(AB) = P(A) \times P(B) \tag{2-4}$$

This is the probability of two independent events occurring together or in succession, which is known as a *joint* probability. This formula is used under conditions of statistical independence.

Page 37

$$P(A \mid B) = P(A) \tag{2-5}$$

This is the formula for conditional probability under conditions of statistical independence. Since independent events are those whose probabilities are not affected by the occurrence of any other events, the probability of A given that B has happened (under statistical independence) is simply the probability of A.

Page 40

$$P(A \mid B) = \frac{P(AB)}{P(B)} \tag{2-6}$$

This formula calculates the conditional probability under statistical dependence of the event A given that B has happened.

Page 42

$$P(AB) = P(A \mid B) \times P(B) \tag{2-7}$$

With this formula, we can calculate joint probabilities under conditions of statistical dependence. It is read "the joint probability of events A and B happening together or in succession equals the probability of event A given that B has happened times the probability of event B."

Exercises

2-1. Which of the following situations are examples of the classical approach, the relative frequency approach, and the subjective approach to estimating probabilities?
a. Life expectancy calculations in the insurance industry.
b. Rolling a 6 on one toss of a single die.
c. Projection of genetic traits in biological experiments.
d. The statement, "The Yankees have a 40 percent chance of winning the pennant."
e. Drawing two aces from a deck of cards without replacement.

2-2. The Singleton Manufacturing Company, Inc., manufactures four fastening products: long fine-thread screws, long coarse-thread screws, short fine-thread screws, and short coarse-thread screws. In the warehouse, there are a number of boxes of mixed screws. You pick up one with 100 screws in it. If there are 46 short screws, 74 screws that are either long or fine-thread, and 30 screws that are long but not fine-thread, what is the probability that a screw picked at random from the box will be:
a. A short or a fine-thread screw
b. A long or a coarse-thread screw
c. A short or a coarse-thread screw

2-3. The Borden County Board of Education assembled the following ethnic breakdown of its student population:

Caucasian American	521
Black American	304
Hispanic surname American	79
Oriental American	46
Native American (Indian)	31
Other	19

Compute the probability that a student selected at random for a television appearance will be:
a. A black American
b. A Caucasian American
c. A Hispanic surname American

2-4. Of the repair jobs that Collie's Machine Shop receives, 30 percent are welding jobs and 70 percent are machining jobs. What are the probabilities that:
a. The next three jobs to come in will be welding jobs?
b. Half of the next six jobs to come in will be machining jobs?

2-5. The fire underwriting department for Southeastern Mutual Property Insurance Company is reviewing last year's fire-loss report to determine if an additional claims adjuster will be required next year. The company will hire this person only if the probability of a fire claim in any of its four areas is above .03. Last year's claims data are:

	Mobile	New Orleans	Atlanta	Nashville
Number of fire claims	40	90	120	60
Number of policies in force	2,000	1,800	3,600	6,000

Do you think the company will hire another claims adjuster?

2-6. An investment counselor is considering three independent speculative investments. He estimates that each of these has a 50 percent chance of going "bust" and losing his capital. He will do worse than break even only if all three investments go "bust." What is the probability that he will at least break even?

2-7. A salesperson is analyzing her customers. She compiles these facts: Based on 200 sales calls last month, she made 60 sales; 110 of the calls were made to urban as opposed to suburban customers. If she expects to call on the same customer list this month in roughly the same order as she did last month, what is the probability of any given call being:
a. A no-sale call?
b. An urban call?
c. A suburban-sale call?

2-8. The Mandy Personal Products Company manufactures personal grooming products for men, including a new hair preparation for redheads. Its intention is to distribute the product free to redheaded men, then survey the users' reactions. Research indicates that 40 percent of adults in the general population are male and that 90 percent of the population has a hair color other than red. Mandy feels that it must have at least 1000 distributions for a valid test. How many persons from the population must it sample before finding 1000 redheaded men? You may assume that hair color and sex are unrelated.

2-9. An operator on one machine must visually inspect items and remove the defective ones. Three different items are produced simultaneously by the machine and move together down a conveyor past the operator. The process is so designed that it is very difficult for him to remove three items at once. The machine was running normally last week, and production data for that period are given below. What is the probability that the three items appearing on the conveyor at the same time will *all* be rejects?

	Item A	Item B	Item C
Rejected	20	110	90
Accepted	980	890	910

2-10. Four small vials (types A, B, C, and D) are produced in sets of four (one of each type) by a machine. They fall down a chute in random order to a conveyor, where they are put in order by an operator. They are then automatically packed. What is the probability that they will come down the conveyor in the proper *A, B, C, D* order, allowing the operator to take a short rest?

2-11. One hundred persons have each purchased a lottery ticket. Seventy-five of the 100 are females and 16 have a college degree. Assuming that any one of the 100 persons is equally likely to win the lottery, and that sex and college education are independent, find the probability that the winner is
a. A male
b. A male without a college degree
c. A male with a college degree

2-12. Suppose you are considering the purchase of stock in IJK Corporation. You feel that if the Dow Jones average rises next year, there is an 80 percent probability that IJK stock will go up. You also feel there is a 60 percent chance of the Dow Jones average increasing next year. What is the probability that *both* the Dow Jones average *and* the price of IJK will rise next year?

2-13. Sylvia Thomas is interested in the potential rise in interest rates in the coming year, as it has a bearing on sales of new homes. She feels that there is a 10 percent probability that both an increase in interest rates and an increase in home sales will occur next year and that there is a 20 percent joint probability that interest rates will *not* rise and new-home sales will increase next year. She thinks there is a 60 percent probability that interest rates will rise. If interest rates *do not* rise in the following year, what is the probability that new-home sales will increase?

2-14. The probability that 100 percent of a 100-person work force will report for work on any given morning is .8. If 100 percent of them do report, the probability that some of them will leave early is only .1. However, since they tend to leave when all do not report due to a decreased level of morale, the probability that some of them will leave when less than 100 percent report is .6. Some of those on the shift just left early to go home. What is the probability that 100 percent of the force reported today?

2-15. As a means of increasing worker morale and performance, the management of an assembly shop was considering a plan providing for job enrichments (such as self-supervision, team working, and the individual selection of working hours). Two groups of 100 workers were selected at random. The first group worked under existing conditions; the second was placed in a separate room and was allowed to function under the proposed job enrichment plan. After a year, management compared the performance ratings of all workers, and found that in the group operating under existing conditions, the performance ratings for 30 employees improved, for 60 employees the ratings remained the same, and for 10 employees the ratings dropped. Within the group working under the job enrichment plan, 40 performance ratings improved, 55 remained the same, and 5 dropped. How should management assess the effects of their job enrichment program on worker morale and performance?

2-16. Suppose you are a wildcat oilwell driller and are considering drilling at a certain site. Based upon past experience, you know there is a 50 percent probability that a well drilled in this area will be profitable, there is a 30 percent probability that it will break even, and a 20 percent probability that it will be a dry well and will cause you to lose your drilling investment. Before deciding on whether to drill, you conduct a scientific study to determine the geological structure. The results of a seismic study show either no structure, open structure, or closed structure. Experience with a large number of oil wells drilled in the past indicates that of all profitable wells, 70 percent have closed structure, 20 percent have open structure, and 10 percent have no structure. Of all breakeven wells, 30 percent have closed structure, 30 percent have open structure, and 40 percent have no structure. Of all dry wells, 20 percent have closed structure, 35 percent have open structure, and 45 percent have no structure. The seismic study is made, and the results indicate a closed structure. Based upon your experience in drilling in this area and the results of the seismic study, what are your revised probability estimates of a profitable, a breakeven, or a dry well?

2-17. A personnel man is considering advertising for a stenographer. He knows from past experience that there is a 5 percent probability that the ad will draw 6 applicants, a 10 percent probability that it will draw 5, a 20 percent probability it will draw 4, a 20 percent probability it will draw 3, a 15 percent probability it will draw 2, a 15 percent probability it will draw 1, and a 15 percent probability it will attract no applicants. He feels that if 6 people apply, he has a 90 percent chance of finding an acceptable stenographer. Similarly, his probability of filling the position from 5 applicants is 80 percent, from 4 applicants is 70 percent, from 3 applicants is 60 percent, from 2 applicants is 30 percent, from 1 applicant is 10 percent, and, of course, if nobody applies, 0 percent. What is the probability that he will fill the position after placing the ad?

2-18. A child chosen at random in a community school system comes from a low-income family 30 percent of the time. Children from low-income families in the community graduate from college only 10 percent of the time. Children not from low-income families have a 40 percent chance of graduating from college. As an employer of people from this community, you are reviewing applicants and note that the first one has a college degree. What is the probability that that person comes from a low-income family?

2-19. The likelihood of getting a completely factual financial statement from credit-card applicants in a Southeastern department store chain is .8. If the applicant's application is factual, the likelihood of the applicant being a good credit risk is .9. If an application is not factual, the probability of the applicant being a good credit risk is only .4. A spot check of applications that you, as credit manager, have approved is begun, and you are informed that the first applicant turned out to be a poor credit risk for the chain. How probable is it that the application was not completely factual?

2-20. You are the marketing manager of a firm that manufactures paper products purchased on a repeat basis by householders. You want to evaluate a campaign of giveaways designed to increase sales and brand loyalty. You test the special campaign against the regular advertising program in two widely separated cities which have about the same demographic characteristics and the same use rates of your products. The population of each city contained 1000 regular users. After a 2-month test, these results were revealed: In the regular advertising area, 250 of the users increased their use, 500 decreased their use, and 250 used about the same amount. In the special campaign area, 350 increased their use, 250 decreased their use, and 400 used about the same. How would you assess the effect of the campaign on product usage and brand loyalty?

2-21. Mel Hanker, a real estate broker, runs an ad describing a piece of property he is handling. From past experience he has the following data about telephone responses to newspaper ads: number of calls; probability of this many calls; probability of a sale, given this many calls.

6 or more calls	.05	.90
5 calls	.10	.75
4 calls	.10	.60
3 calls	.25	.40
2 calls	.15	.20
1 call	.15	.05
No calls	.20	.00

What are the chances that he will sell the property from this ad?

2-22. Ellen Beyer, a real estate broker, is concerned with the behavior of interest rates for the coming year and the effect of these rates on the sale of new homes by her firm. She feels there is a 10 percent probability that both interest rates and her sales will rise next year. She estimates odds of 4 to 1 that sales will increase and rates stay the same. When asked about the chances of interest rates rising, she said, "I think there's about a .3 chance of that happening." If interest rates do not rise next year, what are the chances that Ellen's sales will increase?

Bibliography

Campbell, S. K.: *Flaws and Fallacies in Statistical Thinking* (Englewood Cliffs, N.J.: Prentice-Hall, Inc., 1974).

Freund, J. E.: *Introduction to Probability* (Belmont, Calif.: Dickenson Publishing Company, Inc., 1973).

Goldberg, S.: *Probability—An Introduction* (Englewood Cliffs, N.J.: Prentice-Hall, Inc., 1960).

Hodges, J. L., and **E. L. Lehmann:** *Elements of Finite Probability* (San Francisco: Holden-Day, Inc., Publisher, 1965).

Hoel, P.: *Introduction to Mathematical Statistics,* 4th ed. (New York: John Wiley & Sons, Inc., 1971).

Huff, D.: *How to Lie with Statistics* (New York: W. W. Norton & Company, Inc., 1954).

Levin, R. I.: *Statistics for Management* (Englewood Cliffs, N.J.: Prentice-Hall, Inc., 1978).

Mosteller, F., R. E. K. Rourke, and **G. B. Thomas:** *Probability with Statistical Applications,* 2d ed. (Reading, Mass.: Addison-Wesley Publishing Company, Inc., 1970).

Probability II: distributions

3

1. Introduction to Probability Distributions

Illustrating probability distributions with a coin-toss experiment

The easiest way to introduce probability distributions is to go back for a moment to the idea of a fair coin, which we introduced in Chapter 2. Suppose we toss the coin twice. Table 3-1 illustrates the possible outcomes from this two-toss experiment.

Table 3-1 Possible Outcomes from Two Tosses of a Fair Coin

First toss	Second toss	Number of tails on two tosses	Probability of the four possible outcomes
T	T	2	$.5 \times .5 = .25$
T	H	1	$.5 \times .5 = .25$
H	H	0	$.5 \times .5 = .25$
H	T	1	$.5 \times .5 = \underline{.25}$
			1.00

Presenting the outcome of the coin-toss experiment in an organized form

Now suppose that we were interested in presenting in an organized form the number of *tails* that could possibly result when we toss the coin twice. We could begin by noting in Table 3-1 any outcome which did *not* contain a tail. The only outcome in Table 3-1 which does not contain a tail is the third one: *H, H*. Then we note those outcomes which contain only *one* tail (the second and fourth outcomes in Table 3-1: *T, H,* and *H, T*). Finally we would note any outcome which contained *two* tails. The first outcome in Table 3-1—*T, T*—fits this requirement. Then we would rearrange the outcomes first presented in Table 3-1 to emphasize the number of tails contained in each outcome. This we have done in Table 3-2. We must be careful to remember that Table 3-2 is not the *actual* outcome of tossing a fair coin twice; rather, it is the way in which we would expect our two-

Table 3-2 Possible Number of Tails from Two Tosses of a Fair Coin

Number of tails, T	Tosses	Probability of this outcome, $P(T)$
0	(H,H)	.25
1	$(T,H) + (H,T)$	.50
2	(T, T)	.25

toss experiment to turn out over time. The right-hand column in Table 3-2 is called a *probability distribution* because it lists the outcomes of an experiment and then gives the probabilities we would expect to see associated with each outcome if the experiment were repeated a large number of times. To show a probability distribution in a more formal tabular form, we have slightly rearranged the information in Table 3-2 and retitled it. The probability distribution of the possible number of tails from two tosses of a fair coin is illustrated in Table 3-3. It is useful and quite usual for probability distributions to be expressed graphically as well as in tabular form. If we graph the number of tails we might observe in two tosses of our coin against the probability that this number would happen, we get the graphic presentation of a probability distribution shown in Figure 3-1.

A probability distribution

Graphic and tabular presentation of probability distributions

Table 3-3 Probability Distribution of Possible Number of Tails from Two Tosses of a Fair Coin

Number of tails, T	Probability of this outcome, $P(T)$
0	.25
1	.50
2	.25

Suppose we look at one more example of probability distributions. A financial officer of a company is considering the possible interest rates his company can expect to pay on bonds it intends to issue next week. He feels that interest rates can take on only four possible values. If the financial manager's subjective assessment is like this,

Probability distribution of interest rates

Interest rate	Probability this will happen
$7\frac{1}{2}\%$	.1
$7\frac{5}{8}\%$	.3
$7\frac{3}{4}\%$	.4
$7\frac{7}{8}\%$	.2

then the graph of the probability distribution of his expectations about interest rates the company may likely pay will resemble the one in Figure 3-2.

Before we consider other aspects of probability distributions, we should point out again that a probability distribution is a listing of the probabilities associated with all the possible outcomes that *could* result if the experiment were done. We must also point out that probability distributions can be based on theoretical con-

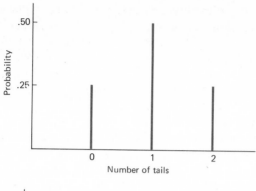

FIGURE 3-1 Probability distribution of possible number of tails from two tosses of a fair coin.

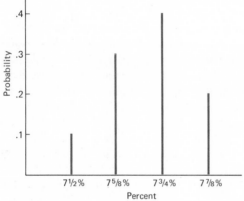

FIGURE 3-2 Probability distribution of interest rates on bonds.

siderations (the toss of a coin) or on subjective assessments of the likelihood of certain outcomes (the financial manager's personal notions about bond interest rates). Probability distributions can also be based on experience; insurance company actuaries determine premiums for life insurance policies by using experience with death rates to establish the probabilities of death among different age groups.

Different bases for probability distributions

2. Types of Probability Distributions

Discrete probability distributions

We classify probability distributions as either *discrete* or *continuous*. A *discrete* probability is allowed to take on only a limited number of values; an example of this would be the financial manager's assessment of possible interest rates on the bond issue next week (7½, 7⅝, 7¾, and 7⅞ percent). In the same sense, the probability that you were born in a given month is also discrete (there are only 12 possible values).

Continuous probability distributions

In a *continuous* probability distribution, the variable under consideration is permitted to take on *any* value within a given range. If, for example, we were examining the concentration of fly ash in smokestacks of industrial plants and we measured this concentration by using parts of fly ash per million parts of air, we would expect quite a continuous range of ppm (parts per million). In plants which had installed precipitators, the value of ppm would be quite small; in plants with no smoke-abatement equipment, the value would be very high. It would be quite normal for the variable ppm to take on an enormous number of values; we would call the distribution of this variable (ppm) a continuous distribution. Other examples of continuously distributed variables would be the dollar amounts in individual accounts receivable held by a company, the absenteeism rates in the 14 plants of a manufacturing company, and the earnings of college graduates 10 years after graduation. Continuous distributions are just convenient ways of representing discrete distributions that have many possible outcomes, all of which are very close to each other.

Continuous distributions are convenient

3. Random Variables

A random variable is a variable that takes on different values as a result of the outcomes of a random experiment. A random variable can be either discrete or continuous. If a random variable is allowed to take on only a limited number of values, it is a *discrete random variable*. If, on the other hand, it is allowed to take on any value within a given range, it is known as a *continuous random variable*.

Discrete and continuous random variables

You can think of a random variable as a value or magnitude that changes from occurrence to occurrence in no predictable sequence. A dairy, for example, has no way of knowing exactly what tomorrow's sales will be. So tomorrow's sales of milk are a random variable. The values of a random variable are the numerical values corresponding to each possible outcome of the random experiment. In the case of the dairy, suppose we know that past daily sales records indicate that the values of the random variable range from sales of 200 to 210 cases daily. In this situation the random variable is a discrete random variable.

Table 3-4 illustrates the number of times each sales level has been reached in the last 100 selling days. To the extent that we believe that the experience of the past 100 days has been typical, we can use this historical record to assign

Assigning probability values to each possible outcome

Table 3-4 Cases Sold during 100 Days

Quantity sold	No. days this quantity sold
200	2
201	3
202	4
203	7
204	9
205	13
206	15
207	21
208	16
209	9
210	1
	100

Normalizing

a probability to each possible level of sales and thereby find a probability distribution. We have done this in Table 3-5 by normalizing the distribution from Table 3-4. *Normalizing* simply means that we took the number of days in the right-hand column of Table 3-4 and divided each value by 100, the number of days for which the record has been kept.

Table 3-5 Probability Distribution of Daily Sales of Milk

Value of random variable, cases	Probability that random variable will take on the particular value
200	.02
201	.03
202	.04
203	.07
204	.09
205	.13
206	.15
207	.21
208	.16
209	.09
210	.01
	1.00

Probability distribution provides information on long-run occurrence

The probability distribution for the random variable "daily sales of milk" is illustrated graphically in Figure 3-3. Notice there that the probability distribution for a random variable provides a probability for each possible value and that these probabilities *must sum to 1.* Table 3-5 shows that both of these requirements have been met. Remember also that Table 3-5 and Figure 3-3 give us information about the long-run occurrence of daily sales of milk we would expect to see if this experiment were repeated.

The Expected Value of a Random Variable

Expected value is a fundamental concept in the study of probability distributions. In the last quarter century, this idea has been put to wide use by managers who have to make decisions under conditions of uncertainty.

Calculating the expected value of a discrete random variable

To calculate the *expected value of a discrete random variable,* we multiply each value that the random variable can take on by the probability of occurrence of that value and then sum these products. We have done this in Table 3-6. The total in Table 3-6 tells us that the expected value of the discrete random variable "daily sales of milk" is 205.89 cases. What does this really mean? It means that over a long period of time, 205.89 is the weighted average daily sales in cases. It does *not* imply that tomorrow's sales of milk will be 205.89 cases.

Meaning of expected value

Expected value as a weighted average of outcomes

The dairy management would find it useful to base its decisions on the expected value of daily sales of milk because the expected value is a *weighted average of the outcomes the dairy expects in the future.* Expected value weights each

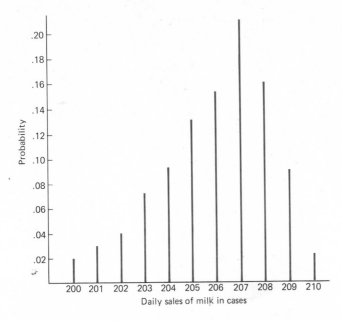

FIGURE 3-3 Probability distribution for the discrete random variable "daily sales of milk."

possible outcome by the probability associated with its occurrence. In this manner, more common occurrences are given more weight than less common ones. As conditions change over time, the dairy management would recompute the expected value of daily sales and then use this new figure as a basis for its decision making. And if the management of our dairy, for example, found through analyzing past sales data that the sales pattern differed for each specific day of the week, their response would be (1) to treat "Monday's sales" as one random variable, "Tues-

Revising the expected value as conditions change

Table 3-6 Finding the Expected Value

(1) Value of random variable, cases	(2) Probability that random variable will take on the particular value	(3) (1) × (2)
200	.02	4.00
201	.03	6.03
202	.04	8.08
203	.07	14.21
204	.09	18.36
205	.13	26.65
206	.15	30.90
207	.21	43.47
208	.16	33.28
209	.09	18.81
210	.01	2.10
	1.00	205.89

day's sales'' as another random variable, and so forth, and (2) to derive an expected value for milk sales for *each* day of the week. The availability of data
would, of course, determine the extent to which they could employ this more
detailed form of analysis.

In our dairy example, management used past sales records as the basis for
calculating the expected value of daily sales of milk. The expected value can also
be derived from management's own subjective assessments of the probability that

the random variable will take on certain values. In that case, the expected value
represents solely the management's personal convictions about the milk market.

In this section, we have worked with probability distributions in tabular form
(Tables 3-3 and 3-5) and in graphic form (Figures 3-1, 3-2, and 3-3). In a number

of situations, however, it will be much more convenient, in terms of the computations that must be done, to represent the probability distribution of a random
variable in *algebraic* form. If we do this, we can do probability calculations by
substituting numerical values directly into an algebraic equation. In the sections
which follow, we shall illustrate situations where this procedure is appropriate as
well as methods for accomplishing it.

4. The Binomial Distribution

One very widely utilized probability distribution of a discrete random variable is
the binomial distribution. This distribution describes many processes of considerable interest to managers. The binomial distribution describes discrete (not continuous) data resulting from an experiment called a *Bernoulli process*. The tossing
of a fair coin a fixed number of times is a Bernoulli process, and the outcomes
of such tosses can be represented by a binomial probability distribution. The

success or failure of college graduates on a job interview aptitude test might also
be described by a Bernoulli process. Conversely, the distribution of the dollar
amounts in a large number of accounts receivable held by one company would
be better measured on a continuous scale of dollars and therefore would not
qualify as a binomial distribution.

Use of the Bernoulli Process

We can use the outcomes of a fixed number of tosses of a fair coin as a good
example of a Bernoulli process. We can describe this process as follows:

1. Each trial (toss) has only *two* possible outcomes: heads or tails, yes or no,
success or failure.

2. The probability of a success on any trial (toss in this case) remains *fixed* over
time. In the case of our fair coin, the probability of heads remains .5 for every toss
no matter how many times the coin is tossed.

3. The trials are *statistically independent;* this means that the outcome of one
toss in this case has no effect on the outcome of any other toss.

Each Bernoulli process has its own *characteristic probability*. Look at a situation where, historically, four-tenths of all persons recruited by the U.S. Army
passed the physical examination. We would say that the characteristic probability
here was .4. In this situation we would be warranted in describing our test results
as Bernoulli only if we felt certain that the proportion of those passing the test
(.4) remained constant over time. The other characteristics of the Bernoulli process
would also have to be met. Specifically, each examination would have to have
only two outcomes (pass or fail) and the results of all examinations would have
to be statistically independent; that is, the outcome of one examination could not
affect the outcome of any other examination.

Formal Symbols for Bernoulli Processes

A bit earlier we noted that it was convenient in many cases to represent the
probability distribution of a random variable in algebraic form. In the case of a
Bernoulli process, the symbol p represents the probability of a success (.4 in the
example of our physical examination). The symbol q (where $q = 1 - p$) is used
to represent the probability of a failure (in our physical examination example,
q would be $1 - .4$, or .6). We use the symbol r to represent a certain number
of successes. (If we wanted to know, for example, what the chances were that
we would get 11 recruits passing the examination, we would use r to represent 11.)
Finally, we use the symbol n to represent the total number of trials. (If, for example,
we were examining 14 recruits, n would equal 14.) In each of the situations we
shall be discussing, n (the number of trials) is fixed before the experiment is begun.

Examples of Bernoulli Processes

Let us start with a very simple example involving the fair coin again. Suppose
we wanted to calculate our chances of getting exactly 2 heads (in any order) on
3 tosses of a fair coin. Using the symbols we have just defined, we would express
this situation like this:

p = characteristic probability or probability of success = .5
$q = 1 - p$ = the probability of failure = .5
r = the number of successes desired = 2
n = the number of trials to be undertaken = 3

It is easy to solve this problem by using the *binomial formula*:

$$\text{Probability of } r \text{ successes in } n \text{ trials} = \frac{n!}{r!(n-r)!} p^r q^{n-r} \qquad (3\text{-}1)$$

This formula probably looks quite complicated, but in fact it can be used quite
easily. First let's explain the symbol !, which means *factorial*. As an example, 3!
means $3 \times 2 \times 1$, or 6. And 5! means $5 \times 4 \times 3 \times 2 \times 1$ or 120. 0! has been

defined as 1. Using the binomial formula to solve our coin-toss problem, we then get:

$$\text{Probability of 2 successes in 3 trials} = \frac{3!}{2!(3-2)!}(.5^2)(.5^1)$$

$$= \frac{3 \times 2 \times 1}{(2 \times 1)(1 \times 1)}(.5^2)(.5^1)$$

$$= \frac{6}{2}(.25)(.5)$$

$$= .375$$

We find, therefore, that the chances of getting 2 heads on 3 tosses of a fair coin are .375.

Water pollution example of a Bernoulli process   Suppose we do one more example using the binomial formula. Some field representatives of the Environmental Protection Agency are doing spot checks of water pollution in streams. Historically, 8 out of 10 such tests produce favorable results, that is, no pollution. The field group is going to perform 6 tests and wants to know the chances of getting exactly 3 favorable results from this group of tests. Let's first define our symbols:

$p = .8$
$q = .2$
$r = 3$
$n = 6$

Now we can use the binomial formula to calculate the desired probability:

$$\text{Probability of } r \text{ successes in } n \text{ trials} = \frac{n!}{r!(n-r)!}p^r q^{n-r} \tag{3-1}$$

$$\text{Probability of 3 favorable tests out of 6} = \frac{6 \times 5 \times 4 \times 3 \times 2 \times 1}{(3 \times 2 \times 1)(3 \times 2 \times 1)}(.8^3)(.2^3)$$

$$= \frac{720}{6 \times 6}(.512)(.008)$$

$$= (20)(.512)(.008)$$

$$= .08192$$

Thus we see that there is less than 1 chance in 10 of getting this particular outcome.

Illustrating the Binomial Distribution Graphically
Up to now, we have dealt with the binomial distribution only by using the binomial formula. The binomial distribution, like any other distribution, can be expressed graphically as well as algebraically.

To illustrate the binomial distribution graphically, let's look at a situation where 5 employees are required to operate a chemical process; the process cannot be started until all 5 work stations are manned. Employee records indicate there is a .4 chance of any one employee being late, and we know that they all come to work independently of each other. Management is interested in knowing the probabilities of 0, 1, 2, 3, 4, or 5 employees being late, so that a decision concerning the number of backup personnel can be made. If we want to draw a probability distribution illustrating this situation, we would use the binomial formula where:

$p = .4$
$q = .6$
$n = 5$ in defining n in this case, we are interested in the number of employees; the fact that there is a chance that none of them will be late does not alter our choice of $n = 5$

We would make a separate calculation for each r from 0 through 5.

Probability of r late arrivals out of n employees $= \dfrac{n!}{r!(n-r)!} p^r q^{n-r}$ (3-1)

Our calculations for r from 0 to 5 in order are then:

$$P(0) = \frac{5!}{0!(5-0)!}(.4^0)(.6^5)$$

$$= \frac{5 \times 4 \times 3 \times 2 \times 1}{(1)(5 \times 4 \times 3 \times 2 \times 1)}(1)(.6^5)$$

$$= \frac{120}{120}(1)(.07776)$$

$$= (1)(1)(.07776)$$

$$= .07776$$

$$P(1) = \frac{5!}{1!(5-1)!}(.4^1)(.6^4)$$

$$= \frac{5 \times 4 \times 3 \times 2 \times 1}{(1)(4 \times 3 \times 2 \times 1)}(.4)(.6^4)$$

$$= \frac{120}{24}(.4)(.1296)$$

$$= .2592$$

$$P(2) = \frac{5!}{2!(5-2)!}(.4^2)(.6^3)$$

$$= \frac{5 \times 4 \times 3 \times 2 \times 1}{(2 \times 1)(3 \times 2 \times 1)}(.4^2)(.6^3)$$

$$P(2) = \frac{120}{12}(.16)(.216)$$

$$= (10)(.03456)$$

$$= .3456$$

$$P(3) = \frac{5!}{3!(5-3)!}(.4^3)(.6^2)$$

$$= \frac{5 \times 4 \times 3 \times 2 \times 1}{(3 \times 2 \times 1)(2 \times 1)}(.4^3)(.6^2)$$

$$= \frac{120}{12}(.064)(.36)$$

$$= (10)(.064)(.36)$$

$$= .2304$$

$$P(4) = \frac{5!}{4!(5-4)!}(.4^4)(.6^1)$$

$$= \frac{5 \times 4 \times 3 \times 2 \times 1}{(4 \times 3 \times 2 \times 1)(1)}(.4^4)(.6^1)$$

$$= \frac{120}{24}(.0256)(.6)$$

$$= (5)(.0256)(.6)$$

$$= .0768$$

$$P(5) = \frac{5!}{5!(5-5)!}(.4^5)(.6^0)$$

$$= \frac{5 \times 4 \times 3 \times 2 \times 1}{(5 \times 4 \times 3 \times 2 \times 1)(1)}(.4^5)(.6^0)$$

$$= \frac{120}{120}(.4^5)(.6^0)$$

$$= (1)(.01024)(1)$$

$$= .01024$$

Graphing binomial probabilities   Now, if we graph the results of these six different calculations, this binomial distribution would appear as shown in Figure 3-4.

Using the Binomial Tables

From the previous example, it is obvious that calculating probabilities using the binomial formula is tedious. Fortunately there are tables available which greatly

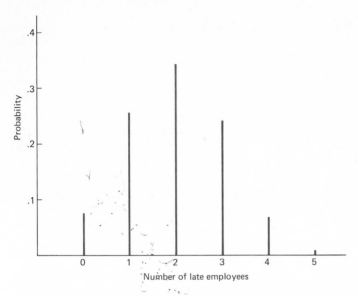

FIGURE 3-4 Binomial probability distribution of the number of late employees.

simplify this work. Appendix Table 2 enables us to determine binomial proba- bilities quickly. Let us illustrate the use of the binomial tables. A large bank hires 15 M.B.A.'s each year and assigns them to the various divisions. After a year's experience, the chances that any one M.B.A. will be performing unsatisfactorily have historically been .3. In this year's group, what are the chances that 8 or more will be performing unsatisfactorily after a year? We can begin to answer this ques- tion by expressing the elements in this problem using the binomial formula symbols:

$p = .3$ probability that any one M.B.A. will perform unsatisfactorily
$q = .7$ $(1 - p)$
$r = 8$ number of unsatisfactory performers in question
$n = 15$ number of persons in the group

Then, since this situation involves 15 trials, we look in Appendix Table 2 for the $n = 15$ table. Since the probability of unsatisfactory performance for any one person is .3, we look through the $n = 15$ table until we find the column where $p = .30$ (this is denoted as 30). We move down that column to the $r = 8$ row where we find the value 0500, which can be interpreted as representing a probabil- ity of .05; this represents the probability of 8 or more unsatisfactory performances.

If our problem had asked us for the probability of *more than 8* unsatisfactory performances in this group, we would simply have looked up the probability of *9 or more,* in this case .0152. If the problem had asked for the probability of *exactly 8* unsatisfactory performances, we would have subtracted the probability of 9 or more (.0152) from the probability of 8 or more (.05); the answer, .0348, would represent the probability of exactly 8 unsatisfactory performances. And if

the problem had asked for the probability of fewer than 8 unsatisfactory performances, we would have subtracted the probability of 8 or more from 1.0 for
an answer of .95.

Care in Using the Bernoulli Process

When we are using the binomial probability distribution, we must be certain that
the three conditions for its use first introduced on page 66 are met. If there is any
chance of more than two outcomes, condition 1 is not satisfied. Condition 2 requires that the probability of the outcome of any trial remain fixed over time.
In many managerial decisions, this is not really the case. It might be usual to
expect that the outcome of a series of trials would have *some* influence on the
characteristic probability over time. Even the most carefully maintained machine
undergoes some very slight wear each time a part is produced on it. Condition 3
requires that the trials of a Bernoulli process be statistically independent. This
condition is also difficult to satisfy in many managerial situations. For example, if
you have been making loans in a bank and you have just turned down the last
10 applicants, it may be difficult to evaluate the creditworthiness of the eleventh
applicant with complete objectivity; in this case, the trials might not be statistically
independent.

The Bernoulli Process with Revision of Prior Probability

Revising prior
probabilities in a
situation described
by a Bernoulli
process

In Chapter 2, we introduced methods for revising prior probabilities in light of new
information. These methods are equally useful in situations described by a Bernoulli process when new information becomes available to the decision maker.
Consider this example. A construction company purchases plywood sheets in
batches of 200 for use in home building. These sheets come in two grades (two
quality levels); grade A sheets are guaranteed to be not more than .5 percent
defective (1 defective sheet in 200); the distribution of defectives in past grade B
batches has been:

Percent defective	P(this outcome)
.5	.20
1.0	.30
10.0	.50

The defectives are repaired by the carpenters before being installed; the labor
cost of each repair is $1. Grade A sheets cost $8 more per batch of 200 than
grade B sheets because of the guaranteed higher quality. The repair cost of using
both grades is shown in Table 3-7.

It would certainly seem from the cost figures in Table 3-7 that using grade A
material is the better alternative and that such continued action would save
$10.80 − $9 = $1.80 per batch. *But,* past data show that grade B batches have

Table 3-7 Cost of Two Grades of Material

Grade A:	.005 defective × 200 pieces × $1		= $1	
	Extra cost per batch for grade A		= 8	
	Total cost per batch of grade A sheets		= $9	

Grade B:	Percent defective	No. of sheets defective	Repair cost	P(this cost)
	.5	1	$1	.2
	1.0	2	$2	.3
	10.0	20	$20	.5

Cost calculations

Expected repair cost per batch of grade B sheets:

$$\$1 \times .2 + \$2 \times .3 + \$20 \times .5 = \$10.80$$

Total cost of using grade B
sheets per batch = $10.80

sometimes been of as high quality as grade A batches; in fact, this has been true 20 percent of the time. Suppose we could sample, for nominal cost, the B batches prior to use; if we felt we had strong evidence that we were dealing with one of the better B batches, then we could use it. On the other hand, if our sampling indicated strongly that we were dealing with one of the poorer B batches (10 percent defective, for example), we could put this batch to some other use and sample another batch. Let us assume that the maximum sample we can take is 50 sheets.

Using this procedure, we sample the next batch of grade B material and find 1 bad sheet in the first 50. We now want to find the following probabilities:

P(.5% defective batch | 1 defective in 50)
P(1.0% defective batch | 1 defective in 50)
P(10.0% defective batch | 1 defective in 50)

Conditional probabilities

At this point, we shall have to employ our knowledge of Bernoulli processes and the binomial probability formula to calculate the probabilities required for the solution to this problem. The three conditional probabilities we require can be stated as follows:

P(1 defective in 50 | a batch which is .5% defective)
P(1 defective in 50 | a batch which is 1.0% defective)
P(1 defective in 50 | a batch which is 10.0% defective)

and the correct values for each of these can be determined from these three binomial probability formulas:

$$\frac{50!}{1!(50-1)!}(.005^1)(.995^{49}) = .1970$$

Correct binomial probabilities

$$\frac{50!}{1!(50-1)!}(.01^1)(.99^{49}) = .3056$$

$$\frac{50!}{1!(50-1)!}(.1^1)(.9^{49}) = .0286$$

Doing the necessary arithmetic with such large values can be cumbersome, so we have used the binomial tables in Appendix Table 2 instead of attempting to do the calculations by hand. We are now in position to compute the joint probabilities as follows:

Joint probabilities

$P(1 \text{ defective in } 50, \text{ and a } .5\% \text{ defective batch}) = .1970 \times .2 = .03940$
$P(1 \text{ defective in } 50, \text{ and a } 1.0\% \text{ defective batch}) = .3056 \times .3 = .09168$
$P(1 \text{ defective in } 50, \text{ and a } 10.0\% \text{ defective batch}) = .0286 \times .5 = \underline{.01430}$
$\qquad\qquad\qquad P(1 \text{ defective in } 50) \qquad\qquad = .14538$

And with this information, we can find our desired probabilities:

$$P(.5\% \text{ defective batch} \mid 1 \text{ defective in } 50) = \frac{.03940}{.14538} = .271$$

$$P(1.0\% \text{ defective batch} \mid 1 \text{ defective in } 50) = \frac{.09168}{.14538} = .631$$

$$P(10.0\% \text{ defective batch} \mid 1 \text{ defective in } 50) = \frac{.01430}{.14538} = .098$$

Conclusion

If we accept this grade B batch, our expected repair cost is $1 \times .271 + \$2 \times .631 + \$20 \times .098 = \$3.49$; thus we should accept this batch as being *less* costly than the price of grade A material, $9.

5. The Poisson Distribution

Poisson distribution describes a number of situations of interest to management

There are many discrete probability distributions, but we will focus on only two of them: the *binomial distribution,* which we have just concluded, and the *Poisson distribution,* which is the subject of this section. The Poisson distribution appears frequently in the literature of management science and finds a large number of managerial applications. It is used to describe a number of managerial situations including the demand (arrivals) of patients at a health clinic, the distribution of telephone calls going through a central switching system, the arrival of vehicles at a toll booth, the number of accidents at an intersection, and the number of looms in a textile mill waiting for service. All these examples have a common characteristic: they can all be described by a discrete random variable that takes on nonnegative integer (whole number) values (0, 1, 2, 3, 4, 5, and so on). The number of cars arriving at a toll booth on the Petersburg Turnpike during some 10-minute period will be 0, 1, 2, 3, 4, 5, and so on; the number of patients who arrive at a physician's office in a given interval of time will also be 0, 1, 2, 3, 4, 5, and so on.

Characteristics of Processes That
Produce a Poisson Probability Distribution

Suppose we use the number of patients arriving at a physician's office during the busiest part of the day as an illustration of Poisson probability distribution characteristics:

1. The average arrivals of patients per 15-minute interval can be estimated from past office data.

2. If we divide the 15-minute interval into smaller intervals of, say, 1 second each, we will see that these statements are true:
   a. The probability that exactly one patient will arrive at the office per second is a very small number and is constant for every 1-second interval.
   b. The probability that two or more patients will arrive within a 1-second interval is so small that we can safely assign it a 0 probability.
   c. The number of patients who arrive in a 1-second interval is independent of where that 1-second interval is within the larger 15-minute interval.
   d. The number of patients who arrive in any 1-second interval is not dependent on the number of arrivals in any other 1-second interval.

Characteristics of processes that produce Poisson probability distributions

It is acceptable to generalize from these conditions and to apply them to other processes of interest to management. If these processes meet the same conditions, then it is possible to use a Poisson probability distribution to describe them.

Calculating Probabilities with the Poisson Distribution

The Poisson distribution is useful in analyzing certain processes that can be described by a discrete random variable. It is usual for the letter X to represent the discrete random variable. X can take on integer values (0, 1, 2, 3, 4, 5, and so on); when we refer to *one* of those specific values that X can take, we use a lowercase *x*. The probability of exactly *x* occurrences in a Poisson distribution is calculated using this formula:

Defining X and x in Poisson probability distributions

$$P(x) = \frac{\lambda^x e^{-\lambda}}{x!}$$

(3-2) **The Poisson formula**

It will perhaps be useful to examine each part of this formula:

λ (the Greek letter lambda) = the average (mean) of the distribution
x = the specific value of the discrete random variable in which we are interested
e = 2.718, the base of natural logarithms

Poisson distribution symbols

An example will help us understand the use of this formula. We are considering an emergency room of a small rural hospital where the past records indicate an average of 5 arrivals daily. The demand for emergency room service at this hospital is distributed according to a Poisson distribution. The hospital administrator wants to calculate the probability of exactly 0, 1, 2, 3, 4, and 5 arrivals. This calculation is simplified by the use of Appendix Table 5, which frees us from having to calculate e's to negative powers. The appropriate calculations for the probabilities of 0, 1, 2, 3, 4, and 5 requests for emergency room service are:

Calculation of probability of 0 through 5 arrivals

$$P(0) = \frac{(5^0)(e^{-5})}{0!}$$

$$= \frac{(1)(.00674)}{1}$$

$$= .00674$$

$$P(1) = \frac{(5^1)(e^{-5})}{1!}$$

$$= \frac{(5)(.00674)}{1}$$

$$= .03370$$

$$P(2) = \frac{(5^2)(e^{-5})}{2!}$$

$$= \frac{(25)(.00674)}{2 \times 1}$$

$$= .08425$$

$$P(3) = \frac{(5^3)(e^{-5})}{3!}$$

$$= \frac{(125)(.00674)}{3 \times 2 \times 1}$$

$$= .14042$$

$$P(4) = \frac{(5^4)(e^{-5})}{4!}$$

$$= \frac{(625)(.00674)}{4 \times 3 \times 2 \times 1}$$

$$= .17552$$

$$P(5) = \frac{(5^5)(e^{-5})}{5!}$$

$$= \frac{(3125)(.00674)}{5 \times 4 \times 3 \times 2 \times 1}$$

$$= .17552$$

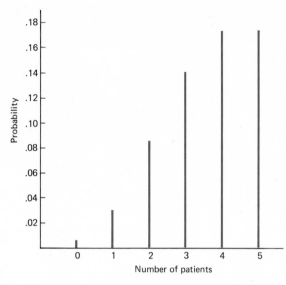

FIGURE 3-5   Poisson probability distribution of demand for emergency room service (0 through 5 calls).

We can use the results of these calculations to answer some questions of interest to Rebecca Rubin, the hospital administrator, as she attempts to provide adequate emergency room staff. If she wanted to know the probability of more than 3 calls for emergency room service on a given day, she could find this answer by adding together the probabilities for 0, 1, 2, and 3 calls and subtracting the result from 1: **Probability of 0, 1, 2, or 3 calls**

$$P(0) = .00674 \qquad P(\text{more than } 3) = 1 - .26511$$
$$P(1) = .03370 \qquad\qquad\qquad = .73489$$
$$P(2) = .08425$$
$$\underline{P(3) = .14042}$$
$$.26511$$

Thus Rebecca sees that she will have to be prepared to have more than 3 calls per day slightly less than three-quarters of the time.

In Figure 3-5, we have illustrated graphically the Poisson probability distribution of demand for emergency room services.

The distribution illustrated in Figure 3-5 is only for 0 through 5 calls for emergency room service; it would, of course, be possible to produce the required probability values (and thus the graphic distribution) for *any* number of calls with additional calculation.

6. The Normal Distribution: A Distribution of a Continuous Random Variable

Up to this point in this chapter we have been concerned with discrete probability distributions. Now we shall turn to cases in which the random variable can take on *any* value within a given range and the probability distribution is continuous.

An important continuous probability distribution is the *normal* distribution. Several mathematicians were instrumental in its development, among them the eighteenth-century mathematician-astronomer Karl Gauss. In honor of his work, the normal probability distribution is often referred to as the *Gaussian* distribution. The normal distribution occupies an important place in management science for two reasons. First, it has properties that make it applicable to a number of managerial situations in which decision makers have to make inferences by drawing samples. Second, the normal distribution comes quite close to fitting the actual observed distribution of many phenomena, including outputs from physical processes and human characteristics (height, weight, intelligence) as well as many other measures of interest to management in the social and natural sciences.

Importance of the normal distribution to management

Characteristics of the Normal Probability Distribution

Characteristics of the normal distribution

Look now at Figure 3-6, a normal distribution. This diagram indicates several important characteristics of a normal probability distribution:

1. The curve has a single peak.

2. It is bell-shaped.

3. The mean (average) lies at the center of the distribution; the distribution is symmetrical around a vertical line erected at the mean.

4. The two tails of the normal probability distribution extend indefinitely and never touch the horizontal axis (it is impossible to illustrate this graphically).

A whole family of normal curves

Of course, most real world distributions don't extend forever in both directions; but for many distributions the normal distribution is a convenient approximation. As a matter of fact, there is not a single normal curve but rather a whole family of normal curves. Figure 3-7 shows three normal probability distributions each of which has the same average (mean); each of these three has different "spreads"—that is, the values in curve *A* tend to cluster or group together very

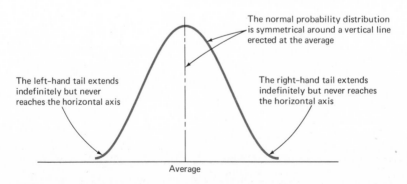

The normal probability distribution is symmetrical around a vertical line erected at the average

The left-hand tail extends indefinitely but never reaches the horizontal axis

The right-hand tail extends indefinitely but never reaches the horizontal axis

Average

FIGURE 3-6 The normal probability distribution

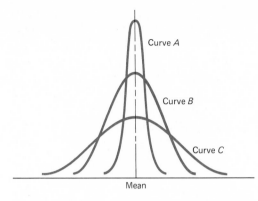

FIGURE 3-7 Three examples of normal probability distributions with the same mean but different spreads.

near the mean, and the values in curve C tend to spread out far from the mean. The values in curve B tend to spread out more than A but less than C. Although the three curves in Figure 3-7 differ in appearance, they are all normal curves.

Normal curves with the same mean and different spreads

Now look at the three curves in Figure 3-8. The values in each of these three curves have the same tendency to cluster about their mean, but the means are all different. Each of the three distributions in Figure 3-8 is *also* a normal distribution.

Normal curves with the same spread but different means

Finally, let us look at the three curves in Figure 3-9; here each distribution has not only a different mean but also different tendency to spread out away from its mean. Each distribution in Figure 3-9 is *also* normal, even though the means and spreads differ. The nine different normal probability distributions illustrated in Figures, 3-7, 3-8, and 3-9 demonstrate that normal curves can describe a large number of groups of data differentiated only by their means and their tendency to spread. Any normal distribution is defined by two measures: the *mean*, which locates the center, and the *standard deviation* which measures the spread around the center.

The normal curve describes many sets of data

The Mean of a Distribution

In our past examples, we have been discussing the *mean* or *average* without formally explaining what the mean is and how to calculate it. Most of us become

Interpreting the mean of a distribution

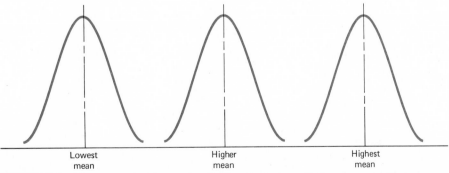

FIGURE 3-8 Three examples of normal probability distribution with the same spread but different means.

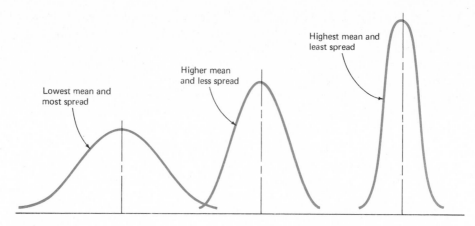

FIGURE 3-9   Three examples of normal probability distributions with different spreads and different means.

familiar with the notion of *average* and we come to accept it as a measure of something, but of what? The average or mean is known as a measure of central tendency, that is, a measure of the center of the data. Take the 30 values in Table 3-8, for example. These represent the daily sales for a used car lot since it was opened last month. We can calculate the *mean* daily sales by dividing the total number of cars sold during the 30-day period by 30:

Calculating the mean

$$\text{Mean sales per day} = \frac{420}{30}$$

$$= 14 \text{ per day}$$

A more formal expression of the calculation of the mean using conventional symbols would be:

Formula for the mean

$$\mu = \frac{\Sigma \, x_i}{n} \tag{3-3}$$

where μ (the Greek letter mu) = the mean of the values in the distribution

n = the number of values used to calculate the mean

x_i = the values of the random variable in the distribution

Mean formula symbols

Σ = the symbol meaning "the sum of"

Table 3-8   Quantity Sold

26	20	5	13	18	13
13	19	7	19	9	22
33	5	10	18	9	9
10	18	3	10	10	7
13	17	13	17	17	17

The mean is a very useful measure. In this case, it gives us a reasonable idea of the average daily sale of used cars. We can see from the 30 values in Table 3-8 that the daily sales tend to be centered around 14. But in many cases, we need to have more information about the distribution than just the mean. Suppose, for example, that you were sent to recruit pilots for an airline with the stipulation that they *average* 6 feet in height. Further, suppose that the first two persons you brought back were 4 feet tall and 8 feet tall; although the mean of this unusual group would be 6 feet,

Values and limitations of the mean as a measure

$$\text{Mean} = \frac{4 + 8}{2}$$

$$= 6 \text{ ft}$$

neither person would make a particularly appropriate pilot. The shorter person could not see out the windshield and the taller person could probably not fit into a standard cockpit. In this case the mean alone is not a good description of the data *because the data tend to spread out too much.* It is clear that in addition to the mean (a measure of the center of the data), we need another measure of the tendency of the data to spread out. This is the subject of the next section.

Problems due to too much spread

The Standard Deviation

There are several measures of the tendency for data to spread out or disperse, but we will restrict our attention to the most commonly used statistical measure of the tendency for data to disperse around their own mean. This measure is called the *standard deviation.* Because we can make important management inferences from past data with this measure, we must learn how to calculate it and what it means.

The standard deviation is calculated by following these five steps:

Calculating the standard deviation

1. Subtract the mean from each value of the data.

2. Square each of the differences obtained in step 1.

3. Add together all the squared differences.

Five steps

4. Divide the sum of all of the squared differences by the number of values.

5. Take the square root of the quotient obtained in step 4.

Let us perform these five operations on the original data from Table 3-8. This has been done in Table 3-9. Note that the standard deviation is expressed in the *same dimensional units* as the mean. If the mean is the average distance (in inches) of the hemline of skirts above the knee, then the standard deviation will also be in inches and will indicate the degree of variation of hemlines around their mean.

A more formal expression of the calculation of the standard deviation using accepted symbols would be:

$$\sigma = \sqrt{\frac{\Sigma (x_i - \mu)^2}{n}}$$ (3-4)

Formula for the standard deviation

Standard deviation
symbols

where σ = standard deviation of values in distribution
μ = mean of values of distribution
n = number of values used to calculate standard deviation
x_i = value of x for each item in distribution

and where Σ = symbol representing "the sum of"

Table 3-9   Finding the Standard Deviation

Step 1 Subtract the mean from each value	Step 2 Square each of the differences	Step 3 Add the squared differences
$26 - 14 = 12$	$12^2 = 144$	144
$13 - 14 = -1$	$-1^2 = 1$	1
$33 - 14 = 19$	$19^2 = 361$	361
$10 - 14 = -4$	$-4^2 = 16$	16
$13 - 14 = -1$	$-1^2 = 1$	1
$5 - 14 = -9$	$-9^2 = 81$	81
$7 - 14 = -7$	$-7^2 = 49$	49
$10 - 14 = -4$	$-4^2 = 16$	16
$3 - 14 = -11$	$-11^2 = 121$	121
$13 - 14 = -1$	$-1^2 = 1$	1
$18 - 14 = 4$	$4^2 = 16$	16
$9 - 14 = -5$	$-5^2 = 25$	25
$9 - 14 = -5$	$-5^2 = 25$	25
$10 - 14 = -4$	$-4^2 = 16$	16
$17 - 14 = 3$	$3^2 = 9$	9
$20 - 14 = 6$	$6^2 = 36$	36
$19 - 14 = 5$	$5^2 = 25$	25
$5 - 14 = -9$	$-9^2 = 81$	81
$18 - 14 = 4$	$4^2 = 16$	16
$17 - 14 = 3$	$3^2 = 9$	9
$13 - 14 = -1$	$-1^2 = 1$	1
$19 - 14 = 5$	$5^2 = 25$	25
$18 - 14 = 4$	$4^2 = 16$	16
$10 - 14 = -4$	$-4^2 = 16$	16
$17 - 14 = 3$	$3^2 = 9$	9
$13 - 14 = -1$	$-1^2 = 1$	1
$22 - 14 = 8$	$8^2 = 64$	64
$9 - 14 = -5$	$-5^2 = 25$	25
$7 - 14 = -7$	$-7^2 = 49$	49
$17 - 14 = 3$	$3^2 = 9$	9
		1,264

Illustration of five
steps in calculating
the standard
deviation

Step 4   Divide the sum of the squared differences by the number of values.

$$\frac{1,264}{30} = 42.13$$

Step 5   Take the square root of the quotient from step 4.

$$\sqrt{42.13} = 6.49 = \text{std. dev.}$$

Relating these symbols to the five numbered steps referred to on page 81, we have:

1. Subtract the mean from each value in the data:

$(x_i - \mu)$

2. Square each of the differences obtained in step 1:

$(x_i - \mu)^2$

3. Add together all the squared differences:

$\Sigma (x_i - \mu)^2$

4. Divide the sum of all the squared differences by the number of values:

$$\frac{\Sigma (x_i - \mu)^2}{n}$$

5. Take the square root of the quotient obtained in step 4:

$$\sqrt{\frac{\Sigma (x_i - \mu)^2}{n}}$$

The standard deviation of the distribution of past daily sales is 6.49 units. Now what does this mean? Just this: There is mathematical proof that (1) approximately 68 percent of all the values in a normal distribution lie within 1 standard deviation (plus or minus) from the mean, (2) about 95 percent of all the values lie within 2 standard deviations (plus or minus) from the mean, and (3) over 99 percent of all the values lie within 3 standard deviations (plus or minus) from the mean; these statements also hold for many nonnormal distributions found in practice. They are illustrated in Figure 3-10. Let's apply them to our data.

If the mean of our past daily sales is 14 and if the standard deviation is 6.49 units, then approximately 68 percent of all future sales will fall between 14 plus 6.49 units and 14 minus 6.49 units, or between 20.49 units and 7.51 units. Similarly, about 95 percent of all future sales will fall between $14 + (2 \times 6.49)$ units and $14 - (2 \times 6.49)$ units or between 26.98 and 1.02 units.

It turns out, however, that very few of the applications we shall make of the normal probability distribution involve intervals of *exactly* 1, 2, or 3 standard deviations (plus and minus) from the mean. What do we do about all those other cases? Fortunately we can refer to statistical tables which have been constructed precisely for these situations. These tables indicate portions of the area under the normal curve that are contained within *any* number of standard deviations (plus and minus) from the mean. No matter what the mean (μ) and the standard deviation (σ) are for a normal probability distribution, the *total* area under the normal curve is 1.00, so that we may think of areas under the curve as probabilities.

It is neither necessary nor possible to have a different table for every possible normal curve. Instead, we can use a table of areas under the curve of a *standard normal probability distribution*. With this table, we can determine the area, or

How to handle deviations other than 1, 2, or 3

Standard normal probability distribution

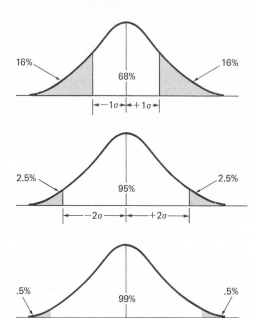

FIGURE 3-10 Approximate areas under intervals of normal curves.

probability, that a normally distributed random variable with any mean and standard deviation will lie within certain distances from the mean. These distances are defined in terms of standard deviations.

Explanation of the standard normal probability distribution

We can understand the standard normal probability distribution by examining the relationship of the standard deviation to the normal curve. Now look at Figure 3-11, where we have illustrated two normal probability distributions, each with a different mean and a different standard deviation. Both area A and area B, the shaded areas under both curves, contain the *identical* proportion of the total area under the normal curve. Why is this true? Because both these areas are defined as being the area between the mean and 1 standard deviation to the right of the mean. *All* such intervals which contain the same number of standard deviations from the mean will in turn contain the same proportion of the total area under the curve for *any* normal probability distribution. Thus it is possible to use one standard normal probability table, Appendix Table 1.

Using the Standard Normal Probability Table

Using the standard normal probability distribution table

Appendix Table 1 illustrates the area under the normal curve between the left-hand tail and any point to the right of the mean. Notice in this table the location of the column labeled z. The value for z is derived from this equation:

Formula for z
$$z = \frac{x - \mu}{\sigma}$$

(3-5)

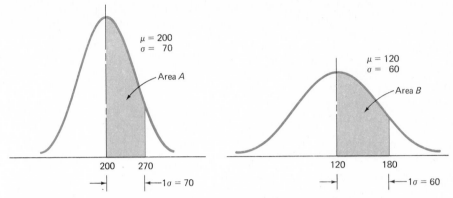

FIGURE 3-11 Two intervals, each one standard deviation to the right of the mean.

where x = the value of the random variable with which we are concerned
  μ = the mean of the distribution of this random variable
  σ = the standard deviation of this distribution
  z = the number of standard deviations from x to the mean of this distribution

Why should we use z instead of "the number of standard deviations"? Because normally distributed random variables take on many *different units* of measure (dollars, parts per million, pounds, time), and since we will use only *one* table, we should talk in terms of *standard units*. This, in fact, really means standard deviations; standard units are given a symbol of z. A glance at Figure 3-12 will show that using z only means that we have changed our scale of measurement on the horizontal axis. **Standard units**

We must work several examples to become comfortable with the use of Appendix Table 1 (Standard Normal Probability Distribution). As our problem environment, let's consider an accounts receivable auditor examining customer accounts for a client. Past records indicate that the mean amount per account is $5000 and that this particular random variable has a standard deviation of $1000.

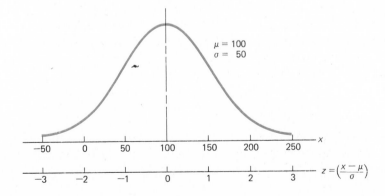

FIGURE 3-12 Normal distribution illustrating relationship of z values and standard deviations.

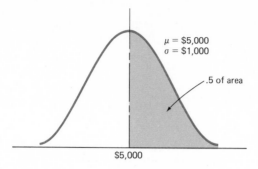

$\mu = \$5,000$
$\sigma = \$1,000$

.5 of area

$5,000

FIGURE 3-13 Distribution of accounts receivable balances. Interval more than $5000 shown in shaded area.

Example of the random variable being greater than the mean

Example 1 What is the probability that an account selected at random will have a balance of *more* than $5000? In Figure 3-13, we see that half the area under the normal curve is located on either side of the mean of $5000; therefore we know that the probability that the random variable will take on a value higher than $5000 is the shaded half, or .5.

Example of the random variable being between the mean and a value larger than the mean

Example 2 What is the probability that an account selected at random will have a balance *between* $5000 and $6500? This situation is shown graphically in Figure 3-14. The shaded area between the mean ($5000) and the x value in which we are interested ($6500) represents this probability. Using Eq. (3-5), we get a z value of:

$$z = \frac{x - \mu}{\sigma} \tag{3-5}$$

$$= \frac{\$6500 - \$5000}{\$1000}$$

$$= \frac{\$1500}{\$1000}$$

$$= 1.5 \text{ standard deviations}$$

If we look up $z = 1.5$ in Appendix Table 1, we find a probability of .93319. Since the area between the left-hand tail of the normal curve and the mean is .5 of the

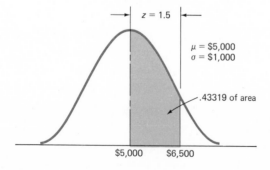

$z = 1.5$

$\mu = \$5,000$
$\sigma = \$1,000$

.43319 of area

$5,000 $6,500

FIGURE 3-14 Distribution of accounts receivable balances. Value between $5000 and $6500 shown in shaded area.

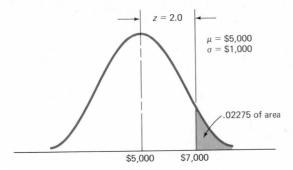

.02275 of area   **FIGURE 3-15** Distribution of
accounts receivable balances.
Interval more than $7000
shown in shaded area.

area, we obtain our answer by subtracting .5 from .93319 and get .43319. The chances of randomly getting an account with between $5000 and $6500 as a balance are slightly higher than .4.

Example 3   What is the probability that an account drawn at random will have a balance of *more* than $7000? Now look at Figure 3-15. We are interested in the shaded area to the right of the value $7000. Using Eq. (3-5), we get a z value as follows:

Example of the random variable being greater than a value which is above the mean

$$z = \frac{x - \mu}{\sigma} \qquad (3\text{-}5)$$

$$= \frac{\$7000 - \$5000}{\$1000}$$

$$= \frac{\$2000}{\$1000}$$

$$= 2 \text{ standard deviations}$$

When we look in Appendix Table 1 for a z value of 2.0, we find there a probability value of .97725. That represents the probability that an account will have a balance *less* than $7000. However, we want the probability that the account will have a balance of *more* than $7000, the shaded area in Figure 3-15. Since the entire area under the normal curve has a value of 1.0, we can find our answer by subtracting .97725 from 1.0; doing this, we get .02275 as our answer.

Example 4   Suppose that our auditors want to know the probability that they will select at random an account with a balance between $5500 and $6500? This probability is represented by the shaded area in Figure 3-16. This time, it will take us two steps to find the required probability. First, we calculate a z value for the $6500 value like this:

Example of the random variable being between two values that are both above the mean

$$z = \frac{x - \mu}{\sigma} \qquad (3\text{-}5)$$

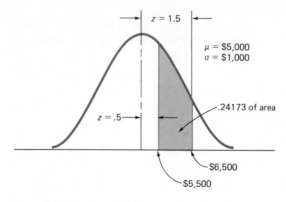

$\mu = \$5,000$
$\sigma = \$1,000$

$z = 1.5$

.24173 of area

$z = .5$

$6,500
$5,500

FIGURE 3-16 Distribution of accounts receivable balances. Interval between $5500 and $6500 shown in shaded area.

$$z = \frac{\$6500 - \$5000}{\$1000}$$

$$= \frac{\$1500}{\$1000}$$

$$= 1.5 \text{ standard deviations}$$

When we look up a z value of 1.5 in Appendix Table 1, we find a probability value of .93319. This is the probability that the random variable will lie between the left-hand tail and $6500 (the probability that it will be *less* than $6500). In step 2 of this solution, we calculate a z value for the $5500 value as follows:

$$z = \frac{x - \mu}{\sigma} \tag{3-5}$$

$$= \frac{\$5500 - \$5000}{\$1000}$$

$$= \frac{\$500}{\$1000}$$

$$= .5 \text{ standard deviation}$$

Appendix Table 1 shows a probability of .69146 for this z value; .69146 is the probability that the random variable will be less than $5500. To answer our question then, we subtract as follows:

<table>
<tr><td rowspan="3">**Solution to the problem**</td><td>.93319</td><td>probability that the random variable will be less than $6500</td></tr>
<tr><td>−.69146</td><td>probability that the random variable will be less than $5500</td></tr>
<tr><td>.24173</td><td>probability that the random variable will lie between $5500 and $6500</td></tr>
</table>

Thus there is slightly less than 1 chance in 4 that our auditor would select at random an account with a balance between $5500 and $6500.

Care in Using the Normal Probability Distribution

Some assumptions made by the normal distribution

Somewhat earlier in this chapter, we noted—as one characteristic of the normal probability distribution—that the tails approach but never touch the horizontal axis. This implies that there is *some* probability (albeit very small) that the random variable can take on enormous values. In the examples just completed, it would be possible for the right-hand tail of a normal curve to assign a very minute probability of an account with a balance of $105,000, for example. An account of this size would lie somewhere more than 100 standard deviations to the right of the mean. It would be hard to believe that, in a company whose accounts receivable had a mean of $5000 and a standard deviation of only $1000, we would find an account with a balance this large. In actual practice, we really do not lose much accuracy by completely ignoring these values far out in the tails of the normal distribution. We must remember, however, that in exchange for the convenience of using this model, we have to accept the fact that it *can* assign impossible values. As a matter of fact, the probability of finding an account with this balance in the distribution we have described begins with over 2000 zeros to the right of the decimal.

Glossary

1. **Probability distribution** List of the outcomes of an experiment with the probabilities we would expect to see associated with these outcomes.

2. **Discrete probability distribution** A probability distribution in which the variable is allowed to take on only a limited number of values.

3. **Continuous probability distribution** A probability distribution in which the variable is permitted to take on any value within a given range.

4. **Random variable** A variable that takes on different values as a result of the outcomes of a random experiment.

5. **Discrete random variable** A random variable allowed to take on only a limited number of values.

6. **Continuous random variable** A random variable allowed to take on any value within a given range.

7. **Expected value** A weighted average of the outcomes of an experiment.

8. **Expected value of a random variable** The multiplication of each value the random variable can take on by the probability of occurrence of that value and the summation of these products.

9. **Binomial distribution** A discrete distribution of the results of an experiment known as a Bernoulli process.

10. **Bernoulli process** A process in which each trial has only two possible outcomes, where the probability of the outcome of any trial remains fixed over time, and where the trials are statistically independent.

11. **Characteristic probability** The probability of success in a Bernoulli process.

12. **Poisson distribution** A discrete distribution where the probability of the occurrence of an event within a very small time period is a very small number, where the probability that two or more such events will occur within the same

small time interval is effectively 0, and where the probability of the occurrence of the event within one time period is independent of where that time period is.

13. Normal distribution   A distribution of a continuous random variable where the curve has a single peak, where it is bell-shaped, where the mean lies at the center of the distribution and the curve is symmetrical around a vertical line erected at the mean, and where the two tails extend indefinitely and never touch the horizontal axis.

14. Mean   A measure of central tendency; that is, a measure of the location of the data.

15. Standard deviation   A measure of the spread of the data around the mean.

16. Standard normal probability distribution   A normal probability distribution where the standard deviations are expressed in standard units.

17. Standard unit   The standard deviation of a standard normal probability distribution.

Review of Equations

Page 67

$$\text{Probability of } r \text{ successes in } n \text{ trials} = \frac{n!}{r!(n-r)!}p^r q^{n-r} \qquad (3\text{-}1)$$

This is the binomial formula. In this formula, p is the characteristic probability (or probability of success), q is $1 - p$, r is defined as the number of successes desired, and n equals the number of trials to be undertaken.

Page 75

$$P(x) = \frac{\lambda^x e^{-\lambda}}{x!} \qquad (3\text{-}2)$$

The probability of getting exactly x occurrences in a Poisson distribution is calculated by the use of this formula. λ is the mean of the distribution, x is the specific value of the discrete random variable in which we are interested, and e is the base of the natural logarithm system.

Page 80

$$\mu = \frac{\Sigma x_i}{n} \qquad (3\text{-}3)$$

With this formula, we find the mean of a random variable. The n represents the number of values we use for this calculation.

Page 81

$$\sigma = \sqrt{\frac{\Sigma (x_i - \mu)^2}{n}}$$ (3-4)

Use this formula to find the standard deviation, a useful measure of dispersion. μ is the mean of the values in the distribution, x_i represents the value of x for each item in the distribution, and n is the number of values used in the calculation of the standard deviation. We refer to the standard deviation in this case as sigma (σ).

Page 84

$$z = \frac{x - \mu}{\sigma}$$ (3-5)

This is the formula for z which is used instead of standard deviations in the standard normal probability distribution table. Because normally distributed random variables take on many different units of measure and because we use only one table for the standard deviation, it is conventional to talk in terms of standard units; z is a standard unit.

Exercises

3-1. Which of the following distributions are discrete and which are continuous?
a. Test scores on college entrance examinations
b. Possible weights of students in a physical education class
c. The number of possible pages in a textbook
d. The barometric pressure at any given time
e. The number of grains of sand on each of the world's beaches

3-2. You are the accounts receivable manager for Occidental Steel, Inc. You know from past experience that 10 percent of your accounts receivable are overdue at any one time and are a continuing source of concern to your boss. You have four accounts receivable statements on your desk as she passes one morning. She instructs you to "bring a couple of those statements into my office and let's get going." You know that if you show up with an overdue statement, she will probably fire you on the spot. What is the probability that of the two statements you have to take in to her, one or both will be past due?

3-3. Assume you are a dealer in refrigerators and have hired a new salesman for a 2-week trial period. At the end of the 2 weeks, you must decide either to release him or to place him permanently on the payroll. Based upon past experience, you estimate that given your prospective salesman's experience, personality, etc., there is a 20 percent probability he will be a superior salesman, a 40 percent probability he will be an average salesman, and a 40 percent probability he will be an inferior salesman. A superior salesman is one who sells a refrigerator to

50 percent of his customers; an average salesman sells to 30 percent of his customers; and an inferior salesman sells to 10 percent of his customers.

After the 2-week period, you note that he has demonstrated refrigerators to a total of 50 customers and has sold refrigerators to 14 of them. Based upon all the information you have, should you retain the man permanently in your employment if your policy is to employ only average or superior salesmen? Assume that the selling of refrigerators is a Bernoulli process.

3-4. Alcoholism is an increasing problem among young executives at Carol and Sloam Advertising Agency. The feeling of the managing partner, Richard Best, is that probably 30 percent of the younger executives have a problem serious enough to impair their work effectiveness. Drinking at lunch is considered by Mr. Best to be prima facie evidence that effectiveness is impaired. While out to lunch one day, Best comes across a table at which four of Carol and Sloam's young executives are sitting. What is the probability that two of them are drinking?

3-5. By very carefully screening loan applicants, the Bank of Halifax County has been able to limit bad-debt losses on consumer loans to 5 percent. What is the probability that at least four of the five loan applicants that you, as a loan officer trainee, have just approved will repay their loan?

3-6. International Foods, Inc., manufacturers of Zesty, a special Italian tomato sauce, were interested in discovering whether consumers could tell the difference between a competitor's more expensive sauce and theirs. Twenty persons are given a sample of Zesty and then a sample of the competitor's sauce. Then they are each asked to identify the competitor's brand. It is customary to hypothesize that there is no difference in the tastes; if this is so, the chances of a person identifying the competitor's brand are .5. What is the probability that 17 of the 20 persons in the test will identify the competitor's brand if the hypothesis is really true? Use the binomial tables to compute your answer.

3-7. Ninety percent of all persons passing a job aptitude test over the last several years have been successful performers on that job. What is the probability that five of the six applicants who have just passed the test will be successful workers?

3-8. The Portland Trailblazers and the Philadelphia 76ers are playing in a best-of-seven series. Based upon past performance, you estimate that Portland would have a 60 percent chance of winning in a single game against Philadelphia. If the winner is the team that wins four games first, what is the probability that Portland will win in a four-game series? What is the probability that Philadelphia will win in a seven-game series?

3-9. A building contractor knows that the probability of rain in his region during any given day in August is 25 percent. He has 2 days' work remaining on a job and there are 4 days during which the work can be done without incurring penalty costs. Assuming he gets no work done on rainy days, what is the probability that he will pay a penalty? Assume that rain on any given day is independent of the fact that it did or did not rain on any other day.

3-10. Tom Shetley and Harriet Dupuis are members of an auditing team in one of the "big eight" firms. Today they are auditing accounts payable balances in a client company where the past audit history indicates there is 1 chance in 50 of finding an error in an accounts payable balance. What are the chances that Tom and Harriet will find an error in the first 15 accounts they examine? What are the chances that they could finish their day's assigned work (20 accounts) without finding any errors?

3-11. City Parking Systems, Inc., operates a parking garage in the downtown area. Cars arrive at the garage during the rush hour at the rate of 30 every 60 minutes. Three garage attendants can handle this level of arrivals, but not too much more. What is the probability of more than 5 arrivals in any 10-minute interval, which would require the help of another garage attendant?

3-12. Sarah Shari is the emergency room supervisor at County General Hospital. As a part of her responsibilities, she plans staffing for the facility. An especially busy period is Saturday night after 9 P.M. It is normal for Sarah to schedule three interns to work during that period; from past experience she knows that this level of staffing can handle the usual load of 4 arrivals per hour. However, in the event arrivals rose much above this level, additional professional help would need to be scheduled. Sarah thinks the distribution of arrivals can be described by the Poisson distribution and would like to know what the chances are of 5, 6, 7, or 8 persons arriving in any 1-hour period, since this would make it necessary to provide another attendant.

3-13. University Medical Center has a backup power generating system that could take over if city power should fail. This standby system actually has two separate generators; if one fails, the other is cut into the system automatically. The probability of a standby generator failing is estimated by the manufacturer to be .00013. What is the probability that two standby generators would fail in succession, leaving the hospital without any power?

3-14. The output of cold-rolled steel pipe of the Valley Tubing Corporation is 20,000 pounds daily, with a standard deviation of 4000 pounds. If any output above 25,000 pounds daily would so tax the materials-handling crew as to cause a shutdown of the entire facility, what is the probability of such an event if the output is normally distributed?

3-15. Control of the heat in a chemical blending process at Universal Products Co., Inc., is absolutely essential. Too much or too little heat during the process produces polyvinyl insulation material that is either too brittle or so flimsy that it cannot support the weight of roofing shingles which are normally laid on top of the insulation. Past processes have produced an output with a compression strength of 150 pounds per square inch and a standard deviation of 25 pounds per square inch. Insulation with a compression strength above 220 pounds per square inch or below 105 pounds per square inch is not usable. What portion of a day's run of 50 tons of insulation will be unusable if the heat control of the process stays at the same level of effectiveness?

3-16. A financial analyst computed the return on stockholder's equity for all the companies listed on the New York Stock Exchange. She found that the mean of this distribution was 10.2 percent, with a standard deviation of 3.2 percent. She is interested in examining further those companies whose return on stockholder equity is between 15.0 percent and 17.5 percent. Of the approximately 1300 companies listed on the exchange, how many are of interest to her?

Bibliography

Childress, R. I.: *Mathematics for Managerial Decisions* (Englewood Cliffs, N.J.: Prentice-Hall, Inc., 1974).

Freund, J. E.: *Introduction to Probability* (Belmont, Calif.: Dickenson Publishing Company, Inc., 1973).

Goldberg, S.: *Probability—An Introduction* (Englewood Cliffs, N.J.: Prentice-Hall, Inc., 1960).

Hodges, J. L., and **E. L. Lehmann:** *Elements of Finite Probability* (San Francisco: Holden-Day, Inc., Publisher, 1965).

Levin, R. I.: *Statistics for Management* (Englewood Cliffs, N.J.: Prentice-Hall, Inc., 1978).

Morgan, B. W.: *An Introduction to Bayesian Statistical Decision Processes* (Englewood Cliffs, N.J.: Prentice-Hall, Inc., 1968).

Mosteller, F., R. E. K. Rouke, and **G. B. Thomas:** *Probability with Statistical Applications,* 2d ed. (Reading, Mass.: Addison-Wesley Publishing Company, Inc., 1970).

Schlaifer, R.: *Probability and Statistics for Business Decisions* (New York: McGraw-Hill Book Company, 1961).

Forecasting

1. Introduction

All managers forecast

Every manager considers some kind of forecast in every decision that he or she makes. Some of these forecasts are quite simple; for example, take the case of the office manager who, on Thursday, forecasts the work load she anticipates for Friday in order to give some of her employees time off. Other forecasts are much more complex; consider the vice-president of finance for an automobile company trying to forecast, a year in advance, the company's seasonal needs for working capital. Still other forecasts have exceptionally long time horizons and deal with **Complexity of forecasts varies** issues much more difficult to quantify; if you manage a company which produces heating and cooling systems for residences, the long-term outlook for energy, energy-related technologies, and government constraints on energy production and use weigh heavily on your company's future.

Accuracy of forecasts

No one forecasts with the accuracy that the users of the forecast would like; nevertheless, decisions must still be made every day, and they get made with the best information that is available, *not* with perfect forecasts. Therefore, the real issue in forecasting turns out to be not whether forecasts are completely accurate but rather how to continue to develop and use the existing forecasting methodology with all its hangups, inaccuracies, and mystical properties.

Management scientists have developed many forecasting techniques in recent years to help managers handle the increasing complexity in management decision making. Each of these techniques has a special use, and the more you understand about these techniques, the better the chances that your forecasting efforts will be successful. The purpose of this chapter is to introduce you to some of the more commonly used forecasting techniques and demonstrate what they can and can't do for managers.

Whether you use one forecasting technique or another, the forecasting *process* stays pretty much the same.

Five steps in the forecasting process

1. Determine the objective of the forecast. (What is its use?)

2. Select the period over which the forecast will be made. (What are your information needs over what time period?)

3. Select the forecasting approach you will use. (Which forecasting technique is most likely to produce the information you need?)

4. Gather the information to be used in the forecast. (Which data will most likely produce forecasts of greatest use to you?)

5. Make the forecast. (Which computational procedures will you have to use?)

The roles of management scientist and manager in this process are critical to the success of forecasting. The forecaster and the manager should collaborate to go over the purpose of the forecast—that is, how it is to be used. If management is undecided about whether to invest $50 million in a new technology, the forecast will take into account changing patterns of technology, sociology, and even politics. On the other hand, the cash forecast for next quarter can disregard long-term financial trends. Management should also make sure that the forecaster understands the system for which the forecast is being made; how sensitive it is to changes in the environment, how much its future direction depends on its past movement, and which factors in the environment seem to affect it most. Without a good working knowledge of the operation, the forecaster is hampered in producing something of value to management.

Roles of the manager and the quantitative specialist

2. Types of Forecasts

There are three basic kinds of forecasts: *judgmental forecasts, extensions of past history,* and *causal forecasting models.* Let's look a bit more closely at each one of these approaches here in a general way; later we shall examine them in more detail.

Three types of forecasts

Judgmental Forecasts

We tend to use these kinds of forecasts when "good" data are not readily available. With a judgmental forecast we are trying to change subjective opinion into a quantitative forecast that we can use. The process brings together, in an organized way, personal judgments about the process being analyzed. Outside experts may be consulted, we can convene a panel of experts to make a combined forecast, or we can ask one of the organized "futurist" organizations (organizations that specialize in the future) what they think about the situation. In each case, we are relying primarily on human judgment to interpret past data and make projections about the future.

Forecasts when good data are unavailable

Extensions of Past History

When we take history as our beginning point for forecasting, it doesn't mean that we think March will be just like January and February; it simply means that *over*

Forecasts based on the past

the short run we believe that future patterns tend to be extensions of past ones and that we can make some useful forecasts by studying past behavior. Unfortunately these kinds of forecasts do very poorly when we try to extend them farther into the future, because the past—although it is often a guide to the future—does not *predict* very accurately the point at which interest rates will rise or decline, the month in which demand for a new dress will begin to fall, or the day on which demand for electric power will be maximum next summer. All these peaks and valleys are called turning points. Even though turning points are of the greatest significance to managers, extending past history too far into the future is not an effective way of determining when they will occur.

Causal Forecasting Models

Forecasts which relate several variables

If considerable historical data are available and if we know the relationship between the variable we want to forecast and other variables that we can observe, it's possible to construct a *causal forecast.* For example, one causal model, *regression,* can be used to relate sales to a number of other environmental factors including the level of GNP, the price level, disposable income, unemployment, and population shifts. Causal models tend to consider a great deal of information; consequently they are among the most expensive forecasting tools to use.

3. Judgmental Forecasting

Delphi Technique

Expert forecasts without disclosure of majority opinion

As forecasts of the social and economic environment become more and more necessary for managerial decision making, expert opinion becomes more widely used to keep us informed about what is likely to happen. One technique that's used to get agreement among the "experts" is the Delphi technique. Here a group of experts is asked for their opinions in an environment in which all of them individually have access to each other's information but in which the majority opinion is *not* disclosed, to prevent it from influencing anyone unduly.

One such Delphi session, concerned with changes in health-care systems, achieved a 90 percent consensus on these predictions:

Delphi forecast of health-care changes

1. By 1998, typical physicians will spend less than 25 percent of their time on direct patient care.

2. By 1991 there will be wide use of computers and monitoring devices attached directly to the patient in the home.

3. By 1988, in all the larger hospitals, pharmacists, or pharmacologically trained personnel, will make "rounds," with physicians acting as drug consultants.

4. By 1990, there will be few if any physicians in "solo" practice.

Of course, experts are wrong from time to time, just like the rest of us. When the first great hydroelectric plant at Niagara Falls, New York, was being designed, proposals were received for direct-current equipment (a traditional power-generation method) and alternating-current equipment (a new technology.) The project promoters consulted England's Lord Kelvin, one of the world's best-known power experts, who advised them strongly not to commit the mistake of using alternating current. The decision makers, however, chose to disregard the expert and selected alternating current, a decision which has worked out well for about 60 years. Just recently, interest in direct current was again renewed by one of the major electrical ·equipment manufacturers.

Everyone makes mistakes

Panel of Experts

This technique differs from the Delphi technique in that there is no secrecy and full communication among panel members is encouraged. Although this process brings to bear the opinion of experts, the group process tends to influence the outcome (social pressure, majority view, and personalities may all combine to produce a consensus which is not reflective of the group's true feelings).

Expert forecasts with full disclosure of information

4. Extensions of Past History

Moving Averages

Averages that are updated as new information is received are generally called *moving averages.* The speed of the response is controlled by adjusting the number of periods we include in the moving average and the weighting we assign to each period. The simplest moving average weights each period equally. For example, if we want to forecast sales for April with a simple 3-month moving average, we would average the sales for January, February, and March. May's forecast would drop January's and add April's figures. Table 4-1 illustrates both a 3-month and a 4-month moving average forecast of Fitch Lumber Company's roof truss sales. Notice from the results how the 4-month moving average forecast is slower to react to the increasing sales; its speed of response is dampened by the extra month's data included in the forecast.

Comparing a 3-month moving average with a 4-month moving average

Neither the 3- nor the 4-month moving average forecast does a very good job forecasting Fitch's roof truss sales. R. B. Fitch, president of the company, says he needs a forecast which responds faster than these two. In this instance, equal weighting for each month may not be the best approach, because newer information is more reflective of the trend of sales. R. B. could try weighting the latest month as heavily as the preceding 2 months and the next-to-last month twice as heavily as the one 3 months ago. If R. B. did this, the forecast for next month (symbolized F) would be based on actual sales for the 3 preceding months as follows:

Weighting a moving average

$$F = \frac{3M_1 + 2M_2 + M_3}{6} \qquad (4\text{-}1)$$

where M_1 = latest month's information

M_2 = information from 2 months ago

M_3 = information from 3 months ago

Table 4-1 Sales of Roof Trusses by Fitch Lumber Company, 3- and 4-Month Moving Average Forecasts

Month	Actual sales (000's)	Three-month moving average forecast	Four-month moving average forecast
Jan.	$10		
Feb.	12		
Mar.	13		
Apr.	16	(10 + 12 + 13)/3 = 11.67	
May	19	(12 + 13 + 16)/3 = 13.67	(10 + 12 + 13 + 16)/4 = 12.75
June	23	(13 + 16 + 19)/3 = 16.00	(12 + 13 + 16 + 19)/4 = 15.00
July	26	(16 + 19 + 23)/3 = 19.33	(13 + 16 + 19 + 23)/4 = 17.75
Aug.	30	(19 + 23 + 26)/3 = 22.67	(16 + 19 + 23 + 26)/4 = 21.00
Sept.	28	(23 + 26 + 30)/3 = 26.33	(19 + 23 + 26 + 30)/4 = 24.50
Oct.	18	(26 + 30 + 28)/3 = 28.00	(23 + 26 + 30 + 28)/4 = 26.75
Nov.	16	(30 + 28 + 18)/3 = 25.33	(26 + 30 + 28 + 18)/4 = 25.50
Dec.	14	(28 + 18 + 16)/3 = 20.67	(30 + 28 + 18 + 16)/4 = 23.00

Comparing unweighted moving averages with weighted moving averages

In Table 4-2, we have applied Eq. (4-1) to R. B.'s situation. When we compare the results of the weighted moving average in Table 4-2 with the simple moving average in Table 4-1, we see that weighting the latest information more heavily generated a much more accurate forecast. The exact weightings to use and the best number of periods of data to include in the forecast are both matters which require quite a bit of experimentation to decide. If you weight the latest month too heavily, you run the risk of having your forecast respond too quickly to what may be a random disturbance in the pattern of sales.

Table 4-2 Sales of Roof Trusses by Fitch Lumber Company, 3-Month Weighted Moving Average Forecast

Month	Actual sales (000's)	Three-month weighted moving average forecast
Jan.	$10	
Feb.	12	
Mar.	13	
Apr.	16	[(3 × 13) + (2 × 12) + (10)]/6 = 12.17
May	19	[(3 × 16) + (2 × 13) + (12)]/6 = 14.33
June	23	[(3 × 19) + (2 × 16) + (13)]/6 = 17.00
July	26	[(3 × 23) + (2 × 19) + (16)]/6 = 20.50
Aug.	30	[(3 × 26) + (2 × 23) + (19)]/6 = 23.83
Sept.	28	[(3 × 30) + (2 × 26) + (23)]/6 = 27.50
Oct.	18	[(3 × 28) + (2 × 30) + (26)]/6 = 28.33
Nov.	16	[(3 × 18) + (2 × 28) + (30)]/6 = 23.33
Dec.	14	[(3 × 16) + (2 × 18) + (28)]/6 = 18.67

In a moving average forecast, new data, as they come in, replace the oldest data. Suppose, however, that R. B. Fitch has 8000 different items in his inventory for which he would like to forecast demand. If he uses a 6-month moving average, somebody has to take the current figure, add it to the five other figures, and compute the new moving average forecast—and this has to be done for all 8000 items. For this many items, R. B. would have to store 48,000 pieces of monthly sales information. If he *weights* the moving average forecast, there is even more work. Many managers like R. B. *see* the increased accuracy of weighted moving average forecasting methods, but the computational burden involved discourages them from doing anything more than equal weighting.

Computational shortcomings of moving averages

Exponential Smoothing

A technique called *exponential smoothing* eliminates some of the computational disadvantages of forecasting with a weighted moving average. Exponential smoothing uses a *single* weighting factor called *alpha*, symbolized α. Just as we tried different moving average methods to get a better forecast, it's possible to experiment with different alphas to improve forecasting accuracy. In many cases the single weighting factor, alpha, may be just as effective as more complex weighting schemes and considerably more efficient computationally.

Using a single weighting factor to minimize computational difficulty

An exponentially smoothed forecast for R. B. Fitch's roof truss sales can be obtained using this formula:

Smoothed forecast
for this month's $= \alpha$ (sales last month)
    sales $\quad\quad + (1 - \alpha)$ (previous forecast of last month's sales)

For example, suppose actual sales *last* month were \$15,000 and we had forecast \$16,000 sales for last month. If we were using an alpha of .4, the forecast for this month's sales would be:

.4(\$15,000) + (1 − .4) (\$16,000) = \$15,600

In Table 4-3, we've shown the computations for an exponentially smoothed forecast of R. B.'s roof truss sales using an alpha of .4. If we compare the smoothed forecast for this month (the right-hand column of Table 4-3) with the actual sales for this month [column (2)], we see that the forecast was slow in reacting to increased sales; additionally, R. B. would notice that even though actual sales turned down in September, the forecast didn't turn down until November. It would be natural for R. B. to suggest that perhaps our choice of alpha was incorrect and suggest that a larger alpha (say, .7) might do a better job of forecasting.

Reaction time of a forecast with $\alpha = .4$

In Table 4-4 we have shown the computations for an exponentially smoothed forecast with an alpha of .7. The forecast this time is more responsive than the one we obtained in Table 4-3. Not only are the forecast sales nearer to actual sales but R. B. would notice that the forecast turned down this time in October, only a month after actual sales declined. Whether .7 is the best weighting factor for R. B. to use

Changing α

Table 4-3   Exponentially Smoothed Forecast of Sales of Roof Trusses by Fitch Lumber Company; $\alpha = .4$; Sales in 000's

Month (1)	Actual sales (2)	Sales last month (3)	α (4)	α (sales last month) (4)(3)	$1 - \alpha$ (5)	Previous forecast of last month's sales (6)	$(1 - \alpha)$ (previous forecast of last month's sales) (5)(6)	Smoothed forecast for this month (4)(3) + (5)(6)
Jan.	$10						A beginning "guess"	
Feb.	12	10	.4	4.0	.6	11	6.6	10.6
Mar.	13	12	.4	4.8	.6	10.6	6.4	11.2
Apr.	16	13	.4	5.2	.6	11.2	6.7	11.9
May	19	16	.4	6.4	.6	11.9	7.1	13.5
June	23	19	.4	7.6	.6	13.5	8.1	15.7
July	26	23	.4	9.2	.6	15.7	9.4	18.6
Aug.	30	26	.4	10.4	.6	18.6	11.2	21.6
Sept.	28	30	.4	12.0	.6	21.6	13.0	25.0
Oct.	18	28	.4	11.2	.6	25.0	15.0	26.2
Nov.	16	18	.4	7.2	.6	26.2	15.7	22.9
Dec.	14	16	.4	6.4	.6	22.9	13.7	20.1

Increasing α is not always the answer   is a matter for experimentation. We should point out to R. B. that larger alphas don't always make for better forecasts. Consider the factory manager who revises production upward or downward depending on changes in demand; each time changes are made, the costs of the changes are proportional to the amount of overtime that is authorized or to the number of factory employees hired or laid off. If much of the fluctuation in demand from month to month appears to be random, this manager may prefer a small alpha resulting in a more dampened response to demand and thus in lower costs of "adjustment."

Trend-adjusted Exponential Smoothing

Adjusting your forecast based on rate of change   R. B. notices from the forecast in Table 4-4 that during the period when the trend of sales was upward (January to August), the forecast was low; during the period when sales were falling (August to December), the forecast was high. He wonders if he can somehow add a trend factor to minimize this effect. In Table 4-5, we've demonstrated the computations for trend-adjusted exponential smoothing, a variation of exponential smoothing which adjusts the forecast based on the rate at which the forecast is changing. From the right-hand column in Table 4-5, R. B. can see that the trend-adjusted forecast comes pretty close to actual sales, although it does "overshoot" actual sales for 2 months after they turn down in August, particularly so in October.

Trend Projections

Fitting a trend line   The final forecasting method under the category of *the extension of past history* which we shall discuss is trend projection, a mathematical method which fits a trend line to a data set of past observations and then projects this line into the future for purposes of estimating. We illustrate this process with another example. R. B.

Table 4-4 Exponentially Smoothed Forecast of Sales of Roof Trusses by Fitch Lumber Company; $\alpha = .7$; Sales in 000's

Month (1)	Actual sales (2)	Sales last month (3)	α (4)	α (sales last month) [(4)(3)]	$1 - \alpha$ (5)	Previous forecast of last month's sales (6)	$(1 - \alpha)$ (previous forecast of last month's sales) [(5)(6)]	Smoothed forecast for this month [(4)(3) + (5)(6)]
Jan.	$10						A beginning "guess"	
Feb.	12	10	.7	7.0	.3	11	3.3	10.3
Mar.	13	12	.7	8.4	.3	10.3	3.1	11.5
Apr.	16	13	.7	9.1	.3	11.5	3.5	12.6
May	19	16	.7	11.2	.3	12.6	3.8	15.0
June	23	19	.7	13.3	.3	15.0	4.5	17.8
July	26	23	.7	16.1	.3	17.8	5.3	21.4
Aug.	30	26	.7	18.2	.3	21.4	6.4	24.6
Sept.	28	30	.7	21.0	.3	24.6	7.4	28.4
Oct.	18	28	.7	19.6	.3	28.4	8.5	28.1
Nov.	16	18	.7	12.6	.3	28.1	8.4	21.0
Dec.	14	16	.7	11.2	.3	21.0	6.3	17.5

Fitch bought some land south of Chapel Hill some years ago and has developed it himself, building homes on it each year. During the last 6 years, his construction record has been as follows:

Year	No. of homes
1974	14
1975	17
1976	18
1977	21
1978	25
1979	26

If this *trend* continues, R. B. would like to estimate the number of homes he will probably build in 1981. To get a quick idea of the trend, we have plotted R. B.'s construction record in Figure 4-1. This graph is commonly called a *scatter diagram*. When we view all these data points together, we can visualize the relationship that exists between the two variables *time* and *number of homes built*. As a result, we can help R. B. see the pattern or relationship by drawing or fitting a straight line through our scatter diagram to represent the relationship. This we have done in Figure 4-2. It is common to draw these lines so that an equal number of points lie on either side of the line. **Examining a trend visually**

    It is more usual to fit a trend line more precisely by using an equation that relates the two variables in this situation, *time* and *number of homes built*. To a statistician, a line fitted to R. B.'s construction record scatter diagram will have a "good fit" if it *minimizes the sum of the squares of the errors* between the estimated points on the line and the actual observed points that were used when we drew it. The farther away a point is from the trend line, the more serious is the error. To penalize large errors, we square the individual errors before we add them to find the total error. Since we are searching for the trend line that gives us the minimum **Fitting a straight line visually** **Fitting a trend line mathematically**

Table 4-5 Trend-adjusted Exponentially Smoothed Forecast of Sales of Roof Trusses by Fitch Lumber Company; $\alpha = .7$; Sales in 000's

Month (1)	Actual sales (2)	Smoothed forecast from Table 4-4 (3)	Change in smoothed forecast from month to month (4)	α (5)	α (change in smoothed forecast) [(5)(4)]	$1-\alpha$ (6)	Old trend (7)	$(1-\alpha)$ (Old trend) [(6)(7)]	Trend adjustment [(5)(4) + (6)(7)]	Trend-adjusted forecast (3) + [(5)(4) + (6)(7)]
Jan.	$10									
Feb.	12	10.3	0	.7	0	.3	0	0	0	10.3
Mar.	13	11.5	1.2	.7	.84	.3	0	0	.84	12.3
Apr.	16	12.6	1.1	.7	.77	.3	.84	.25	1.02	13.6
May	19	15.0	2.4	.7	1.68	.3	1.02	.31	1.99	17.0
June	23	17.8	2.8	.7	1.96	.3	1.99	.60	2.56	20.4
July	26	21.4	3.6	.7	2.52	.3	2.56	.77	3.29	24.7
Aug.	30	24.6	3.2	.7	2.24	.3	3.29	.99	3.23	27.8
Sept.	28	28.4	3.8	.7	2.66	.3	3.23	.97	3.63	32.0
Oct.	18	28.1	−.3	.7	−.21	.3	3.63	1.09	.88	29.0
Nov.	16	21.0	−7.1	.7	−4.97	.3	.88	.26	−4.71	16.3
Dec.	14	17.5	−3.5	.7	−2.45	.3	−4.71	−1.41	−3.86	13.6

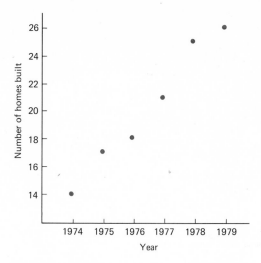

FIGURE 4-1 Construction record for R. B. Fitch Development.

sum of the squares of the errors, this method of fitting a trend is called the *least-squares method.*

The equation for a fitted straight line is:

$$\hat{Y} = a + bX \qquad (4\text{-}3)$$

Meaning of least squares

Equation for a straight line

where $\hat{Y}$ (pronounced Y-hat) = the quantity which is being estimated (the dependent variable "number of homes")

a = the point at which the trend line intercepts the Y axis

b = the rate of change (slope) of the trend line (sales growth per year in R. B.'s case)

X = the independent variable (time in this case)

Statisticians have developed the equations we can use to find the slope and the Y intercept of the best-fitting trend line. The first equation calculates the slope:

$$b = \frac{\Sigma\, XY - n\overline{X}\overline{Y}}{\Sigma\, X^2 - n\overline{X}^2} \qquad (4\text{-}4)$$

Finding the slope of the best-fitting trend line

where b = slope of the best-fitting trend line

X = values of the independent variable (time in this case)

Y = values of the dependent variable (homes in this case)

$\overline{X}$ = the mean of the values of the independent variable

$\overline{Y}$ = the mean of the values of the dependent variable

n = the number of data points (six in our case)

and the second equation calculates the Y intercept:

$$a = \overline{Y} - b\overline{X} \qquad (4\text{-}5)$$

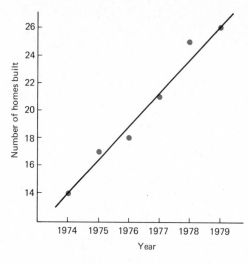

FIGURE 4-2 Straight line fitted through scatter diagram of construction record for R. B. Fitch Development.

Finding the Y intercept of the best-fitting trend line

where a = the Y intercept

b = the slope from Eq. (4-4)

$\overline{Y}$ = the mean of the values of the dependent variable

$\overline{X}$ = the mean of the values of the independent variable

Simplifying the arithmetic

With these two equations, R. B. can find the best-fitting trend line for his set of data points in Figure 4-1. To help him keep track of the inputs necessary for Eqs. (4-4) and (4-5), we have set up the problem in Table 4-6. (To simplify the arithmetic, we have let 1974 be year 0, 1975 be year 1, and so on.) With the information in Table 4-6, we can now use Eqs. (4-4) and (4-5) to find the slope and Y intercept of the best-fitting trend line. The slope is

The slope of R. B.'s trend line

$$b = \frac{\Sigma\, XY - n\overline{X}\,\overline{Y}}{\Sigma\, X^2 - n\overline{X}^2} \tag{4-4}$$

$$= \frac{346 - (6)(2.5)(20.167)}{55 - (6)(2.5)^2}$$

$$= \frac{346 - 302.5}{55 - 37.5}$$

$$= \frac{43.5}{17.5}$$

$$= 2.486$$

And the Y intercept is

The Y intercept of R. B.'s trend line

$$a = \overline{Y} - b\overline{X} \tag{4-5}$$

$$= 20.167 - (2.486)\,(2.5)$$

$$= 20.167 - 6.215$$

$$= 13.952$$

Table 4-6 Calculations and Inputs for Eqs. (4-4) and (4-5) Used in Fitting a Trend Line to R. B. Fitch's Construction Record

Data point (1)	Year (X) (2)	Homes built (Y) (3)	(X)(Y) [(2)(3)]	X^2 [(2)^2]
1	0,(1974)	14	0	0
2	1,(1975)	17	17	1
3	2,(1976)	18	36	4
4	3,(1977)	21	63	9
5	4,(1978)	25	100	16
6	5,(1979)	26	130	25
	$\Sigma X = 15$	$\Sigma Y = 121$	$\Sigma XY = 346$	$\Sigma X^2 = 55$

$$\overline{X} = \Sigma X/n \qquad \overline{Y} = \Sigma Y/n$$
$$= 15/6 \qquad\quad = 121/6$$
$$= 2.5 \qquad\quad\ = 20.167$$

R. B. can estimate the number of homes he will likely be building in 1981 by using the trend-line equation:

$$\hat{Y} = a + bX \qquad\qquad (4\text{-}3)$$

with the values

$a = 13.952$

$b = 2.486$

The trend-line equation appears then as:

R. B.'s trend line

$$\hat{Y} = 13.952 + 2.486X$$

And since he is interested in the forecast for 1981, we can insert 7 in place of X (if 1974 is 0, then 1981 is year 7):

Using the trend line to forecast

$$\hat{Y} = 13.952 + 2.486(7)$$
$$= 13.952 + 17.402$$
$$= 31.35 \text{ homes}$$

With this construction history and using the method of least squares to fit this trend line, R. B. should plan on about 31 homes for 1981.

5. Causal Forecasting Models

A causal model is probably the most sophisticated forecasting model. It takes into account a great deal of information about the relationship between what you are trying to forecast and a number of other variables, including economic measures

Causal models use a lot of information

and social indicators. The most common causal forecasting models are regression, econometric models, and input-output analysis.

Regression model

A *regression model* for forecasting sales would relate sales to a number of other variables all affecting sales. This would be accomplished statistically using a variation of the least-squares method we employed in trend-line analysis. An *econometric model* is a whole system of equations which describes the operation of an economic system, whether it be the economy of a country or the market within a particular industry. These models are very expensive but forecast better than regression models. *Input-output analysis* is concerned with flows of goods among industries in an economy or even flows of service among branches of a large organization. If you are interested in the levels and kinds of inputs necessary to achieve certain levels of outputs, then input-output analysis would be quite useful. These models require a great deal of historical data for their development. The demonstration of econometric models and input-output analysis is far beyond the scope of a text like this, but we can illustrate how a regression model forecasts.

Econometric model

Input-output analysis

Forecasting with a Regression Model

Developing a regression model

R. B. Fitch has been concerned for some time with the overhead costs in his cabinet shop. For some years now he has estimated these costs monthly, using the number of direct labor hours as the independent variable; in recent months, however, he has noticed that the forecasts are off by a considerable amount. He wonders whether adding still another independent variable would improve his forecasts. For the last 7 months, R. B. has kept a record not only of the direct labor hours in the cabinet shop but also of the total number of board feet of lumber used in the operation. These data are shown in Table 4-7, along with the overhead cost for each month.

Adding a second independent variable to improve the forecast

Symbols for a multiple regression model

Whereas in least-squares trend-line fitting, X was the symbol used for the values of the independent variable, now—with more than one independent variable—we will add subscripts to distinguish between them (X_1, X_2). In R. B.'s cabinet shop problem, X_1 will represent the direct labor hours, X_2 the board feet of lumber used, and Y the overhead expense.

Table 4-7 Overhead Cost, Direct Labor Hours, and Quantity of Lumber Used per Month in Fitch Lumber Company's Cabinet Shop

Month	Overhead (000's)	Direct labor hours (000's)	Board feet of lumber used (000's)
Mar.	$3.1	3.9	2.4
Apr.	2.6	3.6	2.1
May	2.9	3.8	2.3
June	2.7	3.9	1.9
July	2.8	3.7	1.9
Aug.	3.0	3.9	2.1
Sept.	3.2	3.8	2.4

In fitting the trend line for R. B., we used an estimating equation:

$$\hat{Y} = a + bX \tag{4-3}$$

but now that we have added another independent variable, we have to add one new term to that equation. The equation we use with two independent variables is

$$\hat{Y} = a + b_1 X_1 + b_2 X_2 \tag{4-6}$$

Multiple regression equation

where $\quad \hat{Y}$ = the estimated value of the dependent variable (overhead cost in R. B.'s case)
a = the Y intercept
X_1 and X_2 = values of the *two* independent variables
b_1 and b_2 = slopes appropriate for X_1 and X_2

To use the least-squares criterion, statisticians have developed these three equations to determine the values of a, b_1, and b_2:

$$\Sigma Y = na + b_1 \Sigma X_1 + b_2 \Sigma X_2 \tag{4-7}$$

$$\Sigma X_1 Y = a \Sigma X_1 + b_1 \Sigma X_1{}^2 + b_2 \Sigma X_1 X_2 \tag{4-8}$$

$$\Sigma X_2 Y = a \Sigma X_2 + b_1 \Sigma X_1 X_2 + b_2 \Sigma X_2{}^2 \tag{4-9}$$

Equations to find the Y intercept and slopes

Keeping track of all the inputs for these three equations is a bit of a problem, so once again, we've set up the problem in tabular form (see Table 4-8).

We can now substitute directly from Table 4-8 into Eqs. (4-7), (4-8), and (4-9), like this:

$$20.3 = 7a + 26.6b_1 + 15.1b_2 \tag{4-7}$$

$$77.22 = 26.6a + 101.16b_1 + 57.41b_2 \tag{4-8}$$

$$44.0 = 15.1a + 57.41b_1 + 32.85b_2 \tag{4-9}$$

Finding a, b_1, and b_2

Solving these equations simultaneously for a, b_1, and b_2, we get

$a = -1.39563$

$b_1 = .74614$

$b_2 = .67696$

We are now able to estimate R. B.'s overhead from Eq. (4-6) if we know the number of direct labor hours (X_1) and the board feet of lumber (X_2) used:

Estimating R. B.'s overhead with our model

$$\hat{Y} = a + b_1 X_1 + b_2 X_2 \tag{4-6}$$

$$= -1.39563 + .74614 X_1 + .67696 X_2$$

Table 4-8 Calculations and Inputs for Eqs. (4-7), (4-8), and (4-9) Used in a Regression Forecast for Fitch Lumber Company's Cabinet Shop Overhead

Month (1)	Overhead (Y) (2)	Direct labor hours (X_1) (3)	Board feet of lumber (X_2) (4)	X_1Y [(3)(2)]	X_2Y [(4)(2)]	X_1X_2 [(3)(4)]	X_1^2 [(3)²]	X_2^2 [(4)²]
Mar.	3.1	3.9	2.4	12.09	7.44	9.36	15.21	5.76
Apr.	2.6	3.6	2.1	9.36	5.46	7.56	12.96	4.41
May	2.9	3.8	2.3	11.02	6.67	8.74	14.44	5.29
June	2.7	3.9	1.9	10.53	5.13	7.41	15.21	3.61
July	2.8	3.7	1.9	10.36	5.32	7.03	13.69	3.61
Aug.	3.0	3.9	2.1	11.70	6.30	8.19	15.21	4.41
Sept.	3.2	3.8	2.4	12.16	7.68	9.12	14.44	5.76
	Σ = 20.3	Σ = 26.6	Σ = 15.1	Σ = 77.22	Σ = 44.00	Σ = 57.41	Σ = 101.16	Σ = 32.85

If, in November, R. B. uses 4.1 thousand labor hours and 2.5 thousand board feet of lumber, the cabinet shop overhead can be estimated as:

$$\text{Overhead} = -1.39563 + .74614(4.1) + .67696(2.5)$$
$$= -1.39563 + 3.06 + 1.69$$
$$= 3.35 \ (\$3350)$$

Glossary

1. **Judgmental forecast** Forecasting method that brings together in an organized way personal judgments about the process being analyzed.

2. **Extension of past history** Forecasting method based on the belief that over the short run, future patterns tend to be extensions of past ones.

3. **Causal forecasting model** Forecasting model which relates the variable to be forecast to a number of other variables that can be observed.

4. **Delphi technique** Forecasting method that brings together a group of experts who have access to each other's opinions in an environment where no majority opinion is disclosed.

5. **Panel of experts** Forecasting method using a group of experts with full disclosure of information and majority opinion.

6. **Moving average** An average that is updated as new information becomes available.

7. **Unweighted moving average** A moving average in which all data used to compute the average are weighted equally.

8. **Weighted moving average** A moving average in which data used to compute the average are given different weights depending generally upon their age.

9. **Exponential smoothing** A forecasting method involving a single weighting factor called alpha.

10. **Trend-adjusted exponential smoothing** A forecasting method where the weighting factor is also used to adjust the forecast based on the rate at which the forecast is changing.

11. **Trend line** A line fitted to sets of data points which describes the relationship between the independent and dependent variables.

12. **Least-squares method** A method of fitting a trend line which minimizes the sum of the squares of the errors between the estimated points on the trend line and the actual observed points that were used to fit the line.

13. **Regression model** A forecasting model which relates the dependent variable (sales, for example) to one or more independent variables (GNP and Index of Economic Activity, for example).

14. **Econometric model** System of equations which describes the operation of an economic system.

15. **Input-output analysis** Models which are concerned with the flows of goods among industries in an economy or among branches of a large organization.

Review of Equations

Page 99

$$F = \frac{3M_1 + 2M_2 + M_3}{6} \tag{4-1}$$

This equation computes a 3-month (or three-period) weighted moving average. M_1 is the latest month's (period's) information, M_2 is the information from 1 month (period) ago, and M_3 is the information from 2 months (periods) ago. In this formulation, the latest information is weighted as heavily as that of the preceding 2 months, and the data of the next to the last month (period) are weighted twice as heavily as those of the month (period) 3 months ago.

Page 101

$$\text{Smoothed forecast} = \alpha(\text{sales last month}) \tag{4-2}$$
$$+ (1 - \alpha)(\text{previous forecast of last month's sales})$$

This is the equation for an exponentially smoothed forecast, with α representing the single weighting factor.

Page 106

$$\hat{Y} = a + bX \tag{4-3}$$

This is the equation for a fitted straight line, where $\hat{Y}$ is the quantity being estimated, a is the Y intercept of the trend line, b is the slope of the trend line, and X is the independent variable.

Page 107

$$b = \frac{\Sigma XY - n\bar{X}\bar{Y}}{\Sigma X^2 - n\bar{X}^2} \tag{4-4}$$

Equation to find the slope of the best-fitting trend line, where X is the values of the independent variable, Y is the values of the dependent variable, $\bar{X}$ and $\bar{Y}$ are the means of the independent and dependent variables respectively, and n is the number of data points.

Page 107

$$a = \bar{Y} - b\bar{X} \tag{4-5}$$

Equation which calculates the Y intercept of the best-fitting trend line, where a is the Y intercept, b is the slope, and $\bar{X}$ and $\bar{Y}$ are the means of the independent and dependent variables respectively.

Page 110

$$\hat{Y} = a + b_1 X_1 + b_2 X_2$$

The least-squares equation with two independent variables, where $\hat{Y}$ is the quantity being estimated, a is the Y intercept, X_1 and X_2 are values of the two independent variables, and b_1 and b_2 are slopes appropriate for X_1 and X_2.

Page 110

$$\Sigma Y = na + b_1 \Sigma X_1 + b_2 \Sigma X_2 \tag{4-7}$$

$$\Sigma X_1 Y = a \Sigma X_1 + b_1 \Sigma X_1^2 + b_2 \Sigma X_1 X_2 \tag{4-8}$$

$$\Sigma X_2 Y = a \Sigma X_2 + b_1 \Sigma X_1 X_2 = b_2 \Sigma X_2^2 \tag{4-9}$$

Equations to determine the values for a, b_1, and b_2 in Eq. (4-6).

Exercises

4-1. Anne Montgomery is the production control manager for United Sleepwear, a producer of fine-quality robes, gowns, and lounge suits. Its business tends to be rather seasonal, with sales quite heavy toward the end of the year, just before the holiday season. Anne has tried several ways of forecasting sales with little success; she has heard of 3-month moving averages and wants to know how accurately this method would have forecast sales compared to the method she used last year. Here are her actual monthly sales for last year. Use a 3-month moving average with equal weighting to forecast sales beginning with April. Then calculate the average absolute error for the 9 months between actual sales and forecast sales.

Jan.	$12,000	July	$18,700
Feb.	12,800	Aug.	20,900
Mar.	13,400	Sept.	24,300
Apr.	15,000	Oct.	29,600
May	16,000	Nov.	34,500
June	17,500	Dec.	41,000

4-2. Using Anne Montgomery's actual sales data from Problem 4-1, forecast sales using a 3-month moving average with these weights: most recent month, 5; next most recent month, 3; oldest month, 2. For the months April through December, calculate the average absolute error between actual sales and forecast sales. What factor has caused this error to change from the one in Problem 4-1?

4-3. Look again at the actual data in Problem 4-1. Using a 2-month unweighted moving average, forecast sales for March through December. Now calculate the average absolute error between forecast sales and actual sales for this period. Which of the three methods you have employed in Problems 4-1, 4-2, and 4-3 is most accurate? Explain this outcome.

4-4. Wayne Daniels is director of the State Fish and Game Department. One of the projects Wayne's office has been reviewing is the seasonal change in the migratory river fish population in South Carolina. By tagging fish and with some fancy statistical sampling methods, Wayne's staff compiled this estimate of the fish population in a 10-mile stretch of the Chatahoochie River last year:

Jan.	34,000,000	July	43,600,000
Feb.	35,200,000	Aug.	41,900,000
Mar.	36,700,000	Sept.	38,200,000
Apr.	44,800,000	Oct.	35,000,000
May	49,200,000	Nov.	34,600,000
June	44,300,000	Dec.	34,200,000

Wayne knows that the river fish population is quite seasonal, being heaviest in the spawning season; he needs a method of estimating changes in the population for purposes of regulating fish catches, river level, and navigation. Use exponential smoothing with an alpha of .3 to forecast the fish population with Wayne's data. Use 34,000,000 as a January guess. Calculate the average absolute error between your forecast and the actual population for the 11 months from February through December.

4-5. With the data from Problem 4-4, forecast the fish population using exponential smoothing with an alpha of .5. Calculate the average absolute error between this forecast and the actual fish population for the 11 months from February through December. Use 34,000,000 as a January guess.

4-6. Using the data from Problem 4-4, forecast the fish population using exponential smoothing with an alpha of .7. Calculate the average absolute error between your forecast and the actual fish population for the 11 months from February through December. Of the three forecasts you have made (Problems 4-4, 4-5, and 4-6), which is the most accurate? Do you think it is possible to produce a more accurate forecast than this using a different alpha? Make a guess about the best alpha without actually doing the forecast. Use 34,000,000 as a January guess.

4-7. Roy Holsten is dean of students at a large Southern university. As one of his responsibilities, he directs the student counseling service, an operation that provides help and advice to students who are having emotional problems resulting primarily from academic pressures. The counseling service is staffed by part-time residents at the medical school, and scheduling these residents has been a real problem for Roy. He knows that peak demand occurs whenever examination pressures are maximum but has been less than truly successful in forecasting these points. He has gathered these data from last year representing requests for counseling from students:

Jan.	688	July	650
Feb.	745	Aug.	670
Mar.	780	Sept.	750
Apr.	790	Oct.	794
May	1,050	Nov.	820
June	870	Dec.	1,120

Using trend-adjusted exponential smoothing with an alpha of .3 and a guess of 688 for the January smoothed forecast, forecast the requests for counseling using Roy's data. Calculate the average absolute error between your forecast and the actual requests for the 11 months from February through December.

4-8. Using the data from Problem 4-7, forecast the requests for counseling using trend-adjusted exponential smoothing with an alpha of .5. For the 11 months from February through December, calculate the average absolute error between this forecast and the actual requests.

4-9. Using the data from Problem 4-7, forecast the requests for counseling using trend-adjusted exponential smoothing with an alpha of .7. For the 11 months from February through December, calculate the average absolute error between this forecast and the actual requests. Of the three forecasts you made (Problems 4-7, 4-8, and 4-9), which was the most accurate? What is your guess about the possibility of producing an even more accurate forecast by changing alpha again?

4-10. The National Association of Mortgage Lending Institutions is trying to determine what relationship exists between the size of the down payment made by a home purchaser and the occurrence of foreclosures. They sampled six sets of 2000 mortgage accounts and found these data:

Size of down payment (percent of price)	5	10	15	20	25	30
Number of foreclosures	120	85	55	30	7	3

Using the least-squares method, develop the trend line that best describes the relationship between size of down payment and foreclosure. Using the line you have fitted, predict the number of foreclosures we would expect if we looked at 2000 accounts where the down payment was 23 percent.

4-11. A University of North Carolina sociologist is investigating what relationship exists between the unemployment rate and the crime rate in major cities. She has gathered, from 9 major cities, these data concerning the number of robberies and assaults per 10,000 residents and the corresponding rate of unemployment in that city:

Percent unemployment	7.2	10.4	9.7	6.8	8.0	5.9	4.8	6.6	5.6
Robberies and assaults per 10,000 residents	7.4	8.6	6.6	5.5	6.9	3.5	2.4	6.9	3.2

Develop a trend line that describes the relationship between crime and unemployment using the least-squares method. If Boston has an unemployment rate of 7.1 percent, estimate its assault and robbery rate per 10,000 residents.

4-12. Ed Davis is a senior marketing analyst with Asheville Knitting Mills, Inc. The new-product development section of the company has just completed testing on a yarn which is fire-retardant, soil-resistant, and impervious to extreme changes in temperature. Ed has been asked to estimate annual demand for this yarn if the offering price is $3.78 a pound. From past experience with similar products, Ed has compiled these data describing the relationship between price and annual demand:

Price	$2.00	$2.50	$3.00	$4.00	$5.00
Annual demand (000 yards)	443	405	372	342	335

Using the least-squares method, develop a trend line that describes the relationship between price and annual demand; use this line to estimate annual sales of the new product.

4-13. Nancy Murray, sales manager of Frocks, Ltd., a high-fashion dress retailer, would like to develop an estimating equation which would predict her sales based on gross national product (GNP) and the index of retail sales. She has gathered these data from previous years:

Year	GNP (trillions)	Index of retail sales	Frocks, Ltd. sales
1978	1.41	117	$1,100,000
1977	1.29	106	970,500
1976	1.24	111	890,000
1975	1.17	101	794,000
1974	1.02	98	704,000

Using the method of least squares for more than one independent variable, determine the estimating equation which best fits these data. If the coming year's GNP is forecast to be $1.51 trillion and the index of retail sales is expected to be 123, estimate Nancy's sales.

4-14. Cal Atwood, placement director for an M.B.A. program, is investigating the relationship between a graduate's academic record, years of work experience, and annual earnings. He has these data for seven graduates of his program:

Academic record (scale of 100)	Years of work experience	Present salary
89	6	$34,000
79	4	26,000
94	7	37,000
82	6	28,000
96	9	42,000
74	2	20,000
67	0	15,000

Using the least-squares method, develop an estimating equation which best fits Cal's data. Using the equation you develop, estimate what earnings a graduate could expect after 5 years of work experience if she left the program with an academic average of 80.

Bibliography

Burrington, R. S., and **D. C. May:** *Handbook of Probability and Statistics with Tables,* 2d ed. (New York: McGraw-Hill Book Company, 1970).

Ezekiel, M., and **K. Fox:** *Methods of Correlation and Regression,* 3d ed. (New York: John Wiley & Sons, Inc., 1959).

Freund, J., and **F. Williams:** *Dictionary/Outline of Basic Statistics* (New York: McGraw-Hill Book Company, 1966).

Harris, R. J.: *A Primer of Multivariate Statistics* (New York: Academic Press, Inc., 1974).

Silk, L. S., and **M. L. Curley:** *A Primer on Business Forecasting with a Guide to Sources of Business Data* (New York: Random House, Inc., 1970).

Decision theory I

5

1. Introduction to Decision Theory

Most decisions involve some uncertainty

Most complex managerial decisions are made with some uncertainty. Managers authorize substantial capital investments with less than complete knowledge about product demand. Government officials make consequential decisions concerning the environment which will affect our lives for years to come, yet precise knowledge about the future is not available to them. A president of a major power company must decide whether to construct a $5 billion nuclear generating plant in the face of extreme uncertainty about future power demand, government regulation, and environmental impacts. Each of these persons must make decisions under uncertain future conditions; in these and other contexts, decision theory provides a rational method for choice.

2. Steps in the Decision Theory Approach

The decision theory approach generally involves three steps; we shall introduce these by using the example of a record and tape manufacturing company considering several alternative methods of expanding its production to accommodate increasing demand for its products.

Step 1

List all the viable alternatives

The first action a decision maker must take is to list all the viable alternatives that must be considered in the decision. In the case of our record and tape manufacturer, company planners indicate that there are only three viable options open to the company:

1. Expand the present plant

2. Build a new plant

3. Subcontract out extra production to other record and tape manufacturers

Step 2

Having identified all the viable alternatives, the decision maker must now list the future events that may occur. Generally, decision makers can identify most future events that *can* occur; the difficulty is identifying which particular event *will* occur. These future events (not under the control of the decision maker) are called *states of nature* in decision theory literature. In this listing, we include everything that *can* happen; we also assume that the states of nature are defined in such a way that only one of them can occur. In the case of our record and tape manufacturer, the greatest uncertainty attaches to future demand for the product. The future events relating to demand are listed as:

Identify the future events that may occur

1. High demand (resulting from high product acceptance)

2. Moderate demand (resulting from reasonable product acceptance but heavy competitive response)

3. Low demand (resulting from low product acceptance)

4. Failure (no product acceptance)

In defining these states of nature, it would be quite usual for the decision maker to attach a dollar or unit volume value to each of the four possible events to define them more accurately.

Step 3

The decision maker now constructs a *payoff table*—a table which shows the payoffs (expressed in profits or any other measure of benefit which is appropriate to the situation) which would result from each possible combination of decision alternative and state of nature. Table 5-1 illustrates the 12 possible payoffs in the record and tape company's expansion decision.

Construct a payoff table

3. The Different Environments in Which Decisions Are Made

Decision makers must function in three types of environments. In each of these environments, knowledge about the states of nature differs.

Table 5-1 Payoff Table for Record-Tape Company Expansion Decision (Payoffs Expressed in Profits Earned over Next 5 Years)

		States of nature (demand)			
		High	Moderate	Low	Failure
Decision maker's alternatives	Expand	$500,000	$250,000	−$250,000	−$450,000
	Build	$700,000	$300,000	−$400,000	−$800,000
	Subcontract	$300,000	$150,000	−$ 10,000	−$100,000

Making decisions under certainty

1. *Decision making under conditions of certainty:* In this environment, only one state of nature exists; that is, there is complete certainty about the future. Although this environment sometimes exists, it is usually associated with *very* routine decisions involving fairly inconsequential issues; even here, it is usually impossible to guarantee complete certainty about the future.

Making decisions under uncertainty

2. *Decision making under conditions of uncertainty:* Here, more than one state of nature exists, but the decision maker has no knowledge about the various states, not even sufficient knowledge to permit the assignment of probabilities to the states of nature.

Making decisions under risk

3. *Decision making under conditions of risk:* In this situation, more than one state of nature exists, but the decision maker has information which will support the assignment of probability values to each of the possible states.

Making choices under certainty

Under conditions of complete certainty, it is easy to analyze the situation and make good decisions. Since certainty involves only *one* state of nature, the decision maker simply picks the best payoff in that *one* column and chooses the alternative associated with that payoff. In Table 5-1, for example, if John Gwin, the president of the company, knew that demand would be *moderate,* he would choose the alternative "build," since that yields him the highest payoff. Similarly, if he knew that demand would be low, he would choose the alternative "subcontract," since even though that generates a loss, it is still his best alternative given that state of nature. In any event, few of us ever enjoy the luxury of having complete information about the future, and thus decision making under certainty is not of consequential interest to us.

4. The Criteria for Decision Making under Uncertainty

Different possible criteria for making decisions under uncertainty

In the case of making decisions under *uncertainty,* John Gwin, the decision maker, knows which states of nature can happen, but he does not have information which would allow him to specify the probability that these states *will* happen. In this situation, there are four criteria John can use to make decisions; we shall examine each of these briefly.

Table 5-2 Payoff Table for Record-Tape Company Expansion Decision (Payoffs Expressed in Profits Earned over Next 5 Years)

		States of nature (demand)			
		High	Moderate	Low	Failure
Decision maker's alternatives	Expand	$500,000	$250,000	−$250,000	−$450,000
	Build	$700,000	$300,000	−$400,000	−$800,000
	Subcontract	$300,000	$150,000	−$ 10,000	−$100,000

The Maximax Criterion

The maximax criterion for decision making under uncertainty provides John with an *optimistic* criterion. If he wanted to use this criterion, he would select the decision alternative which would maximize his maximum payoff. In our problem illustrated in Table 5-1, John first selects the maximum payoff possible for each decision alternative, then chooses the alternative that provides him with the maximum payoff within this group. Table 5-1 is repeated here as Table 5-2 to illustrate this method. In Table 5-2, John has circled the maximum payoff possible for each of the three decision alternatives. The alternative within this group of three which provides the maximum payoff is "build," with an associated payoff over 5 years of $700,000.

Maximax criterion, an optimistic criterion

The Maximin Criterion

The maximin criterion for decision making under uncertainty gives a *pessimistic* criterion. To use this method, John tries to maximize his minimum possible payoffs. He begins by first listing the minimum payoff that is possible for each decision alternative; he would then select the alternative within this group of three which results in the maximum payoff. Table 5-3 repeats Table 5-1. In Table 5-3, John has circled the minimum payoff that is possible for each of the three decision alternatives. The decision alternative within this group of three which provides the maximum payoff is the alternative "subcontract," with an associated payoff of −$100,000 over the next 5 years.

Maximin criterion, a pessimistic criterion

Table 5-3 Payoff Table for Record-Tape Company Expansion Decision (Payoffs Expressed in Profits Earned over Next 5 Years)

		States of nature (demand)			
		High	Moderate	Low	Failure
Decision maker's alternatives	Expand	$500,000	$250,000	−$250,000	−$450,000
	Build	$700,000	$300,000	−$400,000	−$800,000
	Subcontract	$300,000	$150,000	−$ 10,000	−$100,000

The Minimax Regret Criterion

Minimax regret criterion

To introduce this criterion, let us assume that John can step into the future for a minute and look back. Suppose he earlier made a decision to subcontract production of records and tapes (based on the information he had at that time) and it turns out that demand is high. The profit he will make from subcontracting with high demand is $300,000; but had John known demand was going to be high, he would not have subcontracted but chosen instead to "build" with a profit of $700,000. The difference between $700,000 (the optimal payoff "had he known") and $300,000 (the payoff he actually realized from subcontracting) is $400,000 and is known as the *regret* resulting from his decision. Let us look at the calculation of one more regret value. Suppose he had chosen alternative "build" and demand had turned out to be moderate. In this case there would be *no regret* because, as it turned out, the decision alternative "build" is optimum when demand is moderate, and $300,000 is the maximum payoff possible.

In Table 5-4 we show the regret associated with all 12 combinations of decision alternative and state of nature. These regret values are obtained by subtracting every entry in the payoff table (Table 5-1) from the largest entry in its column. Applying the minimax regret criterion requires John to indicate the maximum regret for each decision alternative; he has done this by circling the maximum regret for the three decision alternatives in Table 5-4. Finally, he chooses the minimum of these three regret values ($350,000, $700,000, and $400,000); in this case, $350,000 is his minimum regret value, and this regret is associated with the decision alternative "expand."

The Criterion of Realism

The criterion of realism, a middle-ground criterion

This criterion for decision making under uncertainty is a middle-ground criterion between maximax and maximin—that is, between optimism and pessimism. This compromise requires the president, John Gwin, to specify a coefficient or index of optimism, symbolized α (the Greek letter alpha), where α is between 0 and 1 in value. When he assigns α a value of 0, John is expressing pessimism about nature; an α of 1 indicates John's optimism about nature. To apply this criterion to his record-tape company expansion decision, John first determines both the maximum

Table 5-4   Regret for Each of the 12 Combinations of Decision Alternative and State of Nature for Record-Tape Company

		States of nature (demand)			
		High	Moderate	Low	Failure
Decision maker's alternatives	Expand	$200,000	$50,000	$240,000	($350,000)
	Build	0	0	$390,000	($700,000)
	Subcontract	($400,000)	$150,000	0	0

Table 5-5 Maximum and Minimum Payoffs for Each Decision Alternative for Record-Tape Company (Color Circle = Maximum; Black Circle = Minimum)

		States of nature (demand)			
		High	Moderate	Low	Failure
Decision maker's alternatives	Expand	$500,000	$250,000	−$250,000	−$450,000
	Build	$700,000	$300,000	−$400,000	−$800,000
	Subcontract	$300,000	$150,000	−$ 10,000	−$100,000

Illustration of application of the criterion of realism

and minimum payoff for each decision alternative. John has done this in Table 5-5. The maximum payoff for each decision alternative is circled in color and the minimum payoff in black. Then, for each decision alternative, John computes this value:

$$\text{Measure of realism} = \alpha \text{ (maximum payoff)} + (1 - \alpha) \text{ (minimum payoff)} \qquad (5\text{-}1)$$

Suppose in this example that the president of the company feels fairly optimistic and assigns a value of .7 to α. Under these conditions, the measure-of-realism values for the three decision alternatives are

Expand	.7($500,000) + .3(−$450,000) = $215,000
Build	.7($700,000) + .3(−$800,000) = $250,000
Subcontract	.7($300,000) + .3(−$100,000) = $180,000

The application of the realism criterion in this case suggests that John choose the alternative "build." The advantage of using the criterion of realism is that John is able to introduce his own personal feelings of relative optimism or pessimism into the decision process.

Advantage of the criterion of realism

5. Decision Making under Conditions of Risk: Discrete Random Variables

When we make decisions under conditions of risk, we need information that will enable us to provide probabilities for the various possible states of nature. This information can be past records or simply the subjective judgment of the decision maker; the source is not important as long as this information enables us to shed some light on which state of nature we feel the environment is in. There are three criteria for decision making under risk which we shall study; in order, they are *expected value* (often called the *criterion of Bayes*), the *criterion of rationality* (also called the *principle of insufficient reason*), and the *criterion of maximum likelihood*.

Three criteria for decision making under risk

The Expected Value Criterion

This criterion asks the decision maker to calculate the expected value for each decision alternative (the sum of the weighted payoffs for that alternative, where the weights are the probability values assigned by the decison maker to the states of nature that can happen). This rather formidable-sounding notion is really not difficult and, in fact, we have already used it on page 72 of Chapter 3, when we discussed the problem involving sheets of plywood. Let us introduce it formally here with the example of Beth Perry, who sells strawberries in a market environment where tomorrow's sales of strawberries is a discrete random variable. Later we shall introduce methods that are useful when demand is a continuously distributed random variable.

Example of use of the expected value criterion

Beth purchases strawberries for $3 a case and sells them for $8 a case. This rather high markup reflects the perishability of the item and the great risk of stocking it; the product has no value after the first day it is offered for sale. Beth Perry faces the problem of how many to order today for tomorrow's business.

Cost and price information

A 90-day observation of past sales gives the information shown in Table 5-6. The probabilities are obtained by normalizing the distribution. Sales were 10 cases on 18 of the 90 days; that is, $18/90 = 2/10 = .20$ of the time.

This distribution, too, is discrete and random. There are only four possible values for sales volume, and there is no discernible pattern in the sequence in which these four values occur.

Statement of the problem

If we assume Beth has no reason to believe that sales volume will behave differently in the future, her problem is that of determining how many cases she should buy today for tomorrow's business. If buyers tomorrow call for more cases than the number in stock, Beth's profits suffer by $5 (selling price minus cost) for each sale she cannot make. On the other hand, there are costs which result from the stocking of too many units on any day. Suppose that on a certain day Beth has 13 cases in stock but sells only 10. She makes a profit of $50, $5 per case on 10 cases. But this must be reduced by $9, the cost of the 3 cases not sold and of no value.

Calculating Conditional Profits   One way of illustrating Beth's problem is to construct a table showing the results in dollars of all possible combinations of purchases and sales. The only values for purchases and for sales which have

Table 5-6   Cases Sold during 90 Days

Daily sales	No. days sold	Probability of each number being sold
10	18	.20
11	36	.40
12	27	.30
13	9	.10
	90	1.00

Table 5-7 Conditional Profit Table

Possible demand (sales), cases	Possible stock action			
	10 cases	11 cases	12 cases	13 cases
10	$50	$47	$44	$41
11	50	55	52	49
12	50	55	60	57
13	50	55	60	65

meaning to us are 10, 11, 12, or 13 cases. These were the sales magnitudes. There is no reason for her to consider buying fewer than 10 or more than 13 cases.

Table 5-7, called a *conditional profit table,* shows the profit resulting from any possible combination of supply and demand. The profits can be either positive or negative and are conditional in that a certain profit results from taking a specific stocking action (ordering 10, 11, 12, or 13 cases) and having sales of a specific number of cases (10, 11, 12, or 13 cases).

Conditional profit table

Table 5-7 reflects the losses which occur when stock remains unsold at the end of a day. It does not reflect profit denied Beth because of inability to fill all buyers' requests, that is, because of an out-of-stock condition.

Notice that the stocking of 10 cases each day will always result in a profit of $50. Even when buyers want 13 cases on some days, Beth can sell only 10.

When Beth stocks 11 cases, her profit will be $55 on days when buyers request 11, 12, or 13 cases. But on days when she has 11 cases in stock and buyers buy only 10 cases, profit drops to $47. The $50 profit on the 10 cases sold must be reduced by $3, the cost of the unsold case.

A stock of 12 cases will increase daily profits to $60, but only on those days when buyers want 12 or 13 cases. Should buyers want only 10 cases, profit is reduced to $44; the $50 profit on the sale of 10 cases is reduced by $6, the cost of 2 unsold cases.

The stocking of 13 cases will result in a profit of $65 when there is a market for 13 cases. There will be a $5 profit on each case sold, with no unsold cases. When buyers buy fewer than 13 cases, such a stock action results in profits of less than $65. For example, with a stock of 13 cases and sale of only 11 cases, the profit is $49; the profit on 11 cases, $55, is reduced by the cost of 2 unsold cases, $6.

Derivation of entries for the conditional profit table

Such a conditional profit table does not tell Beth which number of cases she should stock each day in order to maximize profits. It only shows her what the outcome will be *if* a specific number of cases is stocked and a specific number of cases is sold. Under conditions of risk, she does not know in advance the size of any day's market, but she must still decide which number of cases, stocked consistently, will maximize profits over a long period of time.

Value of the conditional profit table

Determining Expected Profits The next step in determining the best number of cases to stock is to assign probabilities to the possible outcomes or profits.

We saw in Table 5-6 that the probabilities of the possible values for sales were as follows:

Cases	Probability
10	.20
11	.40
12	.30
13	.10

Using these probabilities and the information contained in Table 5-7, Beth can now compute the expected profit of each possible stock action.

Expected profit

It was stated earlier that we could compute the expected value of a random variable by *weighting each possible value the variable could take by the probability of its taking on each value.* Using this procedure, Beth can compute the expected daily profit from stocking 10 cases each day, as in Table 5-8.

Calculating expected profit for the four decision alternatives

The figures in column 4 of Table 5-8 are obtained by weighting the conditional profit of each possible sales volume (column 2) by the probability of each conditional profit occurring (column 3). The sum in the last column is the expected daily profit resulting from stocking 10 cases each day. It is not surprising that this expected profit is $50, since we saw in Table 5-7 that stocking 10 cases each day would always result in a daily profit of $50, regardless of whether buyers wanted 10, 11, 12, or 13 cases.

The same computation for a daily stock of 11 units can be made, as we have done in Table 5-9. This tells us that if Beth stocks 11 cases each day, her expected profit over time will be $53.40 per day. Eighty percent of the time the daily profit will be $55; on these days, buyers ask for 11, 12, or 13 cases. However, column 3 tells us that 20 percent of the time, the market will take only 10 cases, resulting in a profit of only $47. It is this fact that reduces the daily expected profit to $53.40.

For 12 and 13 units, the expected daily profit is computed as shown in Tables 5-10 and 5-11, respectively.

We have now computed the expected profit of each of the four stock actions open to Beth. To summarize, these expected profits are as follows:

If 10 cases are stocked each day, expected daily profit is $50.00.

Table 5-8   Expected Profit from Stocking 10 Cases

(1) Market size, cases	(2) Conditional profit		(3) Probability of market size		(4) Expected profit
10	$50	×	.20	=	$10
11	50	×	.40	=	20
12	50	×	.30	=	15
13	50	×	.10	=	5
			1.00		$50

Table 5-9   Expected Profit from Stocking 11 Cases

(1) Market size, cases	(2) Conditional profit		(3) Probability of market size		(4) Expected profit
10	$47	×	.20	=	$ 9.40
11	55	×	.40	=	22.00
12	55	×	.30	=	16.50
13	55	×	.10	=	5.50
			1.00		$53.40

If 11 cases are stocked each day, expected daily profit is $53.40

If 12 cases are stocked each day, expected daily profit is $53.60.

If 13 cases are stocked each day, expected daily profit is $51.40.

The optimum stock action is the one that results in the greatest expected profit. It is the action that will result in the largest daily average profits and thus the maximum total profits over a period of time. In this illustration, the proper number to stock each day is 12 cases, since this quantity will give the highest possible average daily profits under the conditions given.

We have not introduced certainty into the problem facing Beth Perry. Rather, we have used her past experience to determine the best stock action open to her. She still does not know how many cases will be requested on any given day. There is no guarantee that she will make a profit of $53.60 tomorrow. However, if she stocks 12 units each day under the conditions given, she will have *average* profits of $53.60 per day. This is the best she can do, because the choice of any one of the other three possible stock actions will result in a lower average daily profit.

Optimum stock action

Interpretation of this decision alternative

Expected Profit with Perfect Information   Now suppose for a moment that our strawberry retailer, Beth Perry, could remove all uncertainty from her problem by obtaining additional information. Complete and accurate information about the future, referred to as *perfect* information, would remove all uncertainty from the problem. This does not mean that sales would not vary from 10 to 13 cases per day. Sales would still be 10 cases per day 20 percent of the time, 11 cases 40

Perfect information

Table 5-10   Expected Profit from Stocking 12 Cases

(1) Market size, cases	(2) Conditional profit		(3) Probability of market size		(4) Expected profit
10	$44	×	.20	=	$ 8.80
11	52	×	.40	=	20.80
12	60	×	.30	=	18.00
13	60	×	.10	=	6.00
			1.00		$53.60 ← optimum stock action

Table 5-11   Expected Profit from Stocking 13 Cases

(1) Market size, cases	(2) Conditional profit		(3) Probability of market size		(4) Expected profit
10	$41	×	.20	=	$ 8.20
11	49	×	.40	=	19.60
12	57	×	.30	=	17.10
13	65	×	.10	=	6.50
			1.00		$51.40

percent of the time, 12 cases 30 percent of the time, and 13 cases 10 percent of the time. However, with perfect information Beth would know *in advance* how many cases were going to be called for each day.

Calculating expected profit with perfect information   Under these circumstances, Beth would stock today the exact number of cases buyers will want tomorrow. For sales of 10 cases, she would stock 10 cases and realize a profit of $50. When sales were going to be 11 cases, she would stock exactly 11 cases, thus realizing a profit of $55.

Table 5-12 shows the conditional profit values that are applicable to Beth's problem if she has perfect information. Given the size of market in advance for a particular day, she chooses the stock action that will maximize her profits. This means she buys and stocks so as to avoid *all* losses from obsolete stock as well as *all* opportunity losses which reflect lost profits on unfilled requests for merchandise.

Meaning of expected profit with perfect information   She can now proceed to the computation of the expected profit with perfect information. This is shown in Table 5-13. The procedure is the same as that already used. However, you will notice that the conditional profit figures in column 2 of Table 5-13 are the maximum profits possible for each sales volume. For example, when buyers buy 12 cases, Beth will always make a profit of $60 under certainty because she will have stocked exactly 12 cases. With perfect information, then, she could count on making an average profit of $56.50 a day. This is a significant figure because it is the *maximum profit* possible.

Another approach to solving this problem   ***An Alternate Approach: Minimizing Losses***   We have just solved Beth Perry's problem by maximizing her expected daily profit. There is another approach to

Table 5-12   Conditional Profit Table under Certainty

Possible sales, cases	Possible stock actions			
	10 cases	11 cases	12 cases	13 cases
10	$50	—	—	—
11	—	$55	—	—
12	—	—	$60	—
13	—	—	—	$65

Table 5-13 Expected Profit with Perfect Information

(1) Market size, cases	(2) Conditional profit under certainty		(3) Probability of market size		(4) Expected profit with perfect information
10	$50	×	.20	=	$10.00
11	55	×	.40	=	22.00
12	60	×	.30	=	18.00
13	65	×	.10	=	6.50
			1.00		$56.50

this same problem. We can compute the amounts by which maximum profit possible ($56.50) will be reduced under various stocking actions; then we can choose that course of action which will *minimize* these reductions or *losses*.

Two types of losses are involved: (1) *obsolescence losses* are those caused by stocking too many units; (2) *opportunity losses* are those caused by being out of stock when buyers want to buy.

Types of losses

Table 5-14 is a table of conditional losses for Beth. Each value in the table is conditional on a specific number of cases being stocked and a specific number being requested. The values include *not only* those losses from obsolete inventory when the number of cases stocked exceeds the number buyers desire *but also* those opportunity losses resulting from lost sales when the market would have taken more than the number stocked.

Neither of these losses is incurred when the number stocked on any day is the same as the number requested. This condition results in the diagonal row of zeros. Dollar figures *above* any zero represent losses arising from obsolete inventory; in each case the number stocked is greater than the number sold. For example, if 13 cases are stocked and only 10 cases are sold, there is a $9 loss resulting from the cost of the 3 cases unsold.

Interpreting the table of conditional losses

Values *below* the diagonal row of zeros represent opportunity losses resulting from requests that cannot be filled. For example, if only 10 cases are stocked but 13 cases are wanted, there is an opportunity loss of $15. This is represented by the lost profit of $5 per case on the 3 cases requested but not available.

The next step is to assign probabilities to the quantities buyers will be wanting. Table 5-6 gave these probabilities as:

Cases	Probability
10	.20
11	.40
12	.30
13	.10

Applying these probabilities to the information in Table 5-14, we can compute the expected "loss" (reduction from maximum profit possible of $56.50) of each possible stock action. We do this by weighting each of the four possible loss

Computing expected loss

Table 5-14   Conditional Loss Table

Possible sales, cases	Possible stock actions			
	10 cases	11 cases	12 cases	13 cases
10	$ 0	$ 3	$6	$9
11	5	0	3	6
12	10	5	0	3
13	15	10	5	0

figures in each column of Table 5-14 by the probabilities from Table 5-6. For a stock action of 10 cases, the expected loss is computed as in Table 5-15.

The conditional losses in Table 5-15 are taken from Table 5-14 for a stock action of 10 cases. The sum in the last column tells us that if 10 cases are stocked each day, over a long period of time the average or expected loss will be $6.50 a day. There is no guarantee that *tomorrow's* loss will be exactly $6.50.

Expected loss for the four decision alternatives   Tables 5-16 to 5-18 show the computation of the expected loss resulting from decisions to stock 11, 12, and 13 cases, respectively. The optimum stock action is *the one which will minimize expected losses;* this action calls for the stocking of 12 cases each day, at which point the expected loss is minimized at $2.90.

Beth can approach the determination of the optimum stocking action from either point of view, maximizing expected profits *or* minimizing expected losses; both approaches lead to the same conclusion. In Table 5-19, we show that expected profits are *maximized* and expected losses are *minimized* when Beth Perry stocks 12 units daily.

The expected value of perfect information   *Expected Value of Perfect Information*   Assuming Beth could obtain a perfect predictor of future demand, what would be the value of such a predictor to her? She must compare what such additional information costs her with the additional profit she would realize as a result of having the information.

Beth can earn average daily profits of $56.50 if she has perfect information about the future (see Table 5-13). Her best expected daily profit without the predictor is only $53.60 (see Tables 5-8 to 5-11). The difference of $2.90 is the maximum amount she would be willing to pay, per day, for a perfect predictor

Table 5-15   Expected Loss from Stocking 10 Cases

Market size, cases	Conditional loss		Probability of market size		Expected loss
10	$ 0	×	.20	=	$ .00
11	5	×	.40	=	2.00
12	10	×	.30	=	3.00
13	15	×	.10	=	1.50
			1.00		$6.50

Table 5-16 Expected Loss from Stocking 11 Cases

Market size, cases	Conditional loss		Probability of market size		Expected loss
10	$ 3	×	.20	=	$ .60
11	0	×	.40	=	.00
12	5	×	.30	=	1.50
13	10	×	.10	=	1.00
			1.00		$3.10

because that is the maximum amount by which she can increase her expected daily profit. This difference is *the expected value of perfect information* and is referred to as EVPI. There is no sense in paying more than $2.90 for the predictor; to do so would lower the expected daily profit.

Determining what additional information is worth in the decision-making process is a serious problem for managers. In our example, we found that Beth would pay $2.90 a day for a *perfect* predictor. Generalizing from this example, we can say that the expected value of perfect information is equal to the minimum expected loss.

Expected value of perfect information equals minimum expected loss

It is not often, however, that one is fortunate enough to be able to secure a *perfect* predictor; thus, in most decision-making situations, managers are really attempting to evaluate the worth of information which will enable them to make *better* rather than *perfect* decisions.

Items Which Have a Salvage Value In the previous illustration, we assumed that the product being sold was completely worthless if not sold on the day after delivery, the "selling" day. This assumption that it had no salvage value is, of course, not always realistic. If the product *does* have some salvage value, then this amount must be considered in computing conditional profits for each stock action. Consider the case of fresh blueberries which are ordered by the retailer and received on the day before the selling day. They cost $5 per case and sell for $8 per case; any remaining unsold at the end of the day can be disposed of at a salvage price of $2 per case. Observation shows that past sales have ranged from 15 to 18 cases per day; there is no reason to believe that sales volume will take on any other magnitudes in the future.

Salvage value

Table 5-17 Expected Loss from Stocking 12 Cases

Market size, cases	Conditional loss		Probability of market size		Expected loss
10	$6	×	.20	=	$1.20
11	3	×	.40	=	1.20
12	0	×	.30	=	.00
13	5	×	.10	=	.50
			1.00		$2.90 ← optimum stock action

Table 5-18   Expected Loss from Stocking 13 Cases

Market size, cases	Conditional loss		Probability of market size		Expected loss
10	$9	×	.20	=	$1.80
11	6	×	.40	=	2.40
12	3	×	.30	=	.90
13	0	×	.10	=	.00
			1.00		$5.10

Example of decision making with salvage value

Using the same procedures as in Table 5-6, we establish these probabilities for the values sales will take:

Market size	Probability of market size
15	.10
16	.20
17	.40
18	.30
	1.00

The conditional profit table resulting from the above data is Table 5-20. A stock of 15 cases each day will result in daily profits of $45 regardless of whether demand is for 15, 16, 17, or 18 cases. The 15 cases stocked will always be sold but no more than this can be sold on any day.

Calculating conditional profits

A stock of 17 cases each day will result in a profit of $51 on those days when demand is either 17 or 18 cases. So far, the computation of conditional profits is the same as in all our previous examples. However, *any time the number stocked exceeds the demand on the selling day, the computation of conditional profit must take salvage value into consideration.* This happens, for example, when 17 cases are stocked but only 15 cases are sold. Conditional profit in this event is computed as follows:

Profit on the 15 cases sold	$45
Less cost of the 2 cases unsold	−10
	$35
Plus salvage value of 2 cases	+4
Conditional profit	$39

Table 5-19   Expected Profit and Expected Loss

	Stock action			
	10 cases	11 cases	12 cases	13 cases
Expected profit	$50.00	$53.40	$53.60	$51.40
Expected loss	6.50	3.10	2.90	5.10

Optimum (↑ under 12 cases)

Table 5-20 Conditional Profit Table

| Possible demand | Possible stock actions (cases) | | | |
sales; cases)	15	16	17	18
15	$45	$42	$39	$36
16	45	48	45	42
17	45	48	51	48
18	45	48	51	54

Salvage value can also be considered as a reduction in the cost of unsold cases. In our example, the net cost of each *unsold* case is $3, the original cost of $5 less the salvage value of $2. Thus, when 18 cases are stocked but only 16 are sold, the conditional profit is $42; this is $3 per case on the 16 sold less $6, the net cost of the 2 not sold.

The presence of salvage value in an inventory problem does not alter the application of any of the principles discussed earlier in this chapter. It simply means that we must consider its effect on conditional profits and losses. We have just seen that salvage value increases conditional profits because it reduces the losses caused by overstocking.

We proceed just as before in determining the optimum stock action to be taken. The next step is to determine the expect profit of each of the four possible stock actions. This involves weighting the conditional profit figures for each stock action by the probabilities that each will occur and then summing the results for each stock action.

Calculating expected profits for the four decision alternatives

Table 5-21 presents the resulting expected profit figures; the stocking of 17 cases each day is the optimum stock action. Over time, we can realize greater average and total profits by stocking 17 cases each day, even though on some days demand will be for 15, 16, or 18.

In many instances, the salvage value of an unsold item can take on more than one value, depending upon the age of the unsold item; it is not uncommon, for example, for fresh bread to command one price in the supermarket, for "day-old" bread to be sold for a somewhat lower price, and for bread older than 4 days to be nearly worthless. In some instances like this and in more complicated salvage value situations, tabular solutions to the problem become quite complex and cumbersome. In most such situations, operations researchers prefer to use more efficient methods rather than the tabular approach. Let's examine one of these now.

More than one salvage value

Use of Marginal Analysis In many problems, the use of conditional profit and expected profit tables would be difficult because of the number of computations required. Table 5-21 showed 4 possible stock actions and 4 possible sales levels, resulting in a conditional profit table containing 16 possibilities for conditional profits. Suppose there had been 200 possible values for sales volume and an equal number of possible stock actions. There would have been a tremendous number of calculations in determining the conditional and expected profit from each possible combination. The marginal approach avoids this problem of excessive computational work. When an additional unit of an item is bought, two fates are possible: the unit will be sold or it will not be sold. The sum of the probabilities of

Problems with too many conditional profits

Table 5-21 Expected Profit Table

Market size, cases	Probability of market size	Possible stock actions			
		15 cases		16 cases	
		Conditional profit	Expected profit	Conditional profit	Expected profit
15	.10	$45	$ 4.50	$42	$ 4.20
16	.20	45	9.00	48	9.60
17	.40	45	18.00	48	19.20
18	.30	45	13.50	48	14.40
	1.00		$45.00		$47.40

these two events must be 1. For example, if the probability of selling the additional unit is .4, then the probability of not selling it must be .6. The sum? 1.

Probability of selling and not selling an additional unit

If we let p represent the probability of selling one additional unit, then $1 - p$ must be the probability of *not* selling it. If the additional unit is sold, we shall realize an increase in our conditional profits as a result of the profit from the additional unit. We shall refer to this as *marginal profit* and designate it MP. In our salvage value illustration, the marginal profit resulting from the sale of an additional unit is $3, selling price less cost.

Reference to Table 5-21 will illustrate this point. If we stock 15 units each day and daily demand is for 15 or more units, our conditional profit is $45 per day. Now we decide to stock 16 units each day. If the sixteenth unit is sold (and this is the case when demand is for 16, 17, or 18 units), our conditional profit is increased to $48 per day. Notice that the increase in conditional profit does not follow merely from the *stocking* of the sixteenth unit. Under the conditions assumed in the problem, this increase in profit will result *only* when demand is for 16 or more units; this will be the case 90 percent of the time.

Marginal loss

We must also consider the effect on profits of stocking an additional unit and *not* selling it. This reduces our conditional profit. The amount of the reduction is referred to as the *marginal loss* (ML) resulting from the stocking of an item which is not sold.

Reference again to Table 5-21 will illustrate marginal loss. Assume once more that we decide to stock 16 units. Now assume that the sixteenth unit (the marginal unit) is not sold; only 15 units are sold. The conditional profit is now $42; the $45 conditional profit when 15 units were stocked and 15 were sold is now reduced by $3. This $3 is the cost of the unsold unit ($5) less the salvage value ($2).

Rule for stocking additional units

Additional units should be stocked so long as the *expected marginal profit* from stocking each of them is greater than the *expected marginal loss* from stocking each. The size of each day's order should be increased up to that point where the expected marginal profit from stocking one more unit *if it sells* is just equal to the expected marginal loss from stocking that unit *if it remains unsold*.

Possible stock actions			
17 cases		18 cases	
Conditional profit	Expected profit	Conditional profit	Expected profit
$39	$ 3.90	$36	$ 3.60
45	9.00	42	8.40
51	20.40	48	19.20
51	15.30	54	16.20
	$48.60		$47.40

↑ Optimum action

In our illustration, the probability distribution of demand is

Market size	Probability of market size
15	.10
16	.20
17	.40
18	.30
	1.00

This distribution tells us that as we increase our stock, the probability of selling 1 additional unit (this is p) decreases. For example, as we increase our stock from 15 to 16 units, the probablity of selling all 16 is .90. This is the probability that demand will be for 16 units or more. Here is the computation:

Probability that demand will be for 16	.20	**Probability of selling an additional unit**
Probability that demand will be for 17	.40	
Probability that demand will be for 18	.30	
Probability that demand will be for 16 or more units	.90	

With the addition of a seventeenth unit, the probability of selling all 17 units is reduced to .70 (the sum of the probabilities of demand for 17 or 18 units). Finally, the addition of an eighteenth unit carries with it only a .30 probability of our selling all 18 units, because demand will be for 18 units only 30 percent of the time.

The expected marginal profit from stocking and selling an additional unit is the marginal profit of the unit multiplied by the probability that the unit will be sold; this is p(MP). The expected marginal loss from stocking and not selling an additional unit is the marginal loss incurred if the unit is unsold multiplied by the probability that the unit will not be sold; this is $(1 - p)$(ML). From this example we can generalize that the manager in this situation would stock up to the point where:

Expected marginal profit from selling an additional unit

$$p(\text{MP}) = (1 - p)(\text{ML})$$

Point at which
expected profit from
an additional unit
equals expected loss

This equation describes the point at which the expected profit from stocking an additional unit, $p(MP)$, is equal to the expected loss from stocking the unit, $(1 - p)(ML)$. So long as $p(MP)$ is larger than $(1 - p)(ML)$, additional units should be stocked because the expected profit from such a decision is greater than the expected loss.

In any given problem, there will be only *one* value of p for which the maximizing equation will be true. We must determine that value in order to know the optimum stock action to take. We can do this by taking our maximizing equation and solving it for p in the following manner:

$$p(MP) = (1 - p)(ML)$$

Multiplying the two terms on the right side of the equation, we get

$$p(MP) = ML - p(ML)$$

Collecting terms containing p, we have

$$p(MP) + p(ML) = ML$$

or

$$p(MP + ML) = ML$$

Dividing both sides of the equation by $MP + ML$ gives

$$p = \frac{ML}{MP + ML} \tag{5-2}$$

The letter p represents *the minimum required probability of selling at least an additional unit to justify the stocking of that additional unit.* Additional units should be stocked so long as the probability of selling at least an additional unit is greater than p.

We can now compute p for our illustration. The marginal profit per unit is $3 (selling price less cost); the marginal loss per unit is also $3 (cost of each unit less salvage value); thus

Calculation of
minimum
probability

$$p = \frac{ML}{MP + ML} \tag{5-2}$$

$$= \frac{\$3}{\$3 + \$3} = \frac{\$3}{\$6} = .5$$

This value of .5 for p means that in order to make the stocking of an additional unit justifiable, we must have at least a .5 *cumulative* probability of selling that unit. In order to determine the probability of selling each additional unit we

Table 5-22   Cumulative Probabilities of Sales

Sales, units	Probability of this sales level	Cumulative probability that sales will be at this level or greater
15	.10	1.00
16	.20	.90
17	.40	.70
18	.30	.30

consider stocking, we must compute a series of cumulative probabilities as in Table 5-22.

The cumulative probabilities in the right-hand column of Table 5-22 represent the probabilities that sales will reach or exceed each of the four sales levels. For example, the 1.00 which appears beside the 15-unit sales level means that we are 100 percent certain of selling 15 or more units. This must be true because our problem assumes that one of four sales levels will *always* occur.

The .90 probability value beside the 16-unit sales figure means that we are only 90 percent sure of selling 16 or more units. This can be calculated in two ways. First, we could add the chances of selling 16, 17, and 18 units:

Calculating cumulative probabilities for the four decision alternatives

16 units	.20
17 units	.40
18 units	+.30
	.90 = probability of selling 16 or more

Or we could reason that sales of 16 or more units include all possible outcomes except sales of 15 units, which has a probability of .10.

Cumulative probability for 16 units or more

All possible outcomes	1.00
Probability of selling 15	−.10
	.90 = probability of selling 16 or more

The cumulative probability value of .70 assigned to sales of 17 units or more can be established in similar fashion. Sales of 17 or more must mean sales of 17 or of 18 units: so

Cumulative probability for 17 units or more

Probability of selling 17	.40
Probability of selling 18	+.30
	.70 = probability of selling 17 or more

And, of course, the cumulative probability of selling 18 units is still .30 because we have assumed that sales will never exceed 18.

As mentioned previously, the value of p, the cumulative probability, decreases as the levels of sales increase. This increase causes the expected marginal profit to

Cumulative probability for 18 units

decrease and the expected marginal loss to increase until, at some point, our stocking of an additional unit would not be profitable.

We have said that additional units should be stocked so long as the probability of selling at least an additional unit is greater than p. We can now apply this rule to our probability distribution of sales and determine how many units should be stocked.

Expected profit and loss for sixteenth unit

This procedure tells us that we should stock a sixteenth unit because the probability of selling 16 or more is .90, a figure clearly greater than our p of .50. This also means that the expected marginal profit from stocking this unit is greater than the expected marginal loss from stocking it. This can be verified as follows:

$$p(MP) = .90(\$3) = \$2.70 \text{ expected marginal profit}$$
$$(1 - p)(ML) = .10(\$3) = \$0.30 \text{ expected marginal loss}$$

Expected profit and loss for seventeenth unit

A seventeenth unit should be stocked because the probability of selling 17 or more units (.70) is greater than the required p of .50. Such action will result in the following expected marginal profit and expected marginal loss:

$$p(MP) = .70(\$3) = \$2.10 \text{ expected marginal profit}$$
$$(1 - p)(ML) = .30(\$3) = \$0.90 \text{ expected marginal loss}$$

Optimum stock

This is the *optimum* number of units to stock because the addition of an eighteenth unit carries with it only a .30 probability that it will be sold; this is less than our required p of .50. The following figures show why the eighteenth unit should not be stocked:

Expected profit and loss for eighteenth unit

$$p(MP) = .30(\$3) = \$0.90 \text{ expected marginal profit}$$
$$(1 - p)(ML) = .70(\$3) = \$2.10 \text{ expected marginal loss}$$

This tells us that if we stock an eighteenth unit, we will add more to expected loss than we add to expected profit.

Notice that the use of marginal analysis leads us to the same conclusion reached with the use of conditional profit and expected profit tables. Both methods of analysis result in a decision to stock 17 units each period.

In the problem we have just solved, we assumed that daily sales was a random variable; accordingly, we proposed a strategy to follow every day without alteration: stock 17 cases. In actual practice, however, we would no doubt find that daily sales would take on recognizable patterns depending upon the particular day of the week; this seems to invalidate the concept of a random variable. In retail sales, for example, Saturday is generally recognized as being a higher-volume day than, say, Tuesday. Similarly, Sunday retail sales are typically less than those on Friday.

Dealing with recognizable patterns in demand

In situations where there are recognizable patterns in daily sales, we can still apply the techniques we have learned. We would compute an optimal stocking rule for each day of the week. For Saturday, for example, we would use as our input data past sales experience *for Saturdays only*. Each of the other 6 days could be treated

Table 5-23 Expected Value Calculations Using the Criterion of Rationality

Possible demand (cases)	Possible stock actions			
	10 cases	11 cases	12 cases	13 cases
10	$50 × .25 = $12.50	$47 × .25 = $11.75	$44 × .25 = $11.00	$41 × .25 = $10.25
11	50 × .25 = 12.50	55 × .25 = 13.75	52 × .25 = 13.00	49 × .25 = 12.25
12	50 × .25 = 12.50	55 × .25 = 13.75	60 × .25 = 15.00	57 × .25 = 14.25
13	50 × .25 = 12.50	55 × .25 = 13.75	60 × .25 = 15.00	65 × .25 = 16.25
	$50.00	$53.00	$54.00	$53.00

Optimum stock action

in the same fashion. Essentially this approach represents nothing more than recognition of, and reaction to, discernible patterns in what may first appear to be a completely random environment.

The Criterion of Rationality

In decision-making situations where Beth Perry has little or no data on past demand, she could apply the *criterion of rationality* (also known as the principle of insufficient reason). This assumption was first introduced by Jacob Bernoulli. This criterion says that in the absence of any strong information to the contrary, Beth might as well assume that *all states of nature are equally likely.*

Applying the criterion of rationality to Beth Perry's strawberry problem, we see that since there are four possible states of nature (demand for 10, 11, 12, and 13 cases), she should assign a probability of .25 to each of these states. In Table 5-23, we have repeated the conditional profit table first shown in Table 5-7 on page 127, added equal probability weights to the four states of nature, and computed the expected value of the four stocking alternatives. Using this criterion, the optimum stocking decision is 12 cases, with an expected profit of $54.00.

Criterion of rationality

Applying criterion of rationality to previous problem

The Maximum Likelihood Criterion

If Beth wants to use the maximum likelihood criterion, she just selects the state of nature that has the highest probability of occurrence; then, having assumed that this state will occur, she picks the decision alternative which will yield the highest payoff. To demonstrate this criterion, we have repeated in Table 5-24 the information from Table 5-7, adding the probabilities Beth first assigned to the four states of nature. She can see that "demand for 11 cases" with an assigned probability of .4 is the state of nature with the highest probability of occurrence and that the stock action "11 cases" has the highest payoff for that state of nature. In Table 5-24, we have boxed the state of nature "demand for 11 cases" in black and circled the highest-payoff stock action, "11 cases," in color. This decision criterion is rather widely used and will produce valid results when one state of nature is much more probable than any other, and when the conditional values are not extremely

Maximum likelihood criterion

Applying maximum likelihood criterion to previous problem

Table 5-24 Determining the Optimum Stock Action Using the Maximum Likelihood Criterion

Possible demand (cases)	Probability of this demand	Possible stock actions			
		10 cases	11 cases	12 cases	13 cases
10	.20	$30	$28	$26	$24
11	.40	30	㉝	31	29
12	.30	30	33	36	34
13	.10	30	33	36	39

Shortcomings of the maximum likelihood criterion

different; however, it is possible to make some serious errors if we use this criterion in a situation where a large number of states of nature exist and each of them has a small, nearly equal probability of occurrence.

6. Using the Expected Value Criterion with Continuously Distributed Random Variables

Moving from discrete to continuous expected value

All the problems we have worked to this point in this chapter have involved *discrete* random variables. Most real situations, however, are concerned with continuously distributed random variables. It is not difficult to apply what we have learned up to this point to situations where the random variable is continuously distributed. Consider Steve Skeebo, a college senior who sells cherry tomatoes every spring. Steve buys them for $9 a crate and resells them for $16 per crate. If a crate is not sold on the first selling day, it is worth $3 as salvage. Steve's examination of past sales records indicates that demand for this particular item is normally distributed, with a mean of 120 crates daily and a standard deviation of 38 crates. What should Steve's stock be? Steve can use Eq. (5-2) to calculate the minimum required probability of selling at least an additional unit to justify his stocking of that unit with the data he has available:

$$p = \frac{ML}{MP + ML} \qquad (5\text{-}2)$$

$$= \frac{\$6}{\$7 + \$6}$$

$$= \frac{\$6}{\$13}$$

$$= .462$$

Minimum required probability illustrated on a normal distribution

Remember what this probability value means. Steve must be .462 sure of selling at least an additional unit before it would pay him to stock that unit. In Figure 5-1, we have illustrated the .462 probability on a normal distribution of past demand.

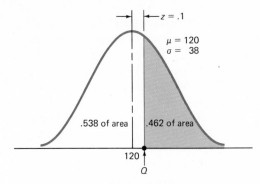

FIGURE 5-1 Continuously distributed random variable "past sales."

The .462 required probability is the shaded area. Steve should stock additional units until he reaches point Q; if he stocks a larger quantity, the probability falls below .462.

Since the shaded area under the normal curve in Figure 5-1 is .462 of the total area under the curve, the open area must be $1.000 - .462$, or .538 of the area under the curve. If we look in Appendix Table 1 (Standard Normal Probability) for .538, we see that the appropriate z value is .1. This means that point Q is .1 standard deviation to the right of the mean. Since we know that the standard deviation of the distribution of past demand for this item is 38 crates, point Q is found as follows:

Point Q = mean + .1 standard deviation

= mean + .1(38 crates)

= 120 crates + 3.8 crates

= 124 crates

The optimum stock for Steve to order is 124 crates.

Determining the optimum stock using the standard normal probability table

7. Utility as a Decision Criterion

Up to this point in this chapter, we have used expected value (expected *profit,* for example) as our decision criterion. This assumed that if the expected profit of alternative A was better than that of alternative B, then the decision maker would certainly choose alternative A. Conversely, if the expected loss of alternative C was greater than the expected loss of alternative D, then it was assumed that the decision maker would surely choose D as the better course of action.

There are situations, however, where the use of expected value as the decision criterion would get one into serious trouble. For example, suppose a businessperson owned a new factory worth, say, $1 million. Suppose further that there is only 1 chance in 1000 (.001) that it will burn down this year. From these two figures we can compute the expected loss:

Shortcomings of expected value as a decision criterion

$.001 \times \$1,000,000 = \$1000 = $ expected loss

Now suppose an insurance representative comes along and offers to insure the building for, say, $1250 this year. Strict use of the notion of minimizing expected losses would dictate that the businessperson refuse to insure the building, since the expected loss of insuring, $1,250, is higher than the expected loss of a fire. But if the businessperson felt that a million-dollar uninsured loss would mean disaster, the expected value would very probably be discarded as the decision criterion and the insurance would be bought at an extra cost of $250 per year per policy ($1250 − 1000). The choice would be *not* to minimize expected loss in this case.

Another example where expected value doesn't work

Let us look at an example a bit closer, perhaps, to students. Suppose you are the typical struggling graduate student with two children and just enough money to get through the semester and a friend offers to sell you a .9 chance at winning $10 for just $1. You would most likely think of the problem in terms of expected values and reason as follows: "Is .9 × $10 greater than $1?" Because $9 (the expected value of the bet) is 9 times greater than the cost of the bet ($1), you might feel inclined to take your friend up on this offer. Even if you lost, the loss of $1 would not affect your situation materially.

Suppose now that your friend offers to sell you a .9 chance at winning $1000 for $100. The question you would now ponder is: "Is .9 × $1000 greater than $100?" Of course $900 (the expected value of the bet) is still 9 times the cost of the bet ($100), but you would more than likely think twice before putting up your money. Why? Even though the pleasure of winning $1000 would be high, the pain of losing your hard-earned $100 might be more than you care to experience.

Suppose, finally, that your friend offers to sell you a .9 chance at winning $10,000 for your total assets, which happen to be $1000. If you use expected value as your decision criterion, you would ask the question "Is .9 × $10,000 greater than $1000?" with the same answer as before, namely, "Yes." The expected value of the bet ($9000) is still 9 times greater than the cost of the bet ($1000), but now you would probably refuse your friend, not because the expected value of the bet is unattractive but because the thought of losing all your assets is competely unacceptable as an outcome.

In these three examples, the student changed the decision criterion away from expected value as soon as the thought of losing $1000 was too painful despite the pleasure to be gained from $10,000. At this point, the student was not considering the expected value but thinking solely of *utility*. In this sense, *utility* refers essentially to the pleasure or displeasure one would derive from certain outcomes. The utility curve of our hypothetical student in Figure 5-2 is linear around the origin ($1 of gain is as *pleasurable* as $1 of loss is *painful* in this region); it turns down rapidly when the potential loss rises to levels near $1000. Specifically, this utility curve shows us that from the point of view of our hypothetical student, the displeasure from losing $1000 is greater than the pleasure from winning many times that amount. The shape of one's utility curve is a product of one's psychological makeup, one's expectations about the future, and the particular decision or act being evaluated. A person can well have one utility curve for one type of situation and quite a different one for the next situation.

Utility

The utility curve

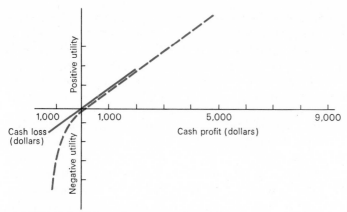

FIGURE 5-2 Utility of various profits and losses.

Different Utilities

The utility curves of three different businesspeople for a decision are shown on the graph in Figure 5-3. We have arbitrarily named these individuals Head, Bell, and Lev. The attitudes of these three individuals are readily apparent from analysis of their utility curves. Head is a cautious and conservative businessman; a move to

Individual utilities

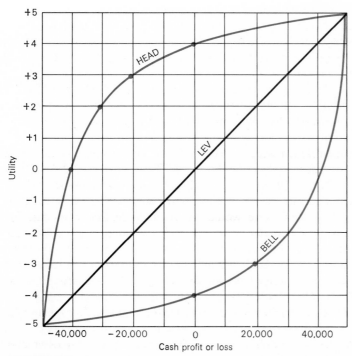

FIGURE 5-3

the right of the zero profit point increases his utility only very slightly whereas a move to the left of zero profit point decreases his utility rapidly. In terms of numerical values, Head's utility curve indicates that going from $0 to $50,000 profit increases his utility by a value of 1 on the vertical scale, while moving into the loss range by only $20,000 decreases his utility by the same value of 1, on the vertical scale. Head will avoid situations where high losses might occur; he is said to be *averse to risk*.

Bell is quite another story. We see from her utility curve that a profit increases her utility by much more than a loss of the same amount decreases it. Specifically, increasing her profits $10,000 (from $40,000 to $50,000) raises her utility from 0 to +5 on the vertical scale, but lowering her profits $10,000 (from $0 to −$10,000) decreases her utility by only .25, from −4 to −4.25. Bell is a player of long shots; she feels strongly that a large loss would not make things much worse than they are now but, on the contrary, that a big profit would be quite rewarding. She will take large risk to earn even larger gains.

Lev, fairly well off financially, is the kind of businessman who would not suffer too greatly from a $50,000 loss nor increase his wealth significantly from a $50,000 gain. He would get about as much pleasure from making an additional $50,000 as he would pain from losing $50,000. Because Lev's utility curve is linear, he can effectively use *expected value* as his decision criterion, whereas Head and Bell must use *utility*. In summary, whereas Lev will act where the expected value is positive, Head will demand a high expected value for the outcome while Bell may act when the expected value is negative.

Only one of the three decision makers should use expected value

Glossary

1. **State of nature**   Future event not under the control of the decision maker.
2. **Payoff table**   Illustration of the payoffs which would result from each possible combination of decision alternative and state of nature.
3. **Decision alternative**   An alternative choice open to the decision maker.
4. **Payoff**   The benefit which accrues from a given combination of decision alternative and state of nature.
5. **Certainty**   The decision environment in which only one state of nature exists.
6. **Uncertainty**   The decision environment in which more than one state of nature exists but in which the decision maker has no knowledge about the various states.
7. **Risk**   The decision environment in which the decision maker has information which will support the assignment of probability values to each of the possible states of nature.
8. **Maximax criterion**   An optimistic criterion which maximizes the maximum payoff.
9. **Maximin criterion**   A pessimistic criterion which maximizes the minimum payoff.

10. Minimax regret criterion A criterion which selects that payoff which minimizes the maximum regret.

11. Criterion of realism A middle-ground criterion between maximax and maximin which requires the decision maker to specify a coefficient or index of optimism.

12. Expected value criterion A criterion which requires the decision maker to calculate the expected value for each decision alternative (the sum of the weighted payoffs for that alternative where the weights are the probability values assigned by the decision maker to the states of nature that can happen).

13. Conditional profit The profit which would result from a given combination of decision alternative and state of nature. Conditional profit is a payoff.

14. Expected profit The summation of the conditional profits for a given decision alternative each weighted by the probability that they will happen.

15. Expected profit with perfect information The expected value of profit with perfect certainty about the occurrence of the states of nature.

16. Obsolescence loss The loss occasioned by stocking too many units and having to dispose of unsold units.

17. Opportunity loss The profit that could have been earned if stock had been sufficient to supply a unit that was demanded.

18. The expected value of perfect information The difference between expected profit (under conditions of risk) and expected profit with perfect information.

19. Salvage value The value of an item after the initial selling day.

20. Marginal profit The profit earned from selling one additional unit.

21. Marginal loss The loss incurred from stocking a unit which is not sold.

22. Expected marginal profit The marginal profit multiplied by the probability of selling that unit.

23. Expected marginal loss The marginal loss multiplied by the probability of not selling that unit.

24. Minimum probability The probability of selling at least an additional unit which must exist to justify stocking that unit.

25. Cumulative probability The probability of selling a given number or greater.

26. Criterion of rationality Criterion used when all states of nature are assumed equally likely; also known as the *principle of insufficient reason*.

27. Maximum likelihood criterion Criterion which selects that state of nature which has the highest probability of occurring and picks the decision alternative which yields the highest payoff for that state.

28. Utility The value of a certain outcome or payoff to someone; the pleasure or displeasure that person would derive from that outcome.

Review of Equations

Page 125

Measure of realism $= \alpha$ (maximum payoff) $+ (1 - \alpha)$ (minimum payoff)   (5-1)

When decision makers would rather not use a completely optimistic or a completely pessimistic decision criterion under uncertainty, the measure of realism allows them to introduce their personal assessment of optimism (α) and thereby find a middle ground between a criterion of optimism and a criterion of pessimism.

Page 138

$$p = \frac{ML}{MP + ML} \tag{5-2}$$

This formula calculates the p or probability, which represents the minimum probability of selling at least an additional unit to justify stocking that unit. In this formulation, MP is the marginal profit if the extra unit is sold and ML is the marginal loss if it is not sold.

Exercises

5-1. Are the following statements made under conditions of risk, certainty, or undertainty?
a. "The investment proposals I am considering have equally likely chances of tripling my money or losing 50 percent of my investment."
b. "These 20,000 pounds of raw material will yield 550 finished products."
c. "Depending on business conditions, our firm will either make or lose money this year."
d. "I know that 20 percent of our accounts are past due. If I select one at random, there is a .2 chance that it will be past due."
e. "If I deposit $10,000 in a savings account, the bank will pay me the prevailing interest rate."

5-2. Virgil Williams is a door-to-door salesman of food products; he uses a three-wheeled cart and moves through the neighborhood selling meat, eggs, some vegetables, and milk. Virgil is considering adding summer sausage; however, because his cart has no refrigeration, any sausage not sold at the end of the day spoils. From his knowledge of his customers, Virgil estimates demand for sausage to be between 0 and 4 pounds daily; using his known cost/price relationship, he has put together this table of profit/loss:

	Number of pounds stocked				
Demand	0	1	2	3	4
0	0	−$2	−$4	−$6	−$8
1	0	3	1	− 1	− 3
2	0	3	6	4	2
3	0	3	6	9	7
4	0	3	6	9	12

Using the maximin decision criterion, how many pounds should Virgil stock?

5-3. Yogurt Hut, Ltd., sells natural yogurt in a college community. Julie Stoneman, the manager, is filling out the orders for next week's supply of yogurt. She is uncertain as to what sales will be. Julie has the table below as a historical representation of profits given certain sales and buying-level combinations.

Weekly sales	Actions		
	Buy 200	Buy 300	Buy 400
200	$50	$25	$ 0
300	50	75	50
400	50	75	100

Using the maximax decision criterion, what advice can you give Julie about quantities of yogurt to buy for next week?

5-4. Mutual Funds of the Northeast has $500,000 available for one of three investment alternatives in the stock market: a blue chip stock offering, a growth stock offering, and a venture stock offering. The investment environment can assume any one of four states and Mutual has no prior information about what the market will do. Mutual's payoff table looks like this:

Type of stock	Stock market trend			
	Boom	Moderate growth	Moderate decline	Collapse
Blue chip	$250,000	$ 75,000	$ 0	−$300,000
Growth	375,000	150,000	− 50,000	− 400,000
Venture	500,000	100,000	− 150,000	− 500,000

Using the minimax regret criterion for decision making, evaluate each alternative and advise Mutual which is preferable.

5-5. The New Era Toy Co., Inc., manufactures wooden children's toys. The company believes that the current trend toward sturdier and simpler toys will continue; thus New Era must decide among three alternative methods of providing for anticipated higher demand for its products. These are completely overhauling the existing plant and installing computerized woodworking machinery, expanding the current plant and adding more machines, or buying a competitor's plant which is available. A fourth alternative would be to limit production to the current plant capacity (do nothing). New Era's payoff table is as follows:

Alternatives	Demand			
	High	Moderate	Low	Failure
Overhaul	$30,000	$10,000	−$ 5,000	−$50,000
Expand	60,000	20,000	− 10,000	− 70,000
Buy	50,000	15,000	− 20,000	− 60,000
Do nothing	3,000	2,000	− 1,000	− 5,000

New Era management has no information as to how demand will be likely to shape up. Using the criterion of realism, with $\alpha = .75$, determine the best choice for New Era under these conditions.

5-6. Here is a distribution of past sales of 8-track tape cartridges for Big Charlie's Stereo Shop.

Quantities buyers bought	Number of days occurred	p(occurrence)	Cumulative probability
20 units	10	.10	1.00
25	30	.30	.90
40	50	.50	.60
60	10	.10	.10

Charlie buys these for $6 each and sells them for $10.
a. If he stocks 25 every day, what will his expected profit per day be?
b. What would the expected profit per day be with a 60-unit stock?
c. What quantity should Charlie buy every day to maximize expected profits?
d. What is the expected value of perfect information for Charlie?

5-7. A veterinarian purchases rabies immunization vaccine on Monday of each week. Because of the characteristics of this vaccine, it must be used by Friday or disposed of. The vaccine costs $7 per dose and the vet charges $10 per dose. In the past, the vet has administered rabies vaccine in the following quantities:

Quantities used per week	Number of weeks this occurred	Probability of occurrence	Cumulative probability
25	15	.4	1.00
40	20	.3	.60
50	10	.2	.30
75	5	.1	.10

Using marginal analysis, determine how many doses the veterinarian should order each week.

5-8. The Captain's Table is a mail-order distributor of fresh lobsters. The company buys these for $3.60 and sells them for $4.50. The per-week shipment distribution is as follows:

Shipments per week	Number of weeks this occurred	Probability of occurrence	Cumulative probability
3,000	5	.05	1.00
5,000	15	.20	.95
8,000	25	.20	.75
12,000	40	.40	.55
18,000	15	.15	.15

The company has been approached by a consulting firm specializing in sales fore-casting. The firm has offered to provide The Captain's Table with a sales forecasting model which will more than double the distributor's present profit by matching purchases with sales. The cost of buying and running this model will be $7500 a week. Should the company buy it? (Expected value is already being used to calculate how many lobsters to order each week.)

5-9. You have undertaken the sponsorship of a racing car and team as part of an advertising campaign. In preparing an expected expense statement for the next race, you have accumulated this information: Complete engines for the race car cost $5000; complete overhauls cost $2000; minor maintenance is essentially a no-cost item since the crew is already salaried. The team completely "blows" an engine (destroys it) in 40 percent of the races; in 30 percent of the races, the engine needs a complete overhaul after the race; 30 percent of the time, the engine needs only minor maintenance. Your data also show the following conditional probabilities for qualifying speeds given the kind of engine repair needed after the race:

Qualifying speed before race	Occurrence of "blown" engines, percent	Occurrence of major overhaul, percent	Occurrence of minor maintenance, percent
Over 175 mph	70	60	10
160–175 mph	20	30	30
Below 160 mph	10	10	60

Your driver, Beauford Johnson, has just qualified for the Dixie 600 at 182.375 mph. What is your expected engine expense for the race?

5-10. You own a citizen's band radio manufacturing company. You buy your crystals from two different sources to guarantee the supply. The normal order is 30,000 crystals. One supply source guarantees not more than 1 percent defectives. The other source has had varying rates according to this table:

Percent defective	Probability of this level
.5	.30
2.0	.50
5.0	.20

Your own assembly-line personnel are able to repair defective crystals at a cost of $2 each. The supply source with the guaranteed defective rate charges $1000 more per order than the other source. Which source provides the lowest cost for your crystal supply?

5-11. Southwestern University feels that four characteristics should be considered when selecting students for admission: grade point average, entrance test score, recommendations, and extracurricular activities. The university further believes that grade point average is four times more important than extracurricular activities, entrance test scores are three times as important as extracurricular activities, and recommendations are twice as important as extracurricular activities. Scores are standardized to a 100-point scale. At this point, there are two vacancies for scholarships; choose two from among these seven students:

Student name	Grade point average	Test score	Recommendation	Extracurricular activities
Steve	75	84	90	80
Celeste	91	88	83	88
Carole	86	93	90	92
Frank	94	90	88	75
Linda	94	84	86	89
Cam	82	70	94	93
Bill	74	89	85	68

5-12. Fred Allen has his own Sno-Cone truck and lives 30 miles from the nearest beach resort. The number of Sno-Cones he sells is highly dependent upon the weather; the most recent forecast indicates a .3 chance of fair weather. If the weather is fair and Fred drives to the beach, he makes $90 per day on average; if he stays home, his profit is $40. If the weather is bad, he makes only $10 at the beach versus $25 at home. Given the latest weather forecast, construct Fred's payoff table and recommend whether he should stay home or drive to the beach. What could Fred afford to pay for a really good forecast of the next day's weather—one which would rarely miss?

5-13. The Alexander Livestock Company receives orders for an average of 6000 dozen quail eggs a week. The standard deviation of weekly orders is 425 dozen. The eggs cost $7 a dozen and are resold for $10. If the eggs are not shipped within a week, their fertility is impaired and Alexander's cannot sell them as first-quality; they can, however, be sold for $1 a dozen. Calculate Alexander's optimum weekly order of eggs.

5-14. Charlie owns a very old truck which he uses for occasional deliveries both in town and out of town. If he delivers out of town, he can average $100 a trip provided that his truck doesn't break down; if it does, repairs, delay, and towing cut his profit to $20. If he stays in town, he makes $60 a trip, but this is reduced to $30 if his truck breaks down. Compute what the probability of a breakdown would have to be for Charlie to be indifferent as to where he delivers.

5-15. Terry's Pro Shop stocks golf equipment. It's the beginning of the season and Terry is deciding how many golf bags to stock. She has used past records to formulate the table below, which illustrates demand expectations and conditional profits (losses) given certain stocking actions. Using the principle of maximum likelihood as a decision criterion, how much inventory should Terry stock?

Demand	Likelihood	Conditional profits (stock actions)					
		2	4	6	8	10	12
2	.1	$50	$ 20	$ 0	−$ 20	−$ 60	−$100
4	.3	50	100	50	0	− 20	− 60
6	.2	50	100	150	120	80	0
8	.2	50	100	150	200	160	120
10	.1	50	100	150	200	250	190
12	.1	50	100	150	200	250	300

5-16. Care, Inc., is a charity meal center which provides indigent families with nourishing food on a daily basis. Each family pays $1 for meals which cost an average of $3 to prepare. If the meals prepared at a given time are not eaten, they go to waste. If more meals are demanded than are fixed, each unfed family is given $3 to buy meals elsewhere. The possible demand for meals and associated costs of preparation and payments to unfed families are these:

Demand	Number of meals prepared					
	4	5	6	7	8	9
4	− 8	−11	−14	−17	−20	−23
5	−11	−10	−13	−16	−19	−22
6	−14	−13	−12	−15	−18	−21
7	−17	−16	−15	−14	−17	−20
8	−20	−19	−18	−17	−16	−19
9	−23	−22	−21	−20	−19	−18

The charity which runs Care, Inc., wants to minimize its expense. If it uses the criterion of rationality, how many meals should it prepare?

5-17. Mr. Wood is approached with an investment opportunity which could result in a profit or loss ranging between −$3000 and +$5000. He is quite rich, and losing up to $2000 will still result in positive utility. In fact, a breakeven situation will result in a rather high level of utility. Plot a utility curve for Mr. Wood.

5-18. Mrs. Slade is approached by an associate with an investment proposition. The maximum profit that she can realize is $25,000, and the maximum loss possible is $20,000. Mrs. Slade feels that a no-gain or loss situation carries a low level of utility. Plot a utility curve for her.

5-19. An investor has $10,000 to invest in common stock. His selection is between companies A and B. He feels that for each of the investments he has a .4 probability of doubling his money and a .6 probability of losing half his money. His choices are: (1) invest the entire amount in either A or B, (2) invest $5000 in one company and not invest the other $5000, (3) invest $5000 in A and $5000 in B, or (4) not invest at all. If his utility values for changes in assets are: ($10,000) = 1, ($5000) = .90, ($2500) = .70, ($0) = .40, (−$2500) = .20, and (−$5000) = 0, what investment plan should he choose to maximize his expected utility? Assume that the rise or fall of either stock is independent of the other's.

5-20. An investor is considering two alternatives for which she has $25,000 to invest. The first is commercial property; the second is stocks. Analysis has revealed that each alternative offers a .3 probability of tripling her investment and a .7 probability of losing 60 percent of the entire amount. Her choices are (1) invest the entire amount in one or the other, (2) invest half her funds in one or the other and keep half, (3) invest half her money in each alternative, or (4) make no investment. She exhibits these utilities for change in her assets: ($50,000) = 1; ($25,000) = .8; ($17,500) = .6; ($0) = .4; (−$7500) = .2; and (−$15,000) = 0. What investment plan should this woman follow to maximize her utility? You may assume that the rise and fall of one investment is independent of the other.

5-21. Caroline Edwards is a great basketball fan and a very wealthy person. She is thinking of buying a professional basketball team. A look at the financial records of the team indicates profits and losses ranging from −$50,000 to $30,000. Because of Caroline's love of the game, the team could lose as much as $30,000 without causing her utility to become negative. If the team breaks even, she will enjoy a high utility level. Plot her utility curve.

5-22. Freddy Jackson is a compulsive gambler. He has several large gambling debts which are past due now. He has managed to borrow $5000 more and is planning to bet this on a single horserace. The horse he is betting on will pay 20:1 for win and decreasing amounts for place and show. If the horse fails to return at least 10:1, Freddy's utility will be negative; a 20:1 return would result in a very high utility for him. Plot Freddy's utility curve.

Bibliography

Baumol, W. J.: *Economic Theory and Operations Analysis,* 3d ed. (Englewood Cliffs, N.J.: Prentice-Hall, Inc., 1972).

Beer, S.: *Management Sciences, The Business Use of Operations Research* (Garden City, N.Y.: Doubleday & Company, Inc., 1968).

Hiller, F. S., and **G. J. Lieberman:** *Introduction to Operations Research,* 2d ed. (San Francisco: Holden-Day, Inc., 1974).

Luce, R. D., and **H. Raiffa:** *Games and Decisions* (New York: John Wiley & Sons, Inc., 1957).

Schlaifer, R.: *Analysis of Decisions under Uncertainty* (New York: McGraw-Hill Book Company, 1969).

Wagner, H. M.: *Principles of Management Science with Applications to Executive Decisions* (Englewood Cliffs, N.J.: Prentice-Hall, Inc., 1970).

Winkler, R. L.: *Introduction to Bayesian Inference and Decision* (New York: Holt, Rinehart and Winston, Inc., 1972).

Decision theory II

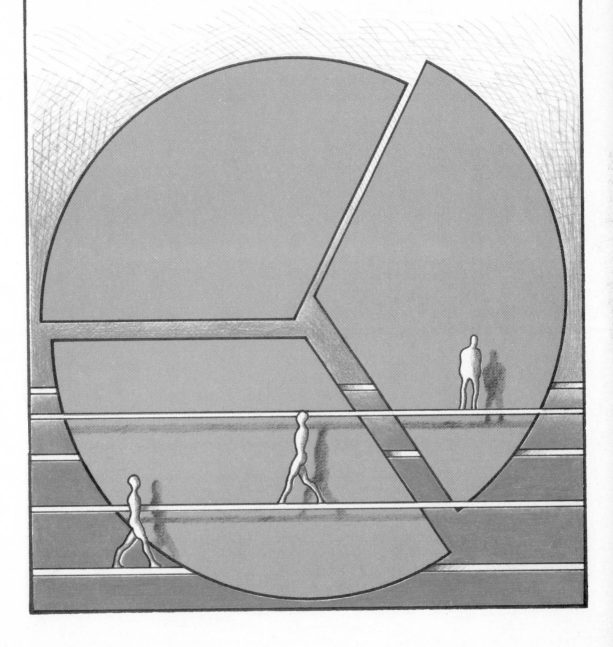

6

1. Supplying the Numbers

What are the alternatives when μ and σ cannot be specified?

The problems treated in Chapter 5 using the normal probability distribution all required one to know both the *mean* and the *standard deviation*. In each of the illustrative problems used in that chapter, these two values (μ and σ) could be computed from available data. But what about the situations where past data are missing or at best incomplete? How does one make use of a probability distribution in these cases? An illustrative problem will help to point out how one can often generate the values that are required using an *intuitive* approach.

Suppose, for example, that you were contemplating the purchase of a machine which replaces manual labor on an operation. The machine will cost $5000 per year to operate and will save $4 for each hour it operates. For it to break even, it must operate at least $5000/$4 = 1250 hours annually. Now if we are interested in the probability that it will actually run more than 1250 hours, we must know something about the distribution of running times, explicitly the *mean* and *standard deviation* of this distribution. But where would we find these figures with no past history of machine operation?

An estimate of the mean

Suppose we went to the supervisor of this operation and asked him to guess the mean running time of the machine. With his close knowledge of the process involved, he would probably be able to give us a "guessed-at" mean; let us say his best estimate here is 1400 hours. But how would he react if you then asked him to give you the *standard deviation* of the distribution? This term is not meaningful to

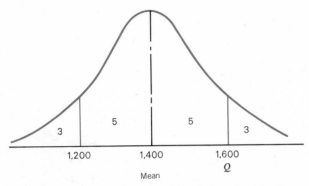

Figure 6-1 Supervisor's estimated distribution of running times.

him and yet, intuitively, he probably has some notion of the dispersion of the distribution of running times. Since most people understand betting odds, let us appeal to him on that basis.

Let us count off an equal distance on each side of his mean, say 200 hours; this gives us an interval from 1200 to 1600 hours. Then let us ask him the question "What are the odds that the number of hours will lie between 1200 and 1600?" If he has had any experience with betting, he should be able to reply. Suppose he says, "I think the odds it will run between 1200 and 1600 hours are 5 to 3." We show his answer on a probability distribution in Figure 6-1.

Using betting odds to get an estimate of the standard deviation

Figure 6-1 indicates exactly what the supervisor replied, that the odds are 5 to 3 the machine will run between 1200 and 1600 hours rather than outside those limits. Now what to do? On the distribution in Figure 6-1, we have called the 1600-hour point on the distribution point Q. We see that the area under the curve to the left of point Q, according to the supervisor's estimates, is $^{13}/_{16}$ of the area under the entire curve, $(3 + 5 + 5)/(3 + 5 + 5 + 3)$. Now see Figure 6-2. Since $^{13}/_{16}$ is approximately .813, let us look in Appendix Table 1 for the value .813. There we find that point Q is .89 standard deviation to the right of the mean.

Converting odds to the standard deviation

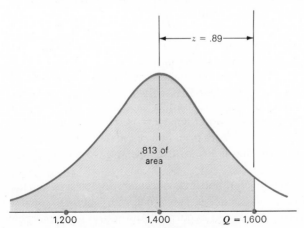

Figure 6-2 Supervisor's estimated distribution of running times.

As the distance from the mean to Q is known to be 200 hours, we see that:

.89 std. dev. = 200 hr

and thus

1 std. dev. = 225 hr

Using the estimated standard deviation to specify risk

Now that we can specify the mean and standard deviation of the distribution of running times, we can calculate the probability of the machine's running less than its breakeven point of 1250 hours. This situation is shown in Figure 6-3. From Appendix Table 1 we find that the area between one tail of the distribution and a point .666 standard deviation past the mean (1250 hours) is about .747 of the total area under the curve. Because this is the probability that the machine will operate *more* than 1250 hours, the chances that it will operate *less* than 1250 hours (its breakeven point) are $1 - .747$, or .253; it would seem that this is not too risky a situation.

Asking for information in terms that are relevant

In this section, we have illustrated with a hypothetical example how one can make use of other people's knowledge about a situation without requiring them to understand the intricacies of various mathematical techniques. Had we expected the supervisor to comprehend the theory behind our calculations or even attempted to explain the theory to him, we might never have been able to benefit from his practical wisdom concerning the situation. In this case (and for that matter, in most others, too) it is wiser to accommodate the ideas and knowledge of other people in one's models than to search until you find a situation which will fit a model that has already been developed.

Questioning the assumption of normality

Finally, before we leave this example, we must remember that we *assumed* the distribution of machine operating hours to be a normal distribution. If we had *strong* information to the contrary, we certainly would be wise to heed that information and not to make the assumption we did. However, in the absence of information to the contrary, it would be reasonable to make the assumption we did. In this case as well, the opinion of the supervisor would be quite useful, and his experience would likely allow him to make some intuitive observation about the symmetry of the distribution.

2. Combining Experience and Numbers

In the previous example, we saw how the extensive experience of our supervisor was "captured" as a probability distribution and used successfully because we were able to communicate with him in language and terms of reference which he understood. We were able to get workable estimates from him of the *mean* and *standard deviation* of the distribution of operating times for the machine we contemplated purchasing.

Combining intuition and statistical evidence

There are many situations in which it becomes necessary to combine the extensive experience and intuition of operating personnel with equally valuable statistical evidence. Specifically, this situation might well arise again in the context of the decision whether to purchase a new machine to be used exclusively for the production of a new product. Clearly, what is needed here is an estimate of the

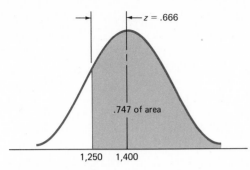

z = .666

.747 of area

1,250   1,400

Figure 6-3 Illustration of probability that machine will operate above breakeven hours.

future sales of the new product on which we can rely with some confidence. But how to get it?

Judgment in this instance is certainly available in the form of the "best estimates" of the sales manager and her staff. So-called hard data in this case might be obtained from a market research survey of the potential demand for the product. In cases such as this, one must be quite certain not to *discard* judgment simply because it is intuitive and similarly not to *accept* statistical survey results just because they involve numerical operations; *both* sources of information are subject to estimating errors. The sensible decision maker prefers in most cases to *combine* the two sources of information as opposed to discarding one or both. Although the underlying mathematical theory is a bit too heady for a text at this level, the procedures by which this combination can be made are easily understood and applied. **Use judgment, don't discard it**

Below, we illustrate the sales manager's probability distribution of monthly sales for the new product. She puts the mean sales volume per month at 110 units, and from the same kinds of questions we asked the supervisor in the previous example, we have been able to calculate the sales manager's standard deviation of monthly sales as 10 units. A recently completed market survey indicates potential monthly sales at 70 units with a standard deviation of 7 units. **One estimate of monthly sales**

Now suppose the financial manager, after considering the capital costs involved and the relevant cost-price relationships, has determined that breakeven volume on the new product is 80 units a month. At this point, the management of the company can reject the new product on the strength of the assumed greater precision of the market survey, they can accept the new product if they choose to consider the more favorable estimate of mean sales given by the sales manager, or they can choose to combine the two estimates (both the means and the standard deviations) to see what implications the combination of judgment and numbers has for the new-product decision. **A second estimate of monthly sales**

Combining estimates like this involves weighting each mean by its *reliability*; that is (without going into the mathematics underlying this operation), we weight each mean by the reciprocal of its standard deviation squared, like this: **Combining two estimates by reliability weighting**

Estimate source	Mean	Std. deviation	(Std. deviation)^2	$\dfrac{1}{(\text{Std. deviation})^2}$
Sales manager	110	10	100	$1/100$
Market survey	70	7	49	$1/49$

$$\text{Combined estimate} = \frac{(\text{est. 1})\left(\begin{array}{c}\text{reciprocal}\\ \text{of std.}\\ \text{deviation 1}\end{array}\right)^2 + (\text{est. 2})\left(\begin{array}{c}\text{reciprocal}\\ \text{of std.}\\ \text{deviation 2}\end{array}\right)^2}{\left(\begin{array}{c}\text{reciprocal of std.}\\ \text{deviation 1}\end{array}\right)^2 = \left(\begin{array}{c}\text{reciprocal of std.}\\ \text{deviation 2}\end{array}\right)^2} \quad (6\text{-}1)$$

$$\text{Combined estimate of mean sales} = \frac{110 \times {}^1\!/_{100} + 70 \times {}^1\!/_{49}}{{}^1\!/_{100} + {}^1\!/_{49}}$$

$$= 83.17 \text{ units}$$

Combining the two estimates of the standard deviation And the combined standard deviation for the two estimates may be approximated by using a formula many will recognize as being that for the harmonic mean:

$$\begin{array}{c}\text{Combined standard}\\ \text{deviation}\end{array} = \frac{\sqrt{2} \leftarrow (\#\text{ of estimates})}{\sqrt{\left(\begin{array}{c}\text{reciprocal of std.}\\ \text{deviation 1}\end{array}\right)^2 + \left(\begin{array}{c}\text{reciprocal of std.}\\ \text{deviation 2}\end{array}\right)^2}} \quad (6\text{-}2)$$

$$\text{Combined standard deviation} = \frac{\sqrt{2}}{\sqrt{({}^1\!/_{10})^2 + ({}^1\!/_7)^2}}$$

$$= 8.11$$

Using combined estimates   The best *combined* estimate of the new product's sales is a mean of slightly higher than 83 units per month and that the standard deviation of the distribution around this mean will be about 8.11 units. Using these two values, the distribution of sales for the proposed product is illustrated in Figure 6-4.

Because one standard deviation for the combined distribution is 8.11 units, we calculate that the breakeven point is $(83 - 80)/8.11$ which is

$$\frac{3}{8.11} \quad \text{or} \quad .37 \text{ standard deviation}$$

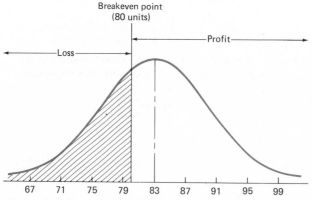

Figure 6-4 Estimated monthly sales in units (combined estimate).

to the left of the mean of the *combined* distribution (83). From Appendix Table 1, we find that the area under the normal curve from one tail to a point .37 standard deviation past the mean is .64431 of the total area. Thus the portion of the area under the curve representing sales volumes less than the breakeven point (loss) is calculated as:

1.0 − .64431   or about .356

and is shown in Figure 6-4 as the shaded area under the curve. On the strength of our combined estimates of the new product's sales, it then appears that chances for a loss are less than .4, not bad odds at all for a new product. Interpreting results

Let us examine the significance of what we have done. Had we proceeded solely on the strength of the market survey, with its mean of a 70-unit monthly sales volume, chances are that we would *not* have proceeded with the introduction of a product which required 80 units monthly just to break even. On the other hand, had we chosen to disregard the market survey and proceed full speed ahead on the strength of our sales manager's 110-unit monthly estimate, we would have failed to see the chance of failure and thus would have made our new-product decision on incomplete information. We chose to do neither. Instead, we combined the considerable experience and "feel" of our sales manager with some valuable quantitative market survey information. Additionally, we looked not only at the *mean* values in each estimate but also at the standard deviations of the estimates. Combining the two means and the two standard deviations, we came to an objective determination of our chances of success on this new product; we chose not to use judgment or quantitative market information alone but to *combine both* to make a better decision. Value of more than one estimate

3. The Normal Probability Distribution and Cost-Volume-Profit Analysis

Cost-volume-profit analysis (often referred to as breakeven analysis) allows management to determine in advance (with at least a worthwhile degree of accuracy) the effects that certain contemplated decisions or expected states of nature will have on revenues, costs, and therefore profits. Of the two variables which determine profits (revenues and costs), management has considerably less control over revenues; thus the estimation of revenues is a good example of decision making under conditions of risk, where management can usually specify a *distribution* of revenues. Sales volume is, in fact, a random variable, and solutions to cost-volume-profit problems which treat it differently are avoiding some of the real issues in decision making. Cost-volume-profit analysis A distribution of revenues can usually be specified Sales volume as a random variable

Let us use as an example a company with these financial data concerning a proposed new product:

Selling price	$7.50
Variable cost/unit	$4.50
Fixed cost/year	$1,500,000

Breakeven point defined   In cost-volume-profit analysis, the breakeven point (the point at which total revenue equals total cost) can be expressed algebraically like this:

$$\text{Breakeven point (in units)} = \frac{\text{total fixed cost}}{\text{price/unit} - \text{variable cost/unit}} \qquad (6\text{-}3)$$

where total fixed costs = indirect costs such as rent, interest on debt, property taxes, insurance, executive salaries, depreciation, and other costs which do not vary with volume

price/unit = selling price charged for the item

variable cost/unit = direct costs per unit which can be charged directly and specifically to the product and which are constant per unit of output regardless of volume

Using Eq. (6-3), we can calculate the breakeven point for the new product like this:

Breakeven point calculated

$$\begin{aligned} \text{Breakeven point (in units)} &= \frac{\text{total fixed cost}}{\text{price/unit} - \text{variable cost/unit}} \qquad (6\text{-}3)\\ &= \frac{\$1,500,000}{\$7.50 - \$4.50}\\ &= \frac{\$1,500,000}{\$3.00}\\ &= 500,000 \text{ units annually} \end{aligned}$$

Variability of the estimate   Now, suppose our sales manager estimates that the mean expected sales volume for the new product for the coming year is 600,000 units. When asked about the variability of this estimate, she indicates chances are 2 to 1 that sales will be within 300,000 of the mean she has estimated. Using the same technique first illustrated in the section of this chapter called "Supplying the Numbers," we can illustrate the distribution of sales our sales manager seems to have in mind in Figure 6-5.

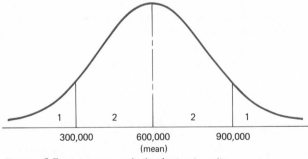

Figure 6-5   Sales manager's distribution in units.

From Figure 6-5 we can see that the area between the left-hand tail of the distribution and the 900,000-unit point is $^5/_6$ or .8333 of the total area under the curve. From Appendix Table 1, we can determine that the 900,000-unit point is about .97 standard deviation to the right of the mean of this distribution. As

.97 standard deviation = 300,000 units
  1 standard deviation = 309,278 units

Converting this to financial terms, we can say that the standard deviation of the *contribution* of this new product (contribution is price per unit less variable cost per unit and is linearly related to volume) is

309,278 units × $3 contribution/unit = $927,834

Figure 6-6 illustrates the distribution of contribution, a variable which is generally of great concern to management. Expected profit from the new product is calculated as follows:

Expected profit = expected sales × contribution/unit − fixed cost
       = 600,000 × $3 − $1,500,000
       = $1,800,000 − $1,500,000
       = $300,000

The standard deviation of contribution has already been calculated to be $927,834. From the distribution in Figure 6-6, a number of financial questions of considerable relevance to managerial decision making can now be answered. These are:

1. *What is the probability of at least breaking even?* In order for the company to lose money on the new product (not break even), profits would have to fall to zero; the zero profit point is equal to a contribution of $1,500,000, or .323 ($300,000/ $927,834) standard deviation to the left of the mean of this distribution. Appendix Table 1 tells us that there is only a .374 chance that contribution would ever be less than $1,500,000; that is about a .626 chance of breaking even.

2. *What is the chance that profits from the new product would be at least $500,000?* The half-million-dollar profit point is equal to a contribution of $2 million, or .216 ($200,000/$927,834) standard deviation to the right of the mean.

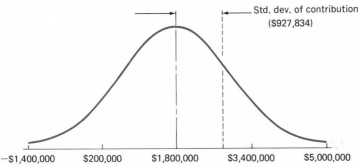

Std. dev. of contribution
($927,834)

−$1,400,000 $200,000 $1,800,000 $3,400,000 $5,000,000

Figure 6-6 Distribution of expected contribution.

Again from Appendix Table 1 we can calculate that the chances are only about .586 of earning less than $2 million contribution; thus we conclude that our chances of bettering a half-million-dollar profit are about .414.

Calculating the probability that losses will be greater than some value

3. *What are the chances that the new product would cause us to lose as much as $250,000?* The $250,000 loss point is a contribution of $1,250,000; this is ($550,000/$927,834) or .593 standard deviation to the left of the mean. Appendix Table 1 indicates that there is only a .277 chance of losing $250,000 or more from this product. In comparing this proposed new product with other uses for resources, under conditions of risk with respect to demand, the management of the company now has these facts at hand:

a. The chance of breaking even on this product is better than .625.
b. The chance of making at least $500,000 on this new product is about .415.
c. The chances of losing $250,000 or more on this venture are only about .277.

Contribution of probability estimates to this decision

With these probability estimates, most managements would consider this alternative to be an attractive one. The contribution that this analysis has made to managerial decision making is simply that it has allowed new-product decisions to be made under market conditions involving risk as to future sales volumes. Whenever questions exist as to the levels of future demand, decision analysis of this type will be of considerable use in choosing among alternatives.

In the foregoing example, we have considered sales volume to be the random variable and have produced a distribution of expected profits accordingly. It is also possible for decision makers to consider fixed costs, variable costs, and price as random variables to test the effect of their variability on profits. When one of these four variables—sales volume, price, variable cost, and fixed cost—is considered a random variable, the analysis is accomplished exactly as we have illustrated it above. However, if all four become random variables *simultaneously,* the statistical calculations are greatly complicated because of (1) the relationships which do exist among the variables and (2) the difficulty of computing a combined standard deviation even when the four variables are assumed to be independent. In any case, even though the problem *can* be handled statistically, it is more properly a part of an advanced analysis in this area.

Assumptions about normality

Finally, before we leave this topic, we should point out that, once again, we have assumed that the random variable "sales volume" is normally distributed. If we have strong reason to suspect that this is not the case, there are more advanced statistical tests which will confirm or deny our suspicions; however, these are beyond the scope of this text.

4. Combining Unit Monetary Values and Probability Distributions

Probability without the expected value of the profit or loss

In the previous examples of the use of the normal probability distribution (our new-product example and our cost-volume-profit example) we have calculated answers in terms of *probabilities;* in the case of the new product, for example, we determined that the chances of a loss were .356; in the cost-volume-profit example, we calculated three probability values: (1) the probability of at least breaking even, (2) the probability of making at least $500,000 profit, and (3) the probability of losing $250,000 or more.

All these probability values we calculated represent useful information to the decision maker; however, in none of the examples above have we determined the *expected value* of the loss or profit, but only whether we would lose or earn a profit.

Both the probability of loss *and* the expected value of that loss are important to the decision maker. Why? Look at the example of Figure 6-4; here we calculated the probability of loss at .356; this looks like more than a safe bet on a new product. But suppose that if sales turn out to be in the loss area (lower than 80 units a month), we could lose from $100,000 to $1,000,000 a year, depending on the specific sales level within that loss area. In a situation such as this, the decision maker needs to know *not only* what his probability of loss is *but also* what the expected dollar value of that loss is (in our problem the loss area is from 80 units per month all the way down to zero unit sales). Let us look now at a procedure for determining such monetary values.

Why expected value of the loss is necessary

Using Unit Loss and Expected Loss

In Figure 6-7, we have illustrated a probability distribution representing management's best estimate of the operating time per year of a proposed new machine. We have assumed that the distribution of operating times will be a normal distribution, with a mean of 1500 hours and a standard deviation of 500 hours. Prior accounting calculations indicate that we would earn a profit on this machine if it operated more than 900 hours annually, that we would break even on this new machine at an operating level of exactly 900 hours a year, and that we would lose $6 per hour for every hour below the breakeven level.

Specifying a unit loss

In Figure 6-8 we have repeated the distribution in Figure 6-7 but added our unit loss line (line *AB*), which we shall describe as a line with a slope of $6 (the per hour loss for each hour of operation below 900). The shaded area in Figure 6-8 represents the probability of the machine operating less than 900 hours annually. Using the methods illustrated earlier, this probability can be determined to be about

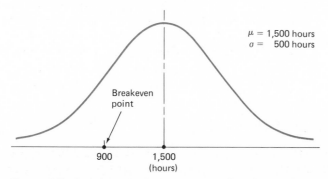

$\mu = 1,500$ hours
$\sigma = 500$ hours

Breakeven point

900   1,500
(hours)

Figure 6-7 Probability distribution of estimated yearly operating hours of proposed new machine.

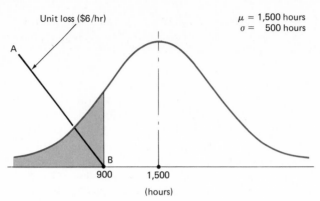

Figure 6-8 Distribution of estimated yearly operating hours with unit loss line illustrated.

Calculating the expected loss using the unit normal loss integral .116. It is at this point that we can employ one of the very useful features of the normal distribution. The availability of Appendix Table 4 (Unit Normal Loss Integral) makes the calculation of the expected loss a very straightforward process. The use of Appendix Table 4 permits us to multiply the $6 unit loss times *every one* of the probabilities between 900 hours and the left-hand tail of the distribution in Figure 6-8 and to sum the total of these multiplications.

This problem, illustrated in Figure 6-8, can be solved with these three steps:

1. First determine how many standard deviations there are between the mean (1500 hours) and the breakeven point (900 hours).

$$\frac{1500 - 900}{500} = 1.2 \text{ standard deviations}$$

2. Next look up the value which corresponds to 1.2 standard deviations in Appendix Table 4 (Unit Normal Loss Integral).

1.2 standard deviations = a table value of .0561

3. Third, to calculate the total expected loss, multiply together the unit loss, the standard deviation of the distribution (in hours), and the value obtained in step 2 from Appendix 4.

$6 \times 500 \times .0561 = $168.30 (expected loss)

Examining the significance of the answer Now let us examine the significance of the value $168.30. Instead of knowing only that there is a .116 chance of losing money on the purchase of this machine due to the variation in estimated operating hours, we can now state this loss in more definitive monetary terms by saying that the expected loss on this purchase is $168.30. But why would a manager authorize the purchase of a machine with an expected loss? Simply because the machine will earn a profit for every hour that it operates *above* 900 hours annually, and, since the probability of its operating more than 900 hours is (1.000 − .116 = .884), this profit is expected to be far larger than the expected loss. All we have done is pinpoint for the manager the total possible extent of his loss because he is unable to specify the distribution of operating hours with more precision.

Relationship between Expected Loss and
EVPI (Expected Value of Perfect Information)

In Chapter 5, we first introduced the idea that there is a maximum price managers should pay for perfect information about the future, and we labeled this value EVPI (the expected value of perfect information). In the example just concluded, let us assume that our manager could buy a perfect predictor, an analysis of the future which would eliminate completely *any* chance of loss; in our example he should be willing to pay up to $168.30 for such "perfect information," but no more. To pay more for perfect information (assuming of course that one can get it in the first place) than the loss which obtains because you lack perfect information is foolish. In our example, the loss we expect to incur with the estimates we have available to us (the estimated mean and standard deviation of the distribution of operating hours) is only $168.30; that is all we would pay to eliminate uncertainty completely (a condition possible only if we had perfect information).

Relationship between expected loss and the expected value of perfect information

How Much Should You Pay for
More Information about the Future?

Knowing that it is all but impossible to purchase "perfect information" about the future leaves one with the problem of how to evaluate new information in terms of what it costs and what it is worth. Lots of new information is available to decision makers in the form of market surveys, forecasts, interviews, and the like, all of which cost money but may reduce one's uncertainty about what the future really holds.

What is information about the future worth

Using the same proposed new-machine example from the section just above, let us suppose that a more detailed analysis of past operating hours of similar machines and a concerted survey of other firms using the same type of machine could together give us additional information about the future. Having this new information would not enable us to predict with complete certainty the number of operating hours, but it would enable us to specify the *distribution* of future operating hours more precisely; more specifically, having additional information (if it is any good) should allow us to reduce the *standard deviation* of the estimated distribution of operating hours, that is, to be more sure about the range of hours within which the machine will likely operate.

To illustrate this point, we shall assume that we have been offered a detailed analysis of operating time of similar machines in organizations similar to ours; the asking price of this new information is $50. This new information is of sufficient quality to enable us to specify the distribution of operating times with greater precision (to be more sure about the range within which our proposed machine will operate). Specifically, it will allow us to reduce our estimate of the standard deviation of the distribution of operating hours from 500 hours to 350 hours. Is the new information worth $50?

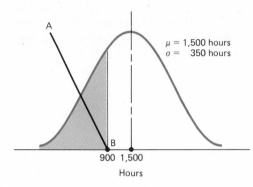

Figure 6-9   Distribution of estimated operating hours possible with new information.

Figure 6-9 illustrates the new distribution of estimated operating hours which would be possible if we purchase the detailed analysis. Using the same three-step procedure we employed before, we can compute the expected loss as follows:

Three steps in the calculation of expected loss

1. First, determine how many standard deviations there are between the mean (1500 hours) and the breakeven point (900) hours:

$$\frac{1500 - 900}{350} = 1.71 \text{ standard deviations}$$

2. Next, look up the value which corresponds to 1.71 standard deviations in Appendix Table 4:

1.71 standard deviations = a table value of .01785

3. To calculate the total expected loss, multiply together the unit loss, the standard deviation of the distribution (in hours), and the value obtained in step 2 from Appendix Table 4:

$6 \times 350 \times .01785 = \$37.49$

We can see from these results that our expected loss (with the new information) is $37.49. This is a reduction in loss from the previous amount—a saving of:

$168.30 - $37.49 = $130.81

Evaluating the cost and worth of new information

As the new information is being offered to us for $50, we should buy it. In this example, the expenditure of $50 will enable us to reduce our expected loss by $130.81, a handsome return on our investment in new information. Even if the cost of the analysis were to rise substantially, it would pay us to go ahead and purchase the information as long as the cost did not rise above $130.81 and as long as the quality of that new information did not diminish. Notice that the more certain we are about the future (the smaller the standard deviation is in relation to the mean of the distribution), the less new information is worth to us. If the manager who is estimating the operating hours of our proposed new machine is almost positive that it will operate exactly 1500 hours, the value of new information is almost zero. If the manager is *absolutely* certain that the new machine in our example of Figure 6-8 would operate *exactly* 1500 hours a year with no chance of this figure being more or less than 1500, the standard deviation would be zero and thus the expected loss zero. In numerical terms, with these assumptions added to the problem in Figure 6-8, expected loss would be

$$\text{Expected loss} = \$6 \times 0 \times 0 \leftarrow$$
$$= \$0$$

As σ gets smaller, $(1500 - 900)/\sigma$ gets larger and the value of UNLI in Appendix Table 4 decreases to zero.

The Expected Value of Sample Information (EVSI)

Managers do not really search for "perfect information"; rather, they evaluate the worth to their organizations of additional information. This additional information may be purchased or provided by adding "experts" to our staff. In the case of quality control, additional information is obtained by taking another sample. In any case, however, the managerial decision is always the same, i.e., how to evaluate the cost of additional information against the expected benefits that information will provide to the decision process. In more formal terminology, the expected value of this new information is often referred to symbolically as EVSI, an acronym for the *expected value of sample information*. Our example just concluded has illustrated how to compute EVSI and how to compare it with the cost of the new information to determine whether it pays to buy more information.

Perfect information and sample information

Unit Monetary Values and
Both Sides of the Normal Distribution

In each of the two examples just completed of combining unit monetary values and the normal probability distribution, we have concerned ourselves only with one side of the probability distribution. More specifically, we calculated in each case the sum of a set of probability values each of which had been multiplied by a constant, $6 in our example. In these two examples, we limited our analysis to that portion of the probability distribution representing potential loss situations.

Using the unit normal loss integral on both sides of the distribution

The procedure that we have employed can be used equally well to analyze the entire set of outcomes represented by a normal distribution, both those that are *favorable* (profits) and those that are *not favorable* (losses). We illustrate this procedure now by using a problem similar to the one involving our proposed purchase of a machine. In the case represented by the distribution in Figure 6-10, we estimate the mean of the distribution of operating hours as 1850 hours and the standard deviation of this distribution as 600 hours. In this particular case, our cost information indicates that we will break even at 1600 operating hours. Below 1600 hours we will lose $15 an hour (line *AB*), and above 1600 hours we will earn $11 an hour from the operation of the machine (line *CB*).

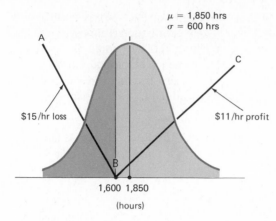

μ = 1,850 hrs
σ = 600 hrs

A

C

$15/hr loss

$11/hr profit

B

1,600 1,850

(hours)

Figure 6-10 Estimated distribution of operating hours illustrated with unit loss and unit profit.

Calculating expected profit, expected loss, and expected net profit

The shaded area of the distribution in Figure 6-10 to the left of the breakeven point (1600 hours) is the loss area. The shaded portion of the distribution to the right of the 1600-hour value is the profit area. Our task this time is twofold; first, we must multiply the $15-per-hour unit loss by each of the probabilities under the normal curve from the 1600-hour value to the *left*-hand tail and sum these; then, we will multiply the $11-per-hour unit profit by each of the probabilities under the curve from the 1600-hour value to the *right*-hand tail and sum these. Knowing the expected loss and the expected profit will allow us to evaluate the "net profit" expected to be earned by the machine simply by subtracting the results in the first step from those in the second.

The procedure is as follows:

(step 1) Expected loss	(step 2) Expected profit
a. $\dfrac{1,850 - 1,600}{600} = .417$ std. dev.	a. $\dfrac{1,850 - 1,600}{600} = .417$ std. dev.
b. Appendix Table 4 value of .417 = .2236	b. Appendix Table 4 value of .417 = .2236
	c. Add .417 to .2236
	$\begin{array}{r} .2236 \\ \underline{.4170} \\ .6406 \end{array}$
c. Expected loss: $15 × 600 × .2236 = $2,012.40	(in two-sided cases such as this when the loss or profit line crosses the mean, the procedure is to *add* the z score to the value in the table)
	d. Expected profit: $11 × 600 × .6406 = $4,227.96

Subtracting step 1 from step 2 ($4227.96 − $2012.40), we get $2215.56, the expected net profit from the machine purchase given our present information about the future. If the value $2215.56, when related to the investment required, represents a return felt by management to be adequate, then they would purchase the machine.

5. Replacement Analysis: Items Which Fail over Time

One area to which decision theory concepts can be applied with considerable effectiveness is the replacement of items which fail in use over time. There are many examples of this situation: light bulbs, heating filters, electric motors, and faucet washers, to name but a few. Although the exact time of failure of these items cannot be known in advance, it *is* possible to specify from past information a probability distribution of the lives of the items, that is, to specify the probability of failure for any future time period. With this probability distribution and with appropriate cost information, it is possible to calculate an optimum replacement policy.

Examples of items which fail in use over time

In replacing heating filters in a facility, there are basically two alternatives:

1. Replace all the filters at the same time

2. Replace the filters as they become clogged

When all the filters are replaced at one time, the labor cost per filter to accomplish this replacement is only a fraction of what it is when filters are replaced on an individual basis as they become inoperative.

Our problem concerns a large federal agency where cost records indicate that the 1000 filters in the facility can be replaced for 25 cents labor cost each if done on a mass replacement basis. If, however, each filter is replaced as it becomes clogged, the labor cost is $1.75 per filter. Since the filters are bought in large quantities, the cost of the filter itself is $.25 under both replacement alternatives. The past behavior of filters (their life expectancy) is given in Table 6-1. From the information in this table, the average life of the 1000 filters is computed like this:

Problem illustrating replacement analysis approach

$$
\begin{array}{rcl}
.10 \times 1\,\text{month} &=& .10\ \text{month}\\
.15 \times 2\,\text{months} &=& .30\ \text{month}\\
.25 \times 3\,\text{months} &=& .75\ \text{month}\\
.30 \times 4\,\text{months} &=& 1.20\ \text{months}\\
.20 \times 5\,\text{months} &=& \underline{1.00\ \text{month}}\\
\text{Average life} &=& 3.35\ \text{months}
\end{array}
$$

If we begin any time period with 1000 filters, we shall be replacing 1000/3.35 = 299 per month over time if we replace them as they fail; at $2 each ($1.75 labor + $.25 filter) our monthly total replacement cost will be $598 ($299 × $2).

Total cost if we replace at failure

Table 6-1 Life Expectancy of Heating Filters

	Month after replacement				
	1	2	3	4	5
Percent of original filters which have failed *by* that month (cumulative)	10	25	50	80	100
Percent of original filters which fail *in* that month	10	15	25	30	20

Perhaps it would be possible to reduce the cost of this operation by replacing all filters at a fixed interval (say, 4 months). Of course, if we did this, we would still have to replace filters which failed during this interval because we must maintain a constant level of airflow. Calculating the number which would have to be replaced each month is not difficult if we introduce a few symbols:

Notation for replacement at fixed interval

N_0 = original number (1000)
N_1 = number replaced at end of month 1
N_2 = number replaced at end of month 2
N_3 = number replaced at end of month 3
N_4 = number replaced at end of month 4
N_5 = number replaced at end of month 5

P_1 = probability of failure during month 1
P_2 = probability of failure during month 2
P_3 = probability of failure during month 3
P_4 = probability of failure during month 4
P_5 = probability of failure during month 5

We can now symbolize the number to be replaced in each month as follows:

Number replaced each month

$N_1 = N_0 \times P_1$
   (The original ones are 1 month old.)
$N_2 = (N_0 \times P_2) + (N_1 \times P_1)$
   (The original ones are 2 months old; filters replaced at the end of month 2 are 1 month old.)
$N_3 = (N_0 \times P_3) + (N_1 \times P_2) + (N_2 \times P_1)$
   (The original ones are 3 months old; those replaced at the end of month 1 are 2 months old; those replaced at the end of month 2 are 1 month old.)
$N_4 = (N_0 \times P_4) + (N_1 \times P_3) + (N_2 \times P_2) + (N_3 \times P_1)$
   (The original ones are 4 months old; those replaced at the end of month 1 are 3 months old; those replaced at the end of month 2 are 2 months old; those replaced at the end of month 3 are 1 month old.)
$N_5 = (N_0 \times P_5) + (N_1 \times P_4) + (N_2 \times P_3) + (N_3 \times P_2) + (N_4 \times P_1)$
   (The original ones are 5 months old; those replaced at the end of month 1 are 4 months old; those replaced at the end of month 2 are 3 months old; those replaced at the end of month 3 are 2 months old; those replaced at the end of month 4 are 1 month old.)

And we can calculate the number of filters to be replaced in each month by replacing the symbols with the appropriate numerical values:

$N_1 = 1000 \times .10$ 　　　　　　　　　　　　　　　　　　　　　$= 100$
$N_2 = (1000 \times .15) + (100 \times .10)$ 　　　　　　　　　　　$= 160$
$N_3 = (1000 \times .25) + (100 \times .15) + (160 \times .10)$ 　　$= 281$
$N_4 = (1000 \times .30) + (100 \times .25) + (160 \times .15) + (281 \times .10)$ 　$= 377$
$N_5 = (1000 \times .20) + (100 \times .30) + (160 \times .25) + (281 \times .15)$
　　　　　　　　　　　　　　　　　　　　$+ (377 \times .10) = 350$

Table 6-2 Labor and Material Cost of Filter Replacement

Replacement at end of	Cost of replacing 1,000 filters at $.50 each	Cost of replacing those which failed at $2 each	Total cost	Cost per month
Month 1	$500	$ 200 (100 × $2)	$ 700	$700
Month 2	500	520 (260 × $2)	1,020	510
Month 3	500	1,082 (541 × $2)	1,582	527
Month 4	500	1,836 (918 × $2)	2,336	584
Month 5	500	2,536 (1,268 × $2)	3,036	607

The various alternatives open to us can be compared by the use of Table 6-2. From Table 6-2 we see that from a total cost standpoint, expense would be less if we replace all filters at the end of 2 months; those which failed during that period we would replace on an individual basis. The total cost saved by this solution would be $598 (the old method) less $510 (the new method), or about $88 per month.

Comparison of cost of alternatives

6. Decision Trees: Graphic Displays of the Decision Theory Process

In Chapter 2 we introduced the idea of a probability tree in connection with the study of joint probabilities; we indicated how this "tree" technique could help us analyze the possible outcomes of three successive coin tosses in terms of the probabilities of the various outcomes. When these "trees" contain both probabilities of outcomes *and* conditional monetary values of those outcomes such that expected values can be computed, the common practice is to refer to them as *decision trees*.

Probability trees and decision trees

Decision Tree Fundamentals

Decision trees are usually drawn with standard symbols; in Figure 6-11 we represent the simple decision of making a choice between going to the movies and staying home and watching TV. The square node symbolizes a decision point; for each alternative it is standard practice to show a circular node from which branches on the tree represent each possible outcome or state of nature which *could* result. In this example, it would be unrealistic to add probability values to the outcomes because we could call up the theater and look in *TV Guide* and find out before the fact what the outcome was going to be. Therefore, in this simple case, we would have nearly perfect information. In Figure 6-12, we have presented a decision problem of similar size, but one which allows us to estimate some probability values representing the likelihood of the outcomes. In this problem, we can also introduce some conditional values; then we can compute expected values for the two alternatives and make a choice using that criterion. We have numbered the two state-of-nature nodes in this illustration.

Decision nodes

State-of-nature nodes

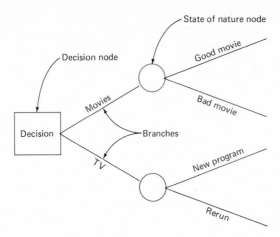

Figure 6-11 Simple decision tree.

Calculating the expected value of a state-of-nature node

Figure 6-13 repeats the decision tree from Figure 6-12 but adds our estimates of what our $1000 stock investment would be worth a year from now and what our savings account would be worth under the two conditions of a rising and a falling stock market. We have assumed that the savings account would pay 5 percent interest and that the stocks pay no dividends. In our simple investment problem, the expected value of a $1000 investment in savings (given our assessment) would remain stable (except for interest) regardless of what happened to the stock market. In Figure 6-13 we have shown the expected value of the two state-of-nature nodes, 1 and 2. Since node 1 has the greater expected value, a decision maker using expected value as his or her decision criterion would choose the branch between the decision node and state-of-nature node 1, that is, "invest $1000 in stocks."

Rollback or foldback procedure

The general process we use in decision tree analysis is to work *backward* through the tree (from right to left), computing the expected value of each state-of-nature node. We then choose the particular branch leaving a *decision* node which leads to the *state-of-nature* node with the highest expected value. This process is known as *rollback* or *foldback*.

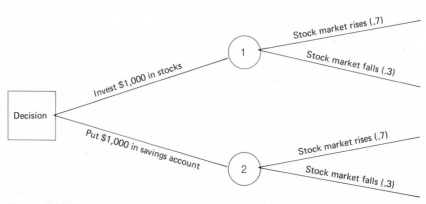

Figure 6-12 Use of decision tree to structure investment decision.

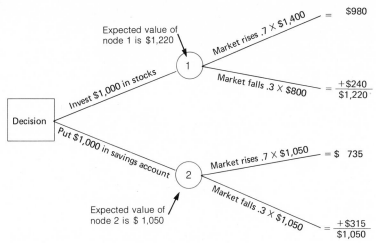

Expected value of
node 1 is $1,220

Market rises .7 X $1,400 = $980

Invest $1,000 in stocks

1

Market falls .3 X $800 = $\frac{+\$240}{\$1,220}$

Decision

Put $1,000 in savings account

2

Market rises .7 X $1,050 = $ 735

Market falls .3 X $1,050 = $\frac{+\$315}{\$1,050}$

Expected value of
node 2 is $ 1,050

Figure 6-13 Use of decision tree to solve investment problem.

Decision Tree Illustrating Plant Investment Problem

The real managerial value of the decision tree type of analysis is obtained when it is used on more complex kinds of problems, those involving not only a greater number of alternatives but also decisions about considerably longer future periods. Consider the following somewhat more complex example.

A more complex
decision tree
problem

Stereo Industries, Ltd., must decide to build a large or a small plant to produce a new turntable which is expected to have a market life of 10 years. A large plant will cost $2,800,000 to build and put into operation, while a small plant will cost only $1,400,000 to build and put into operation. The company's best estimate of a discrete distribution of sales over the 10-year period is

High demand: probability = .5
Moderate demand: probability = .3
Low demand: probability = .2

Probability
estimates

Cost-volume-profit analysis done by Stereo Industries, Ltd., management indicates these conditional outcomes under the various combinations of plant size and market size:

1. A large plant with high demand would yield $1 million annually in profits.

Conditional values

2. A large plant with moderate demand would yield $600,000 annually in profits.

3. A large plant with low demand would lose $200,000 annually because of production inefficiencies.

4. A small plant with high demand would yield only $250,000 annually in profits, considering the cost of the lost sales because of inability to supply customers.

5. A small plant with moderate demand would yield $450,000 annually in profits because the cost of lost sales would be somewhat lower.

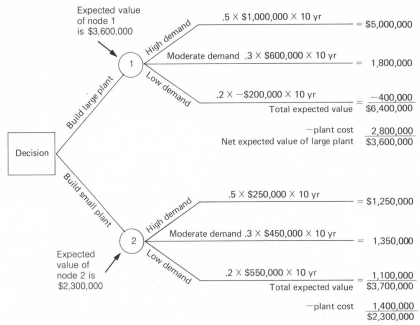

Figure 6-14 Decision tree analysis of Stereo Industries, Ltd., plant expansion alternatives.

6. A small plant with low demand would yield $550,000 annually because the plant size and market size would be matched fairly optimally.

Information on the decision tree
The decision tree in Figure 6-14 illustrates the alternatives graphically. For each of the combinations of plant size and market size, we have indicated (1) the probability that that outcome will happen, (2) the conditional profit the company would receive if that outcome happened, and (3) the expected value of that outcome. Our decision process is the same as before. We work backward through the tree from right to left (using the rollback approach), computing the expected value of each state-of-nature node. We then choose that particular branch leaving a *decision* node which leads to the *state-of-nature* node with the highest expected value.

Conclusions and Assumptions behind Those Conclusions
Choosing the optimum alternative
From our decision tree analysis it appears that building a large plant will produce $1,300,000 more profit over the next 10 years ($3,600,000 − $2,300,000 = $1,300,000) and thus, given the information we have, represents the better alternative for that company. We must remember, however, that some assumptions made in this problem include the following:

Assumptions made in this problem
1. We have allowed only *three* discrete levels of demand in our estimates of the future; demand *could* be continuously distributed.

2. We have permitted only *two* sizes of plant to be built in response to our esti-

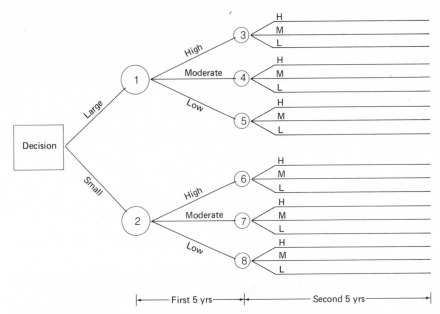

Figure 6-15 Illustration of decision tree with estimates of future demand for two separate time periods.

mates of future demand when, in reality, many different-size plants could be designed and built.

3. We did *not* allow the small plant to be *expanded* (at an additional cost) in response to either moderate or high demand, or the large plant to be sold.

4. We considered the future as one 10-year period; estimates of demand and benefits could be made for each individual year.

5. We considered the profits received in the tenth year equal to those in the first year; that is, we did not use discounting to place more value on benefits to be received in the earlier years. In *this* problem, as a matter of interest, the relative merits of the two alternatives would not have been changed by discounting the future benefits.

Removing Some of the Assumptions in Decision Tree Analysis
Each of the assumptions we made in the problem illustrated in Figure 6-14 could be removed if one were willing to draw a larger decision tree and do more arithmetic. For example, if we had wanted to illustrate our decision analysis in two 5-year periods, with three different estimates of demand for *each* of these two periods, the decision tree would have looked like the one in Figure 6-15.

Our process of analysis for the decision tree in Figure 6-15 would involve these steps:

1. Compute the expected value for state-of-nature nodes 3, 4, 5, 6, 7, and 8.

How to remove the assumptions

The process for analyzing the more complex decision tree

2. Using the probabilities of high, moderate, and low demand for the *first 5 years* and the expected values of nodes 3, 4, and 5, compute the expected value of node 1.

3. Using the probabilities of high, moderate, and low demand for the *first 5 years* and the expected values of nodes 6, 7, and 8, compute the expected value of node 2.

4. Choose the branch leaving the *decision* node which leads to the state-of-nature node (1 or 2) with the higher expected value.

Decision Trees and the Expected Value of New Information

The value of waiting There are many instances in decision making where the best decision is to wait. Waiting, however, is useless as a strategy unless we spend the time learning about the future; specifically, we need to learn about the risk of future alternatives we may face.

Companies with a new product often decide to built a *pilot plant* before construction of a large commercial facility. In this way, the output of the pilot plant (a much smaller facility) provides the company with information on market acceptance, production yields, design engineering problems, and equipment difficulties. The decision tree in Figure 6-16 illustrates the sequence of decision nodes and state-of-nature nodes involved in deciding whether to build a pilot plant to study process yields before commercial mass production is begun.

Probability estimates In Figure 6-16, management has estimated that their pilot plant (if it is built) has a .8 chance of a high yield and a .2 chance of a low yield. *If* the pilot plant does show a high yield, management assigns a probability of .85 that the commercial plant will also have a high yield. *If* the pilot plant shows a low yield, there is only a .1 chance that the commercial plant will show a high yield. Finally, management's best assessment of the yield on a commercial-size plant *without* building a pilot plant first is a .7 chance of high yield. A pilot plant will cost $350,000.

On Figure 6-16, the expected values (EV) of nodes 5, 6, 7, 8, 9, and 10 are shown. Using the rollback procedure, we find that the expected value of node 2 is $8,147,000 (.8 × $10,183,750 + .2 × $0). Our conclusion is that the expected value of the information from the pilot plant is $8,147,000 − $8,117,500 = $29,500. At a cost of $350,000, the pilot plant is not a good idea.

Advantages of the Decision Tree Approach

Five advantages of using a decision tree The decision tree approach we have illustrated enjoys rather wide use today, and for good reason. It has five distinct advantages:

1. *It structures the decision process,* making the user approach decision making in an orderly, sequential fashion.

2. *It requires the decision maker to examine all possible outcomes,* desirable and undesirable ones alike.

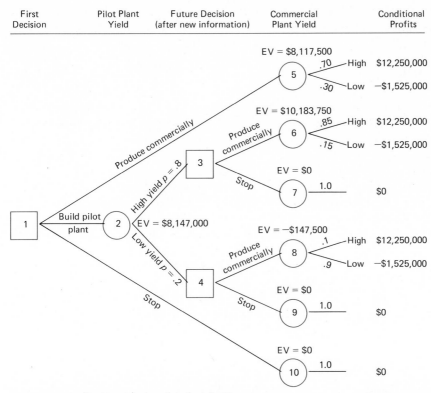

First Decision	Pilot Plant Yield	Future Decision (after new information)	Commercial Plant Yield	Conditional Profits

Figure 6-16 Decision tree for pilot plant decision.

3. *It communicates the decision-making process to others* in a very succinct manner, illustrating each assumption about the future.

4. *It allows a group to discuss alternatives* by focusing on each individual financial figure, probability, and underlying assumption—one at a time.

5. *It can be used with a computer,* so that many different sets of assumptions can be simulated to observe the effect on the final outcome of alterations in these alternatives.

Glossary

1. Reliability   A weight attached to an estimate; the reciprocal of the square of the standard deviation.

2. Cost-volume-profit analysis   Sometimes referred to as breakeven analysis; the systematic analysis of the relationship of profit to changes in fixed costs, variable costs, and volume.

3. Breakeven point   The point (volume) at which total revenue equals total cost.

4. Contribution   Price per unit less variable cost per unit.

5. **Unit normal loss integral** A tabular expression of values necessary for the integration of unit benefits or losses into analyses involving the normal probability distribution.

6. **Expected value of sample information** The expected value of new information in a decision process.

7. **Replacement analysis** Systematic analysis of alternatives available in situations involving items which fail in use over time.

8. **Decision tree** Graphic display of the decision process indicating decision alternatives, states of nature, probabilities attached to the states of nature, and conditional benefits and losses.

9. **Node** Point at which branching can take place on a decision tree.

10. **Decision node** Branching point which requires a decision.

11. **State-of-nature node** Branching point after which more than one state of nature can occur.

12. **Rollback** Also called foldback; method of using decision trees to find optimum alternatives which involves working from right to left in the tree.

Review of Equations

Page 160

$$\text{Combined estimate of means} = \frac{(\text{est. 1})\left(\begin{array}{c}\text{reciprocal}\\\text{of std.}\\\text{deviation 1}\end{array}\right)^2 + (\text{est. 2})\left(\begin{array}{c}\text{reciprocal}\\\text{of std.}\\\text{deviation 2}\end{array}\right)^2}{\left(\begin{array}{c}\text{reciprocal of std.}\\\text{deviation 1}\end{array}\right)^2 + \left(\begin{array}{c}\text{reciprocal of std.}\\\text{deviation 2}\end{array}\right)^2} \quad (6\text{-}1)$$

This formula enables us to combine two estimates which have different means and different standard deviations. In combining estimates, we weight each estimate by its *reliability* (the reciprocal of its standard deviation).

Page 160

$$\text{Combined standard deviation} = \frac{\sqrt{2}}{\sqrt{\left(\begin{array}{c}\text{reciprocal of std.}\\\text{deviation 1}\end{array}\right)^2 + \left(\begin{array}{c}\text{reciprocal of std.}\\\text{deviation 2}\end{array}\right)^2}} \quad (6\text{-}2)$$

To get an estimated combined standard deviation from two individual standard deviations, we use this formula.

Page 162

$$\text{Breakeven point (in units)} = \frac{\text{total fixed cost}}{\text{price/unit} - \text{variable cost/unit}} \quad (6\text{-}3)$$

Using this formula solves for the breakeven point (in units), given a level of fixed cost and price and variable cost data.

Exercises

6-1. Jim Hicks, the general superintendent, asks five of his supervisors to estimate for next year the average operating time of a proposed machine; he also asks each of them to estimate the odds that the machine will operate within plus and minus 300 hours of their estimates of the average. For each of the five, calculate the implied standard deviation of the distribution of operating times:

	Estimated average operating hours	Odds that operating hours will be within plus or minus 300 hours of the estimated average
Supervisor 1	1,000	5 : 1
Supervisor 2	1,200	3 : 5
Supervisor 3	1,400	2 : 1
Supervisor 4	1,600	4 : 5
Supervisor 5	2,000	2 : 3

6-2. A modification of a machine which would cost $10,000 per year in additional operating costs is being considered by Frances McKensie, a superintendent. This modification will reduce variable costs by 5 cents. Her supervisor estimates that the mean production level for this machine is about 260,000 per year. When asked to give odds on production running between 210,000 and 310,000, he indicates that he feels that they would be approximately 3:2. What is the probability that the machine will operate at less than its breakeven point with the modification?

6-3. Jim Tilman, a marketing manager, collects three estimates from three different sources about next year's demand for a new product. Calculate the *combined* mean and standard deviation of the distribution of demand for this product from the following data:

	Estimate of mean sales	Estimate of standard deviation
Salesperson 1	250	50
Salesperson 2	300	80
Salesperson 3	200	30

6-4. From the combined estimate of the mean and standard deviation of sales for the new product in Problem 6-3, calculate the probability that sales of that product next year will fall below 224 units.

6-5. From the combined estimate of the mean and standard deviation of sales for the new product in Problem 6-3, calculate the probability that sales of that product next year will be above 350 units.

6-6. If salesperson number 2 in Problem 6-3 suddenly becomes much more optimistic and revises her estimate to a mean of 500 units and a standard deviation of 150 units, calculate the probability that sales will fall between 200 and 300 units next year, using the combined estimate of the mean and standard deviation from the three sources.

6-7. The ACME Company is contemplating producing a product that would sell for $10 a unit; the per-unit variable cost for this product is $6.60, and the fixed cost per year allocated to this product is $235,000. The sales manager for ACME estimates that annual sales of this product would have a mean of 145,000 with a standard deviation of 25,000 units. Using these data and estimates, answer the following questions:

a. What is the expected profit from this product next year?
b. What is the probability that ACME would lose money on this product next year?

6-8. The IRS regional office conducts an informal survey about the number of tax returns that will be "flagged" for audit in the upcoming tax year. Each of the five auditors makes a guess of the actual number plus an estimate of the odds that the actual number of audited returns will be within plus and minus 400 of the estimate. Their estimates for this year were:

	Estimated flagged returns	Odds of actual returns being within ±400 of the estimate
John Knowles	2,500	2:1
Sarah Hortman	1,000	3:5
Bill Wenslaff	1,800	1:1
Carole Cole	2,100	4:5
Ron Keeton	2,500	1:3

Calculate each auditor's implied standard deviation of the number of flagged returns.

6-9. Your R&D department has just sent you the prototype of a new turntable to be added to your stereo line. As marketing manager, you are interested in some immediate feedback about the likely size of the market for this product. You realize that this informal technique will not produce precise results, but you call the regional sales managers anyhow and describe the turntable to them. You ask each of them for an estimate of market size and corresponding standard deviation. Responses you get are these:

Sales region	Estimate of market size, units	Estimate of standard deviation, units
Northeast	300,000	10,000
Southeast	100,000	50,000
Midwest	25,000	10,000
West	50,000	20,000

Calculate the combined mean and standard deviation for the distribution of demand for the turntable.

6-10. The addition of an automatic welding machine to an auto assembly line is estimated to cost $560,000. Savings in labor per car will be about $4. John Gee, the production manager, estimates the average production rate for the line at 200,000 units annually, with 3:2 odds that production will range from 160,000 to 240,000 cars. What is the probability that this assembly line will operate below the breakeven point after the addition of the new welding equipment?

6-11. The University of the Great Northwest is a private university which, like many private educational institutions, depends on profits from its undergraduate program to support graduate research and teaching activities. The number of graduate students admitted each year is determined by the total "profit" generated by the undergraduate program divided by the "per student loss" of the graduate program. The provost of the university has calculated that variable costs are $3000 per undergraduate student, and the university has fixed costs of $8 million annually. Tuition is $4000 per year. The registrar estimates that the total undergraduate enrollment will average 11,000 students with a standard deviation estimated to be 3000.

a. How much profit will the university show from its undergraduate program next year?

b. If the university loses $1500 per graduate student, how many graduate students can the university admit and still break even?

c. How likely is the university to lose money on its undergraduate program next year?

d. If the university wanted to admit 1500 graduate students next year, how large would the undergraduate program have to be?

6-12. Alan Fulton, marketing vice-president for Burrington Textiles, Inc., was looking over a marketing proposal from his assistant, Roger Smythe. Roger suggested spending $100,000 advertising a new fabric which was unusually stain-resistant. Fulton returned the proposal to Roger with this comment, "If you can convince me that there is at least a .8 chance that this fabric will make twice as much as your proposal will cost, I'll authorize your proposal." After several days of poring over sales projections, Roger projected sales at 6,500,000 yards with a 2:1 chance that the sales would lie between 5.5 and 7.5 million yards. The company would make $.05 per yard. Can Smythe convince his boss?

6-13. The J. L. Beamer Co., Inc., has developed a new apple corer for home canning use and for making applesauce. It is expected to retail for $8.95 and has variable costs of $6.29. The allocated fixed costs are $461,000. Beamer Company market research suggests that annual sales will average 200,000 units; an estimate of the standard deviation of these sales is 40,000 units.

a. What is the expected profit from this product next year?

b. What is the probability that the company will lose money on this product next year?

c. What is the probability of the company making a profit of between $20,000 and $50,000 on this product?

d. What is the chance of the company losing at least $30,000 on this product next year?

6-14. THEIM Machine Company is considering the purchase of a new machine which could generate significant savings by reducing labor costs on a certain operation—conditioned, of course, on the machine's operating above the breakeven number of hours annually. The mean annual operating hours are estimated at 1900 and the standard deviation of the distribution of operating hours has been estimated to be 400 hours. To break even, the machine must operate above 1175 hours annually; for each operating hour less than the breakeven point, THEIM will lose $5.50. What is THEIM'S expected loss next year if the machine is purchased?

6-15. Should THEIM pay $2750 for a detailed analysis of future operating times which will reduce the standard deviation of the distribution of operating hours to 175 hours? What would this new information be worth?

6-16. Suppose the machine THEIM is considering will cost $50,000 installed. THEIM's accountants state that the machine will save $8.50 for each hour it operates above the breakeven point (1175 hours annually). Using the data from Problem 6-14, calculate whether THEIM should purchase the machine if the expected net savings on the $50,000 investment has to be 12 percent.

6-17. The local university laundry is looking at an automatic shirt-pressing machine which will reduce labor cost and bottlenecks in an already overutilized facility. Grant Rogers, the laundry manager, estimates the machine will operate almost two full shifts a year (3600 hours) with a standard deviation of 400 hours. The breakeven point of the machine is 2700 hours a year (with current cost information). Below the breakeven point, the university will lose $8.80 per hour; above the breakeven point, the laundry will earn a net profit of $11.40 an hour. What is the expected profit of this machine if it is purchased?

6-18. Mountain Coal Corporation has a new coal extractor on trial and must either return it or buy it this week. At $100,000, this is an expensive machine, but it saves about $17 per operating hour beyond its breakeven point, 1200 hours annually. Below its breakeven point, however, it loses $9.50 per operating hour. Tom Brandon, mine equipment supervisor, estimates the operating hours to be 1900 annually with a standard deviation of 300. Mountain Coal has an investment hurdle which demands at least a 9 percent return measured as profit/investment. Should the company invest in this machine?

6-19. Lycuming Engine Company produces engines for the light aircraft industry. Tight tolerances require the use of computer-controlled milling machines with cutter heads which wear out according to this table:

Hours in use	300	600	900	1,200
Portion of cutter heads which fail before this time (cumulative)	.10	.25	.55	1.00

Anytime a cutter head fails in use, it ruins the cam shaft it is working on at that time;

the cost of this is $150. The total cost to replace a cutter head is $30, whether the replacement is done when the head fails or during the regular night maintenance period. Should all the cutter heads be replaced after a regular interval? If so, *what* interval?

6-20. Robert Teer, maintenance engineer for a large construction company, is examining alternatives open to him for the replacement of hydraulic hoses on the firm's 100 front-end loaders; each loader uses six hoses, which—from historical maintenance records—fail at this rate:

Months of use	1	2	3	4	5
Percent requiring replacement by that month	5	15	40	80	100

Teer's chief maintenance supervisor says that the "in the field" replacement cost of $50 per hose could be reduced by $20 if all the hoses were replaced at a regular interval during routine maintenance and service. Evaluate the alternatives open to Teer and recommend a course of action.

6-21. The Independent Rent-A-Car Agency is considering periodic replacement of tires for its fleet of 500 cars. It is now following a policy of replacing tires as they wear out at a total cost of $50 per tire. The agency feels that it can cut its total tire replacement cost by using the periodic replacement method, even though the cost per tire replaced will increase to $60. Evaluate these alternatives and make a recommendation to the agency.

Month after replacement	1	2	3	4	5
Percent of original tires which are worn by that month	10	30	60	85	100
Percent of tires which must be replaced in that month	10	20	30	25	15

6-22. Harry Phelps, owner of Harry's Clothing Cupboard, is considering a move from downtown to a new shopping mall. Due to the fact that he has been downtown for 20 years and has built up quite a following there, Harry thinks there is a 20 percent chance his business will decline by $100,000, a 30 percent chance it will remain stable, and a 50 percent chance it will increase by $175,000 due to the quality of sales promotion done by the mall management. Further, the city is considering a downtown revitalization with a mall in front of Harry's store. He believes there is a 70 percent chance this will pass the city council; if it does, he estimates his business should increase by $200,000. If the mall is not built, Harry thinks his downtown business will decline by about $50,000. Time is of the essence; the mall owners need an answer immediately or he will lose any chance to locate there. Construct a decision tree to help Harry decide.

6-23. The investment staff of First Union National Bank is considering four investment alternatives for a client: stocks, bonds, real estate, and savings certificates.

Historic stock patterns indicate that there is a 30 percent chance stocks will decline by 20 percent, 1 chance in 5 they will remain stable, and a 50-50 chance they will increase in value by 10 percent. The stocks under consideration do not pay dividends. The bonds stand a 30 percent chance of increasing in value by 5 percent and a 70 percent chance of remaining stable, and they yield 7 percent. The real estate parcel being considered has a 1 in 10 chance of increasing 25 percent in value, a 1 in 5 chance of increasing 10 percent in value, a 3 in 10 chance of increasing 5 percent in value, a 1 in 5 chance of remaining stable, and a 1 in 5 chance of losing 5 percent of its value. The savings certificates yield $7^1/_2$ percent with certainty. Use a decision tree to structure the alternatives available to the investment staff and, using the expected value criterion, choose the alternative with the highest expected value.

6-24. The Tarheel Manufacturing Company must decide whether to build a large plant or a small one to process a new product with an expected life of 10 years.

Demand may be high during the first 2 years, but if many users find the product unsatisfactory, demand will be low for the remaining 8 years. High demand during the first 2 years may indicate high demand for the next 8 years. If demand is high during the first 2 years and the company does not expand within the first 2 years, competitive products will be introduced, thus lowering the benefits.

If the company builds a large processing plant, it must keep it for 10 years. If they build the small plant, it can be expanded in 2 years if demand is high, or the company can stay in the small plant while making smaller benefits on the small volume of sales.

Estimates of demand are these:

	Probability	
High demand (first 2 years) followed by high demand (next 8 years)	.6	
High demand (first 2 years) followed by low demand (next 8 years)	.1	.7 probability of high demand during first 2 years
Low demand (first 2 years) followed by continuing low demand (next 8 years)	.3	
Low demand (first 2 years) followed by continuing high demand (next 8 years)	0	

Financial costs and profits are these:

A large plant with high demand would yield $1 million annually in profits.

A large plant with low demand would yield $100,000 annually because of production inefficiencies.

A small plant, not expanded, with a low demand would yield annual profits of $200,000 for 10 years.

A small plant during a 2-year period of high demand would yield $450,000 annually; if high demand continued and if the plant were not expanded, this would drop to $300,000 annually for the next 8 years as a result of competition.

A small plant which was expanded after 2 years to meet high demand would yield $700,000 annually for the next 8 years.

A small plant which was expanded after 2 years would yield $50,000 annually for 8 years if low demand occurred during that period.

A large plant would cost $3 million to build and put into operation.

A small plant would cost $1,300,000 to build and put into operation.

Expanding a small plant after 2 years would cost $2,200,000.

Under the conditions stated and with the information furnished, analyze the alternatives to choose the best decision.

Bibliography

Ackoff, R. L., and **M. W. Sasieni:** *Fundamentals of Operations Research* (New York: John Wiley & Sons, Inc., 1968.)

Baumol, W. J.: *Economic Theory and Operations Analysis,* 3d ed. (Englewood Cliffs, N.J.: Prentice-Hall, Inc., 1972).

Beer, S.: *Management Sciences, The Business Use of Operations Research* (Garden City, N.Y.: Doubleday & Company, Inc., 1968).

Hillier, F. S., and **G. J. Lieberman:** *Introduction to Operations Research,* 2d ed. (San Francisco: Holden-Day, Inc., 1974).

Howell, J. E., and **D. Teichroew:** *Mathematical Analysis for Business Decisions,* 2d ed. (Homewood, Ill.: Richard D. Irwin, Inc., 1971).

Luce, R. D., and **H. Raiffa:** *Games and Decisions* (New York: John Wiley & Sons, Inc., 1957).

Schellenberger, R. E.: *Managerial Analysis* (Homewood, Ill.: Richard D. Irwin, Inc., 1969).

Schlaifer, R.: *Analysis of Decision under Uncertainty* (New York: McGraw-Hill Book Company, 1969).

Wagner, H. M.: *Principles of Management Sciences with Applications to Executive Decisions* (Englewood Cliffs, N.J.: Prentice-Hall, Inc., 1970).

Inventory models I

7

Importance of inventory

For many firms the inventory figure is the largest current asset. Inventory difficulties can and do contribute to business failures. When a firm does no more than unintentionally run out of an item, results are not pleasant. If the firm is a retail store, the merchant loses the gross margin on the item. If the firm is a manufacturer, the stockout (inability to supply an item from inventory) could, in extreme cases, bring production to a halt. Conversely, if a firm carries *excessive* inventories, the added carrying cost may represent the difference between profit and loss. Our conclusion must be that skillful inventory management can make a significant contribution to a firm's profit showing.

1. What Functions Does Inventory Perform?

Functions that inventory performs

In any organization, inventories add an operating flexibility that would not otherwise exist. In manufacturing, work-in-process inventories are an absolute necessity unless each individual part is to be carried from machine to machine and those machines set up to produce that single part. Patients in a hospital are really inventory for the physician; true, they are there because they are too sick to be at home, but it must

190

be recognized that having them in one location enables the physician to see all his patients during "rounds." The many functions inventory performs can be summarized as follows:

Smoothing Out Irregularities in Supply

Tobacco is harvested during the late summer months, but the manufacture of tobacco products such as cigarettes and cigars continues throughout the entire year. In cases like this, sufficient raw material must be purchased during the tobacco-producing period to last the entire year; this forces the manufacturer to carry an inventory.

Filling the gap between supply and demand

In a simpler sense, because a truck may go 100 miles without passing a gasoline station, its tanks must carry enough fuel to avoid runouts.

Buying or Producing in Lots or Batches

When the demand for an item will not support its continued production throughout the entire year, it is usually produced in batches or lots on an intermittent basis. During the time when the item is not being produced, sales are made from inventory which is accumulated while the item is being produced. Similarly, a retailer of men's clothing does not purchase a new shirt from the manufacturer each time he sells one; rather, he chooses to carry in his store an inventory of these shirts so that purchasing can be done in larger quantities, thereby allowing lower costs and less paper work.

Making possible lower production costs

Allowing Organizations to Cope with Perishable Materials

The packers of frozen lobster tails operate at peak production capacity only a few months each year; they too must store up or inventory a supply sufficient to last them through a year's anticipated demand until the next lobster season. The entire production process which deals with freezing fresh fruits and vegetables must also give thoughtful consideration to the rate of inventory accumulation and depletion throughout the peak production and sales periods each year.

Items that are not always available

Storing Labor

Although it may be conceptually difficult to think of "inventorying" labor, it is routine practice to do just that. The peak demand for the installation of replacement heating units comes in the fall, just after the old units have been operated for the first time. The manufacturers of heating units store up excess labor by having their workers produce at a designated rate all year long; then, having converted labor into finished heating units, they hold them in inventory until the point when demand increases rapidly. Even if demand exceeds current productive capacity, a manufacturer can supply the difference out of inventory at that time.

Inventory can store labor

2. Inventory Decisions

Two basic decisions
in inventory
management

There are two basic inventory decisions managers must make as they attempt to accomplish the functions of inventory just reviewed. These two decisions are made for *every* item in the inventory:

1. *How much* of an item to order when the inventory of that item is to be replenished

2. *When* to replenish the inventory of that item

SKU
defined

Companies use the term *SKU* (stockkeeping unit) instead of referring to *items*. The typical supermarket stocks about 7000 SKUs of groceries, meats, fruits, vegetables, bakery goods, and nongrocery merchandise.

The next two chapters will introduce you to the more commonly used inventory models which managers use to make the two decisions enumerated above. This chapter will concentrate on using quantitative models to answer the question "How much to order?" Chapter 8 will concentrate on quantitative tools which help managers answer the question "When to order?"

3. Economic Order Quantity: The Basic "How Much to Buy" Model

EOQ defined

The economic order quantity (EOQ) model is the oldest and best-known inventory model; its origins date all the way back to 1915. The purpose of using the EOQ model is to find that particular quantity to order which minimizes total inventory costs. Let us look for a moment at these costs.

Inventory Costs

There are two basic inventory costs, *ordering* costs and *carrying* costs.

Ordering costs are basically the costs of getting an item into the firm's inventory. They are incurred each time an order is placed and are expressed as dollar cost per order. Ordering costs start with the requisition sent to the purchasing office, include all costs of issuing the purchase order and of following it up, continue

Ordering costs

with such steps as receiving the goods and placing them into inventory, and end with the buying firm's paying the supplier. Salaries constitute the major ordering cost; stationery is another ordering cost.

Because we want the *incremental* cost per order, we need cost estimates from the purchasing department, from the receiving warehouse, and from the accounting office covering their operations at two different levels of operation, as shown in Table 7-1. From this table we see that the 2000 additional orders are estimated to cost us $79,000; the incremental cost per order is $79,000/2000 = $39.50.

Carrying costs

Carrying costs, also referred to as holding costs, are basically the costs incurred because a firm owns or maintains inventories. Carrying costs include:

Table 7-1 Ordering Costs

Expense category	Annual salary	At 3,000 orders per year		At 5,000 orders per year	
		Number required	Annual cost	Number required	Annual cost
Purchasing department chief	$20,000	1	$ 20,000	1	$ 20,000
Buyers	12,000	3	36,000	5	60,000
Assistant buyers	10,000	2	20,000	3	30,000
Follow-up persons	9,000	1	9,000	2	18,000
Clerks	9,000	3	27,000	4	36,000
Typists	8,500	2	17,000	3	25,500
Supplies	—	—	500	—	500
Receiving clerks	8,000	2	16,000	3	24,000
Receiving supplies	—	—	300	—	500
Accounts payable clerks	10,000	3	30,000	4	40,000
Accounting supplies	—	—	450	—	750
Total expenses			$176,250		$255,250

Interest on money invested in inventory.

Obsolescence, a cost incurred when inventories go "out of style."

Storage space cost. This may include heat, lights, or refrigeration.

Stores operation, including record keeping, the taking of physical inventory, and protection.

Taxes, insurance, and *pilferage.*

Carrying costs can be expressed as a percentage of average inventory value (say 22 percent per year to hold inventory) or as a cost per unit per time period (say 25 cents per unit per month to hold inventory). Using inventory holding costs as a percentage of the value of the product is convenient because, regardless of the price of a product, the same percentage can be applied. Look at an example. If you calculate that it costs you 25 percent of the value of an item to hold it for a year, then inventory carrying costs on a $12 case of floor-cleaning compound would be .25 × $12 or $3 a year. Inventory holding costs on a six-pack of beer which costs the store $1.20 would be .25 × $1.20, or 30 cents per year.

Expressing carrying costs

Concept of Average Inventory

If a firm buys an item only once for the coming year, if use of the item is constant, and if the last of the item is used on the last day of the year, then the firm's average inventory equals one-half the amount bought; this is the same as saying one-half the beginning inventory. Figure 7-1 shows average inventory under conditions of constant usage.

The EOQ model is generally applicable where the demand for the SKU has

Average inventory

Table 7-2   Identifying the Economic Order Quantity

(1)	Legend	No. orders per year	1	2	3
(2)	$10,000/(1)	$ per order	$10,000	$5,000	$3,333
(3)	(2)/2	Average inventory	5,000	2,500	1,666
(4)	(3) × 12½%	Carrying charges	625	313	208
(5)	(1) × $25	Ordering cost	25	50	75
(6)	(4) + (5)	Total cost/year	$ 650	$ 363	$ 283

a *constant* or *nearly constant* rate. Whereas Figure 7-1 showed a demand situation which was perfectly constant, Figure 7-2 illustrates the case we generally find in practice, one where irregularities do occur.

Which costs are minimized
To minimize inventory costs, management tries to minimize *ordering* costs and *carrying* costs. Having seen how incremental ordering cost, carrying cost, and average inventory are determined, we are now ready to solve for *economic order quantity*. EOQ is that size order which minimizes total annual cost of ordering and carrying inventory. We are assuming conditions of certainty—annual requirements are known.

Tabular Solution for EOQ

Solving for EOQ using a table
Debbie, the owner of Debbie's Boutique, Ltd., estimates that she will sell $10,000 worth of a certain decorator table this year. Her accountants have determined that ordering costs amount to $25 per order and that carrying costs amount to 12½ percent of average inventory. Construction of a table such as Table 7-2 is one approach to identifying the economic order quantity.

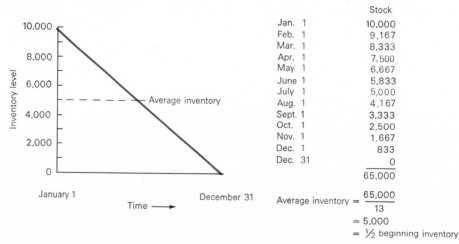

	Stock
Jan. 1	10,000
Feb. 1	9,167
Mar. 1	8,333
Apr. 1	7,500
May 1	6,667
June 1	5,833
July 1	5,000
Aug. 1	4,167
Sept. 1	3,333
Oct. 1	2,500
Nov. 1	1,667
Dec. 1	833
Dec. 31	0
	65,000

$$\text{Average inventory} = \frac{65,000}{13}$$
$$= 5,000$$
$$= \tfrac{1}{2} \text{ beginning inventory}$$

Figure 7-1   Average inventory with constant usage.

4	5	10	20
$2,500	$2,000	$1,000	$500
1,250	1,000	500	250
156	125	63	31
100	125	250	500
$ 256	$ 250	$ 313	$531

↑
Optimum

Note that as cost to carry declines, ordering costs increase. Note also that *total* costs, the figure we want to minimize, are lowest when carrying costs are *equal* to ordering costs. This is the point we always need to determine, because it is always the point of lowest total inventory costs for the year. Table 7-2 shows that Debbie should order this particular SKU 5 times during the year.

Note also that the total costs for ordering 3, 4, and 5 times a year (and also 6 if we had calculated it) are nearly the same. The practical significance of this fact and of the fact that the total cost curve is "dish-shaped" is that *approximate* answers in this situation are often very good ones, varying only slightly from ones we might refer to as *optimum* answers. As long as Debbie orders 3, 4, or 5 times a year, her total inventory cost stays near the minimum.

Precision is not important

Graphic Presentation of EOQ

Figure 7-3 graphs the data from Table 7-2. From the minimum point on the total cost curve in this figure, we can see that the optimum number of orders per year is 5. We can also see that at 5 orders a year, the total ordering cost per year equals

Presenting EOQ graphically

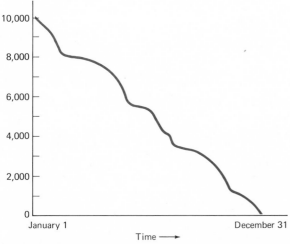

Figure 7-2 Inventory with nearly constant usage.

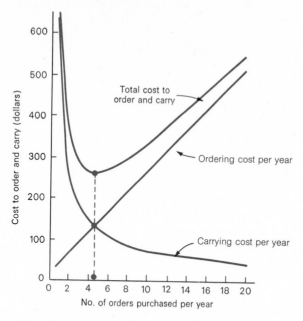

Figure 7-3   Identifying the economic order quantity.

the total carrying cost per year (the two lines cross at this point). You can notice from Table 7-2 that this was also true in the tabular solution. In fact, this is a property of the EOQ model.

Deriving EOQ Formulas

In the following pages, we shall derive *four* EOQ formulas. Each of these produces the same answer, but in different units. Some inventory systems prefer to consider inventory purchasing in terms of *orders per year;* others would rather deal in terms of *units per economic order;* the *number of days' supply* to purchase at one time is a more convenient form for other users; while the *number of dollars per economic order* fits other inventory systems best.

Optimum Number of Orders per Year   To derive this formula,

Let N_o = optimum number of orders per year to minimize total inventory costs
A = total dollar value of the SKU used per year
P = ordering cost per order placed
C = carrying cost expressed as a percentage of average inventory

We have seen that the most economical point as regards total inventory costs is the point where ordering costs are the same in amount as carrying costs. Thus, we can solve for N_o by letting

Total ordering cost/year = carrying cost/year

Total ordering cost/year $= N_o \times P = N_o P$

Carrying cost/year $\quad = \quad \dfrac{A}{N_o} \quad \times \quad \dfrac{1}{2} \quad \times \quad C$

$$\left(\begin{array}{c}\dfrac{\$ \text{ used/year}}{\text{no. orders/year}} \\ = \\ \$ \text{ amount} \\ \text{per order}\end{array}\right) \quad \left(\begin{array}{c}\text{average} \\ \text{inventory} \\ \text{balance} \\ \text{with} \\ \text{constant} \\ \text{usage}\end{array}\right) \quad \left(\begin{array}{c}\text{carrying} \\ \text{cost } \%\end{array}\right)$$

Equating, we get

$$N_o P = \frac{AC}{2N_o}$$

$$2N_o^2 P = AC$$

$$N_o^2 = \frac{AC}{2P}$$

$$N_o = \sqrt{\frac{AC^*}{2P}} \qquad\qquad\qquad (7\text{-}1)$$

Using the formula as derived, we can solve for N_o using the same data seen in Table 7-2 and Figure 7-3:

$$\sqrt{\frac{\$10,000(.125)}{2(\$25)}} = \sqrt{\frac{\$1250}{\$50}} = 5 \text{ orders/year}$$

Optimum Number of Units per Order   Another formula can be derived, this one to give us the optimum number of units to order each time an order is placed.

Deriving a formula where EOQ is defined in units per order

Let R = price of each unit
$\quad N_u$ = optimum number of units per order
$\quad A$ = total dollar value of the SKU used per year
$\quad P$ = ordering cost per order placed
$\quad C$ = carrying cost expressed as a percentage of average inventory

Here we can solve for N_u by letting

Total ordering cost/year = carrying cost/year

$$\dfrac{A/R}{N_u} \qquad \times \qquad P \qquad = \text{total ordering cost}$$

$$\left(\begin{array}{c}\dfrac{\text{no. units used /year}}{\text{no. units /order}} \\ = \\ \text{no. orders/year}\end{array}\right) \qquad (\text{ordering cost/order})$$

* Derivation of this result by the use of calculus is illustrated in the appendix.

$$\frac{A}{(A/R)/N_u} \times \frac{1}{2} \times C = \text{carrying cost/year}$$

$$\left(\begin{array}{c} \dfrac{\text{dollars/year}}{\text{no. orders/year}} \\ = \\ \$/\text{order} \end{array} \right) \left(\begin{array}{c} \text{average} \\ \text{inventory} \\ \text{balance} \\ \text{with} \\ \text{constant} \\ \text{usage} \end{array} \right) \left(\begin{array}{c} \text{carrying} \\ \text{cost } \% \end{array} \right)$$

$$\frac{AP}{RN_u} = \frac{ARC}{2A/N_u}$$

$$\frac{AP}{RN_u} = \frac{RCN_u}{2}$$

$$N_u{}^2 R^2 C = 2AP$$

$$N_u{}^2 = \frac{2AP}{R^2 C}$$

$$N_u = \sqrt{\frac{2AP^*}{R^2 C}} \qquad\qquad (7\text{-}2)$$

Suppose Debbie tells us that this year she plans to sell 40 tables; her cost is $250. You recall that ordering cost per order is $25 and that carrying cost is $12\frac{1}{2}$ percent. Now, substituting our values into our formula, we get

$$\sqrt{\frac{2(10,000)(\$25)}{(\$250)^2(.125)}} = \sqrt{\frac{500,000}{7812.5}} = \sqrt{64}$$

$$= 8 \text{ units/order}$$

Deriving a formula where EOQ is defined in days' supply per order

Optimum Number of Days' Supply per Order   Our third formula tells us how many days' usage Debbie should provide for each time she orders.

Let N_d = optimum number of days' supply per order
  A = total dollar value of the SKU used per year
  P = ordering cost per order placed
  C = carrying cost expressed as a percentage of average inventory
  365 = calendar days per year

Once again,

Total ordering cost/year = carrying cost/year

---

* Derivation of this result by the use of calculus is given in the appendix.

$$\frac{365}{N_d} \quad \times \quad P \qquad\qquad = \text{total ordering cost}$$

$$\left(\begin{array}{c}\text{no. days/year} \\ \overline{\text{no. days/order}} \\ = \\ \text{no. orders/year}\end{array}\right) \quad \left(\begin{array}{c}\text{ordering} \\ \text{cost/order}\end{array}\right)$$

$$\frac{A}{365/N_d} \quad \times \quad \frac{1}{2} \quad \times \quad C \qquad = \text{carrying cost/year}$$

$$\left(\begin{array}{c}\text{dollars/year} \\ \overline{\text{no. orders/year}} \\ = \\ \text{\$/order}\end{array}\right) \quad \left(\begin{array}{c}\text{average} \\ \text{inventory} \\ \text{balance} \\ \text{with} \\ \text{constant} \\ \text{usage}\end{array}\right) \quad \left(\begin{array}{c}\text{carrying} \\ \text{cost \%}\end{array}\right)$$

$$\frac{365P}{N_d} = \frac{AC}{730/N_d}$$

$$\frac{365P}{N_d} = \frac{ACN_d}{730}$$

$$N_d^2 AC = 266{,}450P$$

$$N_d^2 = \frac{266{,}450P}{AC}$$

$$N_d = \sqrt{\frac{266{,}450P*}{AC}} \qquad\qquad (7\text{-}3)$$

Substituting, we get

$$N_d = \sqrt{\frac{266{,}450(\$25)}{(\$10{,}000)(.125)}}$$

$$= \sqrt{5329} = \text{about 73 days' supply}$$

Optimum Number of Dollars per Order Our fourth formula indicates how many dollars' worth of an inventory item Debbie should purchase each time she orders.

Let $N_\$$ = optimum number of dollars per order
   A = total dollar value of the SKU used per year
   P = ordering cost per order placed
   C = carrying cost expressed as a percentage of average inventory

Here again,

Deriving a formula where EOQ is defined in dollars per order

*   Derivation of this result by the use of calculus is given in the appendix.

Total ordering cost/year = carrying cost per year

$$\frac{A}{N_\$} \quad \times \quad P \qquad\qquad = \text{total ordering cost}$$

$$\left(\begin{array}{c}\dfrac{\$/\text{year}}{\$/\text{order}}\\ =\\ \text{no. orders/year}\end{array}\right) \left(\begin{array}{c}\text{ordering}\\ \text{cost/order}\end{array}\right)$$

$$\frac{A}{A/N_\$} \quad \times \quad \frac{1}{2} \quad \times \quad C = \text{carrying cost/year}$$

$$\left(\begin{array}{c}\dfrac{\$/\text{year}}{\text{no. orders/year}}\\ =\\ \$/\text{order}\end{array}\right) \left(\begin{array}{c}\text{average}\\ \text{inventory}\\ \text{balance}\\ \text{with}\\ \text{constant}\\ \text{usage}\end{array}\right) \left(\begin{array}{c}\text{carrying}\\ \text{cost }\%\end{array}\right)$$

$$\frac{AP}{N_\$} = \frac{N_\$C}{2}$$

$$N_\$^2 C = 2AP$$

$$N_\$^2 = \frac{2AP}{C}$$

$$N_\$ = \sqrt{\frac{2AP*}{C}} \tag{7-4}$$

Substituting our values into *this* formula we get

$$N_\$ = \sqrt{\frac{2(\$10,000)(\$25)}{.125}}$$
$$= \sqrt{4,000,000}$$
$$= \$2000 \text{ per order}$$

Comparability of Answers

All four formulas lead us to the same action

Application of the four formulas we have derived for Debbie's Boutique produced these four answers for her:

Optimum number of orders per year   = 5
Optimum number of tables per order   = 8
Optimum number of day's supply to order = 73
Optimum dollars per order   = $2000

* Derivation of this result by the use of calculus is given in the appendix.

All these answers mean the *same* thing, and Debbie would use the formula that produced the answer in a form most siutable for her ordering and inventory system. In any event, she would use only one of the four formulas we have derived.

Assumptions We Have Made

Instead of just handing Debbie one (or all four) of the EOQ formulas we have derived, we ought to be careful to review with her the assumptions under which these formulas work best. First, we've assumed that she can estimate annual demand. Second, we assumed that demand was constant or nearly constant. Third, we assumed that when an order arrives, it arrives all at one time. And finally, we assumed that her cost figures for purchasing and carrying were reasonably accurate. If any of these assumptions is wrong, then applying our EOQ formulas will not generate answers useful to her. Fortunately, there are ways of coping with situations in which these assumptions are not true; we shall present them later in this chapter.

Assumptions made in deriving the EOQ model

Cost Savings with an EOQ Model

Before we provided her with an EOQ model, Debbie ordered these decorator tables once a month in an effort to keep her inventory cost down. Now we've suggested that an optimum purchasing policy is for her to order the tables 5 times a year. What is the difference in the two methods? In Table 7-3, we have illustrated the cost difference between these two methods. Using the EOQ model saves her a little over $100 annually on this one SKU.

How much does the EOQ model save

4. How to Eliminate the Instantaneous Receipt Assumption in EOQ Models

In the EOQ models presented to this point, we have assumed that all the inventory which is ordered arrives *simultaneously*—that the inventory rises to its maximum level instantaneously. Hence the vertical line to represent arrival of a new lot of

Receipt of inventory is not usually simultaneous

Table 7-3 Total Cost of Present and Proposed (EOQ) Inventory Policies for Debbie's Boutique

	12 orders/year	5 orders/year
Annual cost of the tables	$10,000	$10,000
Cost per order (annual cost/number of orders)	833	2,000
Average inventory (cost/order)/2	417	1,000
Annual carrying charge (.125 × average inventory)	52	125
Annual purchasing cost ($25 × number of orders)	300	125
Total cost per year (annual purchasing cost + annual carrying charge)	352	250

Savings = $102

Comparison of two ordering patterns

Graphic illustration of assumed inventory behavior

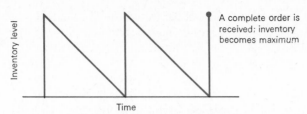

Figure 7-4 Inventory with instantaneous receipt

inventory is as shown in Figure 7-4. In many cases, however, this is not a valid assumption because the vendor delivers the order in partial shipments or portions over a period of time. In such cases inventory is being used while new inventory is still being received, and the inventory *does not* build up immediately to its maximum point. Instead, it builds up gradually when inventory is received faster than it is being used; then it declines to its lowest level as incoming shipments stop and the use of inventory continues. This concept is illustrated in Figure 7-5.

We can express total ordering and carrying costs as follows. If

N_u = optimum lot size in units

and

x = receipt rate in units received daily

then

$$\frac{N_u}{x} = \text{number of days required to receive entire order}$$

If

y = use rate in units used daily

then

Graphic illustration of actual inventory behavior

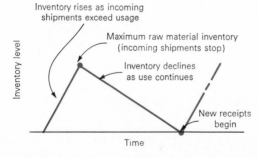

Figure 7-5 Inventory with receipt over time.

$\dfrac{N_u}{x} \times y$ = number of units used during receipt period, and

$N_u - \dfrac{N_u}{x} \times y$ = largest inventory which can accumulate

Because the average inventory is approximately half the maximum inventory, the average inventory in this case would be

$$\tfrac{1}{2}\left(N_u - \dfrac{N_u}{x} \times y\right) = \tfrac{1}{2}N_u\left(1 - \dfrac{y}{x}\right)$$

Let R represent cost per unit and let C represent carrying costs. If carrying costs equal average inventory in units times cost per unit times carrying costs in percent, we get

$$\text{Carrying costs} = \dfrac{N_u}{2}\left(1 - \dfrac{y}{x}\right) \times R \times C$$

$$= \dfrac{RCN_u}{2}\left(1 - \dfrac{y}{x}\right)$$

Total annual carrying costs without instantaneous receipt

And if annual usage in units is symbolized as U and ordering cost as P,

$$\text{Number of lots per year} = \dfrac{U}{N_u}$$

and

$$\text{Total ordering cost} = \dfrac{U}{N_u} \times P$$

Total annual ordering costs without instantaneous receipt

From our previous derivations of EOQ models, we realize that total ordering *and* carrying costs are minimum when the cost to order per year equals the cost to carry per year. Thus, we equate the two expressions we have already defined and solve for N:

$$\dfrac{UP}{N_u} = \dfrac{RCN_u}{2}\left(1 - \dfrac{y}{x}\right)$$

$$RCN_u{}^2\left(1 - \dfrac{y}{x}\right) = 2UP$$

EOQ without instantaneous receipt

$$N_u{}^2 = \dfrac{2UP}{RC(1 - y/x)}$$

$$N_u = \sqrt{\dfrac{2UP*}{RC(1 - y/x)}} \qquad\qquad (7\text{-}5)$$

* Derivation of this result by the use of calculus is illustrated in the appendix.

Table 7-4   Debbie's Estimated Requirements for 7 Weeks

Week	Net requirements
1	0 ⎫
2	0 ⎬ (Zeros reflect inventory already on hand)
3	0 ⎭
4	50
5	30
6	40
7	40

Inventory item: rope hammock

Unit cost: $20.83

Carrying cost: 25%/year $\left(\$20.83 \times \dfrac{.25}{52} = \$.10/\text{unit per week}\right)$

Ordering cost: $20 per order

5. Using EOQ Models When Annual Demand Cannot Be Forecast

Demand forecasting assumptions in the EOQ model

All the formulas we have derived up to this point have required that annual demand be known. In many situations, however, annual demand simply cannot be predicted with any reliability. Demand per week, for example, may be so erratic that one would hesitate to predict annual demand from it; in another situation, we may be dealing with a brand new product, one with absolutely no previous history. So, to predict annual demand is not always possible or prudent. We thus must turn to another approach to EOQ when such is the situation.

Problem illustrating EOQ when annual demand cannot be forecast

Let's go back for a moment to Debbie's Boutique and see how it is possible to use EOQ concepts even when annual demand cannot be forecast accurately. Debbie is interested in applying the EOQ model to a new-model rope hammock which she is stocking; however, all she can give us is her estimated needs for the next 7 weeks. This short-term demand estimate, the cost of ordering, the cost per hammock, and her carrying cost for this item are all illustrated in Table 7-4. The zero net requirements for the first 3 weeks reflect the fact that some inventory is already on hand.

Debbie can still determine her economic order quantity for this SKU in this situation by using an *iterative* (step-by-step) method. She would begin by computing the carrying costs of the four buying alternatives, enough for 4, 5, 6, or 7 weeks' use.

Number of hammocks bought	Carrying cost	
50	(All units used in fourth week)	= $ 0
80	30 units held 1 week	= $ 3
120	$3 (above) plus 40 units held 2 weeks	= $11
160	$11 (above) plus 40 units held 3 weeks	= $23

Carrying cost of four alternatives

Now let us place the carrying costs for the four alternatives beside the ordering costs for the same alternatives:

Number of hammocks bought	Carrying cost	Ordering cost
50	$ 0	$20
80	3	20
120	11	20
160	23	20

Carrying cost and ordering cost for four alternatives

As Debbie increased the number purchased at one time, the carrying charges rose until they were greater than the ordering charges. She knew from our past deriva- tions that the optimum EOQ is where cost to order *equals* cost to carry; so she should order that number of units which equalizes those two costs. The answer lies somewhere between 120 (ordering cost greater than carrying cost) and 160 (carrying cost greater than ordering cost). An approximate EOQ in this situation can be found by some simple interpolation. She knows that the answer is something more than 120 units and that the extra ones, however many there are, we will be carrying in stock for 3 weeks. Her real question then is: "How many units carried in stock for 3 weeks will cause the carrying charges to rise to $20 so as to equal the ordering costs?"

Interpolating to get the EOQ

$$\frac{\$20 - \$11}{\$.10 \times 3 \text{ wk}} = 30 \text{ units}$$

120 + 30 units = 150, the EOQ. This will cover her requirements through 30 units of the seventh week. Sometime prior to that time, another calculation will have to be made. In this procedure, the EOQ will likely be different each time it is cal- culated, but it will still be a completely logical outcome as long as the conditions underlying the need for hammocks are themselves changing from order to order.

6. Using EOQ Models When Cost Information Is Not Available

In all our consideration of economic order quantity formulas to this point, we have assumed that proper use of estimating, accounting, and other cost-finding tech- niques could produce the appropriate values of *carrying cost* and *ordering cost* our formulas have required. Sometimes, however, organizations have not maintained records which would provide a sufficient accounting information base to generate these two *parameters* (values); in other cases, organizations which have not em- ployed formal inventory theory may wish to do so but may not be willing to wait until they have accumulated inventory cost data, and this is often a considerable period of time. And finally, in certain critical situations (severe overstocking or unusually high numbers of purchase orders being written), an organization may want to take immediate action to *improve* the situation, even though that action might not be optimum in the sense of formal inventory theory.

Traditional EOQ models require information that may not be available

EOQ benefits can
be obtained even
when ordering and
carrying costs are
not known

In situations like those reviewed above and in many others, it *is* possible to reap many of the benefits of inventory techniques even when ordering cost and carrying cost are not known and cannot be determined. Although it may first appear that use of inventory models without cost information is impossible, we will show (with a bit of simple algebra) how this *can* be done to provide management with practical answers to complex inventory situations.

There are two approaches to this problem: (1) we can leave the purchasing work load where it is while we minimize the carrying cost or (2) we can leave the inventory where it is while we minimize the purchasing work load.

Developing a Model Which Will Minimize Inventory Levels without Increasing the Purchasing Work Load

Let us begin by repeating Eq. (7-4), which expressed the economic order quantity in *dollars per order:*

Developing a model
to minimize
inventory without
increasing pur-
chasing work load

$$N_\$ = \sqrt{\frac{2AP}{C}} \qquad (7\text{-}4)$$

Now, of the values under the square root sign, organizations generally know or are able to estimate the value of A (the annual dollar use of an item per year). Suppose we separate the right-hand side of Eq. (7-4) into *two* parts, one containing A, the other containing the remaining three terms. Then we have:

$$N_\$ = \sqrt{\frac{2P}{C}} \times \sqrt{A}$$

Even though the value 2 is a numerical constant and is therefore not part of our problem of lack of cost data, we have included it with the other two terms (P and C) just to make the following computations a bit easier.

Now, let us assume the worst possible cost information condition, that is, that we have no way of knowing or finding the values for P and C; therefore, we substitute X for the entire first part above as follows:

$$N_\$ = X\sqrt{A} \qquad (7\text{-}6)$$

At this point, we can do a bit of simple algebra in several steps as follows:

Five steps in the
derivation of the
formula for X

Step 1 Divide both sides of Eq. (7-6) into A:

$$\frac{A}{N_\$} = \frac{A}{X\sqrt{A}}$$

Step 2 Separate the numerator of the *right* side into two parts:

$$\frac{A}{N_\$} = \frac{\sqrt{A} \cdot \sqrt{A}}{X\sqrt{A}}$$

Step 3 Cancel equivalent terms in the numerator and denominator of the right side. This leaves:

$$\frac{A}{N_\$} = \frac{\sqrt{A}}{X}$$

Step 4 Solve for X:

$$X\left(\frac{A}{N_\$}\right) = \sqrt{A}$$

$$X = \frac{\sqrt{A}}{(A/N_\$)}$$

Step 5 Because X will be a constant for any *single* inventory item, it is useful for purposes of this development to consider X as a constant for an *entire inventory* of items; it can therefore be expressed as the ratio of the sums of the numerator and the denominator of the right side:

$$X = \frac{\Sigma\left(\sqrt{A}\right)}{\Sigma\left(A/N_\$\right)} \tag{7-7}$$

Minimizing Debbie's Inventory Level
without Increasing Her Purchasing Work Load

Suppose we have just walked into Debbie's Boutique. She has never made any attempt to apply EOQ models and she has no cost information on purchasing or carrying costs. Her past inventory policy on the five SKUs she stocks was to purchase them quarterly. Table 7-5 illustrates Debbie's inventory situation. What can we do in this situation?

Problem illustrating inventory minimization without any increase in purchasing work load

Table 7-5 Inventory Situation at Debbie's Boutique

SKU	Dollar value used annually	No. of times ordered/yr	Dollars per order	Average inventory balance
Decorator lamp	$10,000	4	$2,500	$1,250
Rattan chair	8,000	4	2,000	1,000
Rope hammock	5,000	4	1,250	625
Brass chafing dish	1,000	4	250	125
Embroidered placemat	600	4	150	75
		20 = total purchasing work load		$3,075 = average inventory balance

Table 7-6 Debbie's Inventory: Minimum Average Inventory Is Achieved Without Increasing Purchasing Work Load

SKU	A ($ used/yr.)	$\sqrt{A}$	X	$X\sqrt{A}$ ($/order)	Ave. inventory ($ per order/2)	No. orders/yr. (A/$ per order)
Decorator lamp	$10,000	100.00	15.815	$1,581.50	$790.15	6.32
Rattan chair	8,000	89.45	15.815	1,414.65	707.33	5.66
Rope hammock	5,000	70.71	15.815	1,118.28	559.14	4.47
Brass chafing dish	1,000	31.64	15.815	500.39	250.20	2.00
Embroidered placemat	600	24.50	15.815	387.46	193.73	1.55
					$2,501.15	20.00

Looking both at Eq. (7-7) and at the information in Table 7-5, we can now solve for X in that equation from the information in the table. First, the *numerator* of Eq. (7-7):

$$\Sigma\,(\sqrt{A}) = \sqrt{\$10,000} + \sqrt{\$8000} + \sqrt{\$5000} + \sqrt{\$1000} + \sqrt{\$600}$$
$$= 100.00 + 89.45 + 70.71 + 31.64 + 24.50$$
$$= 316.30$$

Now the *denominator* of Eq. (7-7):

$$\Sigma\left(\frac{A}{N_\$}\right) = \text{the sum of } \frac{A}{N_\$}; \text{ as } \frac{A}{N_\$} \text{ is the number of orders placed for } one \text{ inventory}$$

item, $\Sigma\left(\dfrac{A}{N_\$}\right)$ must equal the *total* number of orders placed

$$= 20$$

Knowing the values for the numerator and denominator of Eq. (7-7), we can now solve for X in that equation as follows:

$$X = \frac{316.30}{20}$$

$$= 15.815$$

From Eq. (7-6) we saw that the optimum dollar value per order for any single inventory item was:

$$N_\$ = X\sqrt{A} \tag{7-6}$$

Interpreting the results Table 7-6 applies this formula to each of the five SKUs in Debbie's inventory. From the computations represented by this table, we can see that her total average inventory has been reduced from the $3075 of Table 7-5 down to $2501.15, while her total purchasing work load has remained unchanged at 20 orders per year.

(The fact that the number of orders per year for several of her SKUs are not integers is not really relevant. For example, our solution indicates that she should place 6.32 orders per year for lamps; this is nothing more than saying she should order this item every 365/6.32 or 58 calendar days.)

Let us look for a moment at what we have accomplished. Without knowing the value of carrying cost or ordering cost, we have managed to accomplish a significant inventory reduction without increasing purchasing work load. This has been possible because we have used *surrogates* or substitutes for carrying cost and ordering cost. Specifically, we have assumed that whatever the true carrying cost might be, carrying a *lower* inventory ($2501.15) is better than carrying a *higher* inventory ($3075.00). Thus we have really let the value of the average inventory serve as a surrogate for carrying cost. Similarly, we have used the total number of purchase orders written per year as a *surrogate* or substitute for ordering cost; this is nothing more complicated than assuming that if Debbie doesn't write any additional orders, her total cost of operating the procurement function probably won't change.

What has been accomplished

Developing a Model Which Will Minimize the Purchasing Work Load without Increasing the Average Inventory

In the previous section, we were able to minimize the average inventory without increasing the purchasing work load; it is also possible to *minimize the purchasing work load without altering the average level of the inventory*. In situations where temporary shortages of qualified purchasing personnel make exploration of this alternative advantageous, the method to be illustrated represents a very practical alternative. Again, we shall assume that information on carrying costs and ordering costs is not available. We begin by first recalling Eq. (7-6).

Developing a model to minimize purchasing work load without increasing average inventory

$$N_\$ = X \sqrt{A} \tag{7-6}$$

As X is a constant for any single inventory item, it is also a constant for an *entire inventory* of items; thus for the five inventory items of our Debbie's Boutique illustration, we can rewrite (7-6) to:

$$\Sigma N_\$ = (X) \Sigma (\sqrt{A})$$

and solving for X we have:

$$X = \frac{\Sigma (N_\$)}{\Sigma (\sqrt{A})} \tag{7-8}$$

Minimizing Debbie's Purchasing Work Load without Increasing Her Average Inventory

Let us apply Eq. (7-8) to Debbie's inventory in Table 7-5. The numerator of Eq. (7-8) calls for the sum of the dollars per order; this value can be obtained by

Problem illustrating
minimization of
purchasing work
load without
increasing average
inventory
summing the "Dollars per order" column of Table 7-5, or more quickly by simply computing twice the average inventory balance:

$$\Sigma \ (N_\$) = \$2500 + \$2000 + \$1250 + \$250 + \$150$$
$$= \$6150$$

or

$$\Sigma \ (N_\$) = 2 \times \$3075$$
$$= \$6150$$

The denominator of Eq. (7-8) is identical to the numerator of Eq. (7-7) and has previously been computed to be 316.30. Therefore, the required value for X in Eq. (7-8) can now be calculated as:

$$X = \frac{\Sigma \ (N_\$)}{\Sigma \ (\sqrt{A})} \qquad (7\text{-}8)$$

$$= \frac{6150}{316.30}$$

$$= 19.44$$

In Eq. (7-6), we saw that the optimum dollar value per order for any single inventory item was:

$$N_\$ = X\sqrt{A} \qquad (7\text{-}6)$$

Interpreting the
results
Table 7-7 applies this equation to the inventory situation at Debbie's Boutique using the value 19.44 for X just calculated. The results in Table 7-7 indicate that we have achieved about a 20 percent reduction in purchasing work load (measured in terms of the number of orders processed per year) *without* increasing her total average inventory above the $3075 level (there is a slight roundoff error in the calculations, but this is quite normal).

Table 7-7 Debbie's Inventory: Minimizing Her Purchasing Work Load without Increasing Total Average Inventory

SKU	A ($ used/yr)	$\sqrt{A}$	X	$X\sqrt{A}$ ($/order)	Ave. inventory ($ per order/2)	No. orders/year (A/$ per order)
Decorator lamp	$10,000	100.00	19.44	$1,944.00	$ 972.00	5.14
Rattan chair	8,000	89.45	19.44	1,738.91	869.45	4.60
Rope hammock	5,000	70.71	19.44	1,374.60	687.30	3.64
Brass chafing dish	1,000	31.64	19.44	615.08	307.54	1.63
Embroidered placemat	600	24.50	19.44	476.28	238.14	1.26
					$3,074.43	16.27

Conclusion Concerning Options
Open When There Is No Cost Information

We have demonstrated with the preceding two examples how one can still make sensible inventory decisions even in the absence of explicit cost information by using *surrogates* for cost of carrying and cost of ordering. The Debbie's Boutique example used an inventory consisting of only five items to simplify the calculations required; in practice, however, the authors have applied the first approach (minimizing the inventory level without increasing the work load) to an actual inventory of over 16,000 different items with the use of a computer. The analysis resulted in a reduction of nearly 18 percent in the inventory level in a situation where cost information necessary to support the more traditional economic order quantity analysis was completely lacking and where it would be several years before such information might be available.

> Results from using quantitative approaches even when cost information is lacking

It should be noted that the methods illustrated in this section are capable of providing operational answers to *any* desired purchasing work load and average inventory condition desired by management; our two illustrations enabled us to determine the following *two* outcomes:

1. Minimum average inventory without increasing purchasing work load

2. Minimum purchasing work load without increasing total average inventory

Just as a last couple of examples of flexibility, suppose first that Debbie wanted to find what reduction in total average inventory she could achieve *if she were willing to increase her purchasing work load 20 percent a year* (from 20 to 24 orders, in our simplified example). To do this she would have substituted into Eq. (7-7) as follows:

> Alternative answers that may be more useful

$$X = \frac{316.30}{24}$$

$$= 13.18$$

and used the new value of X in a table just as in our Table 7-7.

And finally, if Debbie wanted to determine how much she could reduce her purchasing work load *if she were willing to increase her average inventory by $1000,* she would have substituted into Eq. (7-8) as follows and used it in a table like our Table 7-7:

> More flexibility with this model

$$X = \frac{\$8150^*}{316.30}$$

$$= 25.77$$

---

* Remember that *twice* the increase in average inventory has been added here.

7. Applying the EOQ
Model to Production Processes

The concept that there is one best pattern of ordering to minimize annual inventory costs can be adapted to the production process. For instance, there are many companies which produce certain items among their product lines in lots or batches instead of manufacturing at a constant rate all year long. This method is generally followed because total annual sales of the finished item are not enough to warrant maintaining a production line for the exclusive manufacture of that item on a yearlong continuous basis.

Setup costs   These firms incur a *setup cost* each time a batch is produced. Setup cost is roughly equivalent to the ordering cost per order already treated in this chapter. It consists of:

1. *Engineering cost* of setting up the production lines or machines

2. *Paperwork cost* of processing the work order and authorizing production

3. *Ordering cost* to provide raw materials for the batch or order

Carrying costs   In addition to these setup costs, the company incurs *carrying costs* on the finished product from the time it is manufactured until it is sold. The carrying charges on finished goods consist of the same items constituting the carrying costs on inventory except that the value of finished goods is higher because of the cost of manufacturing, labor, and overhead. We see, then, that the basic concept of an optimum number of batches or runs—the number to minimize total annual production costs for manufacturing of the intermittent type—is quite similar to the concept we have been using for raw material inventories.

Optimum Production Lot Size: Production for Stock

Problem illustrating optimum production lot size   One case where an optimum production lot size can be calculated involves finished goods which are to be placed in stock and then sold at a constant rate until some low level is reached; at that time another lot will be produced. Here the procedure for finding the optimum number of runs per year is the same as in the case of inventory control. The symbols used correspond as shown in Table 7-8. If, for instance, (1) a company produces $40,000 worth of special gears at the factory each year, (2) carrying costs on finished stock are 20 percent per year, and (3) setup cost per production run is $80, then the optimum number of production runs per year for this item would be

$$N_r = \sqrt{\frac{AC}{2S}} = \sqrt{\frac{\$40,000(0.20)}{2(\$80)}} = \sqrt{\frac{\$8000}{\$160}} = \sqrt{50} \qquad (7\text{-}9)$$

= about 7 runs/year

In other words, to minimize total annual cost of setting up to produce these

Table 7-8 Symbols for Computing Production Lot Size for Stock

	Inventory (optimum no. of orders)		Production runs (optimum no./year)
A	Annual use of item in dollars	A	Annual sales of item in dollars (factory cost)
C	Carrying costs as a percent of raw materials	C	Carrying costs as a percent of finished goods
P	Ordering costs per order	S	Setup cost per run
N_0	Optimum no. of orders per year	N_r	Optimum no. of runs per year

Comparability of symbols

gears and of storing them until the gears are sold, the company should manufacture the annual requirement for this item in 7 lots or batches per year. We could, of course, have used other EOQ formulas and derived the answer in terms of optimum number of units per run or in terms of optimum number of months' sales in each run.

Interpreting the results

Optimum Production Lot Size: Simultaneous Production and Sales

Another case in which we can apply the concept of an optimum production lot size is one where the finished goods are being sold while each lot is being produced. In this case, the inventory of finished goods does not build up immediately to its maximum point, as it would in the case of receipt of a complete optimum order of raw materials. Instead, it builds up gradually as goods are produced faster than they are being sold; then it declines to its lowest point as production of a particular batch ceases although sales continue. This concept is illustrated in Figure 7-6.

Table 7-9 shows how the symbols in this situation correspond to those used in calculating inventories. The appropriate formula to use under these conditions is:

$$N_u = \sqrt{\frac{2US^*}{RC(1 - d/p)}}$$

(7-10)

* Derivation of this result by the use of calculus is given in the appendix.

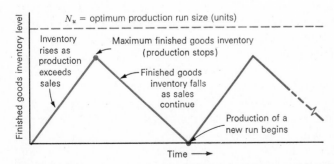

Figure 7-6 Finished goods inventory during simultaneous production and sales.

Table 7-9 Symbols for Computing Lot Size with Simultaneous Sales

	Inventory, Eq. (7-5) (optimum units per lot)		Production runs, Eq. (7-10) (optimum units per run)
U	Annual need in units	U	Annual sales in units
P	Ordering costs per order	S	Setup cost per run
R	Price per unit	R	Factory cost per unit
C	Carrying costs as a percent of raw materials	C	Carrying costs as a percent of finished goods
N_u	Optimum no. of units per order	N_u	Optimum no. of units per run

Comparability of symbols (margin note)

where d is the sales rate in units per day and p is the production rate in units per day. Equation (7-10) corresponds to Eq. (7-5), which was appropriate to use in the case of simultaneous receipt and use of *inventory*.

Problem illustrating production lot size without instantaneous production (margin note)

To apply Eq. (7-10), consider a Napa Valley, California, company that bottles 5000 cases of a particular rosé wine annually. The setup cost per run is $90. Factory cost is $5 per case. Carrying costs on finished goods inventory is 20 percent. Production rate is 100 per day, and sales amount to 14 per day. How many cases should be bottled per production run?

$$N_u = \sqrt{\frac{2(5000)(\$90)}{\$5(.20)(1 - {}^{14}/_{100})}}$$

$$= \sqrt{\frac{\$900,000}{\$1(1 - 0.14)}}$$

$$= \sqrt{\frac{\$900,000}{\$.86}}$$

$$= \sqrt{1,046,000}$$

$= 1023 =$ no. cases/optimum production run (from a practical standpoint, the company would probably set up its bottling line five times a year)

Use of Economic Production Lot Size Models When Cost Information Is Not Available

Using models of production lot size without cost information: a caution (margin note)

Earlier in this chapter, we included a section titled "Using EOQ Models When Cost Information Is Not Available." The concepts brought out there are equally applicable to the production lot size situation when setup costs and carrying costs on finished inventory cannot be determined. One must remember, however, that in the production case, our method would use the "total number of setups per year" as a surrogate for setup cost; in cases where there is no wide variation in the cost of one setup versus another, this method is perfectly suitable. However, in cases where the setups involved in the manufacture of one part cost $500 and the setups involved in the manufacture of another part cost only $5, one would

Table 7-10 Sensitivity of EOQ to Annual Demand

Annual use, units	EOQ, units per economic lot
1,000	$\sqrt{\dfrac{2(\$2,000)(\$10)}{(\$2)^2(.20)}} = 224$
10,000	$\sqrt{\dfrac{2(\$20,000)(\$10)}{(\$2)^2(.20)}} = 707$
100,000	$\sqrt{\dfrac{2(\$200,000)(\$10)}{(\$2)^2(.20)}} = 2,240$
1,000,000	$\sqrt{\dfrac{2(\$2,000,000)(\$10)}{(\$2)^2(.20)}} = 7,070$

Carrying cost: 20%
Ordering cost: $10
Price per unit: $2

Sensitivity shown

have to use the results with caution, remembering that reducing the total number of setups by 20 percent per year is not nearly as meaningful if those reduced are of the $5 variety instead of the $500 variety.

8. Some Conclusions about EOQ Models

Sensitivity of EOQ Models

Let us make a few simple tests to see how sensitive the EOQ formula is to increases in annual demand for any item; then we can attempt to set an inventory policy under these conditions. In Table 7-10, using Eq. (7-2), we have calculated EOQ for four different levels of annual demand. What is the significance of these results? In each case, the annual demand rose by a factor of 10, but a quick calculation indicates that the optimum EOQ rose only by 3.16 (the square root of 10). Of course, because the formula involves a square root and because the only value we altered was in the numerator, this should have been obvious before we completed the calculations. The implications of this simple experiment, however, are quite clear. The size of order, and thus the average inventory held, should rise *only by the square root of the increase in annual sales* of the item. When annual sales are increasing or decreasing, inventory systems which hold a *fixed* percent of anticipated annual sales in inventory cannot be considered optimum.

Sensitivity of the EOQ model to changes in demand

Selective Use of EOQ Formulas

Keep in mind that the EOQ formulas are only tools for use in decision making and that the answers derived from them are only as good as the data fed into the formulas. No company, of course, will use the EOQ formulas to analyze its pur-

EOQ models are not normally used for all SKUs

Table 7-11   Importance of Inventory SKUs

Inventory classification	Degree of capital importance	Percent of inventory items	Percent of annual dollar usage
A	Major	10	80
B	Intermediate	20	15
C	Minor	70	5
		100	100

chasing of *every* SKU it buys (or produces) and stocks. Some distinction must be made between SKUs which account for a large part of the inventory value and those which are of minor importance. The pattern in Table 7-11 is quite common.

Other controls   In the case shown in this table, formulas would be used as an aid in controlling the A group because it is here that management would want to concentrate its effort. Other tools, less technical, would be used for the B SKUs and the C SKUs; for example, management might set rule-of-thumb upper and lower inventory levels. B and C SKUs would seldom be controlled closely because they total only 20 percent of annual dollar usage.

Glossary

1. **SKU**   Stockkeeping unit; a specific different item in an inventory.
2. **EOQ**   Economic order quantity. That particular quantity which, if ordered each time the inventory is replenished, will minimize the total annual cost of ordering and carrying the inventory.
3. **Ordering costs**   The costs of getting an item into the inventory; these costs are incurred each time an order is placed.
4. **Carrying costs**   The costs incurred in maintaining an inventory.
5. **Average inventory**   The average balance of inventory on hand; in the case of constant demand, average inventory is about half maximum inventory.
6. **Instantaneous receipt**   The condition where the entire quantity of inventory which has been ordered arrives at one time.
7. **Iterative process**   A step-by-step process.
8. **Purchasing work load**   Total number of purchase orders written per year; used as a surrogate for total annual ordering cost.
9. **Optimum production lot size**   That particular quantity which, if produced in one production run, will minimize the total annual cost of setting up and carrying finished goods inventory.

Review of Equations

Page 197

$$N_o = \sqrt{\frac{AC}{2P}}$$

(7-1)

This formula will solve for EOQ in terms of the optimum number of orders per year where P = ordering cost, A = annual usage of the SKU in dollars, and C = carrying cost expressed as a percent of average inventory. Instantaneous receipt of inventory is assumed.

Page 198

$$N_u = \sqrt{\frac{2AP}{R^2C}} \tag{7-2}$$

With this formula we can solve for EOQ in terms of the optimum number of units per economic order. The one additional symbol not used in Eq. (7-1) is R, which is the price of each unit. Instantaneous receipt of inventory is assumed.

Page 199

$$N_d = \sqrt{\frac{266{,}450P}{AC}} \tag{7-3}$$

Using the same symbols already defined, we can solve for the optimum number of days' supply per order by using this formula. Instantaneous receipt of inventory is assumed.

Page 200

$$N_\$ = \sqrt{\frac{2AP}{C}} \tag{7-4}$$

This formula will give us the number of dollars per economic order; it uses the same symbols previously defined. This formula, too, assumes instantaneous receipt of inventory.

Page 203

$$N_u = \sqrt{\frac{2UP}{RC(1 - y/x)}} \tag{7-5}$$

By using this formula, we can remove the assumption of instantaneous receipt of inventory which was necessary with Eqs. (7-1) through (7-4). In this formulation, P, R, and C, are as previously defined; U = the annual demand for the SKU in units; y = daily use rate of the SKU; and x = the daily receipt rate of the SKU.

Page 206

$$N_\$ = X\sqrt{A} \tag{7-6}$$

This is Eq. (7-4) with X substituting for $\sqrt{2P/C}$. It is a part of the derivation of an equation useful in situations where cost data concerning carrying costs and ordering costs are not available.

Page 207

$$X = \frac{\Sigma\,(\sqrt{A}\,)}{\Sigma(A/N_\$)} \tag{7-7}$$

Equation (7-7) is used to minimize inventory level without increasing purchasing work load in situations where cost data for carrying and ordering costs are not available. Average inventory serves as a surrogate for carrying charges and purchasing work load serves as a surrogate for ordering cost.

Page 209

$$X = \frac{\Sigma\,(N_\$)}{\Sigma\,(\sqrt{A}\,)} \tag{7-8}$$

We use this formula when we are interested in minimizing the purchasing work load without increasing the average inventory in situations where cost data for carrying and ordering costs are not available. Average inventory serves as a surrogate for carrying charges and purchasing work load serves as a surrogate for ordering cost.

Page 212

$$N_r = \sqrt{\frac{AC}{2S}} \tag{7-9}$$

This formula yields the optimum number of production runs per year to minimize the total annual cost of carrying finished inventory plus setup cost of machines. C is defined as it was in previous EOQ formulas; S = the cost per setup in dollars; A = annual sales of the item in dollars of factory cost.

Page 213

$$N_u = \sqrt{\frac{2US}{RC(1 - d/p)}} \tag{7-10}$$

With this formula we can eliminate the assumption of instantaneous maximum inventory of finished goods inherent in Eq. (7-9). Here we allow for simultaneous production and use of inventory. All the symbols used here have been defined previously except d, which equals the sales rate in units per day, and p, which equals the production rate, also in units per day.

Exercises

7-1. Using the following symbols, derive a formula which will solve directly for the optimum number of weeks' supply to purchase at one time.

P = administrative cost per order
C = carrying charges as a percent of average inventory
A = annual requirement in dollars
X = optimum number of weeks' supply to purchase at one time

7-2. Using the following symbols, derive a formula which will solve directly for N_u.

A = annual requirement in dollars
R = price per unit
P = administrative cost per purchase
C = carrying charges in dollars per unit per year
N_u = units per economic lot

7-3. Central University uses $81,000 annually of a particular reagent in the chemistry department labs. The university purchasing director estimates the purchasing cost at $25 and thinks that the university can hold this type inventory at an annual storage cost of 20 percent of the purchase price. How many months' supply should the purchasing director order at one time to minimize total annual cost of purchasing and carrying?

7-4. Using these symbols, derive a formula which will solve directly for the optimum number of days' supply to purchase at one time:

N_d = optimum number of days' supply per order
U = total number of units used per year
P = ordering cost per order placed
C = carrying cost expressed as a percentage of average inventory value
R = price of each unit
r = receipt rate in units received daily
u = use rate in units used daily

7-5. Cardinal Chemical Company holds its inventory of raw material in special containers, with each container occupying 10 square feet of floor space. There is only 2500 square feet of storage space available. Each year, Cardinal uses 8000 containers of raw material, paying $8 per container. If ordering costs for raw material are $10 per order and annual holding costs are 20 percent of the average inventory value, how much is it worth to Cardinal to increase its raw material storage area?

7-6. The Cardinal Chemical Company of Problem 7-5 has been advised by its supplier of raw material that perhaps it would be of mutual advantage for the supplier to fill its orders incrementally. This plan would call for the supplier to deliver 50 containers per day, beginning immediately when an order is placed and continuing until the order is filled. Under the plan, would the company realize any savings in annual inventory costs?

7-7. A purchasing agent is considering three vendors from whom chemicals may be ordered. Vendor X will sell any amount at $20 per drum. Vendor Y will accept orders for only 800 or more drums but asks only $18 per drum. Vendor Z will accept orders for only 1000 or more drums at $17.50 per drum. Annual usage of the chemicals is 2800 drums, and the usage rate is constant. Inventory carrying costs are 20 percent of the average inventory. If it costs the purchasing agent $200 to place an order, from which vendor should the purchase be made and for what quantities? What will be the annual ordering costs, carrying costs, and purchasing costs for the chemicals?

7-8. The MANN Company uses, in its manufacturing operations, a particular subassembly which it orders from a supplier. The company is able to forecast demand for the subassembly for only about 2 months in advance. The subassembly costs $55.60. The MANN Company estimates its inventory holding cost at 2.25 percent per month and its administrative cost of a purchase order at $27.50. If there are 120 units on hand and the table below indicates the demand estimate for the next 9 weeks, calculate how many subassemblies the company should order if it is now time to place an order.

Week	Estimated demand
1	40
2	50
3	55
4	70
5	80
6	65
7	60
8	50
9	45

7-9. You have been retained as a consultant by a textile company which maintains inventories of 10 items used in its manufacturing process. The company is not able to determine its carrying cost or ordering cost with sufficient reliability to support the use of formal economic order quantity approaches, but it is nevertheless concerned that it is not managing its inventory as effectively as it might. These data concerning use and purchase of the 10 inventory items are available from last year's records:

Item	Dollars used annually	No. purchase orders placed last year
A	$120,000	5
B	80,000	6
C	50,000	6
D	24,000	4
E	10,500	8
F	5,200	6
G	2,400	7
H	1,100	8
I	900	6
J	300	6

Using the data available, answer these questions:

a. Without increasing the purchasing work load, what percentage reduction can you make in the average dollar inventory carried?

b. If the company is willing to increase the purchasing work load by 25 percent, what is the minimum average inventory they can achieve?

c. If they are willing to increase their average inventory by 10 percent, what percentage reduction in purchasing work load can they achieve?

7-10. The First Flite Golf Ball Company stores its rubber winding material in modular containers, each of which measures 4 feet per side. There is a total of 3680 square feet of space available for keeping these containers on hand. Each year, First Flite uses 14,400 containers of rubber winding material in its manufacturing processes, paying $20 for each container. The company estimates its ordering costs at $8 per order, and holding costs are 15 percent of the average inventory value. Calculate what First Flite would be willing to pay to increase its storage area, if anything, and the size of any projected increase.

7-11. The purchasing agent for Jack Spaniel distillery must provide the company with 1800 charred oak barrels each year in which the distillery's fine sour-mash bourbon is aged. The current source of this SKU charges $18 per barrel. The distillery estimates its ordering cost at $175 and figures that it can carry inventory at 2 percent per month of the average balance. The supplier is prepared to ship half of any order immediately and to warehouse the balance at no extra cost to the distillery, shipping this balance as needed. Estimate how many barrels the distillery should order at one time.

7-12. The Soundresearch Corporation assembles stereo components from subassemblies which are contracted to other firms. The company can forecast needs for only about the next 2 months. The particular subsembly of interest to Soundresearch costs $72.40. Soundresearch estimates its holding cost at 3.25 percent per month; its purchasing cost is $70. There are currently 160 subassemblies on hand and the demand estimate for the next 9 weeks is as follows:

Week	Estimated demand
1	45
2	60
3	35
4	70
5	80
6	60
7	70
8	50
9	55

Calculate the number of subassemblies Soundresearch should order if it is now time to place an order.

7-13. You have just been made materials manager of a firm which has been taken over by a large conglomerate. Your new subsidiary has not been particularly well run in terms of inventory management and, as a result, you are unable to obtain precise figures on carrying charges and ordering costs for EOQ models which you would like to apply. By examining last year's records, you find that the seven SKUs used in the manufacturing process had purchase and use records as follows:

SKU	SKU no.	Dollars used/year	No. orders last year
1	112-706	$721,000	4
2	131-J271	461,000	6
3	601-7721	207,000	5
4	66117-I	91,000	7
5	29435706	54,000	9
6	160-7112	26,000	7
7	315-7067	10,000	7

Using the data available, answer these questions:

a. Without increasing the purchasing work load, what percentage reduction can you make in the average inventory carried?

b. If you are willing to increase the purchasing work load by 25 percent, what is the minimum average inventory you can achieve?

c. If you are willing to increase your average inventory by 10 percent, what percentage reduction in purchasing work load can you achieve?

7-14. The Carolina Transport Company owns a fleet of tank trucks which haul petroleum products from the port city of Wilmington to various locations in the state. The company is a big purchaser of truck tires, annual use being estimated at 900. These tires cost Carolina Transport $160 each; Carole Sloan, the purchasing manager, estimates their annual carrying cost at 2 percent a month and their purchase cost at $60. The supplier from whom the company purchases tires has a delivery truck which holds only 12 tires; therefore 12 is the maximum number that can be delivered in a day, since the round-trip haul is over 300 miles. How many times a year should Carolina Transport order tires?

7-15. The Retrieval Systems Company, Inc., is a manufacturer of automatic paging devices used by physicians, lawyers, businesspersons, and others who need to be available on a 24-hour basis. The materials which go into a small "beeper" (paging device) are listed as follows:

SKU	Annual usage	Unit cost	Annual dollars used
H-206	44,000	$.08	$ 3,520
F-2130	214,500	.12	25,740
KLJ-160	4,400	.11	484
J-620	110,000	.06	6,600
M-14562	2,200	.15	330
012-76	264,000	.08	21,120
Z-321	17,600	.09	1,584
LX-002	88,000	.07	6,160

Perform an ABC analysis on Retrieval Systems' inventory. (See Table 7-11.)

7-16. Mr. Monroe Garrett operates an auto parts store. Because of the popularity of the Chevy Suburban wagon, Mr. Garrett estimates that he sells 5 replacement air filters for it on an average day. These cost him $3 each. Mr. Garrett is an astute businessman and feels that every dollar tied up in inventory is a dollar less in his savings account, which draws $5\frac{1}{4}$ percent interest. He figures it takes an order clerk 15 minutes to prepare and call in an order and that the associated paperwork costs 25 cents. An order clerk earns $5 per hour for a 40-hour work week. Mr. Garrett has unused storage space and therefore calculates only interest cost as his carrying charge. How often should Mr. Garrett order this filter?

7-17. Volper Manufacturing Co., makes high-quality hiking and walking boots and shoes. Its heavy winter boot is made with a leather upper, a heavy vinyl sole, a nylon lining, and leather laces. Volper's walking shoe uses a leather upper, rubber sole, and cloth laces. Materials are ordered every 6 months except the leather for uppers, which is ordered every 90 days. Yearly usage of materials is forecast to be as follows: leather, $200,000; vinyl soles, $40,000; rubber soles, $30,000; nylon lining, $30,000; leather laces, $4000; cloth laces $2000. What minimum average inventory can they achieve without adding to their purchasing work load?

7-18. Stylecraft Wood Products Co., produces a number of novelty furniture items for specialty shops. An examination of production records indicates this pattern:

SKU	Value produced/yr.	No. of setups used/yr.
Fern stand	$80,000	5
Bookshelves	50,000	8
Medicine cabinet	30,000	12
Towel rack	20,000	10
Magazine rack	10,000	9
TV table	5,000	10
Ashtray stand	1,000	6

The company records on cost are very poor; as a result, no one seems to be able to determine either the cost of carrying finished inventory or the cost of setups. The shop supervisor ventured that given the current product mix, the time required for setups does not vary significantly from one product to another. Stylecraft is finding it very difficult to employ trained mechanics able to set up machinery, and they have asked you to calculate whether it would be necessary to increase average inventory in order to reduce the total setup work load next year by 20 percent.

Bibliography

Brown, R. G.: *Decision Rules for Inventory Management* (New York: Holt, Rinehart and Winston, Inc., 1970).

Buffa, E. S., and **W. H. Taubert:** *Production-Inventory Systems: Planning and Control,* rev. ed. (Homewood Ill.: Richard D. Irwin, Inc., 1972).

Greene, J. H.: *Production and Inventory Control Handbook* (New York: McGraw-Hill Book Company, 1970).

Hadley, G., and **T. M. Whitin:** *Analysis of Inventory Systems* (Englewood Cliffs, N.J.: Prentice-Hall, Inc., 1963).

Lewis, C. D.: *Scientific Inventory Control* (New York: American Elsevier Publishing Company, Inc., 1970).

Starr, M. K., and **D. W. Miller:** *Inventory Control: Theory and Practice* (Englewood Cliffs, N.J.: Prentice-Hall, Inc., 1962).

Wagner, H. M.: *Principles of Operations Research* (Englewood Cliffs, N.J.: Prentice-Hall, Inc., 1969).

8

Inventory models II

1. Deciding When to Buy: Introduction

The Reorder Point

This chapter deals with the when-to-order decision

Chapter 7 was concerned with the question, "How *much* should we buy when it is time to replenish the inventory of an SKU?" In this chapter we want to introduce quantitative techniques which will help us answer the question, "*When* should we replenish the inventory of that SKU?" This *when-to-order* point is called the *reorder point.*

Lead Time

If you call for home delivery of a pizza and it takes 2 hours for it to arrive, then 2 hours is the *lead time.* If the manager of Debbie's Boutique, Ltd., knows that her supplier of brass candlesticks will deliver 30 calendar days after Debbie places an order, then 30 days is the lead time. In larger organizations, it may require some time for the purchasing office to (1) be notified that the inventory has reached the reorder point and (2) to initiate purchasing action. If so, then the lead time has to be adjusted to reflect these internal factors.

Lead Time Demand

Usage of an SKU *during* the lead time is known as *lead time demand.* If Debbie knows that her average daily sale of this particular candlestick is 2, then lead time demand for this SKU is calculated as 30 days × 2/day or 60 candlesticks. When her stock of this SKU gets near 60, Debbie should reorder this item.

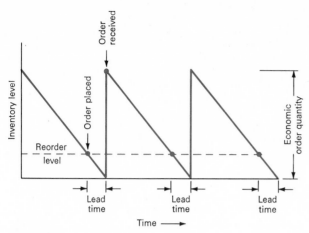

Figure 8-1   Inventory level with constant demand and constant lead time.

Stockouts

If we make the assumption of constant demand and if we assume that lead time is constant, we could represent the reorder situation as in Figure 8-1. But these two assumptions are hardly ever true. Planned demand of a particular SKU can be affected by unexpected market acceptance, by the weather, or by a strike. The lead time varies too; a supplier may run into problems (strikes, floods, breakdowns) or the transportation company may experience delays.

Variations in the lead time or in demand often cause *stockouts,* the condition that exists when the inventory on hand is not sufficient to cover needs. Figure 8-2 graphically shows a stockout when demand (usage) was normal but receipt of goods ordered (delivery) was later than expected. Figure 8-3 graphically shows a stockout when delivery was on schedule but usage was greater than expected.

Stockouts are undesirable because they can be *quite* expensive. Lost sales

Two conditions which produce stockouts

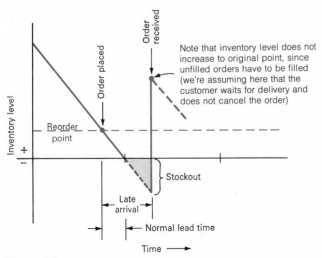

Figure 8-2   Inventory level with constant demand and excessively long lead time.

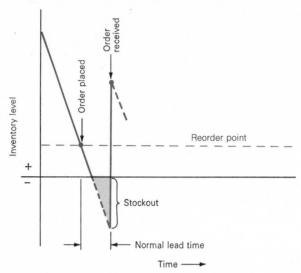

Figure 8-3   Inventory level with excessive demand and constant lead time.

and disgruntled customers are examples of *external* costs. Idle machines and employee ill will are examples of *internal* costs. Management's desire to avoid stockouts leads to further consideration of *when* to order and reorder.

Safety Stock

Two effects of safety stock
The term *safety stock* refers to extra inventory held as a hedge, or protection, against the possibility of a stockout. It is obvious that a safety stock has two effects on a firm's costs. It will *decrease* the costs of stockouts but *increase* carrying costs. The cost of a stockout multiplied by the number of stockouts prevented by the safety stock gives the cost reduction figure. The value of the safety stock multiplied by the carrying cost percentage gives the cost addition figure. Note that this cost addition is continuing—even permanent—in nature because the safety stock is always a part of total inventory. Note also that because the safety stock does not often decline in quantity, we do not divide it by 2 to get average inventory.

2. How to Determine the Optimum Safety Stock Level When Out-of-Stock Costs Are Known

Goals of carrying safety stock
The optimum safety stock to carry is determined in the light of two goals which are somewhat hostile to each other: (1) to minimize the costs of stockouts while also (2) minimizing carrying costs on the safety stock. The decision of how much safety stock to carry is not an easy one. Every approach to this problem has its own limitations. In the next section we shall determine an appropriate level for safety stock. There, we will use the *probability* approach, perhaps the most satis-

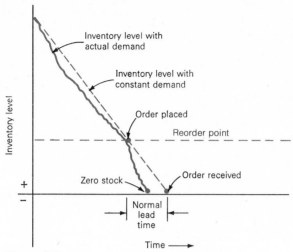

Figure 8-4 Inventory level showing the effect of an increase in demand after the order has been placed.

factory approach developed to date. We shall assume a constant lead time; we shall also assume that each lot ordered is delivered all at one time. Under these assumptions, a stockout can be caused *only* by an increase in demand (usage) *after the reorder point has been reached.* Figure 8-4 illustrates this situation. Note that the stockout resulted from increased demand *after the order to replenish inventory had been placed.* If the increase had occurred *before* the reorder point was reached, a purchase order would have been placed at the moment the inventory level fell to the reorder point. | **Cause of stockout**

Dennis Odle is the production vice-president of Century Electronics Company, a very large manufacturer of printers for computer systems. Each printer uses a fractional horsepower electric motor to drive the roller. Together with one of the company cost accountants, Dennis has estimated that the cost of being out of stock for this particular motor is $50 for each unit Century is short. This cost represents the inconvenience, the cost of reprocessing the printers when the motors finally arrive, and the extra storage cost of holding printers without motors.

Using an EOQ model, Dennis has already calculated the economic order quantity of this motor to be 3600, with an average usage of 50 motors a day. The normal lead time is 6 days. At this point, Dennis would like to know how much safety stock he should carry.

Dennis's first step is to analyze the inventory record card for these motors. By noting the usage during a number of past reorder periods, he can assign a probability to various levels of usage, as shown in Table 8-1. | **Using past inventory records to establish probability of stockouts**

If Dennis reorders when the level of stock falls to 300 units, the company will be safe 81 percent of the time (.68 + .06 + .04 + .03), but it will be out of stock of motors 19 percent of the time (.09 + .07 + .03). Dennis should be quite concerned over this figure of 19 percent.

To *reduce* or avoid this shortage, he could carry some *safety stock.* Dennis

Table 8-1 Probabilities of Usage During Reorder Period

Use during reorder period, units	No. times this quantity was used	Use probability	
150	3	$3/100$, or	.03
200	4	$4/100$, or	.04
250	6	$6/100$, or	.06
300	68	$68/100$, or	.68
350	9	$9/100$, or	.09
400	7	$7/100$, or	.07
450	3	$3/100$, or	.03
	100		1.00

might consider several levels of safety stock and pick the one which yields the lowest total for (1) cost of stockouts plus (2) carrying costs on the safety stock. Thus he could consider carrying a safety stock of:

Specific relationship between safety stock and stockouts

1. *50 units.* This would cover a usage of 350 during the reorder period; Dennis would be out of stock only when usage was 400 or 450 units; .07 + .03 = .1 of the time.

2. *100 units.* This would cover a usage of 350 or 400 during the reorder period; Dennis would be out of stock only when usage was 450 units; this would be .03 of the time.

3. *150 units.* This would cover usage of 350, 400, or 450 during the reorder period; Dennis should never run out of stock with this amount of safety stock. (Remember that the distribution of usage is *discrete.*)

Maximum danger of stockouts is near the reorder point

The danger of being out of stock will occur, of course, when stock is nearing the lowest point, the reorder point; thus we will have to take into consideration the number of times Dennis reorders during the year. Suppose one of the EOQ formulas suggested to him that 5 orders per year is optimum. He will, therefore, be in danger of running out of electric motors 5 times during the year. EOQ thus affects the reorder point.

The costs of being out of stock for the four courses of action (no safety stock, 50 units, 100 units, 150 units) are shown in Table 8-2. If Dennis and the company cost accountant estimate that the cost of carrying one motor in safety stock is $10, then the total annual costs of the four courses of action (stockout cost plus carrying costs on safety stock) would be as shown in Table 8-3. The appropriate safety stock is 100 units.

Adoption of the safety stock policy would change the reorder point. If 100 motors are to be held as safety stock, then the reorder point is determined as follows:

Reorder point = average daily use × lead time + safety stock   (8-1)

In Dennis's situation, the appropriate reorder point would be:

$50 \times 6 + 100 = 400$

Table 8-2 Costs of Being Out of Stock

Safety stock	Probability of being out	Number short	Expected annual cost (no. short × probability of being short that many × cost of being out/unit × no. orders/yr)		Total annual stockout costs
0	.09 when use is 350	50	50 × .09 × $50 × 5	$1,125	
	.07 when use is 400	100	100 × .07 × $50 × 5	1,750	
	.03 when use is 450	150	150 × .03 × $50 × 5	1,125	
					$4,000
50	.07 when use is 400	50	50 × .07 × $50 × 5	$ 875	
	.03 when use is 450	100	100 × .03 × $50 × 5	750	
					1,625
100	.03 when use is 450	50	50 × .03 × $50 × 5	$ 375	375
150	0	0		0	0

3. Setting Safety Stock Levels under Conditions When Out-of-Stock Costs Are Not Known

The Service-Level Concept

In order to use the safety stock model just presented, Dennis was required to furnish a cost of being out of stock per unit. With this value, he was able to determine the relative costs of (1) being out of stock and (2) carrying that amount of additional inventory which minimized the total of these two values. *In many situations, however, it is extremely difficult, if not impossible, to determine the cost per unit of being out of stock.* In a wholesale or retail firm an item bought for stock is sold at a known markup; here we can assume that the cost of being out of stock per unit is at least equal to the markup you would forgo if there were no unit to sell plus loss of goodwill. If the customer will wait for delivery, then perhaps the loss is limited to slightly diminished goodwill.

Using service levels when out-of-stock costs are unknown

In a manufacturing firm, however, the issue is often much more difficult. Because component parts purchased for use in manufacturing are not sold individually, their real value to the process is difficult to determine. If being out of stock on an item causes a production bottleneck, the value of this is hard to assess; it might involve anything from one person's being out of work for a few minutes to the shutdown of an entire plant. Finally, it is unrealistic to assume that being

Table 8-3 Costs of Safety Stock Policies

Safety stock	Cost of being out of stock	Annual carrying costs (no. carried × cost/yr)	Total cost/yr (stockout cost + carrying costs)
0	$4,000	$ 0	$4,000
50	1,625	50 × $10 = $ 500	2,125
100	375	100 × $10 = $1,000	1,375*
150	0	150 × $10 = $1,500	1,500

*$1,375 is the lowest total cost per year; 100 units as safety stock is the optimum quantity.

out of stock 2 units costs twice as much as being out of stock 1 unit; therefore, the out-of-stock cost per unit is not a constant.

Meaning of a service-level policy

We can understand, then, why many companies do not attempt to determine what the cost per unit is of being out of stock. Instead, they adopt what is called a *service-level* policy. Organizations which use this service-level approach simply establish the probability of being out of stock they are willing to "live with"; then they take whatever safety stock action is required to keep the probability of being out of stock at or near this point. For example, a company might adopt a service-level policy of 95 percent on certain items in its inventory; this means that the company wants to be able to supply 95 percent of the requests for those certain items.[1] On what basis is the service level determined? Being in stock 99 percent of the time will obviously cost much more than being in stock only 75 percent of the time. Actually, management must determine what they feel is an acceptable service level; in many cases this is done completely subjectively, although we shall

Source of the service level

show later in this chapter how we can provide management with the *relative carrying costs* associated with any service level. In other cases, industrial practice really determines what choice a single company might make with respect to service level; certain industries adopt a service-level policy which, although not formally agreed to by all firms in that industry, is often adhered to in practice.

A service-level policy is the usual answer when an accurate determination of the cost of being out of stock is impossible; however, even this approach requires a knowledge of both inventory theory and probability theory. Few real organizations can afford a 100 percent service level because it would require a level of safety stock whose cost is too high relative to the cost of being out of stock. Firms generally choose a service level which appears to them to be a reasonable alternative.

Determining the Safety Stock Required for Any Desired Service Level

Demand patterns and safety stock

A company is in danger of being out of stock for an item when the inventory of that item is at its lowest level; this occurs during the reorder period while the replenishment inventory is expected to be on its way. For this reason, determination of safety stock policy under a service-level concept depends upon the consumption of the item during the reorder period. For example, if consumption of an item during past reorder periods was quite constant, then a very small safety stock might enable a company to support a very high service level. Let us suppose in this case that use during past reorder periods averaged 100 units and that this use never went over 110 units. Reordering when the stock level falls to 110 units (a safety stock of 10 units) guarantees that we shall never be out of stock (a service level of 100 percent).

Now suppose, however, that use of an item during past reorder periods averaged 100 units but had gone as high as 300 units on occasion. In this case,

[1]   Actually, this 95 percent applies to the reorder period only. The probability of being able to supply a request, in general, during the entire inventory cycle is much better than 95 percent. In fact, it is near 100 percent prior to the reorder period combined with 95 percent during the reorder period.

if we want to protect against the highest past recorded usage, we must reorder at 300 units, a safety stock of 200 units. Thus, *the pattern of usage during the reorder period determines how large a safety stock is required to support any desired service level.* To provide operational answers for these kinds of inventory problems, we use some of the concepts about probability distributions we introduced in Chapter 3.

Pattern of usage during reorder period determines safety stock needed for any service level

In another one of Century Electronics' products, a liquid cooling device for computers, a small, electrically driven pump is used. Dennis Odle has audited past usage records of *lead time demand*. He is able to provide us with the following information about the probability distribution of lead time demand:

$\mu = 180$ pumps

$\sigma = 30$ pumps

Dennis also thinks that the distribution of lead time demand is such as to allow the use of the normal distribution to approximate its behavior.

Lead time demand is normally distributed

If Dennis wants to maintain a 95 percent service level on this pump, what is the appropriate level of safety stock for him to maintain? We show his situation graphically in Figure 8-5. The shaded area, representing 5 percent of the total area under the curve, is that part of the time he is willing to be out of stock; he is willing to let the probability of being out of stock be 5 percent.

If Dennis reorders at 180 units and carries no safety stock, usage during the reorder period would be above 180 half of the time and he would be out of stock during these periods. Usage, of course, would be under 180 half the time; Dennis would be able to supply pumps during these periods. If he carried no safety stock, then, he would experience a service level of 50 percent.

Raising the service level to 95 percent will compel Dennis to carry some safety stock. Specifically, he will have to reorder at point S; therefore his safety stock will be $S - 180$. How to find S? This is done exactly as in Chapter 3. We know that the area from S to the left-hand tail of the curve equals 95 percent of the area under the curve; so we look for the value .95 in Appendix Table 1 and find that point S is 1.64 standard deviations to the right of the mean. As 1 standard deviation is 30 units, 1.64 standard deviations would be 1.64×30, or about 49 units. Thus we have found that if Dennis carries 49 units of safety stock and reorders when the

Calculating the required safety stock for this service level

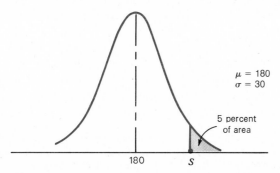

$\mu = 180$
$\sigma = 30$

5 percent of area

180   S

Figure 8-5 Distribution of lead time demand.

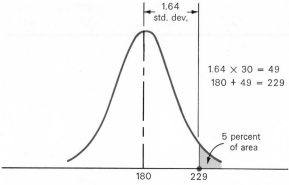

Figure 8-6   Determination of safety stock.

stock level falls to 229 units, he will be able to fill all of the orders received during the reorder time about 95 percent of the time. These conclusions are shown in Figure 8-6.

The Cost of Changing the Service Level

Costs for several service levels

Relationship between cost and service level is not linear

A simple example will illustrate the relationship between the cost of carrying safety stock and increased service levels. In Table 8-4 we have computed the safety stock required to provide several different service levels for an SKU; then we have computed the costs of carrying these different amounts of safety stock. Notice that the right-hand column in Table 8-4 indicates the approximate cost for a *1* percent increase in the service level; notice also how this cost increases very rapidly relative to the increase in the service level desired. Finally, in Figure 8-7 we have graphed the relationship between carrying cost and increases in the service level for the situation in Table 8-4.

You can quickly see from Figure 8-7 that the relationship between cost and

Table 8-4   Cost of Various Service-Level Policies

Service level desired, %	No. of std. dev. to the right of the mean	No. of units of safety stock required	Cost per year of safety stock	Approximate cost of 1% increase in service level
50	.00	0	0	$ 19 = ($190−0)/10
60	.25	38	$ 190	20 = ($390−190)/10
70	.52	78	390	24 = ($630−390)/10
80	.84	126	630	33 = ($960−630)/10
90	1.28	192	960	54 = ($1,230−960)/5
95	1.64	246	1,230	80 = ($1,310−1,230)/1
96	1.75	262	1,310	100 = ($1,410−1,310)/1
97	1.88	282	1,410	130 = ($1,540−1,410)/1
98	2.05	308	1,540	210 = ($1,750−1,540)/1
99	2.33	350	1,750	627 = ($2,315−1,750)/.9
99.9	3.09	463	2,315	

Mean lead time demand = μ = 400
Std. dev. of lead time demand = σ = 150
Cost per year to carry 1 unit of safety stock: $5

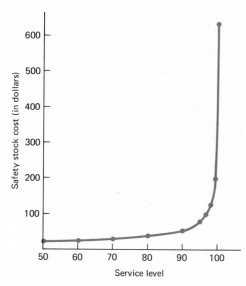

Figure 8-7 Cost of raising service level 1 percent at any service level between 50 and 100

service levels is *not* linear. Because of the enormous cost of raising the service level once it passes about 95 percent, few organizations attempt to achieve service levels above this level unless the SKU is necessary for health and life.

Reasonable service levels in practice

Reordering and Safety Stock in Practice (Two Standard Approaches)

The reordering concepts we have discussed are usually applied in practice in one of two ways: (1) a *fixed reorder point system* or (2) a *fixed review interval system.* The *fixed reorder point system* operates by setting reorder points on all SKUs under system control, just as we have illustrated. Then when the balance on hand of any SKU reaches its reorder point, an order for the economic order quantity is placed with the vendor.

Fixed reorder point systems and fixed review interval systems

A *fixed review interval system,* on the other hand, reviews the inventory status of *every* stockkeeping unit in the system at stipulated intervals, say once every 2 weeks. Such systems rely on past usage data and forecasting models to forecast use during the *next* 2-week interval; the current stock of every SKU plus any quantity in transit and expected to arrive in 2 weeks are compared with their forecast usage during the next review interval; a probability of stocking out during the next 2 weeks is calculated using the methods already illustrated in this chapter. If this probability is above a stipulated level, an order is placed with the vendor for the economic order quantity. If the probability of running out during the coming review period is not of sufficient magnitude, no ordering action is taken until 2 weeks later, when the inventory status is once again reviewed and new probability values are calculated.

Because fixed review interval inventory systems depend for their accuracy on good short-run forecasting methods and because they typically control thousands of SKUs, they require computer support to be effective. Fixed reorder point systems,

Fixed review interval systems generally require a computer

on the other hand, can still be managed by hand as long as the number of SKUs is not too great.

Relationship between Reorder Point and EOQ

EOQ and reorder point related

We have determined the EOQ and the reorder point separately. This is not meant to imply that the two concepts are unrelated. In fact, in the previous section we indicated that a company was more vulnerable to stockouts during the reorder period than at any other time, and here lies the true relationship. As the EOQ *rises* (more units per lot), the company orders fewer times a year; thus the stock moves to low points fewer times a year and the number of times the company is vulnerable to stockouts diminishes. Conversely, as the EOQ *falls* (fewer units per lot), the company orders more times a year; thus the stock moves to low points more times a year and the company finds itself in a vulnerable position more often.

Some more sophisticated mathematical models relate EOQ and reorder point so that an optimum combination of the two results. From our previous discussion of the cost of being out of stock, we can realize that such models must depend upon the precise assessment of such a cost (per time out of stock) and thus are open to criticism.

4. Joint Ordering: More Than One SKU from the Same Supplier Simultaneously

Joint ordering is defined in inventory theory as buying more than one item from the same supplier *at the same time.* The number of items purchased at one time from the same supplier, using a single purchase order or contract, may range from *two* to *hundreds.*

In the previous chapter, we developed economic order quantity models which indicate the appropriate number of items to purchase when the cost of ordering and the cost of holding are known. In the case of *joint ordering,* however, it is usually profitable to modify slightly the traditional EOQ approach because of the effect joint ordering has on the incremental cost per order.

Parts of the purchase order

Using standard purchase order terminology, a purchase order can be divided into two parts: (1) the *header,* which contains all the general information concerning the order (including name and address of supplier, shipping information, price discount information, billing information, and other data relevant to all of the items to be purchased on this one order) and (2) the *line items,* each of which contains specific information relevant to one item being purchased, the quantity of this item, unit price, size, finish, color, and stock number.

Header and Line Item Costs

Two costs in preparing a purchase order

The *header cost* is that cost incurred in preparing the header portion of the purchase order; the *line item cost* is the cost of adding one additional line item to that order. Thus the purchase of one item from a supplier would cause us to incur a header cost *and* a line item cost, whereas the purchase of additional items from that same supplier on the same purchase order would cause us to incur *only* additional line item costs. Put in another way, the cost of preparing the purchase order for the second item purchased (and for the third and others as well) is a bit less than the cost for the first item because the header cost is part of initiating the purchase order and demands the major portion of executive time *and* paperwork, including clerical costs.

Trigger EOQ and Line Item EOQ

Now, although preparation of the purchase order does *not* represent the entire cost of ordering, it *is* true that the ordering cost for the first item is slightly higher than the ordering cost for each additional item on that same order. Therefore, in ordering more than one item from the same supplier on the same purchase order, we should take account of this difference. But how? In practice, inventory managers who employ joint ordering systems normally compute *two* different EOQs for each item they buy in significant quantities: (1) a *trigger* EOQ and (2) a *line item* EOQ. The trigger EOQ is applied if the item triggered the order—if it reached its reorder point first and thus indicated that an order was required. The line item EOQ is applied to all other items the buyer decides to buy from the same supplier on that same purchase order.

Trigger EOQ

Line item EOQ

    From the previous chapter, we know that EOQ is related to the cost of holding and the cost of ordering; we are now considering the effect on EOQ of differing costs of ordering. A lower incremental cost of ordering would dictate that the quantity ordered at one time be less [you can satisfy yourself that this is true by looking at Eq. (7-2) on page 198 and noticing that a lowered value for P in that formula will reduce the value of the entire expression]. We can conclude, therefore, that in operational joint ordering situations, line item EOQs involve lower quantities than trigger EOQs. Now let us apply these concepts to a joint ordering situation.

    Jim Brame is the inventory manager of Brame Specialties, Inc., a wholesale distributor of paper products. Table 8-5 shows the five different SKUs Jim orders from National Paper Company, one of his principal suppliers. For each SKU, Jim has indicated its SKU number, description, reorder point, trigger EOQ, and line item EOQ.

Problem illustrating joint ordering

    Each of the five SKUs comes in cases weighing 100 pounds, and a railroad carload is 80,000 pounds or 800 cases. National is able to offer substantial discounts if Jim orders a full railroad carload. The problem is represented graphically in

Table 8-5 SKUs Jim Brame Orders from National Paper Company

SKU no.	Description	Reorder point	Trigger EOQ	Line item EOQ
1	Paper hand towels (single)	200 cases	300 cases	240 cases
2	Paper kitchen towels	150 cases	250 cases	200 cases
3	Kraft wrapping paper	300 cases	300 cases	240 cases
4	Paper cups	250 cases	350 cases	270 cases
5	Paper hand towels (roll)	50 cases	400 cases	320 cases

Characteristics of the SKUs in this situation

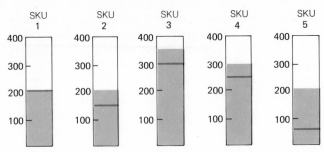

Figure 8-8 Reorder point and present inventory level for five SKUs (reorder point is indicated by the heavy line and the present inventory level by the shaded area).

Figure 8-8, where Jim has shown each SKU with its reorder point and its present inventory level. He can see that SKU 1, paper hand towels (single), has reached its reorder point and thus "triggers" the order from National. Ordering the trigger economic order quantity of that item (300 cases), however, will not fill up the railroad car. *"What other items should he order," "In what order they should be considered,"* and *"What quantities of each should he order"* are the operational questions of interest to Jim Brame in this situation.

Jim must next determine which of the four remaining SKUs is *closest* to its own reorder point; this is the item that is most likely to need replenishing during the delivery period. A look at items 2, 3, 4, and 5 indicates that items 2, 3, and 4 are *all* 50 units away from their reorder points; this looks like a tie situation. But in practice, the difference between actual inventory and reorder point is never measured in units but in *percent excess.* For example, look at items 2 and 3; inventory of both of these items is 50 units above the reorder point; in the case of item 2, the 50 units represent $33^{1}/_{3}$ percent of the reorder point. Using this approach, Jim can see that the present inventory of item 2 gives him considerably more protection than that of item 3. Using the same method of calculation, Jim can also see that the inventory of SKU 4 is 20 percent higher than its reorder point.

Thus SKU 2, 3, and 4 would be considered in the following order: SKU 3 first; SKU 4 second; and SKU 2 last. The inventory of SKU 5 is so far above its reorder point that Jim would order it only if absolutely necessary to fill the railroad car. Jim's solution to this joint ordering problem can be expressed after looking at Table 8-5 and Figure 8-8. He would:

1. First, *order* the trigger EOQ of SKU 1 (300 cases); this leaves 500 cases to fill the railroad car.

2. Next, *order* the line item EOQ of SKU 3 (240 cases); this leaves 260 cases to fill the railroad car.

3. Next, *consider* ordering the line item EOQ of SKU 4 (270 cases); but because this would overfill the railroad car by 10 cases, the order for SKU 4 would have to be reduced to 260 cases.

In the problem above, if Jim were under no pressure to *fill* the railroad car in order to get a substantial discount, chances are he would order only SKU 1 from National at this time. To include quantities of the other items in his order and thus substantially increase his level of inventory would be unprofitable without compensating advantages offered by the supplier.

In some cases, suppliers establish a *minimum dollar value* for orders below which they charge higher unit prices. In cases such as this, the same procedure illustrated above can be employed except that both trigger EOQs and line item EOQs would have to be established in *dollars*.

Dollars versus units

5. How to Evaluate Quantity Discounts Offered by Suppliers

Most suppliers offer buyers incentives in the form of lower unit costs for purchases of larger quantities. It is not difficult to analyze such offers once you understand the idea of EOQ. Let us look first at some of the advantages and disadvantages of buying in larger quantities; then we can show how to evaluate discounts offered by suppliers.

Advantages and Disadvantages of Quantity Buying

Buyers who buy in large quantities may well enjoy some of these advantages claimed for the policy:

Lower unit prices	Lower ordering costs
Cheaper transportation	Fewer stockouts
Mass display by retailers	Preferential treatment by suppliers

But quantity buying can involve these disadvantages;

Higher carrying costs	Older stock
Lower stock turnover	More capital required
Less flexibility	Heavier deterioration and depreciation

Advantages and disadvantages of quantity buying

Cost Comparison Approach to Evaluating Supplier Discounts

Jim Brame buys a specialty printing paper from National Paper Company. Jim's records indicate that he buys 2000 rolls of this SKU annually at $20 a roll. His ordering cost is $50 per order and he estimates his carrying costs at 25 percent of inventory value. Up to this point, National Paper Company has not offered Jim any discount for quantity purchases; therefore Jim has been calculating his EOQ using Eq. (7-2) as follows:

Cost comparison approach to discount evaluation

$$N_u = \sqrt{\frac{2AP}{R^2C}}$$

$$= \sqrt{\frac{2(\$40,000)(\$50)}{(\$20)^2(.25)}}$$

$$= \sqrt{\frac{\$4,000,000}{100}}$$

$$= \sqrt{40,000}$$

$$= 200 \text{ rolls per order} \tag{7-2}$$

Appropriate EOQ Jim realized that, considering the costs of ordering and holding inventory, ordering in lots of 200 rolls minimized his total inventory cost per year for this SKU.

When Jim got to work this morning, there was an announcement from National Paper Company on his desk initiating a new price policy. Table 8-6 shows National's new price policy for this particular SKU. Jim sees from National's announcement that he would have to order at least 500 rolls at one time to qualify for the 3 percent discount; he would have to order at least 1000 rolls at a time to qualify for the larger 6 percent discount. He quickly sees that it would *not* pay him to order more than the minimum quantity which would entitle him to either of **Order only the** these discounts; that is, ordering 600 rolls or 1100 rolls doesn't reduce price below **minimum quantity** what it would be if he ordered 500 or 1000 rolls and only increases his average **which entitles you** inventory.
to the discount

Jim realizes that he will have to determine the total cost of the three alternatives open to him: (1) ordering the EOQ of 200 rolls, (2) ordering 500 rolls at a time, or (3) ordering 1000 rolls at a time. Even without a computer, these calculations **Total cost of the** are not difficult; Jim set up a table similar to Table 8-7 to organize his calculations. **three alternatives** When he finished his calculations, Jim saw that ordering 1000 rolls at one time would result in the lowest annual cost to him ($40,050). He noticed that this alternative represented a reduction in his total annual cost of $41,000 − $40,050, or $950. Since Jim felt quite secure in his estimate of annual demand of 2000 rolls for this SKU, he decided to raise his next order to 1000 rolls. He made a mental **Interpreting the** note however, to keep his eye on the demand for this SKU. "After all," he thought, **results** "if the demand begins to fall, making my 1000-roll order somewhat more risky, I can still save $41,000 − $40,202.50, or $787.50, and only commit myself to 500 rolls at a time."

Table 8-6 Prices Relative to Quantities Ordered

Number of rolls ordered	Discount, percent	Price per roll
1–499	0	$20.00
500–999	3	19.40
1,000–1,999	6	18.80

Table 8-7 Total Annual Cost of Three Purchasing Alternatives

	Quantity ordered at one time		
	200 rolls (EOQ)	500 rolls	1,000 rolls
Ordering cost:			
Price	$20.00	$19.40	$18.80
Dollars in one order	200 × $20 = $4,000	500 × $19.40 = $9,700	1,000 × $18.80 = $18,800
Average inventory ($ per order/2)	$4,000/2 = $2,000	$9,700/2 = $4,850	$18,800/2 = $9,400
Annual carrying cost (average inventory × .25)	$2,000 × .25 = $500	$4,850 × .25 = $1,212.50	$9,400 × .25 = $2,350
Purchasing cost:			
Number of orders/yr (2,000/number per order)	2,000/200 = 10	2,000/500 = 4	2,000/1,000 = 2
Annual purchasing cost (number of orders × $50)	10 × $50 = $500	4 × $50 = $200	2 × $50 = $100
Paper cost:			
Cost of paper (2,000 × price per roll)	2,000 × $20 = $40,000	2,000 × $19.40 = $38,800	2,000 × $18.80 = $37,600
Total cost/yr (carrying cost + purchasing cost + paper cost)	$ 500.00 500.00 40,000.00 $41,000.00	$ 1,212.50 200.00 38,800.00 $40,212.50	$ 2,350.00 100.00 37,600.00 $40,050.00

6. Inventory Management with Planned Stockouts

Up to this point, we have been concerned with methods which *prevent* stockouts. However, in certain situations, management may find it desirable from a cost point of view to not only allow stockouts but to *plan* for them. It is quite common, for example, not to find the sofa you want in the fabric you want at your local furniture store. The shopkeeper will, however, order exactly what you want *if you will wait for delivery.*

Planning for stockouts may be appropriate

Backorders

The specific type of stockout we are concerned with here is called a *backorder.* When we speak of an item being backordered, we imply that:

Backorder assumptions

1. The customer placed an order.

2. The supplier was out of stock in that SKU.

3. The customer does not withdraw the order.

4. The customer waits until the next shipment arrives.

5. The supplier fills the customer's order when the next shipment arrives.

If, however, the customer will *withdraw* the order when the SKU is found to be out of stock, the backorder model we will develop is *not* appropriate.

Development of the Backorder Model

In Figure 8-9, we have illustrated a typical backorder situation.

Graphic presentation of backorder situation

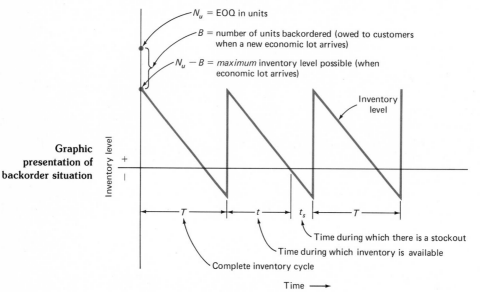

N_u = EOQ in units

B = number of units backordered (owed to customers when a new economic lot arrives)

$N_u - B$ = *maximum* inventory level possible (when economic lot arrives)

Inventory level

Inventory level

$+$

$-$

T t t_s T

Time during which there is a stockout

Time during which inventory is available

Complete inventory cycle

Time $\longrightarrow$

Figure 8-9   Inventory behavior in backorder situations.

Cost in the Backorder Model

The backorder model has the traditional costs plus the cost of backordering

For our inventory model *with backorders,* we will have the same kind of *carrying costs* we had in EOQ models before; we will also have the same kind of *purchasing* or *ordering costs.* But, in addition to these two costs, we will have the additional cost of backordering. Backordering cost is really composed of two different costs: (1) any cost of handling the backorder (special handling, follow-up, labor) and (2) whatever loss of customer goodwill occurs as a result of having to backorder an SKU. It's common in backorder models to express backorder costs as "How much it costs us to have one unit on backorder for a given time period." Of course it's not possible to be precise in calculating this cost, especially when we try to calculate loss of goodwill; but because the EOQ model is not especially sensitive to changes in inputs (look at pages 195 and 215 again), errors in estimates do not prevent us from making reasonably good inventory decisions.

Annual Carrying Cost in the Backorder Model   Look at Figure 8-9. During
the time t when inventory is available, we have a *maximum* inventory of $N_u - B$
units and a minimum inventory of 0 for an average of $(N_u - B)/2$. Since we do
not carry *any* inventory during time t_s, the average inventory during the complete
inventory cycle is

Calculating annual
carrying costs in the
backorder model

$\dfrac{N_u - B}{2}$ units for t of the T time (for that portion of the total inventory cycle represented by the fraction t/T)

plus

0 units for t_s of the T time

which is an average inventory for the total cycle of

$$\text{Average inventory (units)} = \frac{[(N_u - B)/2]t}{T}$$

Let's see whether we can get rid of t and T by expressing them in other terms.

Suppose we let d = daily demand; then, since the maximum inventory was
$N_u - B$, it will be used up in $(N_u - B)/d$ days. Thus,

$$t = \frac{N_u - B}{d}$$

Look now at T. Since N_u units are ordered (and shipped) each inventory cycle,
the length of an inventory cycle must be N_u/d days. Thus,

$$T = \frac{N_u}{d}$$

Now substitute our new expressions for t and T into the average inventory equation:

$$\text{Average inventory} = \frac{\left(\dfrac{N_u - B}{2}\right)t}{T}$$

$$= \frac{\left(\dfrac{N_u - B}{2}\right)\left(\dfrac{N_u - B}{d}\right)}{T} \quad \leftarrow \frac{N_u - B}{d} \text{ substituted for } t$$

$$= \frac{\left(\dfrac{N_u - B}{2}\right)\left(\dfrac{N_u - B}{d}\right)}{\dfrac{N_u}{d}} \quad \leftarrow \frac{N_u}{d} \text{ substituted for } T$$

Average inventory

$$\text{Average inventory} = \frac{\dfrac{(N_u - B)^2}{2d}}{\dfrac{N_u}{d}} \qquad \leftarrow \text{ terms in numerator multiplied}$$

$$= \frac{(N_u - B)^2}{2N_u} \qquad \leftarrow \text{ expression simplified}$$

And if we let C equal the annual carrying cost expressed in dollars/unit/year, total annual carrying cost becomes

$$\text{Annual carrying cost} = \frac{(N_u - B)^2}{2N_u} C \qquad\qquad (8\text{-}2)$$

Annual Ordering Cost in the Backorder Model If we let U equal the annual demand in units, then the number of orders per year is the annual demand divided by the units per economic lot, N_u, or:

Calculating annual ordering cost in the backorder model

$$\text{Number of orders per year} = \frac{U}{N_u}$$

And if we let P equal the purchasing cost per order, annual ordering cost in the backorder model is

Formula for annual ordering cost

$$\text{Annual ordering cost} = \frac{UP}{N_u} \qquad\qquad (8\text{-}3)$$

Annual Backorder Cost In Figure 8-9, we symbolized the maximum number of units backordered B. To find the average number of units backordered throughout the entire inventory cycle, we can use the same logic we used earlier to find the average inventory.

There are *no* units backordered during the time period t (inventory is available). During the period t_s, the number of units backordered goes from a maximum of B to a minimum of 0; during this period, the average number backordered is $B/2$. The number of units backordered for the complete inventory cycle is then:

0 units for t of the T time (for that portion of the total inventory cycle represented by the fraction t/T)

plus:

$\dfrac{B}{2}$ units for t_s of the T time

which is an average units for the total cycle of

$$\text{Average units backordered} = \frac{\left(\dfrac{B}{2}\right) t_s}{T}$$

Again, we can reason that backorders reach their maximum value, B, at a daily demand rate of d; therefore the length of the portion of the inventory cycle in which we *have* backorders is

$$t_s = \frac{B}{d}$$

And, we know that the length of an inventory cycle $T = N_u/d$ days; therefore, let's substitute these values for t_s and T into the expression for the average units backordered. Doing this we get:

$$\text{Average units backordered} = \frac{\left(\dfrac{B}{2}\right)t_s}{T}$$

$$= \frac{\left(\dfrac{B}{2}\right)\left(\dfrac{B}{d}\right)}{T} \quad \leftarrow \frac{B}{d} \text{ substituted for } t_s$$

$$= \frac{\left(\dfrac{B}{2}\right)\left(\dfrac{B}{d}\right)}{\dfrac{N_u}{d}} \quad \leftarrow \frac{N_u}{d} \text{ substituted for } T$$

$$= \frac{\dfrac{B^2}{2d}}{\dfrac{N_u}{d}} \quad \leftarrow \text{terms in numerator multiplied}$$

$$= \frac{B^2}{2N_u} \quad \leftarrow \text{expression simplified}$$

Average units backordered

And if we let V equal the cost to maintain a single unit on backorder status for 1 year (the objective cost of paperwork, etc., plus the subjective cost of lost goodwill), the total annual backorder cost is

$$\text{Annual backorder cost} = \frac{B^2V}{2N_u} \qquad (8\text{-}4)$$

Total Annual Cost Now we have the three costs that we need (annual carrying cost, annual ordering cost, and annual backorder cost) symbolized in Eqs. (8-2), (8-3), and (8-4), respectively. If we add these three equations together, we get the total annual cost of operating an inventory system in which we allow backorders; it is expressed:

$$(8\text{-}2) \quad + (8\text{-}3) + (8\text{-}4)$$

or

Total annual cost of an inventory system that allows backorders $= \dfrac{(N_u - B)^2}{2N_u}C + \dfrac{UP}{N_u} + \dfrac{B^2V}{2N_u}$ $\qquad (8\text{-}5)$

Total annual cost of the system

Using the Backorder Model

Problem illustrating use of the backorder model
Crowell Little is the Ford dealer in Hillsborough, North Carolina. After having the backorder model explained to him, he believes that his situation is one for which the assumptions of this model hold true. Crowell has come up with these estimates:

U (annual demand)	400 units
C (annual carrying cost for inventory expressed as dollars per unit per year)	$800
P (cost per order)	$100
V (cost to maintain 1 unit on backorder status for 1 year)	$150

Trial-and-error solutions
With two decision variables, N_u and B, it becomes unwieldy to find the optimum value for both by a trial-and-error method. However, let's make a couple of trial-and-error runs just to see what's involved.

Crowell would like to use Eq. (8-5) to compute the total annual cost of these two alternatives:

Two alternatives
1. Thirty cars ordered at a time and 15 backorders per cycle ($N_u = 30$ and $B = 15$)

2. Forty cars ordered at a time and 25 backorders per cycle ($N_u = 40$ and $B = 25$)

Here are the calculations for the total cost of operating the inventory system under these two alternatives:

$$\text{Total cost} = \frac{(N_u - B)^2}{2N_u}C + \frac{UP}{N_u} + \frac{B^2V}{2N_u} \tag{8-5}$$

Total cost of first alternative
$$\text{Total cost for alternative 1} = \frac{(30-15)^2}{(2)(30)}\$800 + \frac{(400)(\$100)}{30} + \frac{(15)^2(\$150)}{(2)(30)}$$

$$= (3.75)\$800 + \frac{\$40,000}{30} + \frac{\$33,750}{60}$$

$$= \$3000 + \$1333 + 563$$

$$= \$4896$$

Total cost of second alternative
$$\text{Total cost for alternative 2} = \frac{(40-25)^2}{(2)(40)}\$800 + \frac{(400)(\$100)}{40} + \frac{(25)^2(\$150)}{(2)(40)}$$

$$= (2.81)\$800 + \frac{\$40,000}{40} + \frac{\$93,750}{80}$$

$$= \$2248 + \$1000 + \$1172$$

$$= \$4420$$

Interpreting the results
From these two answers, Crowell knows that alternative 2 (EOQ of 40 cars and backorders = 25 cars) is less expensive than alternative 1 (EOQ of 30 cars and

backorders = 15 cars). But what of the other thousands of possibilities? Would one of them be even less expensive?

Obviously, Crowell doesn't have the time to solve this problem using trial-and-error methods; fortunately, this is not necessary. Using mathematical methods beyond the scope of this book, management scientists have determined that the optimum N_u and B are given by these two equations:

100

$$N_u = \sqrt{\left(\frac{2UP}{C}\right)\left(\frac{C+V}{V}\right)} \qquad (8\text{-}6)$$

$$B = N_u\left(\frac{C}{C+V}\right) \qquad (8\text{-}7)$$

In Crowell's situation, these answers turn out to be

$$N_u = \sqrt{\left[\frac{(2)(400)(\$100)}{\$800}\right]\left(\frac{\$800+\$150}{\$150}\right)}$$

$$= \sqrt{(100)(6.333)}$$

$= 25.166$ cars   (Crowell, knowing that EOQs anywhere near the optimum yield about the same cost, would order 25 cars at a time)   **Backorder EOQ**

$$B = 25.166\left(\frac{\$800}{\$800+\$150}\right)$$

$$= 25.166(.842)$$

$= 21.19$ (Crowell would plan to have 21 cars backordered at the time each shipment of 25 cars, the economic lot, arrived)   **Number of backorders**

Under this optimum alternative, the total annual cost of the inventory system would be

Total annual cost
(EOQ = 25;
backorders = 21)

$$= \frac{(N_u - B)^2}{2N_u}C + \frac{UP}{N_u} + \frac{B^2V}{2N_u}$$

$$= \frac{(25-21)^2}{(2)(25)}\$800 + \frac{(400)(\$100)}{25} + \frac{(21)^2(\$150)}{(2)(25)}$$

$$= \frac{(4)^2}{(2)(25)}\$800 + \frac{\$40,000}{25} + \frac{\$66,150}{50}$$

$$= \$256 + \$1600 + \$1323$$

$$= \$3179 \qquad (8\text{-}5)$$

Comparison with regular EOQ model   If Crowell had used the regular EOQ model *without* allowing for backorders, it turns out that the economic order quantity would be 10 cars, with a total annual cost of ordering and carrying of about $8000; thus a conscious decision to allow for backorders saved Crowell almost $5000 in this case ($8000 − $3179). If, however, Crowell feels strongly that having this many backordered cars (21) when a new shipment arrives might cost him lost sales and bad customer relations, he should take another look at the value he originally set for V.

Some Sensitivity Analysis of the Backorder Model

As V (the cost of backorders) increases and C remains constant, then $C/(C + V)$ in Eq. (8-7) approaches 0. In this case, B (the number of backorders) also approaches 0. In an operational setting, this means simply that if the cost of back-ordering becomes quite high (loss of sales, paperwork cost, and loss of goodwill, for example), then Crowell would allow very few cars to be backordered. If no cars are backordered, then Eq. (8-6) should yield an N_u equal to the N_u in the ordinary EOQ equation. Does it? Look at the expression $(C + V)/V$ in Eq. (8-6); as V gets higher, $(C + V)/V$ approaches 1.0, and Eq. (8-6) becomes an equation for the economic lot size (expressed in units) without backordering.

Now let's hold V (the cost of backordering) constant while we increase C (carrying cost). What happens? As C increases, the expression $C/(C + V)$ in Eq. (8-7) approaches 1.0, indicating that B, the number of backordered cars, equals N_u, the number of cars per lot. This means simply that the high cost of inventory suggests that Crowell hold no cars in inventory; with no cars in inventory, the entire incoming economic lot is backordered (customers are waiting to claim all the cars in that lot when it arrives).

Glossary

1. **Reorder point**   The inventory level at which it is appropriate to replenish stock.

2. **Lead time**   Time (usually measured in days) required for inventory to arrive after an order is placed.

3. **Lead time demand**   Usage of an SKU during the lead time.

4. **Stockout**   when available inventory is not sufficient to satisfy demand.

5. **Safety stock**   Extra inventory held against the possibility of a stockout.

6. **Service level**   The probability (deemed appropriate by a given organization) of being out of stock subtracted from 1; also, the percentage of time that all orders arriving during the reorder period can be satisfied.

7. **Fixed reorder point system**   An inventory system which sets reorder points for all SKUs under the system control and which initiates an order when the inventory reaches that level.

8. **Fixed review interval system**   An inventory system which reviews the inventory status of every SKU under system control at stipulated intervals.

9. **Joint ordering** Process of purchasing more than one SKU from the same vendor simultaneously.

10. **Header** Part of the purchase order containing all the general information concerning the order.

11. **Line item** Part of the purchase order containing information relevant to one SKU being purchased.

12. **Header cost** Cost incurred in preparing the header portion of the purchase order.

13. **Line item cost** Cost incurred in preparing the line item portion of a purchase order for one line item.

14. **Trigger EOQ** Quantity appropriate to purchase of an SKU which initiates the purchasing process by reaching its reorder point.

15. **Line item EOQ** Quantity appropriate to purchase of an SKU which is to be purchased on a purchase order initiated by some other SKU reaching its reorder point.

16. **Discount** Reduction from list or regular price given by a supplier in return for the purchase of great quantities of that SKU.

17. **Backorder** An item ordered but unable to be delivered on which the customer will wait for delivery without canceling the order.

18. **Backorder cost** The cost of handling the backorder (special handling, follow-up, labor) plus whatever loss of goodwill occurs as a result of having to backorder an item.

19. **Annual backorder cost** Total annual cost of handling backorders generated by the inventory system.

Review of Equations

Page 230

Reorder point = average daily use × lead time + safety stock   (8-1)

Multiplying average daily use by the lead time in days would yield the lead time demand; adding safety stock to this to provide for the variation in lead time demand would determine the reorder point.

Page 243

$$\text{Annual carrying cost in the backorder EOQ model} = \frac{(N_u - B)^2}{2N_u} C \qquad (8\text{-}2)$$

Using this formula, we can calculate annual carrying cost in the EOQ model which allows for planned backorders. In this formulation, N_u is the economic lot size in units, B is the quantity backordered during each inventory cycle, and C is the annual carrying cost expressed in percent of average inventory.

Page 244

$$\text{Annual ordering cost in the backorder EOQ model} = \frac{UP}{N_u} \tag{8-3}$$

This formula yields the annual cost of ordering in the EOQ model which allows for backorders. N_u is the same as defined above in Eq. (8-2). U is the annual demand for the SKU in units and P is the cost per purchase order.

Page 245

$$\text{Annual backorder cost in the backorder EOQ model} = \frac{B^2V}{2N_u} \tag{8-4}$$

This expression will give us the annual cost of backorders in the EOQ model which allows for planned backorders. N_u and B are the same as previously defined in Eq. (8-2). V here is the annual cost of a backorder including paperwork cost and any cost attributable to lost sales or lost goodwill.

Page 245

Total annual cost of an EOQ inventory system that allows backorders

$$= \frac{(N_u - B)^2}{2N_u}C + \frac{UP}{N_u} + \frac{B^2V}{2N_u} \tag{8-5}$$

This expression is the sum of the costs introduced in Eqs. (8-2), (8-3), and (8-4). It is the total annual cost of (1) carrying inventory, (2) ordering inventory, and (3) backorders in the system.

Page 247

$$N_u = \sqrt{\left(\frac{2UP}{C}\right)\left(\frac{C+V}{V}\right)} \tag{8-6}$$

Use of this equation solves for the optimum number of units, N_u, per economic lot in an EOQ inventory system which allows for planned backorders.

Page 247

$$B = N_u \left(\frac{C}{C+V}\right) \tag{8-7}$$

This equation yields the optimum number of backordered units, B, which are backordered at the time an economic lot arrives.

Exercises

8-1. A manufacturer of boilers uses $50,000 worth of valves per year. The administrative cost per purchase is $50, and the carrying charge is 20 percent of the average inventory. The company currently follows an optimum purchasing policy but has been offered a .2 percent discount if they purchase five times per year. Should the offer be accepted? If not, what counteroffer should be made?

8-2. Why is it desirable to relate EOQ and reorder point so that an optimum combination of the two results?

8-3. The Logan Company has determined that the cost of being out of stock of motors is $100 for each unit. Their EOQ analysis indicates that they should reorder 10 times each year. Carrying costs are $20 per motor. They are considering dropping the reorder point from 250 to 220. Based on the information in the table below, what would you advise them to do?

Use during reorder period	Probability of stockout
200	.10
220	.08
240	.06
260	.04
280	.02

8-4. The Randall Gear Company has experienced a mean use of 250 gears during past reorder periods with a standard deviation of 50 gears. Assuming a normal distribution of lead time demand, what percentage of the time will stockouts be experienced with a safety stock level of 64 gears?

8-5. Based on the information contained in Problem 8-4, what safety stock would have to be utilized in order to maintain a 95 percent service level?

8-6. Average reorder time for an SKU used by the Dobson Company is 5 days. Average use per day is 20 units. Below are data about use during the reorder period. Optimum number of orders is five per year. If the out-of-stock cost per unit per time is $50 and the carrying charge per unit per year of safety stock is $15, what level of safety stock should be carried?

Usage during past reorder period	Number of times this quantity was used
70	3
80	5
90	22
100	60
110	6
120	4

8-7. Given the following data for an SKU used by the Miller Company, compute the reorder point: (Assume a 250-day work year.)

$$EOQ = 100$$
Average use per day = 4 units
Average reorder period = 25 days
Cost to store one unit per year = $5
Cost of being out of stock per unit per time = $20

Usage during reorder period	Probability of this usage
25	.05
50	.10
75	.15
100	.25
125	.20
150	.15
175	.10

8-8. The Township Distributing Company has maintained an ordering policy for new inventory of power lawn mowers which allows for an 80 percent service level. Mean demand during the reorder period is 100 lawn mowers, and the standard deviation is also 100 mowers. The annual cost of carrying one mower in inventory is $5. The area salespeople have told Township's management that they could expect a $500 improvement in profit (based on current figures of cost per lawn mower) if the service level were increased to 99 percent. Is it worthwhile for Township to make this change?

8-9. Ben's Muffler Repair advertises that they are able to replace a car muffler on the same day a customer brings a car into the shop. If for any reason Ben cannot keep this promise, he pays the customer $100. Ben has found that for LN-70 mufflers, the optimal reorder quantity is 30 mufflers; he orders LN-70 mufflers 10 times a year. As LN-70 mufflers have to be ordered from a manufacturer located a considerable distance away, lead time for his orders is 30 working days, a period of time in which Ben on the average sells 30 LN-70 mufflers. During the past 10 years, 100 orders were placed. There were 10 occasions when Ben sold 32 LN-70s, 5 occasions when he sold 35, and only 1 when he sold 36 during the 30-day order period. On each of the other 84 occasions, he sold 30 or fewer. If it costs Ben $18 a year to hold one LN-70 in safety stock, what should Ben establish as his reorder point for LN-70 mufflers to minimize his costs? At this level of safety stock, how many $100 bills will Ben expect to pay to car owners whose cars require an LN-70 muffler?

8-10. The Dunkers, a professional basketball organization, are planning to construct a new stadium. They estimate that attendance at their games will be normally distributed. About half the time, they feel, attendance will be in excess of 5000 fans, and about 80 percent of the time it will not exceed 6000 fans. If it is their desire to accommodate ticket sales at a 95 percent service level, for what seating capacity should their new stadium be designed?

8-11. A farmer maintains a fresh vegetable stand. He tells his customers that his peas are really fresh because each day he places on the stand only those peas which were picked in the morning. At the end of the day, any peas left unsold are placed on his compost pile. He has 50 regular customers (no more and no less), and each day he figures he has a .20 probability of selling a pound of peas to any customer. Assuming the sale of a pound of peas to a given customer is independent of the actions of any other customer, determine the service level that the farmer maintains in fresh peas if he places 13 pounds of peas on his vegetable stand each morning. At the end of a 30-day selling season for peas, how many pounds of peas should be on the compost pile?

8-12. Assume that you are the purchasing agent for a large retail company which purchases a number of SKUs from the same wholesale supplier. The common shipping unit for these SKUs is cartons, and they are shipped by truck freight. If you are able to order an entire truckload at one time, significant savings result from lower freight rates. A full truckload is 2000 cartons. Inventory data on SKUs ordered from the same wholesaler are as follows:

SKU	Quantity on hand (cartons)	Reorder point (cartons)	Trigger EOQ (cartons)	Line item EOQ (cartons)
A	500	400	450	350
B	350	300	400	300
C	600	600	500	425
D	550	500	600	500
E	105	100	300	200
F	100	75	250	200
G	100	50	350	250
H	200	40	400	300

If you decide to take advantage of the reduced freight rates for a complete truckload, what SKUs should you order and how many cartons of each?

8-13. Radtronics, a manufacturer of microwave ovens, used $75,000 worth of LED readout circuits annually in its production process. Cost per order is $75, and the carrying charge assessed against this classification of inventory is 20 percent of the average balance per year. Radtronics follows an EOQ purchasing system and to date has not been offered any discounts on these LED circuits. Just yesterday, however, the supplier approached Radtronics and indicated that if the company would buy its circuits four times a year, a discount of .1 percent off list price would be given in return. Would you advise Radtronics to accept this offer or to make a counteroffer? If a counteroffer is made, what is the highest price that should be offered to pay for this SKU purchased quarterly?

8-14. The purchasing agent for Jack Spaniel Distillery is considering three sources of supply for oak barrels in which the distillery's fine sour-mash bourbon is aged. The first supplier offers any quantity of barrels at $18.75 each. The second supplier offers barrels in lots of 500 or more at $16.80. The third supplier offers barrels in lots of 800 or more at $16.00 each. The distillery uses 1800 barrels a year at a constant rate. Carrying costs are 10 percent and it costs the purchasing agent $175 to place an order. From which source should this distillery buy its barrels? What will be the total annual cost of buying the barrels, carrying inventory, and performing the necessary purchasing operations?

8-15. Northside General Hospital has instituted an inventory control program for its pharmacy and dispensary; this step has led to a considerable dollar savings in inventory costs. Since a computer was installed, over 90 percent of the hospital's SKUs have been ordered under an EOQ system. The director of supply has computed the cost of carrying inventory at 12 percent per year and the cost of placing an order at $30. The hospital's supplier of surgical thread, which is now one of the optimally ordered SKUs, has just offered a 3 percent discount from list price if the hospital will buy its annual requirement of this item ($8000) in three equally spaced intervals. Should this offer be accepted?

8-16. The Breward County Hospital uses a special drug in emergency situations to relieve shock symptoms. Because of its rather remote location and the need to transport this drug from another hospital, the dispensary places the cost of "stocking out" at $100. By use of EOQ analysis, the hospital's industrial engineer has determined that the drug should be ordered 10 times a year. Because the drug must be stored in carefully controlled conditions, the pharmacist estimates the cost of carrying at $20 per dose per year. In an effort to reduce cost, the hospital is considering dropping the reorder point from 100 to 80 doses. Based on the table below, what would you advise them to do?

Use during reorder period	Probability of a stockout
75	.10
85	.08
95	.06
105	.04
115	.02

8-17. The Eastchester Police Department experiences a mean usage of 160 books of parking tickets during the reorder period for this SKU. The calculated standard deviation of this demand is 26 books of tickets. If demand is normally distributed, what percent of the time will the department experience stockouts if it maintains a safety stock of one case of tickets (24 books)?

8-18. The Kwickie Takeout restaurant has a standing offer to its customers that if Kwickie cannot provide any sandwich on its menu, the customer will be paid $20. Kwickie's optimal order for canned hams (from which it makes ham sandwiches) is 15 hams; the order is placed about 30 times annually. There is a 10-day lead time on ham delivery during which Kwickie sells an average of 15 hams (made up into sandwiches). During the past 5 years, there have been 30 occasions when 17 hams were sold during a reorder period, 15 occasions when 20 hams were sold, and 3 occasions when 25 hams were sold. On all other occasions, there have been 15 or fewer hams sold. If it costs Kwickie $5 per year to hold a ham in cold storage, what should be the established reorder point to minimize costs? At this reorder point, how many $20 offers will Kwickie pay off on?

8-19. In light of a recent referendum allowing dog racing in their state, a group of investors have decided to build and operate a dog track. The investor group has hired a statistician to produce some demand estimates from analyses of other sports operations in the state and similar dog track operations in neighboring states. The statistician reports that attendance can be described by a normal distribution. Additionally, she states that attendance should exceed 12,000 half the time; 80 percent of the time, it should be less than 15,000. If the investors want to plan for a 95 percent service level for their customers, what size track do you recommend they construct?

8-20. Eddie the Egg Man sells fresh eggs from his home. Eddie guarantees to his customers that any eggs bought from his home stand have been laid within 12 hours of the time of purchase (eggs over 12 hours old are sold to a wholesaler who supplies restaurants). Eddie has 20 regular customers, no more no fewer, and each day he figures he has about a 1 in 5 chance of selling a dozen eggs to any customer. Assuming that the sale of a dozen eggs to any customer is independent of the actions of any of the other customers, determine the implied service level Eddie maintains if he places 6 dozen eggs in his home stand each day. At the end of 15 working days, how many dozen eggs will Eddie have sold to the wholesaler?

8-21. Here are data for disposable water-testing kits stocked by a field unit of the Environmental Protection Agency (EOQ = 8 orders/year):

Average daily use	5 kits
Average reorder period	20 days
Cost to store of one kit per year	$6
Estimated out-of-stock cost per kit	$25

Usage during reorder period	Probability of this usage
40	.05
60	.10
80	.15
100	.25
120	.20
140	.15
160	.10

What should the field unit's reorder point be for this SKU?

8-22. Dick Best is the purchasing agent for an automobile asembly plant in Midlands, Michigan. He purchases a number of metal fasteners from the same supplier. These are shipped in cartons by rail freight. If Dick orders an entire carload at a time from this supplier (10,000 cartons), he enjoys considerable freight savings. Inventory data on SKUs ordered from this supplier are as follows:

	(Quantities expressed in cartons)			
SKU	Quantity on hand	Reorder point	Trigger EOQ	Line item EOQ
#10 sheet-metal screw	2,000	1,500	4,000	3,000
2″ metal rivets	1,200	1,200	2,500	2,000
8-32 × 1½″ hex bolts	840	800	1,500	1,000
#4 sheet-metal screws	2,100	1,400	2,500	2,000
$5/16$″ lock washers	1,500	1,000	1,500	1,000
3″ pop rivets	800	500	900	600
1″ hex head nuts	200	100	300	200
10-32 × 2″ hex bolts	3,000	2,800	8,000	5,000
$7/16$″ flat washers	3,000	1,500	4,000	3,000

Suggest for Dick Best the most favorable carload combination of fasteners to order at this time.

8-23. Village Furniture Company deals in rather expensive upholstered sofas and occasional chairs. The company has analyzed its sales records for a particular style sofa and found that annual sales are 90 units. Cost per purchase order is $50, and the carrying charge is $80 per sofa per year. As a rule, retailers of upholstered furniture expect their customers to wait for delivery of the particular SKU they want, and very little goodwill is lost because of this. Rarely have Village's customers canceled orders for sofas. The cost of processing, paperwork, and accounting for the backordered sofas is about $20 a unit per year. What is the economic order quantity for this particular SKU? When the optimum order arrives, how many customers are waiting for their sofas on average? What is the total annual cost of ordering, carrying, and backordering?

8-24. Eugene Montgomery is the sales manager of Miller's Truck Sales in Roxboro, North Carolina. His biggest selling SKU in this year's line is a B-2500 diesel tractor, but the cost of carrying his inventory ($5000/truck/year) makes it desirable to keep the inventory on hand to an absolute minimum. To process the rather substantial amount of paperwork involved in ordering a group of trucks currently costs Gene $200; and the paperwork, accounting, and goodwill cost of backorders is estimated by him to be $200 per year. Gene estimates his sales of the B-2500 to be 60 units this year, and his plans are to order 5 units each month. Can you suggest a better ordering strategy for Gene? What would your plan save him per year if he adopted it?

Bibliography

Arrow, K. J., S. Karlin, and **H. Scarf:** *Studies in the Mathematical Theory of Inventory and Production* (Stanford, Calif.: Stanford University Press, 1958).
Brown, R. G.: *Decision Rules for Inventory Management* (New York: Holt, Rinehart and Winston, Inc., 1970).

Buchan, J., and **E. Koenigsberg:** *Scientific Inventory Management* (Englewood Cliffs, N.J.: Prentice-Hall, Inc., 1963).

Buffa, E. S., and **W. H. Taubert:** *Production-Inventory Systems: Planning and Control,* rev. ed. (Homewood, Ill.: Richard D. Irwin, Inc., 1972).

Hadley, G., and **T. M. Whitin:** *Analysis of Inventory Systems* (Englewood Cliffs, N.J.: Prentice-Hall, Inc., 1963).

Lewis, C. D.: *Scientific Inventory Control* (New York: American Elsevier Publishing Company, Inc., 1970).

Lipman, B. E.: *How to Control and Reduce Inventory* (Englewood Cliffs, N.J.: Prentice-Hall, Inc., 1972).

Starr, M. K., and **D. W. Miller:** *Inventory Control: Theory and Practice* (Englewood Cliffs, N.J.: Prentice-Hall, Inc., 1962).

Linear programming: graphic method

9

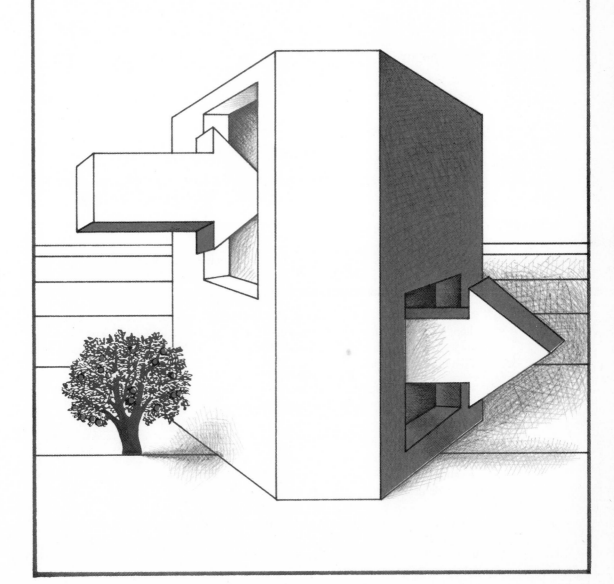

1. Introduction

Applications of Linear Programming

Allocating limited resources   All organizations have to make decisions about how to allocate their resources, and there is no organization which operates permanently with unlimited resources; consequently management must continually allocate scarce resources to achieve the organization's goals, whatever they might be. And organizations can have many goals. Here are a few examples:

Bank application   **1.** A bank wants to allocate its funds to achieve the highest possible return. It must operate within liquidity limits set by regulatory agencies and maintain sufficient flexibility to meet loan demands of its customers.

Advertising application   **2.** An advertising agency wants to achieve the best possible exposure for its client's product at the lowest possible advertising cost. There are a dozen possible magazines in which it can advertise, each one with different advertising rates and differing readership.

Manufacturing example   **3.** A furniture manufacturer wants to maximize its profits. It has definite limits on production time available in its three departments as well as commitments of furniture to customers.

Food-mix problem   **4.** A food economist in a developing country wants to prepare a high-protein food mixture at the lowest possible cost. There are 10 possible ingredients from which protein can be extracted, and each of these is available in different quantities at different prices.

Each of these organizations is attempting to achieve some *objective* (maximize rate of return, maximize exposure at least cost, maximize profits, maximize nutrition), with *constrained resources* (deposits, client advertising budget, available machine time, ingredients).

260

Linear programming is a mathematical technique for finding the best uses of an organization's resources. The adjective *linear* is used to describe a relationship between two or more variables, a relationship which is directly and precisely proportional. In a linear relationship between work hours and output, for example, a 10 percent change in the number of productive hours used in some operation will cause a 10 percent change in output. *Programming* refers to the use of certain mathematical techniques to get the best possible solution to a problem involving limited resources.

What linear programming is

Major Requirements of a Linear Programming Problem

Before looking at a linear programming solution, let us consider the major requirements of a linear programming problem in a specific firm. Assume that the firm is a manufacturer of two types of furniture, tables and chairs.

Four characteristics that a linear programming problem must have

1. There must be an *objective* the firm wants to achieve. The major objective of our manufacturer, we shall assume, is to maximize dollar profits. We recognize that profits are not linearly related to sales volume. The variable that *is* linearly related to sales volume is *total contribution.* You recall that

$$\text{Total contribution} = \left(\begin{array}{c}\text{selling price} \\ \text{per unit}\end{array} - \begin{array}{c}\text{variable cost} \\ \text{per unit}\end{array}\right) \times \left(\begin{array}{c}\text{sales volume} \\ \text{in units}\end{array}\right)$$

Whenever the term *profit* is used in the context of linear programming, it actually refers to *contribution.*

2. There must be *alternative courses of action,* one of which will achieve the objective. For example, should our firm allocate its manufacturing capacity to tables and chairs in the ratio of 50:50? 25:75? 70:30? Some other ratio?

3. *Resources must be in limited supply.* Our furniture plant has a limited number of machine-hours available; consequently, the more hours it schedules for tables, the fewer chairs it can make.

4. *We must be able to express the firm's objective and its limitations as mathematical equations or inequalities, and these must be linear equations or inequalities.* Our furniture maker's objective, dollar profits (P), can be expressed in this simple equation:

$$P = \$8 \text{ (number of tables)} + \$6 \text{ (number of chairs)}$$

Equations and Inequalities

Although less familiar than the equation, the *inequality* is an important relationship in linear programming. How are the two different? Equations, of course, are represented by the well-known equals sign $=$. They are specific statements expressed in mathematical form. Remember our equation in the preceding paragraph: $P = \$8$ (number of tables) $+ \$6$ (number of chairs).

Inequalities   Many business problems, however, cannot be expressed in the form of nice, neat equations. Instead of being precise, specifications may provide only that minimum or maximum requirements be met. Here we need *inequalities;* these are another type of relationship expressed in mathematical form. For example, the statement that the cost of 5 tables and 4 chairs must not exceed \$120 is $5T + 4C \leq$ \$120 when expressed as an inequality. The sign $\leq$ means "is equal to or less than." In this case any value equal to or less than \$120 satisfies the inequality. If this were an equation, the cost of 5 tables and 4 chairs would *equal* \$120, no more, no less. Hence an equation is much more restrictive than a corresponding inequality.

We might have expressed the cost of 5 tables and 4 chairs in still another way. We could have said that the cost of 5 tables and 4 chairs *will be at least* \$120. The sign $\geq$ means "is equal to or greater than." Any value equal to or greater than \$120 would satisfy this inequality.

Most constraints in a linear programming problem are expressed as inequalities As will be seen, they set upper or lower limits; they do not express exact equalities. Thus they permit many possibilities.

2. Graphic Solution to a Maximization Problem

Value of the graphic method   It's possible to solve linear programming problems graphically as long as the number of variables (products, for example) is no more than three. Although practitioners of management science don't generally use the graphic method (other methods to be introduced later are more efficient), it's a good way to begin to develop an understanding of this useful quantitative technique. We've chosen to introduce you to the graphic method by using the example of a small manufacturer of hand-crafted furniture, Dimensions, Ltd., that wants to determine the most profitable combination of products to manufacture given that its resources are limited.

Statement of the Dimensions, Ltd., Problem

Dimensions, Ltd., makes two products, tables and chairs, which must be processed through assembly and finishing departments. Assembly has 60 hours available; finishing can handle up to 48 hours of work. Manufacturing one table requires 4 hours in assembly and 2 hours in finishing. Each chair requires 2 hours in assembly and 4 hours in finishing.

Profit   If profit is \$8 per table and \$6 per chair, the problem is to determine the best possible combination of tables and chairs to produce and sell in order to realize the maximum profit. There are two limitations (also called *constraints*) in the problem: the time available in assembly and the time available in finishing.

Symbols   Let us use T to represent the number of tables and C to represent the number of chairs. The information needed to solve the problem is summarized in Table 9-1.

Table 9-1 Dimensions, Ltd., Problem Information

	Hours required for 1 unit of product		Total hours available
	Tables	Chairs	
Assembly	4	2	60
Finishing	2	4	48
Profit per unit	$8	$6	

First Step

To begin solving the problem, let us restate the information in mathematical form. In order to do this, we must introduce a new term, *objective function*. This term refers to the expression which shows the relationship of output to profit:

$$\$8T = \text{total profit from sale of tables}$$
$$\$6C = \text{total profit from sale of chairs}$$
$$\text{Objective function} = \$8T + \$6C$$

Objective function

Time used in making the two products must certainly not exceed the total time available in the two departments. In other words, the hours required to make 1 table times the number of tables produced—plus the hours required to make 1 chair times the number of chairs produced—must be equal to or less than the time available in each department. Mathematically, this is stated as

Department time constraints

Assembly: $\quad 4T + 2C \leqslant 60$
Finishing: $\quad 2T + 4C \leqslant 48$

The first inequality above states that the hours required to produce 1 table (4 hours) times the number of tables produced (T), plus the hours required to produce 1 chair (2 hours) times the number of chairs produced (C), must be equal to or less than the 60 hours available in assembly. A similar explanation holds for the second inequality. Note that *both* inequalities represent capacity constraints on output and therefore on profit.

In order to obtain meaningful answers, the values calculated for T and C must be positive; they must represent real tables and real chairs. Thus all elements of the solution to a linear programming problem must be equal to or greater than 0 ($T \geqslant 0$, $C \geqslant 0$). This constraint means that the solution must lie in the quadrant in which all values are positive, the first quadrant.

The problem can now be summarized in a mathematical form:

Mathematical summary of the problem

Maximize: $\quad$ Profit $= \$8T + \$6C$

subject to the constraints

$$4T + 2C \leqslant 60$$
$$2T + 4C \leqslant 48$$
$$T \geqslant 0$$
$$C \geqslant 0$$

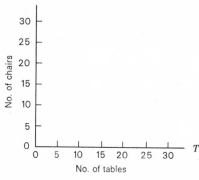

Figure 9-1

Second Step

Graphing the constraints   Plot the constraints in the problem on a graph, with tables shown on the horizontal axis and chairs shown on the vertical axis. Figure 9-1 shows the T and C axes.

The inequality $4T + 2C \leqslant 60$ may be located on the graph by first locating its two terminal points and joining these points by a straight line. The two terminal points for the inequality can be found in the following manner:

1. If we assume that *all* the time available in assembly is used in making chairs (the production of tables is 0), then 30 chairs *could* be made. Thus, if we let $T = O$, then $C \leqslant 30$.

Proof

$$4T \ \ + 2C \leqslant 60$$
$$4(0) + 2C \leqslant 60$$
$$C \leqslant 30$$

If we make the maximum number of chairs, then $C = 30$. Our first point, thus, is $(0,30)$; this point denotes the production of 0 tables and 30 chairs.

2. In order to find the second point, we assume that all the time available in assembly is used in making tables (the production of chairs is 0). Under this assumption we *could* produce 15 tables. Thus, if we let $C = 0$, then $T \leqslant 15$.

Proof

$$4T + 2(C) \leqslant 60$$
$$4T + 2(0) \leqslant 60$$
$$T \leqslant 15$$

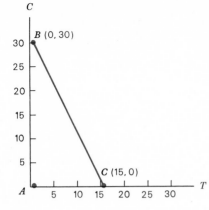

Figure 9-2 Graph of equation $4T + 2C = 60$.

If we make the maximum number of tables, then $T = 15$. Our second point, thus, is (15,0); this point denotes the production of 15 tables and 0 chairs.

Locating these two points (0,30) and 15,0) and joining them results in the straight line shown in Figure 9-2. Now see the same concept shown in Figure 9-3.

Any combination of tables and chairs on line *BC* will use up all the 60 hours available in assembly. For instance, producing 10 tables and 10 chairs [point (10,10) on the graph] will use up 10 (4 hours) + 10 (2 hours) = 60 hours. Suppose, however, that the firm can sell only 5 tables and 15 chairs [point (5,15) on the graph]. This point is not on line *BC,* but this combination *can* be produced without exceeding the 60 hours available: 5 (4 hours) + 15 (2 hours) = 50 hours, and 50 hours $\leqslant$ 60 hours. This point (5,15), or indeed, *any* combination of tables and chairs which lies in the shaded area to the left of line *BC,* can be produced without exceeding the 60 hours available. The shaded area *ABC* is the graphic representation of the inequality $4T + 2C \leqslant 60$ as long as T and C are both greater than 0.

Here are some illustrations. Each of the combinations of tables and chairs is shown as a point on Figure 9-4.

Graphic
representation of
the inequality for
assembly

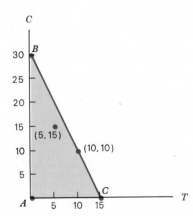

Figure 9-3 Capacity constraint in the assembly department.

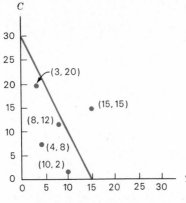

Figure 9-4 Graph of equation $4T + 2C = 60$, with various combinations of T and C shown as points.

4 tables and 8 chairs: $4\,(4) + 2\,(8) = 32$ hr required
10 tables and 2 chairs: $4\,(10) + 2\,(2) = 44$ hr required
3 tables and 20 chairs: $4\,(3) + 2\,(20) = 52$ hr required
8 tables and 12 chairs: $4\,(8) + 2\,(12) = 56$ hr required
15 tables and 15 chairs: $4\,(15) + 2\,(15) = 90$ hr required

Note that the time requirements of the first four combinations fall within the 60 hours available in assembly. The fifth combination *cannot* be produced because the hours needed exceed the hours available.

Graphic representation of the inequality for finishing
A similar explanation applies to the graph of the restraint inequality for finishing; that is, $2T + 4C \leqslant 48$. Line *EF* in Figure 9-5 represents all combinations of tables and chairs which will use up exactly 48 hours ($2T + 4C = 48$). The shaded area *AEF* contains all possible combinations which do not exceed 48 hours ($2T + 4C \leqslant 48$) as long as T and C are both greater than 0; any point, that is, any combination of tables and chairs falling within the shaded area *AEF*, will satisfy the time restriction in the finishing department. Thus the shaded area *AEF* is the graphic representation of the inequality $2T + 4C \leqslant 48$.

In order to complete a table or chair, both departments must be used. This means that the best combination of tables and chairs must fall within the shaded

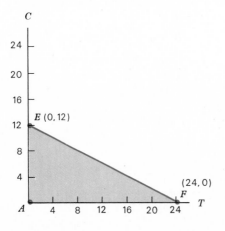

Figure 9-5 Capacity constraint in finishing department.

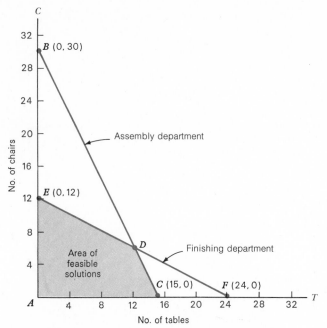

Figure 9-6 Graphic representation of problem constraints.

areas of both Figure 9-3 and Figure 9-5; this best combination must not exceed the available time in either assembly or finishing. To find this common area we must plot the two original inequalities (see Figures 9-3 and 9-5) on the same T and C axes (see Figure 9-6).

The area that does not exceed either of the two departmental constraints (the shaded area *AEDC* in Figure 9-6) contains *all* combinations of tables and chairs satisfying the inequalities.

$$4T + 2C \leqslant 60$$
$$2T + 4C \leqslant 48$$
$$T \geqslant 0$$
$$C \geqslant 0$$

Here are some examples.

Example 1 For 5 tables and 2 chairs

Assembly: $\quad 4T + 2C \quad \leqslant 60$ hr available
$\qquad\qquad 4(5) + 2(2) = 24$ hr required

Finishing: $\quad 2T + 4C \quad \leqslant 48$ hr available
$\qquad\qquad 2(5) + 4(2) = 18$ hr required

The time required to make 5 tables and 2 chairs falls within the time available in both departments (see Figure 9-7).

Two combinations which would satisfy both inequalities

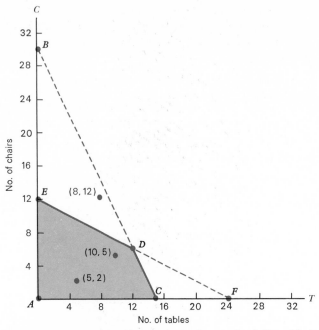

Figure 9-7 Area of feasible solutions, with examples 1, 2, and 3 shown.

Example 2 For 10 tables and 5 chairs

Assembly: $4T + 2C \le 60$ hr available
                $4(10) + 2(5) = 50$ hr required
Finishing: $2T + 4C \le 48$ hr available
                $2(10) + 4(5) = 40$ hr required

The combination 10 tables and 5 chairs also satisfies the two constraints (see Figure 9-7).

Example 3 For 8 tables and 12 chairs

Assembly: $4T + 2C \le 60$ hr available
                $4(8) + 2(12) = 56$ hr required
Finishing: $2T + 4C \le 48$ hr available
                $2(8) + 4(12) = 64$ hr required

The time required to make 8 tables and 12 chairs falls within the time available in assembly but *exceeds* the time available in the finishing department. This combination falls outside the area common to both inequalities in Figure 9-7 and therefore is not possible.

Third Step

Locate point D, because once that point is known, the shaded area $AEDC$ will have been delineated precisely. This is true because we have already three points:

Locating point D

A (0,0) E (0,12) C (15,0)

How can we locate point D? One possibility is to read its location from an accurately drawn graph. Another method, the one we shall be using, is to solve simultaneously the equations of the two lines which intersect to form point D, the only point common to both equations. The equations to be solved are

$$4T + 2C = 60$$
$$2T + 4C = 48$$

Solving for D algebraically

To solve these two equations simultaneously, we multiply the first equation by -2:

Add the second equation:

$$-2(4T + 2C = 60) = -8T - 4C = -120$$
$$+ \quad 2T + 4C = \quad 48$$
$$-6T \qquad = -72$$
$$T = \quad 12$$

Now substitute 12 for T in the second equation:

$$2T + 4C = 48$$
$$2(12) + 4C = 48$$
$$24 + 4C = 48$$
$$4C = 24$$
$$C = 6$$

Point D, thus, is (12,6).

Fourth Step

Test the four corners of the shaded area to see which yields the greatest dollar profit.

Point A: (0,0) $= \$8(0) + \$6(0) = 0$
Point E: (0,12) $= \$8(0) + \$6(12) = \$72$
Point C: (15,0) $= \$8(15) + \$6(0) = \$120$
Point D: (12,6) $= \$8(12) + \$6(6) = \$132$

Testing the corners of the area of feasible solutions

The point which yields the greatest profit is point D ($\$132$).

The concept that the most profitable combination of tables and chairs is found at point D (12,6) can be further amplified by first plotting the objective function $\$8T + \$6C$ (given in the first step) directly on a graph of the feasible solution area.

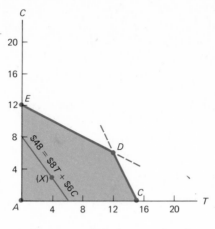

Figure 9-8 Objective function plotted.

A more formal method of determining the optimal point

To accomplish this, we first let profits equal some minimum dollar figure we know we can attain without violating a constraint. In this case we have elected to let profits equal $48, a profit easily attainable. Then the objective function is $48 = $8T + $6C.

We then plot this equation on the graph in Figure 9-8 in the same manner that we originally plotted our constraints (Figure 9-2). First locate two terminal points and then join them with a straight line. When $T = 0$,

$48 = $8(0) + $6C
  C = 8

and when $C = 0$,

$48 = $8T + $6(0)
  T = 6

Iso-profit lines

Figure 9-8 illustrates the area of feasible solutions *(AEDC)* with the profit equation $48 = $8T + $6C drawn in. This line (called an *iso-profit* line) represents all the possible combinations of tables and chairs which would yield a total profit of $48. You might want to check one such combination. For example, point X represents the manufacture of 4 tables and $2^2/_3$ chairs.

$4($8) + $2^2/_3$ ($6) = $48

Suppose we now graph another iso-profit line representing all combinations of tables and chairs which would produce a $96 profit:

$96 = $8T + $6C

When $T = 0$,

$96 = $8(0) + $6C
  C = 16

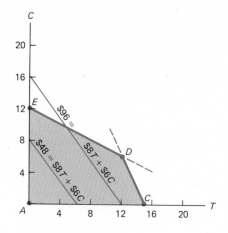

Figure 9-9 Two iso-profit lines plotted.

and when $C = 0$,

$$\$96 = \$8T + \$6(0)$$
$$T = 12$$

Both profit equations ($\$48 = \$8T + \$6C$ and $\$96 = \$8T + \$6C$) are illustrated on the graph in Figure 9-9. Now what is the significance of these parallel iso-profit lines? Simply this: $\$48$ profit will be generated by manufacturing *any* combination of tables and chairs falling on the line $\$48 = \$8T + \$6C$, and a $\$96$ profit will be generated by manufacturing any combination of tables and chairs falling on the line $\$96 = \$8T + \$6C$. [Note, however, that we are limited by problem restrictions to those combinations which fall within the area of feasible solutions (AEDC).]

It is also true that there is *one* parallel iso-profit line which will pass through point D. This particular profit line (line 3) is illustrated in Figure 9-10, together with the first two profit lines. Although most of the combinations of tables and chairs on profit line 3 do not fall within the area of feasible solutions (AEDC), one point does, point D.

The highest iso-profit line

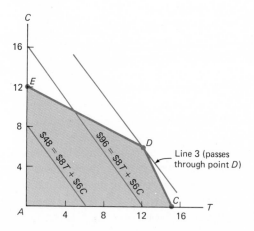

Line 3 (passes through point D)

Figure 9-10 Three iso-profit lines plotted.

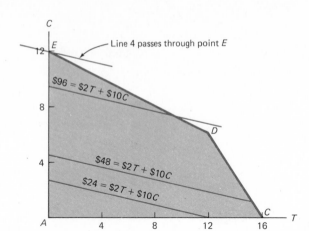

Figure 9-11   Four iso-profit lines plotted for: Profit = $2T + $10C.

The second iso-profit line drawn generated more profit than the first one ($96 versus $48). It is obvious, then, that the iso-profit line which can be located *farthest* from the origin (point A) will contain *all* the combinations of tables and chairs which will generate the greatest possible profit; and as long as at least *one* point on this maximum profit line is still within the area of feasible solutions *(AEDC)*, that point represents the *most profitable combination* of products. Point D lies on iso-profit line 3 and is still within the area of feasible solutions; thus it represents the most profitable combination of tables (12) and chairs (6) for Dimensions to manufacture.

3. Some Technical Issues in Linear Programming

Extreme Points

From our use of the three iso-profit lines in Figure 9-10, you saw that point D generated the highest profit. But now suppose we changed the *profit* for tables and chairs to $2 and $10 respectively and left the department constraints as they were. We have illustrated four new iso-profit lines in Figure 9-11. What is the result? Now you see that the iso-profit line farthest from the origin passes through only one point which is still in the area of feasible solutions, and that is point E. With these two profits, $2 and $10, E is the best combination of products.

One more example will help us develop this idea. Look now at Figure 9-12. Here we've changed the profits for tables and chairs to $12 and $3 respectively. What happened? The iso-profit line farthest from the origin passes through only one point which is still in the area of feasible solutions, and that is point C. With profits of $12 and $3, point C now represents the best combinations of products.

An optimal solution is found at extreme point

We can see from our original problem and the two examples in Figures 9-11 and 9-12 that the optimal solution occurred in each case at one of the corner points of the area of feasible solutions; in linear programming language, we'd say the optimal solution occurs at an *extreme point* in the feasible solution area. Management

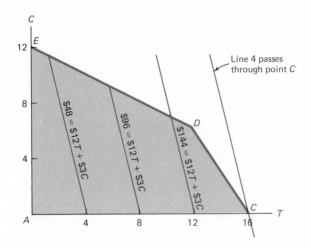

Figure 9-12 Four iso-profit lines plotted for: Profit = $12T + $3C.

scientists have known for some time that if a linear programming problem has an optimal solution, it is found at at least one of the *extreme points*, or "corners," of the feasible solution area. This knowledge makes things easier for us; if we are searching for the optimal solution, we have to evaluate only those solutions that are at the extreme points of the feasible solution area.

Notice that we said above, "If a linear programming problem has a feasible solution. . . ." Is it possible for a linear programming problem to fail to have an optimal solution? The answer is "Yes." There are two ways in which this can happen, and we shall now discuss both.

Infeasibility

Infeasibility means there is *no* solution which satisfies *all* the constraints. Graphically, infeasibility is the case where there is *no* area of feasible solutions which satisfies all constraints. Figure 9-13 shows the problem of Dimensions, Ltd., from earlier in this chapter with two additional constraints: (1) the marketing manager *must* have at least 16 tables and (2) the marketing manager *must* have at least 12 chairs. From Figure 9-13 we see that there is no combination of tables and chairs which will satisfy both areas of feasible solutions (the original production area, *AEDC*, and the new marketing area). Thus there is no feasible solution to this problem *unless* the Dimensions management make available additional capacity in assembly and finishing. How much? Well, to satisfy the marketing manager's constraints, Dimensions needs 16 tables and 12 chairs; according to the problem, this will require 96 hours in assembly and 80 in finishing. Unless these additional resources are made available, the marketing constraints cannot be met.

The case where no solution satisfies the constraints

More resources would be required

Unboundedness

A linear programming problem is unbounded if the solution can be made infinitely large without violating any of the constraints in the problem. If we encounter unboundedness in solving real problems, we know that the problem has not been correctly formulated, since *no* situation permits management an infinitely large

Incorrectly formulated problem

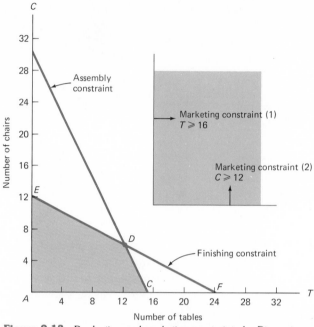

Figure 9-13 Production and marketing constraints for Dimensions, Ltd.

solution and therefore an infinitely large profit. Figure 9-14 shows the Dimensions problem with only *marketing* constraints. In this formulation of the problem, **Iso-profit lines are not constrained** the area of feasible solutions extends indefinitely in both directions. When we begin to draw iso-profit lines through the area of feasible solutions, we quickly see that profit can be as high as we want it (iso-profit line 5 can be followed by any number of higher profit lines we desire).

In addition to *infeasibility* and *unboundedness*, there is one more condition in linear programming which we should take note of at this point; we call this *redundancy*.

Redundancy

More constraints than necessary A constraint which does not affect the feasible area is called a *redundant* constraint. In Figure 9-15 we've shown the Dimensions problem from Figure 9-6, but here a constraint has been added representing the marketing manager's belief that she cannot sell more than 20 chairs. Since the greatest number of chairs that is currently found in the area of feasible solutions, *AEDC*, is 12, the marketing manager's *new* constraint is redundant. If chairs satisfy the finishing constraint, they also satisfy the redundant marketing constraint. Thus the marketing constraint can be removed from the problem. This saves computation time. Unfortunately, in **Problems with redundant constraints** many linear programming problems, redundant constraints are not removed because they have not been recognized as being redundant until after the problem has been solved. With the use of high-speed computers to solve most linear programming problems, redundant constraints are not the problem they once were.

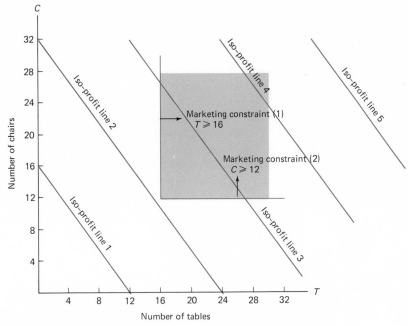

Figure 9-14   Unbounded marketing constraints for Dimensions, Ltd.

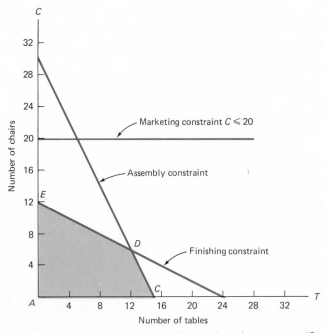

Figure 9-15   Dimensions, Ltd., problem with market constraint ($C \leqslant 20$).

In addition to increasing the computational time, redundant constraints often lead to a condition called *degeneracy*; in the next chapter, we shall show how that situation is handled.

More Than One Optimal Solution

An iso-profit line parallel to a constraint line

Look at the Dimensions situation shown in Figure 9-16; here the iso-profit line farthest from the origin coincides with one of the constraint lines, specifically line *ED*. First we need to satisfy ourselves that at least one optimal solution still lies at an extreme point; in this case *each* of the two extreme points, *E* and *D*, is an optimal solution. In addition to these specific points, *any* point on the line *ED* is an optimal solution too. If the profits from tables and chairs were such as to produce this situa-

Managerial significance of more than one optimal solution

tion, the significance of this to Dimensions is that they have extraordinary flexibility in choosing their product mix, since *any* combination of tables and chairs which lies along line *ED* produces the maximum possible profit for them.

4. Graphic Solution to a Minimization Problem

Graphic linear programming can minimize too

Many problems of interest to managers involve *minimizing* some objective function instead of maximizing one; in these situations too, we can find an optimal solution by using graphic methods.

Hank's Kennel wants to mix up 500 pounds of a special dog food supplement Hank retails. There are two principal ingredients in the mixture, both sources of pro-

A mix problem with two ingredients

tein; let's call these two ingredients P_1 and P_2. P_1, the first source of protein, costs \$5 a pound, and P_2 costs \$8 a pound. Chemical constraints dictate that the mixture contain not more than 400 pounds of P_1 and contain at least 200 pounds of P_2. We can summarize Hank's mixture problem in mathematical form as follows:

Mathematical statement of the problem

Minimize total cost $= \$5\,P_1 + \$8\,P_2$

Subject to the constraints:

$$P_1 \leqslant 400 \text{ pounds}$$
$$P_2 \geqslant 200 \text{ pounds}$$
$$P_1 + P_2 = 500 \text{ pounds} \quad \text{(This ensures that Hank gets the quantity of the mixture he needs)}$$
$$P_1 \geqslant 0$$
$$P_2 \geqslant 0 \quad \text{[This constraint, like the one directly above it, ensures that Hank}$$

gets positive or real values as results; however, since a previous chemical constraint requires P_2 to be greater than 200 pounds $(P_2 \geqslant 200)$, we can say that this constraint $(P_2 \geqslant 0)$ is *redundant;* that is, another constraint is *more* restrictive]

Graphing the constraints

Figure 9-17 is a graph which will allow us to plot P_1 and P_2 on the horizontal and vertical axes, respectively. Looking first at the constraint $P_1 \leqslant 400$ pounds, we can see that a vertical line erected from the 400-pound point on the horizontal axis will

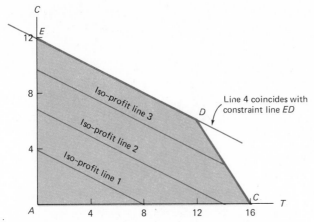

Figure 9-16 Iso-profit line which coincides with a constraint line.

denote the maximum value P_1 can take. Of course, P_1 can take on any value *up to and including* 400 pounds; thus the constraint $P_1 \leq 400$ pounds is properly represented by the striped area to the left of the vertical line *AB* shown in Figure 9-18. *Any* value of P_1 lying on the vertical line or in the striped area to the left of the vertical line will satisfy the constraint $P_1 \leq 400$. **The first constraint**

Now let us look at the second constraint, $P_2 \geq 200$ pounds. If we were to construct a horizontal line *CD* at the 200-pound point on the P_2 axis, we could say that *any* value of P_2 lying on that line or in the space above it would satisfy the constraint $P_2 \geq 200$. This line and the striped space above it are illustrated in Figure 9-19. You will notice that the striped area is constrained only at the bottom (at the 200-pound minimum level), *not* at the top. **The second constraint**

Now what about the third constraint, $P_1 + P_2 = 500$? This ensures that Hank gets the quantity of the mixture that he requires, no more and no less. The equation $P_1 + P_2 = 500$ has been plotted on the graph in Figure 9-20 as the line *EF*. Any combination of P_1 and P_2 which falls on this line will represent exactly 500 pounds of the food supplement and thus satisfy Hank's third constraint. **The third constraint**

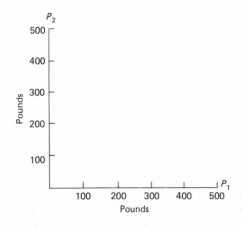

Figure 9-17 Graph indicating ingredients P_1 and P_2.

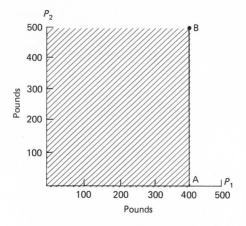

Figure 9-18 Graph of constraint $P_1 \leq 400$ pounds.

As any mixture that Hank produces must satisfy all three constraints; we have illustrated all of them together on the graph in Figure 9-21. This figure shows that any combination of the two ingredients P_1 and P_2 which is *on* the line segment EG will satisfy all *three* constraints; that is,

Such a combination will be exactly 500 pounds.

The amount of P_1 in such a combination will be less than 400 pounds.

The amount of P_2 in such a combination will be more than 200 pounds.

An intuitive solution But there are many combinations of P_1 and P_2 lying on the line segment EG. Which *one* of these will generate the *minimum* cost of producing 500 pounds of the required mixture? One way for Hank to answer this question is to observe that P_2 is the more expensive of the two ingredients ($8/pound) and that it would be best to use the smallest possible amount of this ingredient. The constraint $P_2 \geq 200$ pounds sets the minimum amount of P_2 which must appear in Hank's mixture, 200 pounds; with P_2 being more expensive than P_1, it does not behoove us to include

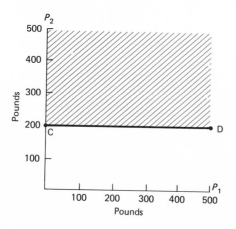

Figure 9-19 Graph of constraint $P_2 \geq 200$ pounds.

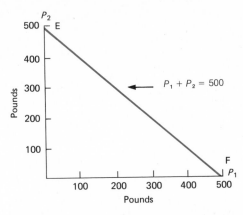

Figure 9-20 Graph of constraint $P_1 + P_2 = 500$ pounds.

more than the minimum amount of P_2 in the final mixture. Thus a bit of simple logic would indicate that the final mixture should consist of 200 pounds of P_2 and 300 pounds of P_1, represented on Figure 9-21 by point G.

Another method of determining the particular combination of P_1 and P_2 on line segment EG which minimizes the total cost of the mixture is to use a variant of the iso-profit lines we employed in the maximization example discussed earlier. Let us call these lines *iso-cost* lines. You will remember that we begin by plotting one such line representing a total cost we *know* we could achieve; with only 500 pounds of the mixture to be produced, it *would* be possible to mix it entirely of P_2 at \$8 per pound; if Hank did this, the total cost would be represented by this equation:

$$\$4000 = \$5P_1 + \$8P_2$$

On the graph in Figure 9-22, we have shown the line segment EG on which

Another method, a variation of iso-profit lines

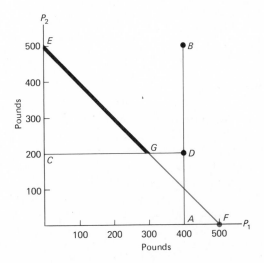

Figure 9-21 Graph of all three constraints.

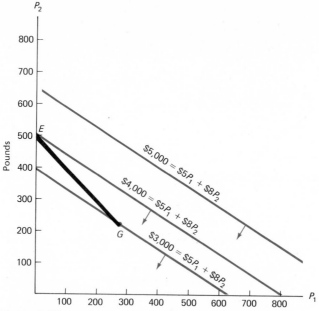

Figure 9-22 Line segment EG illustrated with three iso-cost lines.

Iso-cost lines *any* acceptable mixture must lie; in addition, we have plotted three *iso-cost* lines beginning with a total cost of $5000, then decreasing to a total cost of $4000, and finally the *lowest* iso-cost line, which has at least one point *(G)* on line segment *EG*. The total cost of this third iso-cost line which passes through that point *(G)* is found by solving simultaneously the equations of the two lines which pass through point *G* (lines *EF* and *DC* from Figure 9-21). A simpler method would be to read the coordinates of point *G* directly from the graph in Figure 9-22; regardless of the method chosen, the final solution to Hank's minimizing problem is:

$P_1 = 300$ pounds
$P_2 = 200$ pounds

The optimal solution As P_1 is less than or equal to 400 pounds, it satisfies the original constraint; and because P_2 in the final solution is greater than or equal to 200 pounds, it too satisfies Hank's constraints. Of course, this is a trivial problem, one easily solved in a moment simply by inspecting the ingredient costs and the constraints; however, as will be demonstrated in Chapter 10, in almost all operational applications of linear programming, the complexities of the mixture constraints are such as to make solution by inspection impossible; in this sense, our simple mixture problem serves us as an introduction to the methodology of the more complex solution methods to follow and not as the quickest solution method to the simple problem we have used as an example in this case.

Glossary

1. **Objective**   Goal of the organization.
2. **Constrained resources**   Organizational resources which are limited in quantity to some level.
3. **Linear relationship**   A directly proportional relationship between variables.
4. **Linear programming**   Mathematical technique for finding the best uses of an organization's resources.
5. **Total contribution**   (Selling price per unit − variable cost per unit) × sales volume.
6. **Inequality**   Mathematical expression indicating that minimum or maximum requirements must be met.
7. **Constraint**   A limit on the availability of resources.
8. **Objective function**   Expression which shows the relationship between the variables in the problem and the firm's goal.
9. **Iso-profit line**   A line representing all possible combinations of products which will produce a given profit.
10. **Area of feasible solutions**   That area containing all the possible solutions to the problem which are feasible, that is, those solutions which satisfy all the constraints in the problem.
11. **Extreme point**   A corner of the area of feasible solutions.
12. **Infeasibility**   The condition when there is no solution which satisfies all the constraints in a problem.
13. **Unboundedness**   The condition when the solution to a linear programming problem can be made infinitely large without violating any of the constraints.
14. **Redundancy**   The condition when a constraint exists which does not affect the area of feasible solutions.
15. **Iso-cost line**   A line representing all possible combinations of problem variables which produce the same total cost.

Exercises

9-1. Redikleen Corporation blends solvent from two premixed bases, Donimil and Capilal. Each liter of Donimil costs 80 cents and contains 8 parts kerosene, 10 parts polyvinyl resin, and 6 parts mineral spirits. Capilal costs $1 a liter and contains 6 parts kerosene, 4 parts polyvinyl resin, and 12 parts mineral spirits. Each container of Redikleen solvent must contain at least 24 parts kerosene, 20 parts polyvinyl resin, and 24 parts mineral spirits. Graphically, find the best combination of Donimil and Capilal to meet the requirements for Redikleen solvent at the least cost. What is the cost per liter of the final mix?

9-2. Jim Jones manufactures inexpensive set-it-up-yourself furniture for students. He currently makes two products—bookcases and tables. Each bookcase contributes $6 to profit and each table, $5. Each product passes through two manufacturing points, cutting and finishing. Bookcases take 4 hours a unit in cutting and

4 hours in finishing. Tables require 3 hours a unit in cutting and 5 in finishing. There are currently 40 hours available in cutting and 30 in finishing. Find by graphic linear programming the maximum contribution product mix for Jim.

9-3. Sally Sethness assembles stereo equipment for resale in her shop. She offers two products, turntables and cassette players. She makes a profit of $10 on each turntable and $6 on each cassette. Both must go through two steps in her shop—assembly and bench checking. A turntable takes 12 hours to assemble and 4 hours to bench check. A cassette player takes 4 hours to assemble but 8 hours to bench check. Looking at this month's schedule, Sally sees that she has 60 assembly hours uncommitted and 40 hours of bench checking time available. Use graphic linear programming to find her best combination of these two products. What is the total profit on the combination you found?

9-4. Martin Braudo mixes pet food in his basement on a small scale. He advertises two types of pet food, Diet-Sup and Gro-More. Contribution from Diet-Sup is $1.50 a bag and from Gro-More $1.10 a bag. Both are mixed from two basic ingredients—a protein source and a carbohydrate source. Diet-Sup and Gro-More require ingredients in these amounts:

	Protein	Carbohydrate
Diet-Sup (7-lb bag)	4 lb	3 lb
Gro-More (3-lb bag)	2 lb	1 lb

Martin has the whole weekend ahead of him, but his sources of ingredients have closed. He checks his bins and finds he has 700 pounds of protein source on hand and 500 pounds of carbohydrate in the house. How many bags of each food should he mix to maximize his profits? Use the graphic linear programming method to find this answer.

9-5. Kimbal Draper owns a small perfume shop where she both mixes her own brands and sells other brands. Currently, she is offering two of her own brands, Silent Flower and Mood Swing. Silent Flower makes her $9 an ounce while Mood Swing makes a profit of only $6 an ounce. These two brands are mixed from three essences, E_1, E_2, and E_3. Mixing requirements are

	Essence 1	Essence 2	Essence 3
Silent Flower	.2 oz	.3 oz	.5 oz
Mood Swing	.1 oz	.1 oz	.8 oz

Kimbal checks her essence supply every day. This morning she had 48 ounces of E_1, 30 ounces of E_2, and 60 ounces of E_3. What should she mix today to maximize profits? Use the graphic method to find this answer.

9-6. The King Concrete Company manufactures bags of concrete from beach sand and river sand. Each pound of beach sand costs 6 cents and contains 4 units of fine sand, 3 units of coarse sand, and 5 units of gravel. Each pound of river sand costs 10 cents and contains 3 units of fine sand, 6 units of coarse sand, and 12 units of gravel. Each bag of concrete must contain at least 12 units of fine sand, 12 units of coarse sand, and 10 units of gravel. Graphically, find the best combination of beach sand and river sand which will meet the minimum requirements of fine sand, coarse sand, and gravel at the least cost, and indicate the cost per pound.

9-7. The Central Fabric Company purchases surplus bolts of fabric from two large textile mills, A and B. These fabrics are then sold to the public through fabric stores, discount stores, and direct mail. When Central receives the bolts, it separates them according to the market in which they are sold. Of the fabrics received from textile mill A, 40 percent are sold in fabric stores, 10 percent in discount stores, and 30 percent by direct mail. The fabrics received from textile mill B are 20 percent for fabric stores, 20 percent for discount stores, and 40 percent for direct mail sales. Of the total purchases made from either mill A or mill B, 20 percent of the bolts are unusable and are thrown away. For every 1000 bolts purchased from mill A, Central Fabric realizes a profit of $8000; for every 1000 bolts purchased from mill B, it realizes a profit of $6000. The sales department forecasts that, at most, 1600 bolts can be sold through fabric shops, 7800 through discount stores, and 2600 through direct mail in the coming year. Determine the most profitable numbers of bolts which Central Fabric should purchase from mills A and B, using the graphic method.

9-8. The Riverside Auto Company is planning a promotional campaign intended to bring prospective purchasers of new cars into their showroom. To every prospective buyer who drops by on a given day, Riverside will pay a dollar. Riverside wants to advertise their "Dollar-a-Look" offer to the public, but in order to hold down costs, they want to get as many serious buyers as possible without attracting too many freeloaders. They are considering advertising on one of the television shows. The costs for a commercial on each show, as well as the estimates of drawing power per commercial in terms of serious buyers and freeloaders, are as follows:

TV show	Cost per ad	Number of serious buyers	Number of freeloaders
Western movie	$ 900	800	4,800
Romance movie	1,000	1,000	3,600

There are at most two units of Western and two units of romance movie advertising available. Riverside hopes to keep total costs (advertising plus $1 gifts) at or below $20,000. Using graphic linear programming, determine the optimum plan for drawing as many serious buyers as possible.

9-9. The owner of the Neighborhood Hamburger Stand has decided to operate on a 24-hour basis. Based upon estimates of trade throughout this period, he feels that he requires at least the following number of employees during the given time periods:

Time period	Minimum number of employees required
0:01– 4:00	3
4:01– 8:00	5
8:01–12:00	13
12:01–16:00	8
16:01–20:00	19
20:01–24:00	10

(In this notation, 12:00 is noon and 24:00 is midnight.)

His employees may report for work at midnight, 4 A.M., 8 A.M., noon, 4 P.M., or 8 P.M. Once employees report in, however, they must stay continuously for an 8-hour shift. Set up the objective function and constraint equations which would generate a solution to the problem, but do not attempt the solution itself. You should determine the numbers of employees reporting at each of the six possible reporting times if the total overall number of personnel is to be held to the minimum.

9-10. The Atlantic States Bus Company is considering the problem of allocating buses on three different express routes for the coming year. The following table represents the number of passengers expected on each route and the income received per passenger.

Route	Numbers (in thousands)	Income per passenger
1	300	$20
2	400	14
3	200	16

Atlantic States has three types of buses (A, B, and C) which can be allocated. The following table shows the number of passengers (in thousands) which can be accommodated in a year's time by a bus allocated to each of the routes; it also shows the maximum number of each type of bus which can be made available for use on all routes.

Route	Type of bus		
	A	B	C
1	18	20	6
2	20	23	8
3	19	21	8
Total buses available	18	7	31

The operating cost (in thousands of dollars) of one bus of type A, B, or C allocated to each of the routes is:

Route	Type of bus A	B	C
1	$18	$18	$18 (thousands of dollars)
2	24	22	26
3	20	19	24

Atlantic States estimates that the cost of losing a passenger because of the un-availability of seats is equal to twice the income which would have been received as the fare. Formulate the objective function for the minimum total annual cost solution of this problem, along with the constraint inequalities necessary for its solution. Do not attempt the solution itself.

Bibliography

Gass, Saul I.: *An Illustrated Guide to Linear Programming* (New York: McGraw-Hill Book Company, 1970).

Hughes, Anne J., and **D. E. Grawoig:** *Linear Programming: An Emphasis on Decision Making* (Reading, Mass.: Addison-Wesley Publishing Company, Inc., 1973).

Levin, R. I., and **R. P. Lamone:** *Linear Programming for Management Decisions* (Homewood, Ill.: Richard D. Irwin, Inc., 1969).

Llewellyn, Robert: *Linear Programming* (New York: Holt, Rinehart, and Winston, Inc., 1964).

Naylor, T. H., E. T. Byrne, and **John M. Vernon:** *Introduction to Linear Programming* (Belmont, Calif.: Wadsworth Publishing Company, Inc., 1971).

Stockton, R. S.: *Introduction to Linear Programming* (Homewood, Ill.: Richard D. Irwin, Inc., 1971).

Linear programming: the simplex method

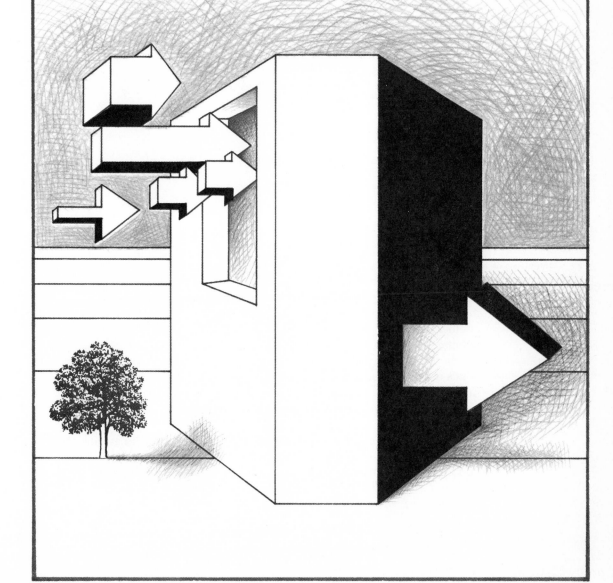

Limitations of graphic method

The decisions most managers face are much more complex than the one Dimensions, Ltd., had to make in its choice between tables and chairs. Most of these decisions involve not two but many variables. Hence, because the graphic method of linear programming is limited to three variables, we have to look to another procedure—the *simplex method*—which offers an efficient means of solving more complex linear programming problems.

Characteristics of the simplex method

In the simplex method, the computational routine is an *iterative* process. To iterate means to repeat; hence, in working toward the optimum solution, the computational routine is repeated over and over, following a standard pattern. Successive solutions are developed in a systematic pattern until the best solution is reached.

Another characteristic of the simplex method is that each new solution will yield a value of the objective function as large as or larger than the previous solution. This important feature assures us that we are always moving closer to the optimum answer. Finally, the method indicates when the optimum solution has been reached.

1. Setting Up the Initial Solution

To demonstrate the simplex method, let us use the Dimensions, Ltd., problem from Chapter 9 so that you can relate the steps in the simplex method to those in the graphic method. We are going to stay with the T = tables and C = chairs notation, since this makes it easier to remember what the variables stand for. Computer linear programming codes permit the user to provide names for the variables (up to 8 characters in some codes). Of course, this would be cumbersome, perhaps impossible, in a problem with 2000 variables, but in the Dimensions, Ltd., problem, remembering the variables is easier with T and C. We shall keep track of slack time by using the notation S_A = slack in assembly and S_F = slack in finishing.

Stated algebraically, the Dimensions, Ltd., problem is:

Maximize: Profit = $\$8T + \$6C$

Subject to: Assembly: $4T + 2C \leqslant 60$

               Finishing: $2T + 4C \leqslant 48$

               All variables $\geqslant 0$

Mathematical statement of the problem

Converting Inequalities to Equations

The first step is to convert the inequalities into equations. Previously, we stated that the best combination of tables and chairs may not necessarily use all the time available in each department. We must therefore add to each inequality a variable which will take up the slack, that is, the time not used in each department. This variable is called a *slack variable*. For example, let

Using slack variables to generate equations from inequalities

S_A = slack variable (unused time) in assembly

S_F = slack variable (unused time) in finishing

S_A is equal to the total amount of time available in assembly (60 hours) less any hours used there in processing tables and chairs. S_F is equal to the total amount of time available in finishing (48 hours) less any hours used there in processing tables and chairs. We can express these two statements in mathematical form by writing equations for the slack variables S_A and S_F as follows:

Assembly: $S_A = 60 - 4T - 2C$

Finishing: $S_F = 48 - 2T - 4C$

By adding the slack variables, we convert the *constraint inequalities* in the problem into *equations*. The slack variable in each department takes on whatever value is required to make the equation relationship hold. Two examples will clarify this point.

Example 1 Assume that in assembly we process 5 tables and 3 chairs.

$S_A = 60 - 4(5) - 2(3)$

    = 34 hr unused time in assembly

Example 2 Assume that in finishing we process 4 tables and 6 chairs.

Examples of slack variables

$S_F = 48 - 2(4) - 4(6)$

    = 16 hr unused time in finishing

By adding a slack variable to each inequality, we convert them into these equations:

Constraint equations $4T + 2C + S_A = 60$ hr
$2T + 4C + S_F = 48$ hr

In the simplex method, any unknown that occurs in one equation *must* appear in all equations. The unknowns that do not affect an equation are written with a zero coefficient. For example, since S_A and S_F represent unused time which yields no profit, these variables are added to the objective function with zero co-efficients. Furthermore, since S_A represents unused time in assembly only, it is added to the equation representing finishing with a zero coefficient. For the same reason $0S_F$ is added to the equation representing the time constraint in assembly. Thus the problem of Dimensions, Ltd., in its final form is:

Maximize: Profit $= \$8T + \$6C + \$0S_A + \$0S_F$

Dimensions, Ltd., problem in final form   Subject to $4T + 2C + S_A + 0S_F = 60$ hr
$2T + 4C + 0S_A + S_F = 48$ hr
All variables $\geqslant 0$

The Simplex Tableau
To make the equations in the problem easier to handle, they can be put into tabular form.

Parts of the simplex tableau and their functions   It will be helpful to describe the simplex tableau and to identify the parts and function of each.

1. See Table 10-1. The two *constraint equations* are shown in the simplex tableau as

	T	C	S_A	S_F
60	4	2	1	0
48	2	4	0	1

Note first that row 1(4, 2, 1, 0) represents the coefficients of the equation $4T + 2C + S_A + 0S_F = 60$, and row 2(2, 4, 0, 1) the coefficients of $2T + 4C + 0S_A + S_F = 48$.

2. Each *variable column* contains all the coefficients of one unknown. For example, under T is written $\binom{4}{2}$, under C is written $\binom{2}{4}$, under S_A is written $\binom{1}{0}$, and under S_F is written $\binom{0}{1}$.

Table 10-1 Parts of the Simplex Tableau

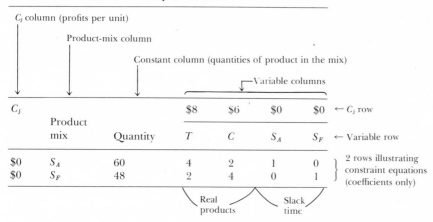

3. The constants (60 and 48) have been placed to the left of the equations. We simply rearrange the terms in the constraint equations to form the simplex tableau.

The First Solution Shown in the Simplex Tableau

In the simplex method, we need to establish an initial solution. The simplest starting solution is for Dimensions, Ltd., to make *no* tables or chairs, have all unused time, and earn no profit. This solution is technically feasible but not financially attractive; it is symbolized:

$T = 0$ no tables
$C = 0$ no chairs
$S_A = 60 - 4(0) - 2(0) = 60$ hr unused
$S_A = 48 - 2(0) - 4(0) = 48$ hr unused

The initial solution for the Dimensions, Ltd., problem

This solution contains only the slack variables S_A and S_F. Substituting the quantities of T, C, S_A, and S_F in the objective function gives the following profit:

Profit $= \$8T + \$6C + \$0S_A + \$0S_F$
$= \$8(0) + \$6(0) + \$0(60) + \$0(48)$
$= 0$

This first feasible solution is shown in the initial simplex tableau as

Product mix	Quantity	T	C	S_A	S_F
S_A	60	4	2	1	0
S_F	48	2	4	0	1

Illustrating the first solution in the simplex tableau

Note that the *product-mix column* contains the variables in the solutions. The variables in the first solution are S_A and S_F (the slack variables). In the *quantity column* we find the quantities of the variables that are in the solution.

Product-mix and quantity columns

S_A = 60 hr available in assembly

S_F = 48 hr available in finishing

First simplex solution is equivalent to a corner point in the graphic solution

Since the variables T and C do not appear in the mix, they are equal to zero. Notice that this first solution (no tables and no chairs) is equivalent to point A in the graphic method of Figure 9-6 on page 267.

Substitution Rates Shown in the Simplex Tableau

The C_j *column* in Table 10-1 contains the profit per unit for the variables S_A and S_F. For example, the zero appearing to the left of the S_A row in Table 10-1 means that profit per unit of S_A is zero.

Explaining the entries in Table 10-1

The last two columns in the initial simplex tableau consist of the coefficients of the slack variables that are added to the constraint inequalities to make them equations.

The fourth and fifth columns consist of the coefficients of the real product variables, T and C. For example, the element 4 in the T column of the table means that if we wanted to make 1 unit of T (to bring 1 table into the solution), we would have to give up 4 hours of S_A in assembly.

Similary, the element 2 in the C column indicates that the manufacturing of 1 unit of C (bringing 1 chair into the solution) would force us to give up 2 hours of S_A in assembly.

The elements in the fourth and fifth columns thus represent rates of substitution.

The element 1 in the S_A column tells us that to bring in 1 hour of S_A (to make 1 hour of S_A available) we would have to give up 1 of the 60 hours of S_A now in the solution. As there are only 60 hours in assembly available, we must give up 1 of the 60 if we want an hour for some other purpose. This is just like taking 1 hour off the top of a pile and adding another to the bottom.

The zero in the S_F column immediately under the S_F means that making 1 hour in finishing available for other purposes has *no* effect on S_A, the amount of slack time in assembly.

In our examination of substitution rates, we have treated *two* types of action:

Two kinds of substitutions

1. The *addition* of real products, T and C into the production schedule or solution

2. The *withdrawal* of time, S_A and S_F, from the total amounts of time available in each of the two departments—withdrawal so as to make time available for other purposes

Adding Two More Rows to the Simplex Tableau

Up to this point, setting up the initial simplex tableau has not involved any computations. We have simply rearranged the problem equations to form the first simplex tableau.

Explaining the Z_j row and the $C_j - Z_j$ row

To find the profit for each solution and to determine whether the solution can be improved upon, we need to add two more rows to the initial simplex tableau: a Z_j row and a $C_j - Z_j$ row. This has been done in Table 10-2. The value in the Z_j row under the quantity column represents the total profit from this particular solution: zero, in this case. In this first solution, we have 60 hours of unused time in assembly ($S_A = 60$) and 48 hours of unused time in finishing ($S_F = 48$). The total profit from this solution is found by multiplying the profit per unit of S_A ($0) by the quantity of S_A in the solution (60 hours) plus the profit per unit of S_F ($0) times the quantity of S_F in the solution (48 hours).

Total profit for the first solution is

Number of unused hours of S_A = 60
Times profit per unit of S_A × $0 = $0

+

Number of unused hours of S_F = 48
Times profit per unit of S_F × $0 = $0
Total profit $0

The four values for Z_j under the variable columns (all $0) are the amounts by which profit would be *reduced* if 1 unit of any of the variables (T, C, S_A, S_F) were added to the mix. For example, if we want to make 1 unit of T, the elements $\binom{4}{2}$ under T tell us we must give up 4 hours of S_A and 2 hours of S_F. But unused time is worth $0 per hour; consequently, there is *no* reduction in profit.

How much profit is lost by adding 1 unit of T to the production schedule or solution?

Number of hours of S_A given up = 4
Times profit per unit of S_A × $0 = $0

Number of hours of S_F given up = 2
Times profit per unit of S_F × $0 = 0
Total profit given up $0

C_j has been defined as profit per unit; for tables (T), C_j is $8 per unit.

Table 10-2 Initial Simplex Tableau Completed (Two Rows Added)

C_j			$8	$6	$0	$0
	Product mix	Quantity	T	C	S_A	S_F
$0	S_A	60	4	2	1	0
$0	S_F	48	2	4	0	1
2 rows	Z_j	$0	$0	$0	$0	$0
added	$C_j - Z_j$		$8	$6	$0	$0

$C_j - Z_j$ is the *net* profit which will result from introducing, that is, adding, 1 unit of a variable to the production schedule or solution. For example, if 1 unit of T adds $8 of profit to the solution *and* if its introduction causes no loss, then $C_j - Z_j$ for $T = \$8$.

The calculation of Z_j's for Table 10-2 follows:

Computation of Z_j row and $C_j - Z_j$ row

Z_j (total profit) $= \$0(60) + \$0(48) = \$0$

Z_j for column $T = \$0(\ 4) + \$0(\ 2) = \$0$

Z_j for column $C = \$0(\ 2) + \$0(\ 4) = \$0$

Z_j for column $S_A = \$0(\ 1) + \$0(\ 0) = \$0$

Z_j for column $S_F = \$0(\ 0) + \$0(\ 1) = \$0$

Calculations of *net* profit per unit of each variable follow:

Variable	Profit/unit — C_j	Profit lost/unit = Z_j	Net profit/unit $C_j - Z_j$
T	$8	$0	$8
C	6	0	6
S_A	0	0	0
S_F	0	0	0

Meaning of the $C_j - Z_j$ row

By examining the numbers in the $C_j - Z_j$ row of Table 10-2, we can see, for example, that total profit can be increased by $8 for each unit of T (tables) added to the mix or by $6 for each unit of C (chairs) added to the mix. Thus a positive number in the $C_j - Z_j$ row ($8 in the case of the T column) indicates that profits *will* be improved by that amount for each unit of T added. On the other hand, a negative number in the $C_j - Z_j$ row would indicate the amount by which profits would *decrease* if 1 unit of the variable heading that column were added to the solution. Hence the optimum solution is reached when no positive numbers remain in the $C_j - Z_j$ row; that is, no more profit can be made.

2. Developing the Second Solution

Is improvement possible?

Now that the initial simplex tableau is established, the next step is to determine how to improve profits.

We now introduce a computation procedure which will generate the correct second and subsequent tableaus of the problem. In this section we shall address ourselves to generating the appropriate values for each iteration of the problem; the section entitled Justification and Significance of All Elements in the Simplex Tableau will demonstrate the logic of the procedures we have followed. The computational procedure for the second solution follows.

Step 1

Determine which variable will add the *most* per unit to profit. The numbers in the $C_j - Z_j$ row tell exactly which product will increase profits most. As stated previously, the presence of positive numbers in the $C_j - Z_j$ row indicates that profit can be improved; the larger the positive number, the greater the improvement possible.

Which variable would add the most per-unit profit?

We select as the variable to be added to the first solution that variable which contributes the most profit per unit. In Table 10-3, bringing in T (tables) will add $8 per unit to profit. The T column is the optimum column.

By definition, the *optimum column* (Table 10-3) is that column which has the largest positive value in the $C_j - Z_j$ row or, stated in another way, that column whose product will contribute the most profit per unit. Inspection of the optimum column tells us that the variable T (tables) should be added to the mix, replacing one of the variables presently in the mix.

Step 2

The next step is to determine which variable will be replaced. This is done in the following manner: divide 60 and 48 in the quantity column by their corresponding numbers in the optimum column and select the row with the smaller nonnegative ratio as the row to be replaced. In this case, the ratios would be:

Which variable will be replaced?

$$S_A \text{ row:} \quad \frac{60 \text{ hr available}}{4 \text{ hr required/unit}} = \widehat{15} \text{ units of } T$$

$$S_F \text{ row:} \quad \frac{48 \text{ hr available}}{2 \text{ hr required/unit}} = 24 \text{ units of } T$$

Since the S_A row has the smaller positive ratio (15:1 rather than 24:1), it is called the *replaced row* because it will be replaced in the next solution by 15 units of T. The elements common to both the S_A and S_F rows *and* the optimum column are called *intersectional elements*. Thus the intersectional element of the row to be replaced (S_A row) is 4, and the intersectional element of the S_F row is 2 (see Table

How many units of the new variable will enter the solution?

Table 10-3 Optimum Column in Initial Simplex Tableau

C_j				$8	$6	$0	$0
	Product mix		Quantity	T	C	S_A	S_F
$0	S_A		60	4	2	1	0
$0	S_F		48	2	4	0	1
	Z_j		$0	$0	$0	$0	$0
	$C_j - Z_j$			$8	$6	$0	$0

Optimum column

Table 10-4 Replaced Row and Intersectional Elements in Initial Simplex Tableau

C_j	Product mix	Quantity	$8 T	$6 C	$0 S_A	$0 S_F	
$0	S_A	60	2	2	1	0	←——Replaced row
$0	S_F	48	4	4	0	1	Intersectional elements
	Z_j	$0	$0	$0	$0	$0	
	$C_j - Z_j$		$8	$6	$0	$0	

↑——Optimum column

10-4). Row replacement means that in the next solution, the variable S_A (unused time) will be replaced by 15 units of T (15 tables).

Step 3

Developing the second tableau

Having selected the optimum column and the replaced row, we can develop the second simplex solution, an *improved* solution.

The first part of the new tableau to be developed is the T row. The T row appears in place of the replaced row (S_A) in Table 10-5. The T row of the new tableau is computed as follows: divide each number in the replaced row (the S_A row) by the intersectional element (4) of the replaced row:

$$^{60}/_4 = 15 \qquad ^4/_4 = 1 \qquad ^2/_4 = ^1/_2 \qquad ^1/_4 = ^1/_4 \qquad ^0/_4 = 0$$

Thus the new T row should be (15, 1, $^1/_2$, $^1/_4$, 0).

This solution is equivalent to one of the corner points of the graphic solution

In Table 10-5, for the first time, there is a nonzero dollar figure in the C_j column ($8 per unit). Also, S_F and its profit per unit ($0) remain in the new tableau. Notice that making 15 tables (our second solution) is equivalent to point C in the graphic solution in Figure 9-6, page 267.

Step 4

To complete the second tableau, we compute new values for the remaining rows. *All* remaining rows of the variables in the tableau are calculated using the formula

Table 10-5 Replacing Row in Second Simplex Tableau

C_j	Product mix	Quantity	$8 T	$6 C	$0 S_A	$0 S_F	
$8	T	15	1	$^1/_2$	$^1/_4$	0	←Replacing row
$0	S_F						
	Z_j						
	$C_j - Z_j$						

$$\begin{pmatrix} \text{Elements in} \\ \text{old row} \end{pmatrix} - \left[\begin{pmatrix} \text{intersectional} \\ \text{element of old row} \end{pmatrix} \times \begin{pmatrix} \text{corresponding elements} \\ \text{in replacing row} \end{pmatrix} \right] = \begin{pmatrix} \text{new} \\ \text{row} \end{pmatrix}$$

Completing the second tableau

Using this formula, the new S_2 row is calculated like this:

Element in old S_F row	—	Intersectional element of S_F row	×	Corresponding element in replacing row	=	New S_F row
48	—	(2	×	15)	=	18
2	—	(2	×	1)	=	0
4	—	(2	×	$1/2$)	=	3
0	—	(2	×	$1/4$)	=	$-1/2$
1	—	(2	×	0)	=	1

The new S_F row as it appears in the second tableau is shown in Table 10-6. The method for computing the Z_j and $C_j - Z_j$ rows (the profit opportunities) has already been demonstrated in developing the initial simplex tableau. The computation of the Z_j row of the second tableau is as follows:

Z_j (total profit) = $8(15) + $0(18) = $120 = total profit of second solution

Z_j for T:	$8(1) + $0(0) = $8	
Z_j for C:	$8($1/2$) + $0(3) = $4	profits given up by
Z_j for S_A:	$8($1/4$) + $0($-1/2$) = $2	introducing 1 unit of
Z_j for S_F:	$8(0) + $0(1) = $0	these variables

Thus the computations above indicate that introducing a unit of T would lose $8 for us. How can this be?

1. We currently make 15 units of T.

2. Production of 15 tables uses up all the time originally available in assembly.

3. To introduce another T we would have to give up 1 of the current 15 T's.

4. Giving up a table would cost us $8.

The new $C_j - Z_j$ row (net profit per unit) is

Variables	Profit/unit C_j	—	Profit lost/unit Z_j	=	Net profit/unit $C_j - Z_j$
T	$8		$8		$0
C	6		4		2
S_A	0		2		−2
S_F	0		0		0

The completed second tableau is shown in Table 10-7. Certainly the total profit from this second solution ($120) is an improvement over the zero profit in the first solution.

The completed second tableau

Table 10-6 Replacing Row and New S_F Row in Second Tableau

C_j			$8	$6	$0	$0
	Product mix	Quantity	T	C	S_A	S_F
$8	T	15	1	$1/2$	$1/4$	0
$0	S_F	18	0	3	$-1/2$	1
	Z_j					
	$C_j - Z_j$					

3. Developing the Third Solution

Is further improvement possible? The presence of a positive number ($2) in the C column of the $C_j - Z_j$ row of the second solution (Table 10-7) indicates that further improvement is possible. Therefore the same process used to develop this solution must be repeated to develop a third solution.

Step 1

Which variable would add the most per-unit profit? A look at the $C_j - Z_j$ row of the second tableau (Table 10-7) shows that C, chairs, contributes a *net* profit of $2 per unit.

$$
\begin{array}{lll}
C_j: & \text{Profit per unit of } C & \$6 \\
Z_j: & \text{Profit lost per unit of } C \quad (-) & 4 \\
\hline
C_j - Z_j: & \text{Net profit per unit of } C & \$2
\end{array}
$$

The optimum column, therefore, in Table 10-7 is the C column. Chairs will now be added, replacing one of the variables, T or S_F, in the second solution.

Step 2

Which variable will be replaced and how many units of the new variable will enter the solution? The replaced row is found as before by dividing 15 and 18 in the quantity column by their corresponding numbers in the optimum column and selecting the row with the smaller ratio as the replaced row.

Table 10-7 Second Simplex Tableau Completed

C_j			$8	$6	$0	$0
	Product mix	Quantity	T	C	S_A	S_F
$8	T	15	1	$1/2$	$1/4$	0
$0	S_F	18	0	3	$-1/2$	1
	Z_j	$120	$8	$4	$2	$0
	$C_j - Z_j$		$0	$2	$-$2	$0

Table 10-8 Optimum Column, Replaced Row, and
Intersectional Elements of Second Tableau

C_j			$8	$6	$0	$0	
	Product mix	Quantity	T	C	S_A	S_F	Intersectional element of C row
$8	T	15	1	½	¼	0	
$0	S_F	18	0	3	−½	1	← Replaced row (S_F)
	Z_j	$120	$8	$4	$2	$0	Intersectional element of S_F row (replaced row)
	$C_j - Z_j$		$0	$2	−$2	$0	

Optimum column

T row: $\dfrac{15}{^1/_2} = 30$

S_F row: $\dfrac{18}{3} = 6$

The S_F row, the one with the smaller ratio, is designated as the replaced row. It will be replaced in the next solution by 6 units of C (chairs). Table 10-8 shows the optimum column, replaced row, and intersectional elements of the second tableau.

Step 3
The replacing row of the third tabelau is computed by dividing each number in the replaced row by the intersectional element of the replaced row.   **Completing the replacing row**

$$\frac{18}{3} = 6 \qquad \frac{0}{3} = 0 \qquad \frac{3}{3} = 1 \qquad \frac{-^1/_2}{3} = -\frac{1}{6} \qquad \frac{1}{3} = \frac{1}{3}$$

Thus the replacing row of the third tableau is (6, 0, 1, − ¹/₆, ¹/₃). It assumes the same row position as the replaced row of the second tableau (see Table 10-9).

Step 4
The new values of the T row are

Element in old T row	−	(Intersectional element of T row	×	Corresponding element of replacing row)	=	New T row	
15	−	(½	×	6)	=	12	**Completing the third tableau**
1	−	(½	×	0)	=	1	
½	−	(½	×	1)	=	0	
¼	−	(½	×	−¹/₆)	=	¹/₃	
0	−	(½	×	¹/₃)	=	−¹/₆	

The new T row is (12, 1, 0, ¹/₃, − ¹/₆). In Table 10-10 it has been added to the third tableau.

Table 10-9   Replacing Row of Third Tableau

C_j			$8	$6	$0	$0	
	Product mix	Quantity	T	C	S_A	S_F	
$8	T						
$6	C	6	0	1	$-1/6$	$1/3$ ←	Replacing row
	Z_j						
	$C_j - Z_j$						

The Z_j's of the third tableau are computed as follows:

Z_j (total profit): $\$8(12) + \$6(6) = \$132 =$ total profit from third solution
Z_j for T: $\$8(1) + \$6(0) = \$8$
Z_j for C: $\$8(0) + \$6(1) = \$6$
Z_j for S_A: $\$8(1/3) + \$6(-1/6) = \$5/3$
Z_j for S_F: $\$8(-1/6) + \$6(1/3) = \$2/3$

The new $C_j - Z_j$ row (net profit per unit) is computed as follows:

Variable	Profit/unit C_j	−	Profit lost/unit Z_j	=	Net profit/unit $C_j - Z_j$
T	$8		$8		$0
C	6		6		0
S_A	0		$5/3$		$-5/3$
S_F	0		$2/3$		$-2/3$

No further improvement is possible; the optimum solution has been reached

The completed third tableau is shown in Table 10-11. As there is no positive $C_j - Z_j$ value, no further profit improvement is possible, thus the optimum solution has been obtained. It is

$$T = 12 \quad C = 6 \quad S_A = 0 \quad S_F = 0$$

This solution is equivalent to one of the corner points in the graphic solution

This solution (12 tables and 6 chairs) is identical to point D in the graphic solution in Figure 9-6 on page 267.

Table 10-10   Replacing Row and New T Row in Third Tableau

C_j			$8	$6	$0	$0
	Product mix	Quantity	T	C	S_A	S_F
$8	T	12	1	0	$1/3$	$-1/6$
$6	C	6	0	1	$-1/6$	$1/3$
	Z_j					
	$C_j - Z_j$					

Table 10-11 Third Simplex Tableau Completed

C_j			$8	$6	$0	$0
	Product mix	Quantity	T	C	S_A	S_F
$8	T	12	1	0	$1/3$	$-1/6$
$6	C	6	0	1	$-1/6$	$1/3$
	Z_j	$132	$8	$6	$5/3$	$2/3$
	$C_j - Z_j$		$0	$0	$-$5/3$	$-$2/3$

Profits will be maximized by making 12 tables and 6 chairs and having no unused time in either department. The variables T and C appear in the product-mix column with their values represented by the corresponding numbers in the quantity column. The variables S_A and S_F do not appear in the product-mix column and therefore are equal to zero.

The Z_j total, $132, represents the profit obtained under the optimum solution. The above solution also can be verified by substitution in the initial problem equations:

Objective function: $Z_j = \$8T + \$6C + \$0(S_A + S_F)$
$$= \$8(12) + \$6(6) + \$0 = \$132$$

Problem constraints: $4T + 2C \leqslant 60$ assembly
$4(12) + 2(6) \leqslant 60$
$60 \leqslant 60$
$2T + 4C \leqslant 48$ finishing
$2(12) + 4(6) \leqslant 48$
$48 \leqslant 48$

Summary of Steps in the Simplex Maximization Procedure
In summary form, the steps involved in the simplex procedure for maximization problems are as follows:

1. Set up the inequalities describing the problem constraints.

2. Convert the inequalities to equalities by adding slack variables.

3. Enter the equalities in the simplex table.

4. Calculate the C_j and Z_j values for this solution.

5. Determine the entering variable (optimum column) by choosing the one with the highest $C_j - Z_j$ value.

6. Determine the row to be replaced by dividing quantity-column values by their corresponding optimum-column values and choosing the smallest nonnegative quotient. (That is, only compute the ratios for rows whose elements in the optimum column are greater than zero; for example, omit ratios like 160/0 and 15/−1.)

The 11 steps in the simplex method of solving a maximizing problem

Table 10-12 Second Simplex Tableau with Each Element Numbered

C_j	Product mix	Quantity	$8 T	$6 C	$0 S_A	$0 S_F
			(1)	(12)	(16)	(8)
					(4)	
$8	T	15	1	$1/2$	$1/4$	0
			(2)	(13)	(17)	(9)
					(5)	
$0	S_F	18	0	3	$-1/2$	1
			(3)	(14)	(18)	(10)
					(6)	
	Z_j	$120	$8	$4	$2	$0
			(15)	(19)	(7)	(11)
	$C_j - Z_j$		$0	$2	-$2	$0

7. Compute the values for the replacing row.

8. Compute the values for the remaining rows.

9. Calculate C_j and Z_j values for this solution.

10. If there is a nonnegative $C_j - Z_j$ value, return to step 5 above.

11. If there is no nonnegative $C_j - Z_j$ value, the final solution has been obtained.

4. Justification and Significance of All Elements in the Simplex Tableau

The logic of the simplex method Up to now, the discussion has centered on the procedures involved in solving a simplex problem. In addition to the solution, however, the simplex method provides us with important information concerning various alternative solutions and the effect of changes in the basic data upon the solutions. Frequently, this information is as valuable and revealing as the answer itself.

In this section we will explain the logic and economic significance of all the elements in the simplex tableau; thus we will give meaning to the procedures learned so far.

In Table 10-12 we have reproduced the second simplex tableau from the preceding section (see Table 10-7) and have numbered each element. Our general interpretation, keyed to each circled number, is as follows.

The Quantity Column

Explaining the two entries in the quantity column of Table 10-12 (1) In the initial simplex tableau (Table 10-2) we noted that T (tables) made the larger contribution per unit to profit and thus should be added to the second solution. To find the quantity to be added, we proceeded as follows:

$$\frac{60 \text{ hr available in assembly}}{4 \text{ hr required/table}} = 15 \text{ tables}$$

We found that 15 was the largest quantity which could be made without violating any of the time restrictions in both departments.

Making 15 tables required all the hours available in assembly (4 hours per unit × 15 units = 60 hours). Thus T replaced S_A in the solution.

②Each of the 15 tables requires 2 hours in finishing. Thus to make 15 tables requires 30 hours (2 hours per unit × 15 units). Since 48 hours are available and only 30 hours are required, we have 18 hours left in finishing.

In the quantity column we see 15 tables, 18 hours, and $120. Including three different types of item in the same column may seem confusing. This quantity column, however, will never be added. The figure 15 is significant as an element of the T row and not as an element of the quantity column. In similar fashion, 18 is an element of the S_F row, and $120 is an element of the Z_j row.

③The $120 represents the total profit from the variables in the product mix.

Number of units of T (tables)	= 15	
Times profit/unit of T	× $8 =	$120
+		
Number of units of S_F (unused hours) =	18	
Times profit/unit of S_F	× $0 =	0
Total profit of second mix		$120

Substitution Rates

④Since 1 unit of T (1 table) requires 4 hours in assembly, the second solution uses up all the 60 hours in assembly. Therefore, the production of anything else in this department would require that some of the tables be given up. For example, if 1 unit of S_A (1 hour) is made available for other purposes, $1/4$ table would have to be given up; or stated in another way, every hour of S_A added to the solution reduces the production of T (tables) by $1/4$ unit.

⑤Reducing the production of T (tables) by $1/4$ unit certainly must have an effect on finishing because *chairs and tables* must be processed through both departments. Because T requires 2 hours per unit in finishing and because adding 1 unit of S_A reduces the production of T (tables) by $1/4$ unit, $1/4 \times 2 = 1/2$ hour is freed in finishing. We can illustrate this another way:

Units of T now in mix	15
If 1 unit of S_A is added to the mix, T is reduced by	$- 1/4$
New quantity of T	$14^3/_4$
2 hr/unit of T required in finishing	$\times\ 2$
Total hr required to make $14^3/_4$ units of T (in finishing)	$29^1/_2$
Total hr required to make $15T$ (2×15)	30
Total hr freed by adding 1 unit of S_A	$1/_2$

Explaining the eight substitution rates in the body of Table 10-12

⑧Adding 1 unit of S_F has no effect (0) on T. Why? Since assembly is the limiting department (all hours have been used), making available 1 hour of S_F in finishing will have no effect on the production of tables. Since 18 hours are still available in finishing, we can make one of them available without reducing our production of tables.

⑨Withdrawing 1 unit of S_F; since there are only 18 hours available in finishing in the second solution, withdrawing 1 hour ($1S_F$) would remove one of the 18 hours now available.

⑫ Here again we have a 1-for-1 substitution; that is, each unit of T added to the production schedule replaces 1 unit of T in the solution. From ① we found that 15 was the largest quantity of tables that could be processed in assembly. Thus, in order to add another table ($1T$) and at the same time satisfy the time restriction in assembly (60 hours available), we must subtract or give up 1 table in order to make the necessary time available.

⑬ Adding 1 unit of T to the production schedule has no effect on S_F. Why? From ⑫ we found that adding 1 table ($1T$) required giving up 1 table ($1T$), so that the net change in finishing must be zero ($1 - 1 = 0$). Since there is no real change in assembly, neither is there any change in finishing. No additional hours are required.

⑯ Adding 1 unit of C (chair) to the program replaces $1/_2T$ (table): a chair ($1C$) requires 2 hours per unit in assembly and a table ($1T$) requires 4 hours. Now, because assembly is the limiting department (time is exhausted), processing 1 chair would require giving up $2/_4$, or $1/_2$, table ($1/_2T$). Stated another way, processing a chair in assembly takes 2 of the 4 hours required to make a table. Thus, for every chair processed in assembly, $1/_2$ table must be given up to provide the necessary 2 hours.

⑰ Adding 1 unit of C (chair) replaces 3 units of S_F (3 hours). The problem originally stated that $1C$ required 4 hours in finishing. How can we justify this apparent inconsistency? First note that adding 1 chair ($1C$) replaces $1/_2$ table (from ⑯). Second, a table requires 2 hours in finishing. Thus giving up $1/_2$ table frees 1 hour in finishing ($1/_2 \times 2$ hours required per unit of $T = 1$ hour). The 4 hours required to make a chair in finishing minus the 1 hour freed equals 3 hours net change. Processing a chair still requires 4 hours per unit: 3 hours plus the 1 hour freed equals the 4 hours required. The inconsistency therefore disappears when we consider the effect of a change not in one department but in both departments. Chairs and tables must be processed in both departments in order to make a completed unit. Thus any change in assembly must have an effect in finishing.

These eight elements represent marginal rates of substitution

In summary, the eight elements we have discussed represent marginal rates of substitution between the variables in the product mix and the variables heading the column. We found that a positive rate of substitution, for example, ⑯, indicates the decrease in T that occurs if 1 unit of C is added to the program. On the other hand, a negative rate of substitution, for example, ⑤, indicates increase in S_F, that is, $1/_2$ hour freed, that occurs if 1 unit of S_A is added to the program.

The Z_j Row

We turn now to an explanation of the elements in the Z_j row; these represent the loss of profit that results from the addition of 1 unit of the variable heading the column.

(6) Adding 1 unit of S_A results in *two* changes: (1) T is decreased by $1/4$ unit (see (4)); (2) S_F is increased by $1/2$ unit ($1/2$ hour freed; see (5)). How much profit would we lose if these two changes took place? Since profit per unit of T is $8 and T is decreased by $1/4$ unit, the profit lost from this change would be $8 × $1/4 T = 2. Because profit per unit of S_F is $0, the increase in S_F by $1/2$ unit results in no gain ($0 × $1/2 S_F = 0). The *total* profit lost, therefore, is the sum of the two changes, or $2 + $0 = 2.

Explaining the four entries in the Z_j row of Table 10-12

The same reasoning process applies to the other elements of the Z_j row. We want to know (1) the changes which occur when 1 unit of the variable heading the column is added, (2) the loss of profit from each change, and (3) the total profit lost, the sum of the losses of each change.

(10) With the addition of 1 unit of S_F:

Change 1	No change in T (see (8))	0
	Profit per unit of T	× $8
	Loss	$0

Change 2	$1S_F$ given up (see (9))	1
	Profit per unit of S_F	× $0
	Loss	0
	Total loss	$0

(14) With the addition of 1 unit of T:

Change 1	$1T$ given up (see (12))	1
	Profit per unit of T	× $8
	Loss	$8

Change 2	No change in S_F (see (13))	0
	Profit per unit of S_F	× $0
	Loss	0
	Total loss	$8

(18) With the addition of 1 unit of C:

Change 1	$1/2 T$ given up (see (16))	$1/2$
	Profit per unit of T	× $8
	Loss	$4

Change 2	$3S_F$ given up (see (17))	3
	Profit per unit of S_F	× $0
	Loss	0
	Total loss	$4

Explaining the four
entries in the $C_j - Z_j$
row of Table 10-12

The $C_j - Z_j$ Row

Each positive number in the $C_j - Z_j$ row represents the net profit obtainable if 1 unit of the variable heading that column were added to the solution. The following examples help to illustrate this point.

(19) The positive number 2 represents the net profit if 1 unit of C (1 chair) were added.

Total profit per unit of C	$6
Less total profit per unit lost (see (18))	− 4
Net profit	$2

So long as there is a positive dollar figure in the $C_j - Z_j$ row, further improvement in profit can and should be made, because for each unit of C added, we can increase the profit of $120 by $2. Element (2) (18 hours) and element (17) (3 hours per chair) indicate that $^{18}/_3$, or 6 chairs can be added.

(15) Total profit per unit of T	$8
Total profit per unit lost (see (14))	− 8
Net profit	$0

For every unit of T added, total profit will not change. The explanation is that we are already producing as many tables as possible under the time restrictions in assembly. If we add 1T to the solution, we must give up 1T. Adding 1 unit of T results in a profit increase of $8, but giving up 1 unit of T results in a profit decrease of $8. Thus nothing is added to total profit.

(11) Total profit per unit of S_F	$0
Total profit per unit lost (see (10))	− 0
Net profit	$0

Each unit of S_F added to the program will not change total profit. Again the explanation is that assembly limits the production of tables to 15. Therefore adding 1 unit of S_F has no effect on T (see (8)). Total profit, then, cannot be increased by adding any units of S_F.

(7) Total profit per unit of S_A	$0
Less total profit per unit lost (see (6))	− 2
Net loss	− $2

A negative number (a net loss) in the $C_j - Z_j$ row indicates the decrease in total profit if 1 unit of the variable heading that column were added to the product mix. In this case, each unit of S_A added to the program will decrease total profit by $2. Why? From (4) we found that for every unit of S_A added, $^1/_4$ table would have to be given up. Profit per unit of S_A is $0, but profit per table is $8. So each S_A added would result in a $2 loss ($8 × $^1/_4$ = $2).

A negative number in the $C_j - Z_j$ row under one of the columns representing time (S_A or S_F) has another interpretation. A negative number here represents the amount of increase in total profit if the number of hours available in that department could be increased by 1. For example, in ⑦, if 1 more hour ($1S_A$) were available in assembly, (that is, if $S_A = 61$ instead of 60 in the initial solution, Table 10-2), then total profit could be *increased* by $2. This can be proved by using the equation from page 290 representing the time restriction in assembly altered to reflect the addition of 1 hour. If

$$4T + 2C + S_A = 61$$

and we let

$$S_A = 0 \quad C = 0$$

(since C and S_A are not in the second solution, they are equal to 0), then

$$4T + 2(0) + 0 = 61$$
$$4T = 61 - 2(0) - 0 = 61$$
$$T = {}^{61}/_4$$

Substituting $T = {}^{61}/_4$ for T in the objective function yields the following total profit:

$$\text{Profit} = \$8T + \$6C + \$0S_A + \$0S_F$$
$$= \$8({}^{61}/_4) + \$6(0) + \$0 + \$0 = \$122$$

Note that making available 1 additional hour in assembly *would* increase total profit by $2.

With this information, Dimensions, Ltd., may want to investigate the possibilities of expanding the capacity in the assembly department.

In summary, a *positive number* in the $C_j - Z_j$ row indicates the amount of increase in total profit possible if 1 unit of the variable heading that column were added to the solution. A *negative number* in the $C_j - Z_j$ row indicates the amount of decrease in total profit if 1 unit of the variable heading that column were added to the solution. A negative number in the $C_j - Z_j$ row *under one of the columns representing time* can be thought of as the amount of increase in total profit obtainable if 1 more hour in the department heading that column were available.

Managerial interpretations of the entries in the $C_j - Z_j$ row

5. The Simplex Solution to a Minimizing Problem

Up to this point in the chapter the discussion has involved a profit maximization problem. The simplex method can also be used in problems where the objective is to minimize costs such as the minimization example of Chapter 9.

Using the simplex method for cost minimization problems

Symbolizing the Problem
Livestock Nutrition Inc. (LNI) produces specially blended feed supplements. LNI currently has an order for 200 pounds of its mixture 141-B. This consists of two ingredients, P (a protein source) and C (a carbohydrate source).

The LNI problem

The first ingredient, P, costs LNI $3 a pound; the second ingredient costs $8 a pound. The mixture can't be more than 40 percent P, and it must be at least 30 percent C. LNI's problem is to determine how much of each ingredient to use to minimize cost.

Cost function   The cost function can now be written as

$$\text{Cost} = \$3P + \$8C$$

One constraint in the problem is that LNI must produce 200 pounds of the mixture—no more, no less. Stated mathematically, this statement becomes

First constraint $P + C = 200$ lb

This equation means that the number of pounds of P plus the number of pounds of C must equal 200 pounds.

Second constraint   The second constraint is that the mixture can't be more than 40 percent P, so we may use less than 80 pounds ($40\% \times 200 = 80$), but we must not exceed 80 pounds. In mathematical language this is written

$$P \leqslant 80 \text{ lb}$$

Third constraint   The third constraint is that the mixture must be at least 30 percent C. Thus we may use more than 60 pounds ($30\% \times 200 = 60$) but not less than 60 pounds. Mathematically, this is expressed

$$C \geqslant 60 \text{ lb}$$

In summary, then, the problem stated in mathematical form is:

Minimize: Cost $= \$3P + \$8C$

Subject to $P + C = 200$ lb

Initial $P \leqslant 80$ lb
mathematical $C \geqslant 60$ lb
statement of the P and $C \geqslant 0$
problem

At this point, it might be helpful to point out that irrespective of whether the goal is to maximize profits or minimize costs, the steps in setting up the problem are similar, and once the first solution is formulated, the procedure is much the same.

An Initial Solution

Getting an initial   Now consider the first constraint in this minimization problem represented by an
solution   equality:

$$P + C = 200 \text{ lb}$$

Remember from the manufacturing problem that our first need was for a solution—*any* technically feasible solution—so that we could start moving toward the final, the optimum, solution. Our first solution in the manufacturing problem netted us zero profit. This was a ridiculous solution profitwise, *but* it served as a starting point or base for improvement and refinement.

In this cost minimization problem, we once again need a starting solution. It too will be ridiculous costwise. It too will be a point of departure in our search for the lowest-cost mixture.

Suppose we decide to let $P = 0$ and $C = 200$ as a first solution; does this solution satisfy all the constraints?

A first solution by inspection

$P + C = 200$
$0 + 200 = 200$
$200 = 200$ weight constraint is satisfied
$P \leqslant 80$
$0 \leqslant 80$ protein constraint is satisfied
$C \geqslant 60$
$200 \geqslant 60$ carbohydrate constraint is satisfied

Shortcomings of finding a first solution by inspection

In a more realistic problem, one involving 12 ingredients (and each with its own constraints), finding a first solution by inspection is almost impossible. Our need, then, is for a simple procedure which will generate a first solution in all problems, no matter how complicated.

Let us start by not putting any P or C into our first solution. Instead, start with 200 pounds of A_1—an *artificial variable* representing a new ingredient.

Artificial variables

$P + C + A_1 = 200$
$0 + 0 + 200 = 200$
$200 = 200$ constraint is satisfied

Just what is A_1? It can be thought of as a very expensive substance ($100 a pound) which could substitute satisfactorily for our end product.

Our first solution, then, consists entirely of 200 pounds of A_1 at $100 per pound. Although this is ridiculous costwise, it does represent a technically feasible solution in that the product *would* fill LNI's customers' needs.

Because of its high price ($100 versus $8 and $3), A_1 must not be present in LNI's optimum solution.

In linear programming terminology, an *artificial variable* is only of value as a computational device; it allows two types of restrictions to be treated, the equality type and the greater-than-or-equal-to type.

The second constraint in this problem is of a type with which we are familiar

$P \leqslant 80$ lb   constraint on protein

Because P in the final solution may turn out to be less than 80 pounds, we must *add* a slack variable in order to form an equation.

$P + S_1 = 80$ lb

The slack variable S_1 represents the difference between 80 pounds of P and the actual number of pounds of P in the final solution.

Finally, there is a third constraint

$C \geqslant 60$ lb   constraint on carbohydrates

A subtracted slack variable

To convert this inequality into an equation, we must *subtract* a slack variable

$C - S_2 = 60$ lb

The subtracted slack variable S_2 represents the amount by which C will exceed 60 pounds in the final solution. For example, if C in the final solution equals 130 pounds, then S_2 must equal 70 pounds in order for the equation to hold. Of course, if C equals 60 pounds in the final solution, then the value of S_2 would have to be 0.

We see at once that if $C = 0$ in the first solution, then $0 - S_2 = 60$, or $S_2 = -60$. This equation is not a feasible one in the first solution because -60 pounds of an ingredient is not possible: -60 makes no more sense than -12 tables or -6 chairs. What shall we do?

One approach is to prevent S_2 from appearing in the first solution. But what takes its place to keep the equation in balance? If C is zero and S_2 is zero in the first solution, then we must introduce a new ingredient, one that is an acceptable substitute for C, one that will take the place of C in the first solution. As in the case of A_1, this new ingredient (A_2) can be thought of as a very expensive substance ($100 a pound). The high price of A_2 assures us that it will never appear in our final solution. Thus the original constraint of $C \geqslant 60$ was first changed to $C - S_2 = 60$ by the subtraction of a slack variable; now the present change revises this into $C - S_2 + A_2 = 60$ by the inclusion of an artificial variable. The equation in the first solution still holds because $C = 0$ and $S_2 = 0$.

Notation for artificial variables

We stated that the artificial variables A_1 and A_2 would be assigned a very high cost, $100 a pound. In many problems, 100 will not be large enough to prevent the artificial variables from being used in the optimal solution. To avoid having to work with extremely large numbers, we let the letter M represent a very large number; this will simplify the calculations to follow.

The cost function and the constraint equations ready for the initial simplex tableau are shown below:

Minimize: Cost $= \$3P + \$8C + \$0S_1 + \$0S_2 + \$MA_1 + \$MA_2$

Subject to
$$P + C + A_1 \qquad\qquad = 200$$
$$P \qquad\quad + S_1 \qquad\quad = 80$$
$$C \qquad - S_2 + A_2 = 60$$
$$P, C, A_1, S_1, S_2, A_2 \geqslant 0$$

We show zero cost for the slack variables S_1 and S_2, and we show $M cost for the artificial variables A_1 and A_2. We also insert the appropriate variables with zero coefficients into the constraint equations.

Here is LNI's problem ready for the simplex solution:

Minimize: Cost = $3P + $8C + $0S_1 + $0S_2 + $MA_1 + $MA_2

Subject to $P + C + A_1 + 0S_1 + 0S_2 + 0A_2 = 200$
$$P + 0C + 0A_1 + S_1 + 0S_2 + 0A_2 = 80$$
$$0P + C + 0A_1 + 0S_1 - S_2 + A_2 = 60$$
$$\text{All variables} \geq 0$$

Final mathematical statement of the LNI problem

First Simplex Tableau for LNI Problem

The first simplex tableau is shown in Table 10-13. Note that the total cost of the first solution, $260M, is extremely high. Since the objective is to minimize costs, the optimum column is found by selecting that column which has the largest *negative* value in the $C_j - Z_j$ row (that column whose value will decrease costs the most). A glance at the $C_j - Z_j$ row shows only two negative values, $3 - $M and $8 - $2M. As $8 - $2M is the larger negative number in the $C_j - Z_j$ row (8 − $2M = −$192 while $3 − $M is only −$97), C is the optimum column.

Look at the $C_j - Z_j$ row to see whether further improvement is possible

The computational procedures for finding the replaced row, the replacing row, all other new rows, the Z_j row, and the $C_j - Z_j$ row are exactly the same as those for the maximization problem.

Computations for the initial tableau Table 10-13 are as follows:

Z_j Row:

$$Z_{total} = \$M(200) + \$0(80) + \$M(60) = \$260M$$
$$Z_P = \$M(1) + \$0(1) + \$M(0) = \$M$$
$$Z_C = \$M(1) + \$0(0) + \$M(1) = \$2M$$
$$Z_{A_1} = \$M(1) + \$0(0) + \$M(0) = \$M$$
$$Z_{S_1} = \$M(0) + \$0(1) + \$M(0) = \$0$$
$$Z_{S_2} = \$M(0) + \$0(0) + \$M(-1) = -\$M$$
$$Z_{A_2} = \$M(0) + \$0(0) + \$M(1) = \$M$$

Table 10-13   Initial Simplex Tableau: LNI Problem

C_j			$3	$8	$M	$0	$0	$M
	Product mix	Quantity	P	C	A_1	S_1	S_2	A_2
$M	A_1	200	1	1	1	0	0	0
$0	S_1	80	1	0	0	1	0	0
$M	A_2	60	0	1	0	0	−1	1 ←
	Z_j	$260M	$M	$2M	$M	$0	−$M	$M
	$C_j - Z_j$		$3 − $M	$8 − $2M	$0	$0	$M	$0

Optimum column (under C) — Replaced row (at A_2)

$C_j - Z_j$ Row:

$C_P - Z_P = \$3 - \$M$
$C_C - Z_C = \$8 - \$2M$
$C_{A_1} - Z_{A_1} = \$M - \$M = \$0$
$C_{S_1} - Z_{S_1} = \$0 - \$0 = \$0$
$C_{S_2} - Z_{S_2} = \$0 - (-\$M) = \$M$
$C_{A_2} - Z_{A_2} = \$M - \$M = \$0$

Replaced Row:

A_1 row: $^{200}/_1 = 200$

Determining the replaced row for the second solution S_1 row: ←——————— since 0 is not positive, this row is not considered (see step 6 on page 301)

A_2 row: $^{60}/_1 = 60$ ← replaced row (smallest quotient)

Second Solution for LNI Problem
The second solution is shown in Table 10-14. Computations for the second simplex tableau are as follows.

Completing the second solution computations   Replacing Row (C):

$^{60}/_1 = 60$
$^{0}/_1 = 0$
$^{1}/_1 = 1$
$^{0}/_1 = 0$
$-^{1}/_1 = -1$
$^{1}/_1 = 1$

A_1 Row: S_1 Row:

$200 - 1(60) = 140$ $80 - 0(60) = 80$
$1 - 1(0) = 1$ $1 - 0(0) = 1$
$1 - 1(1) = 0$ $0 - 0(1) = 0$
$1 - 1(0) = 1$ $0 - 0(0) = 0$
$0 - 1(0) = 0$ $1 - 0(0) = 1$
$0 - 1(-1) = 1$ $0 - 0(-1) = 0$
$0 - 1(1) = -1$ $0 - 0(1) = 0$

Z_j Row:

$Z_{total} = \$M(140) + \$0(80) + \$8(60) = \$140M + \$480$
$Z_P = \$M(1) + \$0(1) + \$8(0) = \$M$
$Z_C = \$M(0) + \$0(0) + \$8(1) = \$8$
$Z_{A_1} = \$M(1) + \$0(0) + \$8(0) = \$M$
$Z_{S_1} = \$M(0) + \$0(1) + \$8(0) = \$0$
$Z_{S_2} = \$M(1) + \$0(0) + \$8(-1) = \$M - \$8$
$Z_{A_2} = \$M(-1) + \$0(0) + \$8(1) = \$8 - \$M$

Table 10-14 Second Simplex Tableau: LNI Problem

C_j	Product mix	Quantity	$3	$8	$M	$0	$0	$M
			P	C	A_1	S_1	S_2	A_2
$M	A_1	140	1	0	1	0	1	-1
$0	S_1	80	1	0	0	1	0	0
$8	C	60	0	1	0	0	-1	1
	Z_j	$140M + $480	$M	$8	$M	$0	$M - $8	$8 - $M
	$C_j - Z_j$		$3 - $M	$0	$0	$0	$8 - $M	$2M - $8

Optimum column   Replaced row

$C_j - Z_j$ Row:

$$C_P - Z_P = \$3 - \$M \leftarrow \text{optimum column}$$
$$C_C - Z_C = \$8 - \$8 = \$0$$
$$C_{A_1} - Z_{A_1} = \$M - \$M = \$0$$
$$C_{S_1} - Z_{S_1} = \$0 - \$0 = \$0$$
$$C_{S_2} - Z_{S_2} = \$0 - \$(M - 8) = \$8 - \$M$$
$$C_{A_2} - Z_{A_2} = \$M - \$(8 - M) = \$2M - \$8$$

Replaced Row:

A_1 row: $^{140}/_1 = 140$
S_1 row: $^{80}/_1 = \ 80 \leftarrow$ replaced row
C row: $\longleftarrow$ not considered since 0 is not positive

Third Solution for LNI Problem

The third simplex tableau is shown in Table 10-15. Computations for the third simplex tableau are as follows.

The third solution for the LNI problem

Replacing Row (P):

$$^{80}/_1 = 80$$
$$^{1}/_1 = 1$$
$$^{0}/_1 = 0$$
$$^{0}/_1 = 0$$
$$^{1}/_1 = 1$$
$$^{0}/_1 = 0$$
$$^{0}/_1 = 0$$

A_1 Row:

$$140 - 1(80) = 60$$
$$1 - 1(1) = 0$$
$$0 - 1(0) = 0$$
$$1 - 1(0) = 1$$
$$0 - 1(1) = -1$$
$$1 - 1(0) = 1$$
$$-1 - 1(0) = -1$$

C Row:

$$60 - 0(80) = 60$$
$$0 - 0(1) = 0$$
$$1 - 0(0) = 1$$
$$0 - 0(0) = 0$$
$$0 - 0(1) = 0$$
$$-1 - 0(0) = -1$$
$$1 - 0(0) = 1$$

Table 10-15 Third Simplex Tableau: LNI Problem

C_j	Product mix	Quantity	$3	$8	$M	$0	$0	$M	
			P	C	A_1	S_1	S_2	A_2	
$M	A_1	60	0	0	1	-1	1	-1	←
$3	P	80	1	0	0	1	0	0	
$8	C	60	0	1	0	0	-1	1	
	Z_j	$60M + $720	$3	$8	$M	$3 - $M	$M - $8	$8 - $M	
	$C_j - Z_j$		$0	$0	$0	$M - $3	$8 - $M	$2M - $8	

Optimum column ——————→   Replaced row

Z_j Row:

$$Z_{total} = \$M(60) + \$3(80) + \$8(60) = \$60M + \$720$$
$$Z_P = \$M(0) + \$3(1) + \$8(0) = \$3$$
$$Z_C = \$M(0) + \$3(0) + \$8(1) = \$8$$
$$Z_{A_1} = \$M(1) + \$3(0) + \$8(0) = \$M$$
$$Z_{S_1} = \$M(-1) + \$3(1) + \$8(0) = \$3 - \$M$$
$$Z_{S_2} = \$M(1) + \$3(0) + \$8(-1) = \$M - \$8$$
$$Z_{A_2} = \$M(-1) + \$3(0) + \$8(1) = \$8 - \$M$$

$C_j - Z_j$ Row:

$$C_P - Z_P = \$3 - \$3 = \$0$$
$$C_C - Z_C = \$8 - \$8 = \$0$$
$$C_{A_1} - Z_{A_1} = \$M - \$M = \$0$$
$$C_{S_1} - Z_{S_1} = \$0 - \$(3 - M) = \$M - \$3$$
$$C_{S_2} - Z_{S_2} = \$0 - \$(M - 8) = \$8 - \$M \leftarrow \text{optimum column}$$
$$C_{A_2} - Z_{A_2} = \$M - \$(8 - M) = \$2M - \$8$$

Replaced Row:

A_1 row $^{60}/_1 = 60 \leftarrow$ replaced row
P row ←————— not considered (0 not positive)
C row ←————— not considered (-1 not positive)

Fourth Solution for LNI Problem

The fourth solution for the LNI problem The fourth simplex tableau is shown in Table 10-16. Computations for the fourth tableau are as follows.

Replacing Row (S_2):

$$^{60}/_1 = 60$$
$$^{0}/_1 = 0$$
$$^{0}/_1 = 0$$
$$^{1}/_1 = 1$$
$$-^{1}/_1 = -1$$
$$^{1}/_1 = 1$$
$$-^{1}/_1 = -1$$

Table 10-16 Fourth Simplex Tableau (Optimum Solution): LNI Problem

C_j	Product mix	Quantity	$3	$8	$M	$0	$0	$M
			P	C	A_1	S_1	S_2	A_2
$0	S_2	60	0	0	1	−1	1	−1
$3	P	80	1	0	0	1	0	0
$8	C	120	0	1	1	−1	0	0
	Z_j	$1,200	$3	$8	$8	−$5	$0	$0
	$C_j - Z_j$		$0	$0	$M—$8	$5	$0	$M

P Row:

$80 - 0(60) = 80$
$1 - 0(0) = 1$
$0 - 0(0) = 0$
$0 - 0(1) = 0$
$1 - 0(-1) = 1$
$0 - 0(1) = 0$
$0 - 0(-1) = 0$

C Row:

$60 - (-1)(60) = 120$
$0 - (-1)(0) = 0$
$1 - (-1)(0) = 1$
$0 - (-1)(1) = 1$
$0 - (-1)(-1) = -1$
$-1 - (-1)(1) = 0$
$1 - (-1)(-1) = 0$

Z_j Row:

$Z_{total} = \$0(60) + \$3(80) + \$8(120) = \$1,200$
$Z_P = \$0(0) + \$3(1) + \$8(0) = \$3$
$Z_C = \$0(0) + \$3(0) + \$8(1) = \$8$
$Z_{A_1} = \$0(1) + \$3(0) + \$8(1) = \$8$
$Z_{S_1} = \$0(-1) + \$3(1) + \$8(-1) = -\$5$
$Z_{S_2} = \$0(1) + \$3(0) + \$8(0) = \$0$
$Z_{A_2} = \$0(-1) + \$3(0) + \$8(0) = \$0$

$C_j - Z_j$ Row:

$C_P - Z_P = \$3 - \$3 = \$0$
$C_C - Z_C = \$8 - \$8 = \$0$
$C_{A_1} - Z_{A_1} = \$M - \$8$
$C_{S_1} - Z_{S_1} = \$0 - (-\$5) = \$5$
$C_{S_2} - Z_{S_2} = \$0 - \$0 = \$0$
$C_{A_2} - Z_{A_2} = \$M - \$0 = \$M$

Since in the fourth tableau (Table 10-16) no negative values remain in the $C_j - Z_j$ row, we have reached the *optimum* solution. It is to use 80 pounds of P and 120 pounds of C. This results in a cost of $1200, the minimum cost combination of P and C which satisfies the constraints in the problem. We have the 200 pounds of our mixture (120 + 80) required. Note that the slack variable S_2 is also in the solution. S_2 represents the amount of C used over the minimum quantity required (60 pounds). Substituting the values for C and S_2 in the constraint equation from page 310, $C - S_2 + A_2 = 60$, we have

$120 - 60 + 0 = 60$
$60 = 60$

Since the artificial variable A_2 is not in the solution, it is equal to zero.

No further improvement is possible; this is the optimum solution

Larger problems are not this easy   Of course this problem could have been solved quickly by visual inspection; unfortunately this is just not the case with most minimization problems. For an example of a much more complex blending problem which cannot be solved by inspection, look at the blending problem discussed in the section of this chapter entitled Applications.

Summary of Steps in the Simplex Minimization Procedure

In summary form, the steps involved in the simplex procedure for minimization problems are as follows:

The 12 steps in the simplex method of solving a minimization problem

1. Set up the inequalities and equalities describing the problem constraints.

2. Convert any inequalities to equalities by adding or subtracting slack variables as necessary.

3. Add artificial variables to any equalities involving negative slack variables and to any equalities which were not obtained by adding slack variables initially.

4. Enter the resulting equalities in the simplex table.

5. Calculate C_j and Z_j values for this solution.

6. Determine the entering variable by choosing the one with the largest negative $C_j - Z_j$ value.

7. Determine the row to be replaced by dividing quantity column values by their corresponding optimum-column values and choosing the smallest nonnegative quotient. (That is, only compute the ratios for rows whose elements in the optimum column are greater than zero; for example, omit ratios like $160/0$ and $15/-5$.)

8. Compute the values for the replacing row.

9. Calculate the values for the remaining rows.

10. Calculate the C_j and Z_j values for this solution.

11. If there is a negative $C_j - Z_j$ remaining, then return to step 6, given above.

12. If there is no negative $C_j - Z_j$ value remaining, the final solution has been obtained.

6. The Dual in Linear Programming

The concept of duality in linear programming   Associated with any linear programming problem is another linear programming problem, called its *dual*. Although the idea of *duality* is essentially mathematical, we shall see in this section that duality has important economic interpretations which can help managers answer questions about alternative courses of action and their relative values.

The Primal and Dual in Linear Programming

Each linear programming maximizing problem has its corresponding dual, a minimizing problem; similarly, each linear programming minimizing problem has *its* corresponding dual, a maximizing problem. As we shall see, it is an interesting feature of the simplex method that we can use it to solve either the original problem (called the *primal*) or the dual; whichever problem we start out to solve, it will also give us the solution to the other problem.

Let's consider an expanded version of the Dimensions, Ltd., problem, now with three departments (assembly, finishing, and packing) and with the capability to make three products: tables (T, at \$2/unit profit), chairs (C, at \$4/unit profit), and bookcases (B, at \$3/unit profit.) The problem can be stated as:

Maximize: $\$2T + \$4C + \$3B$

Subject to
$$3T + 4C + 2B \leq 60 \quad \text{assembly constraint}$$
$$2T + 1C + 2B \leq 40 \quad \text{finishing constraint}$$
$$1T + 3C + 2B \leq 80 \quad \text{packing constraint}$$
$$\text{All variables} \geq 0$$

Table 10-17 contains the solution to this problem, the *primal* problem.

Table 10-17 Solution to the Primal

C_j				$\$2$	$\$4$	$\$3$	$\$0$	$\$0$	$\$0$
	Product mix		Quantity	T	C	B	S_A	S_F	S_P
$\$0$	S_A		60	3	4	2	1	0	0
$\$0$	S_F		40	2	1	2	0	1	0
$\$0$	S_P		80	1	3	2	0	0	1
	Z_j		$\$0$	$\$0$	$\$0$	$\$0$	$\$0$	$\$0$	$\$0$
	$C_j - Z_j$			$\$2$	$\$4$	$\$3$	$\$0$	$\$0$	$\$0$

└─Optimum column

$\theta = {}^{60}/_4 = \boxed{15}$ $\theta = {}^{40}/_1 = 40$ $\theta = {}^{80}/_3 = 26^2/_3$

└─θ (Greek theta) is the standard symbol for ratio

$\$4$	C		15	$^3/_4$	1	$^1/_2$	$^1/_4$	0	0
$\$0$	S_F		25	$^5/_4$	0	$^3/_2$	$-^1/_4$	1	0
$\$0$	S_P		35	$-^5/_4$	0	$^1/_2$	$-^3/_4$	0	1
	Z_j		$\$60$	$\$3$	$\$4$	$\$2$	$\$1$	$\$0$	$\$0$
	$C_j - Z_j$			$-\$1$	$\$0$	$\$1$	$-\$1$	$\$0$	$\$0$

└─Optimum column

$\theta = 15/(^1/_2) = 30$ $\theta = 25/(^3/_2) = \boxed{16^2/_3}$ $\theta = 35/(^1/_2) = 70$

$\$4$	C		$6^2/_3$	$^1/_3$	1	0	$^1/_3$	$-^1/_3$	0
$\$3$	B		$16^2/_3$	$^5/_6$	0	1	$-^1/_6$	$^2/_3$	0
$\$0$	S_P		$26^2/_3$	$-^5/_3$	0	0	$-^2/_3$	$-^1/_3$	1
	Z_j		$\$76^2/_3$	$\$^{23}/_6$	$\$4$	$\$3$	$\$^5/_6$	$\$^2/_3$	$\$0$
	$C_j - Z_j$			$-\$^{11}/_6$	$\$0$	$\$0$	$-\$^5/_6$	$-\$^2/_3$	$\$0$

Primal and dual problems

An expanded Dimensions, Ltd., problem; three products and three departments

Mathematical statement of the problem

Solution to the primal problem

<table>
<tr><td>

Interpreting the $C_j - Z_j$ row of the solution to the primal problem

</td><td>

We see from Table 10-17 that the optimal solution is to produce $6\frac{2}{3}$ chairs, $16\frac{2}{3}$ bookcases, and no tables. The total contribution for this product mix is about $76.67. The values contained under the S_A, S_F, and S_P columns in the $C_j - Z_j$ row indicate that to remove one productive hour from each of the three departments would *reduce* the total contribution respectively by $5/6, $2/3, and $0. This can be taken to mean also that *if* additional capital were available to expand productive time in these three departments, the value (of the increased production) to Dimensions, Ltd., of 1 more hour in each of these departments would be $5/6, $2/3, and $0 respectively. To be more specific about expanding capacity, if adding another hour to each department cost the same, we would add the time to the assembly department, for there it is worth $5/6, which is more than $2/3 or $0. This kind of information is *also* available from a solution to the dual problem.

</td></tr>
</table>

Solving the Dual and Interpreting Its Managerial Significance

<table>
<tr><td>

Focus of the dual problem

</td><td>

The *primal* was concerned with maximizing the contribution from the three products; the *dual* will be concerned with evaluating the time used in the three departments to produce the tables, chairs, and bookcases.

</td></tr>
<tr><td>

Monetary value of resources

</td><td>

Jim Littlefield, the production manager of Dimensions, Ltd., recognizes that the productive capacity of the three departments is a valuable resource to the firm; he wonders whether it would be possible to place a monetary value on its worth. He soon comes to think in terms of how much he would receive from another furniture producer, a renter who wanted to rent all the capacity in Jim's three departments. He reasons along the following lines.

Suppose the rental charges were $A per hour of assembly time, $F per hour of finishing time, and $P per hour of packing time. Then the cost to the renter of *all* the time would be

</td></tr>
<tr><td>

Value of all the resources

</td><td>

$60A + $40F + $80P = total rent paid

And of course the renter would want to set the rental prices in such a way as to *minimize* the total rent he would have to pay; so the objective of the dual is

Minimize: $60A + $40F + $80P

Jim will not rent out his time unless the rent offered enables him to net as much as he would if he used the time to produce furniture for Dimensions, Ltd. This observation leads to the constraints of the dual.

</td></tr>
<tr><td>

Developing the first constraint for the dual

</td><td>

To make one table required 3 assembly hours, 2 finishing hours, and 1 packing hour. The time that goes into making a table would be rented out for $3A + $2F + $1P. If Jim used that time to make a table, he would earn $2 in contribution to profit, so he will not rent out the time unless

$$3A + 2F + 1P \geqslant 2$$

</td></tr>
</table>

and this gives us the first constraint in the dual. Similar reasoning with respect to chairs and bookcases gives us the other two dual constraints,

$$4A + 1F + 3P \geqslant 4$$

and

$$2A + 2F + 2P \geqslant 3$$

The other two constraints for the dual

and of course the rents must be nonnegative.

So the entire dual problem which determines for Jim the value of the productive resources of Dimensions, Ltd., (its plant hours) is

Minimize $\$60A + \$40F + \$80P = $ total rent paid

Subject to $3A + 2F + 1P \geqslant 2$
$4A + 1F + 3P \geqslant 4$
$2A + 2F + 2P \geqslant 3$
$A, F, P \geqslant 0$

Mathematical statement of the dual

In Table 10-18 we have first added appropriate slack and artificial variables and then solved the dual problem. Only the initial tableau and the final tableau (the fifth) are shown in Table 10-18.

The optimum solution to the dual problem in Table 10-18 indicates that the worth to Dimensions, Ltd., of a productive hour in the assembly department is $\$5/6$, in the finishing department $\$2/3$, and in the packing department $\$0$. Of course, these are the same values we got by looking at the $C_j - Z_j$ row in the final tableau of Table 10-17 (the primal problem). Thus when we solved the primal, we also got the solution to the dual. Does solving the dual also give us the solution to the primal? Yes: if we look at the values contained under the S_A, S_F, and S_P columns in the $C_j - Z_j$ row in the final tableau of Table 10-18, we find 0, $6\,{}^2/_3$, and $16\,{}^2/_3$, which are the optimal values for T, C, and B in the primal.

Interpretation of the solution to the dual

Table 10-18   Solution to the Dual (Initial and Final Tableaus)

C_j	Product mix	Quantity	60 A	40 F	80 P	0 S_1	0 S_2	0 S_3	M A_1	M A_2	M A_3
M	A_1	2	3	2	1	-1	0	0	1	0	0
M	A_2	4	4	1	3	0	-1	0	0	1	0
M	A_3	3	2	2	2	0	0	-1	0	0	1
	Z_j	9M	9M	5M	6M	$-$M	$-$M	$-$M	M	M	M
	$C_j - Z_j$		$60 - 9$M	$40 - 5$M	$80 - 6$M	M	M	M	0	0	0

Optimum column

$\theta = {}^2/_3$ $\theta = {}^4/_4 = 1$ $\theta = {}^3/_2$

60	A	${}^5/_6$	1	0	${}^2/_3$	0	$-{}^1/_3$	${}^1/_6$	0	${}^1/_3$	$-{}^1/_6$
0	S_1	${}^{11}/_6$	0	0	${}^5/_3$	1	$-{}^1/_3$	$-{}^5/_6$	-1	${}^1/_3$	${}^5/_6$
40	F	${}^2/_3$	0	1	${}^1/_3$	0	${}^1/_3$	$-{}^2/_3$	0	$-{}^1/_3$	${}^2/_3$
	Z_j	$76{}^2/_3$	60	40	$53{}^1/_3$	0	$-6{}^2/_3$	$-16{}^2/_3$	0	$6{}^2/_3$	$16{}^2/_3$
	$C_j - Z_j$		0	0	$26{}^2/_3$	0	$6{}^2/_3$	$16{}^2/_3$	M	M $- 6{}^2/_3$	M $- 16{}^2/_3$

Choosing which problem to solve, the primal or the dual

We have seen that solving *either* the primal or the dual gets us the solution to *both* problems. Which one should we apply the simplex method to? Computational experience shows that the work necessary to solve linear programs depends primarily on the *number of constraints* in the problem. Suppose we had a problem like Dimensions, Ltd., but with seven departments. The primal problem would have seven constraints, but the dual would have only three (three products). In this case it would be sensible to apply the simplex method to the dual.

Further Economic Interpretations of Duality

Duality has several other useful economic interpretations:

Additional interpretations of the dual

1. Suppose T, C, B is a feasible solution to the primal (that is, a level of output which can be achieved with the current resources) and A, F, P is a feasible solution to the dual (that is, a set of rents which would induce Jim to rent out the plant rather than produce himself). Then

$$\$2T + \$4C + \$3B \leq \$60A + \$40F + \$80P$$

In words, in order to get Jim to rent rather than produce, the rents must total at least as much as he can get by producing.

The objective function value for the optimum answer is the same in both problems

2. Notice that the optimal objective value is the same in both problems ($76 $^2/_3$). This is *always* the case. Whenever the primal has an optimal solution, so does the dual, and the optimal objective values are equal. How can we interpret this? It says that the value to Dimensions, Ltd., of all of its productive resources is precisely equal to the profit the firm can make if it employs these resources in the best way possible. In this way, the profit made on the firm's output is used to derive *imputed values* of the inputs used to produce that output.

Complementary slackness

3. Notice that the dual variable P was equal to zero and that not all the packing time was used. This is entirely reasonable, since if Dimensions, Ltd., already has excess packing time, additional packing time cannot be profitably used and so is worthless. This is half of what is called the *principle of complementary slackness*.

4. Notice that with $A = 5/6$, $F = 2/3$, and $P = 0$, $3A + 2F + 1P = 23/6$. This shows us that the value of the time needed to produce a table is $\$^{23}/_6$. But a table only contributes a profit of $2. Since the time needed to produce a table is worth more than the return on a table, the optimal solution to the primal *does not* produce any tables for Dimensions, Ltd. This is the other half of the *principle of complementary slackness*.

7. Some Technical Issues in the Simplex Method

Technical problems encountered in linear programming

The third section of Chapter 9 was titled Some Technical Issues in Linear Programming. There, we introduced—using graphic methods—some problems encountered in working linear programs and solutions to these problems. Here, we shall consider three such issues—*infeasibility, unboundedness,* and *degeneracy*—in the simplex method. It will be useful for you to review these topics in Chapter 9 before moving ahead.

Infeasibility

What about recognizing infeasibility in the simplex method? If, when you reach the final solution, one or more artificial variables are still in the solution, there is *no* feasible solution to the problem. Why is this true? Remember that in minimization problems we introduced A's into the first solution. A's were expensive substitutes for ingredients which were driven out in later solutions. In the Dimensions, Ltd., problem shown in Figure 9-13, A's would be very expensive *substitute* resources for assembly and finishing hours necessary to meet the marketing constraints. In this case, since there is no feasible solution, A's would not be replaced in later solutions and would show up in the final solution.

When there is no feasible solution

Unboundedness

When we are using the simplex method, how do we recognize unboundedness? Look back for a moment to page 295; there, we illustrated how to determine which variable was to be replaced. Our rule was to *select the row with the smaller or smallest nonnegative ratio.* If there is *no* nonnegative ratio—or if all the ratios are of the form, say, 60/0—then we know the solution is unbounded. Why is this true? If the ratio *is* negative, this means we "get back" something each time we introduce a unit of the new variable; thus we could conceivably keep introducing that variable forever. If the ratio is of the form 60/0, this can be thought of as meaning that an infinite quantity of the entering variable could be introduced. In either case, these are signals that the solution is unbounded, and that generally means we have incorrectly formulated the problem.

When there is no constraint on the solution

Degeneracy

Degeneracy refers to a condition sometimes encountered in solving a linear programming problem. It sounds much worse than it actually is, and there are simple procedures which, if used properly, will make the issue a fairly minor one.

To demonstrate what degeneracy is and the procedure for resolving it, let us consider the following product-mix problem involving two products and three departments:

Ties in theta values

Maximize: $\quad \$5X_1 + \$8X_2$

Subject to $\quad 4X_1 + 6X_2 \leqslant 24$
$\qquad\qquad\ 2X_1 + X_2 \ \leqslant 18$
$\qquad\qquad\ 3X_1 + 9X_2 \leqslant 36$

The first simplex tableau for this problem is illustrated in Table 10-19; the $C_j - Z_j$ row values indicate that X_2 is the variable which will enter the mix in the second solution. When we compute the theta values, we find, however, that we have a

Table 10-19   Problem Illustrating Degeneracy

C_j			$5	$8	$0	$0	$0
	Product mix	Quantity	X_1	X_2	S_1	S_2	S_3
$0	S_1	24	4	6	1	0	0
$0	S_2	18	2	1	0	1	0
$0	S_3	36	3	9	0	0	1
	Z_j	$0	$0	$0	$0	$0	$0
	$C_j - Z_j$		$5	$8	$0	$0	$0

$\theta = {}^{24}/_6 = 4 \qquad \theta = {}^{18}/_1 = 18 \qquad \theta = {}^{36}/_9 = 4 \qquad$ Optimum column

Tie

tie between the first and third rows. Unless we break this tie, there is the theoretical possibility that the simplex method may "run around in circles" and fail to find the optimal solution. To break this tie, we'll choose the third row as the row to be replaced. Table 10-20 shows the rest of the solution. If we had replaced the *first* row in Table 10-19 instead of the third, then we would have found the optimal solution in one less step.

Ties in the $C_j - Z_j$ row   The question may arise here: "What happens if a tie occurs in the $C_j - Z_j$ row?" Such a condition is not called degeneracy, and either of the tied variables may be chosen to enter the next solution. The choice in some cases may affect the number of iterations but never the final objective function value.

8. Objectives Other than Maximizing Contribution

Up to this point, the simplex method has been used to generate the maximum contribution answer for a product-mix problem. But what if the company, for any one of several short-run reasons, is willing to sacrifice contribution to increase output (units)? Linear programming can help here too. In Table 10-21 we solve a simple product-mix problem for the maximum contribution answer. We find the answer to be production of $3^1/_2$ units of X_2 for a maximum contribution (price − variable cost) of $24.50; there are 5 hours left unused in department 1.

Maximizing output instead of contribution   Now to generate that particular solution which maximizes units of output, we must in fact "instruct" the program that we are not concerned with contribution per product but only in the maximum number of units. This can best be done, as shown in Table 10-22, by giving both products an objective coefficient of 1. Then if we maximize, the program will produce the greatest number of units of products. Specifically, it will show a preference toward that product which can be produced in the shortest time. The final tableau in Table 10-22 indicates that to maximize production in units, we should manufacture $6^1/_3$ units of X_1; this increases production from $3^1/_2$ to $6^1/_3$ units but reduces contribution from $24.50 to $19 (that is $3 \times 6^1/_3$). Two hours remain unused in the second department.

For an illustration of another criterion managers might use in the short run,

Table 10-20 Procedure for Solving Degeneracy

C_j			$5	$8	$0	$0	$0
	Product mix	Quantity	X_1	X_2	S_1	S_2	S_3
$0	S_1	0	2	0	1	0	$-2/3$
$0	S_2	14	$5/3$	0	0	1	$-1/9$
$8	X_2	4	$1/3$	1	0	0	$1/9$
	Z_j	$32	$8/3$	$8	$0	$0	$8/9$
	$C_j - Z$		$7/3$	$0	$0	$0	$-$8/9$

$\theta = \dfrac{0}{2} = 0 \qquad \theta = \dfrac{14}{5/3} = \dfrac{42}{5} \qquad \theta = \dfrac{4}{1/3} = 12 \qquad$ Optimum column

$5	X_1	0	1	0	$1/2$	0	$-1/3$
$0	S_2	14	0	0	$-5/6$	1	$4/9$
$8	X_2	4	0	1	$-1/6$	0	$2/9$
	Z_j	$32	$5	8	$7/6$	$0	$1/9$
	$C_j - Z_j$		$0	$0	$-$7/6$	$0	$-$1/9$

let us suppose that this same company wants to keep both departments working at maximum capacity and is willing to forgo some of the contribution to do this. It is possible with linear programming to find this third solution to the sample problem. We must now, of course, "instruct" the program to disregard contribution again, thus the zero C_j's for the X_1 and X_2 variables in the tableaus in Table 10-23. Now, if unused time is very unappealing to us, why not just give S_1 and S_2 a C_j of -1 and use the maximizing program? The program will maximize by getting rid of all the unused time. The results of the solution in Table 10-23 show production of five X_1's and one X_2 for a total contribution of $22 (that is, $3 × 5 + $7 × 1); thus the available time in both departments has been used up (neither S_1 nor S_2 appears in the final solution). There has been a slight reduction in contribution, $22

Minimizing unused time

Table 10-21 Maximum Contribution Solution

C_j			$3	$7	$0	$0
	Product mix	Quantity	X_1	X_2	S_1	S_2
$0	S_1	19	3	4	1	0
$0	S_2	21	3	6	0	1
	Z_j	$0	$0	$0	$0	$0
	$C_j - Z_j$		$3	$7	$0	$0

$\theta = 19/4 = 4 3/4 \qquad \theta = 21/6 = 3 1/2 \qquad\qquad$ Optimum column

$0	S_1	5	1	0	1	$-2/3$
$7	X_2	$3 1/2$	$1/2$	1	0	$1/6$
	Z_j	$24 1/2$	$3 1/2$	$7	$0	$7/6$
	$C_j - Z_j$		$-$1/2$	$0	$0	$-$7/6$

Table 10-22   Maximum Units Solution

C_j	Product mix	Quantity	1	1	0	0
			X_1	X_2	S_1	S_2
0	S_1	19	3	4	1	0
0	S_2	21	3	6	0	1
	Z_j	0	0	0	0	0
	$C_j - Z_j$		1	1	0	0

$\theta = {}^{19}/_3 = 6^1/_3$ $\theta = {}^{21}/_3 = 7$ ⬑———— Optimum column (arbitrarily picked)

1	X_1	$6^1/_3$	1	$^4/_3$	$^1/_3$	0
0	S_2	2	0	2	-1	1
	Z_j	$6^1/_3$	1	$^4/_3$	$^1/_3$	0
	$C_j - Z_j$		0	$-^1/_3$	$^1/_3$	0

versus $24.50; in this solution the number of units produced (6) is slightly less than what we produced in the maximum production solution.

When other criteria are important   One might argue that in the long run there is only one criterion on which a facility should be scheduled, namely, maximization of total contribution; however, in the short run when production is behind, it may be necessary to appease certain good customers by producing more units at some sacrifice of contribution. In other situations it may be highly desirable to keep all the employees working during a period when demand has fallen off temporarily. Accepting a diminution of contribution in both these cases is still sound management, and linear programming can help determine which product mix will best carry out any desired managerial policy.

9. Sensitivity Analysis

Additional managerial interpretations of linear programming   In the sixth section of this chapter (The Dual in Linear Programming), we found the value of additional hours of productive time in both departments. In this section we want to continue the analysis of adding additional resources. In addition, we want to examine the effect of changes in the objective function coefficients (decreased profits, for example) on the optimal solution.

Right-Hand-Side Ranging

Over what range does the shadow price remain valid   In Table 10-24 we have repeated from Table 10-17 the final simplex tableau for the optimal solution to the expanded Dimensions, Ltd., problem. From our previous analysis of the dual, we can see from the $C_j - Z_j$ row of Table 10-24 that adding another hour of S_A (assembly time) will increase profit $5/6, adding another hour of S_F (finishing time) will increase profit $2/3, and adding another hour of S_P (packing time) will leave profit unchanged. These three values ($5/6, $2/3, and $0) are called *shadow prices*. Our problem at this point is to determine how

Table 10-23 Minimum Unused Time Solution

C_j			0	0	-1	-1
	Product mix	Quantity	X_1	X_2	S_1	S_2
-1	S_1	19	3	4	1	0
-1	S_2	21	3	6	0	1
	Z_j		-6	-10	-1	-1
	$C_j - Z_j$		6	10	0	0

$\theta = {}^{19}/_4 = 4^3/_4 \qquad \theta = {}^{21}/_6 = 3^1/_2$ ⬆ Optimum column

-1	S_1	5	1	0	1	$-^2/_3$
0	X_2	$3^1/_2$	$^1/_2$	1	0	$^1/_6$
	Z_j		-1	0	-1	$^2/_3$
	$C_j - Z_j$		1	0	0	$-^5/_3$

⬆ Optimum column

$\theta = {}^5/_1 = 5 \qquad \theta = \dfrac{3^1/_2}{^1/_2} = 7$

0	X_1	5	1	0	1	$-^2/_3$
0	X_2	1	0	1	$-^1/_2$	$^1/_2$
	Z_j	0	0	0	0	0
	$C_j - Z_j$		0	0	-1	-1

many hours of assembly or finishing time we can actually use to earn these potential increased profits. In linear programming we call this *determining the range over which the shadow prices will remain valid.*

Obviously we can't add assembly hours forever or we will violate one of the other two constraints; and using the same logic, we can't add or subtract finishing hours forever or we will violate the assembly or packing constraints. Suppose you want to know the number of hours you can add or remove from the assembly department and still have the shadow price of $5/6 remain valid. The process here is quite like finding the replaced row in the simplex method. To illustrate it, we repeat the S_A column and the quantity column from Table 10-24 and perform the same division (see table at top of page 326) we did in the simplex method.

The least positive quotient (20) is the answer to how much the number of

Table 10-24 Final Simplex Tableau of Expanded Dimensions, Ltd., Problem

C_j			$2	$4	$3	$0	$0	$0
	Product mix	Quantity	T	C	B	S_A	S_F	S_P
$4	C	$6^2/_3$	$^1/_3$	1	0	$^1/_3$	$-^1/_3$	0
$3	B	$16^2/_3$	$^5/_6$	0	1	$-^1/_6$	$^2/_3$	0
$0	S_P	$26^2/_3$	$-^5/_3$	0	0	$-^2/_3$	$-^1/_3$	1
	Z_j	$76^2/_3$	$23/_6$	$4	$3	$5/_6$	$2/_3$	$0
	$C_j - Z_j$		$-$11/_6$	$0	$0	$-$5/_6$	$-$2/_3$	$0

Quantity	S_A		
$6^2/_3$	$^1/_3$	$(6^2/_3)/^1/_3$	$= \boxed{20}$
$16^2/_3$	$-^1/_6$	$(16^2/_3)/-^1/_6$	$= -100$
$26^2/_3$	$-^2/_3$	$(26^2/_3)/-^2/_3$	$= \boxed{-40}$

assembly hours can be decreased. The least negative quotient (40) is the answer to how much the number of assembly hours can be increased. Thus we have found that the shadow price for assembly ($5/6 per hour) is *valid* over a range from *reducing* the assembly hours by 20 to *increasing* them by 40. Since we started with 60 assembly hours, we'd say that the right-hand-side range for assembly was 40 to 100, or (60 − 20) to (60 + 40). Applying the same method to the finishing department will demonstrate that the right-hand-side range there is 15 to 60 hours.

Now what about the packing department? Things are different in this case because *all the packing hours have not been used* (S_P is in the final solution in Table 10-24). With $26^2/_3$ unused hours in packing still in the solution, we see that we can *reduce* the number of packing hours only by $26^2/_3$ before a shortage of packing time occurs; conversely, since we are not using all the packing hours now, we can *increase* them indefinitely without changing the solution to the problem. Thus the right-hand-side range for S_p would be $53^1/_3$ to no limit, $(80 − 26^2/_3)$ to (80 + no limit). Most computer programs used to solve linear programming problems provide the right-hand-side ranges as a part of the output.

Changes in Objective Function Coefficients

Over what range of the objective function coefficient is the optimal solution unchanged?

Variables That Are Not in the Solution   Look again at Table 10-24 on page 325. T (tables) is *not* in the optimal solution. That means that T's C_j (its profitability, $2 a table) is *not* as great as its Z_j (the loss it would produce if it came into the solution, $23/6). This is the same as saying that its $C_j − Z_j$ is negative; −$11/6 in this case. To come into the solution, its profit, C_j, would have to exceed $23/6. This means its profit would have to increase $11/6 ($23/6 − $2) before it would pay Dimensions, Ltd., to produce tables (in this expanded problem). In the case of a minimizing problem, a variable not in the solution would come in if its cost drops *below Z_j*.

Variables That Are Already in the Solution   Suppose Dimensions, Ltd., wanted to know how large or how small the profit for chairs *(C)* could become without changing the optimal solution. To do this, we repeat the C row and the $C_j − Z_j$ rows from the final simplex tableau, Table 10-24, and divide each $C_j − Z_j$ entry (for variables *not* in the solution) by its associated C entry.

$C_j − Z_j$	$−\$^{11}/_6$	$\$0$	$\$0$	$−\$^5/_6$	$−\$^2/_3$	$\$0$
C	$^1/_3$	1	0	$^1/_3$	$−^1/_3$	0
$\dfrac{C_j − Z_j}{C}$	$−\$5.50$			$\boxed{−\$2.50}$	$\boxed{\$2.00}$	

The *least positive* quotient ($2) is the answer to how much the profit per chair could *increase* without changing the solution. The *least negative* quotient ($2.50) is how much the profit per chair could *decrease* without changing the solution. Therefore, the *range* of the profit for C is $1.50 to $6, ($4 − 2.50) to ($4 + 2). Using the same method, the range for B is $2 to $8. What is the value of this information to Dimensions, Ltd.? Just this. The marketing manager now knows what pricing latitude he has (assuming that costs stay the same); that is, in the face of competitive pressure or in the absence of any competition, the marketing manager knows just how much prices can be adjusted without interfering with the optimal solution.

Marketing value of objective function ranging

10. Linear Programming Applications

According to a study of operations research activities, linear programming is the third most widely used among all quantitative techniques.[1] It would be impossible to either list or show all the present or potential applications of this technique; however, to give you some idea of the scope of application of linear programming, we have included this section.

Linear programming is the third most widely used quantitative technique

The number of applications we will present here makes it necessary that we use fairly small problems; it also makes it necessary to omit the actual solutions and concentrate on formulating the problem and setting it up in proper linear programming form. In each case, we shall describe the problem setting, define the variables, and illustrate how the objective function and constraints are written. Following through these applications will not only give you an appreciation of the potential areas of application but also develop your skills in *formulating* linear programming applications; as is the case with most quantitative techniques, computer-assisted solutions are much easier to produce than are correct problem formulations.

Formulating problems is much more difficult than solving them

Finally, we should point out that in each instance, one or the other of the authors has been involved in an active role in each of the applications chosen for inclusion here. We have had to simplify the formulation and reduce the number of variables and constraints, but the problem that remains comes directly from one that we have been involved in during the last 15 years. Although we cannot identify the organizations by name, we have indicated their type of business, their approximate size, and their general geographic location. We felt that this approach rather than the all too common listing of contrived problems would show you how effective and how simple some applications really are.

All the problems here are real ones

Production Smoothing Application

A large private-brand manufacturer of knitted products in Tennessee approached us some years ago looking for help in a situation where seasonal peaks in demand exceeded current production capacity. The manufacturer knew that to meet seasonal demand, earlier production of items would have to be scheduled and the

Matching production and demand with linear programming

---

[1] E. Turban, "A Sample Survey of Operations-Research Activities at the Corporate Level," *Operations Research,* vol. 20, pp. 708–721, 1972.

items then stored; in addition, in this case, both regular time and overtime could be used for production of most items, at a higher labor cost for overtime. The fact that it produced over 3000 different items made this problem quite complex. Here is forecast demand (in plant hours) and available capacity (also in plant hours) both for the *busy* season (last 6 months of the year) and the *slack* season (first 6 months of the year) for one product.

Time period	Forecast demand (hours)	Plant capacity (hours)	
		Regular time	Overtime
First quarter of year	24	28	12
Second quarter of year	29	28	12
Third quarter of year	34	28	14
Final quarter of year	48	28	14
	135	112	52

Since regular-time production and overtime production in any previous quarter could be sold in any later quarter of the year, we defined the variables in the problem this way:

An hour's production in:		For sale in:			
		1st quarter	2d quarter	3d quarter	4th quarter
First quarter:	Regular time	X_1	X_2	X_3	X_4
	Overtime	X_5	X_6	X_7	X_8
Second quarter:	Regular time		X_9	X_{10}	X_{11}
	Overtime		X_{12}	X_{13}	X_{14}
Third quarter:	Regular time			X_{15}	X_{16}
	Overtime			X_{17}	X_{18}
Fourth quarter:	Regular time				X_{19}
	Overtime				X_{20}

Taking into account (1) the per-hour labor cost for regular time or overtime production and (2) the cost of storing an hour's production for varying lengths of time, company cost accountants came up with cost figures applicable to each X variable defined above; here is a simulated set of costs for illustration:

X_1, \$8; X_2, \$9; X_3, \$10; X_4, \$11; X_5, \$12; X_6, \$13; X_7, \$14; X_8, \$15; X_9, \$8; X_{10}, \$9
X_{11}, \$10; X_{12}, \$12; X_{13}, \$13; X_{14}, \$14; X_{15}, \$8; X_{16}, \$9; X_{17}, \$12; X_{18}, \$13; X_{19}, \$8; X_{20}, \$12

The objective function and constraints for a linear programming solution to this problem are:

Formulation		Explanation
$\$8X_1 + \$9X_2 + \$10X_3 + \$11X_4 + \$12X_5 + \$13X_6 +$ $\$14X_7 + \$15X_8 + \$8X_9 + \$9X_{10} + \$10X_{11} +$ $\$12X_{12} + \$13X_{13} + \$14X_{14} + \$8X_{15} + \$9X_{16} +$ $\$12X_{17} + \$13X_{18} + \$8X_{19} + \$12X_{20} = \text{total cost}$		Objective function
$X_1 + X_2 + X_3 + X_4$	≤ 28	Constraint on first-quarter regular-time hours available
$X_5 + X_6 + X_7 + X_8$	≤ 12	Constraint on first-quarter overtime hours available
$X_9 + X_{10} + X_{11}$	≤ 28	Constraint on second-quarter regular-time hours available
$X_{12} + X_{13} + X_{14}$	≤ 12	Constraint on second-quarter overtime hours available
$X_{15} + X_{16}$	≤ 28	Constraint on third-quarter regular-time hours available
$X_{17} + X_{18}$	≤ 14	Constraint on third-quarter overtime hours available
X_{19}	≤ 28	Constraint on fourth-quarter regular-time hours available
X_{20}	≤ 14	Constraint on fourth-quarter overtime hours available
$X_1 + X_5$	$= 24$	Constraint on first-quarter demand
$X_2 + X_6 + X_9 + X_{12}$	$= 29$	Constraint on second-quarter demand
$X_3 + X_7 + X_{10} + X_{13} + X_{15} + X_{17}$	$= 34$	Constraint on third-quarter demand
$X_4 + X_8 + X_{11} + X_{14} + X_{16} + X_{18} + X_{19} + X_{20}$	$= 48$	Constraint on fourth-quarter demand
All variables	≥ 0	

Of course, it just was not that easy. With more than 3000 products, we didn't want to generate a set of constraints for each product, so we grouped products into 17 homogeneous groups (one such group was children's knitted shirts, size 1 to 6X; another was men's thermal underwear, all sizes) and generated a set of constraints like those above for each of the 17 groups. Another problem we had with this formulation was storage. We had taken care of the storage *cost* in the objective function, but *storage space* was limited at this mill. We finally had to establish constraints on the slack variables representing quantities in excess of current demand (quantities stored). We then constrained these variables to an upper limit representing the practical capacity of the company's finished-goods warehouse.

Some problems we had with this situation

Portfolio Selection Application

The investment manager of a state employees' credit union came to a quantitative methods seminar at the authors' university and got quite excited about a linear programming application to his responsibilities. He, like all investment managers, was expected to make decisions regarding types of investments under constraints imposed on him by law, the policies of the credit union, and his own good common sense. In this particular situation, the need to minimize risk limited the investment

Maximizing the return on a portfolio of investments using linear programming

portfolio to preferred stocks, public utility bonds, and U.S. government securities (Federal National Mortgage Association, Federal Intermediate Credit Banks, U.S. Treasury bills, U.S. Treasury notes, etc.). Here's a condensed version of the investment opportunities which were open to our investment manager at the time (he had $250,000 to invest) and the constraints under which he was expected to invest to maximize the return on the credit union's portfolio.

Investment	Symbol	Projected rate of return, percent
Milwaukee Electric Company bonds	X_1	9.1
Florida Gas bonds	X_2	10.3
Federal Intermediate Credit bonds	X_3	6.7
United Industries Preferred	X_4	8.7
Federal Home Loan Bank bonds	X_5	5.9
Consumers Utility bonds	X_6	8.8

Government securities cannot be less than 30% of the investment.
Preferred stocks are limited to at most 20% of the investment.
Public utility bonds must account for at least 40% of the investment.
No one of the three investment possibilities (preferred stocks, utility bonds, or government securities) can account for more than half the investment.

The objective function and constraints required to solve the state employees' credit union investment problem are these:

Formulation		Explanation
$.091X_1 + .103X_2 + .067X_3 + .087X_4 +$		Objective function
$.059X_5 + .088X_6$	= total return	
$X_1 + X_2 + X_3 + X_4 + X_5 + X_6$	= \$250,000	Constraint ensuring that all funds are invested
$X_3 + X_5$	≥ 75,000	Constraint on government securities
X_4	≤ 50,000	Constraint on preferred stocks
$X_1 + X_2 + X_6$	≥ 100,000	Constraint on public utility bonds (minimum)
$X_1 + X_2 + X_6$	≤ 125,000	Constraint on public utility bonds (maximum)
$X_3 + X_5$	≤ 125,000	Constraint on government securities (maximum)
All variables in the problem	≥ 0	

Notice in the state employees' credit union formulation that the 50 percent constraint on preferred stocks is *redundant*, since they are already constrained to a maximum of 20 percent by another constraint.

Some issues that gave us trouble in this situation

We've made some assumptions in the simplified version of the problem used here. First, we've eliminated a problem that could give you some trouble in the real case, that of maturity. No financial institution like this wants all its investments in either short-term securities or very long term securities; some balance must be reached. Therefore, we had to get a consensus from the union board about the maturities they wanted, specifically what percent of their portfolio (or of additions to it) they wanted coming due in each future period. At the time, it looked like we were going to generate about a thousand new constraints, given the way the conversation was going, but we finally got the group to agree on nine different maturities (such as less than 6 months, 6 to 12 months, 1 to 2 years, etc.).

Another simplifying assumption we've made here is that we have treated the new investment of $250,000 as if it were the whole portfolio; that is, we have subjected it to all the constraints the portfolio must meet. In fact, the size of this particular portfolio was over $100 million, and if a new investment or a reinvestment of $1 million were put entirely into preferred stocks, it would hardly violate our third constraint on page 330. What we finally did was to consider all funds which were to be invested or reinvested within a year—not any single investment or single day's investment—as having to meet the constraints. In that way, over time, the entire portfolio will take on the characteristics embodied in the constraints regardless of where you start from.

Ingredient Mix Application

Using linear programming in the sausage plant

For a number of years the university had run a seminar for a state association of food processors. One participant ran a meat processing plant about 100 miles southeast of Chapel Hill. He got quite interested in whether linear programming could be applied to sausage mixing. We'd seen similar applications in the journals for years but had never done one ourselves, so off we went to the sausage plant. This plant manufactured sausage and other meat products. The process involved the purchase of the required ingredients (meats of various kinds and qualities, spices, other additives, and packing material), the blending of these ingredients in specific proportions, and a mechanized packaging operation.

The company advertised several different sausage mixes—Super-Hot, Hot Special, Country Best, Superlean, and so forth—each representing a particular mix of eight very specifically described U.S. Government grades of beef and pork with appropriate spices. These grades and their characteristics were:

Grade and symbol	Percent lean	Cost/pound
Imported beef, IB	95	$1.16
Boneless chuck beef, BCB	80	.99
Boneless carcass beef, BKB	65	.97
Boneless pork butts, BPB	85	.98
Boneless pork picnics, BPP	70	.91
Boneless pork trimmings (A quality), BPTA	50	.82
Boneless pork trimmings (B quality), BPTB	30	.61
Boneless pork fat, BPF	0	.12

The company asked us to figure out for it the least expensive way to mix up a batch (its standard batch of sausage was 1000 pounds) of its Half-n-Half brand. The label on this brand guaranteed that it had a total lean content of 70 percent (that 70 percent of its total weight, exclusive of spices and additives, was either lean pork or lean beef). The label also promised that half the total weight, exclusive of spices and additives, was pork and the other half beef. The company generally always had several thousand pounds of each of the eight grades of meat on hand, so constraints on raw materials were not necessary.

The objective function and constraints necessary to solve this sausage mix problem are:

Formulation		Explanation
\$1.16 IB + \$.99 BCB + \$.97 BKB + \$.98 BPB + \$.91 BPP + \$.82 BPTA + \$.61 BPTB + \$.12 BPF	= total cost	Objective function
IB + BCB + BKB + BPB + BPP + BPTA + BPTB + BPF	= 1,000	Constraint to ensure that we get 1,000 pounds of sausage in the solution
IB + BCB + BKB	= BPB + BPP + BPTA + BPTB + BPF	Constraint ensuring that mixture is half beef, half pork
.95 IB + .80 BCB + .65 BKB + .85 BPB + .70 BPP + .50 BPTA + .30 BPTB + .0 BPF	$\geq$ 700	Constraint ensuring that 70% of the mixture will be lean

We are told the optimal solution will not work

We punched a set of equations similar to these into the Portacom portable terminal we had brought with us, and out came the answer. The plant owner was more than mildly surprised to find that our average cost per pound was about 8 cents less than his historic cost. When he looked at the ingredients in our mix, he laughed and said something like, "It won't hold together." We were sort of mystified and asked him to explain. He pointed out that our mixture had too much BPF (boneless pork fat) to stay together as a mixture. We knew no constraint had been established on this ingredient and asked him to do exactly that. Back in it went; this time we were about 5 cents less than his historic cost, and this time he accepted the mixture as salable. Since we were competing with a man who had been mixing meat products for 30 years, we felt pretty good about the whole thing.

Subsequent work with this company produced some interesting situations. We encountered, for example, the issue of "texture"; that is, one of our optimal solutions didn't "look right" according to the packing plant owner. It turned out that too much BKB (boneless carcass beef) as opposed to chuck or imported beef produced a beef weiner which just had too many visible fat particles, so once again we had to ask the company for another constraint to cover this rather nonmathematical situation.

Cotton Spinning Application

A textile application of linear programming

One of the early experiences we had with linear programming concerned a company about 50 miles from the university which produced cotton yarns used in clothing. Its financial vice-president attended an executive program in Chapel Hill, and the section on quantitative methods really caught his attention. His company had the typical problem of yarn producers called *mill balance*. In the manufacture of yarn, there are two primary operations, carding and spinning. Carding is a process which gets all the cotton fibers arranged in the same direction and spinning turns a loose mat of cotton into a strong yarn by simultaneously pulling and twisting it onto a spindle.

When our friend's mill was producing coarse yarns, the carding operation just could not keep up with spinning. (Each spindle put on so many pounds of coarse yarn per hour that the carding operation fell way behind. Unfortunately, in-process carding output is severely limited.) Alternatively, when the mill was producing fine yarns, the amount of yarn put on per hour by a spindle was so small that the carding operation could supply enough cotton for spinning in only 2 hours a day and consequently shut down a good part of the time. The situation was intolerable from labor's point of view due to the irregular work hours and from management's point of view because it could never really determine what kinds of yarn to produce to maximize contribution. To make matters worse, the mill offered for sale six different thicknesses of yarn (called *counts*); each one of these put a different quantity of yarn per hour on a spindle and had its own profit contribution.

We asked our friend to supply us with (1) the maximum capacity of the carding room in pounds of cotton per shift, (2) the pounds per hour that the six different counts of yarn would put on a spindle, (3) the contribution earned by each of the six counts of yarn, and (4) the number of spindles the company had in operation on its spinning machines (frames).

	Yarn count	Pounds/hour/spindle	Contribution/pound
Coarse	3's = X_1	.78	$.08
	6's = X_2	.61	.11
	8's = X_3	.54	.12
	10's = X_4	.42	.14
	12's = X_5	.31	.15
Fine	16's = X_6	.22	.21

Maximum capacity of carding operation = 20,000 pounds/8-hour shift
Current spindles in operation = 15,000

The objective function and constraints necessary to solve this problem are

Formulation		Explanation
$.08X_1 + $.11X_2 + $.12X_3 + $.14X_4 + $.15X_5 + $.21X_6$	= total contribution	Objective function
$X_1 + X_2 + X_3 + X_4 + X_5 + X_6$	$\leq 20{,}000$	Constraint necessary to ensure that yarn produced does not exceed carding capacity
$\dfrac{X_1}{.78} + \dfrac{X_2}{.61} + \dfrac{X_3}{.54} + \dfrac{X_4}{.42} + \dfrac{X_5}{.31} + \dfrac{X_6}{.22}$	$\leq (15{,}000)(8)$	Constraint necessary to ensure that yarn produced does not exceed spinning capacity in an 8-hour shift

When we presented our friend with the optimum solution to his problem, he was not surprised that it contained *two* counts of yarn; "After all," he said, "anyone who's worked in a cotton mill knows that you can't balance the mill with less than two counts." Our two counts, however, were just different enough from the two he had been using to increase contribution by over $1100 a week.

Using linear programming to cope with a recession

But this isn't the whole story. Shortly after we had done this work, the textile industry suffered quite a recession, our friend included. He asked us if linear programming had anything to say about running a cotton yarn mill in a recession. We took his question to mean, "What counts should I run to keep the mill running as long as possible without creating excessive inventory?" We used a variation of the objective function to maximize labor hours used, and of course the program indicated that he should run the finer counts (the spindles would work the same number of hours but put on less yarn, thus produce less finished goods inventory to carry). Again he didn't seem surprised; "Any fool knows you *fine up* when yarn isn't selling," he said. We were interested in the way in which good common sense, for years before linear programming, had found better ways to accomplish different goals.

Adding other constraints

Later applications of linear programming for this company saw us introduce marketing constraints into the program, both the kind that promise at least a given quantity to a customer and the kind that keep production of a low-selling yarn count to a minimum. Here too, we expanded the number of constraints to consider other manufacturing processes besides carding and spinning, including the way in which the yarn was packaged for sale (called *put up* in the industry), the processes of opening the cotton bales, plying yarns (putting two or more single yarns together to form a plied yarn), and—more recently—blending synthetic fibers with the cotton to produce yarns like the now ubiquitous cotton-polyester blend.

All solutions were done by hand

One final note. In the early years of linear programming application in this firm, it did not have ready access to a computer. All solutions for these kinds of problems were found by hand, one tableau at a time, just like the ones in this chapter. Some of these took as long as 12 hours to hand-compute, but considering the savings that linear programming brought to this company, this was still quite a bargain.

Glossary

1. **Simplex method**   An efficient method for solving a linear programming problem.
2. **Iterative process**   A step-by-step process following a standard pattern.
3. **Slack variable**   Variable used in linear programming to convert an inequality into an equation.
4. **Variable column**   The column of entries under a heading variable in the simplex tableau.
5. **Product-mix column**   Column containing all the variables in a solution in the simplex tableau.

6. **Quantity column** Column in a simplex tableau indicating the quantities of the variables that are in a solution.

7. **C_j column** Column in the simplex tableau which contains the profit or cost per unit for the variable in the solution.

8. **Optimum column** That column in any solution to a maximizing problem which has the largest positive value in the $C_j - Z_j$ row or which has the largest negative value in a minimizing problem.

9. **Replaced row** A row in the simplex tableau which is replaced by the variable entering the new solution.

10. **Intersectional elements** Elements which are common to both the optimum column and the rows representing variables in the solution.

11. **Z_j row** Row containing the opportunity costs of bringing one unit of a variable into the solution of a linear programming problem.

12. **$C_j - Z_j$ row** Row containing the net benefit or loss occasioned by bringing one unit of a variable into the solution of a linear programming problem.

13. **Artificial variable** Computational device used in linear programming to achieve an initial solution to the problem.

14. **Dual** A linear programming problem which is one part of a pair of associated linear programming problems called the primal and the dual.

15. **Primal** A linear programming problem which is one part of a pair of associated linear programming problems called the primal and the dual.

16. **Imputed value** Values of the inputs to a process obtained by valuing the output of that process.

17. **Principle of complementary slackness** Principle relating the use of resources by a variable in a linear programming problem with the profit or value generated by that variable.

18. **Infeasibility** The condition in linear programming when there is no feasible solution to the problem.

19. **Unboundedness** The condition in linear programming where the objective function is not constrained.

20. **Degeneracy** A condition sometimes encountered in solving a linear programming problem where there is a tie in the theta calculations.

21. **Right-hand-side ranging** Procedure used to determine the range over which shadow prices hold.

Exercises

Twenty problems in this section call for a linear programming formulation, the interpretation of an answer, or both. Only three ask for a hand-computed solution. Conceptual skills in formulation and interpretation are extensively reinforced here.

10-1. The Raleigh Fire Department must provide fire protection for the city on a 24-hour basis. Based on past experience with fires, the chief feels that at least the following number of fire fighters must be on duty during the given time periods:

0:01–4:00	40
4:01–8:00	70
8:01–12:00	200
12:01–16:00	120
16:01–20:00	300
20:01–24:00	150

There are 10 fire stations in the city, with each station having no more than 30 people on duty at any given time. The fire fighters report at 4-hour intervals for 8-hour shifts, beginning at 24:00. Each station must have at least three people on duty at all times. Set up the objective function and constraints to determine the minimum number reporting at each of the six reporting times if the total number of employees is to be held to a minimum.

10-2. Carolina Health Services, Inc., is a clinic specializing in four types of patient care: cosmetic surgery, dermatology, orthopedic surgery, and neurosurgery. It has been determined from past records that a patient in each of these specialities contributes to the profit of the clinic as follows: cosmetic, $200; dermatology, $150; orthopedic, $150; and neurosurgery, $250. The physicians are convinced that patients are not being processed in an optimal manner. The clinic has contracted with you to provide a weekly patient processing system. You have been able to determine the following time requirements and limitations:

	Hours required/patient				
Specialty	Lab	X-ray	Therapy	Surgery	Physicians
Cosmetic	5	2	1	4	10
Dermatology	5	8	10	8	14
Orthopedic	2	1	0	16	8
Neurosurgery	4	5	8	10	12
Total hours available per week with present staff and facilities	200	140	110	240	320

The physicians have access to as many of each type of patient as they wish. Additionally, they have limited their cosmetic and orthopedic practice to a combined total of no more than 120 hours a week. Set up the objective function and constraints to find the optimum patient mix on a weekly basis.

10-3. Metropolitan Parcel Service is studying the allocation of trucks on its four different delivery routes for this year. The following table indicates the number of parcels estimated to be delivered on each route and the incomes received from delivery.

Route	Number of parcels (000)	Income/parcel
1	250	$1.20
2	175	2.00
3	360	1.50
4	425	.90

Metropolitan has three types of trucks: light duty, medium duty, and tandem axle. The following table shows the number of parcels (in thousands) which can be accommodated in a year's time by a truck allocated to each of the routes; it also shows the maximum number of each truck type which can be made available for use on all routes.

Route	Type of truck		
	Light	Medium	Tandem axle
1	15	24	96
2	18	36	78
3	12	31	84
4	16	29	84
Total trucks available	21	17	8

The annual operating cost for a truck (thousands of dollars) allocated to each route is as follows:

Route	Type of truck		
	Light	Medium	Tandem
1	$18	$18	$21
2	24	22	24
3	20	19	26
4	24	21	23

Set up the objective function and constraints which will find the maximum total annual profit solution to the trunk allocation.

10-4. A producer of dolomitic limestone for agricultural use has three lime quarries which supply five regional warehouses. The inventory position of each of the quarries this week follows:

Quarry	Tons of lime on hand
1	200
2	100
3	150

Transportation costs per ton from each quarry to each of the regional warehouses are shown in the following table:

Quarries	Cost per ton to warehouse				
	1	2	3	4	5
1	$5	$1	$6	$3	$1
2	2	3	4	5	4
3	4	2	3	2	3

The warehouses need lime for next week in the following quantities:

Warehouse 1:	80 tons
Warehouse 2:	90 tons
Warehouse 3:	100 tons
Warehouse 4:	70 tons
Warehouse 5:	60 tons

Set up the objective function and constraints that will solve for the shipping schedule for next week to minimize the total cost of satisfying the requirements of each of the five warehouses.

10-5. During the coming week a factory can manufacture combinations of the following products:

Product	Contribution per unit
X_1	$3
X_2	4
X_3	5
X_4	2
X_5	6

The manufacturing facilities of the firm are divided into four departments through which the products may or may not have to pass, depending on individual manufacturing requirements. Individual requirements for each product in terms of hours and the total number of available hours in each department are given below:

Product	Hours per unit			
	Dept. 1	Dept. 2	Dept. 3	Dept. 4
X_1	3	8	2	6
X_2	4	3	1	0
X_3	2	2	0	2
X_4	2	1	3	4
X_5	5	4	4	3
Total hours available	700	600	400	900

In addition to the above manufacturing restrictions on output, the following list represents the maximum sales anticipated for each of the five products during the coming week. No production is scheduled for inventory.

X_1:	100 units
X_2:	50 units
X_3:	90 units
X_4:	70 units
X_5:	30 units

Each of the five products is made from five raw materials, A, B, C, D, and E. The following table illustrates the per-unit requirements in pounds for each product and the total availability of each raw material for the coming week:

Product	Pounds per unit				
	A	B	C	D	E
X_1	4	2	0	1	3
X_2	7	4	4	0	4
X_3	6	2	5	7	0
X_4	1	1	6	4	2
X_5	3	0	2	3	4
Total pounds available	1,000	900	300	400	1,600

If the company desires to maximize the contributions of the products to overhead and profit, what should the objective function and constraints be for this problem?

10-6. The Stevens Fertilizer Company markets two types of fertilizer which are manufactured in two departments. Type A contributes $3, and type B contributes $4 per ton.

Department	Hours/ton		Maximum hours worked per week
	Type A	Type B	
1	2	3	40
2	3	3	75

To which department would you give priority for plant expansion funds?

10-7. From a primal problem we know that one unit of X_1, which contributes $6, requires 2 hours in department A and 1 hour in department B. One unit of X_2 contributes $7 and requires 1 hour in department A and 3 hours in department B. Capacity operation for both departments is currently 40 hours. Set up a dual and indicate the worth to the company of another productive hour in each department.

10-8. Lisa's Craft Shoppe manufactures two products in two departments. Product X_1 contributes $6 and takes 6 hours in department 1 and 6 hours in department 2. Product X_2 contributes $14 and takes 8 hours in department 1 and 12 hours in department 2. Department 1 has a capacity of 38 hours, and department 2 has a capacity of 42 hours. Indicate the maximum production level in units and the maximum dollar contribution production level, and show the dollar contribution difference between the two.

10-9. The Jeff Moore Corporation requires trained salespeople to market its construction equipment; sales of this equipment tend to be seasonal. Jeff estimates the following minimum numbers of salespeople during each month of the year (constant for all years).

Month	Minimum salespeople required
January	30
February	20
March	40
April	90
May	110
June	120
July	120
August	100
September	60
October	20
November	20
December	10

After hiring a salesperson, Jeff first sends him or her to a 4-month training school; following his training, the salespeople begin active selling. Although the members of Jeff's sales force receive good salaries, the work is quite strenuous, and Jeff has noted that each month about 10 percent of the active people quit the company. Set up the linear programming objective function and constraints which will allow Jeff to determine the numbers of prospective salespeople who must be admitted into the training program each month for the next 12 months. Jeff wants to hire the least number of new members possible while still maintaining the minimum sales force requirement projected over the entire duration of each month. At the beginning of January, the sales force consists of 50 active salespeople and 90 trainees (30 of whom will become active the first of March and 60 of whom will become active the first of April).

10-10. The Queen City Naval Reserve Unit has been notified that they will have their annual inspection in a month. The skipper of the unit would like to receive as high an overall grading for his unit as possible. He knows that his overall grade will be based on four categories: close order drilling, seamanship, mechanics, and electronics. These categories carry grading weights of 2, 3, 4, and 5, respectively. The grades assigned to these categories are from 0 to 4. So, for example, if the grades were: 1 for drilling, 4 for seamanship, 3 for mechanics, and 0 for electronics, the overall grade would be:

$$\frac{(1)(2) + (4)(3) + (3)(4) + (0)(5)}{2 + 3 + 4 + 5} = \frac{26}{14} = 1.86$$

The skipper has available 30 hours in which to prepare for the inspection, and he estimates that grades for each category could be expected by devoting hours of preparation as follows:

Skipper's Estimate of Preparation-Grade Relationship

Category	Hours of preparation	Grade expected
Close order drilling	0	1
(weight = 2)	2	2
	4	3
	6	4
Seamanship	0	0
(weight = 3)	1	1
	2	2
	3	3
	4	4
Mechanics	0	2
(weight = 4)	8	3
	16	4
Electronics	0	0
(weight = 5)	9	1
	18	2
	27	3
	—	Grade of 4 is not possible.

Set up the linear programming objective function and constraints which will allow the skipper to solve for the number of hours he should devote to each category so as to maximize the expected overall grade for his unit.

10-11. The Township Machine Company is planning to add a new product line and wishes to hire some experienced machinists. The local union hall has advised Township that machinists are categorized in one of three skill levels: expert, normal, and apprentice. An *expert* machinist has at least 10 years of experience and must exhibit a competence to produce 20 pieces a day in the job Township wants to fill. A *normal* machinist must have 6 years of experience and should produce 16 pieces a day. An *apprentice* machinist must have at least a year of experience and should produce 12 pieces a day. The Township Company's union contract calls for wage scales of $40, $30, and $20 per day for the three skill levels. Currently, there are at most 2 expert machinists, 7 normal machinists, and 9 apprentice machinists available for hire. Township has budgeted $2000 a week (5-day week) for machinists' salaries for the manufacture of their new product. Township would like to hire a complement of new workers which will yield them the highest output rate, but would like to keep both the union and present employees happy by ensuring that the total experience of the workers hired represents a seniority level of at least 60 worker-years. Formulate the linear programming objective function and constraints which will solve for the number of machinists of each category that Township should hire to maximize their expected output rate.

10-12. The parents of schoolchildren in Centerville would like to establish racially balanced schools. In order to do this, they have decided to bus some students to other areas of the city. The city has four schools located in areas 2, 5, 7, and 8 of the city, and the schoolchildren reside in one of eight areas. All children residing in a given area who are assigned to the school in that area may walk to school. The following table reflects the numbers of whites and blacks living in each area and the distance from each area to each of the schools.

	Distance to school (miles)				No. of blacks in area	No. of whites in area
Area	2	5	7	8		
1	10	20	30	40	90	30
2	0	30	40	30	110	20
3	20	10	20	30	80	40
4	10	20	30	20	70	70
5	30	0	10	20	40	100
6	20	10	20	10	30	120
7	40	10	0	10	10	130
8	30	20	10	0	10	150
				Total	440	660

Although the Centerville citizens would ideally like to have 40 percent of each school made up of black students, this could be a very expensive plan. They have, therefore, set as a goal that the percentage of blacks in each school be no less than 30 percent and no more than 50 percent. Set up the linear programming objective function and constraints which will allow Centerville to assign their students to schools so that the total number of student miles traveled by bus is a minimum. Each school has a capacity of 300 students.

10-13. The Acme Company has budgeted $250,000 for the development of new products. The possible development plans, expected cost if adopted in the fall, expected yields, and degree of risk (rated from 0 to 10) are as follows:

Plan	Expected cost	Expected yield	Degree of risk
A	$100,000	.20	8
B	50,000	.10	4
C	50,000	.15	10
D	150,000	.10	0

Acme can accept an entire plan at its full cost or it may accept a partial (fractional) plan and still expect a constant yield proportionate to the level of expenditure on the plan. However, the company has decided to limit its total weighted risk (degree of risk times budgeted amount) to 1 million units; i.e., an adopted plan for a $10,000 expenditure with a degree of risk of 7 would be 70,000 risk units. Formulate the linear programming objective function and constraints which will allow Acme to determine the development plan which will net the highest yield.

10-14. The Overseas Shipping Company has just docked an empty ship in a remote port prior to its heading for home. The captain will load some cargo to bring back. This will be his only trip from that port, so he wishes to load that combination of commodities which will yield the largest profit. His ship has three holds (forward, center, and aft), and their capacity limits are:

Hold	Tons	Cubic feet
Forward	2,000	100,000
Center	3,200	140,000
Aft	1,900	95,000

The following list represents the possible commodities which can be taken on in any mix:

Commodity	Amount in tons available	Cubic-foot vol. per ton	Profit per ton
A	7,000	60	$10
B	6,500	50	12
C	4,000	25	8

In order to preserve the trim of the ship, the weight in each hold must be proportional to its weight capacity.

Formulate the objective function and constraints for solving this problem with linear programming.

10-15. Billy Frank Haywood is the bartender at Oceanside Motel. When he checked the supply cabinet this afternoon, it contained these items:

Gin	120 oz
Bourbon	108 oz
Vermouth	60 oz
Scotch	72 oz
Vodka	48 oz

His cabinet also contained cherries, orange slices, lemons, limes, onions, and juices as well as other garnishes which he might need. Billy offers a limited bar menu consisting of six mixed drinks, which he premixes and places on trays. He then circulates through the crowd to sell them. His current bar menu is:

Scotch on the rocks	2 oz scotch
Martini	1.5 oz gin
	.25 oz vermouth
Atomic bomb	1.5 oz scotch
	1.5 oz vodka
Snowdrift	2 oz bourbon
Kentucky colonel	2 oz bourbon
	1 oz vermouth
Steamroller	2 oz gin
	1 oz vodka
	.5 oz scotch

Each drink sells for $2.50 and Billy can sell as many drinks of each kind as he can premix. What should he mix this evening?

10-16. Sailcraft, Inc., is a builder of sailboats in New Bern, North Carolina. The company currently offers three models: the Adventurer (32 ft), the Explorer (42 ft), and the World Cruiser (50 ft). There is currently a large backlog of orders. The production process is in three steps; the number of worker-days required for each step for the three models is

	Forming (fiber glass)	Wood trim (hull and cabin)	Outfitting (rigging and sails)
Adventurer	60	100	80
Explorer	100	240	100
Cruiser	200	360	160

Past profits lead to these expectations of profit: Adventurer, $7500; Explorer, $15,000; World Cruiser, $30,000. Sailcraft currently employs 15 persons in fiber glass forming, 30 in woodworking, and 15 in outfitting; the average worker is on the job 200 working days a year. With this capacity, determine Sailcraft's optimum product mix.

10-17. Goober Gallery markets dry-roasted nut mixes. Ingredients in an 8 oz bag of its four best-selling nut mixes and current prices are as follows:

Cocktail Special, $3	2 oz cashews
	2 oz peanuts
	1 oz Brazils
	1 oz filberts
	1 oz pecans
	1 oz almonds
Deluxe Mix, $3.50	3 oz cashews
	2 oz Brazils
	2 oz pecans
	1 oz almonds
Royal Mix, $4	3 oz cashews
	3 oz pecans
	2 oz filberts
Party Special, $3.50	4 oz pecans
	4 oz peanuts

Prices of ingredients and current stocks of bulk nuts are

	Price per pound	Pounds in stock
Cashews	$2.60	300
Peanuts	1.25	Unlimited
Brazils	2.00	100
Filberts	3.00	75
Almonds	3.50	200
Pecans	2.75	200

The Gallery can't sell more than 20 bags of Royal Mix in the current period or more than 50 bags of the Cocktail Special. Recommend the best product mix to maximize both profit and the number of bags sold.

10-18. North Carolina State Bank is doing funds planning for next year. The bank has essentially five different funds uses, each with a different rate of return as follows:

Signature loans (unsecured)	14%
Installment loans on vehicles (secured with a lien on the vehicle)	11%
Home improvement loans (secured with a second deed of trust)	10%
Miscellaneous installment loans (secured with liens)	12%
U.S. government securities	8%

State banking regulations impose these constraints on North Carolina State Bank's investments:

1. Signature loans cannot exceed 10 percent of total loans.

2. Home improvement loans cannot exceed 50 percent of total secured loans.

3. Signature loans may not exceed the amount invested in U.S. government securities.

4. Investment in U.S. government securities may not exceed 40 percent of total money invested.

State Bank has $25 million to invest next year and wishes to maximize the return on its investment portfolio consistent with banking regulations. Set up the objective function and constraints necessary to solve this problem.

10-19. Treasure Cove is a resort land development near Myrtle Beach, South Carolina. The primary market for lots is within 200 miles of Myrtle Beach, an area served by four radio stations. The developers have decided to limit their advertising campaign to radio spots, since television appears much too expensive for a venture this size. The William Carmichael Agency of Columbia, South Carolina, has been asked to put together a 1-month radio promotional campaign; they, in turn, have retained you as a consultant to help them apportion the client's advertising budget —$5000 in this case—among the four stations. Here are data on cost per spot, availability of spots, and the National Radio Association's listener count per station.

	Cost/30-second spot	Maximum no. of spots available next month	NRA listener count
WFRA (Columbia, S.C.)	$60	34	32,000
WSMB (Charleston, S.C.)	74	29	45,000
WKYT (Florence, S.C.)	46	44	14,000
WLAW (Myrtle Beach, S.C.)	52	30	20,000

The Carmichael Agency wants an allocation of the budget to achieve the highest possible listener count (defined as listeners per 30-second spot) for next month consistent with the client's budget. Set up the objective function and constraints to solve this problem.

10-20. Southland Petroleum operates a refinery in Galveston, Texas, which produces four petroleum products from crude. Refinery and crude oil data are as follows:

Source of crude	Cost per barrel*	Availability (barrels/day)	Density (lb/gallon)	Sulfur content (ounces/barrel)
Texas	$16	12,000	6.1	.05
Pennsylvania	11	18,000	6.9	.03
Offshore	13	15,000	7.1	.04

* A barrel is 55 gallons.

	Refinery yields (percent by volume)				
Source of crude	Gasoline	Diesel	Fuel oil	Kerosene	Residual
Texas	35	15	25	15	10
Pennsylvania	50	15	10	20	5
Offshore	20	25	30	15	10
Selling price	$.51/gal	$.48/gal	$.45/gal	$.43/gal	$.38/gal
Sulfur restriction (ounces/gallon)	.0003	.0006	.0007	.0009	.0007

You may assume that each gallon of refined output from a given source of crude has the same proportional sulfur content as the crude did. Refining costs are $4 a barrel and the total capacity of the refinery is 150,000 gallons of crude a day. Formulate the objective function and constraints necessary to produce the optimum mix of the three crude sources. You may assume that there are no marketing constraints on the five finished products refined.

10-21. Here are the objective function, constraints, and final simplex tableau for a linear programming product-mix problem:

Objective function: $2X_1 + $5X_2 + $8X_3 + $0S_1 + $0S_2 + $0S_3$

Constraints: $6X_1 + 8X_2 + 4X_3 \leqslant 96$
$2X_1 + 1X_2 + 2X_3 \leqslant 40$
$5X_1 + 3X_2 + 2X_3 \leqslant 60$

C_j			$2	$5	$8	$0	$0	$0
	Product mix	Quantity	X_1	X_2	X_3	S_1	S_2	S_3
$5	X_2	$^8/_3$	$^1/_3$	1	0	$^1/_6$	$-^1/_3$	0
$8	X_3	$18^2/_3$	$^5/_6$	0	1	$-^1/_{12}$	$^2/_3$	0
$0	S_3	$14^2/_3$	$^7/_3$	0	0	$-^1/_3$	$-^1/_3$	1
	Z_j		$^{200}/_3$	$5	$8	$^1/_6$	$^{11}/_3$	$0
	$C_j - Z_j$		$-^{194}/_3$	$0	$0	$-^1/_6$	$-^{11}/_3$	$0

a. Comment on the value to the company of adding additional capacity in each of the three departments.

b. Determine the range over which the shadow prices for the slack variables will hold true.

c. Determine the range over which the coefficients of X_2 and X_3 can vary without affecting the optimal solution.

d. What would the contribution per unit of X_1 have to be for it to be in the optimal solution?

e. What are the marketing implications of the answers you have found for parts c and d above?

10-22. From a primal problem we know that a single unit of product 1 contributing $7 requires 3 units of input 1 (an ingredient) and 2 hours of labor. A single unit of output 2, contributing $5, requires 1 unit of input 1 and 1 hour of labor. Capacity of inputs is currently 48 units and there are 40 hours of labor. Set up the dual to this problem and indicate the value to this firm of another unit of input 1 and another labor hour.

10-23. Here are the objective function, constraints, and final simplex tableau for a linear programming–product-mix problem involving four products and three departments:

Objective function: $2X_1 + $4X_2 + $1X_3 + $1X_4 + $0S_1 + $0S_2 + $0S_3$

Constraints: $X_1 + 3X_2 \qquad + X_4 \leqslant 4$
$2X_1 + X_2 \qquad\qquad \leqslant 3$
$X_2 + 4X_3 + X_4 \leqslant 3$

C_j			$2	$4	$1	$1	$0	$0	$0
	Product mix	Quantity	X_1	X_2	X_3	X_4	S_1	S_2	S_3
4	X_2	1	0	1	0	$2/5$	$2/5$	$-1/5$	0
2	X_1	1	1	0	0	$-1/5$	$-1/5$	$3/5$	0
1	X_3	$1/2$	0	0	1	$3/20$	$-1/10$	$1/20$	$1/3$
	Z_j	$6\frac{1}{2}$	$2	$4	$1	$27/20$	$22/20$	$9/20$	$1/3$
	$C_j - Z_j$		$0	$0	$0	$-7/20$	$-22/20$	$-9/20$	$-1/3$

a. Comment on the value to this company of adding additional capacity in each of its three departments.

b. Determine the range over which each of the shadow prices for the slack variables will hold true.

c. Determine the range over which the coefficients of X_1, X_2, and X_3 can vary without affecting the optimal solution.

d. What would the contribution of X_4 have to be for it to be in the optimal solution?

e. What are the marketing implications of the answers you have found for parts c and d above?

Bibliography

Daellenbach, H. G., and **E. J. Bell:** *User's Guide to Linear Programming* (Englewood Cliffs, N.J.: Prentice-Hall, Inc., 1970).

Driebeek, N. J.: *Applied Linear Programming* (Reading, Mass.: Addison-Wesley Publishing Company, Inc., 1969).

Hughes, A. J., and **D. E. Grawoig:** *Linear Programming: An Emphasis on Decision Making* (Reading, Mass.: Addison-Wesley Publishing Company, Inc. 1973).

Levin, Richard I., and **R. P. Lamone:** *Linear Programming for Management Decisions* (Homewood, Ill.: Richard D. Irwin, Inc., 1969).

Naylor, T. H., E. T. Byrne, and **J. M. Vernon:** *Introduction to Linear Programming* (Belmont, Calif.: Wadsworth Publishing Company, Inc., 1971).

Strum, J. E.: *Introduction to Linear Programming* (San Francisco: Holden-Day, Inc., Publisher, 1972).

Thompson, G. E.: *Linear Programming* (New York: The Macmillan Company, 1971).

Special-purpose
algorithms

11

Computational procedures more efficient than the simplex

Some types of linear programming problems can be solved by using more efficient computational procedures than the simplex method. One of the most useful of these special-purpose algorithms is the *transportation method* examined in this chapter. The *assignment problem,* a special case of the more general transportation problem, will also be treated.

Transportation problem

The *transportation problem* is concerned with selecting routes between manufacturing plants and distribution warehouses or between regional distribution warehouses and local distribution outlets. The *assignment* problem, on the other hand, involves assigning employees to tasks, salespersons to territories, contracts to bidders, or jobs to plants. In applying the transportation method and the assignment method, management is searching for a distribution route or an assignment which will optimize some objective; this can be the minimization of total transportation cost, the maximization of profit, or the minimization of total time involved.

Assignment problem

1. The Transportation Method (Demand Equals Supply)

Sources and destinations

As its name implies, the transportation method was first formulated as a special procedure for finding the minimum cost program for distributing homogeneous units of a product from several points of supply *(sources)* to a number of points of demand *(destinations)*. For example, a manufacturer may have 5 plants (sources) and 20 warehouses (destinations), all located at different geographical points. For a specified time period, each source has a given capacity and each destination has a given requirement. Knowing the costs of shipping the product from each source to each destination, the objective is to schedule shipments from sources to destinations in such a way as to minimize the total transportation cost.

The earliest formulation of this basic transportation problem was stated by F. L. Hitchcock in 1941 and later expanded by T. C. Koopmans. The *linear pro-*

gramming formulation was first given by G. B. Dantzig. In 1953, W. W. Cooper and A. Charnes developed the *stepping-stone* method, a special-purpose algorithm for solving the transportation problem. Subsequent improvements led to the computationally easier *modified-distribution* (MODI) method in 1955.

Let us consider the case of the Bass Gravel Company, which has received a contract to supply gravel for three new road projects located in the towns of Greenville, Fountain, and Ayden. Construction engineers have estimated the required amounts of gravel which will be needed at three road construction projects:

Project	Location	Weekly requirement, truckloads
A	Greenville	72
B	Fountain	102
C	Ayden	41
Total		215

The Bass Company has three gravel plants located in the towns of Kinston, Wilson, and Bethel. The gravel required for the construction projects can be supplied by these three plants. Bass's chief dispatcher has calculated the amounts of gravel which can be supplied by each plant:

Plant	Location	Amount available/week, truckloads
W	Kinston	56
X	Wilson	82
Y	Bethel	77
Total available		215

At this point we see that the total amount available is exactly equal to the total amount required. When total supply is equal to total demand, a *balanced condition* is said to exist. Although the balanced case is very unlikely in actual practice, it will enable us to focus on the basic ideas underlying the transportation method. The *unbalanced case,* where supply and demand are unequal, will be discussed later in the chapter.

The company has computed the delivery costs from each plant to each project site. As in the linear programming problems discussed in previous chapters, we assume that the variables in the problem must be linearly related. Thus, in this case, delivery costs per truckload between each plant and project site vary directly with the quantity distributed. These costs are shown in Table 11-1.

In Figure 11-1, we have illustrated this problem graphically. The circles represent the projects and the rectangles represent the gravel pits. Delivery costs per truckload are shown on the arrows which connect each plant with each road construction project.

Given the amounts required at each project and the amounts available at each plant, the company's problem is to schedule shipments from each plant to

Table 11-1 Delivery Costs

	Cost per truckload		
From	To project A	To project B	To project C
Plant W	$ 4	$ 8	$ 8
Plant X	16	24	16
Plant Y	8	16	24

each project in such a manner as to minimize the total transportation cost within the constraints imposed by plant capacities and project requirements. At this point we have all the information necessary to solve Bass's problem.

Step 1: Set Up the Transportation Table

Setting up the transportation table   The transportation table serves the same basic purpose as the simplex table; it provides a framework for presenting all the relevant data in a concise manner and facilitates the search for progressively better solutions. In Figure 11-2 the standard format for the transportation table has been divided into *five* lettered sections—A, B, C, D, and E—each of which will be explained in detail.

Section A   In this part we list the sources of supply, plants W, X, and Y. Each row represents a plant in the table.

Section B   The capacity for each plant is shown in section B. Thus we can think of the rows of the table as representing the capacity constraints. These are also re-

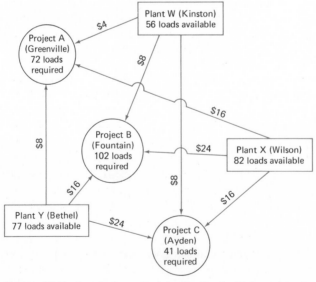

Figure 11-1 Gravel plants, road construction projects, and transportation costs for Bass Gravel Company.

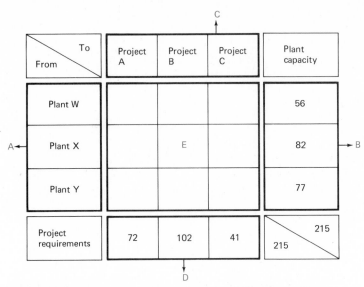

Figure 11-2 Transportation table for Bass Gravel Company problem.

ferred to as the *rim requirements* for the rows. For example, the rim requirement in the first row means that plant W can supply no more than 56 truckloads per week.

Section C The destination points are listed in this section, road construction projects A, B, and C. Each project represents a column in the table.

Section D The requirements for each project are placed in this part. The columns, then, represent the project constraints, or rim requirements, for the columns. For example, the rim requirement for column 1 signifies that project A requires exactly 72 truckloads per week. The total number of rim requirements in our problem is six, three for the rows and three for the columns.

Section E In this section are nine squares, or cells, representing the alternative source-to-destination assignments that could be made. For example, the 56 truckloads per week available at plant W may be used, in whole or in part, to fulfill the requirements of any of the three projects. Any combination of shipments from plant W would be acceptable as long as the total equaled exactly 56 truckloads. Similarly, the 72 truckloads required at project A may be met by any combination of shipments from the various plants as long as the total equals 72.

To complete the table, it will be helpful to add to each square of section E an identification symbol and a delivery cost figure. This has been done in Figure 11-3.

Let us examine square WA located in the upper left-hand corner, repeated in Figure 11-4.

> **Identification symbol and delivery cost**

1. The WA in the upper left-hand corner of the square is the identification symbol. This square represents the combination "plant W to project A" and therefore is identified as square WA.

To From	Project A	Project B	Project C	Plant capacity
Plant W	WA 4 (X_1)	WB 8 (X_2)	WC 8 (X_3)	56
Plant X	XA 16 (X_4)	XB 24 (X_5)	XC 16 (X_6)	82
Plant Y	YA 8 (X_7)	YB 16 (X_8)	YC 24 (X_9)	77
Project requirements	72	102	41	215 215

Figure 11-3 Transportation table with squares identified and delivery costs added.

2. The 4 in the upper right-hand corner is the transportation cost per truckload between plant W and project A. The costs in each subsquare were obtained from Table 11-1.

3. (X_1) represents the number of truckloads shipped from Bass plant W to project A. In other words, all X's in Figure 11-3 denote the number of shipments between each plant and each project. The value of each X will be a positive whole number or zero. If in a particular solution the X value is missing for a square, this means that no quantity is shipped between the plant and project in question.

Step 2: Develop an Initial Solution

Developing an initial solution

Now that the data have been arranged in table form, the next step is to find a solution to the problem in order to provide a starting point leading to the procedure for developing improved solutions. Thus the initial solution in the transportation method serves the same purpose as the initial solution in the simplex method.

Northwest corner rule

A systematic and logical procedure known as the *northwest corner rule* has been developed for setting up the initial solution. Although it does not *have* to be used, this rule offers the advantage of being systematic rather than trial and error. Having a logical procedure is important when using a computer, and for small problems it permits the computations to be delegated to clerical personnel. The northwest corner rule may be stated as follows:

1. Starting at the upper left-hand corner (the northwest corner) of the table, the supply available at each row must be exhausted before moving down to the

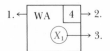

Figure 11-4 Square WA.

To From	Project A	Project B	Project C	Plant capacity
Plant W	WA 4 (56)	WB 8	WC 8	56
Plant X	XA 16 (16)	XB 24 (66)	XC 16	82
Plant Y	YA 8	YB 16 (36)	YC 24 (41)	77
Project requirements	72	102	41	215 215

Figure 11-5 The initial solution to the Bass Gravel Company problem.

next row, and the rim requirement of any column must be exhausted before moving to the right to the next column.

2. Check to see that *all* rim requirements have been satisfied.

The results of this procedure are shown in Figure 11-5.

An explanation of each assignment made in the initial solution shown in Figure 11-5 is made below:

Square WA   Beginning in the upper left-hand corner, we compared the quantity available at plant W (56) with the quantity required at project A (72). Exhausting the supply at plant W, 56 truckloads are shipped to project A. This leaves project A short 16 truckloads. Move down to the second row in the same column to square XA.

Square XA   Plant X has 82 truckloads available. Since project A is 16 short, Bass plant X will ship 16 of its 82 available truckloads to project A. The requirements for project A have now been met. Since plant X has 66 truckloads remaining, we move to the right to the next column to square XB.

Initial solution assignment explained

Square XB   Project B needs 102 truckloads. The remaining 66 truckloads from plant X will then be shipped to project B, leaving project B short 36 truckloads. As the amount available at plant X has been exhausted, we move vertically down to the next row to square YB.

Square YB   Plant Y has 77 truckloads available. Project B needs 36 more truckloads to fully satisfy its requirements. Hence plant Y will ship 36 of its 77 available truckloads to project B. We now move to the right to the next column to square YC.

Square YC   Plant Y has 41 truckloads remaining, which are shipped to project C, requiring 41 truckloads. The schedule of shipments is now complete.

Table 11-2 Initial Solution Illustrated

From plant	To project	Quantity, truckloads/week
W	A	56
X	A	16
X	B	66
Y	B	36
Y	C	41
Total		215

The initial solution, then, includes the five source-destination combinations shown in Table 11-2. The squares in Figure 11-5 where no circled values appear are referred to as *unused squares;* that is, no quantity is shipped between the two points represented by an unused square. These squares therefore are not in the initial solution.

We must now determine the cost of this first solution for the Bass Gravel Co. To do this we multiply the quantities shipped between each source-destination combination in the solution by the respective unit cost. The results are shown in Table 11-3.

Initial solution is feasible

Before proceeding to the next step, several points should be made. The initial solution is a feasible one as all rim requirements have been met; that is, the sum of each row or column is equal to its rim requirement. Initial solutions obtained by using the northwest corner rule can always be recognized by their stairstep appearance, as shown by the path described in Figure 11-5.

Finally, for any solution, the number of used squares must be equal to the total number of rim requirements minus 1. In our first solution, there are 5 used squares or source-destination combinations. The total rim requirements are 6, 1 for each plant (row) and project (column). Thus

The initial solution is not degenerate

Used squares = total rim requirements − 1

$$5 = 6 - 1$$

When *any* solution does not conform to the above rule, a condition referred to as *degeneracy* is said to exist. The procedure for handling a degenerate solution will

Table 11-3 Total Cost of Initial Solution

Source-destination combination	Quantity shipped	×	Unit cost	=	Total cost
WA	56		$ 4		$ 224
XA	16		16		256
XB	66		24		1,584
YB	36		16		576
YC	41		24		984
Total					$3,624

be discussed in a later section. The important point here is that each solution should be tested for degeneracy; that is, the number of used squares must be equal to the total rim requirements minus 1.

Step 3: Test the Solution for Improvement

Having obtained a first solution to the Bass Gravel Co. problem, the next step is to determine whether this solution is the best, or least-cost, solution. The evaluation procedure involves the examination of each unused square in the table to see whether it is more desirable to move a shipment into one of them. The purpose of this evaluation is to determine whether a better schedule of shipments from plants to projects can be developed. Two alternative procedures for evaluating the unused squares will be presented, the *stepping-stone* and *MODI* methods. The stepping-stone method (presented here) is the basis for the MODI method (presented later in the chapter) and provides a good introduction to it.

Testing the initial solution for improvement

Stepping-stone method

    The used squares, those containing circled values, are said to be *in solution* and will be referred to as *stone squares*. In applying the stepping-stone method, we ask this question: "What would happen if *one* truckload of gravel were tentatively shipped or assigned to an unused square?" If this tentative assignment results in a favorable effect (reduces cost), the unused square evaluated then becomes a possible candidate for entering the next solution. This is analogous to the examination of the $C_j - Z_j$ row of the simplex method to determine which variable should be brought into the mix.

Stone squares

    Let us now apply this reasoning to our present problem. In Figure 11-5 we note the square WB is unused. Suppose that we assign 1 truckload to square WB, that is, ship 1 truckload from plant W to project B. In order to make this assignment and still satisfy the capacity restriction (rim requirement) for plant W, we must subtract from square WA 1 truckload so that the total shipments from plant W do not exceed 56. However, if we subtract 1 truckload from square WA, we must then add 1 truckload to square XA in order to meet the rim requirement for project A. Adding 1 truckload to square XA means that we must subtract 1 truckload from square XB in order to satisfy the rim requirement for that row (plant X). Finally, the truckload subtracted from square XB still enables project B requirements to total 102; one truckload had been tentatively added to square WB at the start of the evaluation. The evaluation is now back where it started. These changes in the shipping program can be much more readily seen in Figure 11-6.

    Note that the net change for any row or column is zero; wherever 1 truckload was added to a square, another square was decreased by the same amount.

    The question we now ask is: "What effect will the assignment of one truckload to the unused square WB have on Bass's total cost?" Looking at the path described in evaluating square WB (Figure 11-6), we see that shipping 1 truckload from plant X to project B results in an increase of $8 in distribution costs. The $8 cost per truckload between the two points is given in the upper right-hand corner of square WB. A similar increase from plant X to project A results in an additional cost of $16 (square XA). Likewise, the decrease of 1 truckload between plant W and project A

To From	Project A		Project B		Project C		Plant capacity
Plant W	WA	4	WB	8	WC	8	56
	(56)			+			
Plant X	XA	16	XB	24	XC	16	82
	(16) +		(66)				
Plant Y	YA	8	YB	16	YC	24	77
			(36)		(41)		
Project requirements	72		102		41		215
						215	

Figure 11-6 Adjustment required in evaluating square WB.

Computing the improvement index

reduces total costs by $4 (square WA). In addition, the decrease of 1 truckload between plant X and project B results in a reduction of $24 (square XB). The *net change in costs,* referred to as the *improvement index,* is computed as follows:

Addition to cost:	From plant W to project B	$ 8	
	From plant X to project A	16	$24

Reduction in cost:	From plant W to project A	$ 4	
	From plant X to project B	24	28
			−$4

The same answer can be obtained by following the path used directly and resorting to a sort of shorthand, as follows:

Improvement index for square WB = WB − WA + XA − XB

Now substituting the cost per truckload for each source-destination combination in the above equation, we have

Improvement index for square WB = $8 − $4 + $16 − $24 = − $4

The − $4 means that for *every* truckload shipped from plant W to project B, total transportation costs would be reduced by $4. Because this is true, it would be advantageous to use this route if this were the only choice available. However, the evaluation of other unused squares in our table might bring about an *even greater* reduction. The task remaining then is to evaluate all remaining unused squares.

In *evaluating any unused square,* the following procedure is used:

1. *Choose the unused square* to be evaluated.

Steps in evaluating an unused square

2. Beginning with the selected unused square, *trace a closed path* (moving horizontally and vertically only) from this unused square via stone squares back to the

To From	Project A	Project B	Project C	Plant capacity
Plant W	WA 4 (56) ←	WB 8	WC 8 +	56
Plant X	XA 16 (16) +	XB 24 → (66) −	XC 16	82
Plant Y	YA 8	YB 16 (36) +	YC 24 → (41) −	77
Project requirements	72	102	41	215 215

Figure 11-7 Path used in evaluating square WC.

original unused square. Only one closed path exists for each unused square in a given solution. Although the path may skip over stone or unused squares, corners of the closed path may occur only at the stone squares and the unused square being evaluated. Only the most direct route is used.

3. *Assign plus (+) and minus (−) signs* alternately at each corner square of the closed path, beginning with a plus sign at the unused square. Assign these signs by starting either in a clockwise or counterclockwise direction. The positive and negative signs represent the addition or subtraction of 1 unit (truckload in this case) to a square.

4. *Determine the net change in costs* as a result of the changes made in tracing the path. Summing the unit cost in each square with a plus sign will give the addition to cost. The decrease in cost is obtained by summing the unit cost in each square with a negative sign. Comparing the additions to cost with the decreases will give the improvement index.

5. *Repeat the above steps* until an improvement index has been determined for each unused square.

If all the indices are greater than or equal to zero, an optimal solution has been found. Conversely, if any of the indices is negative, an improved solution is possible.

The above rules were used in tracing the path and determining the improvement index for square WB (Figure 11-6). Let us now evaluate the unused square WC. The traced path used in evaluating this square is shown in Figure 11-7.

The improvement index for unused square WC traced in Figure 11-7 is computed as follows:

Has the optimal solution been found?

$$\text{Improvement index for WC} = \text{WC} - \text{WA} + \text{XA} - \text{XB} + \text{YB} - \text{YC}$$
$$= \$8 - \$4 + \$16 - \$24 + \$16 - \$24$$
$$= -\$12$$

To From	Project A	Project B	Project C	Plant capacity
Plant W	WA [4] (56)	WB [8] −4	WC [8] −12	56
Plant X	XA [16] (16)	XB [24] (66)	XC [16] −16	82
Plant Y	YA [8] 0	YB [16] (36)	YC [24] (41)	77
Project requirements	72	102	41	215 215

Figure 11-8 All unused squares evaluated.

The closed paths and improvement indices for the remaining two unused squares are

Path for square XC: (+)XC → (−)XB → (+)YB → (−)YC
Improvement index for XC = XC − XB + YB − YC
$$= \$16 - \$24 + \$16 - \$24$$
$$= -\$16$$
Path for square YA: (+)YA → (−)XA → (+)XB → (−)YB
Improvement index for YA = YA − XA + XB − YB
$$= \$8 - \$16 + \$24 - \$16$$
$$= \$0$$

We have now completed the evaluation of all unused squares, each of which represents an alternative route that might be taken. The improvement index for each unused square is shown in Figure 11-8.

A brief summary might be helpful at this point. Step 3 called for testing the solution for improvement. In order to do this, the stepping-stone procedure was used to evaluate each unused square. The objective was to determine whether it would be profitable to use some other route, represented by each unused square. If any improvement index is *negative,* the best solution has not been obtained. Our evaluation resulted in three unused squares with negative improvement indices, and so we know that a better solution is possible. The next step, then, is to develop the new solution.

Step 4: Develop the Improved Solution

Developing the improved solution for the Bass Gravel Co. problem

Each negative improvement index represents the amount by which Bass's total transportation costs could be reduced if 1 truckload were shipped by that source-destination combination. In this sense the improvement indices are analogous to

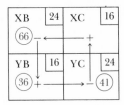

Figure 11-9 Closed path traced in evaluating unused square XC.

the values in the $C_j - Z_j$ row of the simplex method. For example, the improvement index for square XC means that for *every* truckload shipped from plant X to project C, total transportation costs will be reduced by \$16. The question now is: "Given three alternative routes with negative improvement indices (squares WB, WC, and XC), which one shall we choose in developing the improved solution?" We shall select that route (unused square) with the *largest negative improvement index.* In our problem this is square XC, with a negative index of \$16.

Select the route with the largest negative improvement index

Using this route will reduce costs. Bass must now decide how many truckloads to ship via this route, that is, from plant X to project C. To do this, we must reconstruct the closed path traced in evaluating unused square XC. This has been done in Figure 11-9, using only the relevant part of the table.

Now the maximum quantity which Bass can ship from plant X to project C is found by determining the smallest stone in a negative position on the closed path. The closed path for square XC has negative corners at squares XB and YC, and the smaller of these two stones is 41 truckloads per week. To obtain our new solution, we add 41 truckloads to all squares on the closed path with plus signs, and we subtract this quantity from all squares on the path assigned minus signs, as shown in Figure 11-10.

Why did we choose the smallest stone in a negative position on the closed path as the maximum number of truckloads that could be shipped from plant X to project C? Suppose we add 66 truckloads to square XC instead of 41. In order to satisfy our rim requirements, we would have to do the following: add 66 to XC, subtract 66 from XB, add 66 to YB, and subtract 66 from YC. The results are

XC: $0 + 66 = 66$
XB: $66 - 66 = 0$
YB: $36 + 66 = 102$
YC: $41 - 66 = -25$

The computation for square YC shows that Bass Gravel Co. plant Y would ship -25 truckloads to project C. This negative shipment is both meaningless in an actual problem and a violation of the requirement prohibiting the assignment of

XB −	XC +
$66 - 41 =$ (25)	$0 + 41 =$ (41)
YB +	YC −
$36 + 41 =$ (77)	$41 - 41 =$ 0

Figure 11-10 Forty-one loads added and subtracted.

To \ From	Project A	Project B	Project C	Plant capacity
Plant W	WA ⁴ (56)	WB ⁸	WC ⁸	56
Plant X	XA ¹⁶ (16)	XB ²⁴ (25)	XC ¹⁶ (41)	82
Plant Y	YA ⁸	YB ¹⁶ (77)	YC ²⁴	77
Project requirements	72	102	41	215 / 215

Figure 11-11 The second solution.

negative stone squares. As in the simplex method, all values in the solution must be greater than or equal to zero. Hence the maximum quantity which may be brought into a solution is found by determining the smallest stone in a negative position on the closed path of the square with the highest negative improvement index. This quantity is added to all squares on the closed path with plus signs and subtracted from all squares on the path with minus signs. The new improved solution is shown in Figure 11-11.

Note that square YC, which was a stone square in the initial solution, is now an unused square. Square XC has entered the improved solution in place of square YC. As can be seen in Table 11-4, the total transportation cost for the new shipping assignments of our second solution is an improvement upon the cost of the first solution, $2,968 versus $3,624.

Is further improvement possible? We now go back to step 3 to determine whether further improvement is possible. Using the stepping-stone method described in that section, we calculate an improvement index for each unused square in the second solution. The closed path and improvement index for each unused square in Figure 11-11 are shown in Table 11-5.

As previously mentioned, in tracing a closed path, the most direct route may

Table 11-4 Total Cost of Second Solution

Shipping assignments	Quantity shipped	×	Unit cost	=	Total cost
WA	56		$ 4		$224
XA	16		16		256
XB	25		24		600
XC	41		16		656
YB	77		16		1,232
Total transportation cost					$2,968

Table 11-5 Closed Paths and Improvement Indices for Unused Squares of Figure 11-11

Unused square	Closed path	Computation of improvement index
WB	+WB − WA + XA − XB	+ 8 − 4 + 16 − 24 = −4
WC	+WC − WA + XA − XC	+ 8 − 4 + 16 − 16 = +4
YA	+YA − XA + XB −YB	+ 8 − 16 + 24 − 16 = 0
YC	+YC − XC + XB −YB	+24 − 16 + 24 − 16 = +16

require *skipping* over stone squares as well as over unused squares. This occurs in tracing the path for square WC and is shown in Figure 11-12.

    Looking at the improvement indices computed in Table 11-5, we find one negative index for unused square WB, indicating that further improvement is possible. For each truckload assigned to square WB, total costs will be reduced $4. To determine the number of truckloads to be shipped, we select the smallest stone in a negative position on the closed path traced in evaluating square WB (step 4).

$$+ \text{WB} - \text{WA} + \text{XA} - \text{XB} + \longrightarrow - \boxed{56} \longrightarrow + \boxed{16} \longrightarrow - \boxed{25}$$

    As seen above, the smallest stone in a negative position is 25. This quantity is added to all squares on the path with plus signs and subtracted from all squares on the path with minus signs, as shown in Figure 11-13.

    The third improved solution is given in Figure 11-14.

    The total cost of the third solution is shown in Table 11-6.

    Again we go back to step 3 to determine if further improvement is possible. The closed paths and improvement indices for the unused squares in Figure 11-14 are given in Table 11-7. The negative improvement index for square YA indicates that the best solution has not been obtained. Now, following the same procedure discussed in step 4, we find that the maximum quantity to assign to square YA is 31 truckloads; the new solution is given in Figure 11-15. This is indeed the *optimum* solution. The improvement indices for Figure 11-15 are all greater than or equal to zero (see Table 11-8).

Skipping over stone squares

This is the optimum solution

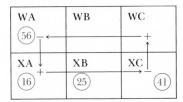

Figure 11-12 Tracing the path for square WC.

WA 56 − 25 = ㉛	WB 0 + 25 = ㉕
XA 16 + 25 = ㊶	XB 25 − 25 = 0

Figure 11-13 25 loads added and subtracted.

To From	Project A	Project B	Project C	Plant capacity
Plant W	WA ⟨4⟩ (31)	WB ⟨8⟩ (25)	WC ⟨8⟩	56
Plant X	XA ⟨16⟩ (41)	XB ⟨24⟩	XC ⟨16⟩ (41)	82
Plant Y	YA ⟨8⟩	YB ⟨16⟩ (77)	YC ⟨24⟩	77
Project requirements	72	102	41	215 / 215

Figure 11-14 The third solution.

The total cost for the optimum solution to the Bass Gravel Co. problem is shown in Table 11-9. Bass might question the use of a somewhat tedious method for solving such a simple problem. Why not use a trial-and-error method? Why not begin by simply choosing the lowest-cost route and using it to the fullest extent? Then we might select the next highest rate and use it to the fullest extent, and so on, until we have satisfied all the requirements for the project. The assumption underlying this thought is that making the best possible choice in each part of the schedul-

Table 11-6 Total Cost of Third Solution

Shipping assignments	Quantity shipped	$\times$	Unit cost	$=$	Total cost
WA	31		$4		$ 124
WB	25		8		200
XA	41		16		656
XC	41		16		656
YB	77		16		1,232
Total transportation cost					$2,868

Table 11-7 Closed Paths and Improvement Indices for Figure 11-14

Unused square	Closed path	Computation of improvement index
WC	+WC − WA + XA − XC	$+8 - 4 + 16 - 16 = +4$
XB	+XB − WB + WA − XA	$+24 - 8 + 4 - 16 = +4$
YA	+YA − WA + WB − YB	$+8 - 4 + 8 - 16 = -4$
YC	+YC − YB + WB −WA + XA − XC	$+24 - 16 + 8 - 4 + 16 - 16 = +12$

ing program will automatically result in the best overall program. An examination of the final solution to our problem indicates that the assumption is not a valid one. Figure 11-15 shows that two of the least-cost routes, squares WA and WC, are *not* included in the optimal solution. Here we recognize the importance of a characteristic of operations research: a problem must be studied in terms of the *total system*, not merely the separate parts. The optimal source-destination combinations are often far from apparent, even in small problems like that of the Bass Gravel Co.

Some least-cost routes may not be in the optimal solution

Alternative Optimal Solutions

Let us examine further the optimal solution to the Bass Gravel Co. problem with particular attention to the improvement index of square XB computed in Table 11-8. The improvement index for square XB is zero. What does this signify? A zero improvement index for an unused square means that if this route were brought into the solution, *the shipping assignments would change yet the total transportation cost would be the same.* Thus, if we were to assign one truckload to unused square XB, the total cost figure would neither increase nor decrease. We can conclude, then, that in addition to our present optimal shipping schedule, another equally profitable schedule exists. To determine what *this* alternative optimal solution is, we follow the same procedure used for bringing any route into the solution (step 4). In this case the maximum number of truckloads that can be assigned to square XB is 41. The alternative solution and its total cost are given in Figure 11-16. The improvement indices are also included.

Are there any other solutions with the same cost?

We see that the total cost is exactly the same as the total cost of the original optimal solution. Also, the improvement indices are positive except for square XA, which equals zero. This is to be expected, as square XA was the one replaced in the original optimal solution. From a practical viewpoint, the existence of alternative optimal solutions gives valuable flexibility to the management of the Bass Gravel Co.

To From	Project A		Project B		Project C		Plant capacity
Plant W	WA	4	WB (56)	8	WC	8	56
Plant X	XA (41)	16	XB	24	XC (41)	16	82
Plant Y	YA (31)	8	YB (46)	16	YC	24	77
Project requirements	72		102		41		215 / 215

Figure 11-15 The optimum solution to the Bass Gravel Company problem.

The MODI Method for Computing Improvement Indices

The *modified distribution method,* referred to as the MODI method, is very similar to the stepping-stone method except that it provides a more efficient means for computing the improvement indices for the unused squares. The major difference between these two methods concerns that step in the problem solution at which the closed paths are traced. In order to calculate the improvement indices for a par-
MODI and stepping-stone methods compared   ticular solution, it was necessary in the stepping-stone method to trace a closed path for each unused square. The unused square with the most improvement potential (the largest negative value) was then selected to enter the next solution.

In the MODI method, however, the improvement indices can be calculated without drawing the closed paths. The MODI method, in fact, requires tracing only *one* closed path. This path is drawn after the unused square with the highest improvement index has been identified. As in the stepping-stone method, the purpose of this path is to determine the maximum quantity that can be assigned to the unused square entering the next solution.

Using the Bass problem, we shall illustrate the procedures used in applying the MODI method. Beginning with the same initial solution obtained by using the
Initial solution obtained by the northwest corner rule   northwest corner rule, the first step is to compute a value for each row and each column in the transportation table. These values depend on the particular solution and are used to compute the improvement indices for the unused squares. Assigning a number to each row and column requires a slight modification in the transportation table. This modification together with the initial solution is shown in Figure 11-17.

In this figure we let R and K represent the row and column values. We have attached a subscript to denote the specific row and column value. In our case, we have R_1, R_2, and R_3 to represent the rows and K_1, K_2, and K_3 to represent the columns. In general, then, we can say:

R_i = value assigned to row i

and

K_j = value assigned to column j

The transportation cost, as in previous tables, is shown in the upper right-hand corner, or subsquare, of each large square.

For identification purposes, we can let

C_{ij} = cost in square ij (the square at the intersection of row i and column j)

Table 11-8   Closed Paths and Improvement Indices for Figure 11-15

Unused squares	Closed path	Computation of improvement index
WA	$+WA - YA + YB - WB$	$+4 - 8 + 16 - 8 = +4$
WC	$+WC - XC + XA - YA + YB - WB$	$+8 - 16 + 16 - 8 + 16 - 8 = +8$
XB	$+XB - YB + YA - XA$	$+24 - 16 + 8 - 16 = 0$
YC	$+YC - XC + XA - YA$	$+24 - 16 + 16 - 8 = +16$

Table 11-9 Total Cost of Optimum Solution for Bass Gravel Co., Problem

Shipping assignments	Quantity shipped	×	Unit cost	=	Total cost
WB	56		$ 8		$ 448
XA	41		16		656
XC	41		16		656
YA	31		8		248
YB	46		16		736
Total transportation cost					$2,744

To / From	Project A		Project B		Project C		Plant capacity
Plant W	WA	4	WB	8	WC	8	56
	+4		(56)		+8		
Plant X	XA	16	XB	24	XC	16	82
	0		(41)		(41)		
Plant Y	YA	8	YB	16	YC	24	77
	(72)		(5)		+16		
Project requirements	72		102		41		215 / 215

Total cost

$$56 \times \$8 = \$ \ 448$$
$$41 \times \$24 = \quad 984$$
$$41 \times \$16 = \quad 656$$
$$72 \times \$8 = \quad 576$$
$$5 \times \$16 = \quad 80$$
$$\overline{\qquad \$2,744}$$

Figure 11-16

R_i / K_j			K_1		K_2		K_3		
	To / From		Project A		Project B		Project C		Plant capacity
R_1	Plant W		WA	4	WB	8	WC	8	56
			(56)						
R_2	Plant X		XA	16	XB	24	XC	16	82
			(16)		(66)				
R_3	Plant Y		YA	8	YB	16	YC	24	77
					(36)		(41)		
	Project requirements		72		102		41		215 / 215

Figure 11-17 Transportation table using MODI method.

For example, C_{12} represents the cost in the square located at the intersection of row 1 and column 2. Now to compute the values for each row and column, we use the formula

Computing values for each row and column

$$R_i + K_j = C_{ij} = \text{cost at stone square } ij \tag{11-1}$$

This formula is applied *only* to the stone squares in a particular solution. Because there are five stone squares in our problem, we must have *five* equations. For the stone square located at the intersection of row 1 and column 1 we write

$$R_1 + K_1 = C_{11}$$

and, as there is a stone square at the intersection of row 2 and column 1,

$$R_2 + K_1 = C_{21}$$

similarly,

$$R_2 + K_2 = C_{22}$$
$$R_3 + K_2 = C_{32}$$
$$R_3 + K_3 = C_{33}$$

Because we are given the cost figure for each square in the table, we can substitute the appropriate value for each C_{ij} in our equations. The results are

$$R_1 + K_1 = 4$$
$$R_2 + K_1 = 16$$
$$R_2 + K_2 = 24$$
$$R_3 + K_2 = 16$$
$$R_3 + K_3 = 24$$

Notice that we have six unknowns and only five equations. Thus this system of equations has several solutions. In order to find a particular solution (a value for each R and K), we shall let $R_1 = 0$. We could have chosen any value for any row or column, but the usual procedure is to let row 1 (R_1) equal zero. This is legitimate since the entire process is a comparative one. In other words, the significance of the row and column values is not their absolute numerical value. We are interested only in comparing the figures, not in the figures themselves.

Solving the row and column equations   To solve the five equations, then, we proceed as follows. If $R_1 = 0$, then

$$R_1 + K_1 = 4$$
$$0 + K_1 = 4$$
$$K_1 = 4$$

Since $K_1 = 4$, then

$$R_2 + K_1 = 16$$
$$R_2 + 4 = 16$$
$$R_2 = 12$$

R_i \ K_j	To \ From	$K_1 = 4$ Project A	$K_2 = 12$ Project B	$K_3 = 20$ Project C	Plant capacity
$R_1 = 0$	Plant W	WA $\quad$ 4 (56)	WB $\quad$ 8	WC $\quad$ 8	56
$R_2 = 12$	Plant X	XA $\quad$ 16 (16)	XB $\quad$ 24 (66)	XC $\quad$ 16	82
$R_3 = 4$	Plant Y	YA $\quad$ 8	YB $\quad$ 16 (36)	YC $\quad$ 24 (41)	77
	Project requirements	72	102	41	215 / 215

Figure 11-18 Initial solution with R and K values for the Bass Gravel Company problem.

Since $R_2 = 12$, then

$R_2 + K_2 = 24$
$12 + K_2 = 24$
$\quad K_2 = 12$

Since $K_2 = 12$, then

$R_3 + K_2 = 16$
$R_3 + 12 = 16$
$\quad R_3 = 4$

Since $R_3 = 4$, then

$R_3 + K_3 = 24$
$4 + K_3 = 24$
$\quad K_3 = 20$

The R and K values need not always be positive; indeed, they may be *positive, negative,* or *zero*. After some practice, computing the R and K values can usually be done mentally instead of writing out each equation as above. The transportation table with the R and K values included is shown in Figure 11-18.

With the row and column values computed, the next step in the MODI method is to evaluate each unused square in the present solution, that is, to compute the improvement indices. Computing the improvement index for any unused square is accomplished in the following manner: from the cost of an unused square subtract the corresponding row value and column value. Stating this rule as a general formula, we have

$$C_{ij} - R_i - K_j = \text{improvement index} \qquad (11\text{-}2)$$

R and *K* may be positive, negative, or zero

If the result is negative, further improvement is possible. When all indices are equal to or greater than zero, the optimal solution has been obtained.

Each unused square in the initial solution (Figure 11-18) can now be evaluated. For example, the route from plant W to project B at the intersection of row 1 and column 2 is one of the unused routes (unused squares) in our initial solution. Using our formula, we have

Unused square 12: $C_{12} - R_1 - K_2 =$ improvement index
$$8 - 0 - 12 = -4$$

Similarly, for the other unused squares we have:

Unused square	$C_{ij} - R_i - K_j$	Improvement index
13	$C_{13} - R_1 - K_3$ $8 - 0 - 20$	-12
23	$C_{23} - R_2 - K_3$ $16 - 12 - 20$	-16
31	$C_{31} - R_3 - K_1$ $8 - 4 - 4$	0

A comparison of these improvement indices with those obtained using the stepping-stone method (see Figure 11-8) shows them to be identical. From this point on, then, the procedure for developing a new, improved solution is identical to the one discussed in the previous sections.

For convenience, the procedure is briefly outlined here.

Procedure for developing an improved solution

1. *Trace a closed path* for the cell having the largest negative improvement index.

2. *Place plus and minus signs* at alternate corners of the path, beginning with a plus sign at the unused square.

3. The smallest stone in a negative position on the closed path indicates the quantity that can be assigned to the unused squares being entered into the solution. *This quantity is added* to all squares on the closed path with plus signs *and subtracted* from those squares with minus signs.

4. Finally, the improvement indices for the new solution *are calculated.*

With this procedure, the second solution to the problem of the Bass Gravel Co. is obtained (Figure 11-19). Notice that it is identical to our second solution found by using the stepping-stone procedure. As we shall see in a moment, this holds true for all solutions.

To evaluate the unused squares of the second solution using the MODI method, we must calculate the R and K values. This must be done with every new solution. Again we begin by letting R_1 equal zero. Using the general formula

R_i \ K_j		$K_1 = 4$	$K_2 = 12$	$K_3 = 4$	
	To \ From	Project A	Project B	Project C	Plant capacity
$R_1 = 0$	Plant W	WA 4 (56)	WB 8	WC 8	56
$R_2 = 12$	Plant X	XA 16 (16)	XB 24 (25)	XC 16 (41)	82
$R_3 = 4$	Plant Y	YA 8	YB 16 (77)	YC 24	77
	Project requirements	72	102	41	215 / 215

Figure 11-19 Second solution to the Bass Gravel Company problem.

$R_i + K_j = C_{ij}$ (the cost at stone square ij), the R and K values are computed as follows:

Stone square 11: $R_1 + K_1 = 4$
$$0 + K_1 = 4$$
$$K_1 = 4$$

Stone square 21: $R_2 + K_1 = 16$
$$R_2 + 4 = 16$$
$$R_2 = 12$$

Stone square 22: $R_2 + K_2 = 24$
$$12 + K_2 = 24$$
$$K_2 = 12$$

Stone square 23: $R_2 + K_3 = 16$
$$12 + K_3 = 16$$
$$K_3 = 4$$

Stone square 32: $R_3 + K_2 = 16$
$$R_3 + 12 = 16$$
$$R_3 = 4$$

Computing R and K values

These R and K values were included in Figure 11-19. In comparing our new R and K values with those obtained in the initial solution (Figure 11-18), we find that all R and K values are the same except for K_3, which is equal to 4 in the second table. Changing the solution changes some if not all of the R and K values. Hence,

Table 11-10   Evaluation of Unused Squares in Second Solution

Unused square	$C_{ij} - R_i - K_j$	Improvement index
12	$C_{12} - R_1 - K_2$	
	$8 - 0\ \ - 12$	
		-4
13	$C_{13} - R_1 - K_3$	
	$8 - 0\ \ - 4$	
		$+4$
31	$C_{31} - R_3 - K_1$	
	$8 - 4\ \ - 4$	
		0
33	$C_{33} - R_3 - K_3$	
	$24 - 4\ \ - 4$	
		$+16$

with every new solution, new values for R and K must be established in order to determine whether further improvement is possible, that is, to calculate the improvement indices.

The evaluation of each unused square of the second solution is shown in Table 11-10. The remaining improved solutons with their respective R and K values are given in Figures 11-20 and 11-21. The improvement indices are also included.

The MODI method may be summarized by the following steps:

Steps in MODI method

11-1. For each solution, *compute the R and K values* for the table using the formula:

$R_i + K_j = C_{ij}$ (the cost at *stone* square *ij*)

Row 1 (R_1) is always set equal to zero.

11-2. *Calculate the improvement indices* for all unused squares using:

C_{ij} (cost of *unused* square) $- R_i - K_j$ = improvement index

R_i \ K_j		$K_1 = 4$	$K_2 = 8$	$K_3 = 4$	
	From \ To	Project A	Project B	Project C	Plant capacity
$R_1 = 0$	Plant W	WA ⁴ ㉛	WB ⁸ ㉕	WC ⁸ +4	56
$R_2 = 12$	Plant X	XA ¹⁶ ㊶	XB ²⁴ +4	XC ¹⁶ ㊶	82
$R_3 = 8$	Plant Y	YA ⁸ −4	YB ¹⁶ ㊻⁷	YC ²⁴ +12	77
	Project requirements	72	102	41	215 / 215

Figure 11-20   Third solution to the Bass Gravel Company problem.

K_j / R_i	To / From	$K_1 = 0$ Project A	$K_2 = 8$ Project B	$K_3 = 0$ Project C	Plant capacity
$R_1 = 0$	Plant W	WA 4 / +4	WB 8 / (56)	WC 8 / +8	56
$R_2 = 16$	Plant X	XA 16 / (41)	XB 24 / 0	XC 16 / (41)	82
$R_3 = 8$	Plant Y	YA 8 / (31)	YB 16 / (46)	YC 24 / +16	77
	Project requirements	72	102	41	215 / 215

Figure 11-21 Optimal solution to the Bass Gravel Company problem.

3. *Select the unused square* with the largest negative index. (If all indices are equal to or greater than zero, the optimal solution has been obtained.)

4. *Trace the closed path* for the unused square having the largest negative index.

5. *Develop an improved solution* using the same procedure as outlined in the stepping-stone method.

6. *Repeat steps 1 to 5* until an optimal solution has been found.

2. The Transportation Method (Demand Not Equal to Supply)

To this point the transportation method has required that supply and demand be equal: the rim requirements for the rows must equal the rim requirements for the columns. This is unlikely. Most real problems are of the so-called *unbalanced* type, where supply and demand are unequal. In such cases, there is a method for handling the inequality.

Unbalanced form of the transportation problem

Demand Less than Supply

Considering the original Bass Gravel Co. problem, suppose that plant W has a capacity of 76 truckloads per week rather than 56. The company would be able to supply 235 truckloads per week. However, the project requirements remain the same. Using the northwest corner rule to establish an initial solution, we get the program shown in Figure 11-22. Obviously the rim requirements for the rows and columns are not balanced. Plant Y still has 20 truckloads available for supply. The method employed to balance this type of problem is to create a fictitious destina-

When demand is less than supply

From \ To	Project A	Project B	Project C	Plant capacity
Plant W	WA 4 (72)	WB 8 (4)	WC 8	76
Plant X	XA 16	XB 24 (82)	XC 16	82
Plant Y	YA 8	YB 16 (16)	YC 24 (41)	77
Project requirements	72	102	41	235 / 215

Figure 11-22 Unbalanced form when demand is less than supply.

An equivalent to the slack variable — tion or project requiring 20 truckloads per week. This fictitious project serves the same purpose as the *slack variable* in the simplex method. Since these truckloads will never be shipped, the transportation costs to this dummy project are equal to zero. An additional column is required to handle the dummy project in the transportation table. Again the northwest corner rule is used to determined the initial solution, as shown in Figure 11-23.

The problem can now be solved using the steps discussed earlier. Let us look, however, at the final table, or optimal solution, to this problem (Figure 11-24). The optimal solution shows a shipment of 20 truckloads to the dummy project. This means that plant X will have an excess of 20 truckloads. With this information, the decision maker knows not only the optimal shipping program but also the plant which should not be utilized at full capacity.

From \ To	Project A	Project B	Project C	Dummy D	Plant capacity
Plant W	4 (72)	8 (4)	8	0	76
Plant X	16	24 (82)	16	0	82
Plant Y	8	16 (16)	24 (41)	0 (20)	77
Project requirements	72	102	41	20	235 / 235

Total cost

$$72 \times \$4 = \$\ 288$$
$$4 \times \$8 = \ 32$$
$$82 \times \$24 = 1,968$$
$$16 \times \$16 = \ 256$$
$$20 \times \$0 = \ 0$$
$$41 \times \$24 = \underline{\ 984}$$
$$\$3,528$$

Figure 11-23 Initial solution for unbalanced problem (demand less than supply).

To From	Project A	Project B	Project C	Dummy D	Plant capacity
Plant W	4	8 (76)	8	0	76
Plant X	16	24 (21)	16 (41)	0 (20)	82
Plant Y	8 (72)	16 (5)	24	0	77
Project requirements	72	102	41	20	235 / 235

Total cost

$76 \times \$8 = \$ 608$
$21 \times \$24 = 504$
$41 \times \$16 = 656$
$20 \times \$0 = 0$
$72 \times \$8 = 576$
$5 \times \$16 = \underline{\quad 80}$
$\$2,424$

Figure 11-24 Optimal solution to unbalanced problem (demand less than supply).

Demand Greater than Supply

Another type of unbalanced condition occurs when total demand is greater than total supply; that is, the customers (projects in our case) require more gravel than the Bass Gravel Co. plants can supply. Again, referring to our sample problem, assume that project A will require 10 additional truckloads per week and that project C estimates additional requirements of 20 truckloads. The total project requirements now would be equal to 245 truckloads, as opposed to the 215 available from the plants. Similar to the previous type of unbalance, the key to solving this problem is to set it up with balanced conditions. To accomplish this, we create a dummy plant having a capacity exactly equal to the additional demand (30 truckloads). The distribution costs from this plant are equal to zero, since no actual deliveries will be made from this dummy plant.

When demand is greater than supply

Use of the dummy source

As can be seen in the initial solution table (Figure 11-25), the inclusion of a dummy plant results in an additional row.

To From	Project A	Project B	Project C	Plant capacity
Plant W	4 (56)	8	8	56
Plant X	16 (26)	24 (56)	16	82
Plant Y	8	16 (46)	24 (31)	77
Dummy	0	0 (30)	0	30
Project requirements	82	102	61	245 / 245

Total cost

$56 \times \$4 = \$ 224$
$26 \times \$16 = 416$
$56 \times \$24 = 1,344$
$46 \times \$16 = 736$
$31 \times \$24 = 744$
$30 \times \$0 = \underline{\quad 0}$
$\$3,464$

Figure 11-25 Initial solution for unbalanced problem (demand greater than supply).

To / From	Project A	Project B	Project C	Plant capacity
Plant W	4	8	8	56
		(56)		
Plant X	16	24	16	82
	(21)		(61)	
Plant Y	8	16	24	77
	(61)	(16)		
Dummy	0	0	0	30
		(30)		
Project requirements	82	102	61	245 / 245

Total cost

$56 \times \$8 = \$\ \ 448$
$21 \times \$16 = \ \ \ 336$
$61 \times \$16 = \ \ \ 976$
$61 \times \$8 = \ \ \ 488$
$16 \times \$16 = \ \ \ 256$
$30 \times \$0 = \ \ \ \ \ \ \underline{0}$
$\$2,504$

Figure 11-26   Optimal solution to the Bass Gravel Company unbalanced problem (demand greater than supply).

Having established the balanced condition, we solve the problem using exactly the same procedure as outlined in the previous sections. The optimal solution to this problem is given in Figure 11-26.

Assumptions in this situation   This particular type of unbalanced problem implies that one or more of the projects will not have its requirements satisfied. In this case, the optimal solution indicates that project B will be short 30 truckloads per *week*, as it receives 30 from the dummy plant. This method, however, *does* distribute all available gravel at the lowest total transportation cost for the Bass Gravel Co.

3. Degeneracy

Degeneracy in the transportation problem   We have pointed out that the total number of stone squares in *any* solution must be equal to the number of rim requirements minus 1. An alternative way of stating this rule is that the number of stone squares in *any* solution must be equal to the number of rows plus the number of columns minus 1. When this rule is not met, the solution is degenerate.

Failure to meet the test for degeneracy in the transportation problem is indicated in *two* ways:

Recognizing degeneracy   **1.** There may be an *excessive* number of stone squares in a solution; the number of stone squares is greater than the number of rim requirements minus 1. This type of degeneracy arises only in developing the initial solution and is caused by an improper assignment or an error in formulating the problem. In such cases, one must modify the initial solution so as to satisfy the rule of rim requirements minus 1.

2. There may be an *insufficient* number of stone squares in a solution. Degeneracy of this type may occur either in the initial solution or in subsequent solutions. It is this type of degeneracy which requires special procedures to resolve the de-

From \ To	A		B		C		Plant capacity
W	WA ㉟	4	WB ⑳	8	WC	8	55
X	XA	16	XB ㉕	24	XC	16	25
Y	YA	8	YB	16	YC ㉟	24	35
Project requirements	35		45		35		115 / 115

Figure 11-27 Degenerate problem: initial solution.

generacy. With an insufficient number of stone squares in a solution, it would be impossible to trace a closed path for each unused square, and in using the MODI method it would be impossible to compute the R and K values.

The procedures for handling degeneracy resulting from an insufficient number of stones will now be presented.

Degeneracy in Establishing an Initial Solution

Let us assume that the plant capacities and project requirements in the original Bass Gravel Co. problem have been changed. Using the northwest corner rule, we obtain the initial solution given in Figure 11-27.

Resolving degeneracy in the initial solution

In this solution we have four stone squares. According to our rule of rim requirements minus 1, we should have five stone squares. Hence the solution is degenerate. This particular case of degeneracy arises when, in using the northwest corner rule, both a column requirement and row requirement are satisfied simultaneously, thus breaking the stairstep pattern. In our case, this occurs in square XB. Of course, the assignment of a value to the final stone square always satisfies the remaining row and column requirements simultaneously, but this will not result in a degenerate solution.

To resolve this degeneracy, we assign a zero stone to one of the unused squares. Although there is a great deal of flexibility in choosing the unused square for the zero stone, the general procedure, when using the northwest corner rule, is to assign it to a square in such a way that it maintains an unbroken chain of stone squares. Figure 11-28 shows the zero stone added to square XC, although it could have been assigned to square YB.

We now have five stone squares; this satisfies the degeneracy test. The problem can now be solved using the same solution procedure with the zero stone square treated just like any other stone square in the solution. This zero stone

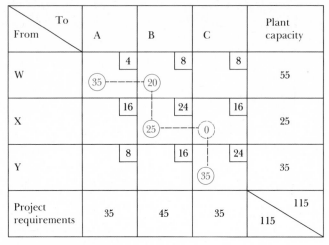

From \ To	A	B	C	Plant capacity
W	4 (35)	8 (20)	8	55
X	16	24 (25)	16 (0)	25
Y	8	16	24 (35)	35
Project requirements	35	45	35	115 \ 115

Figure 11-28 Degeneracy resolved.

square has no meaning in a problem; it is merely a computational device which permits the Bass Gravel Co. to apply the regular solution method.

Degeneracy during Subsequent Solution Stages

Resolving degeneracy in subsequent solutions

The initial solution to another problem is given in Figure 11-29. We observe that the initial solution is not degenerate. The improvement indexes are shown in the unused squares and indicate that an improved solution may be obtained by introducing unused square YB into the next solution. Let us go through the procedure for developing the next solution to this problem and observe what happens. We first trace the closed path for unused square YB and then choose the smallest stone as the quantity to be assigned to unused square YB. This is shown in Figure 11-30.

From \ To	A	B	C	Plant capacity
W	WA 4 (45)	WB 8 (45)	WC 24 +12	90
X	XA 8 +8	XB 4 (30)	XC 8 (30)	60
Y	YA 16 +8	YB 4 −8	YC 16 (30)	30
Project requirements	45	75	60	180 \ 180

Figure 11-29 Degenerate problem: initial solution.

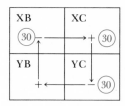

Figure 11-30 Tracing closed path for square YB.

In this case all stones have a value of 30. The results of the assignment of 30 units to square YB are shown in Figure 11-31. When we added 30 units to square YB, the quantities shipped through squares XB and YC were *both* reduced to zero. This will always occur when a tie exists between two or more stone squares when these stones represent the smallest stones on the path in squares assigned a minus sign. Hence in our problem, adding an unused square resulted in the elimination of two stone squares from the previous solution, but in order to satisfy the rule that the number of stone squares equals the number of rim requirements minus 1, we will keep XB as a stone square and only eliminate square YC. We have placed the zero stone in square XB, as shown in Figure 11-32.

In some cases more than two stone squares may be reduced to zero. In such cases we eliminate only one of those squares, so the number of stone squares in the solution still satisfies the rule of rim requirements minus 1. The Bass Gravel Co. problem can now be solved using the standard procedure, which was discussed before.

4. The Assignment Method

Another special-purpose algorithm used in linear programming is the *assignment method*. Like the transportation method, the assignment method is computationally more efficient than the simplex method for a special class of problems. We shall also show that the assignment problem is a special case of the transportation problem. In other words, we can solve an assignment problem using the transportation method.

The Kellum Machine Shop does custom metalworking for a number of local plants. Kellum currently has three jobs to be done (let us symbolize them A, B, and C). Kellum also has three machines on which to do the work (X, Y, and Z). Any one of the jobs can be processed completely on any one of the machines. Furthermore, the cost of processing any job on any machine is known. The assignment of jobs to machines must be on a one-to-one basis; that is, each job will be assigned ex-

A special case of the transportation problem: the assignment problem

XB 30 − 30 = 0	XC 30 + 30 = (60)
YB 0 + 30 = (30)	YC 30 − 30 = 0

Figure 11-31 Thirty units assigned to square YB.

To From	A		B		C		Plant capacity
W	WA	4	WB	8	WC	24	90
	(45)		(45)				
X	XA	8	XB	4	XC	8	60
			(0)		(60)		
Y	YA	16	YB	4	YC	16	30
			(30)				
Project requirements	45		75		60		180 180

Figure 11-32 Degeneracy resolved: subsequent solution stage.

clusively to one and only one machine. The objective is to assign the jobs to the machines so as to minimize total cost.

Number of rows equals number of columns in the assignment problem

The cost data are given in Table 11-11. The number of rows (jobs) equals the number of columns (machines). This is one characteristic of all assignment problems. Another characteristic is that in the optimal solution there will be one and only one assignment in a given row or column of the given assignment table. These characteristics are peculiar to the assignment problem. In the general transportation problem, for example, it is not necessary to have an equal number of sources and destinations; nor does the transportation method require that there be one assignment only in a given row or column of the optimal solution.

Using the Transportation Method to Solve the Assignment Problem

Use the northwest corner rule to get the initial solution

Since each job must be assigned to one and only one machine, we can say that the job requirement for each job is 1 and that the machine capacity for each machine is also 1. This might be the case, for example, when the additional setup expenses are such as to prohibit the partial assignment of machines to more than one job. Given the cost data of Table 11-11, the job requirements, and machine capacities,

Table 11-11 Cost for Each Job-Machine Assignment for Kellum Machine Shop Problem

	Machine		
Job	X	Y	Z
A	$25	$31	$35
B	$15	$20	$24
C	$22	$19	$17

To / From	Machine X	Machine Y	Machine Z	Job requirements
Job A	25 ⓵	31	35	1
Job B	15	20 ⓵	24	1
Job C	22	19	17 ⓵	1
Machine capacity	1	1	1	3 / 3

Figure 11-33 The Kellum assignment problem set up in the transportation table.

we can set up the transportation table given in Figure 11-33, showing the initial solution using the northwest corner rule.

There are three stone squares in this initial solution. However, according to the rule of rim requirements minus 1, we should have five stone squares. Hence we must add two zero stone squares to resolve the degeneracy. This has been done in Figure 11-34.

The Kellum problem can now be solved in the usual manner. Because all the stone squares have a value of 1 or zero, a degenerate solution will result with each subsequent solution. The reason for this can be attributed to the two special characteristics of the assignment problem mentioned in the previous section. Having to cope with the problem of degeneracy at each solution makes the transportation method computationally inefficient for solving an assignment problem.

Why the transportation method is inefficient for the assignment problem

To / From	X	Y	Z	Job requirements
A	25 ⓵	31 ⓪	35	1
B	15	20 ⓵	24 ⓪	1
C	22	19	17 ⓵	1
Machine capacity	1	1	1	3 / 3

Figure 11-34 Degeneracy resolved.

Using the Assignment Method

Assignment method is more efficient

The assignment method, also known as *Flood's technique* or the *Hungarian method of assignment,* provides a much more efficient method of solving assignment problems. There are basically three steps in the assignment method. We present the reasoning underlying each of these steps.

Concept of opportunity cost and opportunity-cost table

Step 1: Determine the Opportunity-Cost Table   Since the assignment method applies the concept of *opportunity* costs, a brief explanation of this concept may be helpful. The cost of any kind of action or decision consists of the opportunities that are sacrificed in taking that action. Many of us go through an opportunity-cost analysis without realizing it. For example, a friend who had been thinking of buying a new house drives by in a brand new car. He promptly starts explaining how nice it is living in an apartment. This is an example of opportunity-cost analysis. If we do one thing, we cannot do another.

Let us now see how this concept plays an important part in the computational mechanics of the assignment method. For convenience, the cost data for the Kellum Machine Shop problem are repeated in Table 11-12.

Suppose we decide to assign job A to machine X. The table shows that the cost of this assignment is $25. Because machine X could just as well process job B for $15, it is clear that our assignment of job A to machine X is not the best decision. Therefore, when we arbitrarily assign job A to machine X, we are in effect sacrificing the opportunity to save $10, ($25 − $15). This sacrifice is more generally referred to as an opportunity cost. In other words, the decision to assign job A to machine X precludes the assignment of job B to machine X, given the restriction that one and only one job can be assigned to a machine. Thus we say that the opportunity cost of the assignment of job A to machine X is $10 with respect to the lowest cost assignment for machine X (or column X). Similarly, a Kellum decision to assign job C to machine X would involve an opportunity cost of $7, ($22 − $15). Finally, since the assignment of job B to machine X is the best assignment, we can say that the opportunity cost of this assignment is zero ($15 − $15).

Job-opportunity costs

More specifically these costs can be called the *job-opportunity costs* with regard to machine X. If we were to subtract the lowest cost of column Y (machine Y) from all the costs in this column, we would have the job-opportunity costs with regard to machine Y. The same procedure in column Z would give the job-opportunity costs for machine Z.

Table 11-12 Cost of Each Job-Machine Assignment for the Kellum Machine Shop Problem

Job	Machine		
	X	Y	Z
A	$25	$31	$35
B	15	20	24
C	22	19	17

Table 11-13 Step 1, Part *a*: Job-Opportunity Table for Kellum Machine Shop Problem

Job	Machine			Computations		
	X	Y	Z	Column X	Column Y	Column Z
A	10	12	18	$25 - 15 = 10$	$31 - 19 = 12$	$35 - 17 = 18$
B	0	1	7	$15 - 15 = 0$	$20 - 19 = 1$	$24 - 17 = 7$
C	7	0	0	$22 - 15 = 7$	$19 - 19 = 0$	$17 - 17 = 0$

Machine-opportunity costs

In addition to these job-opportunity costs, there are *machine-opportunity costs*. We could, for example, assign job A to machine X, Y, or Z. If we assigned job A to machine Y, there is an opportunity cost attached to this decision. The assignment of job A to machine Y costs $31, while the assignment of job A to machine X costs only $25. Therefore the opportunity cost of assigning job A to machine Y is $6, ($31 − $25). Similarly the assignment of job A to machine Z involves an opportunity cost of $10, ($35 − $25). A zero opportunity cost is involved in the assignment of job A to machine X, since this is the best assignment for job A (row A). Hence, we could compute the machine opportunity costs for each row (each job) by subtracting the lowest cost entry in each row from all cost entries in its row.

This discussion on opportunity costs should provide an understanding of the mechanics of the first step in the assignment method, which is to develop the total opportunity-cost table. There are *two* parts to this first step. Part *a* is to subtract the lowest entry in each column of the original cost table from all entries in that column. The resulting new table with computations is given in Table 11-13.

Table 11-13 should be recognized as the job-opportunity table. Now the objective of this first step is to develop a total opportunity-cost table. In other words, we want to consider the machine-opportunity costs also. Part *b* of step 1 accomplishes this, but not in *exactly* the same way as our intuitive analysis. The effect, however, is the same. Part *b* is to subtract the lowest entry in each row of the *table obtained in part a* from all numbers in that row. The new table and computations are shown in Table 11-14.

Step 2: Determine Whether an Optimal Assignment Can Be Made The objective is to assign the jobs to the machines so as to minimize total costs. With the total opportunity-cost table, this objective will be achieved if we can assign the jobs to the machines in such a way as to obtain a total opportunity cost of zero. In other

Table 11-14 Step 1, Part *b*: Total Opportunity-Cost Table for Kellum Machine Shop Problem

Job	Machine			Computations			
	X	Y	Z				
A	0	2	8	Row A:	$10 - 10 = 0$	$12 - 10 = 2$	$18 - 10 = 8$
B	0	1	7	Row B:	$0 - 0 = 0$	$1 - 0 = 1$	$7 - 0 = 7$
C	7	0	0	Row C:	$7 - 0 = 7$	$0 - 0 = 0$	$0 - 0 = 0$

The best possible assignment

words, we want to make the three best possible assignments. *The best possible assignment of a job to a machine would involve an opportunity cost of zero.*

Looking at the total opportunity cost in Table 11-14, we find four squares with zeros, each indicating a zero opportunity cost for that square (assignment). Hence, we could assign job A to machine X and job C to machine Y or Z, all assignments having an opportunity cost of zero. If this were done, however, we could not assign job B to any machine with a zero opportunity cost. The reason here is that assigning job A to machine X precludes the assignment of job B to machine X. If we had a zero in square BY, we could make an optimal assignment. In other words, to make an optimal assignment of the three jobs to the three machines, we must locate three zero squares in the table such that a complete assignment to these squares can be made with a total opportunity cost of zero.

There is a convenient method for determining whether an optimal assignment can be made. This method consists of drawing straight lines (vertically and horizontally) through the total opportunity-cost table in such a manner as to minimize the numbers of lines necessary to cover all zero squares. If the number of lines equals either the number of rows or columns in the table, an optimal assignment can be made and the problem is solved. On the other hand, an optimal assignment cannot be made if the number of lines is less than the number of rows or columns. In this case we must develop a new total opportunity-cost table.

The test for optimal assignment has been applied to our present table and is shown in Table 11-15. It requires only two lines (row C and column X) to cover all the zero squares. Therefore, as there are three rows, an optimal assignment is not possible.

If an optimal assignment cannot be made, modify the opportunity-cost table

Step 3: Revise the Total Opportunity-Cost Table   If an optimal assignment is not feasible, we must modify the total opportunity-cost table by including some assignment not in the rows and columns covered by the lines. Of course, that assignment with the least opportunity cost is chosen; in our problem, this would be the assignment of job B to machine Y with an opportunity cost of 1. In other words we would like to change the opportunity cost for this assignment from 1 to zero.

The procedure for accomplishing this task is as follows: *(a)* select the smallest number in the table not covered by a straight line and subtract this number from all numbers not covered by a straight line; and *(b)* add this same lowest number to the

Table 11-15   Test for Optimal Assignment for Kellum Machine Shop Problem

Job		Machine	
	X	Y	Z
A	0	2	8
B	0	1	7
C	7	0	0 → line 1

line 2

Table 11-16 Revised Opportunity-Cost Table for Kellum Machine Shop Problem

Machine		Computations:	
Job X Y Z			
A 0 1 7		$2 - 1 = 1$ $8 - 1 = 7$	(a) Subtract lowest number
B 0 0 6		$1 - 1 = 0$ $7 - 1 = 6$	from all uncovered numbers
C 8 0 0			line 1

$7 + 1 = 8$

line 2

(b) Add same smallest number to number lying at the intersection of two lines

numbers lying at the intersection of any two lines. The revised total opportunity-cost table and computations of parts *a* and *b* of step 3 are shown in Table 11-16.

The test for optimal assignment described in step 2 is applied again to the revised table. This is shown in Table 11-17.

As the minimum number of lines necessary to cover all zeros is three, and as this number is equal to the number of rows or columns, an optimal assignment can be made. In this case the optimal assignments are A to X, B to Y, and C to Z. In larger problems, however, the assignments may not be readily apparent and we must resort to a more systematic procedure. The first step is to select a row or column in which there is only one zero square. The first assignment is made to that zero square. Lines are then drawn through the column and row in which the zero square is located. From the remaining rows and columns we again select that row or column in which there is only one zero cell. Another assignment is made and lines are drawn through the respective row and column. The procedure is repeated until a complete assignment has been made. The assignment sequence using this procedure in our problem is shown in Figure 11-35.

To calculate the total cost of these assignments for Kellum, we must go back to the original cost table. The computation of total cost is given below:

Assignment	Cost
A to X	$25
B to Y	20
C to Z	17
Total	$62

Table 11-17 Test for Optimal Assignment Applied to Revised Opportunity-Cost Table

Jobs	Machine		
	X	Y	Z
A	0	1	7
B	0	0	6 → line 2
C	8	0	0 → line 3

line 1

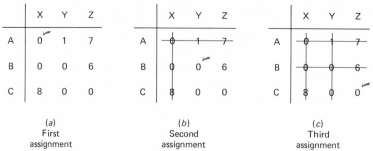

	X	Y	Z
A	0	1	7
B	0	0	6
C	8	0	0

	X	Y	Z
A	0	1	7
B	0	0	6
C	8	0	0

	X	Y	Z
A	0	1	7
B	0	0	6
C	8	0	0

(a)	(b)	(c)
First assignment	Second assignment	Third assignment

Figure 11-35 Assignment sequence.

Summary of the Assignment Method

Summarizing the assignment method

1. *Determine the opportunity-cost table.*
   a. Subtract the lowest entry in each column of the given cost table from all entries in that column.
   b. Subtract the lowest entry in each row of the table obtained in part *a* from all numbers in that row.

2. *Determine whether an optimal assignment can be made.* The procedure is to draw straight lines (vertically and horizontally) through the total opportunity-cost table in such a manner as to minimize the number of lines necessary to cover all zero squares. An optimal assignment can be made when the number of lines equals the number of rows or columns. If the number of lines drawn is less than the number of rows or columns, an optimal assignment cannot be made and the problem is not solved.

3. *Revise the total opportunity-cost table.*
   a. Select the smallest number in the table not covered by a straight line and subtract this number from all numbers not covered by a straight line.
   b. Add this same number to the numbers lying at the intersection of any two lines. Go back to step 2.

Other applications of the assignment method

The assignment method has been applied successfully to a number of situations other than the Kellum job-machine problem we have used as an illustration here. This approach has produced optimum assignments of personnel to job situations requiring specialized talents. Included in successful applications of the assignment method is the assignment of selling personnel to territories, instructors to specialized learning situations, and auditors to client accounts. In order to apply this method successfully, management must be able to determine cost data or other effectiveness measures like the costs in Table 11-12.

Glossary

1. **Transportation problem** Special linear program concerned with selecting optimal routes between sources and destinations.
2. **Source** A point of supply in a transportation problem.

3. **Destination**   A point of demand in a transportation problem.

4. **Stepping-stone method**   A special-purpose algorithm for solving the transportation problem.

5. **Modified distribution method (MODI)**   A computationally more efficient procedure for solving the transportation problem.

6. **Balanced condition**   When total demand is equal to total supply.

7. **Unbalanced case**   Condition in a transportation problem when supply and demand are unequal.

8. **Transportation table**   Tabular framework for solving the transportation problem.

9. **Rim requirements**   Capacity constraints at sources and destinations in the transportation problem.

10. **Northwest corner rule**   A systematic and logical procedure for setting up the initial solution to a transportation problem.

11. **Unused squares**   Squares representing routes where no quantity is shipped between a source and a destination.

12. **Degeneracy**   Condition in the transportation problem when the number of unused squares does not equal the number of rim requirements − 1.

13. **Stone squares**   Used squares in the transportation problem containing circled values that are in solution.

14. **Improvement index**   The net change in cost occasioned by a one-unit change in the quantity shipped.

15. **Assignment problem**   A special case of the transportation problem where the number of columns equals the number of rows and in which there will be one and only one assignment in a given row or column of the assignment table in the optimal solution.

16. **Flood's technique**   Another name given to the assignment method.

17. **Hungarian method of assignment**   Another name given to the assignment method.

18. **Opportunity cost**   The cost of the opportunities that are sacrificed in order to take a certain action.

19. **Job-opportunity costs**   Differences in cost between the best possible assignments of job to machine and the ones chosen (column differences).

20. **Machine-opportunity costs**   Differences in cost between the best possible assignment of machines to jobs and the ones chosen (row differences).

Review of Equations

Page 368

$$R_i + K_j = C_{ij} \tag{11-1}$$

This equation is used to determine row and column values at a stone square in the MODI method of determining improvement indices.

Page 369

$$C_{ij} - R_i - K_j = \text{improvement index} \qquad (11\text{-}2)$$

This formulation is used to compute the improvement index. If the result is negative, further improvement is possible; when all indices are equal to or greater than zero, the optimal solution has been obtained.

Exercises

11-1. Central Construction Company moves materials between three plants and three projects. Project A requires 140 truckloads each week, project B requires 200, and project C requires 80. Plant W can supply 120 loads, X can supply 160, and Y can supply 160. Using the cost information given in the following table, compute the optimal transportation cost using the stepping-stone method.

Cost Information

From	To project A	To project B	To project C
Plant W	$1	$2	$2
Plant X	4	3	5
Plant Y	1	2	3

11-2. T. C. Mellott trucking company has a contract to move 115 truckloads of sand per week between three sand-washing plants, W, X, and Y, and three destinations, A, B, and C. Cost and volume information are given below. Compute the optimal transportation cost using the stepping-stone method.

Project	Requirement per week, truckloads	Plant	Available per week, truckloads
A	45	W	35
B	50	X	40
C	20	Y	40

Cost Information

From	To project A	To project B	To project C
Plant W	$5	$10	$10
Plant X	20	30	20
Plant Y	5	8	12

11-3. Sid Lane hauls oranges between Florida groves and citrus packing plants. His schedule this week calls for 520 boxes with locations and costs as follows:

Grove	Requirement per week	Packing plant	Available per week
A	170	W	130
B	250	X	200
C	100	Y	190

Cost Information

From	To Plant W	To Plant X	To Plant Y
Grove A	$ 2	$ 5	$ 5
Grove B	10	15	10
Grove C	2	4	6

Use the MODI method to find the lowest transportation cost.

11-4. Jack Evans owns several trucks used to haul crushed stone to road projects in the county. The road contractor for whom Jack hauls, N. Teer, has given Jack this schedule for next week:

Project	Requirement per week	Plant	Available per week
A	50	W	45
B	75	X	60
C	50	Y	60

Jack figures his costs from the crushing plant to each of the road projects to be these:

Cost Information

From	To project A	To project B	To project C
Plant W	$4	$3	$3
Plant X	6	7	6
Plant Y	4	2	5

Using the MODI method, compute Jack's optimal schedule (source and destination) for next week and his transportation cost.

11-5. The Advanced Company has three jobs to be done on three machines. Each job must be done on one and only one machine. The cost of each job on each machine is given in the following table. Give the job assignments which will minimize cost.

Cost Information

Job	Machine		
	X	Y	Z
A	$4	$6	$8
B	2	3	4
C	4	8	5

11-6. Coley's Machine Shop has four machines on which to do three jobs. Each job can be assigned to one and only one machine. The cost of each job on each machine is given in the following table. What are the job assignments which will minimize cost?

Job	Machine			
	W	X	Y	Z
A	$18	$24	$28	$32
B	8	13	17	19
C	10	15	19	22

11-7. The Houston Aerospace Company has just been awarded a rocket engine development contract. The contract terms require that at least five other smaller companies be awarded subcontracts for a portion of the total work. So Houston requested bids from five small companies (A, B, C, D, and E) to do subcontract work in five areas (V, W, X, Y, and Z). The bids are as follows:

Cost Information

Company	Subcontract bids				
	V	W	X	Y	Z
A	$45,000	$60,000	$75,000	$100,000	$30,000
B	50,000	55,000	70,000	100,000	45,000
C	60,000	70,000	80,000	110,000	40,000
D	30,000	50,000	60,000	95,000	25,000
E	60,000	55,000	65,000	115,000	35,000

Which bids should Houston accept in order to fulfill the contract terms at the least cost? What is the total cost of the subcontracts?

11-8. An assignment algorithm may be used to solve maximizing assignments as well as minimizing assignments. In either case the procedures covered in this chapter are used to produce a matrix of opportunity costs. To convert a maximizing assignment to its equivalent opportunity-cost matrix, one need only multiply each element in the original matrix by -1 and proceed as if it were a minimizing assignment.

The town of Boulton is putting up for bids four used police vehicles. The town will allow individuals to make bids on all four vehicles but will accept only one bid per individual. Four individuals have made the following bids:

Individual	Vehicle			
	Chevrolet	Ford	Plymouth	AMC
Albert	$1,000	$ 900	$1,100	$ 900
Bruce	1,100	1,000	950	950
Charles	1,050	950	900	1,050
David	1,150	1,000	950	1,000

Which bids should be awarded in order to yield the town the maximum total sales revenue? What will the total revenue be?

11-9. You have begun a business of your own and have decided to produce one or more of products A, B, C, and D. You've approached four banks—W, X, Y, and Z—with your ideas on these projects in order to obtain the necessary financing. The following table reflects the level of financing required for each project, the interest rate each of the banks is willing to charge on loans for each of the projects, and the total line of credit each of the banks is willing to lend you.

| | Project (interest rate) | | | | |
Bank	A	B	C	D	Max. credit
W	6%	8%	9%	7%	$20,000
X	5	5	5	5	10,000
Y	7	6	8	8	20,000
Z	8	9	9	8	30,000
Amount required	$40,000	$30,000	$20,000	$20,000	

As each project should be as attractive profitwise as any other, you've decided to undertake all or part of any number of projects you can at the lowest total payment of interest. Which projects should you adopt and from which banks should you finance them?

11-10. The purchasing agent of the Acme Plumbing Company wishes to purchase 3000 feet of pipe type A, 2000 feet of pipe B, and 3000 feet of pipe C. Three manufacturers (X, Y, and Z) are willing to provide the needed pipe at the costs given below (in dollars per 1000 feet). Acme wants delivery within 1 month. Manufacturer X can produce up to 6000 feet of pipe (total of types A, B, and C). Manufacturer Y can provide 5000 feet, and Manufacturer Z can produce 3000 feet.

| | Type of pipe (cost $/1,000 ft) | | | |
Manufacturer	A	B	C	Available
X	$250	$300	$280	6,000
Y	260	280	290	5,000
Z	300	290	290	3,000
Amount required	3,000 ft	2,000 ft	3,000 ft	

Determine what Acme's least-cost purchasing plan for the pipe should be.

11-11. The Durham Rent-a-Car Company rents car trailers to individuals making one-way moves. Occasionally the company has to redistribute the trailers in order to eliminate a surplus buildup in some cities and a shortage in others. The company currently has 4 too many trailers in Ardsville, 3 too many in Bethel, 6 too many in Canton, and 1 too many in Dover. They would like to shift 5 trailers to Evanston, 3 to Farmington, and 6 to Grove Village. The following table gives mileages between the various sources and destinations:

| Source | Destinations | | | Total available |
	Evanston	Farmington	Grove Village	
Ardsville	50 miles	40 miles	80 miles	4
Bethel	30	10	90	3
Canton	60	100	20	6
Dover	90	90	30	1
Total required	5	3	6	14

How should Durham redistribute the trailers so that total mileage traveled is minimized?

11-12. Ragsdale Textiles has four knitting plants located at Brevard, Flortown, Sillboro, and Siler City. They also own three finishing mills located at Adenton, Buford, and Silverville. The finishing mills have the following yardage requirements per week:

Adenton	1.5 million yards
Buford	.9 million yards
Silverville	2.1 million yards
Total	4.5 million yards

The four knitting mills project this output per week for the next few months:

Brevard	1.1 million yards
Flortown	1.4 million yards
Sillboro	1.2 million yards
Siler City	.8 million yards
Total	4.5 million yards

The delivery costs per 100,000 yards from knitting mill to finishing mills are

| From | Cost per 100,000 yards | | |
	To Adenton	To Buford	To Silverville
Brevard	$150	$200	$200
Flortown	190	260	240
Sillboro	320	220	230
Siler City	180	190	200

Given their information, schedule shipment from each knitting mill to each finishing mill to minimize total transportation cost. Use the transportation method.

11-13. Ed Honey operates four used car lots: Mobile, Biloxi, Ocean Springs, and Pensacola. Ed has found it to be more efficient to operate two large "make ready"

warehouses in Gulfport and Bay Minette and ship the prepared cars by truck to the four lots. The expected demand for cars at his four lots this month is

Mobile	125 cars
Biloxi	110 cars
Ocean Springs	110 cars
Pensacola	165 cars

Each warehouse is expected to receive and make ready these cars during the month:

Gulfport	250 cars
Bay Minette	200 cars

Each of Ed's trucks will haul 5 cars; the cost of a load from each warehouse to each used car lot is:

	Cost per truckload			
From	To Mobile	To Biloxi	To Ocean Springs	To Pensacola
Gulfport	$75	$ 50	$ 50	$150
Bay Minette	90	120	140	75

By using the transportation method and the information given, devise a schedule which will minimize Ed's total transportation costs for the month.

11-14. Charlie's Tuna Cannery produces tuna in two plants, Seattle and Anchorage. Seattle has a capacity of 20,000 cases monthly on regular time and another 5000 cases by using overtime. Anchorage can produce 30,000 cases and 10,000 cases on regular time and overtime respectively. Seattle's production costs are $6 a case on regular time and $9 a case on overtime. Anchorage has costs of $7 and $8 respectively. Tuna can be sold in the same month as canned or stored at a cost of $1 per case per month.

Charlie's two customers, Chicken of the Ocean and Moon-Kist, have the following monthly needs:

	Jan.	Feb.	Mar.	Apr.
Chicken of the Ocean	20,000	30,000	40,000	50,000
Moon-Kist	20,000	40,000	30,000	40,000

Cost per case for shipping from the company's two canneries to the customers is

	To Chicken of the Ocean	To Moon-Kist
Seattle	$2	$3
Anchorage	2	1

Set up the transportation version of a solution to this problem that will minimize Charlie's total production, storage, and transportation costs for this period. Do not work the problem.

11-15. Frosty, Inc. manufactures picnic coolers in three sizes: party size, family size, and storage size. The major restriction on production is labor: party size takes 40 minutes a unit, family size an hour, and storage size 80 minutes a unit. Weekly demand for the coming three weeks has been estimated to be

	Party	Family	Storage
Week 1	150	120	60
Week 2	150	240	120
Week 3	180	180	240

There are no storage costs associated with production which is not shipped, since the plant, for the present time, has considerable unused space. Labor rates are $5 an hour with time and a half for overtime. Labor availability for this production period is

	Regular time	Overtime
Week 1	400 hours	160 hours
Week 2	400 hours	320 hours
Week 3	640 hours	400 hours

Using the transportation method, determine the optimal production schedule for Frosty. (*Hint:* Convert demand from units to hours of production.)

11-16. Mountain Furniture Company produces one product, a handcrafted cane-bottom rocking chair made of maple. From its three plants, Mountain projects this production over the next 2 months: Rock City, 7250 units; Saluda, 10,150 units; Westphal, 4350 units. Mountain wholesales these chairs to specialty stores in New York, Atlanta, Houston, and Los Angeles. Demand for the 2-month period in these four cities is

New York	8,700 chairs
Atlanta	5,800 chairs
Houston	2,900 chairs
Los Angeles	2,175 chairs

Each chair is packed in a separate box after being carefully wrapped with a special cover to prevent marring the finish. Transportation costs from each plant to each distribution point are

From	To New York	To Atlanta	To Houston	To Los Angeles
Rock City	$ 5.60	$12.00	$14.50	$11.00
Saluda	11.00	6.50	4.00	5.00
Westphal	13.50	9.00	5.50	5.50

Use the transportation model to minimize the total shipping cost for this period.

11-17. The purchasing agent for the Town of New Hope, Tennessee, wishes to purchase replacement tires for the town's service vehicles. He needs 300 E78 × 15; 200 D78 × 14; and 300 GR 78 × 15 tires. Three tire suppliers have bid at the prices given below; each says it will supply all or part of the order.

	E78 × 15	D78 × 15	GR78 × 15
Southern Tire Co.	$25	$30	$28
New Hope Tire Co.	26	28	29
Billy's Tire Service	30	29	29

Use the assignment method to determine the least-cost purchasing plan for the purchasing agent.

11-18. Linville Laboratories has just been notified that it has received three government research grants. The laboratory administrator must now assign research directors to each of these projects. There are four researchers available now who are relatively free from other duties. Time required to complete the required research activities will be a function of the experience and ability of the research director who is assigned to the project. The laboratory administrator has this estimate of project completion times (in weeks) for each director-grant combination:

Research directors	Grant		
	1	2	3
Louis Gump	60	90	54
Anne Aitken	54	108	30
Mary Albritton	36	84	18
Ned Powell	72	96	48

Since the three grants have about the same priority, the laboratory administrator would like to assign research directors in a way that would minimize the total time (in weeks) necessary to complete all three grant projects. What assignments should be made?

Bibliography

Dallenbach, H. G., and **E. J. Bell:** *User's Guide to Linear Programming* (Englewood Cliffs, N.J.: Prentice-Hall, Inc., 1970).

Hu, T. C.: *Integer Programming and Network Flows* (Reading, Mass.: Addison-Wesley Publishing Company, Inc., 1969).

Kwak, N. K.: *Mathematical Programming with Business Applications* (New York: McGraw-Hill Book Company, 1973).

Levin, R. I., and **R. Lamone:** *Linear Programming for Management Decisions* (Homewood, Ill.: Richard D. Irwin, Inc., 1969).

Llewellyn, Robert: *Linear Programming* (New York: Holt, Rinehart and Winston, 1964).

Simmons, Donald M.: *Linear Programming for Operations Research* (San Francisco: Holden-Day, Inc., Publisher, 1972).

Strum, Jay E.: *Introduction to Linear Programming* (San Francisco: Holden-Day, Inc., Publisher, 1972).

Integer programming, branch-and-bound method, goal programming, dynamic programming

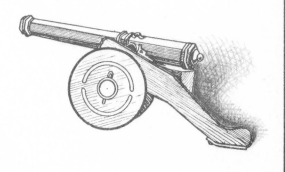

1. Integer Programming

Sometimes noninteger answers don't make sense

In many real situations, solutions to linear programming problems make sense only if they have integer (whole number) values. Quantities like $16^2/_3$ chairs, $78^1/_2$ tables, or 3.46 railroad cars may be unrealistic. Simply rounding off the linear programming solution to the nearest whole numbers may not produce a feasible solution. Take, for example, the optimal linear programming solution to the expanded Dimensions, Ltd., problem first introduced on page 317 of Chapter 10. In the final simplex tableau in Table 10-17, this is given as:

Rounding off noninteger answers is not always feasible

$6^2/_3$ chairs

$16^2/_3$ bookcases

If you round off these quantities to the nearest integer values, 7 chairs and 17 bookcases, you will violate the time constraints in the assembly and finishing departments. In this chapter, we introduce a technique called *integer programming*. This will allow us to find the optimum *integer* solution to a problem without violating any of the constraints.

The Idea of a Cut

Adding a new constraint called a cut

Integer programming is an extension of linear programming; that is to say, we begin by forgetting the integer requirement and solving the problem with the simplex method introduced in Chapter 10. If the solution we find has all integer values, we have found the optimum *integer* solution. If it does not, we continue by adding a new constraint to the problem. This new constraint, called a *cut*, permits the new set of feasible solutions to include *all* the feasible integer solutions for the original constraints, but it does not include the optimal noninteger solution originally found. Look at the expanded Dimensions, Ltd., answer above: $6^2/_3$ chairs and $16^2/_3$ bookcases. A cut would permit the new set of feasible solutions to include solutions like these,

6 chairs   16 bookcases

5 chairs   16 bookcases

6 chairs   15 bookcases

398

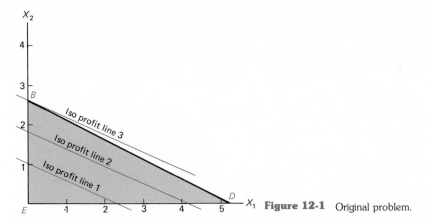

Figure 12-1 Original problem.

but it would exclude the noninteger solution originally found: $6^2/_3$ chairs and $16^2/_3$ bookcases.

Once we have added the cut, we solve the revised problem using the simplex method. If we get an integer solution this time, we are finished. If not, we add still another cut and continue until we find an integer solution. Since we never eliminate any feasible integer solutions from consideration, we hope to find the optimal integer solution to the problem sooner or later. There are many different kinds of cuts; we will discuss *Gomory's fractional cut,* which guarantees an optimal solution.

What to do after adding the new constraint

The Cut Shown Graphically

Look at the simple linear programming problem illustrated in Figure 12-1; there we show the one constraint in the problem, $3X_1 + 6X_2 \leq 16$. The objective function $\$2X_1 + \$5X_2$, is such that point B $(X_1 = 0, X_2 = 2^2/_3)$ is the optimal noninteger solution. Now look at Figure 12-2; here we have added the cut, $X_2 \leq 2$, to the problem. None of the feasible solutions that this cut eliminated, those in the unshaded area ABC, is an integer solution. Therefore the new set of feasible solutions, those in the shaded area $EACD$, still contains *all* the possible integer solutions to the original problem. An examination of the area of feasible solutions $EACD$ shows that the optimal integer solution is point F, $(X_1 = 1, X_2 = 2)$.

What the cut looks like in the graphic solution

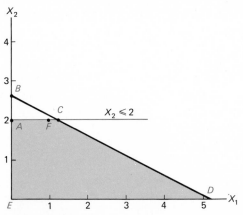

Figure 12-2 Cut $(X_2 \leq 2)$ added.

Table 12-1 Optimal Noninteger Solution

C_j			3	5	0	0
	Product mix	Quantity	T	C	S_1	S_2
5	C	$7/5$	0	1	$2/5$	$-1/5$
3	T	$17/5$	1	0	$-3/5$	$4/5$
	Z_j	$86/5$	3	5	$1/5$	$7/5$
	$C_j - Z_j$		0	0	$-1/5$	$-7/5$

The Integer Programming Algorithm

Let's demonstrate the integer programming algorithm by solving this new Dimensions, Ltd., problem, where the solution must be integer.

Maximize: $\$3T + \$5C$

Subject to: $1T + 4C \leqslant 9$

$\qquad\qquad 2T + 3C \leqslant 11$

Table 12-1 shows the optimal noninteger solution to this problem.

Expressing noninteger values as the sum of an integer and a fraction   To find the cut, we arbitrarily choose one of the noninteger variables in the optimal solution; we choose C. Look now at the row in the final tableau corresponding to C; we must rewrite this row with any noninteger value in it expressed as the sum of an integer and a nonnegative fraction less than 1. Look at these examples of numbers similarly rewritten:

$4/3 = \quad 1 + 1/3$

$5/4 = \quad 1 + 1/4$

$2/3 = \quad 0 + 2/3$

$-2/3 = -1 + 1/3$

Repeating the C row, we have:

Mix	Quantity	T	C	S_1	S_2
C	$7/5$	0	1	$2/5$	$-1/5$

Derivation of the cut algebraically   First we write these values in the C row $(1, 2/5, -1/5, 7/5)$ as the sum of an integer and a nonnegative fraction less than 1:

$(1 + 0)C + (0 + 2/5)S_1 + (-1 + 4/5)S_2 = (1 + 2/5)$

Then we take all the integer coefficients to the right-hand side:

$2/5 S_1 + 4/5 S_2 = 2/5 + (1 - 1C + 1S_2)$

Now, think of this equation in a slightly different form:

$$2/5S_1 + 4/5S_2 = 2/5 + \text{some integer}$$

If the left side is equal to 2/5 *plus* some integer (0, 1, 2, etc.), then the left side by itself must be greater than or equal to 2/5. So we can rewrite:

$$2/5S_1 + 4/5S_2 \geqslant 2/5$$

Now, if we multiply this by −1, we avoid having to deal with subtracted slack variables (which require an artificial variable):

$$-2/5S_1 - 4/5S_2 \leqslant -2/5$$

Adding a slack variable, we get

$$-2/5S_1 - 4/5S_2 + S_3 = -2/5$$

This is the required cut. We add it to the simplex tableau in Table 12-1 and get the new simplex tableau shown in Table 12-2. We have a problem in trying to determine which variable to bring into the second solution in Table 12-2, since all $C_j - Z_j$ values are 0 or negative. Just to get the solution started, divide the negative values in the S_3 row into the corresponding values in the $C_j - Z_j$ row and bring in that variable which has the smallest quotient:

$$S_3: \quad \frac{-1/5}{-2/5} = 1/2 \qquad \frac{-7/5}{-4/5} = \boxed{7/4} \quad \text{(the } S_1 \text{ column gives the smallest quotient, so } S_1 \text{ comes in and } S_3 \text{ goes out)}$$

From this point on, the procedure is the same as in the simplex; in this particular problem, we find the optimal *integer* solution in another tableau, as is shown in Table 12-3. In the tableau in Table 12-3, there are no more positive values in the $C_j - Z_j$ row, so we know the optimal solution has been reached. It is to manufacture 4 tables and 1 chair; this uses all the hours available except for 1 hour in department 1, which appears in the final solution as $1S_1$. The profit earned by this optimal integer solutions is $17, which is only slightly lower than the $86/5 profit earned by the optimal noninteger solution in Table 12-1.

Comparing the integer and noninteger solutions

Table 12-2 Solution to the Integer Problem (First Tableau)

C_j			3	5	0	0	0
	Product mix	Quantity	T	C	S_1	S_2	S_3
5	C	$7/5$	0	1	$2/5$	$-1/5$	0
3	T	$17/5$	1	0	$-3/5$	$4/5$	0
0	S_3	$-2/5$	0	0	$-2/5$	$-4/5$	1
	Z_j		3	5	$1/5$	$7/5$	0
	$C_j - Z_j$		0	0	$-1/5$	$-7/5$	0

Table 12-3 Final Tableau for Integer Solution

C_j	Product mix	Quantity	3 T	5 C	0 S_1	0 S_2	0 S_3
5	C	1	0	1	0	-1	1
3	T	4	1	0	0	2	$-3/2$
0	S_1	1	0	0	1	2	$-5/2$
	Z_j		3	5	0	1	$1/2$
	$C_j - Z_j$		0	0	0	-1	$-1/2$

Although this simple example required only one cut and one simplex iteration to find the optimal integer solution, larger problems may require many cuts and iterations. The general procedure is:

Step 1 Solve the original problem with the simplex algorithm.

Step 2 If the solution has all integer values, it is optimal for the integer program. If not, add a cut obtained from a row which has a noninteger variable in the solution.

Step 3 Pick any solution variable with a negative value to leave the solution. Select the incoming variable as we did in the example on page 401. Do a simplex iteration. If all variables in the new solution are zero or positive, go to step 2; if not, repeat step 3.

2. Branch-and-Bound Method

Enumeration as a decision method Consider the assignment problems we discussed in Chapter 11, where our objective was to assign one job to each machine. Because those have a finite number of possible solutions, it is possible to use *enumeration* as a solution method, that is, to list *all* the possible solutions and pick the one with, for example, the lowest cost. The availability of high-speed computers would lead one to believe that enumeration is a valid operation method even with large problems. However, when you look at the way in which the number of possible solutions increases relative to the size of the problem, you can see that enumeration quickly becomes impossible or at least economically impractical. For example, if there are only eight variables in the problem and each of these has only eight feasible (physically allowable) values, there can be *as many as* $(8)^8$ feasible solutions. Even in a case of this size, using a computer to enumerate all the feasible solutions would be excessively costly and time-consuming.

Branch-and-bound enumerates efficiently For this reason, we shall now introduce you to a technique known as *branch-and-bound,* which, although it uses enumeration, does it so efficiently that only a very small part of the total number of possible solutions need be examined

[1] For a survey of branch-and-bound methods, the reader can see E. L. Lawler and J. D. Wood, "Branch-and-Bound Methods: A Survey," *Operations Research,* vol. 14, pp. 699–719, 1966.

Table 12-4 Cost for Each
Job-Machine Assignment

	Machines			
Jobs	1	2	3	4
A	$90	$ 5	$48	$73
B	69	14	83	86
C	57	93	2	79
D	7	77	75	23

individually. There is quite a large[1] body of literature on this subject and a rapidly increasing number of applications. Although we cannot go into all the nuances and variations of this technique, we can use an assignment problem of the type we have been discussing in this chapter to illustrate how it works.

Conceptually, you can think of branching-and-bounding as a method which keeps dividing up the area of feasible solutions into smaller and smaller parts until that single solution which either minimizes or maximizes some objective function is determined. (The concept of an area of feasible solutions was first developed in Chapter 9, in connection with graphic methods of linear programming.)

Branch-and-Bound Solution to an Assignment Problem

In Table 12-4 we have illustrated a job-machine assignment problem like those in Chapter 11. Here we present four jobs that can each be done on any one of four machines together with the cost of doing each job on each machine. Our objective is to use the branch-and-bound technique to generate the least-cost assignment (that assignment which minimizes the total cost of doing all four jobs). We shall demonstrate the solution to the problem in Table 12-4 in four steps:

Solving a job-machine assignment problem using branch-and-bound

Step 1 Out of the 24 possible solutions, first find a lower bound on the total cost of the assignment—that is, a cost point below which cost could never fall. The assignment which produces this lowest cost need not be a feasible one; there can be more than one job assigned to the same machine. The only purpose of this initial lower-bound calculation is to establish a "floor" below which cost cannot fall. In doing this, we are "bounding" cost on the lower side or setting a lower *bound* on total cost.

Find a lower bound

The quickest way to establish the lowest possible cost is to add the smallest cost in each of the four columns; when we do this we get: $7 + 5 + 2 + 23 = 37$. Because, in this particular assignment of jobs to machines, job D has been assigned to two machines (1 and 4), this assignment is not a feasible one; we must therefore proceed to find the least-cost feasible solution.

Step 2 Next, divide up the process of looking for solutions. Suppose we start by assigning each job in turn to machine 1 and observe the result in each of the four cases in Table 12-5. In each calculation in step 2, once we assigned each of the jobs to machine 1 in turn, we then added the smallest cost in each of the remaining

Dividing up the process of looking for solutions

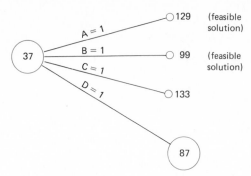

Figure 12-3   Steps 1 and 2 of branch-and-bound solution.

three columns (as in step 1 above) without considering whether doing that would yield a feasible solution. Steps 1 and 2 are expressed in "tree" form in Figure 12-3. The circled value 37 represents the lowest-cost solution obtained in step 1; each of the four solutions obtained in step 2 is shown, and the smallest of these (87) is circled. Because 129 (the lowest-cost solution possible when job A is done on machine 1) is greater than 99, and as 99 is the cost of a known feasible solution, all the other solutions which could be computed when A = 1 are discarded without consideration, as none of them could be lower than 129. The same logic is applied when C = 1, and all possible solutions which could come from that branch of our tree are discarded. In this manner, branch-and-bound evaluates only a very small portion of the total possible alternatives but does not discard one which could be optimal. Specifically, in step 2 we have avoided the evaluation of almost half the possible alternative assignments already.

Half of the possible assignments have been avoided

Step 3   We next consider the lowest-cost branch on the tree in step 2, where job D is assigned to machine 1. (The fact that this cost of 87 does not represent a feasible assignment does not prevent us from searching for other lower-cost solutions on this branch which may be feasible.) In each calculation in this step (Table 12-6), once we had assigned job D to machine 1, we assigned each of the three remaining jobs to machine 2 in turn and added the smallest cost in each of the remaining two columns without considering whether a feasible solution would result. The one feasible assignment which results from this step and produces a total cost of 96 is D = 1, B = 2, C = 3, and A = 4.

In "tree" form, steps 1, 2, and 3 are shown in Figure 12-4.

Table 12-5   Assigning Each Job to Machine 1

Assignment	Lower bound on total cost
A done on machine 1	$90 + 14 + \ 2 + 23 = 129$ (feasible solution)
B done on machine 1	$69 + \ 5 + \ 2 + 23 = \ \ 99$ (feasible solution)
C done on machine 1	$57 + \ 5 + 48 + 23 = 133$
D done on machine 1	$7 + \ 5 + \ 2 + 73 = \ \ 87$

Table 12-6 Assigning Job D to Machine 1

Assignment (when D = 1)	Lower bound on total cost
A done on machine 2	$(7) + [5 + 2 + 79] = 93$
B done on machine 2	$(7) + [14 + 2 + 73] = 96$ (feasible solution)
C done on machine 2	$(7) + [93 + 48 + 73] = 221$

The circled value 93 represents the lowest-cost solution obtained in this step. Each of the other two solutions obtained in this step is also shown. As 221 (the lowest-cost solution possible when D = 1 and C = 2) is greater than 96 (a feasible solution), all the other solutions which could emanate from the D = 1, C = 2 branch of the tree are discarded without further evaluation. Here again, branch-and-bound illustrates how it evaluates only a portion of the possible solutions yet *does not miss one* which might be optimal.

Step 4 We next consider the lowest-cost branch on the tree in step 3, the case where job D is assigned to machine 1 and job A to machine 2. The fact that the cost of 93 does not represent a feasible assignment does not prevent us from searching for *other* lower-cost solutions on this branch which *may* be feasible. The two possible alternative asssignments when D = 1 and A = 2 are shown in Table 12-7.   **The final step**

In tree form, steps 1, 2, 3, and 4 are illustrated in Figure 12-5.

Because both feasible alternatives found in step 4 offer costs higher than 96 (the cost of a known feasible alternative found in step 3), both of those solutions are discarded. The optimal answer to this assignment problem is the $96 feasible solution found in step 3, corresponding to the solution:

D = 1	$ 7
B = 2	14
C = 3	2
A = 4	73
	$96

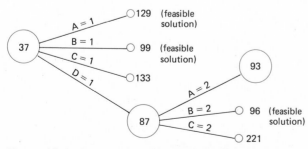

Figure 12-4 Steps 1, 2, and 3 of branch-and-bound solution.

Table 12-7   Assigning D to 1 and A to 2

Assignment (when D = 1 and A = 2)	Lower bound on total cost
B done on machine 3; C done on machine 4	$(12) + [83 + 79] = 174$ (feasible solution)
B done on machine 4; C done on machine 3	$(12) + \ [2 + 86] = 100$ (feasible solution)

A short recapitulation of the four steps may be useful:

Reviewing the four steps in the solution *Step 1*   We established a lower bound on total cost of $37. (This was not a feasible solution, only a beginning point.)

Step 2   We established an upper bound on cost of $99 and a new lower bound of $87. The upper-bound cost of $99 represented a feasible solution but the new lower bound of $87 did not.

Step 3   We established a new upper bound on cost of $96 and a new lower bound of $93. The upper-bound cost of $96 represented a feasible solution but the new lower bound of $93 did not.

Step 4   We evaluated the two possible solutions from the $93 lower bound in step 3 and found both to generate costs higher than the upper-bound cost of $96 established in step 3. Thus step 4 indicated to us that $96 was both the upper bound and lower bound; that is, we had continued to partition our feasible solutions area into smaller and smaller areas until only the $96 solution remained.

There are many computer programs which have been developed to apply the many variations of the branch-and-bound technique with considerable computational efficiency. Using large computers, it is possible to evaluate quite large and complex problems in just a few minutes by using these programs.

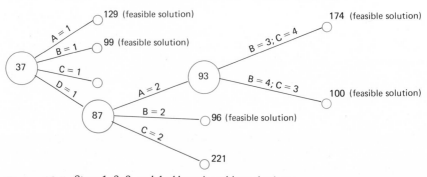

Figure 12-5   Steps 1, 2, 3, and 4 of branch-and-bound solution.

Table 12-8 Optimum Solution to Dimensions, Ltd., Problem

C_j			$8	$6	$0	$0
	Product mix	Quantity	T	C	S_A	S_F
$8	T	12	1	0	$1/3$	$-1/6$
$6	C	6	0	1	$-1/6$	$1/3$
	Z_j	$132	$8	$6	$$5/3$	$$2/3$
	$C_j - Z_j$		$0	$0	$-$5/3$	$-$2/3$

3. Goal Programming

Goal programming applies the linear programming model to situations which contain *multiple* goals or objectives. To introduce this section, let's look back at the original Dimensions, Ltd., problem first introduced in Chapter 9, page 262. The linear programming simplex solution to this problem was presented in Chapter 10, Table 10-11. That solution is repeated here as Table 12-8 for reference. The optimum solution to that problem was to produce 12 tables and 6 chairs for a profit of $132. All hours in assembly and finishing were used.

Some problems have multiple goals

Shortcomings of Linear Programming

A problem with linear programming is that the objective function is measured in only *one dimension*, profit in this case. It's impossible in linear programming to have *multiple goals* in the objective function (say, profit, productivity, and cost) unless they can all be measured in the same units. Organizations generally have *several* goals generally *not* measurable in the same units. These goals may even be conflicting. Suppose, for instance, that Dimensions, Ltd., had these goals:

Shortcomings of linear programming

1. Maximize profit in dollars.
2. Maximize production of tables in units.
3. Maximize production of chairs in units.

In this case the three goals can't be added because dollars and units don't add; in addition, deviating from the optimal solution of 12 tables and 6 chairs will *reduce* profit from the $132 optimum; thus we see that goals 2 and 3 conflict with goal 1.

Making Target Estimates and Ranking Goals

Goal programming asks management to set some estimated targets for each of their goals and to put priorities on them—that is, to rank them in order of importance. Managers who want to use goal programming only have to say which goal they consider more important than another; they do not have to say *how much* more important they consider it.

Setting targets and putting priorities on goals

What goal programming does

When this information is supplied by management, goal programming tries to minimize the deviations from the targets that were set. It begins with the most important goal and keeps on until the achievement of a less important goal would cause management to fail to achieve a more important one.

A Single-Goal Model

A single-goal situation

With only a single goal, say, profit, we could just as easily solve the Dimensions, Ltd., problem using linear programming, but a single-goal model is a good starting point for understanding goal programming. Suppose Dimensions, Ltd., sets its profit goal at $140 in this situation. If we let D_u equal the amount by which the goal is *underachieved* and D_o equal the amount by which the goal is overachieved, we can state the Dimensions, Ltd., problem as a goal programming problem:

Minimize: D_u minimize underachievement of the profit target

Objective function and constraints in a single-goal problem

Subject to: $\$8T + \$6C + D_u - D_o = \$140$ the profit obtained, $\$8T + \$6C$, plus any underachievement minus any overachievement must equal the target

$4T + 2C \leqslant 60$ assembly constraint

$2T + 4C \leqslant 48$ finishing constraint

With the addition of appropriate slack variables, this problem would be ready for solution by the simplex method. The actual answer turns out to be 12 tables and 6 chairs (the same as in the linear programming solution), but the value of the objective function is $8 (the amount by which we underachieved our $140 goal). Of course, we knew that $132 was the maximum profit earnable with these constraints, so missing $140 by $8 was expected. Notice in this formulation that only D_u is in the objective function; therefore, only one entry will appear in the C_j row above the D_u column. This entry will be $1, representing a dollar of deviation.

Equally Ranked Multiple Goals

A multiple-goal problem where all goals are equally desired

Suppose Dimensions, Ltd., states two equally ranked goals, the first to reach a profit goal of $100, the second to produce to meet a table goal of 10. Since these goals are equally ranked, a $1 deviation from the profit target is just as important (in the goal programming model) as a deviation of 1 table. For this formulation, let's use the following notation:

D_{up} = amount by which the profit goal is underachieved

D_{op} = amount by which the profit goal is overachieved

D_{ut} = amount by which the table goal is underachieved

D_{ot} = amount by which the table goal is overachieved

Table 12-9 Initial Solution and Optimal Solution to Dimensions, Ltd., Problem with Two Equally Ranked Goals

C_j	Product mix	Quantity	0 T	0 C	0 S_A	0 S_F	1 D_{up}	0 D_{op}	1 D_{ut}	0 D_{ot}
1	D_{up}	100	8	6	0	0	1	−1	0	0
1	D_{ut}	10	1	0	0	0	0	0	1	−1
0	S_A	60	4	2	1	0	0	0	0	0
0	S_F	48	2	4	0	1	0	0	0	0
	Z_j	110	9	6	0	0	1	−1	1	−1
	$C_j − Z_j$		−9	−6	0	0	0	1	0	1
0	D_{ot}	$2^1/_2$	0	$^3/_4$	0	0	$^1/_8$	$-^1/_8$	−1	1
0	T	$12^1/_2$	1	$^3/_4$	0	0	$^1/_8$	$^1/_8$	0	0
0	S_A	10	0	−1	1	0	$-^1/_2$	$^1/_2$	0	0
0	S_F	23	0	$2^1/_2$	0	1	$-^1/_4$	$^1/_4$	0	0
	Z_j	0	0	0	0	0	0	0	0	0
	$C_j − Z_j$		0	0	0	0	1	0	1	0

The objective function and constraints for the solution to this goal programming problem are

Minimize: $D_{up} + D_{ut}$

Subject to:

$$\$8T + \$6C + D_{up} - D_{op} = \$100 \qquad \text{profit goal}$$

$$T + D_{ut} - D_{ot} = 10 \qquad \text{tables goal}$$

$$4T + 2C \leq 60 \qquad \text{assembly constraint}$$

$$2T + 4C \leq 48 \qquad \text{finishing constraint}$$

$$\text{All variables} \geq 0$$

Objective function and constraints for a problem with multiple equally ranked goals

In Table 12-9, we show the initial solution and the optimal solution to this goal programming problem. We notice from the final tableau that our goal of 10 tables was achieved and bettered ($12^1/_2 - 10 = 2^1/_2$); $2^1/_2$ appears in the final solution as D_{ot} (overachievement of tables). Our profit goal of \$100 was reached (both D_{up} and D_{op} are zero because they are not in the final solution and so profit is exactly \$100). Notice the alternate optimal solutions possible by bringing in C or D_{op}.

Reconciling the answer

Priority-Ranked Multiple Goals

In most cases, one goal is more important to management than another; goal programming can handle this situation too. Suppose Dimensions, Ltd., has established the following goals and has assigned them priorities (P_1, P_2, and P_3, where P_1 is most important) as follows:

A multiple-goal problem where goals are ranked

	Goal	Priority
1.	Produce to meet a table goal of 13.	P_1
2.	Reach a profit goal of $135.	P_2
3.	Produce to meet a chair goal of 5.	P_3

For this formulation, let's use this notation:

D_{up} = amount by which the profit goal is underachieved

D_{op} = amount by which the profit goal is overachieved

D_{ut} = amount by which the table goal is underachieved

D_{ot} = amount by which the table goal is overachieved

D_{uc} = amount by which the chair goal is underachieved

D_{oc} = amount by which the chair goal is overachieved

The objective function and constraints for this version of the Dimensions, Ltd., goal programming problem are:

Objective function and constraints for a problem with multiple ranked goals

Minimize: $P_1 D_{ut} + P_2 D_{up} + P_3 D_{uc}$ the P's used here are called *preemptive priority factors*; in the goal programming algorithm which follows, we assume that the priority ranking is absolute; that is, P_1 goals are so much more important than P_2 goals that P_2 goals will never be achieved until P_1 goals are

Subject to:

$$\$8T + \$6C + D_{up} - D_{op} = 135 \qquad \text{profit goal}$$
$$T + D_{ut} - D_{ot} = 13 \qquad \text{tables goal}$$
$$C + D_{uc} - D_{oc} = 5 \qquad \text{chair goal}$$
$$4T + 2C \leq 60 \qquad \text{assembly constraint}$$
$$2T + 4C \leq 48 \qquad \text{finishing constraint}$$

Table 12-10 presents the initial simplex tableau for this problem.

There are a number of characteristics of this tableau we should explain:

Special characteristics of the goal-programming tableau with ranked goals

1. Notice that there is a separate Z_j and $C_j - Z_j$ row for *each of the $P_1, P_2,$ and P_3* priorities. Since we do not add deviations from the chair goal, for example, to those from the profit goal (the units are different), we need these separate priority rows to keep track of things. It is common practice to illustrate the P rows from *bottom to top* in order of priority.

Table 12-10 Initial Simplex Tableau for Priority-Ranked Dimensions, Ltd., Problem

C_j			0	0	0	0	P_2	0	P_1	0	P_3	0
	Product mix	Quantity	T	C	S_A	S_F	D_{up}	D_{op}	D_{ut}	D_{ot}	D_{uc}	D_{oc}
P_2	D_{up}	135	8	6	0	0	1	-1	0	0	0	0
P_1	D_{ut}	13	1	0	0	0	0	0	1	-1	0	0
P_3	D_{uc}	5	0	1	0	0	0	0	0	0	1	-1
0	S_A	60	4	2	1	0	0	0	0	0	0	0
0	S_F	48	2	4	0	1	0	0	0	0	0	0
P_3	$\begin{cases} Z_j \\ C_j - Z_j \end{cases}$		0	1	0	0	0	0	0	0	1	-1
			0	-1	0	0	0	0	0	0	0	1
P_2	$\begin{cases} Z_j \\ C_j - Z_j \end{cases}$		8	6	0	0	1	-1	0	0	0	0
			-8	-6	0	0	0	1	0	0	0	0
P_1	$\begin{cases} Z_j \\ C_j - Z_j \end{cases}$		1	0	0	0	0	0	1	-1	0	0
			-1	0	0	0	0	0	0	1	0	0

↑In

2. The $C_j - Z_j$ value for any *column* is shown in the priority rows at the bottom of the tableau; for example, the $C_j - Z_j$ value for the T column is contained in the P_2 and P_1 rows at the bottom and is read $-8P_2 - 1P_1$; similarly, the $C_j - Z_j$ value for the C column is read $-1P_3 - 6P_2$.

3. In selecting the variable to enter the mix (T in this case), we start with the most important priority, P_1, and pick the most negative $C_j - Z_j$ value in that row; if there had *not* been a negative $C_j - Z_j$ value in that row, we would have moved up to the next most important priority, P_2, and looked in that row.

4. To determine the variable that is replaced, we use the same procedure we have always used (the theta rule); in this instance, 13/1 is the smallest positive value; therefore the D_{ut} row will be replaced in the next tableau.

5. If we find a negative $C_j - Z_j$ value that has a *positive* $C_j - Z_j$ value in one of the P rows *underneath* it, we disregard it. Such a positive value would mean that deviations from the lower (and more important) goal would be *increased* if we brought in that variable, and this is avoided since it won't lead us to a better solution.

Once the initial simplex tableau is set up, we proceed just as we have done in the simplex method, keeping in mind the five characteristics just discussed. The final simplex tableau for this problem is shown in Table 12-11. Notice there that we still have negative $C_j - Z_j$ values in both the P_2 and P_3 rows (-4 and -2 respectively). However, in both cases there is a positive value in the P_1 row beneath them (1), so we disregard both of them.

Proceeding toward the optimal solution

We notice from the final solution in Table 12-11 that the goals have been met to different extents. Our most important goal (produce 13 tables) was achieved. Our second most important goal (reach $135 profit) was missed (we generated

Interpreting the final solution

only $128 profit); the deviation, however, was slight, something on the order of 5 percent (notice that this deviation shows up as D_{up} in the final solution). Our lowest-ranked goal (produce 5 chairs) was missed by 1 chair; however, this represents a 20 percent deviation. Notice here too that the deviation shows up in the final solution as D_{uc} with a value of 1. Finally, notice that there are 6 hours unused in finishing. Whereas it might seem that these should have been used, remember that to manufacture another chair, for example, would also have required time in assembly, where all the time has been used.

4. Dynamic Programming

What dynamic programming does

Dynamic programming is a quantitative technique used to make a series of *inter-related* decisions. It is concerned with finding a *combination* of decisions which will maximize overall effectiveness. For example, a company may wish to make a series of marketing decisions over time which will provide it with the highest possible sales volume. Another organization may wish to find that series of interrelated production decisions over time which will minimize production cost or minimize the hiring and layoff necessary to achieve some specified production goal.

In Chapter 6, we used decision trees to solve problems that involved probabilities. Dynamic programming can also be used to handle some probabilistic problems, but here we will only show its use in a deterministic problem. The dynamic programming approach divides the problem into a number of subproblems or *stages*. The decision we make at each stage influences not only the next stage but also *every* stage to the end of the problem.

Table 12-11 Final Solution for Priority-Ranked Dimensions, Ltd., Problem

C_j	Product mix	Quantity	0	0	0	0	P_2	0	P_1	0	P_3	0
			T	C	S_A	S_F	D_{up}	D_{op}	D_{ut}	D_{ot}	D_{uc}	D_{oc}
P_2	D_{up}	7	0	0	-3	0	1	-1	4	-4	0	0
0	T	13	1	0	0	0	0	0	1	-1	0	0
P_3	D_{uc}	1	0	0	$-1/2$	0	0	0	2	-2	1	-1
0	C	4	0	1	$1/2$	0	0	0	-2	2	0	0
0	S_F	6	0	0	-2	1	0	0	6	-6	0	0
P_3	Z_j		0	0	$-1/2$	0	0	0	2	-2	1	-1
	$C_j - Z_j$		0	0	$1/2$	0	0	0	-2	2	0	1
P_2	Z_j		0	0	-3	0	1	-1	4	-4	0	0
	$C_j - Z_j$		0	0	3	0	0	1	-4	4	0	0
P_1	Z_j		0	0	0	0	0	0	0	0	0	0
	$C_j - Z_j$		0	0	0	0	0	0	1	0	0	0

Dynamic programming starts with the last stage of the problem and works backward toward the first stage, making optimal decisions at each stage of the problem. In a three-stage problem, for example, the inputs for stage 3 are the outputs of stage 2, and the inputs for stage 2 are the outputs of stage 1. If, by working backward in this way, we can optimize at each stage, then the sequence of decisions we have made will optimize the whole problem.

Whereas linear programming has standard ways to formulate the problems and solve them, there is no such "standard approach" in dynamic programming. It is, instead, sort of a general way of solving large, complex problems by breaking them down into a series of smaller problems which are more easily solved. A good bit of ingenuity is necessary to know when a problem might be solved by using dynamic programming and how that solution should be approached. We think that if you work through the problem we will present in this section, you will have gone quite a way toward the development of those abilities.

Dynamic programming actually works the problem backward

There is no standard approach to dynamic programming

Dynamic Programming Solution to Shortest-Route Problem

John Kottas is the truck dispatcher for an Atlanta transportation company. His firm has been awarded a contract to pick up a number of loads of woven material in Atlanta and transport them to St. Louis. John has looked at a map of the alternative routes between these two points and constructed the highway network in Figure 12-6. The circles (or *nodes*, as they are commonly called) represent the origin (node 1 = Atlanta), the destination (node 10 = St. Louis), and other cities where routes intersect (nodes 2, 3, 4, 5, 6, 7, 8, and 9). The arrows (or *branches*,

A shortest-route problem solved with dynamic programming

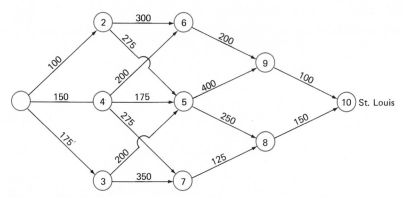

Figure 12-6 Highway network for John Kottas' shortest-route problem.

as they are called) represent highways between the nodes, each with its mileage indicated. John's problem is to find the shortest route from Atlanta to St. Louis.

Now look at Figure 12-7. Here we have broken John's problem into four smaller problems (stages). Each of these stages is described by its distance from St. Louis (measured in branches), and the input and output nodes for each stage

Breaking the original problem into four stages

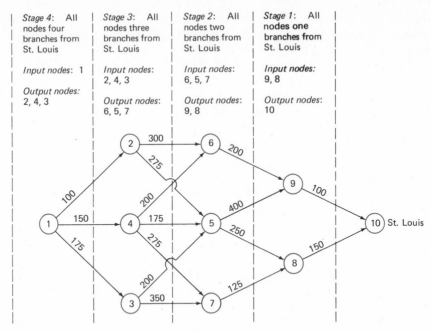

Figure 12-7 Highway network with problem stages, stage inputs, and stage outputs.

are identified. At each of the four stages of John's problem, we need to determine the optimum branch to take to move from each input node to an output node. We begin the solution to John's problem with an examination of the stage 1 problem.

Solving the stage 1 problem

Stage 1 Look at node 8. Since there is only one route from node 8 to St. Louis (node 10), this is the shortest route; the distance is 150 miles. Look now at node 9. Here too there is only one route to node 10, which requires us to travel 100 miles. Thus we have found the optimal route from each input node (8 and 9) to an output node (10). Stage 1 results are:

Input nodes	Output nodes	Route	Shortest distance to St. Louis
8	10	8–10	150
9	10	9–10	100

The solution to stage 1 is shown on the partial network in Figure 12-8 in two rectangular boxes above nodes 8 and 9. The solution is the shortest distance from each of the stage 1 input nodes to St. Louis.

Solving the stage 2 problem

Stage 2 The node we begin with at any stage is not important, so let's start with node 7. There is only one output node for node 7, and that is node 8. We already know (from stage 1) that the shortest distance from node 8 to St. Louis is 150 miles, therefore the shortest distance from node 7 to St. Louis is 275 miles (125 + 150). What about node 6? Again there is only one output node for node 6, and that is

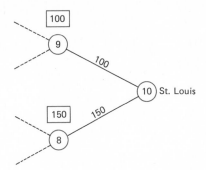

Figure 12-8 Solution to the stage 1 problem.

node 9. From stage 1 results we know that the shortest distance from node 9 to St. Louis is 100 miles, therefore the shortest distance from node 6 to St. Louis is 300 miles (200 + 100). Now look at node 5. There are *two* output nodes for node 5; they are 8 and 9. From stage 1 results we *already* know the shortest route from nodes 8 and 9 to St. Louis, 150 and 100 miles respectively. Therefore the choice of an optimal route between node 5 and St. Louis is either 500 miles (400 + 100) or 400 miles (250 + 150). Route 5–8–10 is the optimal one. Stage 2 results are

Input nodes	Output nodes	Route	Shortest distance to St. Louis
7	8	7–8	275
6	9	6–9	300
5	8	5–8	400

The partial network in Figure 12-9 shows the solution to the stage 2 problem.

Note that we solved the stage 2 problem by using the outputs from the stage 1 problem (the optimum distances 100 and 150 miles). We did *not* have to measure

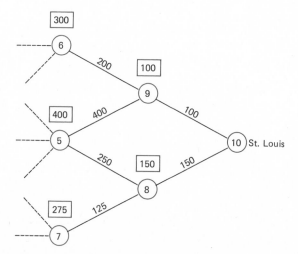

Figure 12-9 Solution to the stage 2 problem.

distances all the way from stage 2 nodes to St. Louis to find the shortest route, only from stage 2 nodes to stage 1 nodes.

Stage 3   We choose to begin here with node 2. Using the optimum answers for nodes 6 and 5 from stage 2 (300 and 400 respectively), we evaluate routes 2-6 and 2-5 and choose 2-6 (300 + 300 is less than 275 + 400). Looking at node 4, we see we have three choices; we use the optimum answers for nodes 6, 5, and 7 from stage 2 (300, 400, and 275 respectively). We evaluate routes 4-6, 4-5, and 4-7 and choose 4-6 (500 is less than either 575 or 550). What about node 3? Here there are two choices, routes 3-5 and 3-7. Using the optimum answers for nodes 5 and 7 from stage 2 (400 and 275 respectively), we choose route 3-5 (600 is less then 625). Stage 3 results are

Input nodes	Output nodes	Route	Shortest distance to St. Louis
2	6	2–6	600
4	6	4–6	500
3	5	3–5	600

Figure 12-10 shows the solution to the stage 3 problem.

Notice here again that we solved the stage 3 problem by using the outputs from the stage 2 problem (the optimum distances 300, 400, and 275 miles). We did *not* have to measure distances all the way from stage 3 nodes to St. Louis to find the shortest route, only from stage 3 nodes to stage 2 nodes.

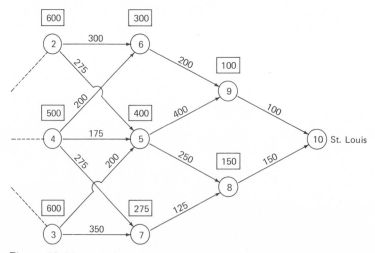

Figure 12-10   Solution to the stage 3 problem.

Stage 4 There is only one input node in stage 4, node 1, so we have three choices (route 1-2, 1-4, or 1-3). Using the output of stage 3 (the optimum distances 600, 500, and 600 miles), we evaluate the three routes and choose 1-4 (650 is less than either 700 or 775). Stage 4 results are

Solving the stage 4 problem

Input nodes	Output nodes	Route	Shortest distance to St. Louis
1	4	1–4	650

Figure 12-11 shows the solution to stage 4 (together with the solutions to the other stages).

The Shortest Route

Now that we have solved the four individual problems, let's go through the network from stage 4 to stage 1 and pick the best decision at each stage. Table 12-12 illustrates this process. You can see that the shortest route between Atlanta and St. Louis is 1-4-6-9-10, with a total distance of 650 miles.

Combining answers from the four stages to find the shortest route

In using dynamic programming to get a solution to this problem, we did not have to enumerate all of the possible paths through this network (and there are 10 of them). Whereas this would not have been such a terrible task for a network this size, think of the work that would be involved if the network had, say, 100

Computational advantage of dynamic programming

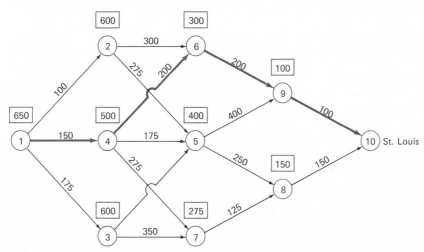

Figure 12-11 Solution to the stage 4 problem.

Table 12-12   Picking the Best Decision at Each Stage

	Input nodes	Output nodes	Route	Shortest distance to St. Louis
Stage 4	1 ⟶ 4		1–4	650
Stage 3	2	6	2–6	600
	4 ⟶ 6	6	4–6	500
	3	5	3–5	600
Stage 2	7	8	7–8	275
	6 ⟶ 9	9	6–9	300
	5	8	5–8	400
Stage 1	8	10	8–10	150
	9 ⟶ 10	10	9–10	100

nodes. Once again, we should emphasize that when using dynamic programming, we did not have to evaluate *all* the paths at each stage as we moved from node 10 back to node 1; instead, we used the output from one stage as the input for a succeeding stage. That's how dynamic programming provides such consequential savings of computation time over other methods.

Glossary

1. Integer programming   Mathematical programming method which generates optimum integer answers to a linear program.

2. Cut   A new constraint added to a linear programming problem as a step in producing the optimum integer solution.

3. Branch-and-bound   An efficient enumeration method for finding the optimum solution to certain types of combinatorial problems.

4. Goal programming   A variation of the simplex algorithm which permits the decision maker to specify target goals in order of their priority.

5. Dynamic programming   Quantitative technique useful in the solution to a problem where there are a number of interrelated decisions to be made.

6. Stage   One of the individual problems which, when taken together, make up a dynamic programming problem.

Exercises

12-1.   The Electric Car Company, Inc., manufactures three vehicles, the Scooter, the Metro, and the Delivery Special. The contributions to profit are $270, $400, and $450 respectively. The battery requirements for each vehicle are as follows: Scooter 1, Metro 2, Delivery Special 3. The charging generators installed on the vehicle are needed in these quantities: Scooter, 2; Metro, 2; Delivery Special, 3. If the Electric Car Company has 100 batteries and 120 generators on hand and no chance to get any more this week, what should the integer product mix be to maximize profit?

12-2. Parke Lane, Ltd., is a custom coachbuilder specializing in 2 types of coachwork: limousine conversion (X_1) and hearses (X_2). The contribution to profit from each of the two products is $3000 and $4000, respectively. The limitations on Parke Lane are strictly labor, since each product is essentially handmade. The production manager has offered these constraints representing time allocations and labor hours available during the next production scheduling period (13 weeks):

$$50X_1 + 36X_2 \leqslant 100,000 \text{ (bodywork)}$$
$$25X_1 + 36X_2 \leqslant 91,000 \quad \text{(interior)}$$
$$X_1, X_2 \geqslant 0$$

Find the integer solution which will maximize Parke Lane's profit for the next scheduling period.

12-3. Curt McLaughlin is an electrical contractor who has just landed the wiring contract for the new Durham Public Library. He has to decide shortly whether to hire one or more apprentice electricians (for 8 hours a day each) or to hire one or more part-time journeyman electricians (for 5 hours a day each). Apprentices can be hired for $5 an hour while part-time journeyman electricians earn a union scale of $11 an hour. Curt wants to limit his extra payroll to $100 a day and to use no more than 20 hours of extra time a day because of limited supervision. He estimates that an apprentice will generate an extra $3 a day in profits and a journeyman part-time electrician $5 a day. Formulate the integer programming problem to help Curt select the optimum number of apprentices and part-time journeymen. Solve the problem as a linear program, and derive the first cut. Do not solve the integer program.

12-4. Imperial Clocks, Inc., is a subcontractor making clock faces for a clock manufacturer. The amounts of brass required, the storage space used (to protect the delicate hand-worked face), the production rates for each face, and the contribution to profit from each clock face are as follows:

	Grandfather	Mantle	Wall	Chime
Pounds of brass per face	5	5	3.75	6.25
Square feet of storage per face	5	6.25	5	3.75
Faces per hour	3.75	7.5	2.5	3.75
Profit per face (dollars)	5.00	6.50	5.00	5.50

Imperial gets a daily allocation of 300 pounds of brass. The company has a total square footage of storage space of 375 for faces, and the plant operates 8 hours a day. All faces produced each day are shipped at the end of the day; this means storage space, material, and production time are shared by all faces. If Imperial must produce integer quantities of faces, find the optimum product mix.

12-5. Here is the final simplex tableau for a product-mix maximizing problem:

C_j			6	14	0	0
	Product mix	Quantity	X_1	X_2	S_1	S_2
0	S_1	10	2	0	1	$-2/3$
14	X_2	3.5	$1/2$	1	0	$1/12$
	Z_j	51	7	14	0	$7/6$
	$C_j - Z_j$		-1	0	0	$-7/6$

Find the integer programming solution to this problem.

12-6. Below is the final simplex tableau for a product-mix maximizing problem:

C_j			1	1	0	0
	Product mix	Quantity	X_1	X_2	S_1	S_2
1	X_1	$6^1/3$	1	$4/3$	$1/6$	0
0	X_2	5	0	4	-1	1
	Z_j	$6^1/3$	1	$4/3$	$1/6$	0
	$C_j - Z_j$		0	$-1/3$	$-1/6$	0

Find the integer programming solution to this problem.

12-7. In an integer programming problem with five variables, where each variable is bounded from below by 0 and from above by 2, what is the maximum number of nodes which can appear on the tree in a branch-and-bound solution?

12-8. Here is a schedule of annual shipping costs for a group of marble quarries and associated monument plants in Tennessee, all owned by the same corporation. Each quarry must supply one plant. Your task is to find an assignment of quarries to plants which will minimize the total shipping cost per year. Use branch-and-bound.

			Quarries		
Plants	Linwood	Sherrard	Johnsonville	Crossville	
Tammerville	11	35	44	24	Cost in
Kingstown	27	20	55	66	000's of
Carrboro	43	35	59	32	dollars
Roseboro	27	32	44	41	

12-9. William Sherrard's Auto-Quick does repairs on foreign cars. William has five mechanics, each of whom specializes in two makes of car but all of whom can work on any make. When he came in this morning, William saw five cars in the service line with repair orders written up. Interestingly, all five were in the shop today for a valve grinding job. William thought a minute about the respective abilities of his mechanics on each make and wrote down these figures:

| | Mechanic | | | | |
	Ham	Lacy	Sam	Sparky	Tuller
Volvo	8	7	6	9	11
Volks	6	9	9	10	9
Fiat	5	7	6	8	6
Saab	8	9	11	6	7
Datsun	9	8	5	5	10

(Hours for a valve job)

Use the branch-and-bound method to help William assign the five cars to the five mechanics so that the total time for all valve jobs is minimum.

12-10. Marcel Robbins is a contractor who currently has four homes under construction in Orange County. Marcel's usual practice is to visit every jobsite once or twice a day to check the progress of the work. He finds himself driving a longer distance than he thinks he should and, over a cup of coffee, has put down these mileages from job to job:

	Marcel's office	Jones job	Whitney job	Parrish job	Hamlin job	Stuart job
Marcel's office	0	4	3	6	2	1
Jones job	2	0	7	3	8	3
Whitney job	5	2	0	1	3	1
Parrish job	3	6	2	0	4	5
Hamlin job	8	6	3	2	0	4
Stuart job	6	2	2	2	5	0

Using the branch-and-bound method, can you find the shortest way for Marcel to leave his office, visit each job, and finish up at his office?

12-11. George Baroff owns George's Bait and Tackle Shop near the Fish River Basin. George sells three types of bait: crickets, red worms, and night crawlers. He figures that he nets $4 a thousand on crickets, $4.50 a thousand on red worms, and $2.40 a thousand on night crawlers. George also knows that it takes 2 cubic feet of potting soil for 1000 crickets, 3 cubic feet for 1000 red worms, and 1 cubic foot for 1000 night crawlers. The secret of George's success in growing bait is his special "bait food," a nutrient mix which he feeds at a rate of 3 gallons a month per 1000 crickets, 3 gallons a month per 1000 red worms, and 2 gallons a month per 1000 night crawlers. George has 100 cubic feet of potting soil and can produce 120 gallons of his bait food a month. He has two equally desirable goals, a target production of 18,000 crickets a month and a profit of $200. Set up the problem as a goal program, and if you have access to a computer, solve it using linear programming.

12-12. Sentimental Lighting, Inc., produces three styles of old-fashioned but currently popular lamps: a desk lamp, a bedside lamp, and a floor lamp. The lamps are all solid brass and are produced in two distinct steps: turning and finishing. The schedule for labor and material inputs and availability for each style is as follows:

	Desk lamp	Bedside lamp	Floor lamp	Availability
Turning labor	1 hr	3 hr	1.5 hr	2,000/mo
Finishing labor	1.5 in.	1.5 in.	4 in.	1,000/mo
Brass	4 lb	3 lb	6 lb	3,000/mo

Contribution to profit for the styles is $35, $40, and $65 respectively. Sentimental has two equally desirable goals: minimizing the idle time in finishing and making a monthly profit of $20,000. Set up the problem as a goal program, and if you have access to a computer, solve it using linear programming.

12-13. Pat Penland has just purchased the boat building firm of Elliot and Smith from the family who had run it for 70 years. She got quite a deal on the sale (low price, high leverage, etc.) but had to agree to these conditions: (1) she has to manufacture a total of at least four boats this year, (2) she has to use up the stock of lumber that is on hand, (3) she has to keep the boat finishing crew busy at least half of the time, and (4) she must show a profit of at least $10,000 in a year or the family will foreclose. Here is a table of the boats she can make, with lumber requirements, labor requirements, contribution, and resource availability:

	28′ Sport Fisherman	36′ Twin Cabin Cruiser	42′ Flying Bridge	Availability
Assembly labor	1,800 hr	2,300 hr	3,000 hr	8,000 hr
Finishing labor	900 hr	1,150 hr	1,300 hr	4,000 hr
Lumber	5,000 bd ft	8,000 bd ft	9,500 bd ft	19,000 bd ft
Profit	$3,000	$5,000	$6,000	

The Elliot and Smith families insist that Pat Penland achieve these goals in the order they appear here: 1, 2, 3, 4. Set up the complete first goal programming tableau to solve this problem.

12-14. Alice North is a history major at Boston Eastern College. Her class schedule requires her to travel quite a distance between two tightly scheduled classes because they are in different buildings at opposite ends of the campus. There are a number of possible routes from the Old West building (class number 1) to Old East building (class number 2). Last weekend, after being late five times for the second class, Alice timed the various legs of the route and prepared the chart below, in which the numbers represent times in minutes. By using dynamic programming, see whether you can figure out a route which will permit Alice to get from her first class to the next one in less than 10 minutes.

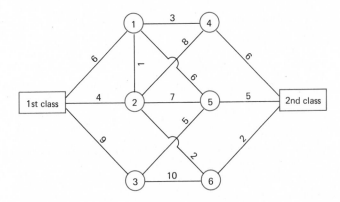

12-15. Jack Behrman has the soft-drink concession for all home Tarheel football games. He has 8 students to assign to 3 areas of the stadium. In the table below, Jack estimates the profits that can be made with different assignments:

Number of persons assigned	End zones	North stands	South stands
0	$ 0	$ 0	$ 0
1	45	15	30
2	90	30	60
3	135	60	90
4	180	120	120
5	180	150	150
6 or more	180	150	180

Use dynamic programming to help Jack assign his crew to maximize his profit per game.

12-16. You are an astronaut of the first manned space mission to Mars. During the only extravehicular excursion on that planet, your motorized ground transport breaks down a considerable distance from your space ship. Because of oxygen limitations, you can carry only 25 kilograms of equipment back to the ship by hand and still make it safely. The transport contains several important pieces of scientific equipment with irreplaceable readings which have been gathered on this one and only extravehicular excursion. A quick inventory reveals the following list of equipment, to which you have assigned an "importance factor" based on the value of information contained.

Item	Weight (kgs)	Importance
1	4	5
2	7	6
3	5	4
4	6	7
5	8	3 (least important)
6	4	8 (most important)

You have put together a makeshift sling which will hold any *volume* of equipment; the sling weighs 1 kilogram. Use dynamic programming to make up a list of items to carry which will maximize the total importance factor and still meet the weight constraint.

12-17. Bernard Richter is the president of a textile concern with mills in four southeastern states. He is currently in a mill which is the farthest one from his home office. He is traveling on the corporate jet. Since each state's mills are under the supervision of the same production officer, a visit to any one of them should give a typical picture of conditions in all the mills in that state. Bernard decides that on the way back to the home office he will visit one mill in each state for a surprise inspection. He wants to conserve fuel and intends to fly the absolute minimum number of air miles on this return trip. He gets out the sectional air chart and pencils in this sketch.

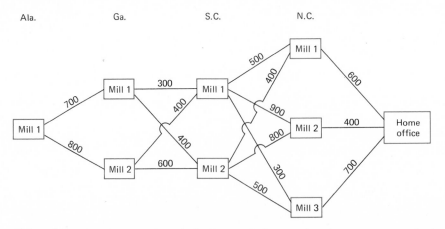

Using dynamic programming, help Bernard choose the shortest route which will meet his plan. The numbers on his sketch are in statute miles.

Bibliography

Bellman, R. E.: *Adaptive Control Processes: A Guided Tour* (Princeton, N.J.: Princeton University Press, 1961).
———: *Dynamic Programming* (Princeton, N.J.: Princeton University Press, 1957).
Hadley, G.: *Nonlinear and Dynamic Programming* (Reading, Mass.: Addison-Wesley Publishing Company, Inc., 1964).
Howard, R. A.: *Dynamic Programming and Markov Processes* (Cambridge, Mass.: The M.I.T. Press, 1960).
Lee, Sang M.: *Goal Programming for Decision Analysis* (Philadelphia: Auerbach Publishers, 1972).
Plane, D. R., and **C. McMillan, Jr.:** *Discrete Optimization* (Englewood Cliffs, N.J.: Prentice-Hall, Inc., 1971).

13

Simulation

1. Introduction

Simulation defined

Simulation is a quantitative procedure which describes a process by developing a model of that process and then conducting a series of organized trial-and-error experiments to predict the behavior of the process over time. Observing the experiments is very much like observing the process in operation. To find out how the real process would react to certain changes, we can produce these changes in our model and simulate the reaction of the real process to them.

Airplane example

For instance, in designing an airplane, the designer can solve various equations describing the aerodynamics of the plane. Or, if those equations are too difficult to solve, a scale model can be built and its behavior observed in a wind tunnel. In simulation, we build mathematical models which we cannot solve and run them on trial data to simulate the behavior of the system.

Mathematical Solutions versus Simulation

Many mathematical solutions involve assumptions

In the case of a number of problems, we have been able to find a mathematical solution. We found the *economic order quantity* in Chapter 7, the simplex solution to a linear programming problem in Chapter 10, and a branch-and-bound solution in Chapter 12. However, in each of those cases the problem was simplified by certain assumptions so that the appropriate mathematical techniques could be employed. It is not difficult to think of managerial situations so complex that mathematical solution is impossible given the current state of the art in mathematics. In these cases, simulation offers a reasonable alternative.

Solving problems mathematically requires simplification

If we insist that all managerial problems have to be solved mathematically, we may find ourselves *simplifying* the situation so that it *can* be solved; sacrificing realism to solve the problem can get us in real trouble. Whereas the assumption of normality in dealing with a distribution of inventory demand may be reasonable, the assumption of linearity in a specific linear programming environment may be totally unrealistic.

In many cases, the solutions which result from simplifying assumptions are suitable for the decision maker; in other cases, they simply are not. Simulation is an appropriate substitute for mathematical evaluation of a model in many

428

situations. Although it too involves assumptions, they are manageable. The use of simulation enables us to provide insights into certain management problems where mathematical evaluation of a model is not possible.

Use of Simulation

Some mathematicians insist that simulation should be used only as a "last ditch" approach, that is, when nothing else seems to work. Despite attitudes like this, it turns out that simulation is one of the most widely used management science techniques. A survey on quantitative techniques used in the corporate planning processes of the 1000 largest companies in the United States indicated that simulation was the most widely used method; some 29 percent of the respondents indicated that they employed simulation studies in their corporate planning. Compare this, for example, with 21 percent who said they used linear programming and only 12 percent who reported using inventory theory in the same process.[1] Another study of the nonacademic members of the Operations Research Society of America showed that, to practicing management scientists, simulation had the third highest value of all the quantitative techniques in use.[2] It would seem, therefore, that simulation, despite its lack of mathematical elegance, is one of the most widely used quantitative techniques employed by management.

Simulation is one of the most widely used quantitative techniques in corporate planning

Reasons for Using Simulation

Among the reasons why management scientists would consider using simulation to solve management problems are these:

Why we use simulation

1. Simulation may be the only method available because it is difficult to observe the actual environment. (In space flight or the charting of satellite trajectories, it is widely used.)

2. It is not possible to develop a mathematical solution.

3. Actual observation of a system may be too expensive. (The operation of a large computer center under a number of different operating alternatives might be too expensive to be feasible.)

4. There may not be sufficient time to allow the system to operate extensively. (If we were studying long-run trends in world population, for instance, we simply could not wait the required number of years to see results.)

5. Actual operation and observation of a system may be too disruptive. (If you are comparing two ways of providing food service in a hospital, the confusion that would result from operating two different systems for long enough to get valid observations might be too great.)

[1] F. C. Weston, "O. R. Techniques Relevant to Corporate Planning Function Practices, an Investigative Look," *Operations Research Bulletin,* vol. 19, suppl. 2, Spring 1971.
[2] R. E. Shannon and W. E. Biles, "The Utility of Certain Curriculum Topics to Operations Research Practitioners," *Operations Research,* vol. 18, no. 4, July-August, 1970.

Shortcomings of Simulation

Disadvantages of using simulation

Use of simulation in place of other techniques, like everything else, involves a trade-off, and we should be mindful of the disadvantages involved in the simulation approach. These include the facts that

1. Simulation is not precise. It is *not* an optimization process and does not yield an *answer* but merely provides a set of the system's responses to different operating conditions. In many cases, this *lack* of precision is difficult to measure.

2. A good simulation model may be very expensive. Often it takes years to develop a usable corporate planning model.

3. Not all situations can be evaluated using simulation; only situations involving uncertainty are candidates, and without a random component, all simulated experiments would produce the same answer.

4. Simulation generates a way of evaluating solutions but does not generate solutions themselves. Managers must still generate the solutions they want to test.

Steps in the Simulation Process

Eight steps in using simulation

All effective simulations require a great deal of planning and organization. Although simulations vary in complexity from situation to situation, in general you would have to go through these steps:

1. Define the problem or system you intend to simulate.

2. Formulate the model you intend to use.

3. Test the model; compare its behavior with the behavior of the actual problem environment.

4. Identify and collect the data needed to test the model.

5. Run the simulation.

6. Analyze the results of the simulation and, if desired, change the solution you are evaluating.

7. Rerun the simulation to test the new solution.

8. Validate the simulation; that is, increase the chances that any inferences you draw about the real situation from running the simulation will be valid.

2. Simulation Applications

Three actual problems solved with simulation

The problems to which simulation has been applied successfully are far too numerous to list here. It is useful at this point, however, to give you some idea of the variety of managerial situations in which this technique has been able to aid the decision process. Each of the situations which we will now describe represents an actual problem in which the authors have been involved during the last few years.

The Home-Heating-Oil Simulation

John Adams, the president of a petroleum products distribution firm in eastern North Carolina, attended a university seminar in quantitative techniques. John became interested in the possibility of using simulation to test the relative effectiveness of several alternative methods of dispatching his eight home-heating-oil delivery trucks. He served over three thousand residential customers in his marketing area; these residences had oil tanks ranging in capacity from 55 to 1000 gallons. John's trucks ranged in size from 1000 to 5000 gallons, and his bulk plant (the terminal where he stored his heating oil) had a tank capacity of 150,000 gallons. John had one transport truck (used to haul heating oil from the port of Wilmington) but could lease others if necessary.

John was well aware that periods of low temperature put a strain on his whole delivery system. His eight trucks could not keep up with residential usage; there was confusion and inefficiency around the bulk plant; and additional transport trucks had to be leased at unfavorable short-term rates. There seemed to be three alternatives. One was to increase truck and bulk plant equipment and personnel so that capacity would be equal to the maximum cold-weather demand; John knew this would be quite expensive and had already calculated the additional investment in equipment alone to be near $140,000. A second alternative was to deliver heating oil to residences more frequently—that is, to keep customers' tanks more nearly full so that demand during low-temperature periods would be lessened. A third alternative was to replace all the small 55-gallon tanks (at company expense) to significantly increase the efficiency of the delivery trucks. (Fewer stops per day and more gallons delivered per stop would significantly increase the capacity of the delivery fleet.) John also knew that combinations of alteratives two and three were another possibility.

It seemed clear to us that solving this problem mathematically was impossible (or at least beyond our mathematical abilities). Therefore we developed a simulation model of John's system which included these elements:

1. The bulk plant
2. The customers
3. Varying residential tank sizes
4. Local delivery trucks
5. Transport trucks (owned and leased)
6. Employees
7. Heating-oil consumption based on temperature

Simulating a distribution system

Three alternatives to be evaluated

The elements in the model simulation

We simulated several alternative delivery systems over a wide range of demand conditions. The results persuaded us that John should adopt a combination of alternatives two (more frequent delivery) and three (replacement of small 55-gallon tanks). By replacing about 450 small tanks at a cost near $70,000 and by increasing the frequency of deliveries to the point that the average customer's tank was 45 percent full, we were able to *reduce* the number of local delivery trucks by two and effect a comparable saving in personnel as well. Our simulation indicated that even with this reduced local delivery capacity, John's system could withstand a prolonged drop in temperatures. In three winters (one of which was the most severe on record), John's new system has operated quite effectively.

The Carpet-cutting Application

The production vice-president of a regional carpet manufacturing company attended our executive program. One day he asked if we had ever done any work with "carpet cutting." Soon after that we were in the mill observing the operation. Carpet was manufactured in 175-foot rolls, all 12 feet wide. This company stocked over two hundred different styles and colors of carpet; usually there were multiple rolls or pieces of rolls of each style and color on hand in the warehouse. Incoming orders for carpet called for lengths ranging from about 8 feet all the way up to an entire roll (175 feet). Incoming orders were delivered to the cutting room, where cutting-machine operators attempted to match existing rolls with incoming orders in such a way that the unusable piece left at the end of the roll (the remnant) would be as small as possible. You can get an idea of the significance of unusable remnants if you consider that the average price per lineal foot of the carpet was about $18 and that any remnant under 3 feet was thrown away; remnants between 3 feet and 6 feet were sold for about a third of the regular price. The cost of unusable remnants was amounting to almost $250,000 a year.

The cutting-machine operators pointed out to us that there were hundreds of ways you could fill an order for a piece of carpet: (1) cut it from the longest roll of the required style and color; (2) cut it from the roll which would leave the shortest piece left over; (3) find two orders which would use up an entire roll or piece of a roll; and so on. To complicate matters, our friend also wanted us to find out whether it would be economical to collect carpet orders for more than 1 day (2 days, 3 days, etc.) before cutting them, his idea being that the more orders you had, the better match of orders and rolls you could make. Of course, you would have to be willing to risk the wrath of those customers who would be kept waiting longer.

We studied the operation at some length and constructed a simulation model of the system. The components of this model included:

1. The production operation (the manner in which carpets were delivered to the cutting operation, frequency, etc.)

2. The distribution of incoming orders (size, color, style)

3. The inventory (rolls in sizes, colors, styles)

4. The cutting process (time, employees)

5. The prices of sold carpet and remnants

We simulated the cutting operation under a wide number of different possible "cutting rules"; each simulation run was for 1000 days, a period deemed long enough to represent a typical order and production pattern. Each time we ran another simulation, we kept track of the effect on inventory, remnants, labor cost, and revenues from sold carpets and remnants. For each different set of cutting rules we evaluated, we allowed carpet orders to accumulate for 1, 2, and 3 days, the last being the maximum that management was willing to try for fear of antagonizing customers.

Our results showed that the accumulation of orders beyond two days had no appreciable effect on reducing remnants, a fact that pleased the customer service manager greatly. We did find a set of seven cutting rules which appeared to be superior to any other set we simulated; application of these rules reduced remnants by 21 percent. Although this may not seem much of a victory, you must remember (1) that the carpet-cutting operation was staffed by intelligent people who had tried different cutting rules for the last 50 years, and (2) a 21 percent reduction in remnants amounted to a saving of over $50,000 annually.

What the simulation showed

The Public School Planning Application

One of the authors had been engaged to conduct a beginning operations research course for the senior administrators of a large metropolitan school system in the Northeast. One day the superintendent (a participant in the course) indicated how difficult it was to deal with his school board on certain long-range planning issues and asked whether simulation had anything to offer in such a situation. It seemed that the board was always asking questions like, "What would happen if enrollments began to grow at 9 percent a year instead of 6 percent a year?" Or, "How many years do you think it will be before the population shifts enough to warrant making this elementary school into an adult education center?" There was a whole series of these mathematically impossible "how," "when," and "what if" questions.

Planning for a school system with simulation

Difficult questions

It was not long before work was underway on a large simulation model of the public school system. With it, the superintendent hoped to be able to do a better job of long-range planning in his very complex environment. The model had to accommodate variables like these:

1. Enrollments (by grade, kindergarten through grade 12)

2. Teacher-pupil ratios

3. Classroom capacities

4. Salaries

5. District population

Variables in the simulation model

6. Number of schools (including capacities)

7. Number of teachers by subject, function, or grade

8. Construction cost

9. Transportation equipment

10. Warehousing and repair facilities

11. Administrative personnel by grade and function

12. Service personnel (maintenance, custodial, etc.)

Over a year of work went into this model; the variables (like the 12 above) had to be related in it. The model had to be able to accept demographic data and, with them, forecast the effects on the school system of future changes in the environment. And the superintendent insisted that the simulation model be in a form that would allow it to be run during school board meetings to test the effect of alternative assumptions about the future.

Answering two interesting questions with simulation

We were present one evening when two very interesting decisions were made as a result of this simulation. A school board member wanted to know why building costs for a proposed elementary school were so high; she was rather impatient while the superintendent explained that a school had to last for about 50 years and that costly construction was necessary to achieve that goal. "But," she said, "are there going to be any kids in that neighborhood in 20 years?" The superintendent asked us to run the model, making some projections about school-age populations from present demographic data and the trends that were a part of the model. It took less than 6 minutes to punch the cards, make a run, and bring the results back to the board room. "It turns out," the superintendent announced, "that our simulator (as he called it) projects fewer than .1 school-age child per household for that district within 20 years." In the ensuing discussion, the board decided to provide for the enrollment in that district with temporary classroom buildings.

In a later discussion of the Coleman report (a study of effects of sociological variables on learning), the board questioned the cost of altering the teacher-pupil ratio. Now that sounds like a simple question, but when you consider that to answer it you have to begin with a change in class size and then calculate the effects of that change on teachers, classrooms, buildings, equipment, salaries, administrative personnel, transportation, and benefits—to name only a few of the variables affected—you can see what a task is involved in answering that question. The "simulator" was able to estimate within a few minutes that the cost of decreasing the size of elementary school classes by *one* pupil would be approximately $7,300,000 per year, a disclosure which quickly ended further discussion.

3. A Hand-computed Simulation

Developing a hand-computed simulation of an operating room

In this section, we shall introduce you to simulation by using an example which can be simulated manually, that is, done without using a computer. This example concerns the scheduling of patients in a hospital operating room. In the next

Table 13-1 Wednesday Operating Schedule,
Room No. 3

Time	Activity	Expected time
8:00 A.M.	Appendectomy	40 min
8:40	Cleanup	20 min
9:00	Laminectomy	90 min
10:30	Cleanup	20 min
10:50	Kidney removal	120 min
12:50 P.M.	Cleanup	20 min
1:10	Hysterectomy	60 min
2:10	Cleanup	20 min
2:30	Colostomy	100 min
4:10	Cleanup	20 min
4:30	Lesion removal	10 min
4:40	Cleanup	20 min

section, we shall introduce three more simulations which are too complex to be done by hand and therefore require use of a computer.

Wake Memorial Hospital Simulation

Wednesday's schedule for operating room number 3 at Wake Memorial Hospital is as shown in Table 13-1. From looking at this schedule, the head operating room nurse concludes that it may not be possible to finish with the operating and cleanup schedule by 5 P.M., the time at which this operating room must be available for emergency night service.

The Wake Memorial simulation described

The hospital management analyst, Margaret Sheeran, suggests that simulation might indicate whether the schedule for Wednesday is workable and, if not, what changes could be made in it. Margaret reviews the operating room records for the past few months and finds that patients do not always arrive at the operating room at the scheduled time. They often have to wait for pre-op medication to be administered, sometimes operating room transportation personnel are late, and from time to time physicians forget to order the patient moved from the floor to the operating room. Margaret's investigation of the operating room log indicates that arrival expectations are about as shown in Table 13-2. Margaret finds that operating times also vary according to surgical difficulties encountered, differences in surgical skills, and the effectiveness of the surgical team in general. An analysis of operations scheduled over the past few months produces the results shown in Table 13-3, which gives a good indication of this variation. Margaret also recognizes that any variation in the expected cleanup time will affect the schedule and checks the

Variation in the patient arrival schedule

Variation in operating times

Table 13-2 Arrival Expectations

Patient arrives on time	.50 probability
Patient arrives 5 minutes early	.10 probability
Patient arrives 10 minutes early	.05 probability
Patient arrives 5 minutes late	.20 probability
Patient arrives 10 minutes late	.15 probability

Table 13-3 Operation Time Expectations

Operation is completed in the expected time	.45 probability
Operation is completed in 90% of the expected time	.15 probability
Operation is completed in 80% of the expected time	.05 probability
Operation is completed in 110% of the expected time	.25 probability
Operation is completed in 120% of the expected time	.10 probability

Variation in cleanup time

records once again. Here she finds that, about half the time, the cleanup crew finishes in 10 minutes. The rest of the time, it takes them 30 minutes. With her data collected, she is ready to begin the simulation.

Generating the Variables in the System (Process Generators)

Process generators for the simulation

Margaret needs a way to generate arrival times, operating times, and cleanup times. The methods she uses to do this are called *process generators*. She decides to use a *random number table,* Appendix Table 7. A random number table is the output we would expect to get from sampling a *uniformly distributed random variable,* a random variable where all of its values (digits from 0 through 9 in this case) are equally likely.

Process generator for arrival times

Generating Arrival Times Margaret decides to use the *first two* digits of each 10-digit number in Appendix Table 7 as her process generator for arrival times. Since there are 100 possible two-digit numbers from 00 through 99, she relates these two-digit numbers to arrival variation like this:

Random numbers	Arrival	
00 through 49	On time	(.50 probability)
50 through 59	5 min early	(.10 probability)
60 through 64	10 min early	(.05 probability)
65 through 84	5 min late	(.20 probability)
85 through 99	10 min late	(.15 probability)

Process generator for operating times

Generating Operating Times Now Margaret decides to use the *last two* digits of each 10-digit number in Appendix Table 7 as her process generator for operating times. She relates these two-digit numbers to operating times in this way:

Random numbers	Operating times	
00–44	On-time completion	(.45 probability)
45–59	Completion in 90% of expected time	(.15 probability)
60–64	Completion in 80% of expected time	(.05 probability)
65–89	Completion in 110% of expected time	(.25 probability)
90–99	Completion in 120% of expected time	(.10 probability)

Process generator for cleanup times

Generating Cleanup Times Since there are only *two* values the random variable takes on here, Margaret decides to use the *fourth* digit of each 10-digit number in Appendix Table 7 as her process generator. If it's an odd number, she'll let that represent a 10-minute cleanup; an even number would represent a 30-minute cleanup.

The Simulation

Margaret proceeds with the simulation. First, she generates an arrival-time deviation for the first patient; then she generates an operating-time deviation for the first operation; finally, she generates a cleanup time for that operation. She continues with this process until the last operation has been performed and the operating room cleaned up for the final time that day. The results of her simulation are shown in Table 13-4.

Doing the simulation

From Margaret's simulation, it appears that the scheduled operations can be completed and the room vacated by 5 P.M. In fact, her simulation indicates that the day's schedule ends at 4:45 P.M., a few minutes early.

Interpreting the results

Table 13-4   Results of Simulation of Activity in Operating Room No. 3

Random number	First two digits	Last two digits	Fourth digit	Meaning	Outcome
15	X			On-time arrival of appendectomy patient	Appendectomy begun at 8 A.M.
96		X		Appendectomy completed in 120% of expected time (48 min)	Appendectomy completed at 8:48 A.M.
1			X	Cleanup done in 10 min	Room ready for second operation at 8:58 A.M.
9	X			On-time arrival of laminectomy patient (9 A.M.)	Laminectomy begun at 9 A.M.
82		X		Laminectomy completed in 110% of expected time (99 min)	Laminectomy completed at 10:39 A.M.
8			X	Cleanup done in 30 min	Room ready for third operation at 11:09 A.M.
41	X			On-time arrival of kidney patient (10:50 A.M.)	Kidney removal begun at 11:09 A.M.
56		X		Kidney removal completed in 90% of expected time (108 min)	Kidney removal completed at 12:57 P.M.
2			X	Cleanup done in 30 min	Room ready for fourth operation at 1:27 P.M.
75	X			Hysterectomy patient arrives 5 min late (1:15 P.M.)	Hysterectomy begun at 1:27 P.M.
68		X		Hysterectomy completed in 110% of expected time (66 min)	Hysterectomy completed at 2:33 P.M.
7			X	Cleanup done in 10 min	Room ready for fifth operation at 2:43 P.M.
00	X			On-time arrival of colostomy patient (2:30 P.M.)	Colostomy begun at 2:43 P.M.
58		X		Colostomy completed in 90% of expected time (90 min)	Colostomy completed at 4:13 P.M.
9			X	Cleanup done in 10 min	Room ready for sixth operation at 4:23 P.M.
72	X			Lesion patient arrives 5 min late (4:35 P.M.)	Lesion operation begun at 4:35 P.M.
40		X		On-time completion of lesion operation (10 min)	Lesion operation completed at 4:45 P.M.
5			X	Cleanup done in 10 min	Operating room schedule for Wednesday completed at 4:55 P.M.

Assumptions and Caveats

Margaret simulated the day's operation only once, and it may be dangerous for us to draw general conclusions from such a short simulation. If she had repeated the day's simulation several times using different random numbers, then we could feel better about generalizing from her results. Margaret also assumed that the variables in this simulation (arrival deviation, operating time deviation, and cleanup deviation) were independent of each other. If this is not the case, her simulation is not a valid one. Finally, Margaret used *discrete* distributions of the three variables. In actual practice, were computation time not such a problem, continuously distributed random variables would be appropriate.

Taking care with assumptions

4. Computer Simulation

It is difficult, if not impossible, to perform simulations without a computer. In Margaret's simulation of an operating room, she limited her simulation to 1 day and performed it only one time. Imagine what work would be involved if she simulated that one operating room for a month or simulated the entire 12-operating-room suite at Wake Memorial Hospital for a month's time. Because hand-computed simulations are so expensive and so tedious, real simulations are done almost exclusively on a computer.

Shortcomings of hand-computed simulations

One of the most efficient computer simulation languages is GPSS (General Purpose Simulation System) developed by IBM. We've used GPSS in the three computer simulations which follow. GPSS has these characteristics, which are found in almost *every* simulation situation:

GPSS computer simulation language

1. *Transactions.* Transactions are the units of traffic or flow that move through the system. In the operating room example, these would be the patients. Transactions in the three simulations to come will be ships, inventory items, and airplanes.

2. *Facilities and storages.* Transactions move from point to point in a system; these points at which units stop or move along are called *facilities* and *storages*. In the hospital simulation, the operating room was a facility. In the airport simulation in this section, a runway is a facility. In the ship simulation we will present shortly, the harbor is a storage, because it can be occupied by a number of units.

3. *Waiting lines.* Because a facility is occupied by only one unit at a time, a waiting line generally develops. Patients waiting for an operating room form a waiting line.

4. *Time.* Time measures the progress of units through the system.

In each case, we begin by first describing the situation we are simulating; then we present a flow chart (a graphic illustration of the flow of units through the system). Finally, we show the results of the simulation and discuss the implications of the simulation output.

Descriptions, flow chart, results, and implications

Inventory Control Simulation

Bill Perrault, a new operations research analyst for the Conner Wholesaling Corporation, is investigating the inventory situation of his company's 24-inch self-propelled rotary mower. The mean and standard deviation of the normally distributed demand for this product are 20 and 5 units a day respectively. Lead time on reorders is normally distributed, with mean and standard deviation in working days being 6 and 1 respectively. Reorder quantities are in multiples of 100, since the manufacturer ships this mower only in truck lots.

A simulation of various combinations of inventory policies

Bill wants to estimate the number of units of lost sales per week and the average inventory on hand which would result from reorder points of 120, 140, and 160 mowers, *each* combined with reorder quantities of 100 and 200 units. The structure of Bill's simulation model to estimate these statistics is shown in Figure 13-1, on page 441.

What would losses and inventory levels be under various combinations?

After initializing the stock on hand (setting up a beginning inventory) at the beginning of the simulation, the program cycles through a common series of steps for each business day. First, a random number is selected to determine the day's demand value. If demand can be filled in its entirety, it is subtracted from stock on hand. Otherwise lost sales are recorded and stock is set equal to zero. Next, any orders due in during the day are added to stock before recording the stock on hand at the end of the day. To keep track of when orders are due, the program maintains an "event" file, which is simply a list of order due dates. When the "clock" (a counter) is incremented to a value equal to the due date of an order, that order will be added to stock. In the reorder division block, stock on hand is compared to the reorder point. If a reorder is necessary, a random number is used to draw a lead time and the due date is posted to the event file. This cycle repeats until the specified number of days elapse.

Description of the inventory simulation

Note that two assumptions are implicit in Bill's simulation. When sales are lost, they are lost entirely and do not reappear when stock becomes available later. Also, orders are received and reorder decisions made only at the *end* of each day. Both these assumptions are a matter of convenience and can easily be modified to reflect other conditions.

Bill makes two important assumptions

The problem was programmed in GPSS-V and run on an IBM 370 system with these results:

Reorder point	Reorder quantity	Average weekly lost sales in units	Average on-hand stock in units
120	100	10.375	44.455
140	100	7.565	50.033
160	100	6.055	56.583
120	200	3.285	97.439
140	200	.765	119.673
160	200	.015	138.439

GPSS-V

Runs were made for 500 business days for each reorder-point–reorder-quantity combination. The same series of random numbers was used in each run to ensure comparability of results. Each run started with the stock on hand equal to the reorder point and with no orders due in.

When Bill checked the results, he saw that higher reorder points, higher reorder quantities, or both generate fewer lost sales, and that lost sales seemed to be inversely related to on-hand stocks; of course, he knew all this before he ran the simulation. Since Bill wants to determine the cost of being out of stock and the cost of carrying inventory, he can use the simulation to find a least-cost combination of reorder point and quantity.

Harbor Simulation

Everett Gardner is a U.S. Navy management scientist assigned to the analysis section of a large harbor installation. He wants to study the waiting-time distribution for ships using this harbor. Everett spends some time analyzing past harbor records and comes up with these figures:

Interarrival time in hours (time between arriving ships)	Cumulative frequency with which these times occur
0–6	.1
6.1–12	.2
12.1–18	.9
18.1–24	1.0

Everett notices that arriving ships move into an unloading complex which can handle only one ship at a time. Unloading time is variable due to the different cargoes involved; it ranges over a period of 12 to 16 hours, uniformly distributed.

Figure 13-2 shows the flow chart Everett made for the simulation he has decided to use to study the harbor operation. He plans to simulate the waiting time experienced by a sample of 500 ships. Here again, Everett uses a simulation clock and an event file (Figure 13-2, on page 443). The clock is simply a counter that is incremented by the number of time units between consecutive arrivals. The event file is a list of the times at which the two types of events in the simulation (arrivals and unloadings) will occur.

To initialize the simulation, the event file is loaded with two events. In order to operate the program, the first ship arrival and the first unloading completion must be scheduled and placed on the event file. Then the clock is advanced to the first event (which is the arrival).

If an arrival event is "due," the program schedules the next future arrival before processing the current arrival. This procedure keeps the simulation moving. The next step is to check to see whether the unloading complex is free. If so, an unloading completion event is placed on the event file. If the complex is *not* free, an entry is made in a waiting-line file in order to record the time at which waiting begins.

When an unloading completion event is due, the program first records the unloading time in a "service" file to keep the unloading times separate from the waiting times. If the completion is the 500th, the simulation stops. Otherwise the waiting-line file is checked to see whether another ship is waiting to unload. If so,

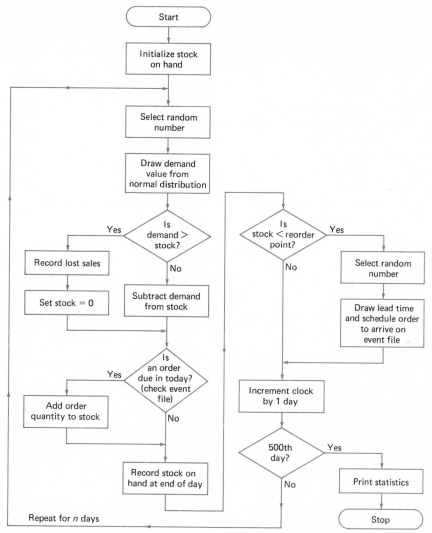

Figure 13-1 Flow chart for Bill Perrault's inventory control simulation.

a random number is used to schedule an unloading completion on the event file. The waiting time of the ship is compiled in the waiting-line file by posting the unloading start time to that file (unloading start time minus arrival time in the waiting line equals waiting time). The program then returns to process the next event.

    This program was written in GPSS-V and run on an IBM 370 system. The simulation was first run for 100 ship completions to "warm up" the model—that is, to wash out the effects of starting the simulation with no ships in line or being unloaded. After the warmup period, statistics were collected for the next 500 ship completions. Here are the results:

Results of Everett's simulation

Upper limit (hours) of waiting time	Observed frequency	Percent of total	Cumulative percentage
6	150	29.99	29.9
12	74	14.79	44.7
18	53	10.59	55.3
24	52	10.39	65.7
30	41	8.19	73.9
36	33	6.59	80.5
42	19	3.79	84.3
48	17	3.33	87.7
54	23	4.59	92.3
60	21	4.19	96.5
66	8	1.59	98.1
72	5	.99	99.1
78	4	.79	100.0

Interpreting the results of the simulation

The program printed out some summary statistics which indicated that the mean of the waiting time was 20 hours with a standard deviation of 18.65 hours. The unloading complex was in use 97.5 percent of the time and unloading time averaged 14 hours per ship. A maximum of 6 ships were waiting to unload at any one time. Everett reported to his commanding officer that the high utilization rate of the unloading complex coupled with the high waiting time seemed to indicate the need for increasing the capacity of the facility. He asked for some additional cost data and authorization to do further simulation studies.

Raleigh-Durham Airport Simulation

Simulating airport arrivals and departures

The Raleigh-Durham airport has two runways available. During the rush period from 8 to 10:05 A.M., 12 takeoffs and 12 landings must be scheduled. Jay Klompmaker, an operations research analyst, wants to evaluate the following proposed scheme: takeoffs will be scheduled every 10 minutes beginning at 8 A.M. and landings every 10 minutes beginning at 8:05 A.M. These are the times when planes are scheduled to enter the active runway (for takeoff) or to announce that they are less than 500 yards from the runway threshold on final landing approach. Planes may be late in arriving at the runway for takeoff due to maintenance, passenger loading delays, or taxi clearance delays; they may be late in landing because of weather, air-traffic-control delays, or late departure. Jay has been able to gather these probability distributions of lateness:

Takeoffs		Landings	
Number of minutes late	Probability	Number of minutes late	Probability
0	.4	0	.3
1–5	.3	1–5	.2
6–10	.2	6–10	.2
11–20	.05	11–20	.2
21–30	.05	21–30	.05
>30	0	30–40	.05
		>40	0

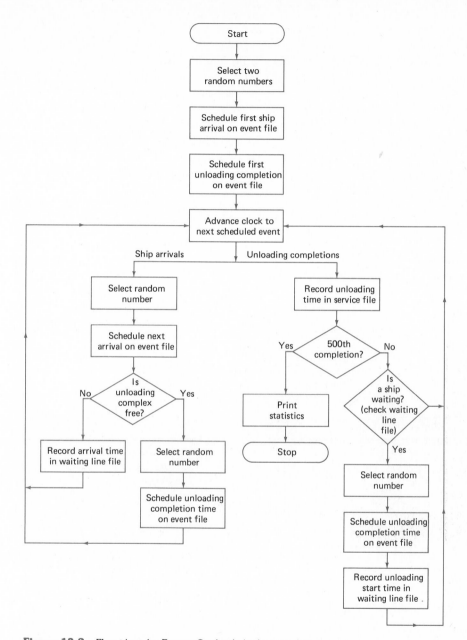

Figure 13-2 Flow chart for Everett Gardner's harbor simulation.

Jay notices that once a plane arrives at the runway for either a takeoff or a landing, an average of 10 minutes of runway time is required to complete the takeoff or landing and free the runway for another plane. Runway time is variable and uniformly distributed from 8 to 12 minutes.

Jay has been told that the schedule management is proposing is tentative; before it is released, management wants to estimate the runway utilization and the delays encountered by both takeoffs and landings. Jay develops the simulation flow-charted in Figure 13-3 and plans to evaluate 25 days of operation under the proposed schedule. His program starts by loading all scheduled takeoffs and landings and the simulation stop time (10:05 A.M.) to the event file. Thereafter, one of four events can occur: (1) a scheduled takeoff or landing, (2) a "ready" for takeoff or landing, (3) a completion of a takeoff or landing; or (4) the arrival of the simulation stop time. After these events are processed for a given day, the program is reset for the next day. Notice from the flow chart that the simulation does not always stop at 10:05 A.M. If planes are still waiting for a runway or are late in getting ready to use a runway, the program finishes such processing before stopping the day's run.

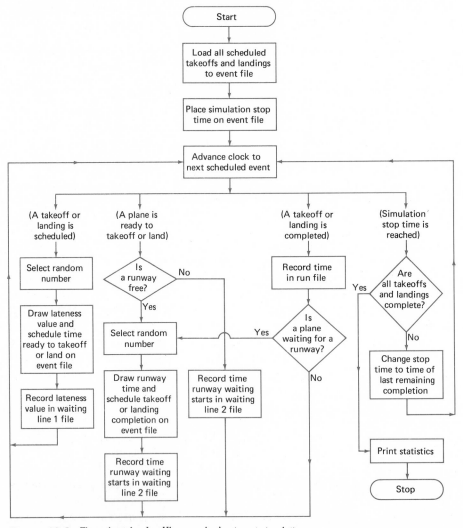

Figure 13-3   Flow chart for Jay Klompmaker's airport simulation.

These were Jay's results for 25 days:

Day	Runway utilization	Takeoffs		Landings	
		Minutes late arriving at runway	Minutes late waiting till runway free	Minutes late arriving at runway	Minutes late waiting till runway free
1	.837	2.4	3.4	8.0	2.7
2	.875	1.3	3.8	8.6	4.6
3	.834	4.7	8.1	8.2	10.2
4	.796	1.9	2.6	9.3	4.4
5	.876	1.8	4.0	8.7	4.2
6	.776	2.4	6.0	14.9	5.0
7	.794	1.3	1.8	7.4	2.5
8	.854	4.7	3.8	9.7	5.2
9	.796	4.6	2.1	9.2	4.1
10	.844	4.5	4.1	11.6	2.7
11	.927	2.9	3.0	4.5	2.3
12	.860	4.1	3.3	5.3	1.3
13	.773	5.4	2.4	4.2	2.6
14	.856	6.3	1.3	4.9	2.6
15	.778	5.5	.8	11.5	1.8
16	.828	3.4	2.0	11.8	2.5
17	.847	6.1	4.8	5.8	5.9
18	.849	5.6	6.3	7.6	5.8
19	.835	1.2	2.2	4.3	2.6
20	.799	3.1	2.3	8.2	2.2
21	.834	5.3	6.2	7.4	5.0
22	.840	3.1	5.7	8.9	8.0
23	.872	3.7	5.3	3.6	4.8
24	.891	2.2	2.8	6.1	2.3
25	.888	1.3	1.2	5.2	2.6

Jay observed that the average number of minutes spent waiting for takeoff once a plane reached the runway was 3.57, a figure well within the tolerance of airlines during rush periods. He also noticed that the time spent waiting (circling) while a runway was being freed up for landing was 3.82 minutes during the rush period; this latter figure was also well within the expectations of the airlines. Jay reported to the airport authority that it looked as though the proposed schedule would operate satisfactorily.

Interpreting the results

Glossary

1. **Simulation** Quantitative procedure which conducts a series of organized trial-and-error experiments on a model of a process to predict the behavior of that process over time.

2. **Process generator** A method used to generate a distribution which is used in a simulation.

3. **Random number table** A table of numbers that simulates the output that one would get from sampling a uniformly distributed random variable.

4. GPSS   General Purpose Simulation System. A computer language developed by IBM Corporation.

5. Transaction   Unit of traffic or flow in a GPSS simulation.

6. Event file   A computer file maintained in a simulation which indicates when certain events are to take place.

7. Clock   A counting device in a simulation which indicates the passage of time.

Exercises

13-1. John Pringle farms several thousand acres of corn in Iowa. He is concerned about the yields per acre he can expect from this year's corn crop. This is the probability distribution John estimates for yields, given current weather conditions:

Yield in bushels/acre	Probability
120	.13
140	.31
160	.49
180	.07

The expected value of the yield per acre is 150 bushels. However, John would like to see a simulation of the yields he might get. Using random numbers, draw a sample of the yields per acre that John might expect over the next 10 years for weather conditions similar to those he is now experiencing.

13-2. John Pringle (from Problem 13-1) is also interested in the effect of market-price fluctuations on his farm revenue. He makes this estimate of per-bushel prices for corn:

Price/bushel	Probability
$2.00	.10
2.10	.10
2.20	.30
2.30	.20
2.40	.20
2.50	.10

Using random numbers, simulate both the yield and the price John might expect to get over the next 10 years and combine these two into his revenue per acre. You may assume that prices are independent of yields (at least for one farm producer).

13-3. Sam Douglas, branch administrator of People's Bank and Trust Co., is thinking of opening a drive-in facility in a suburban location in Wallace, Virginia. A market research study has projected these interarrival times at the branch:

Time between arrivals (minutes)	Probability
1	.17
2	.25
3	.25
4	.20
5	.13

The bank plans for one teller's window at this branch. The teller can service customers at this rate:

Service time (minutes)	Probability
1	.10
2	.30
3	.40
4 (maximum)	.20

Before signing the contract for construction, Sam would like to know how much space to allow for waiting cars. He is also concerned about the mean waiting time for arriving customers. Simulate operation of the facility for an arriving sample of 50 cars and indicate to Sam how many spaces he should plan for. Suppose the location has space only for six cars; how many customers would be turned away due to lack of space? What is the mean waiting time in your sample?

13-4. Refer to the harbor simulation on page 440 of the text. Simulate the first 10 unloading completions at the harbor. Assume that there is one ship in service at the start of your simulation, with completion scheduled for 7 hours from the start of your simulation. Assume that your next ship will arrive in 3 hours from the start of your simulation. When using the frequency distribution given in the text for the harbor problem, interpolate between the class limits of the times.

For example, suppose you use the random numbers 00 to 09 to represent interarrival times of 0 to 6 hours. If you draw the random number 04, that would represent an interarrival time of 2.7 hours for the next ship. That is, when a ship arrives and you draw 04, the next ship is scheduled to arrive at 2.7 hours from the current arrival. This interpolation formula may be useful:

$$Y - Y_1 = \frac{Y_2 - Y_1}{X_2 - X_1}(X - X_1)$$

where X = the random number chosen
 Y = the number of hours we wish to find
 Y_1 = the lower limit of the interval of hours in which Y is included
 Y_2 = the upper limit of the interval of hours in which Y is included
 X_1 = the lower limit of the interval of random numbers in which X is included
 X_2 = the upper limit of the interval of random numbers in which X is included

In this example,

$X = 04$
Y = an unknown number of hours between 0 and 6
$Y_1 = 0$
$Y_2 = 6$
$X_1 = 00$
$X_2 = 09$

and $Y - Y_1 = \dfrac{Y_2 - Y_1}{X_2 - X_1}(X - X_1)$

$Y - 0 = \dfrac{6 - 0}{9 - 0}\ (4 - 0)$

$= 2.67$ hours

In this problem, rounding to the next tenth of an hour is acceptable; hence we would schedule the next ship arrival at 2.7 hours.

For the service times, you can interpolate between 12 and 16 hours. When the tenth ship is complete, compute for Everett Gardner the mean and standard deviation of the waiting time. How do they compare with those found on page 442 of the text?

13-5. Refer to the inventory control problem on page 439 of the text. Simulate the following inventory policy for 25 days: Order 100 units when the stock on hand reaches 180 units. Do not place another order until the previous order has been received. Compute the average weekly lost sales in units (use 5-day working weeks) and compute the average inventory on hand. Start your simulation with 180 units on hand and no order due in. Use this table in your simulation:

			Areas under the normal curve to the left of z				
z	Area	z	Area	z	Area	z	Area
−3.0	.0013	−1.5	.0668	.1	.5398	1.6	.9452
−2.9	.0019	−1.4	.0808	.2	.5793	1.7	.9554
−2.8	.0026	−1.3	.0968	.3	.6179	1.8	.9641
−2.7	.0035	−1.2	.1151	.4	.6554	1.9	.9713
−2.6	.0047	−1.1	.1357	.5	.6915	2.0	.9772
−2.5	.0062	−1.0	.1587	.6	.7257	2.1	.9821
−2.4	.0082	− .9	.1841	.7	.7580	2.2	.9861
−2.3	.0107	− .8	.2119	.8	.7881	2.3	.9893
−2.2	.0139	− .7	.2420	.9	.8159	2.4	.9918
−2.1	.0179	− .6	.2741	1.0	.8413	2.5	.9938
−2.0	.0228	− .5	.3085	1.1	.8643	2.6	.9953
−1.9	.0287	− .4	.3446	1.2	.8849	2.7	.9965
−1.8	.0359	− .3	.3821	1.3	.9032	2.8	.9974
−1.7	.0446	− .2	.4207	1.4	.9192	2.9	.9981
−1.6	.0548	− .1	.4602	1.5	.9332	3.0	.9987
		0	.5000				

To use the above table, draw a four-digit random number. Put a decimal point in front of that number and use it to enter the area column of the table. Find the closest value of z. Multiply the value of z by either sales or lead time and add the result to the mean of either sales or lead time to get a simulated value. (For example, assume you drew 0806. That corresponds to -1.4 standard deviations. From the problem, we saw that the standard deviation of sales was 5 units, so $-1.4 \times 5 = -7$ units. And $20 - 7 = 13$. So we take 13 units as the sampled sales value.)

In your calculations, if the simulated value of demand or lead time comes out to be a fraction, round to the nearest whole number before recording the result. Round *after* the deviation has been added to the mean, as in the example above.

13-6. Repeat Problem 13-5, but this time use a new reordering rule. Order 100 units when the stock on hand *plus* stock on order reaches 180 units. More than one order may thus be outstanding at one time. Use the same random numbers for this problem as for Problem 13-5. Did the new rule reduce lost sales or average on-hand stock? What would you expect to happen?

13-7. An assembly line at Triem Electric Motor has three work stations. The time required for each station to complete its operation on the motor is as follows:

	Probabilities		
Time (minutes)	Station 1	Station 2	Station 3
4	.25	.10	.05
5	.25	.30	.25
6	.25	.40	.25
7	.25	.20	.45

The times given are the only values the operation times take on. Simulate the flow of 10 motors through the assembly line. What is the average time it takes a motor to go through all three operations?

13-8. Bob Headen's company plans to introduce a new device for automobiles to warn the driver of the proximity of the car in front. Bob can follow two different engineering strategies to develop the product. These two strategies have different probability distributions for development time, as follows:

	Strategy	
Development time	1	2
6 mo	.1	.3
9 mo	.3	.4
12 mo	.6	.3

Strategy 1 will require a $500,000 investment and will result in a variable cost per unit of $7.50. Strategy 2 will require a $1,900,000 investment and will result in a variable cost per unit of $7.25. The product will sell for $10. Bob believes that the sales volume of the product depends on the development time, since the industry is highly competitive. Bob has formulated the table below, which gives estimated sales volumes for the life of the product and the probability distributions.

	Development time (months)		
Unit sales volume	6	9	12
1,000,000	.2	.4	.5
1,500,000	.8	.6	.5

Simulate 10 trials for introducing the new product for each engineering strategy. What is Bob's expected profit for each strategy? What would you recommend to Bob?

13-9. Cal Atwood's construction company will incur a penalty of $10,000 a day for every day he is late completing a road construction project. The project is due to be completed in 15 more days. The remaining four activities Cal has to complete are arranged like this:

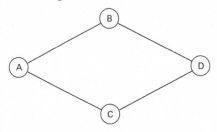

Activities B and C can begin as soon as activity A is completed. Activity D can begin as soon as both B and C are completed.

Cal has estimated these activity times (in days) for the four remaining parts of the project as follows:

Activity A		Activity B		Activity C		Activity D	
Time	Probability	Time	Probability	Time	Probability	Time	Probability
6	.4	5	.2	4	.3	1	.1
7	.1	6	.5	5	.5	2	.1
8	.1	7	.3	6	.2	3	.2
9	.1					4	.3
10	.1					5	.1
11	.1					6	.1
12	.1					7	.1

Simulate three completions of Cal's project. Determine the expected penalty for each simulation.

13-10. The main cargo hoist engine on the Fruit Carrier, a ship which runs between Guatemala City and Fort Lauderdale, Florida, has two bearings that fail periodically. The life of the first bearing is normally distributed, with mean and standard deviation of 80 and 15 operating hours respectively. The life of the second bearing is also normally distributed, with mean and standard deviation of 100 and 20 operating hours. The first bearing costs $60 and the second $40. When either bearing fails, it costs the Fruit Carrier owners $50 in labor charges to install a new one. If both bearings were installed at once, the labor charge would be only $60. Simulate 1000 hours of the operation of the hoist on the Fruit Carrier. Compare replacing only one bearing at a time to replacing both bearings whenever one fails. Which policy involves the least cost in your sample? Use the normal distribution discussed in Problem 13-5 to draw your samples.

13-11. The Western National Bank has agreed to finance the working capital needs of Hi-Fi Ltd., a stereo wholesaler, for the next month. To complete the loan agreement, Hi-Fi Ltd. must estimate the maximum loan required. Daily receipts are normally distributed with a mean of $50,000 and a standard deviation of $12,000. Disbursements are also normally distributed, with a mean and standard deviation of $48,000 and $3000 respectively. Simulate the cash flow of Hi-Fi Ltd. for 15 working days. What is the maximum loan required? Assume that any beginning cash balance will not be available to meet disbursements and that Hi-Fi Ltd. must rely on daily operations to pay its bills. Use the normal distributior introduced in Problem 13-5.

13-12. A traffic signal operates in the east-west direction in the following intervals during the rush hour: green for 60 seconds, yellow for 5 seconds, red for 30 seconds, green for 60 seconds, etc. Cars arrive with these interarrival times:

Direction from	Mean time between arrivals (seconds)
N	.9
S	.7
E	.3
W	.3

Draw a flow chart similar to that for the airport simulation on page 444 of the text to fit this situation. Use the "event file" concept and include two files to collect maximum line length during yellow and red lights. Assume that the first car to arrive after a yellow light flashes on drives through the light. All others stop. Avoid excessive detail and concentrate on the logical checks the flow chart must allow for to record statistics properly.

Bibliography

IBM Corporation: *Bibliography on Simulation* (White Plains, N.Y.: IBM Corporation, 1966).
Maisel, H., and **G. Gnugnoli:** *Simulation of Discrete Stochastic Systems* (Chicago: Scientific Research Associates, Inc., 1972).

Meier, R. C., W. T. Newell, and **H. L. Pazer:** *Simulation in Business and Economics* (Englewood Cliffs, N.J.: Prentice-Hall, Inc., 1969).

Mize, J. H., and **J. G. Cox:** *Essentials of Simulation* (Englewood Cliffs, N.J.: Prentice-Hall, Inc., 1968).

Naylor, T. H., J. L. Balintfy, D. S. Burdick, and **K. Chu:** *Computer Simulation Techniques* (New York: John Wiley & Sons, Inc., 1966).

Schmidt, J. W., and **R. E. Taylor:** *Simulation and Analysis of Industrial Systems* (Homewood, Ill.: Richard D. Irwin, Inc., 1970).

Waiting lines

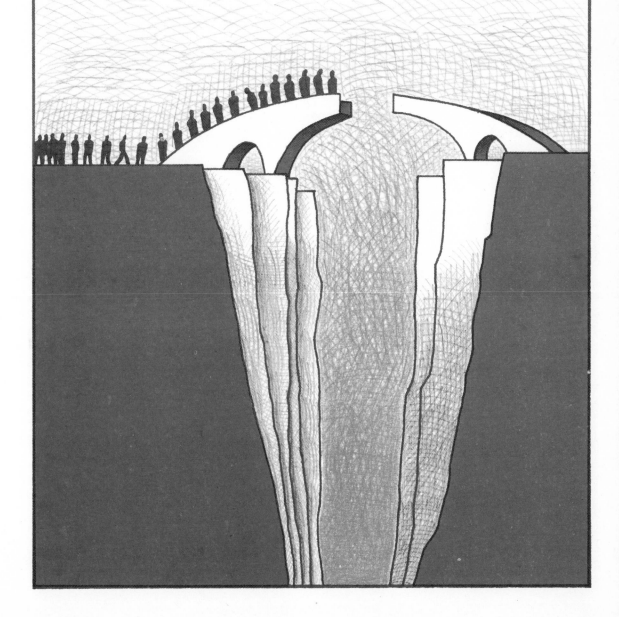

1. Introductory Queuing Ideas

In almost every organization there are examples of processes which generate *waiting lines,* referred to as *queues.* Such waiting lines occur when some employee, part, machine, or unit must wait for service because the servicing facility, operating at capacity, is temporarily unable to provide that service.

Everyday examples of waiting lines—the individual's point of view

If you travel by airline, you have first-hand experience with several types of waiting lines. To buy your ticket, you may have had to stand in line at the travel agent's office. When you arrive at the airport, you stand in line to check your bags; then you stand in line again to get a seat assignment. You line up once more for a security check and then again in the boarding lounge before entering the airplane. When you are inside the plane, you wait for those ahead of you to take their seats. When the plane leaves the gate, it may wait in line for takeoff clearance; when it arrives at its destination, it may circle for some time waiting for landing clearance. And finally, when a gate is assigned and you disembark, you may wait for your baggage to arrive and then for ground transportation. It's possible to be a member of at least 10 queues on one such trip.

The organization's point of view

And consider for a moment the *airline's* queuing experience for that same trip. The plane you rode in has to "wait in line" for fueling, inspection, a particular gate, a specific flight route, and assigned crew, food loading, verified passenger

454

Figure 14-1 A queuing system.

count, and taxi and takeoff clearance for each trip; no wonder airlines are also concerned with queuing, for poorly managed waiting lines result in underutilized equipment and dissatisfied customers.

The pioneering work in the field of queuing theory was done by A. K. Erlang, a Danish engineer associated with the telephone industry. Early in this century Erlang was doing experiments involving the fluctuating demand for telephone facilities and its effect upon automatic dialing equipment. It was not until the end of World War II that this early work was extended to other more general problems involving queues or waiting lines.

Pioneering work in queuing theory

You see the operation of a simple queue at the single checkout counter of your neighborhood convenience store when you drop by on the way home to pick up a six pack. Figure 14-1 illustrates the operation of the checkout counter. In this simple situation, if the convenience store operator wants to minimize the length of the waiting line that would normally form at the single checkout counter, another cash register and another checker can be added. If the queues that form are still too long, more counters can be added. Each addition, of course, adds to expense, but at the same time, each further reduces the time customers have to wait for service. The manager tries to hit a happy medium where waiting lines are short enough to minimize customer ill will, but it is clearly not practical to provide such extensive service facilities that no waiting line, or queue, can ever develop. In effect, our manager *balances* the increased cost of additional facilities against the customer ill will which increases as the average length of the queue increases.

A simple queuing system

The manager's view of a solution

There are many industrial applications of queuing theory in which the cost of time lost by the personnel in the waiting line *and* the cost of additional facilities can be determined accurately. In many of these problems, we can arrive at a solution which provides the lowest total cost of (1) the lost time of persons waiting for service plus (2) the wages of persons who provide the service. Let us look at such a situation.

Typical machine shop application of queuing theory

In the typical machine shop, the expensive cutting tools required in the machining processes are kept in a central location often referred to as a tool crib. This crib is manned by one or more persons who check out the tools required by the machinists in the shop. The machinist who requires a certain tool proceeds to the tool crib, presents a tool authorization to the attendant, and is issued the required tool. The machinist then goes back to work, does the job, and finally goes back to the tool crib and checks in the tool; if required, the machinist then draws another for the next job to be performed. Because some of the tools involved in work of this kind are very expensive, this procedure is necessary to ensure adequate control of the tool inventory.

Two kinds of costs   During the time machinists wait in line at the tool crib for service, they are idle; a loss is incurred by the company. This type of loss is measurable because it is simply the amount of time workers are required to wait multiplied by the wages they receive per hour. By the same token, when the employees who staff the tool crib are idle because no machinist is requiring service, their wages represent a loss to the company.

Possible alternatives   One way to reduce the waiting time of the machinists is to provide sufficient tool crib attendants so that no queue is allowed to form. Since the machinists may arrive in bunches from time to time, this will take quite a few attendants. During the time when no machinists arrived for service, the entire combined wages of this large group of attendants would be a loss. What we need is a workable solution which takes into account all the factors in the problem *and* determines the ratio of tool crib attendants to machinists which will yield the lowest total cost. This type of situation can best be illustrated by using the figures in Table 14-1, collected by observing the operation over an extended period of time under several different staffing alternatives.

From Table 14-1 it seems that *two* crib attendants will minimize the total cost of (1) the machinists' lost time plus (2) the crib attendants' wages. Having fewer or more than two attendants will raise this total cost.

Observation versus analytical solutions   In a real industrial situation, of course, no one wants to observe the operation for the extended period of time necessary to acquire these figures. That would be an unnecessary waste of time and money when the same solution to the problem can be obtained using some quantitative techniques associated with queuing theory. These we shall develop and discuss later.

The problem of the tool crib attendants and the machinists represents, of

Table 14-1   Tool Crib System under Several Alternatives

	Number of attendants			
	1	2	3	4
Number of arrivals of machinists during 8-hr shift	100	100	100	100
Average time each machinist spends waiting for service (minutes)	10	6	4	2
Total time lost by machinists during 8-hr shift (minutes)	1,000	600	400	200
Machinists' average pay (hourly)	$12	$12	$12	$12
Value of machinists' lost time	$200	$120	$80	$40
Tool crib attendants' average pay (hourly)	$6	$6	$6	$6
Total pay of tool crib attendants for 8-hr shift	$48	$96	$144	$192
Machinists' lost time plus tool crib attendants' pay	$248	$216	$244	$232

Behavior of tool crib under alternative staffing patterns

↑——— Optimum no. of tool crib attendants = 2

Table 14-2 Some Applications of Queuing Theory

Situation	Queue or waiting line	Service facility
Food service	Patrons waiting to eat	Waiters
Gasoline station	Motorists waiting for service	Attendants
Dentist's office	Patients	Dentist
Textile mill	Loom waiting for repairs	Loom fixer
Parts warehouse	Mechanics drawing out parts	Parts attendants
Assembly line	Employees waiting for the unfinished assembly	Employees currently processing the assembly
Class registration	Students waiting to register	Faculty registrars
Tunnel	Drivers waiting to enter tunnel	Toll booth attendants
Job interview	Applicants	Interviewer

course, only one application of queuing theory. Consider the illustrations in Table 14-2 which lists cases where application of this useful technique can provide optimum solutions to common managerial problems. These are just a few of the many opportunities for the application of the theory of queues or waiting lines.

2. Queuing Objectives and Cost Behavior

In the tool crib example illustrated in Table 14-1, our objective was to minimize the *total* cost of (1) time lost by the arrivals waiting for service *and* (2) the cost of providing that service. We observed from that example that as we provided more attendants, the average time each machinist spent waiting for service decreased. This reduction in waiting time and its associated cost was achieved, however, by increasing the cost of service (the wages paid to the added attendants). **Costs involved in queuing systems**

The basic relationships between and among the elements involved in queuing problems can be illustrated graphically. In Figure 14-2, we show the relationship between the level of service provided and the cost of *waiting time*. We observe that as the level of service is increased (as more attendants are provided in our tool crib, for example), the cost of time spent waiting by the machinists decreases. In Figure 14-3, we illustrate graphically the relationship between the level of service **Waiting costs**

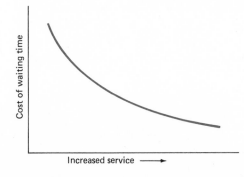

Figure 14-2 Relationship between level of service and cost of waiting time.

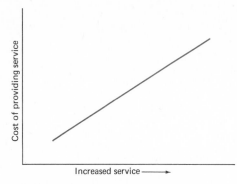

Figure 14-3 Relationship between level of service and cost of providing service.

Service costs   and the cost of *providing that service.* In this case, we observe that as the level of service increases, so does the cost of providing that increased service; in our tool crib example, each additional tool crib attendant was paid $48 a day in wages. Combining these two input costs with the queuing decision has been accomplished in Figure 14-4. Here the cost of the time spent waiting by the arrivals has been added to the cost of providing service to establish a *total expected cost* for the

Total costs   operation of the facility. From Figure 14-4 we see that the total expected cost is minimum at a level of service which we have denoted with the symbol H. Thus the objective of the techniques which we explain in the remainder of this chapter is really to determine that particular level of service which minimizes the total cost of providing service *and* waiting for that service. Although conceptually this may appear to be a simple notion, the various possible ways in which arrivals can appear and be serviced, the many possible ways in which arrivals can be selected for service, and the multitude of possible physical layouts of service facilities make the problem a difficult one. Let us turn now to an understanding of some of the terms used in the study of waiting lines.

3. Standard Language and Definitions for Waiting Lines

Population, queue, and service facility   We will be dealing in some detail with three parts of queuing systems: (1) the calling population (you were a part of this population when you entered the convenience store we used as an example earlier); (2) the queue or waiting line itself (you became a part of this when you selected your purchase and walked to the checkout counter); and (3) the service facility (in our example, this was the single checkout counter). Each of these three parts has characteristics described in specific language.

Characteristics of the Calling Population

The calling population   This part of a queuing system has three characteristics we shall deal with:

1. Size of the calling population

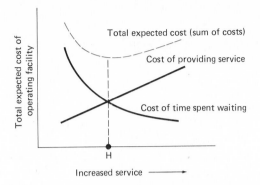

Figure 14-4 Total cost of operating service facility.

2. Arrival characteristics of the calling population

3. Behavior of the calling population

Let's look at each of these in turn.

Size of the Calling Population Calling populations can be either *infinite* or *finite*. Examples of practically *infinite* calling populations include cars arriving at toll booths, patients arriving at the emergency room of a large hospital, and 20,000 students lined up on registration day. These are actually finite populations but they are very very large, and for mathematical convenience we treat them as infinite. When calling populations are infinite, it is much easier to apply quantitative techniques to their analysis. *Finite* calling populations, on the other hand, would be represented by a group of three looms in a weaving mill that require operator service from time to time, or a small taxi fleet of four cars which visit a repair facility from time to time. How to tell the difference between finite and infinite calling populations? Generally, if the probability of an arrival is greatly changed when one member of the calling population is receiving service, we consider the calling population to be *finite.* After all, if one of the four taxis is already in the shop, chances that another will arrive while it is being repaired are rather drastically reduced.

Finite and infinite calling populations

Arrival Characteristics of the Calling Population Members of the calling population arrive at the service facility either in some organized pattern or in random order. When arrivals are random, we have to know the probability distribution describing arrivals, specifically the *time between arrivals.* Management scientists have demonstrated that random arrivals are often best described by the Poisson distribution, which we discussed in some detail in Chapter 3. Of course, arrivals are not always Poisson, and we need to be certain that the Poisson distribution is appropriate before we use it.

Organized or random arrivals

Behavior of the Calling Population Calling populations and their individual members have different attitudes about "getting into line." Most of us routinely skip a gas station when we see most of the pumps busy (in queuing theory this is

Attitudes about getting into a waiting line

called *balking*), and yet we may willingly wait in line several hours for tickets to a good rock concert. Whether you would support it or not, many queuing models assume that the calling population is rather patient and willing to wait.

Characteristics of the Queue (Waiting Line)

Limited or unlimited length

It is common practice to describe queue characteristics in terms of the maximum length to which the queue can grow. This length is classified either as *limited* or *unlimited.* Limited queue lengths are usually due to lack of space (on a very cold night, the waiting line for a restaurant may be limited to the number of people who can crowd into the entrance hall) or to the attitude of the members of the calling population (some folks just don't like to wait in lines). When we can assume the queue can grow to *infinite* length, life is much simpler for the management scientists.

Characteristics of the Service Facility

In examining the characteristics of a service facility, we are interested in three things:

Layout, queue discipline, and service time distribution

1. The physical layout of the queuing system

2. The queue discipline

3. The appropriate probability distribution describing service times

A few words about each of these is in order.

Channel and phase

The Physical Layout of the Queuing System   Physical layout of a queuing system is described by the terms *channel* and *phase*. A *single-channel* system has one service facility, while a *multichannel* system has more than one parallel service facility. If the gas station you stop at has one pump, it is a single-channel system; if it has more than one pump, we would classify it as a multichannel system. Now what about phase? *Phase* refers to the number of servers you need to receive service from. In a *single-phase* system, you are serviced by one person, as when you bring your car in for a tuneup. But if you wreck your car, thereby requiring the services (in order) of a mechanic, a body repairer, and a front-end aligner (all in the same repair shop), you are entering a *multiphase* system. To help you keep channels and phases straight, Figure 14-5 shows several examples of each.

Priority queue discipline

The Queue Discipline   Here we're referring to which unit in the calling population receives service. Two classifications are used: *priority* and *first come, first served.* In priority disciplines, there are two subclassifications: *preemptive* and *nonpreemptive.* Preemptive discipline permits members of the calling population to interrupt members already receiving service. If the president of your company dashes into the company cafeteria, asks if you would mind stepping out of line

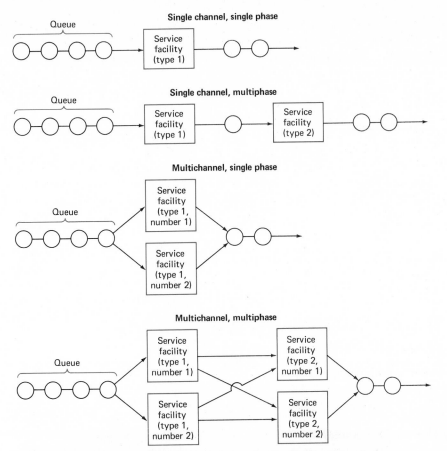

Figure 14-5 Physical layouts of queuing systems described by channel and phase.

so he can make an important meeting, and you do so, you understand preemptive priority discipline. Nonpreemptive queue discipline arranges the queue so that the member with the highest priority gets the first *open* service facility.

First come, first served queue discipline does not assign priorities and serves the queue member who got there first. Combinations of these queue disciplines are very much in evidence. Consider the express line at the supermarket for shoppers with fewer than five items; it is operated on a queue discipline of first come, first served *once you get in the line;* however, this express line does provide a high-priority channel for those shoppers with few items.

First come, first served queue discipline

The Appropriate Probability Distribution Expressing Service Times It's possible for service times to be constant (each member of the queue requires the same time to be serviced) or random. If service times are randomly distributed, we have to find out what probability distribution best describes their behavior. In many cases where service times are random, management scientists have found that they are best described by the *exponential probability distribution.* If service

Distributions of service time

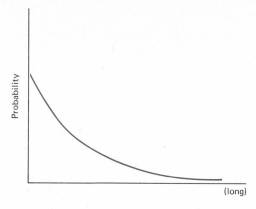

(long)

Figure 14-6 Exponential distribution of service times.

times are exponentially distributed and arrivals Poisson distributed, the mathematics necessary to study waiting line behavior is somewhat easier to develop and use. Figure 14-6 illustrates an exponential probability distribution of service times; from this we see that the probability of long service times is rather small.

4. Elementary Queuing System: Constant Arrival and Service Times

The case in which *both* the arrival rate and the servicing rate are constant can be illustrated with the following examples:

Example 1: No Queue, Idle Time

Examples of constant arrival and service rates

Assume that arrivals occur at the constant rate of 10 per hour, 10 arrivals each hour and every hour, occurring precisely every 6 minutes. Assume also that services can be performed at a constant rate of 12 per hour every hour. With this situation, a queue will not form because the servicing facility can handle with ease the entire arrival work load. In fact, we can easily calculate that the servicing facility will be idle $^2/_{12}$, or 16.67 percent, of the time because arrivals need only $^{10}/_{12}$ of servicing capacity.

Example 2.: No Queue, No Idle Time

Assume now that arrivals occur at a constant rate of 10 per hour, 10 arrivals each hour and every hour, occurring at 6-minute intervals during that hour. Assume also that services can be and are performed at a constant rate of 10 per hour every hour. With this situation, a queue cannot form because arrivals are serviced at the same rate at which they arrive. Also in this situation, there will be no idle time in the servicing facility because it must operate at full capacity to handle the arrivals.

Example 3: Queue Forms, No Idle Time

Assume now that arrivals occur at a constant rate of 10 per hour, occurring every 6 minutes during that hour. Assume also that services are performed at a constant rate of 8 per hour *every* hour. With this situation, a queue will form and grow because the input rate is higher than the ability of the servicing facility to handle it. The queue of unserviced arrivals builds up at the rate of 2 units per hour, the excess of arrivals over serviced items. At the end of 7 hours, for instance, we would normally expect to see 14 units in the queue.

Thus the assumption of *constant* arrival and service times makes quite easy the calculation of whether a queue will form and what its length will be after any period of time. If, however, we move to the more usual case in which both arrivals and services are not constant, in which they happen at other than precise intervals, the problem and the calculations become more difficult. For instance, if we allow arrivals and services to be randomly distributed, even though the servicing facility has a capacity greater than the average arrivals, a group of items arriving at the same time for service may form a temporary queue. And, of course, by the same token, a temporary reduction in arrivals may enable the service facility to catch up, to remove a queue that had previously formed. The next few sections are devoted to models which permit us to analyze queuing systems more complex than these three examples.

5. Single-Channel Queuing Model: Poisson Distributed Arrivals and Exponentially Distributed Service Times

The queuing model we are about to present fits situations where these conditions are satisfied:

1. The number of arrivals per unit of time are described by a Poisson distribution.

2. Service times are described by an exponential distribution.

3. Queue discipline is first come, first served.

4. The calling population is infinite.

5. There is *one* channel.

6. The mean arrival rate is less than the mean service rate.

Six conditions for the use of this model

If these six conditions are met, it's possible to analyze a queuing system with a series of equations which management scientists have derived. These equations make use of the following symbols:

L_s = mean length of the system (number of units in the queue plus number being served)

L_q = mean length of the queue (number in the queue)

Symbolic notation for single-channel queuing model

W_s = mean time spent waiting in the system (queue time plus service time)

W_q = mean time spent waiting in the queue (time in the queue)

A = mean arrival rate of units per unit of time (say, an hour)

S = mean service rate (number of units served per unit of time, say, an hour)

P_w = probability that an arriving unit must wait for service (facility is busy)

Equations for Single-Channel Model

These equations have been derived by management scientists for the single-channel model satisfying the six conditions on page 463.

Equations for use in the single-channel queuing model

1. L_s = mean length of the system = $\dfrac{A}{S - A}$ (14-1)

2. L_q = mean length of the queue = $\dfrac{A^2}{S(S - A)}$ (14-2)

3. W_s = mean time spent waiting in the system = $\dfrac{1}{S - A}$ (14-3)

4. W_q = mean time spent waiting in the queue = $\dfrac{A}{S(S - A)}$ (14-4)

5. P_w = probability that the service facility is busy (utilization factor) = $\dfrac{A}{S}$ (14-5)

Metrolease example of single-channel queuing system

Let's consider the case of Metrolease Furniture Rental in Raleigh, North Carolina, with one warehouse serving its four stores in the area. The warehouse has only one loading dock manned by a three-person crew. President Jerry Fox has observed that at certain times several of his trucks are waiting in the yard to be loaded, yet at other times the three-person crew is idle. Jerry has done some preliminary analysis and feels sure the warehouse loading system fits the six conditions on page 463. His records indicate that the average arrival rate, A, is 4 trucks per hour, and the average service rate, S, is 6 trucks per hour. What can we tell Jerry about the appropriateness of adding another crew, or even two more crews, to increase the service rate at his single loading dock?

Economic interpretation of Metrolease results

In Table 14-3, we've used these formulas to calculate the effect of increased numbers of crews on the warehouse operation. On Jerry's advice, we have assumed that work capacity is proportional to the number of crews. From Table 14-3, it is clear that adding additional crews reduces both the number of trucks waiting and the time they wait. But this has been accomplished only by assuming that additional crews were available. What of the economics of this situation? Jerry says his trucks

Table 14-3 Effect on Warehouse Operation of Number of Crews

	1 crew	2 crews	3 crews
Mean number of trucks in the system	2	.5	.286
Mean number of trucks in the queue	1.33	.166	.063
Mean time spent in the system by a truck	.5	.125	.071
Mean time spent in the queue by a truck	.333	.042	.016
Probability that service facility is busy (utilization factor)	.666	.333	.222

Table 14-4 Total System Cost per Day under Three Alternatives

	Truck cost/day	Crew cost/day	Total cost/day
1 crew	$2 \times 8 \text{ hr} \times \$20 = \$320$	$3 \times \$6 \times 8 \text{ hr} = \$144$	$464
2 crews	$.5 \times 8 \text{ hr} \times \$20 = \$80$	$6 \times \$6 \times 8 \text{ hr} = \$288$	$368
3 crews	$.286 \times 8 \text{ hr} \times \$20 = \$46$	$9 \times \$6 \times 8 \text{ hr} = \$432$	$478

cost $20 an hour to operate and he pays the members of his loading crew $6 an hour each. In Table 14-4, we've shown the cost of idle truck time and of warehouse crew wages for the three alternatives we are examining.

Jerry ought to add another crew to the warehouse operation. It will not only reduce cost by $464 − $368 or $96 a day but will still leave the utilization factor at .333; this means that Jerry's crews will have, on average, $5^1/_3$ hours a day to spend on other productive work.

Results of queuing analysis of Metrolease

6. Multiple-Channel Queuing Model: Poisson Distributed Arrivals and Exponentially Distributed Service Times

Most queuing situations are *not* limited to one channel but involve situations where two or more channels are available and where members of the calling population form a single queue and wait for any *one* of the channels to become available for service. Banks and airline counters that ask customers to wait in a single line and then assign them to the first open teller or ticket agent are common examples of this situation. The multiple-channel queuing model we will now introduce fits situations where these conditions are satisfied:

1. The number of arrivals per unit of time are described by a Poisson distribution.

Six conditions for the use of this model

2. Service times are described by the same exponential distribution for all channels.

3. Queue discipline is first come, first served.

4. The calling population is infinite.

5. There is *more* than one channel.

6. The mean arrival rate is less than the mean service rate times the number of channels.

If these six conditions are met, we can analyze multiple-channel queuing systems with the following five equations which management scientists have derived.

Equations for Multiple-Channel Model

Equations for use in the multiple-channel queuing model

1. L_s = mean length of the system = $\dfrac{AS(A/S)^k}{(k-1)!(kS-A)^2}P_0 + \dfrac{A}{S}$ (14-6)

(All these symbols except P_0 and k) have been previously defined on page 464.

P_0 = the probability that there will be zero units in the system (Appendix Table 6 allows you to look up this value.)

k = the number of channels in the system

(! means *factorial*; $3! = 3 \times 2 \times 1 = 6$)

2. L_q = mean length of the queue = $L_s - \dfrac{A}{S}$ (14-7)

(L_s was obtained in Eq. 14-6)

3. W_s = mean time spent waiting in the system = $\dfrac{L_s}{A}$ (14-8)

4. W_q = mean time spent waiting in the queue = $\dfrac{L_q}{A}$ (14-9)

(L_q was obtained in Eq. 14-7.)

5. P_w = probability that the service facility is busy, i.e., that *all* channels are simultaneously busy (utilization factor)

$$= \frac{1}{k!}\left(\frac{A}{S}\right)^k \frac{kS}{kS-A}P_0$$ (14-10)

Metrolease example of multiple-channel queuing system

Let's take another look at Jerry Fox's furniture leasing operation. At his Durham showroom, Jerry has two rental "windows"; these are cashier stations where his customers arrange for payment after they have chosen their furniture. Jerry notices that most of the time customers have to wait in front of these windows; he cannot put a cost on their waiting time, but he says he's willing to consider opening another cashier's window (which will cost him $40 per day) if this will reduce the average time a customer spends in the payment system by about half. He figures the present customer load at 8 per hour and each cashier can service 5 customers an hour. What help can we give him now?

Table 14-5 Effect on Payment System of Number of Cashiers

	Two cashiers	Three cashiers	
Mean number of customers in the system	4.444	1.913	**Results of queuing analysis of Metrolease**
Mean number of customers in the queue	2.844	.313	
Mean time spent in the system by a customer	.556	.239	
Mean time spent in the queue by a customer	.356	.039	
Probability that all the cashiers are busy (utilization factor)	.711	.274	

In Table 14-5, we have used the multiple-channel formulas, Eqs. (14-6) through (14-10), to calculate the effect of increasing the number of cashier windows from two to three in Jerry's showroom. In using the multiple-channel formulas, we remember that S (5 in Jerry's case) is the service rate for *each* channel.

From Table 14-5 we can see that adding a third cashier reduced a customer's time in the system from .556 hours to .239 hours. This is more than a 50 percent reduction in waiting time, which was the condition under which Jerry would spend another $40 per day for the third cashier. We also see that with three cashiers, customers spend most of their time being waited on and very little (.039 hour) waiting in line. In this problem, as in many managerial situations, Jerry was *not* able to put a precise cost on customer waiting time, but by stating the conditions under which he would add another cashier, he in effect is saying "Reduction of waiting time to half is worth $40 a day to me in good will." Having made this subjective determination, he was able to make use of this particular queuing model.

Economic interpretation of Metrolease results

7. Other Queuing Situations

The two models we have introduced (single-channel and multiple-channel) are only the basic two queuing models. There are many variations of these. Some of the conditions that operations researchers have to contend with in queuing situations include these:

1. Distributions of service times that are not exponential

2. Distributions of the number of arrivals per unit of time that are not Poisson

3. Finite queues

4. Queue disciplines other than first come, first served (priority systems)

5. Customers or shipments which arrive in large batches instead of one at a time

A number of possible queuing situations

In many of these situations, quantitative models have been developed which allow waiting lines to be analyzed; however, there are still a large number of waiting-line situations which are so complex that there are just no quantitative models which can help us analyze them. In many of these situations, simulation can be used effectively. In the next section, we shall introduce a *hand-computed* simulation of a waiting-line situation. In practice, simulating a complex queuing system by hand would be nearly impossible, and we would turn to a computer to perform the simulation; however, some experience with a fairly simple queuing simulation will be useful reinforcement of the material first introduced in Chapter 13.

8. Simulation of a Queuing System

Valdese Machine Tool example of queuing simulation

The Valdese Machine Tool Company operates an inventory warehouse which issues raw material to supervisors. Currently, two persons are assigned to operate the system. The number of supervisors who use the warehouse is 10. Beth James, a senior member of the operations department, believes that the line of supervisors which develops at the warehouse every day is inefficient. She realizes from her knowledge of queuing models that the number of supervisors is probably too small to be represented by an infinite queue; she also has come to the conclusion that the distribution of the number of arrivals per unit of time is not Poisson; neither is the distribution of service times exponential. She realizes that, with a multiple-channel queuing situation which doesn't meet those conditions, finding a mathematical model is almost impossible. Therefore she decides to simulate the system.

No mathematical model is available

Observation

Beth observed the operation of the warehouse for 1-hour periods spread over a month. These 1-hour periods were scheduled at random during the day in order to get a reasonable cross section of activity. She gathered the following data during her observations:

Observation of the system

Length of service time, minutes	Number
8	15
9	30
10	45
11	60
Total requests	150

Average time between requests: 5 min
Total number of requests for service observed: 150

In addition to recording the above data, Beth divided her observation time into 5-minute intervals and recorded the number of shop supervisors who arrived during each interval. The mean was one arrival within each 5-minute period.

Arrivals and service times

At the completion of the observation period, Beth tabulated the results of her observations as follows:

Percentage distribution of service times; $\quad$ $^{15}/_{150} = 10\%$ $\quad$ (8 min)
$^{30}/_{150} = 20\%$ $\quad$ (9 min)
$^{45}/_{150} = 30\%$ $\quad$ (10 min)
$^{60}/_{150} = 40\%$ $\quad$ (11 min)

Weighted average of service times:	10% × 8 min =	0.8 min
	20% × 9 min =	1.8 min
	30% × 10 min =	3.0 min
	40% × 11 min =	4.4 min
Average service time:		10.0 min

With this information, Beth is ready to simulate the operation of the materials warehouse using a table of random digits, Appendix 7.

Simulating Arrivals

Beth first considers the task of simulating the arrivals of shop supervisors at the materials warehouse. She knows that supervisors arrive randomly, although the mean arrival rate is about one every 5 minutes. Because she is dealing with 10 digits (0, 1, 2, 3, 4, 5, 6, 7, 8, 9), she selects one of these (7) and lets it represent an arrival.

Using random numbers to simulate arrivals

Now if she breaks the simulation down into a number of 5-minute periods of operation and goes through a different list of random 10-digit numbers for each simulated period, the number of 7s she finds in each 10-digit random number will represent the number of arrivals during that period.

Beth simulated arrivals at the materials warehouse for a total of 24 five-minute periods. This is not necessarily the optimum period of simulation, but the procedure is identical whether the number of periods is 10, 20, or even 100.

To illustrate the procedure of simulating arrivals, let's reproduce the first 12 ten-digit numbers from Appendix Table 7 and note the number of 7s appearing in each. Beth reads from left to right *across* the five columns of random digits.

1581922396	None	4637567488	2	7055508767	3
2068577984	2	0928105582	None	6472382934	1
8262130892	None	7295088579	2	4112077556	2
8374856049	1	9586111652	None	3440672486	1

Using the number of arrivals she has just computed for the first 12 five-minute periods and using the same technique to compute the number of arrivals during the *next* 12 five-minute periods, Beth has simulated the arrival of shop supervisors at the warehouse. Results for all 24 periods of simulation are shown in Table 14-6.

Simulating Service Times

Having simulated the arrivals at the warehouse, she now turns attention to a simulation of the service times that would be required by each of the above arrivals. Beth recalls the distribution of service times she originally observed:

Minutes	Percent
8	10
9	20
10	30
11	40

Using random numbers to simulate servicing

Table 14-6   Simulated Arrivals for 24 Periods

Period number	Number of arrivals	Period number	Number of arrivals
1	0	13	0
2	2	14	0
3	0	15	1
4	1	16	4
5	2	17	1
6	0	18	1
7	2	19	1
8	0	20	0
9	3	21	0
10	1	22	1
11	2	23	0
12	1	24	2

Because she is still working with the same random digits (0, 1, 2, 3, 4, 5, 6, 7, 8, 9), she could divide them up in this sequence:

Let 0 represent the arrival of a supervisor requiring a service time of 8 minutes.

Let 1 and 2 represent the arrival of a supervisor requiring a service time of 9 minutes.

Let 3, 4, and 5 represent the arrival of a supervisor requiring a service time of 10 minutes.

Let 6, 7, 8, and 9 represent the arrival of a supervisor requiring a service time of 11 minutes.

Simulating arrivals for all 24 observation periods   Because Beth has 1 chance in 10 of getting a 0, it represents a .1 probability. Because she has 2 chances in 10 of getting either a 1 or a 2, they represent together a .2 probability. Because she has 3 chances in 10 of getting 3, 4, or 5, they represent together a .3 probability. Because she has 4 chances in 10 of getting a 6, 7, 8, or 9, they represent together a .4 probability. In this manner Beth is able to simulate the behavior of randomly distributed service times using a table of random numbers.

To illustrate this procedure, let's go back to the first 5-minute period of simulation in Table 14-6 and look at the arrivals. There were no arrivals during the first 5-minute period.

Looking at the second 5-minute period of simulated activity, Beth sees that there were two arrivals. To simulate their service times, she turns to the table of random digits. For arrival simulation, Beth elected to use the random digits beginning at the left-hand side of the fourth from bottom row of the table. The first two random digits on this row are 9 and 8. According to her earlier conventions, the first two arrivals require 11 minutes each for servicing.

To repeat this process for clarity, Beth turns to the third 5-minute period and notices from Table 14-6 that there were no arrivals during this time; so on she goes to the fourth period, when there was one arrival. The third random digit in that row is 4, signifying that this particular arrival required 10 minutes for servicing. If there are no arrivals, Beth does *not* skip a number. She has completed Table 14-7 by working through the above process for all 24 periods of simulation. Each arrival has been assigned a circled number.

Table 14-7 Simulated Service Times for 24 Periods

Period number	Number of arrivals	Service time of each
1	0	
2	2	① ② 11 min, 11 min
3	0	
4	1	③ 10 min
5	2	④ ⑤ 11 min, 10 min
6	0	
7	2	⑥ ⑦ 9 min, 10 min
8	0	
9	3	⑧ ⑨ ⑩ 10 min, 10 min, 11 min
10	1	⑪ 11 min
11	2	⑫ ⑬ 10 min, 8 min
12	1	⑭ 11 min
13	0	
14	0	
15	1	⑮ 11 min
16	4	⑯ ⑰ ⑱ ⑲ 10 min, 11 min, 11 min, 11 min
17	1	⑳ 9 min
18	1	㉑ 8 min
19	1	㉒ 11 min
20	0	
21	0	
22	1	㉓ 11 min
23	0	
24	2	㉔ ㉕ 9 min, 11 min

Illustration of arrivals and their service times

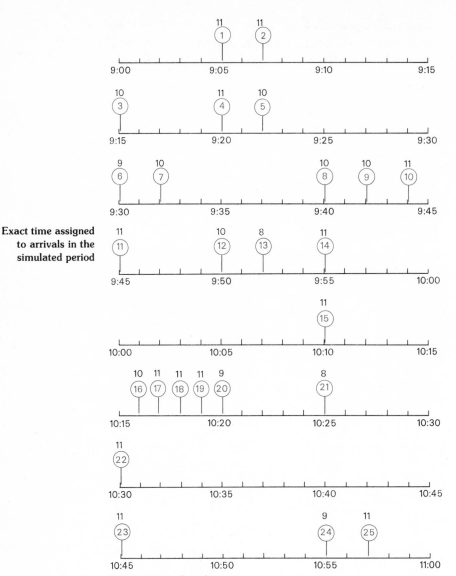

Exact time assigned to arrivals in the simulated period

Figure 14-7 Arrivals.

Simulating the Operation

First come, first served queue discipline

Now that Beth has simulated both the arrivals at the warehouse and the service time required for each arrival, she is ready to simulate the entire operation of the warehouse. She wants to determine the optimum number of attendants in the warehouse in order to minimize the total cost of warehouse operation *plus* time lost by waiting on the part of the supervisors.

She uses as her queue discipline the first come, first served rule: the super-

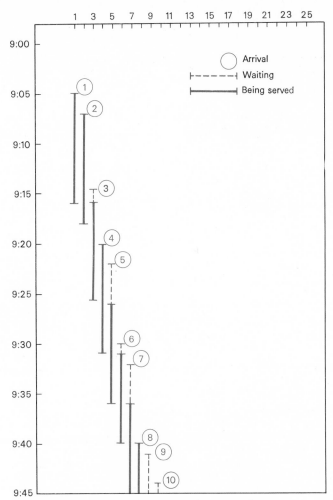

Figure 14-8 Warehouse operation with two attendants.

visors are served as they arrive. The best method to illustrate the overall operation is to use a time scale covering the entire period of simulation. Since the 24 simulated 5-minute periods are so long as to require a pull-out page if placed end to end, we shall get around this by using time scales placed under each other on a single page, each unit or segment representing 15 minutes; eight such representative scales will be required. Beth begins the simulation at, say, 9 A.M. To make it easier to refer to arrivals, she uses the circled numbers assigned to them in Table 14-7. Directly below each circled arrival is its service time.

Format of the simulation

To establish a routine for arrivals within each 5-minute period of simulation, Beth makes these assumptions:

1. If there is *one* arrival, it will be assumed to occur at the beginning of the 5-minute period.

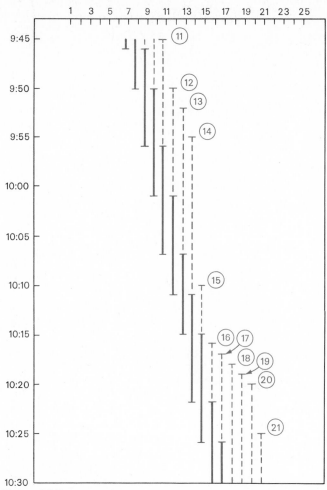

Figure 14-8   (Continued.)

2. If there are *two* arrivals, one will be assumed to arrive at the beginning of the period and the other at the beginning of the third minute during the period.

Rules for handling arrivals

3. If there are *three* arrivals, one will be assumed to arrive at the beginning of the period, the second at the beginning of the third minute, and the third at the beginning of the fifth minute.

4. If there are *four* arrivals, they will be assumed to arrive at the beginning of the second, third, fourth, and fifth minutes.

Assumptions Beth makes

To avoid dealing with fractional minutes, Beth elects to set up the pattern assumed above. She knows that the power of simulation lies in its ability to treat situations and events as they actually happen—to avoid forcing them into arbitrary distribution or behavior patterns. Ideally, she knows that the distribution of arrivals

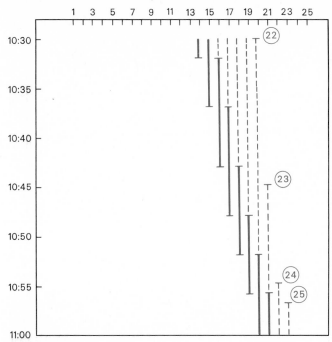

Figure 14-8 (Concluded.)

within the 5-minute period should be based on *observed* patterns of behavior; however, this information was not recorded, so she must make some assumptions and she chooses the ones above.

Figure 14-7 illustrates the arrival of all the supervisors who used the service facility during the 2-hour period of simulated activity. Beth first tries to operate the warehouse with two attendants.

To illustrate the actual behavior of the system, Beth uses a diagram in which each minute of time is represented in the left-hand margin. Beside each minute she shows each arrival, the time it is serviced, its service time, and the time it waits if waiting is necessary. This diagram is shown in Figure 14-8. Because there are two attendants in the warehouse; they can service two supervisors simultaneously. You will notice from Figure 14-8 that only *two* solid lines may appear at any one time, since there are only two attendants in the warehouse.

Determining the Optimum Number of Attendants

Beth gathers her results. If she counts the total length (in minutes) of all the waiting time, she sees that it totals 213 minutes, or an average waiting time per arrival of 213/25 = 8.52 minutes. To convert her findings into dollars she assigns a wage rate to both the warehouse staff and the supervisors:

Economic outcome of one manning alternative

Hourly wage rate for warehouse attendants = $5

Hourly wage rate for supervisors = $9

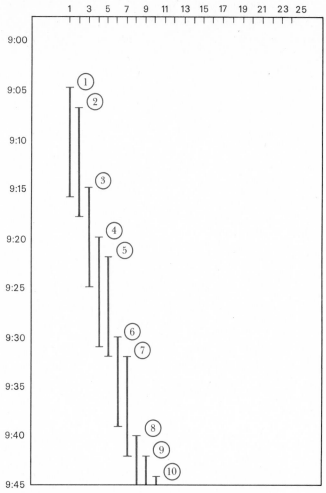

Figure 14-9 Warehouse operation with three attendants.

Now, if the average time between arrivals was 5 minutes (page 468), the supervisors must make 96 trips to the warehouse daily (8 hours per day × 12 trips per hour). And if the average waiting time is 8.52 minutes per trip, total waiting time is 8.52 × 96 = 817.9 minutes, or 13.63 hours of lost time daily.

The supervisors' time costs $9 per hour; therefore, the daily cost of lost time is 13.63 hours × $9 = $122.67. Add to this the cost of the two warehouse attendants (8 hours × $5 per hour × 2 people = $80) and Beth gets the total cost of operating the warehouse in this manner:

Cost of lost time of supervisors	$122.67
Wages of attendants	80.00
Total daily cost	$202.67

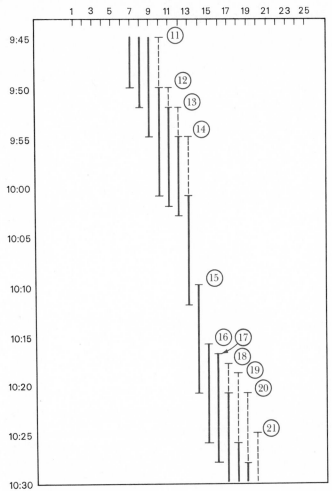

Figure 14-9 (Continued.)

Is two, then, the optimum number of attendants to assign to the warehouse? There is only one way Beth can be sure, and that is to simulate the system with *three* attendants.

Exact time assigned to arrivals in the simulated period

Beth has done this in Figure 14-9 in exactly the same manner as before, except that now she has allowed three solid lines to exist simultaneously because three supervisors can now be serviced at the same time.

Again she counts the total number of minutes of lost waiting time, which in this case totals 47 minutes. This is equivalent to 47/25, or 1.88 minutes lost per arrival. With 96 arrivals per day, the total time lost is 96×1.88, or 180.48 minutes, which equals approximately 3 hours per day.

Economic consequences of three-person manning

Cost of lost time of supervisors $3 \times \$9$ = $ 27
Wages of attendants $8 \times \$5 \times 3 =$ 120
   Total daily cost $147

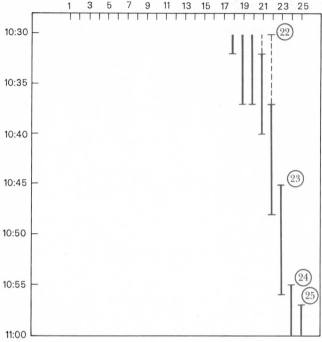

Figure 14-9   (Concluded.)

Consideration of four-person manning   This is lower than that incurred with two attendants; thus it is the better alternative. But what about the possibility that using four attendants would lower costs still more? Should Beth simulate this too?

Suppose that four attendants did somehow manage to remove *all* waiting time on the part of the supervisors. If this were the case, costs would be as follows:

Cost of lost time of supervisors	0 hr × \$9 = \$ 0
Wages of attendants	8 × \$5 × 4 = 160
Total daily cost	\$160

This clearly results in an alternative that is less attractive financially than having three attendants. Thus, in this problem, Beth finds from her simulation of the queuing system that the best staffing for the warehouse is three attendants.

Glossary

1. **Waiting line or queue**   A group of arrivals waiting for service.
2. **Calling population**   The population from which the queue forms.
3. **Service facility**   The facility which provides service to the waiting line.
4. **Waiting time**   Time spent in the queue or in the queue plus being serviced.

5. **Infinite calling population** Calling population where the probability of an arrival is not changed when one member of the population is receiving service.

6. **Finite calling population** Calling population where the probability of an arrival is changed when one member of the population is receiving service.

7. **Balking** Situation when a member of the calling population refuses to join the queue.

8. **Limited queue length** Situation where the waiting line is restricted to some maximum length.

9. **Unlimited queue length** Situation where there are no restrictions on the maximum length of the waiting line.

10. **Single-channel system** Queuing system where there is one service facility.

11. **Multiple-channel system** Queuing system with more than one parallel service facility.

12. **Single-phase system** Queuing system where service must be received from only one station.

13. **Multiphase system** Queuing system where service must be received from more than one station in order.

14. **Priority queue discipline** System in which members of the calling population may have different priorities entitling them to service either on a *preemptive* basis (when they can interrupt members already receiving service) or a *nonpreemptive* basis (where they hold a priority over other members of the calling population but cannot interrupt a member already receiving service).

15. **First come, first served queue discipline** System in which the queue member who arrived first is served first.

Review of Equations

(For all equations in this section, A = arrival rate and S = service rate.)

Page 464

$$L_s = \text{mean length of the system} = \frac{A}{S - A} \tag{14-1}$$

Using this equation will compute the mean number of units in the system (including the one being serviced) in the single-channel case where arrivals per unit of time are Poisson distributed and service times exponentially distributed.

Page 464

$$L_q = \text{mean length of the queue} = \frac{A^2}{S(S - A)} \tag{14-2}$$

This equation will give the mean length of the queue in the single-channel case with Poisson distributed arrivals and exponentially distributed service times.

Page 464

$$W_s = \text{mean time spent waiting in the system} = \frac{1}{S-A} \qquad (14\text{-}3)$$

Using this equation will produce the average time spent waiting in the system (including the time spent in the queue and the time being serviced for the single-channel case with Poisson arrival times and exponential service times).

Page 464

$$W_q = \text{mean time spent waiting in the queue} = \frac{A}{S(S-A)} \qquad (14\text{-}4)$$

To calculate the average time a unit spends waiting in the queue in a single-channel case, we use this equation. Arrivals must be Poisson distributed and service times exponential.

Page 464

$$P_w = \text{probability that the service facility is busy (utilization factor)} = \frac{A}{S} \qquad (14\text{-}5)$$

To calculate the probability that the service facility is busy and that an arriving unit in the single-channel case will have to wait, we use this equation in cases where arrivals are Poisson distributed and service times exponential.

(In the next five equations, k = the number of channels in the system and P_0 = the probability that there will be zero units in the system found from Appendix Table 6.)

Page 466

$$L_s = \text{mean length of the sytem} = \frac{AS(A/S)^k}{(k-1)!(kS-A)^2}P_0 + \frac{A}{S} \qquad (14\text{-}6)$$

We use this equation to compute the mean number of units in a multiple-channel queuing system, including the unit being serviced. Arrivals per unit of time must be Poisson distributed and service times exponentially distributed.

Page 466

$$L_q = L_s - \frac{A}{S} = \text{mean length of the queue} \qquad (14\text{-}7)$$

This equation yields the mean length of the queue in a multiple-channel queuing model where the Poisson distribution describes arrivals and the exponential distribution service times.

Page 466

W_s = mean time spent waiting in the system = $\dfrac{L_s}{A}$ (14-8)

Using this equation gives us the average time a unit spends waiting in a multiple-channel system (including the time being serviced) with Poisson arrivals and exponential service times.

Page 466

W_q = mean time in the queue = $\dfrac{L_q}{A}$ (14-9)

To calculate the mean time a unit spends waiting in the queue in a multiple-channel system, we use this equation. Arrivals must be described by a Poisson distribution and service times by an exponential distribution.

Page 466

P_w = probability that the service facility is busy, i.e., that all channels are simultaneously busy (utilization factor)

$= \dfrac{1}{k!}\left(\dfrac{A}{S}\right)^k \dfrac{kS}{kS-A}P_0$ (14-10)

If we want to find the probability that all the channels in a multiple-channel queuing system are simultaneously busy, we use this equation. Arrivals must be described by a Poisson distribution and service times by an exponential distribution.

Exercises

14-1. Ernie's Super Service has a special bay in the service station which is set up to perform state inspection on customer's cars. The state inspection law requires that all cars be inspected during the month of January or pay a late fee. The cars arrive at Ernie's at an average rate of four an hour in a pattern which can be described by a Poisson distribution. The attendant in the inspection bay can inspect an average of six cars an hour. Inspection times are exponentially distributed. Ernie was overheard to make this statement, "If I could reduce the average time a customer has to wait by a third, I would open another inspection bay." Would opening a second bay achieve Ernie's goal?

14-2. The Mastercraft Machine Company operates a warehouse which services its mechanics. The mechanics are observed to arrive at the warehouse at the random arrival rate of 12 per hour. The one warehouse attendant currently assigned is able to service these arrivals at the uniform rate of 8 per hour. The observer has also recorded data which indicate that on the average there are two arrivals during any 10-minute period. If the attendant is paid $5 per hour and each mechanic is paid $8 per hour, use the simulation method to determine the optimum number of attendants to assign to the warehouse to minimize total cost.

14-3. Trucks arrive at a facility to be unloaded in a pattern which can be characterized by the Poisson distribution. The average rate of arrivals is 36 per hour, and the level of service is exponentially distributed with a mean service rate of 39 trucks per hour. The drivers make $9 each hour and do not unload the trucks. How much expense, on the average, is incurred by the trucking company for idle time on the part of each driver for each visit to the facility?

14-4. The arrival of employees at a tool crib can be described by a Poisson distribution. Service times are exponentially distributed. The rate of arrivals averages 45 machinists each hour, while an attendant can serve an average of 50 men each hour. The machinists are paid $8 per hour, while the attendants are paid $5 per hour. Find the optimum number of attendants to place in the crib.

14-5. The Big Value Market has 10 counters. The average time spent per customer by each clerk is 5 minutes. Average arrivals per hour during three types of activity periods have been calculated, and customers have been surveyed to determine how long they are willing to wait during each type of period.

Type of period	Arrivals per hour	Store's average waiting time target
Peak	110	15
Normal	60	10
Low	30	5

a. How many counters should be open during each type of period?
b. What assumptions must be made in calculating your answers?

14-6. The personnel manager of the Acme Machine Shop needs to hire a mechanic to fix a certain type of lathe when in need of repair. Breakdowns on the lathes are Poisson distributed and occur on the average at two per hour. Any lathe out of service, either being repaired or waiting to be repaired, costs the company $20 per hour. The personnel manager can consider hiring either one of two applicants or both. The first applicant is a very speedy worker who can repair these types of lathes exponentially at an average rate of three per hour and expects to be paid $6 per hour. The second applicant also repairs lathes exponentially but is somewhat slower, performing on the average two repairs per hour and expecting a wage of $4 per hour. Which of the two applicants should be hired to minimize total cost?

14-7. The owner of the Crow's Nose frozen pea factory is considering the layout of processing equipment to package and freeze a grade of peas for consumers. Each day a quantity of peas is harvested and sent to "vineries" where the peas are removed from the pods. From there, they are trucked to the frozen pea factory. Arrivals at the factory are Poisson distributed with a mean arrival of five trucks per hour. The owner of the factory knows that peas are quite perishable and should not be left on the loading dock for too long before they are processed. He figures that if the waiting time before processing can be kept below 4 hours on the average, then the peas will have an adequate level of freshness for processing. Assuming that the processing and freezing of peas is exponentially distributed, determine the minimum average service rate (in truckloads per hour) that the factory must be designed to accommodate.

14-8. Dr. Walter McFall, a dentist, schedules his patients for $1/_2$-hour visits; he can, on the average, finish work on his patients in the half-hour allotted. His process time per patient is variable, however, and approximates a normal distribution (1 std. dev. = 15 min). The patients sometimes come early or late, and occasionally they do not show up at all. Dr. McFall figures the probability that a given patient will not show up is .10. The probability of the patient being on time is .50. The probability of arrivals $1/_2$ hour early or $1/_2$ hour late is .20 for each individual. Simulate Dr. McFall's schedule for an 8-hour (16 scheduled patients) day. Assume Dr. McFall takes patients on a first come, first served basis except that when two or more arrive at the same time, he takes the one with the earlier scheduled appointment.

14-9. The Downtown Photographic Studio has taken some proofs of a number of schoolchildren and has scheduled the parents to come into the studio to view the proofs. After viewing the proofs, the parents decide to buy prints or not to buy them. If they decide to buy, then a representative of the studio spends a certain amount of time going over the various types of photos available, their costs, etc., and takes the order. The parents' decision on whether to buy follows a binomial distribution with the probablity .50 that they will buy. The studio has decided to schedule six sets of parents to come into the studio every hour for an 8-hour period. The distribution of times spent servicing parents who buy the prints is as follows:

Time spent	Probability of occurrence
10 min	.10
15 min	.20
20 min	.50
25 min	.10
30 min	.10

Assume that the parents are taken first come, first served, and that a given set of parents who would normally buy prints becomes discouraged if the line of those waiting to see a representative is three or more. Simulate the system for the 8-hour period when there are two service representatives. Simulate the system with one server. If servers are paid $20 a day and profit from an average customer is $10, which of the two options (one or two servers) is better?

14-10. The registrar at Western University is making plans for fall registration. The final step in the registration process is the Bursar's Office, which determines the fees owed by each student. Students arrive at the Bursar's Office in a pattern which is well described by a Poisson distribution at an average rate of 500 an hour. A single clerk in the office can perform the necessary check at a mean rate of 60 an hour where the service times are exponentially distributed. If the registrar thinks that on average students should not have to wait longer than 30 minutes in the line, how many clerks should she schedule for registration?

14-11. Charlotte's lunch break is only 30 minutes. Her favorite restaurant is the Carolina Coffee Shop, but it is also the favorite of many other people and there is often a line at the door. Charlotte knows that she can wait in line no more than 5 minutes if she is to get back to work on time. If persons arrive at the Carolina Coffee Shop at an average rate of 30 an hour in a manner than can be described by a Poisson distribution and if the restaurant can serve 36 customers an hour with service times that are exponentially distributed, will Charlotte be able to eat there and still get back to work on time?

14-12. Fast-Foto is a rapid film processor with drive-up depositories scattered around metropolitan Minneapolis. Jerry Dana, the owner, guarantees 24-hour delivery on processing. Film is picked up at each depository frequently and delivered to the processing center. Arrivals at the processing center are described by a Poisson distribution with a mean of 500 rolls an hour. Jerry has a single processing machine which has a capacity of 600 rolls of film an hour and on which the service times are exponentially distributed. Jerry is thinking of changing his guarantee to 4-hour delivery. He has space to add up to two more processing machines. He charges an average of $3 a roll for processing and estimates his total costs at $2.50 a roll. He thinks his current business would increase by 50 percent if he could advertise 4-hour delivery. Additional costs incurred by this guarantee (increased pickups and maintenance, for example) would raise his cost per roll by 15 cents with each new machine brought on line. For example, adding a second machine would raise cost to $2.65. Should Jerry add machines to meet his new guarantee if he requires that his total profits must remain at least as high as before?

14-13. Gwin Lumber Company has a logging operation near Crossville, Tennessee. Cut logs are skidded from the cut site to a logging road where a crew loads log trucks. Gwin has sufficient log trucks to ensure that there is always an empty one (or more than one) available for loading. Loaded skidders arrive at the truck at an average rate of 3 per hour in a manner that is described by the Poisson distribution. A crew of 5 can take care of 4 skidders an hour with service times that are exponentially distributed. Gwin wants a less costly way to load, since it costs $40 an hour to operate a skidder, loaded or empty. There is a hydraulic off-loader on the market which can service 7 skidders an hour. It will cost twice as much as the manual crew, each of whose 5 members gets $3.50 an hour. A second alternative for Gwin is to add another crew, but this will also call for the addition of a supervisor at $5 an hour. Another crew could service as many skidders as the original crew. Which of these alternatives is the less costly for Gwin?

14-14. Charlie Gearing's U-Fill-Em and Quicki-Wash gives a free car wash with each fill-up of gasoline. After paying for the gas, customers get in line to be cycled through either of two car washers. The response to this promotional idea has been so great that the car-wash line is interfering with the operation of the gas pumps, causing problems for Charlie. Charlie notes that arrivals for the car wash average 30 an hour and can be described by a Poisson distribution; he also notes that each car wash can service 20 cars an hour with exponentially distributed service times. Charlie is willing to increase the number of car washers until he has decreased the mean length of the waiting line by half. How many car washers does Charlie need to meet this goal?

14-15. The Orange County Community Health Center is responsible for administering oral polio vaccine to school-age children. The center is set up in such a way that parents, with their children, form a single line from which they are served by any one of several nurses on duty. The service is offered once a week, and on that day the mean Poisson arrival rate is 70 an hour. The director of the center knows that most of the parents are employed and have taken time off from work to bring the children for shots. The director wishes to limit the average waiting time in line to no more than 10 minutes. If a single nurse can administer polio shots at a mean exponential rate of 30 an hour, how many nurses should the director schedule to meet his goal?

14-16. Harold Richards is chief of police in Carrboro, North Carolina. All telephone calls coming into the station are routed to a single switchboard and then forwarded to any available detective. Chief Richards knows that many callers hang up when put on hold; he wants to minimize this occurrence. The mean Poisson arrival rate for incoming calls is 20 an hour. By observation, Chief Richards has determined that a detective can handle 10 calls an hour with exponential service times. If there are five detectives currently on duty, what is the probability that a caller will have to be put on hold? What number of detectives would have to be on duty for this probability to be less than .02?

14-17. At Burger-Biggie, four order windows serve a single waiting line. The average Poisson arrival rate is 50 customers an hour; each of the four windows can serve 30 persons an hour with exponentially distributed service times. Cathy Leutze, the manager of Burger-Biggie, would like to reduce the number of serving windows to save on operating costs, but she does not want to interfere too drastically with the speed of the service. Cathy feels that it is OK for customers to wait in line as long as a minute before getting waited on, but no longer. Can she close down one or more of the serving windows?

14-18. Steve's Laundromat advertises "Never more than a 5-minute wait for one of our washing machines." Steve has 15 machines installed and two-thirds of them are functioning at all times. Each machine can wash four loads an hour with exponentially distributed service times. Customers arrive at the single front entrance at an average Poisson rate of 18 an hour, with one load of washing. Is Steve in danger of being accused of false and misleading advertising?

Bibliography

Feller, W.: *An Introduction to Probability Theory and Its Applications,* 3d ed. (New York: John Wiley & Sons, Inc., 1968), vol. I.

Lee, A. M.: *Applied Queuing Theory* (London: Macmillan & Co., Ltd., 1966).

Morse, P. M.: *Queues, Inventories and Maintenance: The Analysis of Operational Systems and Variable Demand and Supply* (New York: John Wiley & Sons, Inc., 1958).

Newell, G. F.: *Applications of Queuing Theory* (London: Chapman & Hall, Ltd., 1971).

Panico, J. A.: *Queuing Theory: A Study of Waiting Lines for Business, Economics and Science* (Englewood Cliffs, N.J.: Prentice-Hall Inc., 1969).

Saaty, T. L.: *Elements of Queuing Theory* (New York: McGraw-Hill Book Company, 1961).

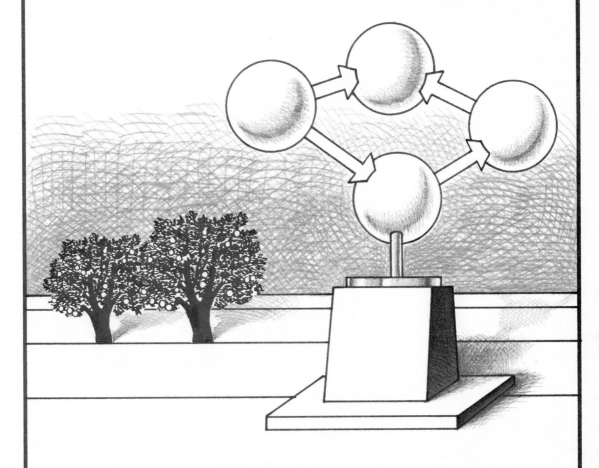

Network models

15

Networking techniques have broad application

The techniques to be introduced in this chapter have been applied successfully to a wide range of significant management problems. The Polaris missile project was planned with the aid of PERT (program evaluation and review technique), which we shall study in this chapter. CPM (critical path method) was successfully used by one of the authors to plan and coordinate the activities of two governments as they cooperated in an earthquake relief project in Turkey. Other uses of network models include the planning of traffic flows to minimize congestion in cities, the determination of the shortest pickup and delivery routes for package handling companies like United Parcel Service, and even finding the best layout for the water system in a new residential subdivision.

1. PERT (Program Evaluation and Review Technique)

Development of PERT

PERT was developed in the 1950s by the Navy Special Projects Office in cooperation with Booz, Allen and Hamilton, a management consulting firm. It was specifically directed at planning and controlling the Polaris missile program, a massive project which had 250 prime contractors and over 9000 subcontractors. Imagine the problems faced by the project director in attempting to keep track of hundreds of thousands of individual tasks on this project. The introduction of PERT into the Polaris project helped management answer questions like these:

Questions that PERT helps answer for management

1. When will the project be finished?

2. When is each individual part of the project scheduled to start and finish?

3. Of the hundreds of thousands of "parts" of the project, which ones must be finished on time to avoid being late?

4. Is it possible to shift resources to *critical* parts of the project (those that *must* be finished on time) from other *noncritical* parts of the project (parts which can be delayed) without affecting the overall completion time of the project?

5. Among all the hundreds of thousands of parts of the project, where should management concentrate its efforts at any one time?

Pioneer Audio Example of PERT

Pioneer Audio has completed the design and testing of a new type of hi-fi speaker, the Response 1000, which they think can be produced and distributed at a price that will give them the strongest market position in the industry. Ken Vaughn, Pioneer's president, is quite concerned that this speaker get the best possible promotion, and he has had a number of meetings with Rollie Tillman, Pioneer's promotion and advertising director. Rollie plans an extensive promotion campaign involving specially prepared literature, training of the field sales force, media releases, and actual demonstrations in selected stores nationwide. Rollie knows that this involves a lot of coordination and that a slipup will mean trouble not only for the Response 1000 speaker project but also for him.

Using PERT to plan the introduction of a new hi-fi speaker

An Activity List Rollie put together a careful list of all the different activities involved in the promotional campaign for the new Response 1000 speaker. This list is shown in Table 15-I. For each activity he identified, Rollie also identified its *immediate predecessors,* that is, the activities that must immediately precede a given activity. For example, in Table 15-1, Rollie noted that activity K, the training program, has as its immediate predecessors activities H and J; this simply indicates that the training program cannot be conducted without both the training material having been prepared and the participating store managers having been screened and selected. Similarly, activity L, the simultaneous in-store introduction of the Response 1000, cannot be accomplished without G (the in-store promotion materials), I (the preintroduction media campaign), and K (the training program) all having been completed.

Preparing the activity list

Precedence relations among activities

Drawing the Networks With his list of activities carefully checked to make sure that all the activities were included and all the predecessors correctly identified, Rollie then drew the graph in Figure 15-1. This shows not only all the activities in Table 15-1 but also all the predecessor relationships among the activities in the network.

Drawing the network to display precedence relationships graphically

From Figure 15-1 you can see that a PERT network is simply a network of numbered circles connected by arrows. In PERT, we call the circles *nodes* and the arrows *branches.* The arrows represent the activities in the project, and the nodes are the start and the finish of those activities. If all the activities leading to a node are finished, that node can be called an *event*; in the Response 1000 network, circle 8

Nodes and branches

Table 15-1 List of Activities for the Response 1000 Promotion Campaign

Activity symbol	Activity description	Immediate predecessors
A	Develop the advertising plan (a detailed plan of projected radio, television, and newspaper advertising)	—
B	Develop the promotion and training materials plan (a detailed study of the materials that will be required for training the store managers and for the final in-store introduction)	—
C	Develop the training plan (the design of the training program that the store managers will undertake prior to the final in-store introduction)	—
D	Schedule the radio, television, and newspaper advertisements that will appear prior to the final introduction	A
E	Develop the advertising copy that will be required	A
F	A "dummy" activity (one that takes no time) which simply indicates activity I can't begin until activity E has been completed: explained at the bottom of this page	E
G	Prepare promotion materials which will be used during the in-store introduction	B
H	Prepare materials which will be used in the store manager training program	B
I	Conduct the preintroduction advertising campaign in the media	D, F
J	Screen and select the store managers who will undergo training	C
K	Conduct the training program	H, J
L	The final in-store introduction of the Response 1000	G, I, K

(which we call node 8 in network language) can be called event 8 only when activities G, I, and K are complete.

The meaning of a dummy activity

Dummy Activities in PERT   Rollie showed one *dummy activity* in the network, activity F. What does this mean? Had he not used that format, it might have appeared that activities D and E had the *same* starting and ending nodes, like this:

However, in PERT we avoid this by putting in a dummy activity F so that the same network can be drawn like this:

The dummy activity in PERT lets us draw networks with proper precedence relationships. The dummy activity F indicates that activity I *cannot* begin until *both* D and E are completed. These dummy activities exist solely for the purpose of establishing precedence relationships and are not assigned any time.

Dummy activities take no time

Activity Times in a PERT Network   In PERT, *time* is usually expressed in calendar weeks. The basic reason for not using smaller units is that most of the activities in a PERT network will take considerable time to accomplish.

Expressing time in PERT networks

To express the time required to complete an activity in the PERT system, we first estimate the number of working days required to do this work and then divide this by the number of working days per week. For example, if we have an activity that is expected to require 10 working days and our normal working week is 5 days, then we would say in the PERT system that this activity is expected to require 2 calendar weeks. Times are usually expressed to one decimal place.

Because of the uncertainty associated with projects which have never been done in the same way before, the estimated time for an activity is really better described by a probability distribution than by a single estimate.

The originators of PERT were faced with the problem of finding a particular kind of probability distribution; they wanted a distribution of activity times with the four characteristics listed on the next page.

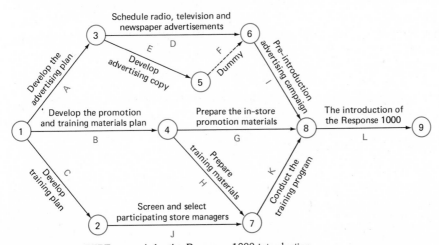

Figure 15-1   PERT network for the Response 1000 introduction.

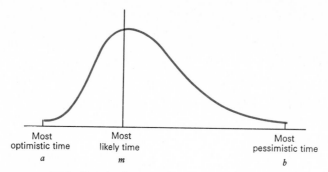

Figure 15-2 Beta distribution with symbols for time estimates.

Characteristics of the distribution used to express the variation in time

1. A small probability (1 in 100) of reaching the *most optimistic time* (shortest time), symbolized *a*

2. A small probability (1 in 100) of reaching the *most pessimistic time* (longest time), symbolized *b*

3. One and only one *most likely time* which would be free to move between the two extremes mentioned in 1 and 2 above, symbolized *m*

4. The ability to measure *uncertainty* in the estimating

The beta distribution

The *beta distribution* was picked because it has all four of these attributes. Figure 15-2 illustrates a beta distribution with the time designations under the curve.

After these three time estimates have been made, they must be combined into a single workable time value. This is done algebraically, using a weighted average,

$$t = \frac{a + 4m + b}{6} \tag{15-1}$$

where *t* equals the expected time for the activity.

Studies have been made of the accuracy and validity of *t* computed by formula (15-1). One study showed that in most PERT situations, the error in *t* from calculating it with Eq. (15-1) was small enough to make the method quite satisfactory in most cases.[1]

To describe the variation or dispersion in the uncertain activity times in a PERT network, we use the standard deviation of the activity times. Because we have three time estimates for each activity, we can calculate a standard deviation for that activity. The difference between the *a* time and the *b* time represents the distance from the extreme left-hand end to the extreme right-hand end of a distribution of possible activity times. This distance is about ±3 standard deviations; therefore, *b* − *a* = 6 standard deviations.

Thus

$$1 \text{ std. dev. for an activity} = \frac{b - a}{6} \tag{15-2}$$

[1] K. R. MacCrimmon and C. A. Ryavec, "An Analytical Study of the PERT Assumptions," Memo RM-3408-PR, RAND Corporation, Santa Monica, Calif., December 1962.

Table 15-2 Expected Time and Standard Deviation for Activities in the Response 1000 Project

Activity	a (most optimistic time)	m (most likely time)	b (most pessimistic time)	(a + 4m + b)/6 (expected time)	(b − a)/6 (activity std. dev.)
A	1	2	3	2	.33
B	1	2	3	2	.33
C	1	2	3	2	.33
D	1	2	9	3	1.33
E	2	3	10	4	1.33
F		(Dummy activity)		0	0
G	3	6	15	7	2.00
H	2	5	14	6	2.00
I	1	4	7	4	1.00
J	4	9	20	10	2.67
K	1	2	9	3	1.33
L	4	4	4	4	0

Activity Times for the Response 1000 Rollie Tillman made his best guess of the *most likely time* for each of the 11 activities in the Response 1000 project; then he indicated how uncertain he was by providing the estimates of the *most pessimistic* and *most optimistic time* for each activity as well. These are shown in Table 15-2 along with the expected times, calculated using Eq. (15-1), and the standard deviation for each activity, calculated using Eq. (15-2).

Notice that in the case of activity L (the actual in-store introduction), there is no uncertainty about this time, since Rollie plans for a 4-week introduction. Notice also that Rollie's uncertainty is reflected in the standard deviation of the activity times; in the case of some activities—A, B, and C, for example—the standard deviation is quite small; in others, however (look at J), the standard deviation is quite large.

Finding the Critical Path For Rollie to estimate how long the Response 1000 project will require, he will have to determine the *critical path* of this network. A path is defined as a sequence of connected activities that leads from the beginning of the project (node 1) to the end of the project (node 9). Since the work described by *all* the paths must be done before the project is considered complete, Rollie must find that path that requires the most work, the *longest* path through the network; this is called the *critical path*. If Rollie wants to *reduce* the time for the Response 1000 project, he will have to shorten the critical path; that is, he will have to reduce the time of one or more activities on that path—but first he has to *find* it.

When the network is larger, it is very tedious, often impossible, to find the critical path by listing all the paths and picking the longest one. We need a more organized method. We start at node 1 with a starting time we define as zero; we then compute an *earliest start time* and an *earliest finish time* for each activity in the network. Look at activity A with an expected time of 2 weeks:

Calculating expected times and standard deviations of those times for the project activities

Reflecting uncertainty in the network

Defining the critical path

Significance of the critical path

An efficient way to find the critical path

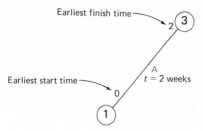

To find the earliest finish time for any activity, we use this formula:

Earliest finish time = earliest start time + expected time $\qquad$ (15-3)

$$EF \quad = \quad ES \quad + \quad t$$

Now Rollie must find the ES time and the EF time for *all* the activities in the Response 1000 network.

The Earliest-Start-Time Rule Since no activity can begin until *all* its predecessor activities are complete, the earliest start time for an activity *leaving* any node is equal to the largest earliest finish time of all activities *entering* that same node. Look at the first few activities in the Response 1000 network:

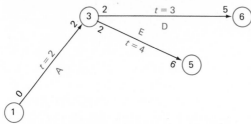

**Concept of the
forward pass in
PERT**
In this instance, the *earliest start time* for activities D and E is 2, the *earliest finish time* for activity A. Using this procedure we make what is called a *forward pass* through the network to get all the ES and EF times shown in Figure 15-3. Rollie can see right away from the earliest finish time for activity L that it's going to take 19 weeks to finish this project, and that's only if all the activities run on schedule.

The Latest-Finish-Time Rule The second step in finding the critical path is for Rollie to compute a *latest start time* and *latest finish time* for each activity. This is
**Concept of the
backward pass in
PERT**
done by using what is called a *backward pass*; that is, we begin this time at the completion point, node 9, and—using a latest finish time of 19 weeks for that activity (which we found in our forward pass method)—compute the *latest finish time* and *latest start time* for every activity. What is latest finish time? It is simply the latest time at which an activity can be completed without extending the completion time of the network. In the same sense, the latest start time is the latest time at which an activity can begin without extending the completion time of the project. In a more formal sense, LS can be computed with Eq. (15-4) on page 495.

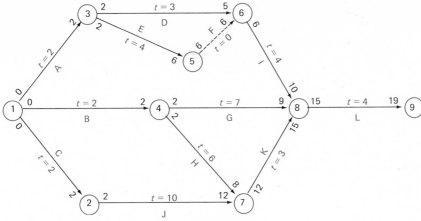

Figure 15-3 Response 1000 network with all earliest start (ES) and all earliest finish (EF) times.

Latest start time = latest finish time − expected time
           LS   =   LF   −   t

15-4. For example, given the latest finish time for activity 9 of 19 weeks, then

LS (for activity 9) = 19 − 4
                    = 15

In Figure 15-4 we've shown the LS and LF times for all of the activities in the network.

A formal statement of the *latest-finish-time rule* would be that the latest finish time for an activity entering any node is equal to the smallest latest starting time for all activities leaving that same node. Look at node 4 in Figure 15-4. The latest finish time for activity B entering that node is 6, the smaller starting time for the two activities leaving node 4.

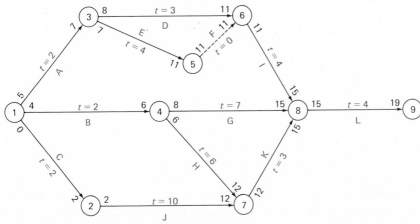

Figure 15-4 Response 1000 network with all latest start and all latest finish times.

Table 15-3 Determination of Critical Path for Response 1000 Project

Activity	Earliest start	Latest start	Earliest finish	Latest finish	Slack (LS − ES or LF − EF)	Activity on critical path
A	0	5	2	7	5	
B	0	4	2	6	4	
C	0	0	2	2	0	Yes
D	2	8	5	11	6	
E	2	7	6	11	5	
F			(Dummy activity)			
G	2	8	9	15	6	
H	2	6	8	12	4	
I	6	11	10	15	5	
J	2	2	12	12	0	Yes
K	12	12	15	15	0	Yes
L	15	15	19	19	0	Yes

Concept of slack in PERT

Now by comparing the *earliest start time* with the *latest start time* for any activity (that is, by looking at when it *can* be started compared with when it *must* be started), we see how much free time, or *slack*, that activity has. Slack is the length of time we can delay an activity without interfering with the project completion. We can also determine slack for any activity by comparing its *earliest finish time* with its *latest finish time.* Look at activity A on the network in Figures 15-3 and 15-4.

LF − EF for activity A = 7 − 2 = 5

LS − ES for activity A = 5 − 0 = 5

The formal statement of these two methods is:

$$\text{Slack} = \text{LF} - \text{EF} \quad \text{or} \quad \text{LS} - \text{ES} \quad\quad\quad (15\text{-}5)$$

Defining the critical path in terms of slack

In Table 15-3, we have shown LF, EF, LS, ES, and slack for all the activities in the Response 1000 network. Those activities without any slack are C, J, K, and L. None of these can be delayed without delaying the whole project. The *critical path* for the Response 1000 project is C-J-K-L. Rollie will have to watch these four activities especially closely; any delay in any one of them will cause a delay in the project completion. Delays in other activities (A, B, D, E, G, H, and I) will not affect on-time project completion (19 weeks) unless the delay is greater than the slack time an activity has. For example, it is O.K. for activity G (preparation of in-store promotion materials) to fall 6 weeks behind schedule because it has 6 weeks of slack; but if it falls *more* than 6 weeks behind schedule, it will delay completion of the Response 1000 project.

Probability Estimates in PERT So far, we've considered the activity times as fixed. Let's now examine the effect of uncertainty in Rollie's time estimating process on completion dates. Rollie knows that the critical path is C-J-K-L, with an expected total time of 19 weeks. Now look back at Table 15-2 on page 493 where Rollie computed a standard deviation for each activity. If the activity times on the critical path are statistically independent, the standard deviation of the earliest finish time of the network is given by the formula:

Standard deviation of the earliest finish time of the network (of the critical path on that network)

$$= \sqrt{\left(\begin{array}{c}\text{std. dev.}\\\text{for first}\\\text{activity}\end{array}\right)^2 + \left(\begin{array}{c}\text{std. dev.}\\\text{for second}\\\text{activity}\end{array}\right)^2 + \left(\begin{array}{c}\text{std. dev.}\\\text{for third}\\\text{activity}\end{array}\right)^2 + \left(\begin{array}{c}\text{std. dev.}\\\text{for fourth}\\\text{activity}\end{array}\right)^2}$$

$$= \sqrt{(.33)^2 + (2.67)^2 + (1.33)^2 + (0)^2} \tag{15-6}$$

$$= \sqrt{.1089 + 7.1289 + 1.7689 + 0}$$

$$= \sqrt{9.01}$$

$$= 3.00$$

Suppose Rollie wants to know the chances that he'll be able to finish the project in 20 weeks. PERT assumes that the distribution of the total project completion time is normal; this permits us to draw the distribution in Figure 15-5, where we've shown the earliest finish time of the network (19 weeks) and the completion time Rollie has on his mind now (20 weeks). We know the standard deviation of the critical path is 3 weeks, thus the distance from the mean to 20 weeks is

$$\frac{20 - 19}{3} = .33 \text{ standard deviation}$$

If we look in Appendix Table 1 for the area under a normal curve from the left-hand tail to a point .33 standard deviation above the mean, we find the answer .62930. Thus there is better than a 60 percent chance that Rollie will finish in less than 20 weeks.

What Did Rollie Find?   Use of PERT in this instance provides Rollie Tillman with some useful information about the Response 1000 project:

1. The expected project completion time is 19 weeks.

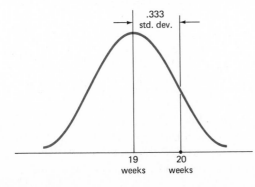

Figure 15-5 Distribution of project completion times for response 1000 project.

2. There is a better than 60 percent chance of finishing before 20 weeks. Rollie can also determine the chances of meeting any other deadline if he wishes.

Information provided by PERT

3. Activities C, J, K, and L are on the critical path; they must be watched more closely than the others, for if they fall behind, the whole project falls behind.

4. If extra effort is needed to finish the project on time, and if resources on one activity can possibly be used on another to reduce time, Rollie can *borrow* resources from any activity *not* on the critical path; these include A, B, D, E, G, H, and I.

5. Activities not on the critical path (A, B, D, E, G, H, and I) can fall behind by varying amounts (their slack times) without causing the project to be late.

6. The earliest starting and finishing times for all activities in the project is known from Figures 15-3 and 15-4.

Network Replanning and Adjustment

Three methods of replanning and readjusting a network

PERT cannot be considered a sterile process of calculating times, drawing networks, and figuring slack time values; it is a dynamic process involved with change, with readjustment, with the formulation of new networks when there are changes in schedules, and with constant revision of plans to achieve better performance in the light of changing conditions. For this reason the process of readjusting and replanning a PERT network is of prime importance to us. Three methods are considered.

Interchanging Resources   When similar resources are employed on several different paths of a network, it is often possible *to switch resources from noncritical paths to the critical path* and thus effect a time savings in the overall network.

Relaxing the Technical Specifications   A second method of reducing the time required to complete a certain project would be to *relax some of the technical specifications governing the project.* For instance, if one of our technical requirements for a certain project is that paint must be allowed to dry for .4 week between coats and we want to put two coats of paint on a certain building, our network might look something like this:

Activity A represents putting on the first coat, activity B represents the drying time, and activity C represents putting on the final coat. If we relax the technical specifications somewhat, perhaps to .3 week or about 2 days between coats, we can obviously reduce the time necessary to complete the work. The extent to which this can be done is severely restricted in many cases. Take, for instance, the process of pouring concrete. If the specifications call for concrete to cure (a process often called setup) for 5 days before a load is put on it and we arbitrarily reduce this specification to 2 days, we may experience disastrous results when the finished concrete is put under load.

Changing the Arrangement of Activities Suppose that a particular finished part must go through three machining operations before completion. If these parts were sent through the machine shop in batches of 100 and we wanted all pieces to travel along together, we would represent the process on a chart like this:

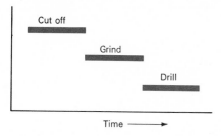

Activities which look like this are called *series-connected* in PERT terminology, meaning that one must be completed before the next can be begun. But, when a few parts have gone through the cutoff process, what would be wrong with sending them along to the grinder instead of waiting for the entire batch of 100 to be processed at the cutoff station? When a few units have gone through the grinding process, what would be wrong with sending them along to the drill presses instead of waiting until the entire batch has been processed? The rearranged activities portrayed below reflect a considerable saving in time.

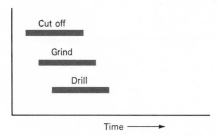

2. CPM (Critical Path Method)

Next to PERT, the critical path method (CPM) of planning and controlling projects has enjoyed the widest use among all the systems that follow the networking principle. CPM was developed in 1957 by J. E. Kelly of Remington Rand and M. R. Walker of Du Pont to help schedule maintenance in chemical plants.

Background of CPM

The fundamental departure of CPM from PERT is that CPM brings more prominently into the planning and control process the concept of *cost*. When time can be estimated rather well and when costs can be calculated rather accurately in advance (labor and materials for a construction project, for example), CPM may be superior to PERT. But when there is an extreme degree of uncertainty and when

How CPM is different from PERT

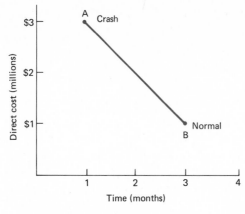

Figure 15-6 Crash time and cost compared with normal time and cost for one segment of the Durham-Chapel Hill expressway project.

control over time outweighs control over costs (as in launching the spacelab, for example), PERT may well be the better choice. The networking principles involved in CPM are like those in the PERT system.

Time Estimating in CPM

Normal and crash time

Under the CPM system, *two* time and cost estimates are indicated for each activity in the network; these two are a *normal* estimate and a *crash* estimate. The *normal* estimate of time approximates the most likely time estimate in PERT. Normal cost is that associated with finishing the project in the normal time. The *crash* time estimate is the time that would be required if *no* costs were spared in reducing the project time. Crash cost is the cost associated with doing the job on a crash basis so as to minimize completion time.

Rob Teer is the project director for Nello Teer Co. on the new Durham-Chapel Hill expressway. Rob has represented one segment of the project with the time-cost graph shown in Figure 15-6.

The vertical axis represents the cost of completing one segment of the project, and the horizontal axis represents the time required for completion. Normal estimates call for 3 months and $1 million. Suppose a crash effort would complete the work in 1 month at a crash cost of $3 million. The line AB on Figure 15-6 is called a *time-cost curve*.

Crashing a Project

Steps in crashing a project

To crash a project successfully, we examine the network, note its activities, and compare normal costs with crash costs for each activity. Our goal is to find those activities on the critical path where time can be cut substantially with minimum extra dollars spent. Our goal is the greatest reduction in project time for the least increase in project cost.

Catch basin crashing example

Figure 15-7 shows one of Rob Teer's networks for a small part of the Durham-Chapel Hill expressway project, a concrete catch basin to control runoff water at a busy intersection; all times are normal times. Table 15-4 contains the time-cost information for this small project.

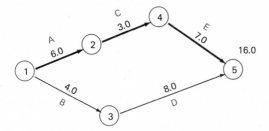

Figure 15-7 Catch basin network with all normal times.

In Figure 15-7, path A-C-E is the critical path. The earliest finish time for the project is 16 weeks, and total costs under normal times are $35,000. Now look at Figure 15-8, the catch basin project with *all* crash times; now the earliest finish time is 10 weeks and the cost is $47,000.

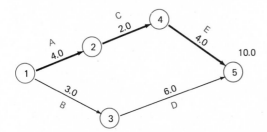

Figure 15-8 Catch basin project with crash times for all the activities.

Rob wonders if the project time can be reduced to 10 weeks *without* increasing costs $12,000, ($47,000 − $35,000). Now look at Figure 15-9.

Figure 15-9 shows the network with activities E, C, D, and A crashed; activity B is the only activity not crashed. Table 15-5 recaps the crashing program. Notice that we began by crashing the least expensive activity, E; we then turned our attention to the next least expensive activity, C and crashed that. At this point both paths through the network (A-C-E and B-D) require 12 weeks; thus further reduction of project time will require reducing activities on *both* paths. On path B-D the least expensive activity to crash is D; thus we crash that to 6 weeks. A similar 2-week reduction on the upper path (A-C-D) can be achieved by crashing activity A to 4 weeks. At this point all activities on the path (A-C-E) have been crashed to their

Can you reduce project time without crashing all activities?

Crashing the least expensive activity first

Table 15-4 Calculation of the Cost of Crashing Catch Basin Project

| Activity | Time, weeks | | Cost | | Cost to reduce per week |
	Normal	Crash	Normal	Crash	
A	6.0	4.0	$10,000	$14,000	$2,000
B	4.0	3.0	5,000	8,000	3,000
C	3.0	2.0	4,000	5,000	1,000
D	8.0	6.0	9,000	12,000	1,500
E	7.0	4.0	7,000	8,000	333
		Total costs	$35,000	$47,000	

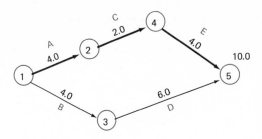

Figure 15-9 Activities E, C, D, and A crashed on Catch basin project.

minimum and further crashing on the lower path (B-D) will not produce any further benefit.

Crashing a CPM Network with Linear Programming

Using linear programming to crash a network

It is possible to find the best crash schedule for a CPM network by using linear programming. To illustrate this, we will use Rob Teer's project from Figure 15-7 and the project data in Table 15-4.

The first thing we do is define the variables; we let X = the time that an event will occur (measured in weeks after the project begins); in Rob's project we would define:

Defining the variables

X_1 = the time event 1 will occur
X_2 = the time event 2 will occur
X_3 = the time event 3 will occur
X_4 = the time event 4 will occur
X_5 = the time event 5 will occur

And we let Y = the number of weeks by which an activity is crashed—that is, the number of weeks we *reduce* that activity's normal time. So we have Y's like this:

Y_A = number of weeks we *reduce* the normal time of activity A
Y_B = number of weeks we *reduce* the normal time of activity B
Y_C = number of weeks we *reduce* the normal time of activity C
Y_D = number of weeks we *reduce* the normal time of activity D
Y_E = number of weeks we *reduce* the normal time of activity E

Table 15-5 The Network in Figure 15-7 and Table 15-4 after Crashing

	Project duration	Total network cost
1. Original network	16.0	$35,000
2. Crash activity E to 4.0 weeks	13.0	36,000
3. Crash activity C to 2.0 weeks	12.0	37,000
4. Crash activity D to 6.0 weeks	12.0	40,000
5. Crash activity A to 4.0 weeks	10.0	44,000

Since we want to crash the project at minimum cost, the objective function is:

Minimize $2000 Y_A + $3000 Y_B + $1000 Y_C + $1500 Y_D + $333 Y_E

The objective
function

(Cost coefficients from Table 15-4)

Now what about the constraints? Look at event 2 in Figure 15-7. If event 1 began at time zero, then X_2 (the time for event 2) can be described this way:

Writing the
constraints

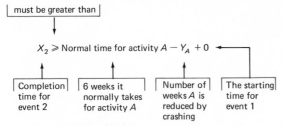

Putting in the normal time for activity A of 6 weeks, we have:

$$X_2 \geqslant 6 - Y_A + 0 \qquad (1)$$

And the constraint for event 3 is developed the same way:

$$X_3 \geqslant 4 - Y_B + 0 \qquad (2)$$

Since activity C begins with event 2 (and not zero, as was the case with the two previous examples), we write the constraint for X_4 this way:

$$X_4 \geqslant 3 - Y_C + X_2 \qquad (3)$$

And since two activities lead into event 5, we'll need *two* constraints there:

$$X_5 \geqslant 7 - Y_E + X_4 \qquad (4)$$
$$X_5 \geqslant 8 - Y_D + X_3 \qquad (5)$$

So far we have five constraints. What about the maximum crashing that can be done? Activity times cannot be reduced forever. From Table 15-4, the maximum values for the Y variables is the difference between the normal and crash times:

$$Y_A \leqslant 2 \qquad (6)$$
$$Y_B \leqslant 1 \qquad (7)$$
$$Y_C \leqslant 1 \qquad (8)$$
$$Y_D \leqslant 2 \qquad (9)$$
$$Y_E \leqslant 3 \qquad (10)$$

And, of course, Rob wants to finish his project in 10 weeks, so we need to write one more constraint on the project completion time:

$$X_5 \leqslant 10 \qquad (11)$$

Optimum answer to
Rob's crashing
problem

If we minimize our objective function under these 11 constraints, we'll get the optimum Y values (you should notice that the X values do not appear in the objective function because they merely indicate when an event occurs and do not themselves incur any costs; only the Y variables represent cost to Rob).

If we add the constraint that all variables must be ≥ 0 and solve this linear programming problem (and it is a large one to be computed by hand, so we would use one of the canned computer programs to do it), the optimum answer turns out to be exactly the one we got using our original approach on page 500. The value of the objective function (the total crashing cost) is \$9000, (\$44,000 − \$35,000); Y_A is 2; Y_B is 0; Y_C is 1; Y_D is 2; and Y_E is 3.

Indirect and Utility Costs in Project Crashing

Other kinds of costs
in crashing a
network

Remember that in crashing this project to its lowest possible time at the minimum possible cost, we have taken into account only the *direct* costs associated with the project. Labor, materials, and such are essentially costs that vary directly with the time required to complete the work. Nothing has been said about (1) *indirect* costs (the overhead costs that go on throughout the entire project) or (2) costs sometimes referred to as *utility* costs (e.g., penalties for being late and bonuses for finishing the project early). The behavior of these two types of costs can certainly influence the decision about the desirability of crashing a project.

Assume that a contracting firm in its original contract promised delivery in 12 weeks; assume further that the firm agreed to pay a penalty of \$10,000 per week if delivery was made later than 12 weeks. Thus, when the firm sees that the work cannot be finished before 16 weeks, it faces a possible total penalty of \$40,000. No doubt the contractor would be glad to incur crashing costs that would reduce the time to 12 weeks as long as they were less than \$40,000. On the other hand, there is no reason why additional money should be spent to reduce the project time to under 12 weeks unless the reduction in indirect costs were greater than the crashing costs.

3. PERT/Cost

Including cost
control in
networking

When they were originally developed, PERT and CPM were both time-oriented; that is, they were designed to allow project planners to produce time schedules for the planning and monitoring of complex projects. In neither case was cost a major consideration, even though CPM did include the concepts of *direct cost, indirect cost,* and *utility cost,* each of which has been explained earlier in this chapter.

Earlier users of PERT and CPM noticed the need for these techniques to concern themselves with project cost control as well as time control; and in the early sixties, after the publication of a United States government manual entitled *DOD and NASA Guide, PERT/Cost Systems Design,* most military and research contracts required the use of PERT/Cost on the part of the contractor. Today, there are many different versions of this early project cost accounting technique; we shall illustrate one.

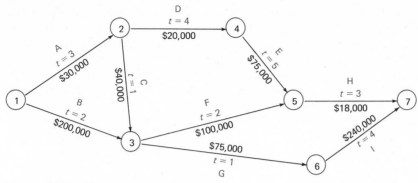

Figure 15-10 Nine-activity project network.

Costing by Activities

The foundation of the PERT/Cost system is the measurement and control of costs by "work packages"; we would have called these *groups of activities* in our earlier discussion of networking. These activities generally represent parts of a project for which responsibility is easily determined; in the original *DOD and NASA Guide*, the lowest-level work package was limited to no more than $100,000 in cost and could not require more than 3 months' estimated completion time; subsequent variations of the PERT/Cost technique have been considerably more flexible in defining such limits.

Work packages

Estimating Project Costs by Activity

Managers should know the amounts of money that are to be expended for each activity over the planned duration of the project; one usually assumes that the expenditures for each activity are made at a constant rate during that activity, although with the use of computers this simplifying assumption can be dropped. To get an idea of how the project times and costs are set up, look at Figure 15-10. Here we have shown a project involving nine activities; for each activity we have given its estimated duration (in months) and the total estimated cost of the activity. In Table 15-6, we show earliest start time, latest start time, duration (in months), total cost, and cost per month for all activities in the network.

How much is to be spent on each activity

Project Budgeting Choices

Now, from a technological point of view, the project director has a choice concerning when he can begin each activity in this project; for example, he could begin each activity at its *earliest start time*. Figure 15-11 illustrates the funds committed under this alternative; but the project director could wait to begin each activity until its *latest start time*. What is the difference? Figure 15-12 shows the cumulative amounts of money which would be spent during the project if *every* activity were to begin on a late start basis. One can see from this figure that beginning *all* the activities on a late start basis allows the project to continue on schedule but reduces the average commitment of funds spent on the project considerably. For example,

Choices open to the project director

Activity	Month 1	2	3	4	5	6	7	8	9	10	11	12	13	14	15
A	$ 10,000	$ 10,000	$ 10,000												
B	100,000	100,000													
C				$ 40,000											
D				5,000	$ 5,000	$ 5,000	$ 5,000								
E								$ 15,000	$ 15,000	$ 15,000	$ 15,000	$ 15,000			
F					50,000	50,000									
G					75,000										
H													$ 6,000	$ 6,000	$ 6,000
I						60,000	60,000	60,000	60,000						
Total	110,000	110,000	10,000	45,000	130,000	115,000	65,000	75,000	75,000	15,000	15,000	15,000	6,000	6,000	6,000
Cumula-tive	110,000	220,000	230,000	275,000	405,000	520,000	585,000	660,000	735,000	750,000	765,000	780,000	786,000	792,000	798,000

Figure 15-11 Project cost with early starts (monthly and cumulative totals shown).

Month

Activity	1	2	3	4	5	6	7	8	9	10	11	12	13	14	15
A	$10,000	$10,000	$10,000												
B									$100,000	$100,000					
C										40,000					
D				$ 5,000	$ 5,000	$ 5,000	$ 5,000								
E								$15,000	15,000	15,000	$ 15,000	$ 15,000			
F											50,000	50,000			
G											75,000				
H													$ 6,000	$ 6,000	$ 6,000
I												60,000	60,000	60,000	60,000
Total	10,000	10,000	10,000	5,000	5,000	5,000	5,000	15,000	115,000	155,000	140,000	125,000	66,000	66,000	66,000
Cumula-tive	10,000	20,000	30,000	35,000	40,000	45,000	50,000	65,000	180,000	335,000	475,000	600,000	666,000	732,000	798,000

Figure 15-12 Project cost with late starts (monthly and cumulative totals shown).

Table 15-6 Activity Information for Nine-Activity Project Network

Activity	ES	LS	Duration (months)	Total cost	Cost/month
A	0	0	3	$ 30,000	$ 10,000
B	0	8	2	200,000	100,000
C	3	9	1	40,000	40,000
D	3	3	4	20,000	5,000
E	7	7	5	75,000	15,000
F	4	10	2	100,000	50,000
G	4	10	1	75,000	75,000
H	12	12	3	18,000	6,000
I	5	11	4	240,000	60,000
				Total cost $798,000	

at the end of 8 months, using the late start alternative would have committed only $65,000 to the project, as opposed to the $660,000 which would have been spent had the director begun all activities at their early start date. At any month, the dif-

Differences between committed funds for both alternatives — ference between the cumulative totals on Figures 15-11 and 15-12 represents money which has not been committed to the project and is thus available for other purposes; in our example, this is a sizable sum. A quick calculation indicates that, under the early start alternative, the *average funds committed* at any one time over the life of the project are $560,733; this may be compared to $269,066, which would be committed under the late start option. Figure 15-13 illustrates the general relationship between funds commitment under the early start and that under the late start option.

Control of Project Costs with PERT/Cost

Comparisons of cost in PERT/Cost — The use of PERT/Cost in project management allows one to go a bit beyond the traditional comparison of actual with budgeted costs. Since this technique deals with time and cost, one can compare, in addition, *scheduled* work with *completed* work. Generally costs are coded according to activity; at the time costs are gathered,

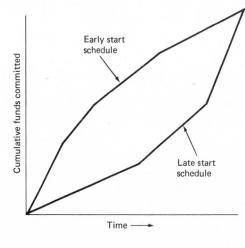

Figure 15-13 General relationship between funds commitment under early start and late start options.

estimates are made on the proportion of that activity that has been completed. If our original assumption that cost and time are directly proportional is true, then comparison between cost incurred and work completed yields information vital to project control. Specifically, if an activity has incurred 75 percent of its budgeted cost but is only 55 percent completed, we have what is usually called a *budget overrun*. It is quite usual for project managers to receive reports which answer pertinent questions including:

1. What is the expected completion time?

2. Is the activity now on schedule?

3. What are the budget overruns on each activity?

4. Is the situation getting better or worse each reporting period?

Typical questions answered by PERT/Cost reports

4. Network Scheduling with Resource Limitations

Up to this point in our discussion of networking techniques, we have assumed that an activity can begin just as soon as all those activities which must precede it have been completed. This assumption is predicated on *there being sufficient resources available to perform all the work defined by the activities.* In our adjustment and replanning of PERT networks earlier in this chapter, we juggled starting times of activities; nonetheless, we still assumed there were resources sufficient to do all the work scheduled on a given day. In practice, this is often *not* the case.

What happens when there are not sufficient resources

Problem with Limited Resources

In Figure 15-14 we have illustrated a network with nine activities; the format of this network is different from the format of those we have presented previously in *two* ways:

1. It uses curved lines for activities; this eliminates the need for zero-time activities and thus simplifies our network.

Differences between this network and previous ones

2. Each activity is identified in three ways: *first* by an identification letter (A), (B), (C), etc., *then* by the estimated duration of that activity in weeks, and *finally* by the number of people we assumed would be available to work on that activity when we estimated its duration.

We can show our network in Figure 15-14 in another, perhaps more useful form by plotting each activity on a schedule graph with a horizontal time scale; this has been accomplished in Figure 15-15. There the duration of each activity is represented by the length of that activity's line; the description on each activity represents its letter designation and the number of people it is assumed will work on that

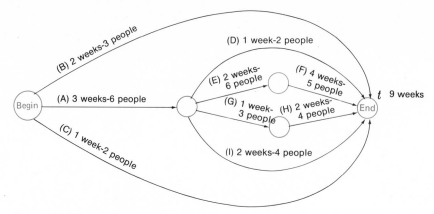

Figure 15-14   Network for problem with limited resources.

activity at one time (crew size). The bottom row of Figure 15-15 is the total number of people scheduled to work in any one week. We can see from this total that we will require from 5 to 15 people, depending upon which week we are scheduling. But suppose the supply of workers is constrained—suppose we have only nine people available for work during this period; what alternatives are open to us?

A Method for Resource Leveling

Use of a personnel loading chart in resource leveling

Often a quick way to solve our personnel scheduling problem is to show it first in graphic form; if we plot the number of people working in any week against time, we produce the *personnel loading chart* illustrated in Figure 15-16. If we have just 9 people available for work, we can see several things from this chart: first, we notice that we will be *short* of workers during the first, fourth, and fifth weeks; we also see that nine people are *exactly sufficient* to perform the work scheduled during the second and sixth weeks; finally, we see that we have a *surplus* of workers for the work we have scheduled during the third, seventh, eighth, and ninth weeks. We can see that our task is to rearrange the schedule so that, insofar as possible, we even out the peaks and valleys without scheduling more work than nine people

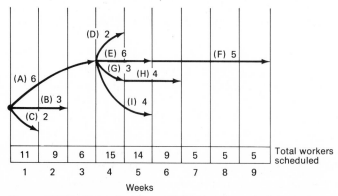

Figure 15-15   Network of Figure 15-14 plotted on schedule graph.

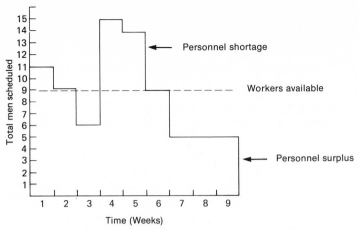

Figure 15-16 Personnel loading chart for schedule graph in Figure 15-15.

can do and without violating any of the precedence relationships in the network. It may not be possible to so rearrange the network and still finish in 9 weeks, but under the present circumstances we do not even have sufficient personnel for the *first* week's scheduled work.

A surplus and a shortage of workers at different times

Heuristic Programming as a Method

Although the scheduling problem we are using as an illustration can be solved quite quickly by hand, when there is a large number of activities, it is generally impossible to enumerate all the answers (and thus find the optimum one) even with a large computer. For this reason, we typically use *heuristic programs* to solve these kinds of combinatorial problems. A *heuristic rule* is really a "rule of thumb" that works, and when you have a collection of these rules of thumb, they are generally referred to as a *heuristic program*. Quite a few heuristic programs for leveling network schedules have been developed during the last few years. As a matter of fact, people have been using heuristic programs throughout all recorded history; these take the form of such rules of thumb as these: get in the back of the shortest line; never try to leave town on Friday at 5 P.M.; and look after only the exceptional problems and leave all the others to your subordinates. Our approach to rescheduling in this sample problem is really nothing more complex than these simple examples.

Heuristic programs

Our heuristic approach generally looks first at the activities that have the most slack and attempts to delay them as long as possible without delaying the completion of the entire project. For example, if we delayed the start of activity (C) (it has the greatest slack time), then activities (A) and (B) could begin simultaneously and yet not violate our personnel limit of nine workers. If we continue to apply this method, we can achieve the revised schedule graph illustrated in Figure 15-17. Notice that when an activity is delayed in order to achieve a better schedule, the time during which it is delayed is represented by a dotted line. Notice also that when we reached the end of the third week, we had a *choice* among delaying activ-

A heuristic approach to rescheduling

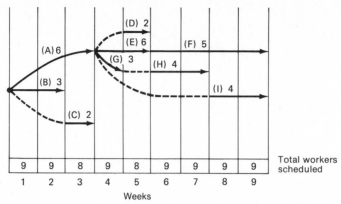

Figure 15-17   Revised schedule graph.

ities (D), (G), and (I); in this case we chose activity (I), even though it had somewhat less slack than the other two, because its personnel requirement of four workers would fit quite nicely with that of activity (F). The network we used for an example was a very simple one, and yet we are unable to come up with a perfectly balanced schedule with nine people working all the time; we perhaps will have to be content with having too little work for our crew during the third and fifth weeks, but even this can be considered a very good balance. Generally, given the complexities of projects on which these types of techniques are used and considering the amount of time required to achieve balance among resources, most project managers would be happy with far less success than we had with our sample project.

5. The Maximal-Flow Problem

What the maximal-flow problem does   In a network with one *source node* (point of entry) and one *output node* (point of exit), the maximal-flow problem seeks to find the maximum flow (whether it be cars, planes, fluids, or electricity) which can enter the network at the source node, flow through it, and exit at the output node in a given period of time. Let us use Durham, North Carolina, as our example of the maximal-flow problem. Normally, north-south traffic around Durham would use Interstate 85, but I-85 will be out of commission for extensive roadway repairs for 2 weeks and the North Carolina **A highway capacity problem**   Highway Commission engineers need to find out whether alternative routes (through the city) will safely handle the 6000 cars an hour that normally use I-85 going south. Look at Figure 15-18, in which we have illustrated these north-south routes through the city. The numbers beside the nodes indicate the traffic flow of **What the activity notation means about flow**   the branches (streets in this case) in thousands of cars per hour. The 6 on branch 1-2 means that street has a capacity of 6000 cars an hour heading toward node 2. The 0 on branch 1-2 means that the highway engineers do not want *any* cars going toward the source node, 1. Look at branch 3-5; 5000 cars an hour can move in the direction of node 5 and 4000 an hour can move along this branch in the direc-

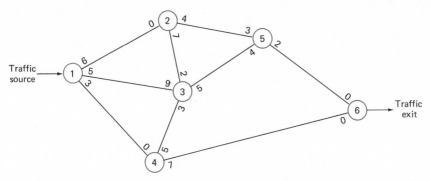

Figure 15-18   City street network for Durham, N.C., with flow capacities.

tion of node 3. The zeros on branches 5-6 and 4-6 indicate that the highway engineers do not want traffic heading from node 6 toward either node 5 or node 4 or simply that these streets are one-way.

The Maximal-Flow Algorithm
We can find the maximal flow by these steps:

1. Find a path from the source to the exit with flow capacity on *all* branches of that path (flow capacity would be designated by a positive number on the branch, next to the node you are moving from). If you can't find such a path, you already have the optimal solution.

   How to find the maximal flow in the network

2. Find the branch on your path with the smallest flow capacity (let us call this capacity *C*); increase the flow on this path by:
   a. *Decreasing* the capacity in the direction of flow of all branches on this path by *C*
   b. *Increasing* the capacity in the reverse direction of all branches on this path by *C*

This procedure sounds much more difficult than it actually is, so let's get started with the Durham traffic flow network.

Three steps in the solution to the Durham traffic network

Step 1   Suppose we begin with path 1-2-5-6. (Actually it doesn't matter which path you choose, for you will eventually get the maximal flow regardless of this first choice.) Branch 5-6, with a flow capacity of 2, has the smallest flow capacity on this path. If we decrease the capacity in the direction of flow by 2 and increase it in the reverse direction by 2, we get the network in Figure 15-19.

Step 2   Now look at path 1-4-6; the smallest flow on this path is branch 1-4 with flow capacity 3. When we decrease the flow capacity in the direction of flow by 3 and increase it in the reverse direction by 3, we get the network in Figure 15-20.

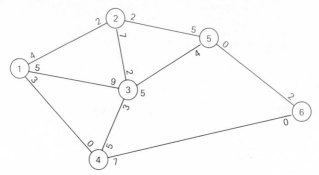

Figure 15-19 Step 1 in maximal-flow algorithm.

Step 3 Can we find another path with positive flow capacity? Yes, path 1-3-4-6 has positive flow capacity and the branch with the smallest capacity on this path is 3-4, with a flow capacity of 3. When we decrease the flow capacity in the direction of flow by 3 and increase it in the reverse direction by 3, we get the network in Figure 15-21.

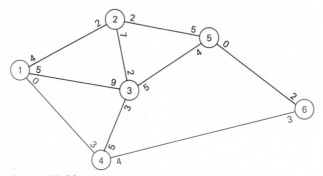

Figure 15-20 Step 2 in maximal-flow algorithm.

There is no path in Figure 15-21 with positive flow capacity on all its branches; therefore we have found the maximal flow for the network. Of course, it may be a bit difficult to recognize it from all the numbers in Figure 15-21, but in Table 15-7 we have shown you an easy way to see exactly where the flow of cars goes. This

Table 15-7 Flow Assigned to Each Branch by the Maximal-Flow Algorithm

		Branches					
	1–2	1–3	1–4	3–4	2–5	4–6	5–6
Step 1 ($C = 2$)	2				2		2
Step 2 ($C = 3$)			3			3	
Step 3 ($C = 3$)		3		3		3	
Total flow assigned	2	3	3	3	2	6	2

Flow assigned in the network

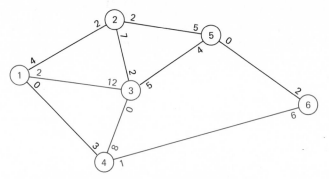

Figure 15-21 Step 3 in maximal-flow algorithm.

table indicates how much flow was assigned by each of the three steps it took us to get the maximal flow.

Figure 15-22 shows the assigned flows from Table 15-7 on the network. It turns out, then, that the city street route has a maximum capacity of 8000 cars per hour, which is well above the 6000 an hour that the Interstate normally carries. It should be feasible, then, to reroute the traffic through the city. Notice from Figure 15-22 that two branches (streets in our case) were assigned no traffic at all, and yet the network taken as a whole manages to produce the maximum traffic flow.

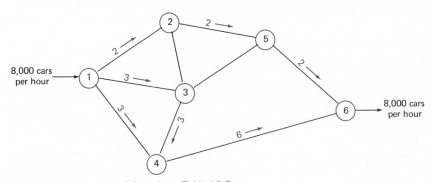

Figure 15-22 Assigned flows from Table 15-7.

6. The Minimal Spanning Tree Problem

The minimal spanning tree problem is concerned with finding a way to reach *all* the nodes in a network from some particular node (a source) in such a way that the total length of all the branches used is minimum. There are two methods we can use, Prim or Kruskal. The Kruskal algorithm is better for small hand-computed networks but inefficient for larger networks, so let us use the Prim method, which works on networks of all sizes.

Suppose we introduce the Prim algorithm with the example of Alan Fine, a real estate developer who has just planned a small subdivision of rural homes,

Focus of the minimal spanning tree problem

each quite some distance from the other. Alan is planning the water system for his development, and at this stage he is not obliged to lay the water lines beside the roads; in fact, after he eliminates routes which would cross streams and those which would involve considerable tunneling, the routes open to him for his water lines are those shown in Figure 15-23.

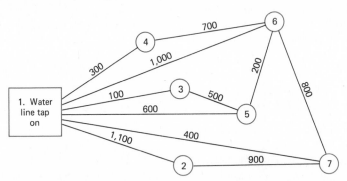

Figure 15-23 Alan Fine subdivision showing distances for possible water line routes.

Minimal Spanning Tree Algorithm

Five steps in the minimal spanning tree algorithm

The minimal spanning tree algorithm operates by joining the nearest unconnected node to nodes that are already connected; of course, for this to happen in the first place, we arbitrarily connect two nodes to begin the process.

Step 1 Construct a table of distances between nodes. Alan made up the one illustrated as Table 15-8. Since some nodes cannot be connected to others, we show this by entering the letter M in the table. M here has the same meaning it did in linear programming—that is, a very large number.

Step 2 Select any node to begin the algorithm; indicate that this node is connected by some appropriate mark (we shall use an X) and delete the column headed by this node. (Now look at Table 15-9 on page 518.)

Step 3 Find the smallest number in all the rows marked with an X and circle it. The column containing this circled number indicates the new connected node.

Table 15-8 Distances between Nodes for Alan Fine Subdivision

From node	To node						
	1	2	3	4	5	6	7
1	0	1,100	100	300	600	1,000	400
2	1,100	0	M	M	M	M	900
3	100	M	0	M	500	M	M
4	300	M	M	0	M	700	M
5	600	M	500	M	0	200	M
6	1,000	M	M	700	200	0	800
7	400	900	M	M	M	800	0

Step 4 Mark the newly connected node with an X and delete the column headed by this node.

Step 5 Repeat steps 3 and 4 until all the nodes have been connected.

Figure 15-24 shows the optimum answer from Table 15-9. In the figure, the closest routes are those that were circled when we finished the final step in the table. The length of the minimal spanning tree is the sum of all the lengths of the circled values in Table 15-9; in this case 2400 feet of water line will be required to connect all the homes in Alan's development.

Optimum answer

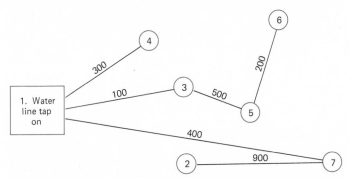

Figure 15-24 Minimal spanning tree for Alan Fine subdivision.

7. The Shortest-Route Problem

In the shortest-route problem, we are trying to find the shortest route from a source to a destination through a connecting network; the destination may be any other node in the network. This is the problem faced by any organization that delivers or picks up material from a number of points. Take, for example, Eban Merritt, the operator of a fleet of trucks, who has contracted to deliver a number of loads of lumber from Chapel Hill to Toledo, Ohio. In Figure 15-25 we've shown the possible routes Eban's trucks can take along with the distances in miles between each node. Of course, with a problem this small it would be an easy matter to list all the possible routes and choose the shortest; but just as we found in PERT networks, when the problem becomes more complex, that kind of solution method becomes useless.

Eban Merritt shortest-route example

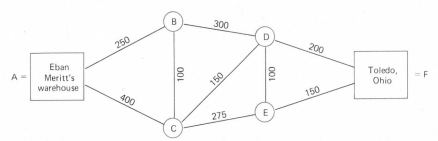

Figure 15-25 Network for Eban Merritt shortest-route problem (the lengths of the branches are not proportional to the distances).

Table 15-9 Solution to Alan Fine Minimal Spanning Tree Problem

	Connected		1	2	3	4	5	6	7
Step 2: Select node 1 to begin the algorithm; indicate with an X that it is connected and delete column 1. *Step 3:* Find the smallest number in the marked row (100) and circle it.	X	1		1,100	(100)	300	600	1,000	400
		2		0	M	M	M	M	900
		3		M	0	M	500	M	M
		4		M	M	0	M	700	M
		5		M	500	M	0	200	M
		6		M	M	700	200	0	800
		7		900	M	M	M	800	0
Step 4: Mark row 3 with an X and delete column 3. *Step 3:* Find the smallest number in all the marked rows (300) and circle it.	X	1		1,100		(300)	600	1,000	400
		2		0		M	M	M	900
	X	3		M		M	500	M	M
		4		M		0	M	700	M
		5		M		M	0	200	M
		6		M		700	200	0	800
		7		900		M	M	800	0
Step 4: Mark row 4 with an X and delete column 4. *Step 3:* Find the smallest number in all the marked rows (400) and circle it.	X	1		1,100			600	1,000	(400)
		2		0			M	M	900
	X	3		M			500	M	M
	X	4		M			M	700	M
		5		M			0	200	M
		6		M			200	0	800
		7		900			M	800	0
Step 4: Mark row 7 with an X and delete column 7. *Step 3:* Find the smallest number in all the marked rows (500) and circle it.	X	1		1,100			600	1,000	
		2		0			M	M	
	X	3		M			(500)	M	
	X	4		M			M	700	
		5		M			0	200	
		6		M			200	0	
	X	7		900			M	800	
Step 4: Mark row 5 with an X and delete column 5. *Step 3:* Find the smallest number in all the marked rows (200) and circle it.	X	1		1,100				1,000	
		2		0				M	
	X	3		M				M	
	X	4		M				700	
	X	5		M				(200)	
		6		M				0	
	X	7		900				800	
Step 4: Mark row 6 with an X and delete column 6. *Step 3:* Find the smallest number in all the marked rows (900) and circle it.	X	1		1,100					
		2		0					
	X	3		M					
	X	4		M					
	X	5		M					
	X	6		M					
	X	7		(900)					
Step 4: Mark row 2 with an X and delete column 2. All the nodes have been connected; this is the optimum answer.	X	1							
	X	2							
	X	3							
	X	4							
	X	5							
	X	6							
	X	7							

Shortest-Route Algorithm

Applying the shortest-route algorithm

We begin by constructing a list for each node in the network of the branches leading out of that node. It is not necessary to include branches leading *into* Chapel Hill or *out of* Toledo. Each branch is identified by a two-letter symbol; the first letter is the node a branch leaves from and the second letter is the node it goes to. Directly beside the symbol we indicate the length of that branch. These branches are arranged in ascending order of the branch lengths. In Table 15-10 we show such a list for Eban Merritt's route problem. The process we will use fans out from the origin (node A), identifying the shortest route to each of the nodes in the network in the ascending order of their distances from the origin. Let's begin by finding the nearest node to the origin.

Identifying the branches

Table 15-10 Branches Leading out of Each Node in Shortest-Route Network

A	B	C	D	E	F
AB-250	BC-100	CB-100	DE-100	ED-100	
AC-400	BD-300	CD-150	DC-150	EF-150	
		CE-275	DF-200	EC-275	
			DB-300		

Step 1 Only two branches lead away from the origin; branch AB is the shorter. Therefore node B is the nearest node to the origin. We indicate *above* node B that the shortest distance is 250 miles. Results of this step are

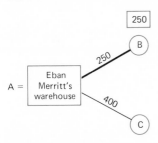

Step 2 The second nearest nodes to the origin are those nearest A and B. These are C and D. D is 300 miles from B and C is 100 miles from B. We choose C, and indicate below C that the shortest distance from the origin to C is 350 miles. This is shown as:

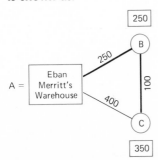

Step 3 The third nearest nodes to the origin are those nearest B and C. These are D and E. There are two ways to get to D: from B and from C. B + 300 = 550 and C + 150 = 500; we pick branch CD. Now look at node E. E is C + 275 = 625. We conclude that node D is the nearest one to B or C, and we indicate that by entering 500 miles above node D like this:

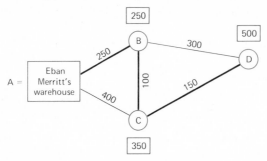

Step 4 The fourth nearest nodes to the origin are those nearest C and D. These are E and F. There are two ways to get to E, from C and D. C + 275 = 625 and D + 100 = 600; we pick branch DE. Now look at node F. F and D + 200 = 700. We conclude that node E is the nearest one to C and D, and we indicate this by entering 600 below node E. It is represented as:

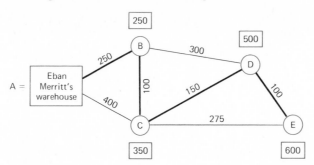

Final step **Step 5** The fifth nearest nodes to the origin are those nearest D and E. Only one node, F qualifies. We compare branch DF (500 + 200) and branch EF (600 + 150) and choose DF. We write 700 above node F, and we illustrate the completed shortest route like this:

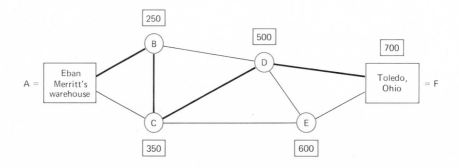

We see from this last network that the shortest route is A-B-C-D-F, with a total distance of 700 miles.

Glossary

1. **PERT (Program Evaluation and Review Technique)**   A networking system developed in the 1950s, useful in planning and control projects.

2. **Immediate predecessor**   An activity that must immediately precede a given activity in a project.

3. **Activity list**   A list of all the activities in a project.

4. **Branches**   Term used to refer to the activities in a network.

5. **Nodes**   The circles in a network representing the beginning and ending of activities.

6. **Event**   A node when all the activities leading to that node have been completed.

7. **Dummy activity**   Activity which requires no time and which is used to establish a precedence relationship in a network.

8. **Most optimistic time**   The shortest possible time in which an activity is likely to be completed, symbolized a.

9. **Most pessimistic time**   The longest possible time in which an activity is likely to be completed, symbolized b.

10. **Most likely time**   The time that the activity would most likely take if it were repeated time and time again, symbolized m.

11. **Beta distribution**   Continuous distribution of a random variable which is used in time estimating in PERT.

12. **Expected time for an activity**   Time calculated using the weighted average $(a + 4m + b)/6$.

13. **Critical path**   Longest path through a network.

14. **Earliest start time**   Earliest time at which an activity can begin.

15. **Earliest finish time**   Earliest time at which an activity can end.

16. **Forward pass**   Process moving from left to right in a network to define all the earliest start and finish times.

17. **Latest start time**   Latest time at which an activity can begin without extending the completion time of the network.

18. **Latest finish time**   Latest time at which an activity can be completed without extending the completion time of the network.

19. **Slack**   Free time in a network. Formally defined as $LF - EF$ or $LS - ES$.

20. **Series-connected activities**   Activities related in such a way that one must be finished before the other can begin.

21. **CPM (critical path method)**   Networking method developed in 1957 which adds the concept of cost to the PERT format.

22. **Normal time**   Time required to finish an activity if it is done in the normal manner.

23. **Crash time**   Time required to finish an activity if special efforts are made to reduce the time to a minimum.

24. **Crashing**   Method used to reduce the time in a network at the least cost.
25. **Direct costs**   Costs which vary directly with the time required to complete the work.
26. **Indirect costs**   Overhead costs which go on throughout the entire project.
27. **Utility costs**   Penalties for being late and bonuses for being early.
28. **PERT/Cost**   Project management system developed by the United States government which measures and controls costs by use of work packages.
29. **Budget overrun**   Condition when an activity has expended a greater proportion of its estimated cost than its degree of completion would justify.
30. **Personnel loading chart**   Graph of available personnel plotted against time.
31. **Heuristic rule**   A rule of thumb that works.
32. **Heuristic program**   A collection of heuristic rules.
33. **Source node**   A point of entry in a maximal-flow problem.
34. **Output node**   A point of exit in a maximal-flow problem.
35. **Flow**   Movement along a branch in a maximal-flow problem.

Review of Equations

Page 492

$$t = \frac{a + 4m + b}{6}$$

(15-1)

With this formula, we can find the expected time for an activity in a PERT network by taking a weighted average of a (the most optimistic completion time), m (the most likely completion time), and b (the most pessimistic completion time).

Page 492

$$\text{Standard deviation of an activity} = \frac{b - a}{6}$$

(15-2)

This calculates the standard deviation of the expected time for a PERT activity. The most pessimistic time is b and the most optimistic time is a.

Page 494

Earliest finish time = earliest start time + expected time   (15-3)

If you add the expected time for an activity to that activity's earliest start time, you get the earliest time at which we could expect that activity to be completed (its earliest finish time).

Page 495

Latest start time = latest finish time − expected time   (15-4)

If you subtract the expected time for an activity from that activity's latest finish time, you get the latest start time for that activity, that is, the latest time at which the activity can begin without delaying completion of the network.

Page 496

$$\text{Slack} = \text{LF} - \text{EF} \quad \text{or} \quad \text{LS} - \text{ES} \tag{15-5}$$

Slack is equal to the difference between the latest finish time and the earliest finish time or—calculated another way—the difference between the latest start time and the earliest start time.

Page 497

Standard deviation of the earliest finish time of a network with four activities on its critical path

$$= \sqrt{\left(\begin{array}{c}\text{std. dev.}\\\text{for first}\\\text{activity}\end{array}\right)^2 + \left(\begin{array}{c}\text{std. dev.}\\\text{for second}\\\text{activity}\end{array}\right)^2 + \left(\begin{array}{c}\text{std. dev.}\\\text{for third}\\\text{activity}\end{array}\right)^2 + \left(\begin{array}{c}\text{std. dev.}\\\text{for fourth}\\\text{activity}\end{array}\right)^2} \tag{15-6}$$

The standard deviation of the earliest finish time of a network is found by taking the square root of the sum of the standard deviations squared of the individual activities on the critical path of that network.

Exercises

15-1. A project has the following characteristics:

Activity	Time	Predecessors
A	3	None
B	2	A
C	4	A
D	5	B
E	3	C
F	6	D

Construct a PERT network and compute the earliest start time for each activity.

15-2. A project plan is as follows:

Activity	Time	Predecessors
A	3	None
B	1	None
C	4	A
D	4	B
E	5	B
F	2	D
G	3	E

Construct a PERT network and compute the latest start time for each activity.

15-3. A project has the following schedule:

Activity	Predecessors	Time	Activity	Predecessors	Time
A	None	4	G	E	4
B	None	1	H	E	8
C	A	1	I	G	1
D	B	1	J	H	2
E	B	6	K	I, J	5
F	C, D	5	L	F	7

Construct a PERT network and compute ES, LS, and slack time for each activity; find the critical path.

15-4. A project has the following characteristics:

Activity	Most optimistic time	Most likely time	Most pessimistic time	Predecessors
A	.5	1	2	None
B	1	2	3	A
C	1	3	5	A
D	3	4	5	B
E	2	3	4	C
F	3	5	7	C
G	4	5	6	D, E
H	6	7	8	F
I	2	4	6	G, H
J	5	6	8	G, H
K	1	2	3	I
L	3	5	7	J

Construct a PERT network and compute the probability that the project will be completed within 30 weeks.

15-5. A complex project has the following characteristics:

Activity	Predecessors	Time	Activity	Predecessors	Time
A	None	1	K	J, F	5
B	None	2	L	H, G, K	10
C	None	3	M	H, G, K	11
D	C	4	N	J, F	1
E	B, D	3	O	I, L	9
F	C	8	P	J, F	3
G	B, D	2	Q	I, L	8
H	A, E	4	R	O, M, N	4
I	A, E	3	S	O, M, N	6
J	B, D	6	T	Q, R	2

Construct a PERT network, compute EF, LF, and S for all events. Find the EF for the network-ending event. What is the probability that the project could be completed in 20 percent less time than the indicated EF time?

15-6. Set up a linear program to find the earliest finish time for this project.

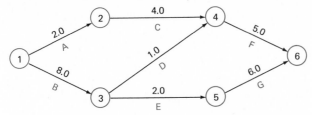

15-7. The following list of activities must be accomplished in order to complete a construction project:

Activity	Time (weeks)	Predecessors
A	2	None
B	3	None
C	4	A, B
D	1	B
E	5	A
F	3	C
G	2	E, F
H	7	D, F
I	6	G, H
J	3	I

Construct the PERT diagram for this project. *Note:* This diagram will require dummy activities. Compute the expected project completion time, and early start, late start, and slack for each activity.

15-8. One criticism of PERT's use of probability is that the probability of a project's completion on a given date is based upon the standard deviation of activities along the critical path. Yet, the probability of completion by the same date along a noncritical path may be a lesser value. Consider, for example, the following project.

Activity	Most optimistic time	Most likely time	Most pessimistic time	Predecessors
A	3	6	9	None
B	2	5	8	None
C	2	4	6	A
D	2	3	10	B
E	1	3	11	B
F	4	6	8	C, D
G	1	5	15	E

First, find the critical path and its standard deviation. What is the probability that the activities in the critical path will be completed by 18 weeks? Then compute the standard deviation of path B-E-G. What is the probability that this noncritical path will be completed by 18 weeks?

15-9. Assume you are the project manager of the project whose schedule is described in Problem 15-3. The project has progressed to the end of week 10 and the status is as follows:

Activities completed: A, B, C, D, E, and F. The remainder of the activities have not been completed, but G, H, and L can be started at the beginning of the following week. The project must be completed at the end of week 22. You have the choice of crashing certain activities. With the schedule as it now stands, what possible management actions might you take to hold the project completion at week 22?

15-10. The convention for constructing a PERT network uses arrows to designate activities and circles to designate events. The critical path method (CPM) sometimes employs a different convention where arrows represent precedence requirements and circles represent the activities. A network using this particular CPM convention would appear as:

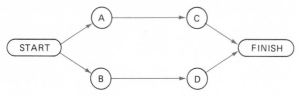

where:

CPM activity	Function or relationship to PERT
START	Dummy to indicate START (zero time)
A	Same as PERT activity
B	Same as PERT activity
C	Same as PERT activity
D	Same as PERT activity
FINISH	Dummy to indicate FINISH (zero time)

Draw the network diagram of Problem 15-7 above, using this CPM convention.

15-11. On the top of page 527 are data and a network diagram for a project. Using the CPM method, crash this project to its minimum possible length at the lowest possible total direct cost. (Assume that for this problem there are no indirect or utility costs.)

15-12. To the project in Problem 15-11, add indirect costs of $2000 per week and a utility cost (a penalty of $5000 per week against the contractor for each week beyond 25 weeks required for completion). What is the least costly completion schedule the contractor should attempt to achieve on this project?

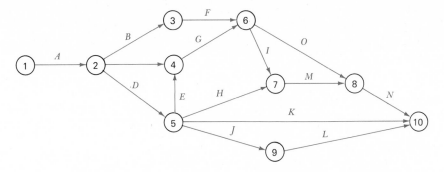

Activity	Normal time (weeks)	Crash time (weeks)	Normal cost (dollars)	Crash cost (dollars)
A	3.0	1.0	$11,000	$17,000
B	6.0	3.0	6,000	9,000
C	5.0	4.0	3,000	5,000
D	8.0	2.0	7,000	31,000
E	2.0	1.0	1,000	6,000
F	11.0	3.0	13,000	17,000
G	10.0	7.0	9,000	13,500
H	5.0	1.0	4,000	14,000
I	3.0	2.0	5,000	8,500
J	9.0	4.0	3,000	5,000
K	4.0	1.0	8,000	8,900
L	3.0	2.0	9,000	16,000
M	8.0	3.0	15,000	19,000
N	2.0	1.0	7,000	13,000
O	11.0	4.0	20,000	24,200

15-13. For the project illustrated below and at the top of page 528, produce a schedule of funds that will be required each month and determine the lowest average commitment of funds it is possible to obtain during the project, using a late start approach to each activity. (Use a simple average, *not* a time-weighted average, in your calculations.)

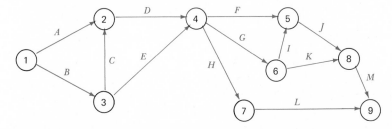

15-14. Refer to the resource leveling problem illustrated in Figure 15-14 in the text. Suppose the number of workers available during this period were increased to 11; what effect, if any, would this have on the total number of weeks required for completion of this project?

Activity	Duration (months)	Total cost
A	3	$ 60,000
B	1	10,000
C	5	20,000
D	4	40,000
E	6	120,000
F	6	180,000
G	7	35,000
H	4	80,000
I	2	30,000
J	1	5,000
K	1	40,000
L	3	90,000
M	2	18,000

15-15. Refer again to the resource leveling problem illustrated in Figure 15-14 in the text. From this figure, we can see that we have an unbalanced work force (5 to 15 people working at different times). Suppose labor constraints prevented us from employing fewer than seven or more than eight people; what effect would these constraints have on the time required to complete this project?

15-16. Sam Stone is the plant manager for the Burlington Hosiery Mill, Inc. From time to time, Sam must send out information for controlling the production process to each work station supervisor for use by the employees at that station. Since delivery of the information involves quite a bit of walking, Sam is interested in installing a pneumatic tube system to reach all the work stations. Sam has drawn the following diagram showing distances in feet from his office to the work stations and indicating possible paths from one station to another. (Walls and stairs prevent direct connection of all work stations.) Using the minimal spanning tree algorithm, show Sam the most economical (shortest length) system to install.

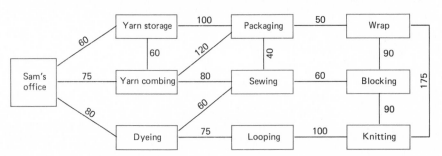

15-17. Joe Ferner has just been caught by a surprise OSHA inspection, and one of the violations for which he was cited dealt with the absence of a sprinkler system in his electric-motor manufacturing plant. Business hasn't been too good lately and Joe is caught between the prospect of a large fine or the cost of installing a sprinkler system. The factory has this floor plan:

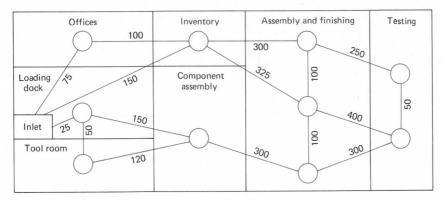

The circles indicate required sprinkler outlets in each area. In the interest of economy, Joe wants the least possible number of feet of piping. He has indicated the distances between sprinkler outlets in his sketch. Using the minimal spanning tree algorithm, which route will satisfy Joe's needs?

15-18. Dr. Clyde Carter, Chief of Emergency Services at Orange General Hospital, is concerned about the length of time it takes the hematology labs to process blood samples in emergency situations. He has full authority to direct the route blood samples take through the lab process to ensure the minimum total processing time possible. At Dr. Carter's request, the Director of the Hematology Lab has provided the accompanying schematic of the possible routes; the numbers shown are the time in minutes from one work station to another. By using the shortest-route algorithm, calculate the minimum possible time for processing a blood sample through the lab. You may assume that any route will produce a comparable test; different routes simply indicate different test machines with different capacities.

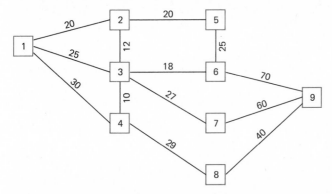

15-19. Lissette Edwards is an installer for the Burlington Telephone Company. She has been handed a service request for installation of a phone in an office building in the business district. When she arrives at the building, Lissette notices that the office which submitted the request is all the way across the building from the telephone junction box. In the interest of saving time and material, she calls you with a brief description of the situation and estimates of the distances involved. You sketch out the plan and it looks something like this. The black lines represent existing conduit through which Lissette can pull a telephone line. Using the shortest-route algorithm, advise Lissette which route to use. (Distances in feet.)

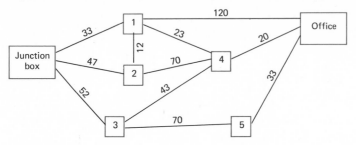

15-20. City Planning and Architectural Associates have been commissioned to design the new soccer stadium for the Miami Warhawks. Their design has the parking lot separated from the stadium with a single gate leading to the stadium (for security reasons). Within the gate, there are a number of possible routes through landscaped gardens to the single stadium entrance. The network through the gardens looks like this (numbers show capacity in thousands of persons per hour):

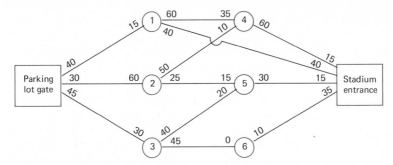

Using the maximal-flow algorithm, what is the hourly capacity of the system to move spectators into the stadium? Charlie Willis, owner of the Warhawks, phoned to say that if the system couldn't accommodate 100,000 fans coming into the stadium during 1 hour, the architects should start redesigning. Will City Planning have to redesign?

15-21. General Carter Williams, Jr., is commander of the aggressor army in the current war games being conducted at Fort John McHenry. He wants to launch a sneak attack on the defender army but needs to be assured of enough troop movement capability to carry off the attack, since an unsuccessful venture here would spell defeat for his forces, not to mention a personal blow. His aides have drawn the following illustration of possible routes from the aggressor army headquarters to the defender headquarters, showing the troop capacity which each route will handle (men per hour). General Carter feels that if he cannot move 22,000 men an hour along the attack routes, his plan is not workable. Should he devise another plan?

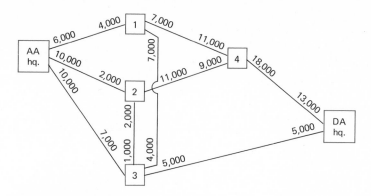

Bibliography

Evarts, H. F.: *Introduction to PERT* (Boston: Allyn and Bacon, Inc., 1964).

Ford, L. R. Jr., and **D. R. Fulkerson:** *Flows in Networks* (Princeton, N.J.: Princeton University Press, 1962).

Hillier, F. S., and **G. J. Lieberman:** *Introduction to Operations Research* (San Francisco: Holden-Day, Inc., 1974).

Levin, R. I., and **C. A. Kirkpatrick:** *Planning and Control with PERT/CPM* (New York: McGraw-Hill Book Company, 1966).

Miller, R. W.: *Schedule, Cost, and Profit Control with PERT* (New York: McGraw-Hill Book Company, 1963).

Wiest, J. D., and **F. K. Levy:** *A Management Guide to PERT/CPM* (Englewood Cliffs, N.J.: Prentice-Hall, Inc., 1969).

Markov analysis

16

Definition and early use of Markov analysis

Markov analysis is a method of analyzing the *current* behavior of some variable in an effort to predict the *future* behavior of that same variable. This procedure was developed by the Russian mathematician, Andrei A. Markov early in this century. He first used it to describe and predict the behavior of particles of gas in a closed container. As a management tool, Markov analysis has been successfully applied to a wide variety of decision situations. Perhaps its widest use is in examining and predicting the behavior of consumers in terms of their brand loyalty and their switching from one brand to another. Another interesting application of Markov analysis has been to the study of the life of newspaper subscriptions. A more recent application of this technique has been to the study of accounts receivable behavior, that is, to the study of customers as they change from "current account," through "30 days overdue," to "60 days overdue," and then to "bad debt." In each of these applications, management is interested in predicting what the future will bring (number of bad debts, for example, in the accounts receivable application) by analyzing what the current behavior is (propensity of customers to move from current account to various past due categories).

Current uses of this tool

1. Introduction to Brand-Switching Analysis

Brand switching

The basics of Markov analysis are best demonstrated with a brand-switching problem. There are three dairies in a community which supply all the milk consumed: Abbot's Dairy, Branch Dairy Products Company, and Carter Milk Products, Inc.

534

Table 16-1 Net Changes in Customers

| | Number of customers | |
Dairy	June 1	July 1
A	200	220
B	500	490
C	300	290

For simplicity, let's refer to them hereafter as A, B, and C. Each of the dairies knows that consumers switch from dairy to dairy over time because of advertising, dissatisfaction with service, and other reasons. If all three dairies maintain records of the number of their customers *and* the dairy from which they obtained each new customer, we have all the ingredients necessary for the application of this management tool.

Consumer behavior

Let us further suppose that Table 16-1 illustrates the movement of customers from one dairy to another over an observation period of 1 month. To further simplify the mathematics necessary, we shall assume that no new customers enter and no old customers leave the market during this period.

Assumptions we make

Casual observation may suggest that a total of 20 customers switched during the month: 10 from B to A and 10 from C to A. However, more detailed inspection may not support this initial inference. Suppose, for instance, that Table 16-2 is the true explanation of the exchange of customers among the three dairies. From it we see that 20 customers were gained by dairy A in a somewhat complex movement of customers involving all three dairies, a movement sometimes referred to in marketing as *brand switching*.

Casual versus detailed observation of brand switching

Each dairy needs details about brand switching if it is to do the best marketing job possible. If dairy B, for example, designs a promotional campaign under the impression that it is the only dairy losing customers *and* that it is losing them only to dairy A, B is operating under a false assumption. In fact, dairy B is not just losing 10 customers per month; rather, each month it is *gaining 40* new customers from the other two dairies and *losing 50* old customers to the other two dairies.

Problems with casual observations

Similarly, suppose that dairy A, noticing that it is gaining 20 customers each month, concentrates solely on efforts to lure additional customers away from its competitors. What dairy A has overlooked is its own losses of 40 customers per

Table 16-2 Actual Exchanges of Customers

| | June 1 | Changes during June | | July 1 |
Dairy	customers	Gain	Loss	customers
A	200	60	40	220
B	500	40	50	490
C	300	35	45	290

month. Perhaps some attempt to reduce this loss of 40 customers per month would be as effective dollarwise as efforts to capture additional customers from B and C.

The upshot of this whole matter is that simple analysis in terms of net gain or net loss of customers is inadequate for intelligent management. What management needs is a more detailed analysis concerning the rate of gains from and losses to *all competitors*. With such data, management can make an effort to:

Management uses of brand-switching analysis

1. Predict the share of market sellers will have at some future time

2. Predict the rate at which sellers will gain or lose their shares of market in the future

3. Predict whether or not some market equilibrium (constant or level market shares) will obtain in the future

4. Analyze a seller's promotion efforts in terms of exactly what effects they are having on gain and loss of market share

Markov analysis offers us just such a tool for marketing analysis. By employing this tool of management, we are able to draw more accurate conclusions about our marketing position, both present and future. Without it, we tend to be in the position of dairy A when A knew that 20 customers per month were being gained but did not know that this gain was the net result of an interchange of customers among all three dairies.

Transition probabilities

To move beyond this simple analysis and into the use of Markov analysis, we will have to compute *transition probabilities* for all three of our dairies. Transition probabilities are nothing more than the probabilities that a certain seller (a dairy, in this instance) will retain, gain, and lose customers. In other words, dairy B observes from Table 16-3 that it loses 50 customers this month; this is the same as saying that it has a probability of .9 of retaining customers; similarly, dairy A has a probability of .8 of retaining its customers; dairy C has a probability of .85 of retaining its customers. These transition probabilities for the retention of customers are calculated in Table 16-3.

Retention, gain, and loss

At this point, we have some measure of the proportion of old customers each dairy retains each month, but we have not said anything about the rates at which the three dairies gain new customers each month. Calculation of a complete set of these transition probabilities would require data on the flow of customers among all the dairies. Data of this sort demand good record keeping and take the form of Table 16-4.

Table 16-3   Transition Probabilities for Retention of Customers

Dairy	June 1 customers	Number lost	Number retained	Probability of retention
A	200	40	160	$160/200 = .8$
B	500	50	450	$450/500 = .9$
C	300	45	255	$255/300 = .85$

Table 16-4 Flow of Customers

Dairy	June 1 customers	Gains			Losses			July 1 customers
		From A	From B	From C	To A	To B	To C	
A	200	0	35	25	0	20	20	220
B	500	20	0	20	35	0	15	490
C	300	20	15	0	25	20	0	290

At this point, all the basic data are grouped in one table. We are able to observe not only the net gain or loss for any of the three dairies but also the interrelationship between the gains and losses of customers by each of the dairies. For instance, it is now quite clear that dairy A gains the majority of its new customers from B. We can reason more intelligently from Table 16-4 concerning these interrelationships than we could when we knew only the net gain or loss by each of the dairies.

2. Matrix Illustration of Transition Probabilities

The next step in the application of Markov analysis is to convert Table 16-4 into a more concise form where all the gains and losses are converted into transition probabilities. Transition probabilities are displayed in a pattern called a *matrix;* therefore it is necessary at this point to introduce some material on *matrix algebra* which will allow you to proceed with the Markov analysis material which follows.

Use of matrix algebra in Markov analysis

Matrices

A *matrix* can be defined as an array of numbers arranged into rows and columns. A matrix, taken as a whole, *has no numerical value.* The numbers in a matrix, however, may represent useful business data. When seen as an entire unit, such data may be of considerable help in the solution to certain problems. Here is a matrix with two rows and three columns:

$$\begin{pmatrix} 1 & 2 & 4 \\ 3 & 5 & 6 \end{pmatrix}$$ Columns ↓

Rows →

It would be referred to as a 2×3 matrix. (The number of rows always precedes the number of columns when describing the dimensions of a matrix.)

Rows and columns

To illustrate a management use of matrices, let us assume a simple condition in international trade; that is, countries X and Y import steel from countries A, B, and C. Country X receives 100 tons annually from A, 200 tons annually from B, and 400 tons annually from C. Y receives 300 tons annually from A, 500 tons annually from B, and 700 tons annually from C. In this written form, it is difficult to

Presenting data with a matrix

visualize the flow of steel from suppliers to users, but if the conditions are expressed in matrix form, the flows of steel are easily indicated as follows:

$$\text{Users} \begin{array}{c} \\ X \\ Y \end{array} \begin{array}{ccc} & \text{Suppliers} & \\ A & B & C \\ \begin{pmatrix} 100 & 200 & 400 \\ 300 & 500 & 700 \end{pmatrix} \end{array}$$

The first column in the matrix indicates the total shipments from country A to both users. The second column indicates the total shipments from country B, and the third column indicates the total shipments from country C. The first row indicates the total sources of country X's requirements, and the second row indicates the total sources of country Y's requirements. In this matrix form, the conditions are more easily visualized; the entire situation can be represented briefly, and the relationships are quite evident. Although this is not the *only* use we can make of matrices, further uses will have to wait until we have had some practice in understanding and dealing with matrices.

Here are several different matrices with size indicated beside each.

Matrices of different size

$$\begin{pmatrix} 2 & 1 \\ 4 & 6 \end{pmatrix} \qquad 2 \times 2$$

$$\begin{pmatrix} 1 \\ 6 \end{pmatrix} \qquad 2 \times 1$$

$$(1 \quad 2 \quad 6) \qquad 1 \times 3$$

$$\begin{pmatrix} -1 & 4 & 6 & 2 \\ 7 & 0 & -3 & 8 \end{pmatrix} \qquad 2 \times 4$$

$$\begin{pmatrix} 1 \\ -4 \\ 8 \end{pmatrix} \qquad 3 \times 1$$

The location of an individual element within any matrix can be described by indicating the row and column (in that order) in which the element appears. Below, the location of each element in the matrix is described by its row and column location.

Individual elements in a matrix

$$\begin{pmatrix} 1 & 2 & 7 \\ -1 & 4 & 6 \\ 3 & 5 & 8 \end{pmatrix}$$

	Row	Column
1 = element 1, 1	1	1
−1 = element 2, 1	2	1
3 = element 3, 1	3	1
2 = element 1, 2	1	2
4 = element 2, 2	2	2
5 = element 3, 2	3	2
7 = element 1, 3	1	3
6 = element 2, 3	2	3
8 = element 3, 3	3	3

Matrix Multiplication

Two matrices can be multiplied together if the *number of columns* in the first matrix equals the *number of rows* in the second matrix. If this condition is not met, multiplication is impossible. Here are two matrices, **A** and **B**, with their dimensions (the number of rows and columns) indicated directly beneath each of them:

Multiplying two matrices

Matrix **A**   Matrix **B**

$$\begin{pmatrix} 2 & 1 \\ 4 & 3 \end{pmatrix} \times \begin{pmatrix} 3 & 1 \\ 2 & 1 \end{pmatrix}$$

$$2 \times \boxed{2} \leftarrow = \rightarrow \boxed{2} \times 2$$

If the two circled numbers (the number of columns in matrix **A** and the number of rows in matrix **B**) are equal, multiplication *is* possible. This rule is a basic definition in matrix algebra. Its logic will become obvious later in the exposition when you attempt to multiply matrices which do not conform to the rule. This rule will *always* be satisfied when the two matrices to be multiplied are square and both of the same size.

If two matrices placed side by side, as matrices **A** and **B** are below, do not satisfy the rule and thus cannot be multiplied, a swap of positions may qualify them for multiplication:

Matrix **A**   Matrix **B**

$$\begin{pmatrix} 2 \\ 4 \\ 9 \end{pmatrix} \times \begin{pmatrix} 1 & 3 & 7 \\ 4 & 2 & 2 \end{pmatrix} \qquad \textit{cannot be multiplied}$$

$$3 \times \boxed{1} \leftarrow \neq \rightarrow \boxed{2} \times 3$$

Matrix **B**   Matrix **A**

$$\begin{pmatrix} 1 & 3 & 7 \\ 4 & 2 & 2 \end{pmatrix} \times \begin{pmatrix} 2 \\ 4 \\ 9 \end{pmatrix} \qquad \textit{can be multiplied}$$

$$2 \times \boxed{3} \leftarrow = \rightarrow \boxed{3} \times 1$$

Here are several pairs of matrices. The number of columns in the first matrix in each case is compared with the number of rows in the second matrix, and a decision is made as to whether they can be multiplied:

$$\begin{pmatrix} 1 & 2 & 6 \\ 3 & 1 & 4 \end{pmatrix} \times \begin{pmatrix} 1 \\ 2 \\ 6 \end{pmatrix} \qquad \textit{can be multiplied}$$

$$2 \times \boxed{3} \leftarrow = \rightarrow \boxed{3} \times 1$$

$$(1 \quad 3 \quad 6) \times \begin{pmatrix} 1 \\ 7 \\ -2 \end{pmatrix} \qquad \textit{can} \text{ be multiplied}$$

$$1 \times \boxed{3} \leftarrow = \rightarrow \boxed{3} \times 1$$

$$\begin{pmatrix} 1 & 2 & 3 \\ 1 & 2 & 6 \end{pmatrix} \times \begin{pmatrix} 1 & 2 \\ 3 & 1 \end{pmatrix} \qquad \textit{cannot} \text{ be multiplied}$$

$$2 \times \boxed{3} \leftarrow \neq \boxed{2} \times 2$$

$$\begin{pmatrix} 2 & 1 & 3 \\ 3 & 4 & 4 \\ 2 & 1 & 6 \end{pmatrix} \times \begin{pmatrix} 1 \\ 2 \\ 6 \\ 3 \end{pmatrix} \qquad \textit{cannot} \text{ be multiplied}$$

$$3 \times \boxed{3} \leftarrow \neq \rightarrow \boxed{4} \times 1$$

Here are two matrices **A** and **B**. The number of *columns* in matrix **A** equals the number of *rows* in matrix **B**; thus they can be multiplied:

Matrix **A**   Matrix **B**

$$\begin{pmatrix} 5 \\ 6 \end{pmatrix} \times (4 \quad 3)$$

Rows   Columns

$$2 \times \boxed{1} \leftarrow = \rightarrow \boxed{1} \times 2$$

Dimensions of the answer   If we compare the *outer two* numbers of their dimensions, we get some useful information. The outer two numbers in the dimensions indicate the size of the matrix which we shall get as an answer; in the last example the answer will be a 2×2 matrix. Here are the same two matrices with their outer dimensions circled:

Matrix **A**   Matrix **B**

$$\begin{pmatrix} 5 \\ 6 \end{pmatrix} \times (4 \quad 3)$$

$$\boxed{2} \times 1 \qquad 1 \times \boxed{2}$$

Rows   Cols.

The outer dimension of matrix **A** indicates the number of rows in the answer. The outer dimension of matrix **B** indicates the number of columns in the answer.

Doing the multiplication   The actual multiplication is quite simple now that we know the size of the answer. If a 2×2 matrix will result, it must contain four elements. Let's show (first in symbolic form, then by numbers) how the multiplication is carried out. To obtain any element in the answer, first determine the *row* and *column* location of that element in the answer. For example, here's how the element *24* was computed in the answer. This element is in the *second row* and the *first column*. To compute it, we simply multiplied the *second row of matrix* **A** by the *first column of matrix* **B**; that is, $6 \times 4 = 24$.

Matrix **A** Matrix **B**   Matrix **C**

$$\begin{pmatrix} a \\ b \end{pmatrix} \times (c \quad d) = \begin{pmatrix} a \times c & a \times d \\ b \times c & b \times d \end{pmatrix}$$

$$\begin{pmatrix} 5 \\ 6 \end{pmatrix} \times (4 \quad 3) = \begin{pmatrix} 20 & 15 \\ 24 & 18 \end{pmatrix}$$

Matrix **A** Matrix **B**	Calculations	Location of figure in answer
Row 1 (5) × col. 1 (4)	$5 \times 4 = 20$	Row 1, col. 1
Row 1 (5) × col. 2 (3)	$5 \times 3 = 15$	Row 1, col. 2
Row 2 (6) × col. 1 (4)	$6 \times 4 = 24$	Row 2, col. 1
Row 2 (6) × col. 2 (3)	$6 \times 3 = 18$	Row 2, col. 2

What about the multiplication of two matrices **A** and **B** where the product contains only one element? Its location is 1, 1 (row 1 and column 1). The multiplication process involves the multiplication of the first (and only) row of matrix **A** by the first (and only) column of matrix **B**. In this and all multiplications of matrices, in each step we are always multiplying some *row* of the first matrix by some *column* of the second matrix:

An answer with just one element

$$\begin{matrix} \text{Matrix} & & \text{Matrix} & & \text{Matrix} \\ \mathbf{A} & \times & \mathbf{B} & = & \mathbf{C} \end{matrix}$$

$$(3 \quad 2 \quad 1) \times \begin{pmatrix} 4 \\ 5 \\ 6 \end{pmatrix} = \text{answer}$$

$$1 \times 3 \qquad\qquad 3 \times 1$$

In this case the row and column involved both contain three elements. The multiplication is illustrated first by symbols, then by numbers.

$$(a \quad b \quad c) \times \begin{pmatrix} d \\ e \\ f \end{pmatrix}$$

$$ad + be + cf = \text{answer}$$

$$(3 \quad 2 \quad 1) \times \begin{pmatrix} 4 \\ 5 \\ 6 \end{pmatrix}$$

$$\begin{matrix} (3 \times 4) & + & (2 \times 5) & + & (1 \times 6) & = & \text{answer} \\ 12 & + & 10 & + & 6 & = & 28 \end{matrix}$$

Here are three final examples of matrix multiplication:

Example 1

Matrix **A**   Matrix **B**   Matrix **C**

$$\begin{pmatrix} 2 & 3 \\ -1 & 4 \end{pmatrix} \times \begin{pmatrix} 5 & 6 \\ 7 & -2 \end{pmatrix} = \begin{pmatrix} 31 & 6 \\ 23 & -14 \end{pmatrix}$$

Matrix A	Matrix B	Calculations	Location of figure in answer
Row 1 (2 3)	× col. 1 $\begin{pmatrix} 5 \\ 7 \end{pmatrix}$	$2(5) + 3(7) = 31$	Row 1, col. 1
Row 1 (2 3)	× col. 2 $\begin{pmatrix} 6 \\ -2 \end{pmatrix}$	$2(6) + 3(-2) = 6$	Row 2, col. 2
Row 2 (−1 4)	× col. 1 $\begin{pmatrix} 5 \\ 7 \end{pmatrix}$	$-1(5) + 4(7) = 23$	Row 2, col. 1
Row 2 (−1 4)	× col. 2 $\begin{pmatrix} 6 \\ -2 \end{pmatrix}$	$-1(6) + 4(-2) = -14$	Row 2, col. 2

Example 2

Matrix **A**   Matrix **B**   Matrix **C**

$$\begin{pmatrix} 2 & 1 & -6 \\ -1 & 4 & 3 \\ 6 & 1 & -5 \end{pmatrix} \times \begin{pmatrix} 3 \\ -5 \\ 7 \end{pmatrix} = \begin{pmatrix} -41 \\ -2 \\ -22 \end{pmatrix}$$

Matrix A	Matrix B	Calculations	Location of figure in answer
Row 1 (2 1 −6)	× col. 1 $\begin{pmatrix} 3 \\ -5 \\ 7 \end{pmatrix}$	$2(3) + 1(-5) + (-6)(7) = -41$	Row 1, col. 1
Row 2 (−1 4 3)	× col. 1 $\begin{pmatrix} 3 \\ -5 \\ 7 \end{pmatrix}$	$(-1)(3) + 4(-5) + 3(7) = -2$	Row 2, col. 1
Row 3 (6 1 −5)	× col. 1 $\begin{pmatrix} 3 \\ -5 \\ 7 \end{pmatrix}$	$6(3) + 1(-5) + (-5)(7) = -22$	Row 3, col. 1

Example 3

Matrix A	Matrix B	Matrix C

$$\begin{pmatrix} 1 & 4 & -2 \\ 3 & 2 & 0 \\ 6 & 5 & 7 \end{pmatrix} \times \begin{pmatrix} -3 & 8 & -5 \\ 0 & 9 & -4 \\ -1 & 10 & 11 \end{pmatrix} = \begin{pmatrix} -1 & 24 & -43 \\ -9 & 42 & -23 \\ -25 & 163 & 27 \end{pmatrix}$$

Matrix A	Matrix B	Calculations	Location of figure in answer
Row 1 $(1 \quad 4 \quad -2) \times$ col. 1	$\begin{pmatrix} -3 \\ 0 \\ -1 \end{pmatrix}$	$1(-3) + 4(0) + (-2)(-1) = -1$	Row 1, col. 1
Row 1 $(1 \quad 4 \quad -2) \times$ col. 2	$\begin{pmatrix} 8 \\ 9 \\ 10 \end{pmatrix}$	$1(8) + 4(9) + (-2)(10) = 24$	Row 1, col. 2
Row 1 $(1 \quad 4 \quad -2) \times$ col. 3	$\begin{pmatrix} -5 \\ -4 \\ 11 \end{pmatrix}$	$1(-5) + 4(-4) + (-2)(11) = -43$	Row 1, col. 3
Row 2 $(3 \quad 2 \quad 0) \times$ col. 1	$\begin{pmatrix} -3 \\ 0 \\ -1 \end{pmatrix}$	$3(-3) + 2(0) + 0(-1) = -9$	Row 2, col. 1
Row 2 $(3 \quad 2 \quad 0) \times$ col. 2	$\begin{pmatrix} 8 \\ 9 \\ 10 \end{pmatrix}$	$3(8) + 2(9) + 0(10) = 42$	Row 2, col. 2
Row 2 $(3 \quad 2 \quad 0) \times$ col. 3	$\begin{pmatrix} -5 \\ -4 \\ 11 \end{pmatrix}$	$3(-5) + 2(-4) + 0(11) = -23$	Row 2, col. 3
Row 3 $(6 \quad 5 \quad 7) \times$ col. 1	$\begin{pmatrix} -3 \\ 0 \\ -1 \end{pmatrix}$	$6(-3) + 5(0) + 7(-1) = -25$	Row 3, col. 1
Row 3 $(6 \quad 5 \quad 7) \times$ col. 2	$\begin{pmatrix} 8 \\ 9 \\ 10 \end{pmatrix}$	$6(8) + 5(9) + 7(10) = 163$	Row 3, col. 2
Row 3 $(6 \quad 5 \quad 7) \times$ col. 3	$\begin{pmatrix} -5 \\ -4 \\ 11 \end{pmatrix}$	$6(-5) + 5(-4) + 7(11) = 27$	Row 3, col. 3

Standard Form for Illustrating
the Matrix of Transition Probabilities

Standard form for brand-switching problems

Now that we have completed our very brief introduction to matrices and matrix multiplication, let us return to the brand-switching example first introduced on page 534. In the matrix of transition probabilities below, we have included for each dairy the retention probability *and* the probability of its loss of customers to its two competitors. The rows in this matrix show the retention of customers and the loss of customers; the columns represent the retention of customers and the gain of customers. These probabilities have been calculated to three decimal places.

Retention and loss

$$
\begin{array}{c c c c}
 & A & B & C \\
A & .800 & .100 & .100 \\
B & .070 & .900 & .030 \\
C & .083 & .067 & .850 \\
\end{array}
\quad \downarrow \; \text{Retention and gain}
$$

Below is a matrix of the same dimensions as the one above illustrating exactly how each probability was determined:

$$
\begin{array}{c c c c}
 & A & B & C \\
A & {}^{160}/_{200} = .800 & {}^{20}/_{200} = .100 & {}^{20}/_{200} = .100 \\
B & {}^{35}/_{500} = .070 & {}^{450}/_{500} = .900 & {}^{15}/_{500} = .030 \\
C & {}^{25}/_{300} = .083 & {}^{20}/_{300} = .067 & {}^{255}/_{300} = .850 \\
\end{array}
$$

The *rows* of the matrix of transition probabilities can be read as follows:

Interpreting the rows

Row 1 indicates that dairy A retains .8 of its customers (160), loses .1 of its customers (20) to dairy B, and loses .1 of its customers (20) to dairy C.

Row 2 indicates that dairy B retains .9 of its customers (450), loses .07 of its customers (35) to dairy A, and loses .03 of its customers (15) to dairy C.

Row 3 indicates that dairy C retains .85 of its customers (255), loses .083 of its customers (25) to dairy A, and loses .067 of its customers (20) to dairy B.

Reading the *columns* yields the following information:

Interpreting the columns

Column 1 indicates that dairy A retains .8 of its customers (160), gains .07 of B's customers (35), and gains .083 of C's customers (25).

Column 2 indicates that dairy B retains .9 of its customers (450), gains .1 of A's customers (20), and gains .067 of C's customers (20).

Column 3 indicates that dairy C retains .85 of its customers (255), gains .1 of A's customers (20), and gains .03 of B's customers (15).

With the information in this form, basic relationships can more easily be observed. In addition, through the use of matrix algebra we will be able to do the four management jobs listed on page 536.

Stability of the Matrix of Transition Probabilities

Markov analysis is concerned with the *patronage* decisions of consumers; it involves how many consumers are buying from which dairies. A basic assumption is that consumers do not shift their patronage from dairy to dairy to dairy at random; instead, we assume that choices of dairies to buy from in the future reflect choices made in the past.

Assumptions about brand switching

A *first-order* Markov process is based on the assumption that the probability of the next event (customers' choices of vendors *next* month, in this case) depends upon the outcomes of the last event (customers' choices *this* month) and not at all on any earlier buying behavior. A *second-order* Markov process assumes that customer choices next month may depend upon their choices during the immediate past 2 months (or other buying period, if months are not used). In turn, *a third-order* process is based upon the assumption that customers' behavior is best predicted by observing and taking account of their behavior during the past 3 months (or other appropriate buying periods).

The mathematics of first-order Markov processes is not difficult. In second- and third-order processes, however, the computations become more cumbersome and difficult. Studies suggest that using first-order assumptions for prediction purposes is not invalid, particularly if data appear to indicate that customer choices follow a fairly stable pattern, that is, if the matrix of transition probabilities remains stable. Because they have proved to be reliable predictors of future behavior, we shall limit our treatment to processes of the first order.

First-order Markov processes are good predictors

3. Prediction of Market Shares for Future Periods

Let us return to our three dairies and assume that the matrix of transition probabilities remains fairly stable and that the July 1 market shares are these: A = 22 percent, B = 49 percent, C = 29 percent. Managers of the three dairies would benefit, of course, from knowing the market shares that would occur in some future period.

Predicting future shares

To calculate the probable share of the total market likely to be held by each of the dairies on August 1 (the month is our basic data-gathering period), we would simply set up the July 1 market shares as a matrix and multiply this matrix by the matrix of transition probabilities as follows:

	Probable
July 1	Transition	August 1
market shares	probabilities	market shares

$$(.22 \quad .49 \quad .29) \times \begin{pmatrix} .800 & .100 & .100 \\ .070 & .900 & .030 \\ .083 & .067 & .850 \end{pmatrix} = (.234 \quad .483 \quad .283)$$

Total = 1.00   Total = 1.000

The matrix multiplication is explained in detail below.

Matrix multiplication in detail

Row 1 × column 1:

A's share of market × A's propensity to retain its customers = $.22 \times .800 = .176$
B's share of market × A's propensity to attract B's customers = $.49 \times .070 = .034$
C's share of market × A's propensity to attract C's customers = $.29 \times .083 = \overline{.024}$

A's share of market on August 1 = $.234$

Row 1 × column 2:

A's share of market × B's propensity to attract A's customers = $.22 \times .100 = .022$
B's share of market × B's propensity to retain its customers = $.49 \times .900 = .441$
C's share of market × B's propensity to attract C's customers = $.29 \times .067 = \overline{.020}$

B's share of market on August 1 = $.483$

Row 1 × column 3:

A's share of market × C's propensity to attract A's customers = $.22 \times .100 = .022$
B's share of market × C's propensity to attract B's customers = $.49 \times .030 = .015$
C's share of market × C's propensity to retain its customers = $.29 \times .850 = \overline{.246}$

C's share of market on August 1 = $.283$

The probable market share on September 1 can also be calculated by squaring the matrix of transition probabilities and multiplying the squared matrix by the July 1 market shares:

Predicting shares two periods in the future; two different methods

$$\text{Method 1:} \quad (.22 \quad .49 \quad .29) \times \begin{pmatrix} .800 & .100 & .100 \\ .070 & .900 & .030 \\ .083 & .067 & .850 \end{pmatrix}^2 = \begin{array}{l} \text{probable Sept. 1} \\ \text{market shares} \end{array}$$

or by multiplying the matrix of transition probabilities by the market shares on August 1:

$$\text{Method 2:} \quad (.234 \quad .483 \quad .283) \times \begin{pmatrix} .800 & .100 & .100 \\ .070 & .900 & .030 \\ .083 & .067 & .850 \end{pmatrix} = \begin{array}{l} \text{probable Sept. 1} \\ \text{market shares} \end{array}$$

First method explained

Method 1

We can explain the logic behind method 1 this way. By squaring the original matrix of transition probabilities, we have in fact calculated the probabilities of retention, gain, and loss which can be multiplied by the original market shares (22, 49, and 29 percent) to yield the market shares which will obtain on September 1. To obtain, for example, the column 1-row 1 term X in the product, we multiply row 1 by column 1:

$$\begin{pmatrix} .800 & .100 & .100 \end{pmatrix} \times \begin{pmatrix} .800 \\ .070 \\ .083 \end{pmatrix} = \begin{pmatrix} X \end{pmatrix}$$

Row 1 × column 1:

A's propensity to retain its own customers times A's propensity to retain its own customers equals that proportion of its original customers it holds for both periods $.8 \times .8 = .64$

Details of squaring the matrix of transition probabilities

+

B's propensity to gain customers from A times A's propensity to gain customers from B equals A's regain of its own customers from B $.1 \times .07 = .007$

+

C's propensity to gain customers from A times A's propensity to gain customers from C equals A's regain of its own customers from C $.1 \times .083 = .0083$

We get the X term in the product by adding together the results of the three calculations:

.6400
.0070
.0083
―――
.6553 = portion of A's original customers A retains on September 1

In similar fashion, the other eight terms in the square of the matrix can be explained and calculated. The resulting matrix for use in method 1 is

$$\begin{pmatrix} .6553 & .1767 & .1680 \\ .1215 & .8190 & .0595 \\ .1416 & .1256 & .7328 \end{pmatrix}$$

To complete method 1, we multiply the squared matrix by the July 1 market shares:

Completing method 1

$$(.22 \quad .49 \quad .29) \times \begin{pmatrix} .6553 & .1767 & .1680 \\ .1215 & .8190 & .0595 \\ .1416 & .1256 & .7328 \end{pmatrix}$$

with the result

A	.245	
B	.477	probable market shares on September 1
C	.278	
Total	1.000	

For clarity, we shall explain the multiplication of the first row by the first column in detail:

$$(.22 \quad .49 \quad .29) \times \begin{pmatrix} .6553 \\ .1215 \\ .1416 \end{pmatrix} = (.245)$$

Matrix details of completing method 1 A's original market share times A's propensity to retain its own customers after two periods equals A's share of its original customers on September 1

$$.22 \times .6553 = .144$$

+

B's original market share times A's propensity to gain B's original customers after two periods equals A's share of B's original customers on September 1

$$.49 \times .1215 = .060$$

+

C's original market share times A's propensity to gain C's original customers after two periods equals A's share of C's original customers on September 1

$$.29 \times .1416 = .041$$

Adding the results of the three calculations, we get

.144
.060
.041
_____
.245 = A's probable market share on September 1

Method 2

Second method of computing market shares two periods in the future Multiplication of the *original* matrix of transition probabilities by the August 1 market shares yields the same result as method 1. We shall reproduce the two matrices and explain one of the multiplications, as follows:

$$(.234 \quad .483 \quad .283) \times \begin{pmatrix} .800 & .100 & .100 \\ .070 & .900 & .030 \\ .083 & .067 & .850 \end{pmatrix}$$

Row 1 × column 1:

Matrix details of second method A's share of market at the end of the last period times A's propensity to retain its own customers equals A's retained share of its own customers it had at the end of the last period

$$.234 \times .800 = .187$$

+

B's share of market at the end of the last period times A's propensity to gain customers from B equals A's gain of the customers B had at the end of the last period

$$.483 \times .070 = .034$$

+

C's share of market at the end of the last period times A's propensity to gain customers from C equals A's gain of the customers C had at the end of the last period

$$.283 \times .083 = .024$$

.187
.034
.024
———
.245 = A's probable share of market on September 1

     Method 1 has some natural advantage over method 2. If we want to go from **Advantage of**
the initial period to the third period, for instance, we do *not* have to go through the **method 1**
intermediate steps if we use method 1. We simply proceed as follows.

Market shares after three periods:

                          Matrix of transition
July 1 market shares   probabilities cubed

$$(.22 \quad .49 \quad .29) \times \begin{pmatrix} .800 & .100 & .100 \\ .070 & .900 & .030 \\ .083 & .067 & .850 \end{pmatrix}^3 = \text{probable market shares on October 1}$$

And, of course, if we want the market shares which will occur after six periods, we
would set up the problem as follows:

Market shares after six periods:

                          Matrix of transition
                          probabilities to the
July 1 market shares   sixth power

$$(.22 \quad .49 \quad .29) \times \begin{pmatrix} .800 & .100 & .100 \\ .070 & .900 & .030 \\ .083 & .067 & .850 \end{pmatrix}^6 = \text{probable market shares on January 1}$$

Of course, raising a matrix to the sixth or an even higher power is no easy job if
you must do the calculations by hand. Computer programs are available, however,
which will perform this otherwise onerous task in a matter of a few seconds.

     To summarize the uses of the two alternative methods of computing market **Advantage of**
shares for future periods, we would obviously employ method 1 if we simply **method 2**
wanted the market shares for the specified future period, while we would choose
method 2 if we wanted to observe the changes which were occurring in the market
shares during all the intervening periods.

4. Equilibrium Conditions

Equilibrium defined It is quite reasonable to assume in our dairy problems that a state of equilibrium might be approached in the future regarding market shares; that is, the exchange of customers under equilibrium would be such as to continue—to freeze—the three market shares which obtained at the moment equilibrium was reached. Of course, equilibrium can result *only* if no dairy takes action which alters the matrix of transition probabilities. From a marketing point of view, we would want the answer to this question: "What would the three final or equilibrium shares of the market be?"

A One-Dairy Equilibrium
To illustrate equilibrium, assume a new matrix of transition probabilities:

Retention and loss →

	A	B	C
A	.90	.05	.05
B	.15	.75	.10
C	0	0	1.0

Retention and gain ↓

One dairy gets all the customers Because C never loses any customers and because both other dairies *do* lose customers to C, it is only a question of time until C has all the customers. In Markov terminology this would be called a *sink* or *basin* of one state, meaning that one of our dairies (C) eventually gets all the customers. C is also called an *absorbing state*.

A Two-Dairy Equilibrium
A second type of equilibrium could occur. To illustrate this, here is a new matrix of transition probabilities:

	A	B	C
A	.90	.05	.05
B	0	.50	.50
C	0	.50	.50

Two dairies get all the customers One can easily see that in time, dairy B and dairy C capture *all* A's customers. Why is this true? Because A loses .05 of its customers to B and .05 to C and does not regain any new customers from either B or C. As B and C both have the same probability of retaining customers (.50), they must eventually divide up the market. This would be referred to as a sink or basin of two states. That is, two dairies, B and C, eventually share all the customers in the whole market.

A Three-Dairy Equilibrium
We could, of course, have a type of equilibrium where no sink or basin exists. Here no one dairy gets *all* the customers—no two dairies capture the entire market. But some final or equilibrium condition develops and continues in which the market

shares will not change *so long as the matrix of transition probabilities remains the same.* Our original three-dairy problem illustrates this third type of equilibrium. To find out what the final or equilibrium shares of the market will be with our original problem, let us proceed as follows:

$$\begin{array}{c} & A & B & C \\ \begin{array}{c} A \\ B \\ C \end{array} & \begin{pmatrix} .800 & .100 & .100 \\ .070 & .900 & .030 \\ .083 & .067 & .850 \end{pmatrix} \end{array} = \begin{array}{c} \text{original matrix of} \\ \text{transition probabilities} \end{array}$$

Now, A's share of the market in the equilibrium period (let us label this unspecified future period the eq. period) equals

.800 times the share A had in the (eq. -1) period (the period immediately preceding equilibrium)

$+ .070$ times the share B had in the (eq. -1) period
$+ .083$ times the share C had in the (eq. -1) period

We can write this relationship as an equation:

$$A_{eq.} = .800A_{eq.-1} + .070B_{eq.-1} + .083C_{eq.-1} \qquad (16\text{-}1)$$

And, of course, we can write two more equations illustrating the shares of market B and C will have in the equilibrium period.

$$B_{eq.} = .100A_{eq.-1} + .900B_{eq.-1} + .067C_{eq.-1} \qquad (16\text{-}2)$$
$$C_{eq.} = .100A_{eq.-1} + .030B_{eq.-1} + .850C_{eq.-1} \qquad (16\text{-}3)$$

In the early periods, the gains and losses from dairy to dairy are usually of fairly high magnitude. But as equilibrium is approached, the gains and losses become smaller and smaller until just before equilibrium they are infinitesimally small. This concept is not a unique one; many phenomena behave in this manner. For instance, Figure 16-1 shows the graph of a number (100) being divided in half at several stages. In the case of our Markov process, the changes in market shares between the equilibrium period and the period just preceding it are so slight that they may for mathematical purposes be treated as equal; that is, $A_{eq.} = A_{eq.-1}$. This allows us to rewrite our three equations as follows:

$$A = .800A + .070B + .083C \qquad (16\text{-}1)$$
$$B = .100A + .900B + .067C \qquad (16\text{-}2)$$
$$C = .100A + .030B + .850C \qquad (16\text{-}3)$$

Because the sum of the three market shares equals 1.0, we can add another equation

$$1.0 = A + B + C \qquad (16\text{-}4)$$

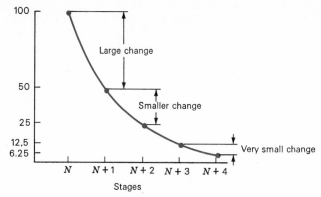

Figure 16-1 Dividing a number in half by stages. As equilibrium is approached, the changes become smaller and smaller.

In Eqs. (16-1) to (16-3) we have similar terms on both sides of the equality sign, so that we can reduce these equations to

$$0 = -.200A + .070B + .083C \qquad (16\text{-}1)$$
$$0 = .100A - .100B + .067C \qquad (16\text{-}2)$$
$$0 = .100A + .030B - .150C \qquad (16\text{-}3)$$
$$1.0 = A + B + C \qquad (16\text{-}4)$$

Solving the equilibrium equations As we have four equations and only three unknowns, we can drop any one of the first three equations [we drop Eq. (16-3)] and solve the remaining three equations simultaneously for the equilibrium market shares.

$$0 = -.200A + .070B + .083C \qquad (16\text{-}1)$$
$$0 = .100A - .100B + .067C \qquad (16\text{-}2)$$
$$1 = A + B + C \qquad (16\text{-}4)$$

Step 1 Multiply Eq. (16-2) by .7 and add it to Eq. (16-1).

$$
\begin{array}{ll}
0 = -.200A + .070B + .083C & (16\text{-}1) \\
0 = .070A - .070B + .047C & (16\text{-}2) \times .7 \\
\hline
0 = -.130A \ + .130C & \\
\end{array}
$$
$$.130A = .130C$$
$$A = C$$

Step 2 Multiply Eq. (16-2) by 2 and add it to Eq. (16-1)

$$
\begin{array}{ll}
0 = -.200A + .070B + .083C & (16\text{-}1) \\
0 = .200A - .200B + .134C & (16\text{-}2) \times 2 \\
\hline
0 = \ -.130B + .217C & \\
\end{array}
$$
$$.13B = .217C$$
$$B = 1.67C$$

Step 3 Repeat Eq. (16-4)

$1 = A + B + C$

Because $A = C$, then

$1 = C + B + C$

and because $B = 1.67C$,

$1 = C + 1.67C + C$
$1 = 3.67C$
$C = .273 = C$'s equilibrium market share

Because $A = C$

$A = .273 = A$'s equilibrium market share

and because $1 = A + B + C$,

$1 = .273 + B + .273$
$1 = B + .546$
$B = .454 = B$'s equilibrium market share

Are you skeptical that an equilibrium has actually been reached? If so, let's prove it. Multiply the equilibrium market share (A, .273; B, .454; C, 273) by the matrix of transition probabilities:

Checking that equilibrium has been reached

$$(.273 \quad .454 \quad .273) \times \begin{pmatrix} .800 & .100 & .100 \\ .070 & .900 & .030 \\ .083 & .067 & .850 \end{pmatrix} = (.273 \quad .454 \quad .273)$$

Just a word about the equilibrium market shares we have calculated. They are based upon the assumption that the matrix of transition probabilities remains *fixed*, that the propensities of all three dairies to retain, gain, and lose customers do not change over time. In many cases this may be somewhat invalid, but no harm is done even so. For the period during which the transition probabilities are stable, we can calculate an equilibrium which will result. Then, if we have good reason to believe that the transition probabilities are indeed changing because of some action by management, we can use the new transition probabilities and calculate the equilibrium market shares which will result. In that manner, we are essentially using Markov analysis as a short- or intermediate-run tool.

Assumptions about equilibrium

Relationship of Market Shares and Equilibrium

An interesting fact about Markov analysis is that the final equilibrium will be the same (provided the transition probabilities remain fixed) *regardless* of the initial market shares held by various producers or suppliers. That is to say, we will always

Going from initial market shares to equilibrium shares; some observations

end with the same final proportion of customers no matter what the original shares were. For example, if three suppliers have as their current shares of market

A = 30%
B = 60%
C = 10%

and the matrix of transition probabilities is

$$
\begin{array}{c c c c}
 & A & B & C \\
A & .90 & .10 & 0 \\
B & .05 & .80 & .15 \\
C & .20 & .20 & .60 \\
\end{array}
$$

then, by using the technique for determining the equilibrium market shares discussed in the previous section, we can determine that the equilibrium market shares would be A, .476; B, .381; C, .143.

If, on the other hand, the initial market shares were

A = 20%
B = 45%
C = 35%

The matrix of transition probabilities determines equilibrium
the equilibrium market shares for the three firms would still be the same (A, .476; B, .381; C, .143) as long as the matrix of transition probabilities did not change. You can satisfy yourself that this is true by noting that the market shares were *not* used in explaining the equilibrium process; only the matrix of transition probabilities enters into the determination of equilibrium.

Of course, the nearer the initial market shares happen to be to the final or equilibrium market shares, the faster equilibrium will be approached. If the beginning shares for three firms are

A = 35%
B = 40%
C = 25%

and the final or equilibrium shares will be

A = 30%
B = 35%
C = 35%

we can see that the process will approach equilibrium much faster than if the initial market shares are

A = 10%
B = 75%
C = 15%

simply because in the former case, less change needs to occur to get close to the final equilibrium. In the latter case, for instance, firm A needs to acquire sufficient customers to bring its market share from 10 percent to its equilibrium share of 30 percent, whereas in the former case, A would move only from 35 to 30 percent before equilibrium is approached.

Speed with which an equilibrium is approached

If this concept that the initial market shares have no bearing on the final equilibrium shares still appears a bit difficult to accept, consider the following example:

$$
\begin{array}{c c c c}
 & A & B & C \\
A & \begin{pmatrix} 1.0 & 0 & 0 \\ B & .3 & .6 & .1 \\ C & .1 & .2 & .7 \end{pmatrix}
\end{array}
$$

One can immediately see that *regardless of the initial market shares held by these three firms,* firm A will eventually get all the customers: A does not lose any of the customers gained from B and C. Thus, though beginning with only 5 percent of the customers, A will eventually have 100 percent of the customers. Of course, the higher the initial percentage of customers held by firm A, the faster equilibrium will be approached.

5. Use of Markov Analysis in Marketing Strategy

Evaluating Alternative Strategies

To illustrate how Markov analysis is helpful in determining marketing strategy, consider the following situation. For three competing sellers, the matrix of transition probabilities is as follows:

A problem in the use of Markov analysis

Retention and loss
⟶

$$
\begin{array}{c c c c}
 & A & B & C \\
A & \begin{pmatrix} .2 & .6 & .2 \\ B & .1 & .5 & .4 \\ C & .2 & .3 & .5 \end{pmatrix}
\end{array}
$$
Retention and gain ↓

If the marketing strategies of these three firms do not change so as to affect the matrix of transition probabilities, we could reasonably expect equilibrium market shares of A, .156; B, .434; C, .410.

In an effort to better his rather poor showing, seller A might consider two new marketing strategies.

Two possible strategies

Strategy 1 Seller A might try to retain more of his own customers. Assume that strategy 1 increases retention from 20 to 40 percent, and assume that this change consists in A's reducing his loss of customers to seller B.

A's first strategy, increase retention

The new matrix of transition probabilities is

$$
\begin{array}{c c c c}
 & A & B & C \\
A & \begin{pmatrix} .4 & .4 & .2 \\ .1 & .5 & .4 \\ .2 & .3 & .5 \end{pmatrix} \\
B \\
C
\end{array}
$$

The new equilibrium market shares work out to be A, .2; B, .4; and C, .4. A's showing now is better; but even though A's campaign was specifically directed against B, note that firm C suffered somewhat. Why? C gains new customers from A and B but more from B than from A. Now that B gets fewer of A's customers as a result of A's strategy, C's gain from B (.4) will represent a smaller number. We should not be too surprised that C's fortunes are not more drastically affected as a result of A's action; C does get back from A some of the customers A takes from B.

A's second startegy, getting more customers from C

Strategy 2   As an alternative, seller A might direct his marketing efforts at capturing a greater share of the buyers who switch from C. Suppose that A's campaign is designed to induce .4 of those who switch from C to move to A, instead of the .2 who now do.

The matrix of transition probabilities now becomes

$$
\begin{array}{c c c c}
 & A & B & C \\
A & \begin{pmatrix} .2 & .6 & .2 \\ .1 & .5 & .4 \\ .4 & .1 & .5 \end{pmatrix} \\
B \\
C
\end{array}
$$

If we calculate the equilibrium market shares which would result from this type of strategy, we find them to be A, .233; B, .391; and C, .376.

We infer from this example that if the costs of the two programs are the same, clearly strategy 2 is the better one. Again in the case of strategy 2, notice that even though A's encroachment efforts were not directed against B at all, B suffers loss of customers as a result of A's marketing program directed against C. Why? B used to get .3 of C's customers each month. Now that A's efforts have been successful in getting .4 of C's customers, B's share of switchers is reduced to .1. Again, we should not be too surprised at seeing that B's share does not shrink drastically; B will eventually get back from A some of the new customers A was successful in taking away from C.

Assumptions We Have Made

Assumptions we have made

In setting up our dairy problem at the beginning of this chapter, we assumed, in order to simplify the mathematics, that no old customers *leave* the market and no new customers *enter* the market during the time period involved. We know that this is seldom the case. What, then, about the more realistic experience, in which new customers do move in and begin patronizing dairies and old customers do disappear from or drop out of the market? In these circumstances, the effects of the additions and the losses on (1) the market shares obtaining in immediately future periods and (2) the market shares at equilibrium would depend on three variables:

1. The dairy from which each newcomer begins to buy

2. The dairy from which each consumer was buying at the moment he or she ceased to be a customer

3. The extent to which the brand loyalty of each newcomer differs from the brand loyalty pattern obtaining at the time of his or her entry into the market as a customer

Source of Information

Perhaps you have been wondering how the firms we have been referring to can get the data needed for application of Markov analysis to their marketing problems. One solution is for a firm to buy the services of a marketing research organization. Some of these organizations collect information about brand loyalty and brand switching for clients. For example, the Market Research Corporation of America has established a sample of United States families who record and report all purchases of certain branded products to MRCA. Because the buying units constituting this consumer panel reveal which brands they buy, MRCA data can be used in Markov analysis. Some individual sellers ought to be in a position to collect the brand preference information each would need in order to make use of Markov analysis.

Where to get brand-switching information

6. Other Uses of Markov Analysis

Our discussion of Markov analysis has been limited to its use in brand-share analysis and prediction. Granted, this *is* a leading use of the technique; there are, however, other areas in which the application of Markov analysis has produced significant contributions. We shall examine several of these.

Equipment Repair Application of Markov Analysis

Kenan Rand is the Coca-Cola dealer in Hillsborough, Virginia. His warehouse manager inspects his soft drink crates (these are the wooden crates that hold 24 bottles) each week and classifies them as "just rebuilt this week," "in good working condition," "in fair condition," or "damaged beyond use." If a crate is damaged beyond use, it is sent to the repair area, where it is usually out of use for a week. Kenan's warehouse records indicate that this is the appropriate matrix of transition probabilities for his soft drink crates:

Analyzing equipment repair alternatives

	Rebuilt	Good	Fair	Damaged
Rebuilt	0	.8	.2	0
Good	0	.6	.4	0
Fair	0	0	.5	.5
Damaged	1.0	0	0	0

Transition probabilities for crates, alternative 1

Costs Kenan's accountant tells him that it costs $2.50 to rebuild a crate, and the company incurs a loss of $1.85 in production efficiency each time a crate is found to be damaged beyond use. This efficiency is lost because broken crates slow down the truckloading process.

To calculate the expected weekly cost of both rebuilding *and* loss of production efficiency, we need the equilibrium probabilities of Kenan's matrix. Using the method previously illustrated, these have been found to be

Equilibrium probabilities

Rebuilt $1/6 = .167$

Good $1/3 = .333$

Fair $1/3 = .333$

Damaged $1/6 = .167$

The average weekly cost of rebuilding and loss of production efficiency is then:

Costs under first alternative

Rebuilding cost   Damage (out of use) loss

$1/6 \times \$2.50 \quad + 1/6 \times \$1.85 = \$.725$ per crate per week

Suppose now that Kenan wants to consider rebuilding crates whenever they are inspected and found to be in *fair* shape. This eliminates the possibility of a crate being damaged. In this instance, the new matrix of transition probabilities would be

	Rebuilt	Good	Fair
Rebuilt	0	.8	.2
Good	0	.6	.4
Fair	1.0	0	0

Transition probabilities for crates, alternative 2

The equilibrium probabilities for this matrix have been found to be

Equilibrium probabilities

Rebuilt $1/4 = .25$

Good $1/2 = .50$

Fair $1/4 = .25$

The average weekly cost of rebuilding and loss of production efficiency under these circumstances is

Rebuilding cost	Damage (out of use) loss	

$1/4 \times \$2.50 +$ 0 $= \$.625$ per crate per week

Rebuilding crates as soon as they are found to be in "fair" shape will save Kenan a little over 10 cents per crate per week in this case. Since Kenan owns over six thousand crates, this is a substantial saving for him. You have probably already recognized that we used Markov analysis here to solve a "replacement type" problem; earlier, in Chapter 6, we solved a similar problem by the use of a somewhat less elegant method.

Employee Productivity Application of Markov Analysis

United Industries, a manufacturer of women's sleepwear, classifies its sewing operators into four categories depending upon their productivity during the preceding month; 1 is the lowest category and 4 the highest. Historically, the sewing work force has been distributed across the four categories as follows: $1 = 30\%$, $2 = 35\%$, $3 = 25\%$, $4 = 10\%$. Seven months ago, United introduced a new organizational system into its Mt. Gilead plant, one of its largest units, with 450 operators. The new system groups the operators into voluntary work units which not only elect their own supervisors but also determine their own work schedules. Production records kept since the new plan was adopted have enabled Bill Haywood, Plant Manager, to construct this matrix of transition probabilities illustrating month-to-month changes in employee productivity:

		Lowest			Highest
		1	2	3	4
Lowest	1	.5	.3	.2	0
	2	.3	.4	.3	0
	3	.1	.2	.2	.5
Highest	4	.1	.1	.1	.7

Bill would like to know what to expect in the way of productivity distribution of the work force as a result of the new organizational system. Further, he would like to know the long-run benefit per month of this system considering that operators earn an average of $700 a month and productivity losses for the four categories of employee are 40 percent, 25 percent, 15 percent, and 5 percent respectively for categories 1, 2, 3, and 4.

Using the method we first introduced on page 550, we can determine that the equilibrium probabilities of Bill Haywood's matrix are these

Highest	1	.247
	2	.241
	3	.192
Lowest	4	.320

Table 16-5   Cost Comparison of Old and New Organization System

	Employee category	Percent of employees	Productivity loss		
Old organizational system	1	30	× 40%	=	12.00%
	2	35	× 25	=	8.75
	3	25	× 15	=	3.75
	4	10	× 5	=	.50
					25.00%
	25% × $700/mo × 450 employees = $78,750				
New organizational system	1	24.7	× 40%	=	9.88%
	2	24.1	× 25	=	6.03
	3	19.2	× 15	=	2.88
	4	32.0	× 5	=	1.60
					20.39%
	20.39% × $700/mo × 450 employees = $64,229				

Analysis of cost of alternatives (margin note)

Bill now sets up Table 16-5 to calculate the monthly productivity losses under the new and the previous system; it appears that the new organization system has the potential to save United over $14,000 per month in productivity losses in its Mt. Gilead plant.

Accounts Receivable Application of Markov Analysis

Accounts receivable analysis (margin note)

Markov analysis has been successfully applied to accounts receivable analysis, specifically to the estimation of that portion of the accounts receivable which will eventually become uncollectible (become bad debts). We can illustrate this application by considering Milton's Clothing Cupboard, a clothing store catering to college students. Milton divides his accounts receivable into two classifications: 0–60 days old and 61–180 days old. Accounts which are more than 180 days old are written off by Milton (considered bad debts). Milton follows the general practice of classify- *Classification of accounts* (margin note) ing a customer's account receivable according to the oldest unpaid bill in the account (this is referred to in accounting as the "total balance" method of aging accounts because the customer's total balance is classified in the aging category of that customer's oldest unpaid bill). This method of aging accounts receivable permits an account which is *now* in the 61–180 day category to appear next month in the 0–60 day category if the customer pays an older bill in his or her account during the month. Milton currently has $6500 in accounts receivable; from analysis of his past records, he has been able to provide us with this matrix of transition probabilities (the matrix can be thought of in terms of what happens to *one dollar* of accounts receivable):

Transition probabilities for $1 of accounts receivable (margin note)

	Paid	Bad debt	0–60 days	61–180 days
Paid	1	0	0	0
Bad debt	0	1	0	0
0–60 days	.5	0	.3	.2
61–180 days	.4	.3	.2	.1

Three features of this matrix of transition probabilities need to be discussed. First, notice the black circled element, 0. This indicates that $1 in the 0–60 day category cannot become a bad debt in 1 month's time. Now look at the two red circled elements; each of these is 1, indicating that, in time, *all* the accounts receivable dollars will either be paid or become bad debts. But in our previous discussions of equilibrium conditions in Markov analysis, we never computed equilibrium probabilities when any *retention* probability was equal to 1, because we knew the process would end up with that company or category having all of the market (or in this case all the dollars). It is true that eventually *all* the dollars *do* wind up either as paid or bad debts, but Milton *would* benefit from knowing the probability that a dollar of 0–60 day or 61–180 day receivables would eventually find its way into *either* paid bills or bad debts. Determining these four probabilities of interest to Milton is done in four steps:

All dollars end in two states

Finding the probabilities of those two states

Step 1 First, we partition Milton's original matrix of transition probabilities into four matrices, each identified by a letter:

$$\begin{pmatrix} 1 & 0 & 0 & 0 \\ 0 & 1 & 0 & 0 \\ .5 & 0 & .3 & .2 \\ .4 & .3 & .2 & .1 \end{pmatrix} \qquad I = \begin{pmatrix} 1 & 0 \\ 0 & 1 \end{pmatrix} \qquad O = \begin{pmatrix} 0 & 0 \\ 0 & 0 \end{pmatrix}$$

$$K = \begin{pmatrix} .5 & 0 \\ .4 & .3 \end{pmatrix} \qquad M = \begin{pmatrix} .3 & .2 \\ .2 & .1 \end{pmatrix}$$

Step 1: partition of the matrix

Step 2 We subtract matrix M from matrix I to get a new matrix we have called R. Matrices with the same dimensions (the same number of rows and columns) can be subtracted from each other by subtracting elements which appear in the same location in each matrix. In this case the subtraction is:

$$\begin{matrix} I & M & R \end{matrix}$$

$$\begin{pmatrix} 1 & 0 \\ 0 & 1 \end{pmatrix} - \begin{pmatrix} .3 & .2 \\ .2 & .1 \end{pmatrix} = \begin{pmatrix} .7 & -.2 \\ -.2 & .9 \end{pmatrix}$$

Step 2: subtract two matrices

Step 3 We find the *inverse* of matrix R. The function of an inverse and the process for obtaining it can be illustrated by multiplying the matrix $(1 \quad 2)$ by the matrix $\begin{pmatrix} 2 & 3 \\ 4 & 5 \end{pmatrix}$ to produce a new matrix. This multiplication has been accomplished below using the same multiplication methods illustrated earlier in the chapter:

Step 3: find the inverse of R

$$(1 \quad 2) \times \begin{pmatrix} 2 & 3 \\ 4 & 5 \end{pmatrix} = (10 \quad 13)$$

$$1 \times \boxed{2} \leftarrow = \rightarrow \boxed{2} \times 2$$

Multiplying the *inverse* of the 2 × 2 matrix (steps in computing the inverse follow in just a moment) by the new matrix $(10 \quad 13)$ will produce the original matrix $(1 \quad 2)$.

An inverse is formed by performing certain procedures on the original matrix. There are three of these procedures, each involving the rows of the matrix:

Row operations for finding an inverse

1. One *row* can be *interchanged* with another *row*.

2. A *row* can be *multiplied* by a *constant*.

3. A *multiple of a row* can be *added* to or *subtracted* from another *row*.

To invert a matrix, we first place beside it an identity matrix of the same size. (An identity matrix is a square matrix whose diagonal is composed entirely of 1's and in which the remainder of the terms are 0's.) Row procedures are then performed on both matrices *simultaneously*. When the original matrix has been altered by these procedures so that it becomes an identity matrix, the identity matrix which was originally placed there will be the inverse. In short, then, the object is to convert the original matrix into an identity matrix by performing the row procedures upon it. Let's now illustrate the inversion of a 2×2 matrix.

Original matrix	Identity matrix	Steps performed
$\begin{pmatrix} 2 & 3 \\ 4 & 5 \end{pmatrix}$	$\begin{pmatrix} 1 & 0 \\ 0 & 1 \end{pmatrix}$	1. Place identity matrix next to original matrix.
$\begin{pmatrix} 1 & 3/2 \\ 4 & 5 \end{pmatrix}$	$\begin{pmatrix} 1/2 & 0 \\ 0 & 1 \end{pmatrix}$	2. Multiply row 1 by $1/2$ (procedure 2).
$\begin{pmatrix} 1 & 3/2 \\ 0 & -1 \end{pmatrix}$	$\begin{pmatrix} 1/2 & 0 \\ -2 & 1 \end{pmatrix}$	3. Multiply row 1 by 4 and subtract it from row 2 (procedure 3).
$\begin{pmatrix} 1 & 3/2 \\ 0 & 1 \end{pmatrix}$	$\begin{pmatrix} 1/2 & 0 \\ 2 & -1 \end{pmatrix}$	4. Multiply row 2 by (-1) (procedure 2).
$\begin{pmatrix} 1 & 0 \\ 0 & 1 \end{pmatrix}$	$\begin{pmatrix} -5/2 & 3/2 \\ 2 & -1 \end{pmatrix}$	5. Subtract $3/2$ row 2 from row 1 (procedure 3).

Finding the inverse (margin label)

Since the original matrix is now an identity matrix, we know our process is complete. Thus the inverse of the original matrix is

$$\begin{pmatrix} -5/2 & 3/2 \\ 2 & -1 \end{pmatrix}$$

Checking the inverse We can check our calculations by multiplying the inverse by the matrix $(10 \quad 13)$ to see if the multiplication will produce the original matrix, $(1 \quad 2)$.

$$(10 \quad 13) \times \begin{pmatrix} -5/2 & 3/2 \\ 2 & -1 \end{pmatrix} = (1 \quad 2)$$

Using the procedure we've just illustrated, the inverse of matrix R $\begin{pmatrix} .7 & -.2 \\ -.2 & .9 \end{pmatrix}$, is found to be $\begin{pmatrix} 1.5254 & .3390 \\ .3390 & 1.1864 \end{pmatrix}$.

Step 4 We multiply this inverse by matrix K from step 1. This multiplication is

$$\begin{pmatrix} 1.5254 & .3390 \\ .3390 & 1.1864 \end{pmatrix} \begin{pmatrix} .5 & 0 \\ .4 & .3 \end{pmatrix} = \begin{pmatrix} .8983 & .1017 \\ .6441 & .3559 \end{pmatrix}$$

Step 4: multiply matrix K by the inverse of matrix R

Let's now interpret the answer from step 4 for Milton. The top row in the answer is the probability that $1 of his accounts receivable in the 0–60 day category will end up in the "paid" and "bad debt" categories. Specifically, there is a .8983 probability that $1 currently in the 0–60 day category will be paid and a .1017 probability that it will eventually become a bad debt. Now the second row. These two entries represent the probability that $1 now in the 61–180 day category will end up in the "paid" and the "bad debt" categories. He can see from this row that there is a .6441 probability that $1 currently in the 61–180 day category will be paid and a .3559 probability that it will eventually become a bad debt.

Interpreting the answer

If Milton wants to forecast the future of his $6500 of accounts receivable, he first determines how much of the total is in each category, 0–60 days and 61–180 days. In this instance his accountant tells him that $4500 is in the 0–60 day category and $2000 is in the 61–180 day category. Milton then sets up this matrix multiplication:

Forecasting accounts receivable behavior

$$(\$4500 \quad \$2000) \begin{pmatrix} .8983 & .1017 \\ .6441 & .3559 \end{pmatrix} = (\$5330.55 \quad \$1169.45)$$

Milton should interpret this answer to mean that $5330.55 of his current accounts receivable is likely to wind up being paid and $1169.45 is likely to become bad debts. If he follows the standard practice of setting up a reserve for "doubtful" accounts, his accountant would set up $1169.45 as the best estimate for this category.

Glossary

1. **Markov analysis** A method of analyzing the current behavior of some variable to predict the future behavior of that variable.

2. **Brand switching** Movement of customers from one supplier to another.

3. **Transition probabilities** Probabilities that suppliers will retain customers, gain customers, and lose customers from one period to another.

4. **Matrix** Array of numbers arranged into rows and columns.

5. **First-order Markov process** Markov process in which the probability of occurrence of the next event depends only upon the outcome resulting from the last event.

6. **Second-order Markov process** Markov process in which the probability of occurrence of the next event depends upon the outcomes resulting from the last two events.

7. **Third-order Markov process** Markov process in which the probability of occurrence of the next event depends upon the outcomes resulting from the last three events.

8. Equilibrium   A position that a Markov process reaches in the long run after which no further net change occurs.

9. Sink, basin, or absorbing state   A state in a Markov process which is never left once it is entered.

10. MRCA   Market Research Corporation of America, an organization which supplies market share data to industry.

Review of Equations

Page 551

$$A = X A + Y B + Z C \qquad (16\text{-}1)$$
$$B = U A + V B + W C \qquad (16\text{-}2)$$
$$C = R A + S B + T C \qquad (16\text{-}3)$$
$$1.0 = A + B + C \qquad (16\text{-}4)$$

These are the general forms of the equations which determine the equilibrium shares in a three-supplier market share application of Markov analysis. The coefficients X, Y, Z, U, V, W, R, S, and T are obtained from the matrix of transition probabilities. Since there are four equations and only three unknowns (A, B, and C), we drop any one of the first three equations.

Exercises

16-1. Ancient Times Distillery is one of the two largest bourbon distilleries in the eastern United States. Their market analysts are currently investigating the brand loyalty of Ancient Times in relation to the loyalty of their major competitor, Jack Donalds, and to all other bourbons considered as a single group. A questionnaire filled out by 1000 bourbon drinkers indicates the following marketing patterns. In a typical month, Ancient Times retains 85 percent of its customers while losing 5 percent to Jack Donalds and 10 percent to all other bourbons. Jack Donalds retains 90 percent of its customers while losing 5 percent to Ancient Times and 5 percent to all other bourbons. All the other bourbons, taken as a group, retain 80 percent while losing 10 percent each to Ancient Times and Jack Donalds. What can Ancient Times plan on as an equilibrium share of market?

16-2. Three radio stations compete for advertising shares of market (call them A, B, and C). At the end of last year, A had 20 percent of the market. Its competitors, stations B and C, each had 40 percent of the market. During last year, sales were $100 million, and station A had a net income of 5 percent on its sales. Both these figures are expected to remain the same for next year. Station A's manager suggests that if A would spend an additional $100,000 during next year on selling, A would retain 85 percent of its customers while gaining 8 percent of B's customers and 7 percent of C's. Company B is expected to retain 85 percent of its customers while gaining 10 percent from A and 3 percent from C. Company C is expected to retain 90 percent of its customers while gaining 5 percent from A and 7 percent from B. Should company A make the additional expenditure for selling?

16-3. Assume that run-proof pantyhose were introduced on the market simultaneously by three companies. The three firms, F, B, and C, launched their respective brands in January. At the start, each company had approximately one-third of the market. During the year, these developments took place:

Company F retained 80 percent of its customers; it lost 12 percent to B, lost 8 percent to C.

Company B retained 70 percent of its customers; it lost 20 percent to F, lost 10 percent to C.

Company C retained 90 percent of its customers; it lost 5 percent to F, lost 5 percent to B.

Assume that the market does not expand.
a. What share of the total market is likely to be held by each company at the end of the year?
b. Predict what the long-run market shares will be at the equilibrium state if buying habits do not change.

16-4. A large department store has secured a breakdown on the transition among three categories of accounts receivable by its customers.

	Jan. 1	From pay on time	From delinquent	From bad debt	Feb. 1
Pay on time	300	285	20	10	315
Delinquent	750	10	700	50	760
Bad debts	450	5	30	390	425

What percentage of credit customers will be classified in each category on April 1? Assume that no new credit customers are included.

16-5. An organization dependent upon volunteer help is divided into three divisions and allows free movement of personnel between any two. Between June and September, personnel movement was as indicated in the table.

Div.	June	Gains			Sept.
		From 1	From 2	From 3	
1	30	29	2	4	35
2	60	1	57	3	61
3	40	0	1	33	34

What percentage of the volunteers will be working for each division in December?

16-6. Assume that radial tires were introduced on the market by three companies at the same time. When they were introduced, each firm had an equal share of the market, but during the first year, the following changes in market share took place:

Company A retained 80 percent of its customers; it lost 5 percent to B and 15 percent to C.

Company B retained 90 percent of its customers; it lost 10 percent to A and none to C.

Company C retained 60 percent of its customers; it lost 20 percent to A and 20 percent to B.

Assume that the market will not expand and that buying habits will not change.
a. What total share of the market is likely to be held by each company at the end of next year?
b. Predict what the equilibrium market state will be.

16-7. The Over-the-Road Trucking Company periodically inspects the bearings on its trucks and categorizes them in one of four states (1 through 4):

State 1—new bearings

State 2—lightly worn bearings

State 3—moderately worn bearings

State 4—worn-out bearings

If the company replaces a set of bearings during inspection, it costs $50. If, however, a truck in service develops bad bearings, the company estimates the cost to be $250. Based on past experience, it has been found that a set of bearings which is new at a given inspection has a .9 probability of being in state 2 and a .1 probability of being in state 3 by the next inspection. A set of bearings classified as state 2 has a .6 probability of remaining in state 2, a .3 probability of going to state 3, and a .1 probability of wearing out by the next inspection date. A set of bearings classified as state 3 has a .7 probability of remaining in state 3 and a .3 probability of wearing out by the next inspection. The company has decided to either (1) replace all bearings in state 2 or worse at each inspection or (2) replace all bearings in state 3 or worse at each inspection. Which policy will result in lower cost?

16-8. The Ridgefield Hospital specializes in heart patients and serves an area in which there is zero population growth (a Markov process with deaths can have a change-of-state system where for each death there is also a birth). From past history, it is known that each month about .001 of the population of 100,000 served by the hospital have heart attacks and are admitted to the hospital. By the end of the first month after being admitted, a patient has a 60 percent probability of being released from the hospital, a 20 percent probability of staying in the hospital another month, and a 20 percent probability of dying during the month. For those who stay the second month, there is a 90 percent probability of their being released by the end of the second month and a 10 percent probability of their dying during the second month. Solve for the equilibrium values showing the number of patients in the hospital who have had heart attacks within one month, the number of patients in their second month of recovery, and the number of patients who die each month from heart attacks.

16-9. The Better-Made Company employs four classes of machine operators (A, B, C, and D); all new employees are hired as class D and, through a system of promotion, may work up to a higher class. Currently there are 200 class D, 150 class C, 100 class B, and 50 class A employees. The company has signed an agreement with the union specifying that 20 percent of all employees in each class are to be promoted one class in each year. Statistics show that each year 20 percent of the class D employees are separated from the company by retirement, resignation, death, etc. Similarly, 10 percent of class C, 10 percent of class B and 20 percent of class A employees are also separated. After the union agreement has been in effect for one year, how many of each class of employees should the company expect to have in its employ? (Assume that for each employee lost, the company will hire a new class D employee.)

16-10. The Centerville Hospital has a policy of keeping 200 pints of blood in inventory. The blood, if not used within four time periods, is thrown away. In the past, there has been no set policy on the use of blood, and each pint was taken randomly from the inventory when needed. The hospital found that there was a .30 probability of a pint of blood being used in a given period and a .70 probability of its remaining in inventory into the next period. Lately, the hospital has become concerned about the shortage of blood donors. It is considering the adoption of a policy which requires that all blood drawn from inventory be the oldest (FIFO). If the hospital adopts the new policy, how many fewer donations per period will be required to maintain the 200-pint inventory level if every donor gives one pint?

16-11. In the town of Ramsville, a life insurance salesperson has computed the following statistics:

1. There are 100 births and deaths each year.

2. A newborn child has a .95 probability of reaching age 20.

3. A 20-year-old has an .85 probability of reaching age 40.

4. A 40-year-old has a .75 probability of reaching age 60.

5. A 60-year-old has a .40 probability of reaching age 80.

6. An 80-year-old has a .04 probability of reaching age 100.

7. No one lives to age 120.

After a long period of time, what will be the population of Ramsville, and what percentage of the population will be in each of the age brackets?

16-12. A university study of population mobility in the Midwest has revealed the following yearly trends among urban, suburban, and rural families. Of those families in urban locations at the beginning of the year, 50 percent will remain there, 30 percent will move to suburban locations during the year, and 20 percent will move to rural locations. Of those families in suburban locations, 60 percent will remain there, 35 percent will move to an urban location, and 5 percent will move to a rural location. Seventy percent of rural families will remain there; 20 percent will move to urban locations and 10 percent to suburban locations. If the population distribution is currently 40 percent urban, 40 percent suburban, and 20 percent rural, what will the distribution look like in 2 years?

16-13. The Tarheel Telephone Company, a small private system which serves a university community, is well known for the unreliable nature of its equipment on rainy days. This Father's Day began with a downpour in the area served by TTC. A graduate student in business who was working part-time for TTC quickly formulated this matrix showing the likelihood of the trunk lines being "open," "busy," or "down" from one minute to the next. Because of the loss of customer good will if the phones are out of order on a day like Father's Day, when many calls are made, the manager of TTC wants to know what the equilibrium state of the system will be.

	Open	Busy	Down
Open	.4	.2	.4
Busy	.2	.6	.2
Down	.3	.5	.2

Can you provide her with this information?

16-14. In January, Major Motors, the nation's largest auto manufacturer, was warned by the FTC that if its share of the automobile market went above 65 percent, antitrust action would be initiated against the company. At that time Major Motors had 50 percent of the market. Its chief competitors, Ferd Motors and Kisler, had 25 percent and 10 percent respectively, with the rest being divided among other manufacturers, primarily foreign. Major Motors' market analysts were able to devise this transition matrix of market shares for yearly changes:

	MM	Ferd	Kisler	Others
MM	.7	.1	.05	.15
Ferd	.1	.8	0	.1
Kisler	.15	.1	.7	.05
Others	.2	.1	.1	.6

Will Major Motors face antitrust action? When?

16-15. Semiconductor Research Corporation has divided its accounts receivable into four classes based on the size of the average purchase made by the account and the length of time the account has been a customer. SRC labels these accounts new accounts, regular accounts, preferred accounts, and priority accounts, ranging from smallest and newest to largest and oldest. Over time, accounts are moved through the four classes. Currently there are 190 new accounts, 130 regular accounts, 120 preferred accounts, and 75 priority accounts. Historical evidence shows that each year, 20 percent of the new accounts become inactive for one reason or another. Similarly, 15 percent of the regular accounts, 10 percent of the preferred accounts, and 30 percent of the priority accounts also become inactive. SRC has a goal of moving 15 percent of each class of account into the next highest class by the end of the year. Assuming that for each account that becomes inactive, SRC finds a new account to replace it, how many of each class of account will SRC have at the end of the year if it reaches its goal?

16-16. Pedal Power, Inc., sells bicycles in competition with two other shops in a university community. Reports from the local Chamber of Commerce indicate that Pedal Power has about 25 percent of the local market, while its two competitors, The Bicycle Shop and Wheels, Unlimited, have about 40 percent and 35 percent respectively. Pedal Power had a profit last year of 6 percent of its sales in a total market of approximately $1 million sales. An M.B.A. class in marketing at the local university offered Pedal Power its advice as a part of a project. The class feels that $10,000 invested in more well-directed advertising by Pedal Power would create this matrix of transition probabilities:

	Pedal Power	Bicycle Shop	Wheels
Pedal Power	.85	.10	.05
Bicycle Shop	.08	.85	.07
Wheels	.07	.03	.90

If Pedal Power wants to get a return on the $10,000 within a year, should it take the students' advice?

16-17. Northeast Electrical is a company specializing in appliances. Many of Northeast's sales are on the installment basis; as a result much of the firm's working capital is tied up in accounts receivable. Although most of the firm's customers make their payments on time, a certain percentage of the accounts are always overdue and some few customers never pay, thereby becoming bad debts. Northeast Electrical's experience is that when a customer is two or more payments behind, the account will generally turn into a bad debt. In these cases, Northeast discontinues credit to the customer and writes the account off as a bad debt. At the beginning of each month, the accounts receivable manager reviews each account and classifies it as paid, current (being paid on time), overdue (one payment behind), or bad debt. The accounts receivable manager has provided this transition matrix from last month's data and this month's data:

		State of a dollar this month			
		Paid	Current	Overdue	Bad debt
State of a dollar last month	Paid	1.0	0	0	0
	Current	.4	.3	.3	0
	Overdue	.5	.2	.2	.1
	Bad debt	0	0	0	1.0

If Northeast now has $20,000 in the current category and $14,000 in the overdue classification, how much will eventually be paid and how much should they plan to write off as bad debts?

Bibliography

Blumenthal, R.: *Markov Processes and Potential Theory* (New York: Academic Press, Inc., 1968).

Derman, C.: *Finite State Markov Decision Processes* (New York: Academic Press, Inc., 1970).

Freedman, David: *Markov Chains* (San Francisco: Holden-Day, Inc., 1971).

Kemeny, J. G., A. Schleifer, Jr., J. L. Snell, and **G. L. Thompson:** *Finite Mathematics with Business Applications,* 2d ed. (Englewood Cliffs, N.J.: Prentice-Hall, Inc., 1972).

Martin, J. J.: *Bayesian Decision Problems and Markov Chains* (New York: John Wiley & Sons, Inc., 1967).

Quantitative methods: past, present, future

17

A great deal of change has occurred in management science during the last quarter century. From the humble beginnings described in Chapter 1, the discipline has undergone incredible growth, especially during the last 10 years. The literature, applications, number of practitioners, successes, *and* failures have all increased significantly. In this final chapter, we shall briefly consider where we have been, what things look like today, and where we seem to be going.

1. Three Phases of Growth

One of the most succinct reviews of the phases through which management science has developed was written by John F. Magee. A brief look, then, at the characteristics of each of these phases as Magee outlines them.

The Primitive Phase

Well-defined problems

Magee places this phase between 1941 and 1960. He notes that the problem solvers were interested in practical operational problems. He characterizes these problems as being well defined and capable of being handled by the smaller, less sophisticated computers available then. People who worked in the field tended to come from other disciplines: chemistry, statistics, mathematics, physics. Interestingly, only very few universities even offered formal training in operations research.

The Academic Phase

Significant growth in university programs

In the early 1960s, the number of universities offering programs in operations research grew over 500 percent. Magee points out that in this phase, people with some operations research experience began to be found at the higher corporate levels in private enterprise. The increasing speed and availability of computers were of great help during this time. Magee notes that research during the 1960s tended to be academic; that is, it was more concerned with developing theory than with finding workable applications. From the practitioner's point of view, however, the

1960s were humbling, since it was during this time that the limitations of operations research and the organizational problems of introducing new ideas became evident.

The Maturing Phase

Magee describes the maturing phase as a time when balance between theory and practice was obtained. He suggests that even though evidence of such concerns was noted years ago, the real thrust toward *practice* and *applications* did not come until the 1970s. Magee's own ideas about the maturing phase are these:

Balancing theory with practice

1. More realistic understanding by both managers and management scientists of what the management sciences can and cannot accomplish.

2. More attention paid to getting the facts . . . compared with development of abstract techniques.

3. Less attention to finding optimum answers, more to developing processes and evolving successively better answers adapted to evolving circumstances.

4. Better integration of behavioral, functional, and quantitative analysis . . . .[1]

2. Development of Quantitative Techniques in Organizations (Successes and Problems)

Over the last 20 years, researchers have, from time to time, studied the use and status of operations research in both public and private organizations. Their aim is to discern what is being used, how successfully, and what trends seem to be developing. Here is a look at some of these studies.

What is used and how successfully

The Schumacher and Smith Study
(Trends in Use of Operations Research)

In the mid 1960s, a study was conducted to determine trends in industrial utilization of operations research. Researchers hoped to reveal any trends related to the organization and size of OR groups, to the characteristics of OR staff personnel, and to changes in the areas of application.

Determining trends in utilization of operations research

Questionnaires were mailed to 168 companies employing from 2000 to 500,000 persons. Of the 65 firms responding, 49, or approximately 75 percent, were engaged in OR activities. In connection with the results obtained, a prominent philosophy in defining OR programs emerged. Points made most frequently indicated the belief that OR is problem-oriented, that it is involved not only with problem formulation and solutions but also with implementation, and that it is a continuous effort as opposed to being a one-time project.

The study also indicated that:

[1] J. F. Magee, "Progress in the Management Sciences," *TIMS Interfaces,* vol. 3, February 1973.

1. A trend appears to exist toward the separation of OR departments from other departments.

2. More economics majors, business majors, and industrial engineers, especially at the graduate level, are becoming involved in OR work.

3. There has been a substantial increase in the use of consultant services in industry.

4. Increased activity in all areas of application indicates the impact of OR in various areas of management.

5. The use of OR techniques has been accompanied by increased utilization of electronic data processing equipment in industry.

The researchers concluded their study by reflecting upon the problems faced in implementing OR. The two biggest problems are (1) gaining the confidence of management and (2) the lack of effective communication with operating personnel. Concerning the outlook for OR in industry, the general consensus indicates continued growth.[2]

The Radnor, Rubenstein, and Bean Study
(Location and Problems of Operations Research Activities)

Determining organizational location of OR and organizational receptivity to OR

A study of 66 major United States corporations, conducted in the late 1960s, had two objectives: (1) to determine the location of OR activities within organizations and (2) to examine problems of OR receptivity in organizations. Here are *three* findings:

1. During the 16-year period covered by the study, the percentage of OR activities domiciled in the top management and planning areas grew from zero to 42 percent.

2. Early in the 16-year period, 25 percent of the OR groups reported to Engineering or to Research and Development. This figure had shrunk to about 10 percent by the end of the period.

3. At the end of the study period, less than 1 percent of the organized OR activities reported to Marketing.

Because of the nature of their work, Engineering and Research and Development were logical locations for an organization's initial OR activities. Other areas within the organization, however, caught up rapidly and eventually passed the two pioneer areas in the control of corporate OR groups. So much for location.

As for receptivity, the study reported these explanations for poor relations between corporate OR groups and their in-house clients or parent organizations:

1. Poor project results

2. Use of highly technical terminology

[2] Charles C. Schumacher and Bernard E. Smith, "A Sample Survey of Industrial Operations Research Activities II," *Operations Research,* vol. 13, no. 6, November–December 1965.

3. Unsatisfactory experience with outside OR consultants

4. Unorthodox or unbusinesslike appearance of OR personnel

5. Identification with a highly specialized functional area

6. Inability to demonstrate cost effectiveness

7. Method of allocating project costs

8. Differences in planning horizons[3]

The Radnor, Rubenstein, and Tansik Study
(Client Support and Top Management Support)

Two of the three authors involved in the study just referred to were involved in another more comprehensive analysis of implementing quantitative techniques in organizations. It differs from previous work in several ways: (1) it includes research and development along with management science/operations research implementation studies, and (2) it includes governmental agencies along with corporate enterprises. Data in the article came primarily from studies in approximately 100 United States business and government organizations. The article analyzes *two* key factors: (1) level of client support and (2) level of top management support, and it attempts to correlate these factors with implementation success/failure of R&D and OR recommendations. Several cases are also presented to illustrate the effects of these two key factors. The article also presents an implementation model reflecting varied recommended implementation strategies as a function of organization goals.

Although the authors of this study do not find methods which will *assure* implementation success, they do suggest approaches which will increase the chance of success. These include:

1. Assuring that there is a clear and recognized need for the results at the time the project is undertaken.

2. Involving of the ultimate user of the results early in the process and maintaining communication with the user throughout the project.

3. Focusing of the direction or strategy for the project in an individual or small group that can review progress and make decisions about changes in direction or level of effort.

4. Having top management support and enthusiasm.

5. Allowing or encouraging researchers to follow projects into applications and make careers there, if they so desire.[4]

[3] M. Radnor, A. H. Rubenstein, and A. S. Bean, "Integration and Utilization of Management Science Activities in Organizations," *Operational Research Quarterly,* vol. 19, June 1968.

[4] Michael Radnor, Albert H. Rubenstein, and David A. Tansik, "Implementation in Operations Research and R&D in Government and Business Organization," *Operations Research,* vol. 18, November–December 1970.

The Radnor and Neal Study (Operations Research Is Maturing)

In 1970, another study was done which extended the results of Radnor's earlier work. This study included over a hundred large United States corporations and came to these conclusions:

OR seems to be reaching maturity

1. The field of operations research was exhibiting signs of maturity.

2. A definite trend toward diffusion of operations research capabilities throughout firms existed.

3. The actual process of performing an operations research study had become more routine, formalized, accepted.

4. Management acceptance of operations research was increasing.

5. Operations research activities tended to be located organizationally with the management information system in the firm.[5]

3. Extent of Use of Quantitative Techniques in Organizations

A number of surveys have been conducted over the last 10 years for the express purpose of determining what kinds of quantitative techniques are being used and where they are being used. Let us take a moment a look at some of them.

The Turban Study (Operations Research at the Corporate Level)

Perhaps the broadest survey of operations research success to be undertaken in recent years was accomplished by Professor Efraim Turban, who presents the findings of a national survey of OR departments at the corporate level. Questionnaires were sent to 475 of *Fortune*'s list of top 500 companies. His survey presents statistics on the following questions:

1. Name of OR department and to whom it reports

2. Degree of acceptance of the OR department by other organizational segments

3. Self-appraisal of the OR department

4. Information of the OR department makeup (i.e., size, educational level, age, turnover, salary, etc.)

5. Cost benefits of OR activities

6. Breakdown of activities by project—past, present, and future

7. Use of OR tools and techniques

8. Implementation of the OR projects

[5] Michael Radnor and R. Neal, "The Progress of Management-Science Activities in Large U.S. Industrial Corporations," *Operations Research*, vol. 21.

Turban concludes from his study that operations research activities have made an impressive gain at the corporate level in the United States. From less than 5 percent of United States corporations which had a special OR unit at their headquarters at the end of the 1950s, he forecast that about two-thirds of these corporations would have a unit by the mid-1970s. OR projects currently under way are quite diversified; there is a trend to move from simple projects on lower organizational levels to more sophisticated projects involving higher levels of the organization as well as environmental factors. The techniques most often used are statistical analysis, simulation, and linear programming. Projects last about 10 months on the average and involve about 2.5 researchers.[6]

The Gershefski Study (Information on Use of Corporate Models)

One research project was aimed at determining the extent to which corporate models were being used. This study by George Gershefski of the Sun Oil Company presents statistical results of an industrywide survey on use of corporate models. This survey yields interesting data regarding applications of OR but is somewhat limited since it is restricted to only one model—the corporate model. A corporate model can be any number of things, depending on whose model you are talking about, but, in general, the models considered as such are reasonably extensive information systems aimed primarily at providing financial and planning information to top-level managers. The survey was designed to broach the following questions:

Determining the extent of use of corporate models

1. How prevalent are corporate models?

2. What are the anticipated advantages of a corporate model?

3. What applications are being made?

4. How well do models work?

5. What approaches can be used in developing a corporate model?

6. How much manpower is required to develop a corporate model?

7. What are the structural characteristics of a corporate model?

Gershefski's findings indicated that 65 percent of the companies developed models which began by considering the total corporation but in very little detail. Only 35 percent chose to start by looking at a part of the company in detail with the idea of proceeding to develop a total corporate model function by function.

The typical projection period considered was 5 years, but periods ranged from 1 to 12 years. Seventy-two percent of the companies considered a year as the time period of interest. However, 13 percent considered a quarter and 15 percent utilized a month as the time period.

[6] Efraim Turban, "A Sample Survey of Operations-Research Activities at the Corporate Level," *Operations Research,* vol. 20, no. 3, May–June 1972.

Some statistics on
the use of corporate
models

Ninety-five percent of the models were of the case-study, simulation type. Only 5 percent were mathematical programming or optimization models. Eighty-eight percent of the models were deterministic in nature; 12 percent were stochastic in nature (considered a probability distribution). Ninety-four percent were computerized.[7]

The Cook and Russell Study (Extent of Usage in 1974)

Cook and Russell[8] report that in 1974 they mailed questionnaires to 240 of the *Fortune* 500 companies. From 105 responses (including 84 companies that engaged in these kinds of activities), they found these percentages of responding companies using the following quantitative techniques: linear programming (95 percent), computer simulation (88.4 percent), inventory control models (90.7 percent), PERT/CPM (90.7 percent), transportation method (75.3 percent), queuing theory (57.8 percent), branch-and-bound method (63.7 percent), dynamic programming (50 percent), integer programming (51.4 percent), Markov analysis (43.1 percent). Their survey did not allow for statistics to be gathered on the use of statistical techniques.

4. The Future Decision Environment

Changes We Are Likely to See

Looking at the
future

It's always risky to predict the future, but given today's information, there are some trends which can be projected.

Consumers We should see not only a growing number of consumers (at a diminished rate, though) but a rising standard of living as well. The consumer should live a longer and healthier life. A number of dread diseases will be brought

Changes in
consumers

under better control and newer drugs and medical techniques will continue to be developed. Education will continue its growth, with new attention on adult consumers and new educational technologies at all levels. The focus should shift slightly from degree programs to more technical training. Increased leisure time will represent an enormous potential for consumption.

Changes in
organizations

Organizations Both public and private organizations will get larger and more complex. The scope of their activities will continue to increase and we may see more and more superagencies like HEW, HUD, ERDA, and the like. The complexity of the problems which face society will require large organizational efforts, complex interactions, and massive planning and control systems. The line between public and private organizations will become less clear as government plays a larger and larger role in society.

[7] George W. Gershefski, "Corporate Models—The State of the Art," *Management Science,* vol. 16, no. 6, February 1970.

[8] Thomas A. Cook and Robert A Russell, *Introduction to Management Science,* Prentice-Hall, Inc., Englewood Cliffs, N.J., 1977, p. 437.

Markers New markets will continue to emerge. Regional economic units will continue to appear and expand. The European Common Market model will probably reappear in other areas of the world. The OPEC countries' wealth will continue to represent a major international market for both goods and technology. Consumption in the public sector market will increase more rapidly than in the private sector. Large public sector consumers like health, education, welfare, and social services will continue to grow. The whole set of urban problems (education, transportation, environment, housing, and the control of the environment) will require enormous resources and new approaches to the decision process.

Changes in markets

Production The rate at which new products appear will accelerate, requiring more complex production systems. Automation will go far beyond what we see today. The automated production line will become the automated factory, work hours will be reduced, and production-line technology will become more sophisticated and specialized. More and more attention will be focused on the technology of service industries as opposed to product manufacturing industries.

Changes in production systems

Demand for Quantitative Techniques

The future will see continued reliance on—and intelligent use of —techniques such as those presented in this book. Other and newer valuable techniques will undoubtedly be developed and put to use. When these tools *and* high-speed computers are used together, great strides are possible in the solution of complex problems.

Demand for quantitative techniques will increase

Organizations will make increasing use of the formal techniques of modeling in attempting to describe their environments and to develop intelligent decision rules to cope with environmental problems. The standard decisions concerning product mix will be made largely through mathematical programming models such as those introduced in Chapters 9, 10, 11, and 12. Executives will cope with complex project management and control headaches by using variants of the networking ideas presented in Chapter 15. Actual management of such customer use facilities as bridges, tunnels, parking areas, highways, rail systems, and airline traffic control systems will be accomplished partially through the use of queuing models based on the ideas in Chapter 14 and implemented with the help of huge computing facilities. Large inventory systems will operate automatically, quite independent of human inputs, for long periods of time; the systems will provide desired service levels for customers. These will reflect refinements of the basic inventory techniques illustrated in Chapters 7 and 8.

Increased use of probability theory and the ideas in Chapters 2 and 3 will be necessary to cope with increasing complexity and less certainty about future events. Forecasting, the subject of Chapter 4, will enjoy a much wider use as newer, more accurate techniques are developed. Almost all decisions will eventually be subjected to the more refined analysis introduced in Chapters 5 and 6. And the speed of change will cause us to rely more on change-predicting models like those of Chapter 16.

The size and complexity of future problems will demand that managers resort to the most advanced quantitative tools available. The *future* use of quantitative tools and computers will be an extension and an enlargement of *present* use.

5. Problems as Quantitative Analysis Tries to Provide Answers

Views of writers on progress versus potential

Let's examine some views of several writers in the field of quantitative methods on *two* matters: (1) how they see management scientists impeding their own progress and (2) how they see managers failing to take proper advantage of the potential of the technology available.

The literature of the last 15 years provides many insights into the problems of successfully applying quantitative methods in organizations.

Roles for Management Scientists

Management scientists seem not to agree among themselves about their role. Donald Heany of General Electric suggested that management scientists question their role and objectives.

Practitioners question their role

> Is 'management science' merely a synonym for 'applied mathematics'? A set of techniques and nothing more? Is the scope of our interest restricted to well-structured problems, those amenable to quantitative tools of analysis? Can one aspire to enterprise models embracing work going on at the top echelons of business organizations as long as managers and scientists are miles apart in terminology, interests, and perspective?[9]

Human Factors

Practitioners do not understand managers

Another test of good management science is the attention given to human factors. Churchman said that "the missing ingredient in the process of implementation is the understanding of the manager. Any research team that fails to study the manager and his personality may very well fail to bring about a recommended change."[10] Management scientists have failed always to be aware of their role vis-à-vis managers and their subordinates; management scientists have not always realized that their work will be successful only if they gain the confidence of the operating personnel for themselves *and* for their concepts, methodology, and solutions.

[9] D. F. Heany, "Is TIMS Talking to Itself?," *Management Science,* vol. 12, no. 4, December 1965.
[10] C. W. Churchman, "Managerial Acceptance of Scientific Recommendations," *California Management Review,* Fall 1964.

Implementation

Heany[11] considers the problem of implementation. Some management scientists seem to have neither the patience nor the diplomatic skill to get their output used. Their allegiance seems to be to truth, and they think that truth should be its own advocate. Their attitude is that their contribution ends with discovery and that selling or interpreting or implementing should not be part of their task. Management scientists must guard against just making black or white choices based upon figures; they must make decisions by building upon the technical factors *and* the consideration of the human factors involved.

Some practitioners lack patience and diplomacy

The Role of Information

Churchman[12] cites another problem with management scientists. "One of the central problems of management science is the lack of understanding of the role of information in decision making." The management scientist must distinguish between "data" and "information." Data do not become information until someone recognizes a need to know, and uses the data to become informed. Management scientists have done far too little research on the value of information. Such value lies in *how* it is used, and the information *must* be used to increase the knowledge of the executive. "Knowledge is a sensitivity to changes in one's environment. It is the ability of a decision maker to adjust his decisions to changes in the the situations that confront him."[13] But Louis Rader has stated[14] that management scientists have failed to make enough allowance for error circuits to detect changes in the environment and thus have constructed models with rigid structures which were capable of being shattered by uncertainty or change.

Practitioners do not understand the role of information

The Manager as a Facilitator and a Constraint

Rader suggests[15] that the biggest roadblock to further progress in the management sciences probably is the manager. Most managers are in their fifties; they completed their education a quarter of a century ago and were taught by people who had completed *their* education 25 years before that; their entry into the business world predated the production, scientific, and technological revolutions of World War II and thereafter.

Managers are a constraint

In addition, Churchman[16] argues that management science is still new and strange to most managers; that people tend to mistrust that which they do not understand; that some managers may feel threatened by certain modern analytical techniques. Managers thus may fear operations research projects because

[11] Op. cit., p. 35.
[12] Op. cit., p. 31.
[13] Ibid., pp. 32 and 33.
[14] Louis T. Rader, "Roadblocks to Progress in the Management Sciences and Operations Research." *Management Science,* vol. 11, no. 6, February 1965.
[15] Ibid.
[16] Op. cit.

they may become upset, their rules may be reexamined, and their private fiefdoms may be subjected to an intense and searching scrutiny. This may tend to limit managers from giving their wholehearted support to the study.

Managers may feel their intuition is being questioned

There is a defense of management, says Morris,[17] that in its more extreme form claims that management is not scientific, cannot become scientific, and even if it could, ought not to become scientific. Managers may claim that they find it impossible to verbalize the mental processes that they use to reach a decision; therefore, they describe their thought processes as judgmatic, intuitive, implicit, artistic, or subconscious. Managers of this type may feel that they have no need for management science because their intuition, developed and tested by experience, has usually produced good results.

Managers do not understand management science

This argument by Morris is a corollary to one advanced by Churchman[18] when he states that the missing gap for many managers is the lack of someone or something to take the information that is available and to translate it into a decision system that will provide the information needed. Churchman says,[19] "Of course, one could say that the difficulty is that the available information is in one location, the analysis is in another (the head of the management scientist), and the decision making is in a third. One might feel that if all three of these components could be combined into one unit, the problem could be solved." Most of the blame for this situation must fall on the managers; in many cases, they seem unwilling to put forth the effort to gain a thorough understanding of the work of the management scientist and seem to be more willing to live with a problem they cannot solve than to implement a solution they do not understand.

Factors Which Lead to Success or Failure

What determines the success of management science's implementation

Mr. Allan Harvey, a management consultant with the Dasol Corporation, reports the results of his work in the implementation of management science solutions. He summarizes the implementation success/failure of management science solutions his company has recommended to 31 past clients. In spite of his position as "recommender," the author reports that among the 31 companies, only 11 of the management science team's recommendations were successfully implemented, 12 were partially successful, and 8 were failures.

The survey seeks answers to the question, "What factors lead to success or failure in implementing OR-based recommendations?" The factors considered are management characteristics, problem characteristics, and characteristics related to the management science team and their recommended solution.

Choice of manager affects OR success

Mr. Harvey suggests strongly that if OR organizations want to be more successful in applying new techniques or new technology to existing problems, either of two alternative courses of action will significantly improve results. One thing they can do is to use the kind of information developed in this study to pick the kinds of managers and the kinds of "experts" who are more likely to get results,

[17] W. T. Morris, "Intuition and Relevance," *Management Science,* vol. 14, no. 4, December 1967.
[18] Op. cit.
[19] Ibid.

and to define problem areas in a way that is likely to increase the chances of getting successful action. This policy will enable them to focus energies on efforts that are likely to lead to significant solutions.

The other alternative is to identify the human and organizational problems in advance and take whatever action is necessary to deal with them *effectively* in a way that will assure effective action on these critical problems. It is in this way that the kind of study here reported provides a framework within which many more specific studies of implementation factors can find a productive application.[20]

Science and Management, the Relationship

On the subject of relaxing or removing the constraints to further development of management science, Charnes and Cooper[21] cite a "mutual understanding position" as one approach toward this goal. This position of mutual understanding makes an "effort to bring about the successful union of managers and researchers." The argument is that science and management must *not* be separated. The two writers claim that there is a move toward this position and that this may cause management and management science to evolve to a point where a distinction is no longer valid.

Both parties must understand each other

Hertz[22] discusses this convergence of science and management and says that management scientists cannot point the finger to a shadowy "they" and say that "they" will not accept recommendations, nor can management scientists admonish themselves to communicate with "them." On the contrary, management scientists must learn to be the "they" of whom they speak. Hertz cites *four* responsibilities of management scientists:

1. To realize that when management is changed at the same time the environment of management is changed, there must be an attempt to predict the future environment that will stem from their work

2. To provide for universal education in the management sciences

3. To mobilize the scarce management science resources to attack nontrivial problems

4. To undertake their work in the spirit of the unity of science and management

Practitioners, Theoreticians, and Educators

Perhaps the best summary of approaches and opportunities which are likely to generate long-run success in the implementation of operations research techniques has been advanced by Professor Harvey M. Wagner. He looks at the future of operations research from three points of view: those of (1) the *practitioner,* (2) the

There are three parties to the long-run success of OR

[20] Allan Harvey, "Factors Making for Implementation Success and Failure," *Management Science,* vol. 16, no. 6, February 1970.

[21] A. Charnes and W. W. Cooper, "Management Sciences and Management: Some Requirements for Further Development," *Management Science,* vol. 13, no. 2, October 1966.

[22] David B. Hertz, "The Unity of Science and Management," *Management Science,* vol. 11, no. 8, April 1965.

theoretician, and (3) the *educator.* In Wagner's terms, the principal opportunities available to *practitioners* are to:

1. Improve the mechanics of applying operations research so as to reduce the resource costs for developing, analyzing, and implementing OR models.

2. Devise diagnostic techniques to predict accurately the economic benefits that will accrue from a proposed OR application.

3. Expand the purview of OR into new areas of management, including formulating a corporation's growth strategy, structuring organizational responsibilities, bridging cultural gaps within a company, improving a company's profit performance, designing management information systems, and delineating the enterprise's public responsibilities.

The challenges open to management science *theoreticians* are to:

1. Develop insightful models that sidestep the axiom of managerial rationality.

2. Propose analytic concepts that enable managers to deal with the future as reality.

3. Build practical models for treating day-to-day operating problems.

4. Find new ways to exploit the full power of computers.

5. Explore approaches to model building that encompass principles of behavioral science.

The recommendations made to *educators* are that they:

1. Assess the appropriate mix between professional and technical training to best prepare students for having a practical influence on managerial decision making.

2. Examine the relative merits of the various approaches to OR higher education that have been in vogue for over a decade.

Wagner is not *confident* that OR professionals will pursue these tasks with vigor and complete them with dispatch, but he remains *hopeful* that the OR profession's fundamental commitment to seek improvements in society continually will direct its energies to solving problems of vital significance.[23]

Building Links, a Necessary Step

Management science has grown away from managers

C. Jackson Grayson, Jr., suggests that management science has grown so remote from live managers and so unmindful of their problems that it has lost much of its usability. He suggests that many managers have become disillusioned about management science and are unwilling to consider it seriously as a working tool for problem solution.

[23] Harvey M. Wagner, "The ABC's of OR," *Operations Research,* vol. 19, no. 5, September–October 1971.

Professor Grayson believes that management science *can* make a contribution to management but not before the scientists begin the process of building a bridge between themselves and practicing managers. Grayson agrees that:

1. Management scientists have had some impact on real-world operations and managers.

2. Some management science tools have been successfully applied.

3. Managers do tend to give more conscious thought to their decision making than in previous years.

4. Management scientists have highlighted areas for further research by indicating how abysmal our knowledge about decision making is.

5. Both the faculty and students of business schools have gained some added prestige for being more "scientific."

But he contends that the real payoffs from management science have been extremely small—even smaller if one compares them with the revolution that was promised in the early years of the discipline. In his own experience as head of the Price Commission from 1971 to 1973, he reports that he rejected completely the use of any management science techniques because of:

1. A shortage of time

2. The inaccessibility of data

3. The considerable resistance to change of his personnel

4. The excessively long time it takes management scientists to respond to needs of the organization

5. The invalidating assumptions often made by management scientists

Grayson suggests that inside operating organizations management science people should not be isolated but rather should be sprinkled throughout the organization, and that managers should demand *implementation* by management scientists. He suggests three approaches at the university level which he feels would significantly improve the success ratio of applications; he suggests that students and faculty go outside academe for problems, that management science people stop tackling problems, and that faculty members plan to get out of the universities for meaningful periods of time to get direct, real-world experience.[24]

Management scientists should be decentralized

Two Recent Views of Where We Should Be Moving

Donald Rice, a recent president of TIMS, challenged management scientists to direct their efforts at the public sector. He sees these problems as intractable and of such consequential concern to society that we should approach them with

A president of TIMS talks

[24]C. Jackson Grayson, Jr., "Management Science and Business Practice," *Harvard Business Review,* vol. 51, no. 4, July–August 1973.

The real problems
are in the public
sector

Management
science must
enhance a
manager's intuitive
abilities

our best technology—in this case, quantitative analysis. Rice shares his view with many who believe that private industry has gone much farther and has been much more successful than public sector enterprises in defining and solving its problems. Rice admits that public sector problems are characterized by multiple, often conflicting objectives, but he asserts that the need is greatest in that area.[25]

Milan Zeleny, writing in *Computers and Operations Research,* maintains that management scientists need to be more effective than efficient, that the biggest challenge for management scientists is to develop new ideas that will enhance the *intuitive* powers of managers. Zeleny says that most of the quantitative techniques have been around from the beginning of operations research applications years ago and that the transition to a *new management science* will require a whole new attitude on the part of practitioners.[26]

Conclusion

Quantitative methods have proved themselves in business and government at least to the point where there can no longer be any excuse for a student graduating from a university program in business or public administration without being conversant with both the *techniques* of management science and the *constraints* on their effective use.

The problems that private and public organizations face in the next decade are mind-boggling in scope. Much new managerial technology must be brought to bear on these problems before they will yield solutions which can be implemented in a practical manner.

It is no longer possible for organizations to avoid researching the potential usefulness of the techniques presented in this book to their policy and operating problems. Past successes indicate a large potential for further application of quantitative techniques.

Managers at all levels in organizations require additional education in this field, and students entering organizations from university curricula in administration must have a working knowledge of the ideas presented herein if they are to contribute effectively to the solution of organizational problems; to that end this book was written.

[25] Donald B. Rice, "Message from the President," *OR/MS Today,* vol. 3, September 1975.
[26] Milan Zeleny, "Notes, Ideas and Techniques: New Vistas of Management Science," *Computers and Operations Research,* vol. 2, 1975.

The standard normal probability distribution

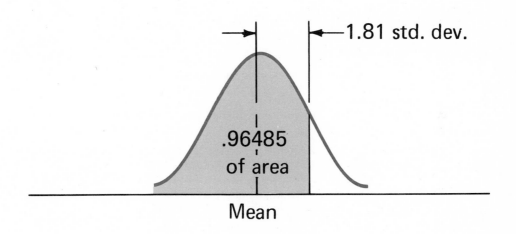

.96485 of area

1.81 std. dev.

Mean

Directions: To find the area under the normal curve between the left-hand end and any point, determine how many standard deviations that point is to the right of the mean, then read the area directly from the body of the table. *Example:* The area under the curve from the left-hand end to a point 1.81 standard deviations to the right of the mean is .96485 of the total area under the curve.

AREAS UNDER THE NORMAL CURVE

Third row of Z

First to depth of Z

	.00	.01	.02	.03	.04	.05	.06	.07	.08	.09
0.0	.50000	.50399	.50798	.51197	.51595	.51994	.52392	.52790	.53188	.53586
0.1	.53983	.54380	.54776	.55172	.55567	.55962	.56356	.56749	.57142	.57535
0.2	.57926	.58317	.58706	.59095	.59483	.59871	.60257	.60642	.61026	.61409
0.3	.61791	.62172	.62552	.62930	.63307	.63683	.64058	.64431	.64803	.65173
0.4	.65542	.65910	.66276	.66640	.67003	.67364	.67724	.68082	.68439	.68793
0.5	.69146	.69497	.69847	.70194	.70540	.70884	.71226	.71566	.71904	.72240
0.6	.72575	.72907	.73237	.73536	.73891	.74215	.74537	.74857	.75175	.75490
0.7	.75804	.76115	.76424	.76730	.77035	.77337	.77637	.77935	.78230	.78524
0.8	.78814	.79103	.79389	.79673	.79955	.80234	.80511	.80785	.81057	.81327
0.9	.81594	.81859	.82121	.82381	.82639	.82894	.83147	.83398	.83646	.83891
1.0	.84134	.84375	.84614	.84849	.85083	.85314	.85543	.85769	.85993	.86214
1.1	.86433	.86650	.86864	.87076	.87286	.87493	.87698	.87900	.88100	.88298
1.2	.88493	.88686	.88877	.89065	.89251	.89435	.89617	.89796	.89973	.90147
1.3	.90320	.90490	.90658	.90824	.90988	.91149	.91309	.91466	.91621	.91774
1.4	.91924	.92073	.92220	.92364	.92507	.92647	.92785	.92922	.93056	.93189
1.5	.93319	.93448	.93574	.93699	.93822	.93943	.94062	.94179	.94295	.94408
1.6	.94520	.94630	.94738	.94845	.94950	.95053	.95154	.95254	.95352	.95449
1.7	.95543	.95637	.95728	.95818	.95907	.95994	.96080	.96164	.96246	.96327
1.8	.96407	.96485	.96562	.96638	.96712	.96784	.96856	.96926	.96995	.97062
1.9	.97128	.97193	.97257	.97320	.97381	.97441	.97500	.97558	.97615	.97670
2.0	.97725	.97784	.97831	.97882	.97932	.97982	.98030	.98077	.98124	.98169
2.1	.98214	.98257	.98300	.98341	.98382	.98422	.98461	.98500	.98537	.98574
2.2	.98610	.98645	.98679	.98713	.98745	.98778	.98809	.98840	.98870	.98899
2.3	.98928	.98956	.98983	.99010	.99036	.99061	.99086	.99111	.99134	.99158
2.4	.99180	.99202	.99224	.99245	.99266	.99286	.99305	.99324	.99343	.99361
2.5	.99379	.99396	.99413	.99430	.99446	.99461	.99477	.99492	.99506	.99520
2.6	.99534	.99547	.99560	.99573	.99585	.99598	.99609	.99621	.99632	.99643
2.7	.99653	.99664	.99674	.99683	.99693	.99702	.99711	.99720	.99728	.99736
2.8	.99744	.99752	.99760	.99767	.99774	.99781	.99788	.99795	.99801	.99807
2.9	.99813	.99819	.99825	.99831	.99836	.99841	.99846	.99851	.99856	.99861
3.0	.99865	.99869	.99874	.99878	.99882	.99886	.99899	.99893	.99896	.99900
3.1	.99903	.99906	.99910	.99913	.99916	.99918	.99921	.99924	.99926	.99929
3.2	.99931	.99934	.99936	.99938	.99940	.99942	.99944	.99946	.99948	.99950
3.3	.99952	.99953	.99955	.99957	.99958	.99960	.99961	.99962	.99964	.99965
3.4	.99966	.99968	.99969	.99970	.99971	.99972	.99973	.99974	.99975	.99976
3.5	.99977	.99978	.99978	.99979	.99980	.99981	.99981	.99982	.99983	.99983
3.6	.99984	.99985	.99985	.99986	.99986	.99987	.99987	.99988	.99988	.99989
3.7	.99989	.99990	.99990	.99990	.99991	.99991	.99992	.99992	.99992	.99992
3.8	.99993	.99993	.99993	.99994	.99994	.99994	.99994	.99995	.99995	.99995
3.9	.99995	.99995	.99996	.99996	.99996	.99996	.99996	.99996	.99997	.99997

The cumulative binomial distribution

The following tables describe the cumulative binomial distribution; a sample problem will illustrate how they are to be used.

Problem

What is the probability that an inspector will find *8 or more* defects in inspecting a lot of 15 pieces when the probability that any one piece is defective is .30?

Steps

1. In binomial distribution notation, the elements in this problem can be represented as follows:

$n = 15$ number of pieces to be inspected
$p = .30$ probability that any one piece will be defective
$r = 8$ number of defects in question

2. Since the problem involves 15 trials or inspections, first find the table corresponding to $n = 15$.

3. The probability of a defect in any one piece is .30; thus we must look through the $n = 15$ table until we find the column where $p = 30$.

4. We then move down the $p = 30$ column until we are opposite the $r = 8$ row.

5. The answer there is found to be 0500; this is interpreted as being a probability value of .0500.

Note

The problem asked for the probability of *8 or more* defects; had it asked for the probability of *more than 8* defects, we would have looked up the probability of *9 or more* defects.

589

CUMULATIVE BINOMIAL DISTRIBUTION

$n = 1$

P R	01	02	03	04	05	06	07	08	09	10
1	0100	0200	0300	0400	0500	0600	0700	0800	0900	1000

P R	11	12	13	14	15	16	17	18	19	20
1	1100	1200	1300	1400	1500	1600	1700	1800	1900	2000

P R	21	22	23	24	25	26	27	28	29	30
1	2100	2200	2300	2400	2500	2600	2700	2800	2900	3000

P R	31	32	33	34	35	36	37	38	39	40
1	3100	3200	3300	3400	3500	3600	3700	3800	3900	4000

P R	41	42	43	44	45	46	47	48	49	50
1	4100	4200	4300	4400	4500	4600	4700	4800	4900	5000

$n = 2$

P R	01	02	03	04	05	06	07	08	09	10
1	0199	0396	0591	0784	0975	1164	1351	1536	1719	1900
2	0001	0004	0009	0016	0025	0036	0049	0064	0081	0100

P R	11	12	13	14	15	16	17	18	19	20
1	2079	2256	2431	2604	2775	2944	3111	3276	3439	3600
2	0121	0144	0169	0196	0225	0256	0289	0324	0361	0400

P R	21	22	23	24	25	26	27	28	29	30
1	3759	3916	4071	4224	4375	4524	4671	4816	4959	5100
2	0441	0484	0529	0576	0625	0676	0729	0784	0841	0900

P R	31	32	33	34	35	36	37	38	39	40
1	5239	5376	5511	5644	5775	5904	6031	6156	6279	6400
2	0961	1024	1089	1156	1225	1296	1369	1444	1521	1600

P R	41	42	43	44	45	46	47	48	49	50
1	6519	6636	6751	6864	6975	7084	7191	7296	7399	7500
2	1681	1764	1849	1936	2025	2116	2209	2304	2401	2500

$n = 3$

P R	01	02	03	04	05	06	07	08	09	10
1	0297	0588	0873	1153	1426	1694	1956	2213	2464	2710
2	0003	0012	0026	0047	0073	0104	0140	0182	0228	0280
3				0001	0001	0002	0003	0005	0007	0010

P R	11	12	13	14	15	16	17	18	19	20
1	2950	3185	3415	3639	3859	4073	4282	4486	4686	4880
2	0336	0397	0463	0533	0608	0686	0769	0855	0946	1040
3	0013	0017	0022	0027	0034	0041	0049	0058	0069	0080

P R	21	22	23	24	25	26	27	28	29	30
1	5070	5254	5435	5610	5781	5948	6110	6268	6421	6570
2	1138	1239	1344	1452	1563	1676	1793	1913	2035	2160
3	0093	0106	0122	0138	0156	0176	0197	0220	0244	0270

P	31	32	33	34	35	36	37	38	39	40
R										
1	6715	6856	6992	7125	7254	7379	7500	7617	7730	7840
2	2287	2417	2548	2682	2818	2955	3094	3235	3377	3520
3	0298	0328	0359	0393	0429	0467	0507	0549	0593	0640

P	41	42	43	44	45	46	47	48	49	50
R										
1	7946	8049	8148	8244	8336	8425	8511	8594	8673	8750
2	3665	3810	3957	4104	4253	4401	4551	4700	4850	5000
3	0689	0741	0795	0852	0911	0973	1038	1106	1176	1250

$$n = 4$$

P	01	02	03	04	05	06	07	08	09	10
R										
1	0394	0776	1147	1507	1855	2193	2519	2836	3143	3439
2	0006	0023	0052	0091	0140	0199	0267	0344	0430	0523
3			0001	0002	0005	0008	0013	0019	0027	0037
4									0001	0001

P	11	12	13	14	15	16	17	18	19	20
R										
1	3726	4003	4271	4530	4780	5021	5254	5479	5695	5904
2	0624	0732	0847	0968	1095	1228	1366	1509	1656	1808
3	0049	0063	0079	0098	0120	0144	0171	0202	0235	0272
4	0001	0002	0003	0004	0005	0007	0008	0010	0013	0016

P	21	22	23	24	25	26	27	28	29	30
R										
1	6105	6298	6485	6664	6836	7001	7160	7313	7459	7599
2	1963	2122	2285	2450	2617	2787	2959	3132	3307	3483
3	0312	0356	0403	0453	0508	0566	0628	0694	0763	0837
4	0019	0023	0028	0033	0039	0046	0053	0061	0071	0081

P	31	32	33	34	35	36	37	38	39	40
R										
1	7733	7862	7985	8103	8215	8322	8425	8522	8615	8704
2	3660	3837	4015	4193	4370	4547	4724	4900	5075	5248
3	0915	0996	1082	1171	1265	1362	1464	1569	1679	1792
4	0092	0105	0119	0134	0150	0168	0187	0209	0231	0256

P	41	42	43	44	45	46	47	48	49	50
R										
1	8788	8868	8944	9017	9085	9150	9211	9269	9323	9375
2	5420	5590	5759	5926	6090	6252	6412	6569	6724	6875
3	1909	2030	2155	2283	2415	2550	2689	2834	2977	3125
4	0283	0311	0342	0375	0410	0448	0488	0531	0576	0625

$$n = 5$$

P	01	02	03	04	05	06	07	08	09	10
R										
1	0490	0961	1413	1846	2262	2661	3043	3409	3760	4095
2	0010	0038	0085	0148	0226	0319	0425	0544	0674	0815
3		0001	0001	0003	0006	0012	0020	0031	0045	0063	0086
4						0001	0001	0002	0003	0005

P	11	12	13	14	15	16	17	18	19	20
R										
1	4416	4723	5016	5296	5563	5818	6061	6293	6513	6723
2	0965	1125	1292	1467	1648	1835	2027	2224	2424	2627
3	0112	0143	0179	0220	0266	0318	0375	0437	0505	0579
4	0007	0009	0013	0017	0022	0029	0036	0045	0055	0067
5				0001	0001	0001	0001	0002	0002	0003

P	21	22	23	24	25	26	27	28	29	30
R										
1	6923	7113	7293	7464	7627	7781	7927	8065	8196	8319
2	2833	3041	3251	3461	3672	3883	4093	4303	4511	4718
3	0659	0744	0836	0933	1035	1143	1257	1376	1501	1631
4	0081	0097	0114	0134	0156	0181	0208	0238	0272	0308
5	0004	0005	0006	0008	0010	0012	0014	0017	0021	0024

CUMULATIVE BINOMIAL DISTRIBUTION (*Continued*)

P R	31	32	33	34	35	36	37	38	39	40
1	8436	8546	8650	8748	8840	8926	9008	9084	9155	9222
2	4923	5125	5325	5522	5716	5906	6093	6276	6455	6630
3	1766	1905	2050	2199	2352	2509	2670	2835	3003	3174
4	0347	0390	0436	0486	0540	0598	0660	0726	0796	0870
5	0029	0034	0039	0045	0053	0060	0069	0079	0090	0102

P R	41	42	43	44	45	46	47	48	49	50
1	9285	9344	9398	9449	9497	9541	9582	9620	9655	9688
2	6801	6967	7129	7286	7438	7585	7728	7865	7998	8125
3	3349	3525	3705	3886	4069	4253	4439	4625	4813	5000
4	0949	1033	1121	1214	1312	1415	1522	1635	1753	1875
5	0116	0131	0147	0165	0185	0206	0229	0255	0282	0313

$n = 6$

P R	01	02	03	04	05	06	07	08	09	10
1	0585	1142	1670	2172	2649	3101	3530	3936	4321	4686
2	0015	0057	0125	0216	0328	0459	0608	0773	0952	1143
3		0002	0005	0012	0022	0038	0058	0085	0118	0159
4				0001	0002	0003	0005	0008	0013
5										0001

P R	11	12	13	14	15	16	17	18	19	20
1	5030	5356	5664	5954	6229	6487	6731	6960	7176	7379
2	1345	1556	1776	2003	2235	2472	2713	2956	3201	3446
3	0206	0261	0324	0395	0473	0560	0655	0759	0870	0989
4	0018	0025	0034	0045	0059	0075	0094	0116	0141	0170
5	0001	0001	0002	0003	0004	0005	0007	0010	0013	0016
6										0001

P R	21	22	23	24	25	26	27	28	29	30
1	7569	7748	7916	8073	8220	8358	8487	8607	8719	8824
2	3692	3937	4180	4422	4661	4896	5128	5356	5580	5798
3	1115	1250	1391	1539	1694	1856	2023	2196	2374	2557
4	0202	0239	0280	0326	0376	0431	0492	0557	0628	0705
5	0020	0025	0031	0038	0046	0056	0067	0079	0093	0109
6	0001	0001	0001	0002	0002	0003	0004	0005	0006	0007

P R	31	32	33	34	35	36	37	38	39	40
1	8921	9011	9095	9173	9246	9313	9375	9432	9485	9533
2	6012	6220	6422	6619	6809	6994	7172	7343	7508	7667
3	2744	2936	3130	3328	3529	3732	3937	4143	4350	4557
4	0787	0875	0969	1069	1174	1286	1404	1527	1657	1792
5	0127	0148	0170	0195	0223	0254	0288	0325	0365	0410
6	0009	0011	0013	0015	0018	0022	0026	0030	0035	0041

P R	41	42	43	44	45	46	47	48	49	50
1	9578	9619	9657	9692	9723	9752	9778	9802	9824	9844
2	7819	7965	8105	8238	8364	8485	8599	8707	8810	8906
3	4764	4971	5177	5382	5585	5786	5985	6180	6373	6563
4	1933	2080	2232	2390	2553	2721	2893	3070	3252	3438
5	0458	0510	0566	0627	0692	0762	0837	0917	1003	1094
6	0048	0055	0063	0073	0083	0095	0108	0122	0138	0156

$n = 7$

P R	01	02	03	04	05	06	07	08	09	10
1	0679	1319	1920	2486	3017	3515	3983	4422	4832	5217
2	0020	0079	0171	0294	0444	0618	0813	1026	1255	1497
3		0003	0009	0020	0038	0063	0097	0140	0193	0257
4				0001	0002	0004	0007	0012	0018	0027
5								0001	0001	0002

P	11	12	13	14	15	16	17	18	19	20
R										
1	5577	5913	6227	6521	6794	7049	7286	7507	7712	7903
2	1750	2012	2281	2556	2834	3115	3396	3677	3956	4233
3	0331	0416	0513	0620	0738	0866	1005	1154	1313	1480
4	0039	0054	0072	0094	0121	0153	0189	0231	0279	0333
5	0003	0004	0006	0009	0012	0017	0022	0029	0037	0047
6					0001	0001	0001	0002	0003	0004

P	21	22	23	24	25	26	27	28	29	30
R										
1	8080	8243	8395	8535	8665	8785	8895	8997	9090	9176
2	4506	4775	5040	5298	5551	5796	6035	6266	6490	6706
3	1657	1841	2033	2231	2436	2646	2861	3081	3304	3529
4	0394	0461	0536	0617	0706	0802	0905	1016	1134	1260
5	0058	0072	0088	0107	0129	0153	0181	0213	0248	0288
6	0005	0006	0008	0011	0013	0017	0021	0026	0031	0038
7					0001	0001	0001	0001	0002	0002

P	31	32	33	34	35	36	37	38	39	40
R										
1	9255	9328	9394	9454	9510	9560	9606	9648	9686	9720
2	6914	7113	7304	7487	7662	7828	7987	8137	8279	8414
3	3757	3987	4217	4447	4677	4906	5134	5359	5581	5801
4	1394	1534	1682	1837	1998	2167	2341	2521	2707	2898
5	0332	0380	0434	0492	0556	0625	0701	0782	0869	0963
6	0046	0055	0065	0077	0090	0105	0123	0142	0164	0188
7	0003	0003	0004	0005	0006	0008	0009	0011	0014	0016

P	41	42	43	44	45	46	47	48	49	50
R										
1	9751	9779	9805	9827	9848	9866	9883	9897	9910	9922
2	8541	8660	8772	8877	8976	9068	9153	9233	9307	9375
3	6017	6229	6436	6638	6836	7027	7213	7393	7567	7734
4	3094	3294	3498	3706	3917	4131	4346	4563	4781	5000
5	1063	1169	1282	1402	1529	1663	1803	1951	2105	2266
6	0216	0246	0279	0316	0357	0402	0451	0504	0562	0625
7	0019	0023	0027	0032	0037	0044	0051	0059	0068	0078

$$n = 8$$

P	01	02	03	04	05	06	07	08	09	10
R										
1	0773	1492	2163	2786	3366	3904	4404	4868	5297	5695
2	0027	0103	0223	0381	0572	0792	1035	1298	1577	1869
3	0001	0004	0013	0031	0058	0096	0147	0211	0289	0381
4			0001	0002	0004	0007	0013	0022	0034	0050
5							0001	0001	0003	0004

P	11	12	13	14	15	16	17	18	19	20
R										
1	6063	6404	6718	7008	7275	7521	7748	7956	8147	8322
2	2171	2480	2794	3111	3428	3744	4057	4366	4670	4967
3	0487	0608	0743	0891	1052	1226	1412	1608	1815	2031
4	0071	0097	0129	0168	0214	0267	0328	0397	0476	0563
5	0007	0010	0015	0021	0029	0038	0050	0065	0083	0104
6		0001	0001	0002	0002	0003	0005	0007	0009	0012
7									0001	0001

P	21	22	23	24	25	26	27	28	29	30
R										
1	8483	8630	8764	8887	8999	9101	9194	9278	9354	9424
2	5257	5538	5811	6075	6329	6573	6807	7031	7244	7447
3	2255	2486	2724	2967	3215	3465	3718	3973	4228	4482
4	0659	0765	0880	1004	1138	1281	1433	1594	1763	1941
5	0129	0158	0191	0230	0273	0322	0377	0438	0505	0580
6	0016	0021	0027	0034	0042	0052	0064	0078	0094	0113
7	0001	0002	0002	0003	0004	0005	0006	0008	0010	0013
8									0001	0001

CUMULATIVE BINOMIAL DISTRIBUTION (*Continued*)

P	31	32	33	34	35	36	37	38	39	40
R										
1	9486	9543	9594	9640	9681	9719	9752	9782	9808	9832
2	7640	7822	7994	8156	8309	8452	8586	8711	8828	8936
3	4736	4987	5236	5481	5722	5958	6189	6415	6634	6846
4	2126	2319	2519	2724	2936	3153	3374	3599	3828	4059
5	0661	0750	0846	0949	1061	1180	1307	1443	1586	1737
6	0134	0159	0187	0218	0253	0293	0336	0385	0439	0498
7	0016	0020	0024	0030	0036	0043	0051	0061	0072	0085
8	0001	0001	0001	0002	0002	0003	0004	0004	0005	0007

P	41	42	43	44	45	46	47	48	49	50
R										
1	9853	9872	9889	9903	9916	9928	9938	9947	9954	9961
2	9037	9130	9216	9295	9368	9435	9496	9552	9602	9648
3	7052	7250	7440	7624	7799	7966	8125	8276	8419	8555
4	4292	4527	4762	4996	5230	5463	5694	5922	6146	6367
5	1895	2062	2235	2416	2604	2798	2999	3205	3416	3633
6	0563	0634	0711	0794	0885	0982	1086	1198	1318	1445
7	0100	0117	0136	0157	0181	0208	0239	0272	0310	0352
8	0008	0010	0012	0014	0017	0020	0024	0028	0033	0039

$n = 9$

P	01	02	03	04	05	06	07	08	09	10
R										
1	0865	1663	2398	3075	3698	4270	4796	5278	5721	6126
2	0034	0131	0282	0478	0712	0978	1271	1583	1912	2252
3	0001	0006	0020	0045	0084	0138	0209	0298	0405	0530
4			0001	0003	0006	0013	0023	0037	0057	0083
5						0001	0002	0003	0005	0009
6										0001

P	11	12	13	14	15	16	17	18	19	20
R										
1	6496	6835	7145	7427	7684	7918	8131	8324	8499	8658
2	2599	2951	3304	3657	4005	4348	4685	5012	5330	5638
3	0672	0833	1009	1202	1409	1629	1861	2105	2357	2618
4	0117	0158	0209	0269	0339	0420	0512	0615	0730	0856
5	0014	0021	0030	0041	0056	0075	0098	0125	0158	0196
6	0001	0002	0003	0004	0006	0009	0013	0017	0023	0031
7						0001	0001	0002	0002	0003

P	21	22	23	24	25	26	27	28	29	30
R										
1	8801	8931	9048	9154	9249	9335	9411	9480	9542	9596
2	5934	6218	6491	6750	6997	7230	7452	7660	7856	8040
3	2885	3158	3434	3713	3993	4273	4552	4829	5102	5372
4	0994	1144	1304	1475	1657	1849	2050	2260	2478	2703
5	0240	0291	0350	0416	0489	0571	0662	0762	0870	0988
6	0040	0051	0065	0081	0100	0122	0149	0179	0213	0253
7	0004	0006	0008	0010	0013	0017	0022	0028	0035	0043
8			0001	0001	0001	0001	0002	0003	0003	0004

P	31	32	33	34	35	36	37	38	39	40
R										
1	9645	9689	9728	9762	9793	9820	9844	9865	9883	9899
2	8212	8372	8522	8661	8789	8908	9017	9118	9210	9295
3	5636	5894	6146	6390	6627	6856	7076	7287	7489	7682
4	2935	3173	3415	3662	3911	4163	4416	4669	4922	5174
5	1115	1252	1398	1553	1717	1890	2072	2262	2460	2666
6	0298	0348	0404	0467	0536	0612	0696	0787	0886	0994
7	0053	0064	0078	0094	0112	0133	0157	0184	0215	0250
8	0006	0007	0009	0011	0014	0017	0021	0026	0031	0038
9				0001	0001	0001	0001	0002	0002	0003

P	41	42	43	44	45	46	47	48	49	50
R										
1	9913	9926	9936	9946	9954	9961	9967	9972	9977	9980
2	9372	9442	9505	9563	9615	9662	9704	9741	9775	9805
3	7866	8039	8204	8359	8505	8642	8769	8889	8999	9102
4	5424	5670	5913	6152	6386	6614	6836	7052	7260	7461
5	2878	3097	3322	3551	3786	4024	4265	4509	4754	5000
6	1109	1233	1366	1508	1658	1817	1985	2161	2346	2539
7	0290	0334	0383	0437	0498	0564	0637	0717	0804	0898
8	0046	0055	0065	0077	0091	0107	0125	0145	0169	0195
9	0003	0004	0005	0006	0008	0009	0011	0014	0016	0020

$$n = 10$$

P	01	02	03	04	05	06	07	08	09	10
R										
1	0956	1829	2626	3352	4013	4614	5160	5656	6106	6513
2	0043	0162	0345	0582	0861	1176	1517	1879	2254	2639
3	0001	0009	0028	0062	0115	0188	0283	0401	0540	0702
4			0001	0004	0010	0020	0036	0058	0088	0128
5					0001	0002	0003	0006	0010	0016
6									0001	0001

P	11	12	13	14	15	16	17	18	19	20
R										
1	6882	7215	7516	7787	8031	8251	8448	8626	8784	8926
2	3028	3417	3804	4184	4557	4920	5270	5608	5932	6242
3	0884	1087	1308	1545	1798	2064	2341	2628	2922	3222
4	0178	0239	0313	0400	0500	0614	0741	0883	1039	1209
5	0025	0037	0053	0073	0099	0130	0168	0213	0266	0328
6	0003	0004	0006	0010	0014	0020	0027	0037	0049	0064
7			0001	0001	0001	0002	0003	0004	0006	0009
8									0001	0001

P	21	22	23	24	25	26	27	28	29	30
R										
1	9053	9166	9267	9357	9437	9508	9570	9626	9674	9718
2	6536	6815	7079	7327	7560	7778	7981	8170	8345	8507
3	3526	3831	4137	4442	4744	5042	5335	5622	5901	6172
4	1391	1587	1794	2012	2241	2479	2726	2979	3239	3504
5	0399	0479	0569	0670	0781	0904	1037	1181	1337	1503
6	0082	0104	0130	0161	0197	0239	0287	0342	0404	0473
7	0012	0016	0021	0027	0035	0045	0056	0070	0087	0106
8	0001	0002	0002	0003	0004	0006	0007	0010	0012	0016
9							0001	0001	0001	0001

P	31	32	33	34	35	36	37	38	39	40
R										
1	9755	9789	9818	9843	9865	9885	9902	9916	9929	9940
2	8656	8794	8920	9035	9140	9236	9323	9402	9473	9536
3	6434	6687	6930	7162	7384	7595	7794	7983	8160	8327
4	3772	4044	4316	4589	4862	5132	5400	5664	5923	6177
5	1679	1867	2064	2270	2485	2708	2939	3177	3420	3669
6	0551	0637	0732	0836	0949	1072	1205	1348	1500	1662
7	0129	0155	0185	0220	0260	0305	0356	0413	0477	0548
8	0020	0025	0032	0039	0048	0059	0071	0086	0103	0123
9	0002	0003	0003	0004	0005	0007	0009	0011	0014	0017
10								0001	0001	0001

P	41	42	43	44	45	46	47	48	49	50
R										
1	9949	9957	9964	9970	9975	9979	9983	9986	9988	9990
2	9594	9645	9691	9731	9767	9799	9827	9852	9874	9893
3	8483	8628	8764	8889	9004	9111	9209	9298	9379	9453
4	6425	6665	6898	7123	7340	7547	7745	7933	8112	8281
5	3922	4178	4436	4696	4956	5216	5474	5730	5982	6230
6	1834	2016	2207	2407	2616	2832	3057	3288	3526	3770
7	0626	0712	0806	0908	1020	1141	1271	1410	1560	1719
8	0146	0172	0202	0236	0274	0317	0366	0420	0480	0547
9	0021	0025	0031	0037	0045	0054	0065	0077	0091	0107
10	0001	0002	0002	0003	0003	0004	0005	0006	0008	0010

$$n = 11$$

P	01	02	03	04	05	06	07	08	09	10
R										
1	1047	1993	2847	3618	4312	4937	5499	6004	6456	6862
2	0052	0195	0413	0692	1019	1382	1772	2181	2601	3026
3	0002	0012	0037	0083	0152	0248	0370	0519	0695	0896
4			0002	0007	0016	0030	0053	0085	0129	0185
5					0001	0003	0005	0010	0017	0028
6								0001	0002	0003

CUMULATIVE BINOMIAL DISTRIBUTION (*Continued*)

P→	11	12	13	14	15	16	17	18	19	20
R										
1	7225	7549	7839	8097	8327	8531	8712	8873	9015	9141
2	3452	3873	4286	4689	5078	5453	5811	6151	6474	6779
3	1120	1366	1632	1915	2212	2521	2839	3164	3494	3826
4	0256	0341	0442	0560	0694	0846	1013	1197	1397	1611
5	0042	0061	0087	0119	0159	0207	0266	0334	0413	0504
6	0005	0008	0012	0018	0027	0037	0051	0068	0090	0117
7		0001	0001	0002	0003	0005	0007	0010	0014	0020
8							0001	0001	0002	0002

P→	21	22	23	24	25	26	27	28	29	30
R										
1	9252	9350	9436	9511	9578	9636	9686	9730	9769	9802
2	7065	7333	7582	7814	8029	8227	8410	8577	8730	8870
3	4158	4488	4814	5134	5448	5753	6049	6335	6610	6873
4	1840	2081	2333	2596	2867	3146	3430	3719	4011	4304
5	0607	0723	0851	0992	1146	1313	1493	1685	1888	2103
6	0148	0186	0231	0283	0343	0412	0490	0577	0674	0782
7	0027	0035	0046	0059	0076	0095	0119	0146	0179	0216
8	0003	0005	0007	0009	0012	0016	0021	0027	0034	0043
9			0001	0001	0001	0002	0002	0003	0004	0006

P→	31	32	33	34	35	36	37	38	39	40
R										
1	9831	9856	9878	9896	9912	9926	9938	9948	9956	9964
2	8997	9112	9216	9310	9394	9470	9537	9597	9650	9698
3	7123	7361	7587	7799	7999	8186	8360	8522	8672	8811
4	4598	4890	5179	5464	5744	6019	6286	6545	6796	7037
5	2328	2563	2807	3059	3317	3581	3850	4122	4397	4672
6	0901	1031	1171	1324	1487	1661	1847	2043	2249	2465
7	0260	0309	0366	0430	0501	0581	0670	0768	0876	0994
8	0054	0067	0082	0101	0122	0148	0177	0210	0249	0293
9	0008	0010	0013	0016	0020	0026	0032	0039	0048	0059
10	0001	0001	0001	0002	0002	0003	0004	0005	0006	0007

P→	41	42	43	44	45	46	47	48	49	50
R										
1	9970	9975	9979	9983	9986	9989	9991	9992	9994	9995
2	9739	9776	9808	9836	9861	9882	9900	9916	9930	9941
3	8938	9055	9162	9260	9348	9428	9499	9564	9622	9673
4	7269	7490	7700	7900	8089	8266	8433	8588	8733	8867
5	4948	5223	5495	5764	6029	6288	6541	6787	7026	7256
6	2690	2924	3166	3414	3669	3929	4193	4460	4729	5000
7	1121	1260	1408	1568	1738	1919	2110	2312	2523	2744
8	0343	0399	0461	0532	0610	0696	0791	0895	1009	1133
9	0072	0087	0104	0125	0148	0175	0206	0241	0282	0327
10	0009	0012	0014	0018	0022	0027	0033	0040	0049	0059
11	0001	0001	0001	0001	0002	0002	0002	0003	0004	0005

$n = 12$

P→	01	02	03	04	05	06	07	08	09	10
R										
1	1136	2153	3062	3873	4596	5241	5814	6323	6775	7176
2	0062	0231	0486	0809	1184	1595	2033	2487	2948	3410
3	0002	0015	0048	0107	0196	0316	0468	0652	0866	1109
4		0001	0003	0010	0022	0043	0075	0120	0180	0256
5				0001	0002	0004	0009	0016	0027	0043
6							0001	0002	0003	0005
7										0001

P→	11	12	13	14	15	16	17	18	19	20
R										
1	7530	7843	8120	8363	8578	8766	8931	9076	9202	9313
2	3867	4314	4748	5166	5565	5945	6304	6641	6957	7251
3	1377	1667	1977	2303	2642	2990	3344	3702	4060	4417
4	0351	0464	0597	0750	0922	1114	1324	1552	1795	2054
5	0065	0095	0133	0181	0239	0310	0393	0489	0600	0726
6	0009	0014	0022	0033	0046	0065	0088	0116	0151	0194
7	0001	0002	0003	0004	0007	0010	0015	0021	0029	0039
8					0001	0001	0002	0003	0004	0006
9										0001

P	21	22	23	24	25	26	27	28	29	30
R										
1	9409	9493	9566	9629	9683	9730	9771	9806	9836	9862
2	7524	7776	8009	8222	8416	8594	8755	8900	9032	9150
3	4768	5114	5450	5778	6093	6397	6687	6963	7225	7472
4	2326	2610	2904	3205	3512	3824	4137	4452	4765	5075
5	0866	1021	1192	1377	1576	1790	2016	2254	2504	2763
6	0245	0304	0374	0453	0544	0646	0760	0887	1026	1178
7	0052	0068	0089	0113	0143	0178	0219	0267	0322	0386
8	0008	0011	0016	0021	0028	0036	0047	0060	0076	0095
9	0001	0001	0002	0003	0004	0005	0007	0010	0013	0017
10						0001	0001	0001	0002	0002

P	31	32	33	34	35	36	37	38	39	40
R										
1	9884	9902	9918	9932	9943	9953	9961	9968	9973	9978
2	9256	9350	9435	9509	9576	9634	9685	9730	9770	9804
3	7704	7922	8124	8313	8487	8648	8795	8931	9054	9166
4	5381	5681	5973	6258	6533	6799	7053	7296	7528	7747
5	3032	3308	3590	3876	4167	4459	4751	5043	5332	5618
6	1343	1521	1711	1913	2127	2352	2588	2833	3087	3348
7	0458	0540	0632	0734	0846	0970	1106	1253	1411	1582
8	0118	0144	0176	0213	0255	0304	0359	0422	0493	0573
9	0022	0028	0036	0045	0056	0070	0086	0104	0127	0153
10	0003	0004	0005	0007	0008	0011	0014	0018	0022	0028
11				0001	0001	0001	0001	0002	0002	0003

P	41	42	43	44	45	46	47	48	49	50
R										
1	9982	9986	9988	9990	9992	9994	9995	9996	9997	9998
2	9834	9860	9882	9901	9917	9931	9943	9953	9961	9968
3	9267	9358	9440	9513	9579	9637	9688	9733	9773	9807
4	7953	8147	8329	8498	8655	8801	8934	9057	9168	9270
5	5899	6175	6443	6704	6956	7198	7430	7652	7862	8062
6	3616	3889	4167	4448	4731	5014	5297	5577	5855	6128
7	1765	1959	2164	2380	2607	2843	3089	3343	3604	3872
8	0662	0760	0869	0988	1117	1258	1411	1575	1751	1938
9	0183	0218	0258	0304	0356	0415	0481	0555	0638	0730
10	0035	0043	0053	0065	0079	0095	0114	0137	0163	0193
11	0004	0005	0007	0009	0011	0014	0017	0021	0026	0032
12				0001	0001	0001	0001	0001	0002	0002

$$n = 13$$

P	01	02	03	04	05	06	07	08	09	10
R										
1	1225	2310	3270	4118	4867	5526	6107	6617	7065	7458
2	0072	0270	0564	0932	1354	1814	2298	2794	3293	3787
3	0003	0020	0062	0135	0245	0392	0578	0799	1054	1339
4		0001	0005	0014	0031	0060	0103	0163	0242	0342
5				0001	0003	0007	0013	0024	0041	0065
6						0001	0001	0003	0005	0009
7								0001	0001	0001

P	11	12	13	14	15	16	17	18	19	20
R										
1	7802	8102	8364	8592	8791	8963	9113	9242	9354	9450
2	4270	4738	5186	5614	6017	6396	6751	7080	7384	7664
3	1651	1985	2337	2704	3080	3463	3848	4231	4611	4983
4	0464	0609	0776	0967	1180	1414	1667	1939	2226	2527
5	0097	0139	0193	0260	0342	0438	0551	0681	0827	0991
6	0015	0024	0036	0053	0075	0104	0139	0183	0237	0300
7	0002	0003	0005	0008	0013	0019	0027	0038	0052	0070
8			0001	0001	0002	0003	0004	0006	0009	0012
9								0001	0001	0002

CUMULATIVE BINOMIAL DISTRIBUTION (*Continued*)

P R	21	22	23	24	25	26	27	28	29	30
1	9533	9604	9666	9718	9762	9800	9833	9860	9883	9903
2	7920	8154	8367	8559	8733	8889	9029	9154	9265	9363
3	5347	5699	6039	6364	6674	6968	7245	7505	7749	7975
4	2839	3161	3489	3822	4157	4493	4826	5155	5478	5794
5	1173	1371	1585	1816	2060	2319	2589	2870	3160	3457
6	0375	0462	0562	0675	0802	0944	1099	1270	1455	1654
7	0093	0120	0154	0195	0243	0299	0365	0440	0527	0624
8	0017	0024	0032	0043	0056	0073	0093	0118	0147	0182
9	0002	0004	0005	0007	0010	0013	0018	0024	0031	0040
10			0001	0001	0001	0002	0003	0004	0005	0007
11									0001	0001

P R	31	32	33	34	35	36	37	38	39	40
1	9920	9934	9945	9955	9963	9970	9975	9980	9984	9987
2	9450	9527	9594	9653	9704	9749	9787	9821	9849	9874
3	8185	8379	8557	8720	8868	9003	9125	9235	9333	9421
4	6101	6398	6683	6957	7217	7464	7698	7917	8123	8314
5	3760	4067	4376	4686	4995	5301	5603	5899	6188	6470
6	1867	2093	2331	2581	2841	3111	3388	3673	3962	4256
7	0733	0854	0988	1135	1295	1468	1654	1853	2065	2288
8	0223	0271	0326	0390	0462	0544	0635	0738	0851	0977
9	0052	0065	0082	0102	0126	0154	0187	0225	0270	0321
10	0009	0012	0015	0020	0025	0032	0040	0051	0063	0078
11	0001	0001	0002	0003	0003	0005	0006	0008	0010	0013
12							0001	0001	0001	0001

P R	41	42	43	44	45	46	47	48	49	50
1	9990	9992	9993	9995	9996	9997	9997	9998	9998	9999
2	9895	9912	9928	9940	9951	9960	9967	9974	9979	9983
3	9499	9569	9630	9684	9731	9772	9808	9838	9865	9888
4	8492	8656	8807	8945	9071	9185	9288	9381	9464	9539
5	6742	7003	7254	7493	7721	7935	8137	8326	8502	8666
6	4552	4849	5146	5441	5732	6019	6299	6573	6838	7095
7	2524	2770	3025	3290	3563	3842	4127	4415	4707	5000
8	1114	1264	1426	1600	1788	1988	2200	2424	2659	2905
9	0379	0446	0520	0605	0698	0803	0918	1045	1183	1334
10	0096	0117	0141	0170	0203	0242	0287	0338	0396	0461
11	0017	0021	0027	0033	0041	0051	0063	0077	0093	0112
12	0002	0002	0003	0004	0005	0007	0009	0011	0014	0017
13							0001	0001	0001	0001

$$n = 14$$

P R	01	02	03	04	05	06	07	08	09	10
1	1313	2464	3472	4353	5123	5795	6380	6888	7330	7712
2	0084	0310	0645	1059	1530	2037	2564	3100	3632	4154
3	0003	0025	0077	0167	0301	0478	0698	0958	1255	1584
4		0001	0006	0019	0042	0080	0136	0214	0315	0441
5				0002	0004	0010	0020	0035	0059	0092
6						0001	0002	0004	0008	0015
7								0001	0001	0002

P R	11	12	13	14	15	16	17	18	19	20
1	8044	8330	8577	8789	8972	9129	9264	9379	9477	9560
2	4658	5141	5599	6031	6433	6807	7152	7469	7758	8021
3	1939	2315	2708	3111	3521	3932	4341	4744	5138	5519
4	0594	0774	0979	1210	1465	1742	2038	2351	2679	3018
5	0137	0196	0269	0359	0467	0594	0741	0907	1093	1298
6	0024	0038	0057	0082	0115	0157	0209	0273	0349	0439
7	0003	0006	0009	0015	0022	0032	0046	0064	0087	0116
8		0001	0001	0002	0003	0005	0008	0012	0017	0024
9						0001	0001	0002	0003	0004

P	21	22	23	24	25	26	27	28	29	30
R										
1	9631	9691	9742	9786	9822	9852	9878	9899	9917	9932
2	8259	8473	8665	8837	8990	9126	9246	9352	9444	9525
3	5887	6239	6574	6891	7189	7467	7727	7967	8188	8392
4	3366	3719	4076	4432	4787	5136	5479	5813	6137	6448
5	1523	1765	2023	2297	2585	2884	3193	3509	3832	4158
6	0543	0662	0797	0949	1117	1301	1502	1718	1949	2195
7	0152	0196	0248	0310	0383	0467	0563	0673	0796	0933
8	0033	0045	0060	0079	0103	0132	0167	0208	0257	0315
9	0006	0008	0011	0016	0022	0029	0038	0050	0065	0083
10	0001	0001	0002	0002	0003	0005	0007	0009	0012	0017
11						0001	0001	0001	0002	0002

P	31	32	33	34	35	36	37	38	39	40
R										
1	9945	9955	9963	9970	9976	9981	9984	9988	9990	9992
2	9596	9657	9710	9756	9795	9828	9857	9881	9902	9919
3	8577	8746	8899	9037	9161	9271	9370	9457	9534	9602
4	6747	7032	7301	7556	7795	8018	8226	8418	8595	8757
5	4486	4813	5138	5458	5773	6080	6378	6666	6943	7207
6	2454	2724	3006	3297	3595	3899	4208	4519	4831	5141
7	1084	1250	1431	1626	1836	2059	2296	2545	2805	3075
8	0381	0458	0545	0643	0753	0876	1012	1162	1325	1501
9	0105	0131	0163	0200	0243	0294	0353	0420	0497	0583
10	0022	0029	0037	0048	0060	0076	0095	0117	0144	0175
11	0003	0005	0006	0008	0011	0014	0019	0024	0031	0039
12		0001	0001	0001	0001	0002	0003	0003	0005	0006
13										0001

P	41	42	43	44	45	46	47	48	49	50
R										
1	9994	9995	9996	9997	9998	9998	9999	9999	9999	9999
2	9934	9946	9956	9964	9971	9977	9981	9985	9988	9991
3	9661	9713	9758	9797	9830	9858	9883	9903	9921	9935
4	8905	9039	9161	9270	9368	9455	9532	9601	9661	9713
5	7459	7697	7922	8132	8328	8510	8678	8833	8974	9102
6	5450	5754	6052	6344	6627	6900	7163	7415	7654	7880
7	3355	3643	3937	4236	4539	4843	5148	5451	5751	6047
8	1692	1896	2113	2344	2586	2840	3105	3380	3663	3953
9	0680	0789	0910	1043	1189	1348	1520	1707	1906	2120
10	0212	0255	0304	0361	0426	0500	0583	0677	0782	0898
11	0049	0061	0076	0093	0114	0139	0168	0202	0241	0287
12	0008	0010	0013	0017	0022	0027	0034	0042	0053	0065
13	0001	0001	0001	0002	0003	0003	0004	0006	0007	0009
14										0001

$$n = 15$$

P	01	02	03	04	05	06	07	08	09	10
R										
1	1399	2614	3667	4579	5367	6047	6633	7137	7570	7941
2	0096	0353	0730	1191	1710	2262	2832	3403	3965	4510
3	0004	0030	0094	0203	0362	0571	0829	1130	1469	1841
4		0002	0008	0024	0055	0104	0175	0273	0399	0556
5			0001	0002	00·06	0014	0028	0050	0082	0127
6					0001	0001	0003	0007	0013	0022
7							0001	0002	0003

P	11	12	13	14	15	16	17	18	19	20
R										
1	8259	8530	8762	8959	9126	9269	9389	9490	9576	9648
2	5031	5524	5987	6417	6814	7179	7511	7813	8085	8329
3	2238	2654	3084	3520	3958	4392	4819	5234	5635	6020
4	0742	0959	1204	1476	1773	2092	2429	2782	3146	3518
5	0187	0265	0361	0478	0617	0778	0961	1167	1394	1642
6	0037	0057	0084	0121	0168	0227	0300	0387	0490	0611
7	0006	0010	0015	0024	0036	0052	0074	0102	0137	0181
8	0001	0001	0002	0004	0006	0010	0014	0021	0030	0042
9					0001	0001	0002	0003	0005	0008
10									0001	0001

CUMULATIVE BINOMIAL DISTRIBUTION (*Continued*)

P	21	22	23	24	25	26	27	28	29	30
R										
1	9709	9759	9802	9837	9866	9891	9911	9928	9941	9953
2	8547	8741	8913	9065	9198	9315	9417	9505	9581	9647
3	6385	6731	7055	7358	7639	7899	8137	8355	8553	8732
4	3895	4274	4650	5022	5387	5742	6086	6416	6732	7031
5	1910	2195	2495	2810	3135	3469	3810	4154	4500	4845
6	0748	0905	1079	1272	1484	1713	1958	2220	2495	2784
7	0234	0298	0374	0463	0566	0684	0817	0965	1130	1311
8	0058	0078	0104	0135	0173	0219	0274	0338	0413	0500
9	0011	0016	0023	0031	0042	0056	0073	0094	0121	0152
10	0002	0003	0004	0006	0008	0011	0015	0021	0028	0037
11			0001	0001	0001	0002	0002	0003	0005	0007
12									0001	0001

P	31	32	33	34	35	36	37	38	39	40
R										
1	9962	9969	9975	9980	9984	9988	9990	9992	9994	9995
2	9704	9752	9794	9829	9858	9883	9904	9922	9936	9948
3	8893	9038	9167	9281	9383	9472	9550	9618	9678	9729
4	7314	7580	7829	8060	8273	8469	8649	8813	8961	9095
5	5187	5523	5852	6171	6481	6778	7062	7332	7587	7827
6	3084	3393	3709	4032	4357	4684	5011	5335	5654	5968
7	1509	1722	1951	2194	2452	2722	3003	3295	3595	3902
8	0599	0711	0837	0977	1132	1302	1487	1687	1902	2131
9	0190	0236	0289	0351	0422	0504	0597	0702	0820	0950
10	0048	0062	0079	0099	0124	0154	0190	0232	0281	0338
11	0009	0012	0016	0022	0028	0037	0047	0059	0075	0093
12	0001	0002	0003	0004	0005	0006	0009	0011	0015	0019
13					0001	0001	0001	0002	0002	0003

P	41	42	43	44	45	46	47	48	49	50
R										
1	9996	9997	9998	9998	9999	9999	9999	9999	10000	10000
2	9958	9966	9973	9979	9983	9987	9990	9992	9994	9995
3	9773	9811	9843	9870	9893	9913	9929	9943	9954	9963
4	9215	9322	9417	9502	9576	9641	9697	9746	9788	9824
5	8052	8261	8454	8633	8796	8945	9080	9201	9310	9408
6	6274	6570	6856	7131	7392	7641	7875	8095	8301	8491
7	4214	4530	4847	5164	5478	5789	6095	6394	6684	6964
8	2374	2630	2898	3176	3465	3762	4065	4374	4686	5000
9	1095	1254	1427	1615	1818	2034	2265	2510	2767	3036
10	0404	0479	0565	0661	0769	0890	1024	1171	1333	1509
11	0116	0143	0174	0211	0255	0305	0363	0430	0506	0592
12	0025	0032	0040	0051	0063	0079	0097	0119	0145	0176
13	0004	0005	0007	0009	0011	0014	0018	0023	0029	0037
14			0001	0001	0001	0002	0002	0003	0004	0005

Square roots (1-400)

Appendix **3**

SQUARE ROOTS (1 to 400)

1	1.00	41	6.40	81	9.00	121	11.00	161	12.69
2	1.41	42	6.48	82	9.06	122	11.05	162	12.73
3	1.73	43	6.56	83	9.11	123	11.09	163	12.77
4	2.00	44	6.63	84	9.17	124	11.14	164	12.81
5	2.24	45	6.71	85	9.22	125	11.18	165	12.85
6	2.45	46	6.78	86	9.27	126	11.23	166	12.88
7	2.65	47	6.86	87	9.33	127	11.27	167	12.92
8	2.83	48	6.93	88	9.38	128	11.31	168	12.96
9	3.00	49	7.00	89	9.43	129	11.36	169	13.00
10	3.16	50	7.07	90	9.49	130	11.40	170	13.04
11	3.32	51	7.14	91	9.54	131	11.45	171	13.08
12	3.46	52	7.21	92	9.59	132	11.49	172	13.11
13	3.61	53	7.28	93	9.64	133	11.53	173	13.15
14	3.74	54	7.35	94	9.70	134	11.58	174	13.19
15	3.87	55	7.42	95	9.75	135	11.62	175	13.23
16	4.00	56	7.48	96	9.80	136	11.66	176	13.27
17	4.12	57	7.55	97	9.85	137	11.70	177	13.30
18	4.24	58	7.62	98	9.90	138	11.74	178	13.34
19	4.36	59	7.68	99	9.95	139	11.79	179	13.38
20	4.47	60	7.75	100	10.00	140	11.83	180	13.42
21	4.58	61	7.81	101	10.05	141	11.87	181	13.45
22	4.69	62	7.87	102	10.10	142	11.92	182	13.49
23	4.80	63	7.94	103	10.15	143	11.96	183	13.53
24	4.90	64	8.00	104	10.20	144	12.00	184	13.56
25	5.00	65	8.06	105	10.25	145	12.04	185	13.60
26	5.10	66	8.12	106	10.30	146	12.08	186	13.64
27	5.20	67	8.19	107	10.34	147	12.12	187	13.67
28	5.29	68	8.25	108	10.39	148	12.17	188	13.71
29	5.39	69	8.31	109	10.44	149	12.21	189	13.75
30	5.48	70	8.37	110	10.49	150	12.25	190	13.78
31	5.57	71	8.43	111	10.54	151	12.29	191	13.82
32	5.66	72	8.49	112	10.58	152	12.33	192	13.86
33	5.74	73	8.54	113	10.63	153	12.37	193	13.89
34	5.83	74	8.60	114	10.68	154	12.41	194	13.93
35	5.92	75	8.66	115	10.72	155	12.45	195	13.96
36	6.00	76	8.72	116	10.77	156	12.49	196	14.00
37	6.08	77	8.77	117	10.82	157	12.53	197	14.04
38	6.16	78	8.83	118	10.86	158	12.57	198	14.07
39	6.25	79	8.89	119	10.91	159	12.61	199	14.11
40	6.32	80	8.94	120	10.95	160	12.65	200	14.14

201	14.18	241	15.52	281	16.76	321	17.92	361	19.00
202	14.21	242	15.56	282	16.79	322	17.94	362	19.03
203	14.25	243	15.59	283	16.82	323	17.97	363	19.05
204	14.28	244	15.62	284	16.85	324	18.00	364	19.08
205	14.32	245	15.65	285	16.88	325	18.03	365	19.11
206	14.35	246	15.68	286	16.91	326	18.06	366	19.13
207	14.39	247	15.72	287	16.94	327	18.08	367	19.16
208	14.42	248	15.75	288	16.97	328	18.11	368	19.18
209	14.46	249	15.78	289	17.00	329	18.14	369	19.21
210	14.49	250	15.81	290	17.03	330	18.17	370	19.24
211	14.53	251	15.84	291	17.06	331	18.19	371	19.26
212	14.56	252	15.87	292	17.09	332	18.22	372	19.29
213	14.59	253	15.91	293	17.12	333	18.25	373	19.31
214	14.63	254	15.94	294	17.15	334	18.28	374	19.34
215	14.66	255	15.97	295	17.18	335	18.30	375	19.36
216	14.70	256	16.00	296	17.20	336	18.33	376	19.39
217	14.73	257	16.03	297	17.23	337	18.36	377	19.42
218	14.76	258	16.06	298	17.26	338	18.38	378	19.44
219	14.80	259	16.09	299	17.29	339	18.41	379	19.47
220	14.83	260	16.12	300	17.32	340	18.44	380	19.49
221	14.87	261	16.16	301	17.35	341	18.47	381	19.52
222	14.90	262	16.19	302	17.38	342	18.49	382	19.54
223	14.93	263	16.22	303	17.41	343	18.52	383	19.57
224	14.97	264	16.25	304	17.44	344	18.55	384	19.60
225	15.00	265	16.28	305	17.46	345	18.57	385	19.62
226	15.03	266	16.31	306	17.49	346	18.60	386	19.65
227	15.07	267	16.34	307	17.52	347	18.63	387	19.67
228	15.10	268	16.37	308	17.55	348	18.65	388	19.70
229	15.13	269	16.40	309	17.58	349	18.68	389	19.72
230	15.17	270	16.43	310	17.61	350	18.71	390	19.75
231	15.20	271	16.46	311	17.64	351	18.74	391	19.77
232	15.23	272	16.49	312	17.66	352	18.76	392	19.80
233	15.26	273	16.52	313	17.69	353	18.79	393	19.82
234	15.30	274	16.55	314	17.72	354	18.81	394	19.85
235	15.33	275	16.58	315	17.75	355	18.84	395	19.87
236	15.36	276	16.61	316	17.78	356	18.87	396	19.90
237	15.39	277	16.64	317	17.80	357	18.89	397	19.92
238	15.43	278	16.67	318	17.83	358	18.92	398	19.95
239	15.46	279	16.70	319	17.86	359	18.95	399	19.98
240	15.49	280	16.73	320	17.89	360	18.97	400	20.00

Unit normal loss integral

The following table presents the unit normal loss integral. In the example below, to determine the expected loss from point Q to the lefthand tail of the distribution when the loss per unit is C and the standard deviation of the distribution is σ,

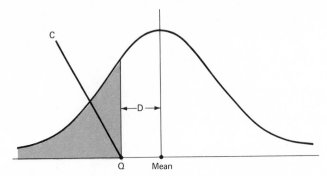

1. Determine distance D (the distance between point Q and the mean expressed in standard deviations).

2. Look up the value corresponding to D standard deviations in the unit normal loss integral table in this appendix (call this value $UNLI$).

3. Multiply together: $C \times \sigma \times UNLI$.

UNIT NORMAL LOSS INTEGRAL

D	.00	.01	.02	.03	.04	.05	.06	.07	.08	.09
.0	.3989	.3940	.3890	.3841	.3793	.3744	.3697	.3649	.3602	.3556
.1	.3509	.3464	.3418	.3373	.3328	.3284	.3240	.3197	.3154	.3111
.2	.3069	.3027	.2986	.2944	.2904	.2863	.2824	.2784	.2745	.2706
.3	.2668	.2630	.2592	.2555	.2518	.2481	.2445	.2409	.2374	.2339
.4	.2304	.2270	.2236	.2203	.2169	.2137	.2104	.2072	.2040	.2009
.5	.1978	.1947	.1917	.1887	.1857	.1828	.1799	.1771	.1742	.1714
.6	.1687	.1659	.1633	.1606	.1580	.1554	.1528	.1503	.1478	.1453
.7	.1429	.1405	.1381	.1358	.1334	.1312	.1289	.1267	.1245	.1223
.8	.1202	.1181	.1160	.1140	.1120	.1100	.1080	.1061	.1042	.1023
.9	.1004	.09860	.09680	.09503	.09328	.09156	.08986	.08819	.08654	.08491
1.0	.08332	.08174	.08019	.07866	.07716	.07568	.07422	.07279	.07138	.06999
1.1	.06862	.06727	.06595	.06465	.06336	.06210	.06086	.05964	.05844	.05726
1.2	.05610	.05496	.05384	.05274	.05165	.05059	.04954	.04851	.04750	.04650
1.3	.04553	.04457	.04363	.04270	.04179	.04090	.04002	.03916	.03831	.03748
1.4	.03667	.03587	.03508	.03431	.03356	.03281	.03208	.03137	.03067	.02998
1.5	.02931	.02865	.02800	.02736	.02674	.02612	.02552	.02494	.02436	.02380
1.6	.02324	.02270	.02217	.02165	.02114	.02064	.02015	.01967	.01920	.01874
1.7	.01829	.01785	.01742	.01699	.01658	.01617	.01578	.01539	.01501	.01464
1.8	.01428	.01392	.01357	.01323	.01290	.01257	.01226	.01195	.01164	.01134
1.9	.01105	.01077	.01049	.01022	.$0^2$9957	.$0^2$9698	.$0^2$9445	.$0^2$9198	.$0^2$8957	.$0^2$8721
2.0	.$0^2$8491	.$0^2$8266	.$0^2$8046	.$0^2$7832	.$0^2$7623	.$0^2$7418	.$0^2$7219	.$0^2$7024	.$0^2$6835	.$0^2$6649
2.1	.$0^2$6468	.$0^2$6292	.$0^2$6120	.$0^2$5952	.$0^2$5788	.$0^2$5628	.$0^2$5472	.$0^2$5320	.$0^2$5172	.$0^2$5028
2.2	.$0^2$4887	.$0^2$4750	.$0^2$4616	.$0^2$4486	.$0^2$4358	.$0^2$4235	.$0^2$4114	.$0^2$3996	.$0^2$3882	.$0^2$3770
2.3	.$0^2$3662	.$0^2$3556	.$0^2$3453	.$0^2$3352	.$0^2$3255	.$0^2$3159	.$0^2$3067	.$0^2$2977	.$0^2$2889	.$0^2$2804
2.4	.$0^2$2720	.$0^2$2640	.$0^2$2561	.$0^2$2484	.$0^2$2410	.$0^2$2337	.$0^2$2267	.$0^2$2199	.$0^2$2132	.$0^2$2067
2.5	.$0^2$2004	.$0^2$1943	.$0^2$1883	.$0^2$1826	.$0^2$1769	.$0^2$1715	.$0^2$1662	.$0^2$1610	.$0^2$1560	.$0^2$1511
2.6	.$0^2$1464	.$0^2$1418	.$0^2$1373	.$0^2$1330	.$0^2$1288	.$0^2$1247	.$0^2$1207	.$0^2$1169	.$0^2$1132	.$0^2$1095
2.7	.$0^2$1060	.$0^2$1026	.$0^3$9928	.$0^3$9607	.$0^3$9295	.$0^3$8992	.$0^3$8699	.$0^3$8414	.$0^3$8138	.$0^3$7870
2.8	.$0^3$7611	.$0^3$7359	.$0^3$7115	.$0^3$6879	.$0^3$6650	.$0^3$6428	.$0^3$6213	.$0^3$6004	.$0^3$5802	.$0^3$5606
2.9	.$0^3$5417	.$0^3$5233	.$0^3$5055	.$0^3$4883	.$0^3$4716	.$0^3$4555	.$0^3$4398	.$0^3$4247	.$0^3$4101	.$0^3$3959
3.0	.$0^3$3822	.$0^3$3689	.$0^3$3560	.$0^3$3436	.$0^3$3316	.$0^3$3199	.$0^3$3087	.$0^3$2978	.$0^3$2873	.$0^3$2771
3.1	.$0^3$2673	.$0^3$2577	.$0^3$2485	.$0^3$2396	.$0^3$2311	.$0^3$2227	.$0^3$2147	.$0^3$2070	.$0^3$1995	.$0^3$1922
3.2	.$0^3$1852	.$0^3$1785	.$0^3$1720	.$0^3$1657	.$0^3$1596	.$0^3$1537	.$0^3$1480	.$0^3$1426	.$0^3$1373	.$0^3$1322
3.3	.$0^3$1273	.$0^3$1225	.$0^3$1179	.$0^3$1135	.$0^3$1093	.$0^3$1051	.$0^3$1012	.$0^4$9734	.$0^4$9365	.$0^4$9009
3.4	.$0^4$8666	.$0^4$8335	.$0^4$8016	.$0^4$7709	.$0^4$7413	.$0^4$7127	.$0^4$6852	.$0^4$6587	.$0^4$6331	.$0^4$6085
3.5	.$0^4$5848	.$0^4$5620	.$0^4$5400	.$0^4$5188	.$0^4$4984	.$0^4$4788	.$0^4$4599	.$0^4$4417	.$0^4$4242	.$0^4$4073
3.6	.$0^4$3911	.$0^4$3755	.$0^4$3605	.$0^4$3460	.$0^4$3321	.$0^4$3188	.$0^4$3059	.$0^4$2935	.$0^4$2816	.$0^4$2702
3.7	.$0^4$2592	.$0^4$2486	.$0^4$2385	.$0^4$2287	.$0^4$2193	.$0^4$2103	.$0^4$2016	.$0^4$1933	.$0^4$1853	.$0^4$1776
3.8	.$0^4$1702	.$0^4$1632	.$0^4$1563	.$0^4$1498	.$0^4$1435	.$0^4$1375	.$0^4$1317	.$0^4$1262	.$0^4$1208	.$0^4$1157
3.9	.$0^4$1108	.$0^4$1061	.$0^4$1016	.$0^5$9723	.$0^5$9307	.$0^5$8908	.$0^5$8525	.$0^5$8158	.$0^5$7806	.$0^5$7469
4.0	.$0^5$7145	.$0^5$6835	.$0^5$6538	.$0^5$6253	.$0^5$5980	.$0^5$5718	.$0^5$5468	.$0^5$5227	.$0^5$4997	.$0^5$4777
4.1	.$0^5$4566	.$0^5$4364	.$0^5$4170	.$0^5$3985	.$0^5$3807	.$0^5$3637	.$0^5$3475	.$0^5$3319	.$0^5$3170	.$0^5$3027
4.2	.$0^5$2891	.$0^5$2760	.$0^5$2635	.$0^5$2516	.$0^5$2402	.$0^5$2292	.$0^5$2188	.$0^5$2088	.$0^5$1992	.$0^5$1901
4.3	.$0^5$1814	.$0^5$1730	.$0^5$1650	.$0^5$1574	.$0^5$1501	.$0^5$1431	.$0^5$1365	.$0^5$1301	.$0^5$1241	.$0^5$1183
4.4	.$0^5$1127	.$0^5$1074	.$0^5$1024	.$0^6$9756	.$0^6$9296	.$0^6$8857	.$0^6$8437	.$0^6$8037	.$0^6$7655	.$0^6$7290
4.5	.$0^6$6942	.$0^6$6610	.$0^6$6294	.$0^6$5992	.$0^6$5704	.$0^6$5429	.$0^6$5167	.$0^6$4917	.$0^6$4679	.$0^6$4452
4.6	.$0^6$4236	.$0^6$4029	.$0^6$3833	.$0^6$3645	.$0^6$3467	.$0^6$3297	.$0^6$3135	.$0^6$2981	.$0^6$2834	.$0^6$2694
4.7	.$0^6$2560	.$0^6$2433	.$0^6$2313	.$0^6$2197	.$0^6$2088	.$0^6$1984	.$0^6$1884	.$0^6$1790	.$0^6$1700	.$0^6$1615
4.8	.$0^6$1533	.$0^6$1456	.$0^6$1382	.$0^6$1312	.$0^6$1246	.$0^6$1182	.$0^6$1122	.$0^6$1065	.$0^6$1011	.$0^7$9588
4.9	.$0^7$9096	.$0^7$8629	.$0^7$8185	.$0^7$7763	.$0^7$7362	.$0^7$6982	.$0^7$6620	.$0^7$6276	.$0^7$5950	.$0^7$5640

Example of table notation: .$0^4$5848 = .00005848.

SOURCE: Robert O. Schlaifer, *"Introduction to Statistics for Business Decisions,"* McGraw-Hill Book Company, 1961.

Values of $e^{-\lambda}$ for computing Poisson probabilities

λ	$e^{-\lambda}$	λ	$e^{-\lambda}$	λ	$e^{-\lambda}$	λ	$e^{-\lambda}$
0.1	0.90484	2.6	0.07427	5.1	0.00610	7.6	0.00050
0.2	0.81873	2.7	0.06721	5.2	0.00552	7.7	0.00045
0.3	0.74082	2.8	0.06081	5.3	0.00499	7.8	0.00041
0.4	0.67032	2.9	0.05502	5.4	0.00452	7.9	0.00037
0.5	0.60653	3.0	0.04979	5.5	0.00409	8.0	0.00034
0.6	0.54881	3.1	0.04505	5.6	0.00370	8.1	0.00030
0.7	0.49659	3.2	0.04076	5.7	0.00335	8.2	0.00027
0.8	0.44933	3.3	0.03688	5.8	0.00303	8.3	0.00025
0.9	0.40657	3.4	0.03337	5.9	0.00274	8.4	0.00022
1.0	0.36788	3.5	0.03020	6.0	0.00248	8.5	0.00020
1.1	0.33287	3.6	0.02732	6.1	0.00224	8.6	0.00018
1.2	0.30119	3.7	0.02472	6.2	0.00203	8.7	0.00017
1.3	0.27253	3.8	0.02237	6.3	0.00184	8.8	0.00015
1.4	0.24660	3.9	0.02024	6.4	0.00166	8.9	0.00014
1.5	0.22313	4.0	0.01832	6.5	0.00150	9.0	0.00012
1.6	0.20190	4.1	0.01657	6.6	0.00136	9.1	0.00011
1.7	0.18268	4.2	0.01500	6.7	0.00123	9.2	0.00010
1.8	0.16530	4.3	0.01357	6.8	0.00111	9.3	0.00009
1.9	0.14957	4.4	0.01228	6.9	0.00101	9.4	0.00008
2.0	0.13534	4.5	0.01111	7.0	0.00091	9.5	0.00007
2.1	0.12246	4.6	0.01005	7.1	0.00083	9.6	0.00007
2.2	0.11080	4.7	0.00910	7.2	0.00075	9.7	0.00006
2.3	0.10026	4.8	0.00823	7.3	0.00068	9.8	0.00006
2.4	0.09072	4.9	0.00745	7.4	0.00061	9.9	0.00005
2.5	0.08208	5.0	0.00674	7.5	0.00055	10.0	0.00005

Value of p_0

Probability of Zero Units in the System (P_0)

$\dfrac{A}{kS}$	\multicolumn{10}{c}{Number of Channels (k)}									
	1	2	3	4	5	6	7	8	9	10
.02	.98000	.96078	.94176	.92312	.90484	.88692	.86936	.85214	.83527	.81873
.04	.96000	.92308	.88692	.85214	.81873	.78663	.75578	.72615	.69768	.67032
.06	.94000	.88679	.83526	.78663	.74082	.69768	.65705	.61878	.58275	.54881
.08	.92000	.85185	.78659	.72614	.67032	.61878	.57121	.52729	.48675	.44933
.10	.90000	.81818	.74074	.67031	.60653	.54881	.49659	.44933	.40657	.36788
.12	.88000	.78571	.69753	.61876	.54881	.48675	.43171	.38289	.33960	.30119
.14	.86000	.75439	.65679	.57116	.49657	.43171	.37531	.32628	.28365	.24660
.16	.84000	.72414	.61837	.52720	.44931	.38289	.32628	.27804	.23693	.20190
.18	.82000	.69492	.58214	.48660	.40653	.33959	.28365	.23693	.19790	.16530
.20	.80000	.66667	.54795	.44910	.36782	.30118	.24659	.20189	.16530	.13534
.22	.78000	.63934	.51567	.41445	.33277	.26711	.21437	.17204	.13807	.11080
.24	.76000	.61290	.48519	.38244	.30105	.23688	.18636	.14660	.11532	.09072
.26	.74000	.58730	.45640	.35284	.27233	.21007	.16200	.12492	.09632	.07427
.28	.72000	.56250	.42918	.32548	.24633	.18628	.14082	.10645	.08045	.06081
.30	.70000	.53846	.40346	.30017	.22277	.16517	.12241	.09070	.06720	.04978
.32	.68000	.51515	.37913	.27676	.20144	.14644	.10639	.07728	.05612	.04076
.34	.66000	.49254	.35610	.25510	.18211	.12981	.09247	.06584	.04687	.03337
.36	.64000	.47059	.33431	.23505	.16460	.11505	.08035	.05609	.03915	.02732
.38	.62000	.44928	.31367	.21649	.14872	.10195	.06981	.04778	.03269	.02236
.40	.60000	.42857	.29412	.19929	.13433	.09032	.06064	.04069	.02729	.01830
.42	.58000	.40845	.27559	.18336	.12128	.07998	.05267	.03465	.02279	.01498
.44	.56000	.38889	.25802	.16860	.10944	.07080	.04573	.02950	.01902	.01226
.46	.54000	.36986	.24135	.15491	.09870	.06265	.03968	.02511	.01587	.01003
.48	.52000	.35135	.22554	.14221	.08895	.05540	.03442	.02136	.01324	.00820
.50	.50000	.33333	.21053	.13043	.08010	.04896	.02984	.01816	.01104	.00671

.52	.48000	.31579	.19627	.11951	.07207	.04323	.02586	.01544	.00920	.00548
.54	.46000	.29870	.18273	.10936	.06477	.03814	.02239	.01311	.00767	.00448
.56	.44000	.28205	.16986	.09994	.05814	.03362	.01936	.01113	.00638	.00366
.58	.42000	.26582	.15762	.09119	.05212	.02959	.01673	.00943	.00531	.00298
.60	.40000	.25000	.14599	.08306	.04665	.02601	.01443	.00799	.00441	.00243
.62	.38000	.23457	.13491	.07750	.04167	.02282	.01243	.00675	.00366	.00198
.64	.36000	.21951	.12438	.06847	.03715	.01999	.01069	.00570	.00303	.00161
.66	.34000	.20482	.11435	.06194	.03304	.01746	.00918	.00480	.00251	.00131
.68	.32000	.19048	.10479	.05587	.02930	.01522	.00786	.00404	.00207	.00106
.70	.30000	.17647	.09569	.05021	.02590	.01322	.00670	.00338	.00170	.00085
.72	.28000	.16279	.08702	.04495	.02280	.01144	.00570	.00283	.00140	.00069
.74	.26000	.14943	.07875	.04006	.01999	.00986	.00483	.00235	.00114	.00055
.76	.24000	.13636	.07087	.03550	.01743	.00846	.00407	.00195	.00093	.00044
.78	.22000	.12360	.06335	.03125	.01510	.00721	.00341	.00160	.00075	.00035
.80	.20000	.11111	.05618	.02730	.01299	.00610	.00284	.00131	.00060	.00028
.82	.18000	.09890	.04933	.02362	.01106	.00511	.00234	.00106	.00048	.00022
.84	.16000	.08696	.04280	.02019	.00931	.00423	.00190	.00085	.00038	.00017
.86	.14000	.07527	.03656	.01700	.00772	.00345	.00153	.00067	.00029	.00013
.88	.12000	.06383	.03060	.01403	.00627	.00276	.00120	.00052	.00022	.00010
.90	.10000	.05263	.02491	.01126	.00496	.00215	.00092	.00039	.00017	.00007
.92	.08000	.04167	.01947	.00867	.00377	.00161	.00068	.00028	.00012	.00005
.94	.06000	.03093	.01427	.00627	.00268	.00113	.00047	.00019	.00008	.00003
.96	.04000	.02041	.00930	.00403	.00170	.00070	.00029	.00012	.00005	.00002
.98	.02000	.01010	.00454	.00194	.00081	.00033	.00013	.00005	.00002	.00001

Random number table (2500 random digits)

2,500 RANDOM DIGITS

1581922396	2068577984	8262130892	8374856049	4637567488
0928105582	7295088579	9586111652	7055508767	6472382934
4112077556	3440672486	1882412963	0684012006	0933147914
7457477468	5435810788	9670852913	1291265730	4890031305
0099520858	3090908872	2039593181	5973470495	9776135501
7245174840	2275698645	8416549348	4676463101	2229367983
6749420382	4832630032	5670984959	5432114610	2966095680
5503161011	7413686599	1198757695	0414294470	0140121598
7164238934	7666127259	5263097712	5133648980	4011966963
3593969525	0272759769	0385998136	9999089966	7544056852
4192054466	0700014629	5169439659	8408705169	1074373131
9697426117	6488888550	4031652526	8123543276	0927534537
2007950579	9564268448	3457416988	1531027886	7016633739
4584768758	2389278610	3859431781	3643768456	4141314518
3840145867	9120831830	7228567652	1267173884	4020651657
0190453442	4800088084	1165628559	5407921254	3768932478
6766554338	5585265145	5089052204	9780623691	2195448096
6315116284	9172824179	5544814339	0016943666	3828538786
3908771938	4035554324	0840126299	4942059208	1475623997
5570024586	9324732596	1186563397	4425143189	3216653251
2999997185	0135968938	7678931194	1351031403	6002561840
7864375912	8383232768	1892857070	2323673751	3188881718
7065492027	6349104233	3382569662	4579426926	1513082455
0654683246	4765104877	8149224168	5468631609	6474393896
7830555058	5255147182	3519287786	2481675649	8907598697
7626984369	4725370390	9641916289	5049082870	7463807244
4785048453	3646121751	8436077768	2928794356	9956043516
4627791048	5765558107	8762592043	6185670830	6363845920
9376470693	0441608934	8749472723	2202271078	5897002653
1227991661	7936797054	9527542791	4711871173	8300978148
5582095589	5535798279	4764439855	6279247618	4446895088
4959397698	1056981450	8416606706	8234013222	6426813469
1824779358	1333750468	9434074212	5273692238	5902177065
7041092295	5726289716	3420847871	1820481234	0318831723
3555104281	0903099163	6827824899	6383872737	5901682626

2,500 RANDOM DIGITS (*Continued*)

9717595534	1634107293	8521057472	1471300754	3044151557
5571564123	7344613447	1129117244	3208461091	1699403490
4674262892	2809456764	5806554509	8224980942	5738031833
8461228715	0746980892	9285305274	6331989646	8764467686
1838538678	3049068967	6955157269	5482964330	2161984904
1834182305	6203476893	5937802079	3445280195	3694915658
1884227732	2923727501	8044389132	4611203081	6072112445
6791857341	6696243386	2219599137	3193884236	8224729718
3007929946	4031562749	5570757297	6273785046	1455349704
6085440624	2875556938	5496629750	4841817356	1443167141
7005051056	3496332071	5054070890	7303867953	6255181190
9846413446	8306646692	0661684251	8875127201	6251533454
0625457703	4229164694	7321363715	7051128285	1108468072
5457593922	9751489574	1799906380	1989141062	5595364247
4076486653	8950826528	4934582003	4071187742	1456207629

SOURCE: Dudley J. Cowden and Mercedes S. Cowden, *Practical Problems in Business Statistics*, 2d ed., © 1963, by permission of Prentice-Hall, Inc., Englewood Cliffs, N.J.

Derivation of EOQ formulas

Appendix **8**

Chapter 7

Page 197

Total cost:

$$N_0 P + \frac{AC}{2N_0}$$

$$\frac{dTC}{dN_0} = P - \frac{AC}{2N_0{}^2}$$

Setting first derivative equal to zero and solving for N_0,

$$P - \frac{AC}{2N_0{}^2} = 0$$

$$P = \frac{AC}{2N_0{}^2}$$

$$2N_0{}^2 P = AC$$

$$N_0{}^2 = \frac{AC}{2P}$$

$$N_0 = \sqrt{\frac{AC}{2P}} \tag{7-1}$$

Page 198

Total cost:

$$\frac{AP}{RN_u} + \frac{RCN_u}{2}$$

$$\frac{dTC}{dN_u} = \frac{-AP}{RN_u{}^2} + \frac{RC}{2}$$

Setting first derivative equal to zero and solving for N_u,

$$\frac{-AP}{RN_u{}^2} + \frac{RC}{2} = 0$$

$$\frac{RC}{2} = \frac{AP}{RN_u{}^2}$$

$$R^2CN_u{}^2 = 2AP$$

$$N_u{}^2 = \frac{2AP}{R^2C}$$

$$N_u = \sqrt{\frac{2AP}{R^2C}}$$

(7-2)

Page 199

Total cost:

$$\frac{365P}{N_d} + \frac{AC}{730/N_d}$$

$$\frac{dTC}{dN_d} = -\frac{365P}{N_d{}^2} + \frac{AC}{730}$$

Setting first derivative equal to zero and solving for N_d,

$$\frac{-365P}{N_d{}^2} + \frac{AC}{730} = 0$$

$$\frac{AC}{730} = \frac{365P}{N_d{}^2}$$

$$N_d{}^2AC = 266{,}450P$$

$$N_d{}^2 = \frac{266{,}450P}{AC}$$

$$N_d = \sqrt{\frac{266{,}450P}{AC}}$$

(7-3)

Page 200

Total cost:

$$\frac{AP}{N_\$} + \frac{N_\$C}{2}$$

$$\frac{dTC}{dN_\$} = \frac{-AP}{N_\${}^2} + \frac{C}{2}$$

Setting first derivative equal to zero and solving for $N_\$$,

$$\frac{-AP}{N_\$^2} + \frac{C}{2} = 0$$

$$\frac{C}{2} = \frac{AP}{N_\$^2}$$

$$N_\$^2 C = 2AP$$

$$N_\$^2 = \frac{2AP}{C}$$

$$N_\$ = \sqrt{\frac{2AP}{C}} \tag{7-4}$$

Page 203

Total cost:

$$\frac{UP}{N_u} + \frac{RCN_u}{2}\left(1 - \frac{y}{x}\right)$$

$$\frac{dTC}{dN_u} = \frac{-UP}{N_u^2} + \frac{RC}{2}\left(1 - \frac{y}{x}\right)$$

Setting first derivative equal to zero and solving for N_u,

$$\frac{-UP}{N_u^2} + \frac{RC}{2}\left(1 - \frac{y}{x}\right) = 0$$

$$\frac{RC}{2}\left(1 - \frac{y}{x}\right) = \frac{UP}{N_u^2}$$

$$\frac{N_u^2 RC}{2}\left(1 - \frac{y}{x}\right) = UP$$

$$N_u^2 RC\left(1 - \frac{y}{x}\right) = 2UP$$

$$N_u^2 = \frac{2UP}{RC(1 - y/x)}$$

$$N_u = \sqrt{\frac{2UP}{RC(1 - y/x)}} \tag{7-5}$$

Page 213

Total cost:

$$\frac{US}{N_u} + \frac{RCN_u}{2}\left(1 - \frac{d}{p}\right)$$

$$\frac{dTC}{dN_u} = -\frac{US}{N_u{}^2} + \frac{RC}{2}\left(1 - \frac{d}{p}\right)$$

Setting first derivative equal to zero and solving for N_u,

$$\frac{-US}{N_u{}^2} + \frac{RC}{2}\left(1 - \frac{d}{p}\right) = 0$$

$$\frac{RC}{2}\left(1 - \frac{d}{p}\right) = \frac{US}{N_u{}^2}$$

$$\frac{N_u{}^2 RC}{2}\left(1 - \frac{d}{p}\right) = US$$

$$N_u{}^2 RC\left(1 - \frac{d}{p}\right) = 2US$$

$$N_u{}^2 = \frac{2US}{RC\left(1 - \frac{d}{p}\right)}$$

$$N_u = \sqrt{\frac{2US}{RC\left(1 - \frac{d}{p}\right)}}$$

(7-10)

Functional list of text exercises

Appendix **9**

This table lists all the exercises in the text according to the functional area of the organization they apply to (i.e., accounting, finance, marketing, organization behavior, production, etc.). Problems which apply to not-for-profit organizations (i.e., education, government, public and social services, etc.) are also arranged under those categories.

To find a linear programming application in marketing, for example, look in the marketing section for problem numbers beginning with the chapter number, 9 (Linear Programming: Graphic Method) or 10 (Linear Programming: The Simplex Method). To find a not-for-profit application of waiting lines, look under the not-for-profit heading or under any of the specific not-for-profit areas for problems beginning with the chapter number, 14 (Waiting Lines). Where appropriate, exercises are listed jointly.

An annotated list of chapter titles for those chapters which have exercises follows:

2. Probability I   Introduction to probability; basic concepts; marginal, joint, and conditional probabilities; statistical independence and dependence; Bayes' revisions of prior probabilities.

3. Probability II   Introduction to probability distributions; types of probability distributions; random variables; binomial, Poisson, and normal distributions.

4. Forecasting   Types of forecasting, judgmental forecasting, extensions of past history, causal forecasting, moving averages, exponential smoothing, trend adjusted exponential smoothing, least-squares trend-line fitting, multiple regression.

5. Decision Theory I   Steps in decision theory; different decision environments; certainty; uncertainty; risk; decision making under certainty, uncertainty, and risk; use of discrete random variables; continuously distributed random variables; utility as a criterion.

6. Decision Theory II   Supplying the numbers of decision theory, combining experience and numbers, normal distribution and cost-volume-profit analysis, combining unit monetary values and probability distributions, items which fail over time, decision trees.

7. Inventory Models I   Functions of inventory, inventory decisions, basic EOQ models, eliminating the instantaneous receipt assumption, use of EOQ when annual demand can't be forecast, use of EOQ when cost information is not available, applying EOQ to production problems.

8. **Inventory Models II**   Deciding when to buy, reorder points, safety stock when out-of-stock cost is and is not known, joint ordering, evaluation of discounts, planned stockouts, the backorder model.

9. **Linear Programming: Graphic Method**   Graphic solution to maximizing and minimizing problems.

10. **Linear Programming: The Simplex Method**   Simplex solution to maximizing and minimizing problems; the dual; infeasibility, unboundedness, and degeneracy; objectives other than profit maximization; right-hand-side ranging and objective function ranging.

11. **Special-Purpose Algorithms**   Transportation method, assignment method.

12. **Integer Programming, Branch-and-Bound Method, Goal Programming, and Dynamic Programming.**

13. **Simulation**   Introduction to simulation, advantages and disadvantages, process generators, hand-computed simulation, computer simulation.

14. **Waiting Lines**   Queuing objectives and cost behavior, language of queues, single-channel model, multiple-channel model, simulation of a queuing system.

15. **Network Models**   PERT, CPM, network scheduling with resource limitations, maximal flow problem, minimal spanning tree problem, shortest-route problem.

16. **Markov Analysis**   Brand switching, transition probabilities, predicting future market shares, equilibrium, using Markov analysis in the determination of marketing strategy, other uses of Markov analysis.

Accounting: 3-2, 3-10, 6-1, 6-8, 15-16, 16-4, 16-15, 16-17
Aerospace: 11-7, 12-16
Agriculture: 13-1, 13-2
Alcoholism: 3-4
Banking: 3-5, 5-1, 10-18, 13-3, 13-11
Auditing: 3-10, 6-8
Construction: 3-9, 6-20, 6-24, 10-19, 11-1, 11-4, 12-3, 12-10, 13-9, 15-1, 15-2, 15-3, 15-4, 15-5, 15-7, 15-9, 15-11, 15-12, 15-13, 15-14, 15-15, 15-20
Credit: 2-19, 3-2, 3-5, 4-10, 5-1, 13-11, 16-17
Crime: 4-11, 8-17, 14-16
Education: 2-3, 2-18, 3-1, 4-7, 4-8, 4-9, 4-14, 5-11, 6-11, 6-17, 7-3, 10-12, 12-14, 14-10, 16-12
Environment—Natural Resources: 4-4, 4-5, 4-6, 5-13, 8-21, 15-17
Extraction (Minerals, Mining, Oil): 2-16, 6-18, 10-20, 13-1, 13-2
Finance: 2-6, 2-12, 2-13, 2-19, 2-22, 3-16, 5-1, 5-4, 5-17, 5-18, 5-19, 5-20, 6-23, 10-18, 12-13
Games (Cards, Dice, Lotteries): 2-1, 2-11, 5-22
Health Affairs (Hospitals, Physicians, Veterinarians): 3-12, 3-13, 5-7, 8-15, 8-16, 10-2, 14-8, 14-15, 15-18, 16-8, 16-10, 16-11

Index